D1238348

GERONTOLOGY

Perspectives and Issues

SECOND EDITION

Kenneth F. Ferraro, PhD, is Professor of Sociology and Director of the Gerontology Program at Purdue University, West Lafayette, Indiana. He has conducted research on a number of topics in gerontology, including health status, images of aging, and fear of crime, and his work has been supported by grants from the AARP Andrus Foundation and the National Insitute on Aging. His current research interests focus on health status assessment and ethnic differences in health and health service use across the life course.

Dr. Ferraro has published approximately 50 papers in professional journals or books. His articles appear in a variety of journals, including the *Journal of Gerontology: Social Sciences*, *Journal of Health and Social Behavior*, *Journal for the Scientific Study of Religion*, *Public Opinion Quarterly*, *Research on Aging*, *Social Forces*, and *Sociological Inquiry*. He has served as a member of the Human Development and Aging study section (subcommittee 2) at the National Institutes of Health and on the editorial boards of the *Journal of Gerontology: Social Sciences* and *Journal of Health and Social Behavior*.

GERONTOLOGY
Perspectives and Issues

SECOND EDITION

Kenneth F. Ferraro, PhD
Editor

Springer Publishing Company

Springer Publishing Company, Inc.
536 Broadway
New York, NY 10012-3955

Cover design by Margaret Dunin
Acquisitions Editor: Bill Tucker
Production Editor: Kathleen Kelly

97 98 99 00 01 / 5 4 3 2 1

Library of Congress Cataloging-in-Publication Data

Gerontology : perspectives and issues / Kenneth F. Ferraro, editor. — 2nd ed.

p. cm.

Includes bibliographical references and index.

ISBN 0-8261-6661-X

1. Geronotology—United States. I. Ferraro, Kenneth F.

HQ1064.U5G43 1997

305.26′0973—dc21 97-2443

CIP

Printed in the United States of America

CONTENTS

PREFACE

A common ritual for prefacing a book on gerontology or social gerontology is to note that the field is necessarily *multidisciplinary*. Although this fact has been implanted in our minds during our educational experience and given deference at professional meetings, most of us retreat to our disciplines to do our work. Rarely do books on gerontology carry over this interest in the multidisciplinary character of the field to the table of contents and thereafter. This book attempts to do just that, recognizing that this first axiom of the field is not ready for the academic museum.

The first edition of this book was born in the multidisciplinary gerontology program at Northern Illinois University. The second edition was developed and field-tested in a multidisciplinary gerontology program at Purdue University. Although I was delighted with the success of the first edition, several changes were made to make the second edition more useful to a diverse gerontological community. In particular, fresh chapters have been added on caregiving, social policy debates, and the economic status of the older population.

Real problems have existed in selecting text material for the cornerstone course of many gerontology programs, a multidisciplinary course on aging. Many universities and colleges have such a course, in which an integrated, multidisciplinary approach is emphasized. However, books suitable for such instruction are in short supply. We have plenty of books written by psychologists or sociologists with token chapters on biology or physiology. We also have other excellent handbooks in the field, but these are typically focused narrowly for scholars in certain disciplines.

This volume is not intended to be an encyclopedia or handbook on gerontology but rather a cogent and comprehensive review of theoretical and empirical research in gerontology. I have sought by all means to keep the multidisciplinary character of gerontology central in its organization and content. The authors of the individual chapters are experts in their own fields. Our disciplines include biology, psychology, sociology, anthropology, political science, medicine, nursing, social work, and health education. Despite this diversity of expertise, each author has a keen interest in aging and a serious commitment to understanding how life may be shaped to aid the well-being of older adults.

I imagine that this book will find a variety of uses. I see it as ideal for a multidisciplinary course, but it may also be used as a supplement for a discipline-based course such as the psychology or sociology of aging. There I would expect it to stretch the scope of inquiry. As Allan Bloom noted in his best-seller, *The Closing of the American Mind* (1987) we have all too frequently permitted education to regress to a conglomeration of specialized—and sometimes isolated—information. I hope that this volume, and the field of gerontology more generally, will offer an area of inquiry that stretches the American mind to integrate and synthesize. Whatever its use, I think that the sophistication and clarity of the chapters will make it helpful for audiences at both advanced undergraduate and graduate levels.

The book is organized into four major sections. The two introductory chapters in part I are designed to articulate a "gerontological imagination" and systematically consider the most current demographic information regarding the aging of the American population. Part II articulates the dominant perspectives for the multidisciplinary study of aging. The object under investigation is the same, but the various lenses used in these chapters to view the object embellish our understanding of it. Part III considers the role of older adults in major social institutions. Part IV takes up a number of salient issues related to older adults that are confronting modern societies. Again, a variety of disciplines are brought to bear on these issues, and considerable insight is offered for confronting them in the future.

KENNETH F. FERRARO
West Lafayette, Indiana

FOREWORD TO THE FIRST EDITION

This ambitious book provides a readable introduction to major themes and issues in contemporary gerontology. The organizing concept is "the gerontological imagination," a concept that is intended to suggest the multidisciplinarity of the field and the complementarity of theory and research in the various disciplines with salient interests in human aging. In the gerontological imagination both aging processes and the experience of aging are embedded in and affected by specific social and cultural contexts. Hence, one is not surprised by the observation that people age differently or by the conclusion that some processes of aging and the experience of aging are modifiable. In the gerontological imagination one entertains the possibility of inventing the future of aging, not just discovering what Nature reveals when scientific investigators inquire.

This book is notably free of excessive disciplinary jargon. The chapters on biology and neurogerontology are good illustrations of biology for nonbiologists. The other substantive chapters—on psychology, sociology, and anthropology—are fair summaries of major disciplinary interests in aging. For all chapters the references are current and reasonably comprehensive. The editor's choice of disciplinary applications—families, religion, politics, work and retirement, and long-term care—will appeal to interests of a broad range of readers. So will the editor's choice of illustrative "contemporary issues," which range from minority populations, caregiving, and crime to abuse and death.

Students interested in human aging will be stimulated by this illustration of the gerontological imagination at work.

George L. Maddox
Duke University

ACKNOWLEDGMENTS

Rituals for acknowledging assistance in creating a book generally dictate that one first offer appreciation to colleagues and then thanks to family members, especially a spouse, at the end. I choose to violate this ritual. Although I am indeed grateful to my colleagues, my wife, Linda, has consistently gone beyond expectations in stimulating my work and offering immediate consultation on scholarly or editorial matters. In fact, she *is* one of my finest colleagues—and a great person too. Thanks also to Charisse, Nathan, and Justin for giving me some time on the home computer.

A number of people served as reviewers for individual chapters, providing rich critiques and constructive comments. To begin, many of the contributors consented to read related chapters; this not only helped those chapters but also the integration of the entire volume. In addition, a number of other colleagues rendered thorough critiques; some at my request, others at the contributor's request.

I express my heartfelt appreciation for comments and suggestions on chapters to W. Andrew Achenbaum, Karen Altergott, Russell Buenteo, Dinnie Chao, Janet Cosby, Gary Deimling, James Ellor, Nancy Esker, Anne Foner, T. Neal Garland, Kristen Garner, Linda George, Bert Hayslip, Cary Kart, Randy LaGrange, Laura Laughlin, Wendy Looman, Keryn Maybeck, Catherine McCarthy, Rose Olson, Wilma Phillips, Kimberly Plake, Leonard Poon, Ruth Relos, George Roth, John Rhoads, Matilda White Riley, David Saarnio, Dorothy Schur, William Serow, Jack Spencer, John Stolte, and Aloen Townsend. In addition, I owe a debt of thanks to recent students in my seminar, entitled "Social Gerontology," at Purdue University. Their written comments on various chapters greatly improved the manuscript.

Also, though not directly related to this project, I appreciate the support of the National Institute on Aging (AG11705), which helped me to focus on my research and writing, some of which is presented herein. The research done on changes in the field of gerontology with Su-Rong Chan (chapter 19) was supported by a Special Initiatives Fellowship from the Graduate School of Purdue University.

I thank Evelyn Douthit, Barb Puetz, and Tara Booth for word-processing, graphic, and clerical help. Donita Ames and Ryan Nalepinski handled a myriad of details, including library and clerical work.

Finally, I would like to thank my contributors, who graciously complied when I asked them to revise or shorten their chapters. Cutting or changing the written word is not always done without some ego loss, but I have been graced with a noble lot of contributors.

K. F. F.

CONTRIBUTORS

Victor S. Alpher received the PhD degree from Vanderbilt University and is a consulting psychologist to the Memorial Geriatric Evaluation and Resources Center, Memorial Healthcare System, in Houston. His major interests are attachment, identity, and interpersonal behavior from a life-span perspective.

Charles M. Barresi is Professor Emeritus of Sociology, University of Akron, and resides in Palm Harbor, Florida. Dr. Barresi specializes in social gerontology, urban sociology, and sociological theory. His recent research focuses on aging and ethnicity.

David M. Bass, PhD, is Assistant Director of Research at the Margaret Blenkner Research Center of The Benjamin Rose Institute, Cleveland. He has conducted numerous studies of the effects of chronic illness on aged persons and their family members. Special areas of interest include the utilization and impact of formal services, and social support, the effect of Alzheimer's disease on family members, bereavement, and the organization of long-term care.

Su-Rong Chan received an MS degree in sociology from Purdue University in 1993. She has worked as Director of the Older Adult and Life Enrichment Program at Legend Learning and Family Resource Center in San Jose, California, and is now employed at Sprint.

Sharon A. DeVaney, PhD, is Assistant Professor of Consumer Sciences and Retailing at Purdue University. Her research interests hinge on the economics of aging and health in later life.

Daniel P. Doyle received his PhD from the University of Washington and is Professor of Sociology, University of Montana. Professor Doyle's major interests are criminology and aging.

Ruth E. Dunkle received her PhD and MSW degrees from Syracuse University and is currently Professor and Associate Dean of the School of Social Work, University of Michigan. Her research interests and publications have been in the areas of mental health, language impairment of the elderly, and service utilization for impaired adults.

Anne-Claire I. France received her PhD at Vanderbilt University and is Director of Clinical Information Systems for Memorial HealthNet Providers, Inc., Memorial Healthcare System, Houston. Her major research interests are experimental design and outcome measurement in research on older adult cognitive development and interpersonal behavior.

Christine L. Fry, PhD, is Professor of Anthropology, Loyola University, Chicago. She is the author of numerous articles and chapters on cross-cultural aging, including a book entitled, *The Aging Experience: Diversity and Commonality across Cultures.*

T. Daniel Griffiths, PhD, is Professor of Biological Sciences, Northern Illinois University. His areas of specialization are radiation biology, physiology, molecular biology, and aging. He has received several grants awarded by the Radiation Research Society and the National Cancer Institute.

Cary S. Kart, PhD, is Professor of Sociology, University of Toledo. He is the author of numerous articles and books related to aging and health, including *The Realities of Aging* (Allyn & Bacon).

Charles F. Longino Jr. received his PhD in sociology from the University of North Carolina and is currently Wake Forest Professor of Sociology and Public Health, Wake Forest University. His work on the demography of aging, especially migration among older adults, is widely recognized.

Nancy Kubitz Matheson received the PhD degree in psychology at the University of Akron and is a research analyst at the American Institutes for Research.

Joel S. Milner received his PhD in experimental clinical psychology from Oklahoma State University. At Northern Illinois University he is Professor of Psychology and Coordinator of the Family Violence Research Program. Dr. Milner serves as Associate Editor for the journal *Violence and Victims* and is a member of the National Institute of Mental Health Criminal and Violent Behavior Research Review Committee.

David O. Moberg, PhD, is Professor Emeritus of Sociology, Marquette University. He wrote *Spiritual Well-Being: Background and Issues* for the 1971 White House Conference on Aging and is the author of numerous chapters in books and articles in professional and religious journals on subjects related to religion and aging.

Elizabeth Mutran, PhD, is Associate Professor of Health Education, University of North Carolina, Chapel Hill. She received the Reuben Hill Award from the National Council on Family Relations for her article "Intergenerational Support Activities and Well-Being of the Aged: An Examination of Symbolic Interactionist and Exchange Perspectives," which appeared in *American Sociological Review.*

Linda S. Noelker, PhD, is Associate Director for Research at The Benjamin Rose Institute and Director of the Institute's Margaret Blenkner Research Center, Cleveland. For the past 20 years she has conducted applied aging research on the nature and effects of family care for frail elders and patterns of service use by the elderly. She has published widely on support networks for the elderly, the well-being of family caregivers, predictors of service use, and the nature of social relationships in nursing homes.

Lisa Schwartz Park received the PhD degree in psychology at the University of Akron and is an Executive Development Counselor for K-Mart Corporation.

Donald C. Reitzes received his PhD at Indiana University and is Professor of Sociology, Georgia State University. He specializes in social psychology, sociological theory, and urban studies. He is corecipient, with Elizabeth Mutran, of the Reuben Hill Award from the National Council on Family Relations.

Harvey L. Sterns, PhD, is Professor of Psychology, Director of the Institute of Life Span Development and Gerontology, and chairperson of the PhD program in industrial gerontological psychology at the University of Akron. He is also Research Professor of Gerontology at Northeastern Ohio Universities' College of Medicine and Co-director, Western Reserve Geriatric Education Center. His research and teaching interests include training and retraining, career development, cognitive and motor skills, and aging.

Judith Treas is Professor of Sociology at the University of California, Irvine. She received the PhD degree in sociology at UCLA and is the author of numerous articles on population, aging, family, and inequality.

Susan N. Walker is Professor and Chair of Gerontological, Psychosocial, and Community Health Nursing at the University of Nebraska Medical Center at Omaha. Her areas of specialization include gerontological nursing and health promotion.

James F. Willott, PhD, is Professor of Psychology, Northern Illinois University. He is widely recognized for his research on presbycusis and is currently supported by a MERIT (Method to Extend Research In Time) award from the National Institute on Aging.

PART I

Introduction to Gerontology

Forty is the old age of youth;
fifty is the youth of old age.
—Victor M. Hugo (1802–1885)

Part I addresses two fundamental questions: (1) What common intellectual ground do investigators share when engaged in gerontology, the systematic study of aging? (2) What are the major characteristics of America's older population?

Ferraro addresses the first question in chapter 1 by articulating seven tenets of a gerontological imagination. One of these tenets, that aging involves a series of transitions from birth to death, may be what Victor Hugo had in mind in the quotation above. Treas and Longino describe the aging of American society in chapter 2 by considering demographic data on population growth, life expectancy, migration, and socioeconomic status. Some dramatic changes are on the horizon, and their review also gives valuable insight for planning our future society.

CHAPTER 1

The Gerontological Imagination

Kenneth F. Ferraro

It has been noted by scholars interested in research on aging that gerontology is a field of study that currently lacks a paradigm—that is, a fundamental image of its subject matter, (Achenbaum, 1987, 1995; Maddox, 1987). The lack of a paradigm is not unusual for social sciences, but it is not as common in the physical sciences. As Ritzer (1975) points out, most of the behavioral sciences possess a number of paradigms. In a situation in which there are several paradigms in a field, there is competition and intellectual conflict among scientists as to the fundamental image of the subject of study. Despite considerable divergence within a field characterized as a multiple-paradigm science, there are obviously many unifying concepts, methodologies, and strategies for interpretation. Yet these do not necessarily constitute a shared paradigm.

Whereas gerontology is a multidisciplinary enterprise, special problems arise in the articulation of its fundamental image of aging. The purpose of this chapter is to identify clearly some of the key elements in the conceptual framework utilized in the scientific study of aging. In addition, this chapter seeks to (1) stimulate thought in the field of gerontology toward developing a paradigm within the field and (2) provide the basic ideas and themes that currently guide scientific research on aging.

To approach this task from a different perspective, one might ask, what is a gerontologist? Although many would agree that a gerontologist is a person who engages in the scientific study of aging, our consensus of what constitutes professional education for gerontologists is weak at best. Efforts to standardize curriculum for preparing a gerontologist have been hotly debated. While the Association for Gerontology in Higher Education has been vigorously pursuing the question of developing standards for curriculum and "certification," others have countered that such an endeavor is ill-advised, for a couple of reasons. First, because we do not yet have a paradigm for gerontology, it is unlikely that we can effectively shape educational standards for this field. In other words, the paradigm must precede the education standards. Second, some would argue that there is no such professional role properly labeled "gerontologist." Rather, because gerontology is multidisciplinary and must remain so, what we want to aid is professional development in those primary disciplines—sociology, psychology, nursing, and social work, as examples—with accompanying expertise in gerontology.

I choose to sidestep the issue of whether gerontologists do or should exist in order to focus on the more relevant question in the development of gerontology, specifically *what fundamental image needs to be fostered for anyone studying aging, regardless of his or her professional background or aspirations?* That is, cannot we as biologists, sociologists, health educators, and political scientists find some common ground for our intellectual work? Ideally, we want a set of axioms from which other thoughts and ideas can be developed.

When we think of the possibility of a paradigm for gerontology, we are not implying that all the details of this emerging science are known. Rather, a paradigm describes a *way of thinking* or general organizing principles that map the field. At its broadest level of conceptualization, Ritzer (1975) states, a paradigm serves several functions:

1. It defines what entities are (and are not) the concern of a particular scientific community.
2. It tells the scientist where to look (and where not to look) in order to find the entities of concern to him.
3. It tells the scientist what he can expect to discover when he finds and examines the entities of concern to his field. (p. 5)

Within sociology, my own major discipline, C. Wright Mills (1959) attempted to carve out a way of thinking about social life. His book *The Sociological Imagination* is not an encyclopedia of sociology, but it remains one of the finest treatises on how sociologists think about the social world. In other words, a clearly articulated paradigm is the most efficient way of coming to understand a field. Also, as Kuhn (1962) and Ritzer (1975) point out, a clearly articulated paradigm aids the cumulative development of a science, either by incremental development or by revolution.

Although paradigms may change, the goal here is to articulate an analytic framework for the study of aging *at this time* so that it may be challenged, strengthened, and/or refocused. This effort is purposively integrative. As Boyer (1990) asserts, this type of integrative work emphasizes the need for scholars to give meaning to isolated facts, placing them in perspective. "By integration, we mean making connections across the disciplines, placing the specialties in larger context, illuminating data in a revealing way, often educating nonspecialists, too" (p. 18).

The analytic framework developed here may be described as the *gerontological imagination*. The gerontological imagination is an awareness of the process of human aging that enables one to understand the scientific contributions of a variety of researchers studying aging. In addition, this awareness allows people (not just gerontology scholars) to comprehend the links between biological, behavioral, and social structure factors that influence human aging. It is by definition a multidisciplinary sensitivity to aging that incorporates the common stock of knowledge from the core disciplines engaged in research on aging. The basic elements of a gerontological imagination can be viewed as representative of a culture of scientific thinking on aging. This scientific culture has changed and is continuing to change. Thus, before articulating the premises of the gerontological imagination, it may be helpful to review briefly some of the major developments in this scholarly ethos.

DEVELOPMENT OF GERONTOLOGY AS A SCIENCE

Achenbaum (1987, 1995) traces the foundation of contemporary gerontology to the first three decades of the 20th century, when aging was no longer to be regarded by scientists as simply "senile pathology" but as a "normal" stage of life albeit replete with problems. Leading thinkers of that time, including G. Stanley Hall and John Dewey, challenged researchers in their respective fields to study old age systematically, especially the common *problems* associated with growing older. During those early years it could be argued that the conception of aging as a personal and social problem dominated the images of researchers studying this subject.

Coupled with this "aging as a problem" orientation was an early recognition that the study of aging involved several disciplines, especially medicine, psychology, and sociology. As such, "no single discipline could preempt the fledgling field of gerontology" (Achenbaum, 1987, p. 5). What followed in subsequent decades was a subdivision of gerontology into a few academic specialties while still placing great emphasis on studying the problems of older people. As Achenbaum further notes, the subdivision between the biomedical and social sciences deepened and created a substantial chasm that persists to this day (Achenbaum & Levin, 1989). Countervailing trends of research linking biomedical and social science can be observed today, although they are still relatively rare.

The 1950s and 1960s brought to the fore certain challenges to the "aging as a problem" orientation in gerontology. Although calling it a revolution in the structure of scientific thought on aging seems to inflate the scope of the tension, gerontology's fundamental image of study was to undergo serious change. Cumming and Henry's (1961) controversial, almost inflammatory, theory of disengagement and the Duke longitudinal studies of normal aging focused the debate (Maddox, 1987). At stake was the image of older people and aging per se. What resulted by the 1970s was a reorientation to the study of aging as a *normal* process that entailed so much more than just problems. Surely, human aging poses problems and challenges, but it offers certain advantages to the individual and society (Palmore, 1979). Also with this shift came an emphasis on studying the *process of aging*, not just the characteristics of older people.

The impact of longitudinal studies on our stock of knowledge has been vital to reshaping our image of aging. The 1980s and 1990s were decades in which research based on panel studies or cohort analyses (cross-sequential designs) became more frequent in this booming literature. Also, advances on the methodological front similarly showed that what was often assumed to be an aging effect was, in fact, not. In addition, longitudinal methods and the empirical generalizations based on them anchored gerontology in a *normal-aging paradigm*. Many scholars agree that the normal-aging paradigm is dominant in the 1990s, but there have been criticisms that gerontology is still too heavily shaped by research on Alzheimer's disease—what Adelman (1995) calls the "Alzheimerization of aging." Although studies of disease continue to shape much of the biomedical research, there is at the same time a strong emphasis on normal aging, heterogeneity, and modifiability of aging processes (Maddox, 1987). It is within this context that the elements of a contemporary gerontological imagination grew.

ELEMENTS OF A GERONTOLOGICAL IMAGINATION

I articulate seven key tenets of a gerontological imagination. I reiterate that these are working ideas about our *current* state of knowledge. They may need refocusing or additions as knowledge about aging, especially human aging, continues to accumulate.

Aging and Causality

Aging is not a cause of all age-related phenomena. One of the basic ideas in the study of research methodology is that only certain conclusions can be drawn from certain types of research activities. Readers familiar with the logic of experimental designs will recognize that there are special problems with the conclusion that correlated variables have a causal relationship in one direction or the other. Although the details of that epistemological issue are not relevant for our current concerns, we should be aware that caution should be exercised in interpreting *age-related* phenomena as being *caused* by age.

Within gerontology there is widespread dissatisfaction with the use of age as a causal independent variable. This is especially the case in developmental research. Age is a very important marker of life events, life transitions, social context, and resources, but age in and of itself is an impotent causal variable. Jack Botwinick (1978) has stated this most eloquently:

> Age, as a concept, is synonymous with time, and time in itself cannot affect living function, behavior or otherwise. Time does not "cause" anything; it does not have physical dimensionality to impinge upon the sensorium. . . . Time is a crude index of many events and experiences and it is these indexed events which are "causal." (p. 307)

Even at the biological level, "aging" is an impotent causal variable. It is not the passage of time that causes cellular or organic changes. Consider the classic Hayflick (1965) experiments on normal diploid human cells. Hayflick observed that regardless of the age of the donor, such cells could proliferate in culture only a finite number of times. In other words, it was not aging per se that was related to cell structure and reproduction but the number of passages such cells underwent. Cunningham and Brookbank (1988) sum it up nicely: "the limit on the number of cell doublings in vitro implies that there may be a predetermined life span of cells outside the body that *is independent of changes occurring with time* in the body as a whole" (p. 64; emphasis added).

Another way to consider this issue is that aging frequently gets a bad name for things it did not cause. Professor Willott raises this question in the context of contemporary research on neurogerontology (see chapter 4 of this volume). He notes that aging is often considered a "gremlin" that steals vitality and intellectual power from individuals. However he notes that it is not really the passage of time—aging—that causes various declines in human performance but rather that other processes—biological, neuropsychological, social—are the real explanatory variables in understanding age-related changes. Although many people will continue to conceptualize aging as a gremlin or thief of human vitality and performance, there is now a considerable body of research indicating that this gremlin may be tamed or subdued through interventions of various sorts.

When one is interested in identifying aging effects, one of the first considerations that a good gerontologist raises is the possibility of cohort (or generational) effects that are known to be age-related. (A cohort refers to a set of people born [or experiencing some other event] at the same time.) It may not be growing older per se that brings about differences in the degree of political conservatism in a given society; perhaps the time at which individuals were born is more important in shaping these dispositions. People who experienced the politically formative years of 18 to 27 during the Depression of the 20th century in America are probably going to have a different political and economic outlook than those who experienced those same politically formative years during the times of economic prosperity in the 1950s and 1960s.

Before one jumps to the conclusion that a cohort is a better variable to explain age-related differences, it should be pointed out that cohort in and of itself is similar to aging in that it is limited to marking or indexing events in gerontological research. Knowing when a person was born does not give us a wholly adequate picture of the causal relationships among these variables. However, it indexes certain life events, historical experiences, and cultural forms that are probably the "real" causal agents. In that sense, discerning differences between age, period (sometimes referred to as time of measurement), and cohort effects is vital to our understanding of human aging. However, one should maintain a healthy skepticism about attributions of certain changes in human performance or social relationships to aging.

In summary, age is a useful categorizing variable in age-related differences for any phenomena under study. Such knowledge of age differences is important in the cumulative development of knowledge on a subject. However, knowledge that age is related to certain criteria is not satisfactory in an explanatory scientific enterprise. A gerontological imagination can grow only when there is a healthy skepticism about age as a causal variable.

Aging as a Life Process

Aging is a life process, not a death process. However, aging is related to mortality in several ways, whether in social, psychological, or biological life. Death often gives aging a bad name. Many might regard such a statement as humorous, but it is nonetheless true. It is vitally important to be able to separate death processes from life processes when one is interested in studying the process of aging. In historical perspective the high prevalence of death among older people is a relatively recent trend among "modern" societies. I conceptualize aging as a life process primarily because of the need to distinguish various types of causal effects in age-related research.

An excellent illustration of how death processes may make the aging process look bad derives from the concept of terminal drop. Kleemeier (1962) pioneered this concept by studying the relationship between test performance and survival. He observed declines in test scores of men on several occasions over the course of 12 years; however, what was most striking was that the decline was much greater for those who died after one of the data collection periods than for those who survived during that same interval.

Contemporary gerontologists have come to identify terminal drop (or terminal change) as referring to decrements in social, psychological, or biological functioning that are not functions of time *since birth*—age—but of the amount of time *before death*. Researchers hold that terminal drop indicates that there is a determinant chain of behavioral changes that are really due to a death process (Jarvik, 1975; Riegel & Riegel, 1972). Distinguishing between aging effects and terminal drop is critical for our image of the aging process, especially during the later years. Riegel and Riegel (1972) suggested that if we eliminate people who do not survive at least 5 years after testing from the analysis of age differences, many of the so-called age declines derived from cross-sectional research would disappear (see also Botwinick, 1977; White & Cunningham, 1988).

Thanatology, the study of death and dying, is an intellectual enterprise separate from gerontology. Although it is helpful to be aware of death and dying in the study of aging, we are not primarily interested in those processes. Instead, we are interested in distinguishing between aging and death processes in order to better understand each one.

Aging as Transitions

Aging involves a series of transitions from birth to death, with both advantages and disadvantages. According to Riley (1985), "Aging is a lifelong process of growing up and growing *older* from birth to death, moving through all the strata in society; it is not simply growing *old* beyond some arbitrary point in the life course" (p. 374). As noted earlier, gerontology as a field has changed from just studying older people to studying the process of growing older. Critical to the gerontological imagination is an awareness that aging is a lifelong process involving transitions from birth to death (Elder, 1994). This has come to be widely recognized as a *life span perspective on aging.* Gerontologists who do not use a life span (or a life course) framework are no doubt disadvantaged in their conceptual and empirical endeavors.

Aging in society involves numerous transitions, as others expect certain things of individuals at certain ages. Certain roles must be taken up, while other activities and roles are laid down. Thus, while age, as a variable measured in chronological years, increases at equal intervals, aging, as a life process involving transitions, is not necessarily so linearly smooth. Rather, much of what we know about the life course is at certain seasons of an individual's life, and certain ages play more pivotal roles than others in shaping the individual's biological, psychological, and social life. Turning 16, 21, 50, 65, or 100 all have special meanings in American society, and there are various other ages throughout the world that are similarly recognized as pivotal in the life course. If we are interested in the process of growing older, we would be wise to recognize earlier transitions in a person's life as well as the social context of transitions throughout the life course. Also, the very process of aging varies in sociocultural space and time (Elder, 1994).

As noted earlier, gerontology used to function out of a problem orientation in studying the aging process. Although we recognize that aging poses certain challenges and disadvantages for the individual, it must also be recognized that there are countervailing trends. Specifically, various societies hold special advantages for older adults, although we rarely recognize them in the drone of disadvantages with which we are so often faced. Palmore (1979) has articulated some of the advantages of aging for both society and the individual. Examples for society include more law-abiding behavior, greater political participation, and more voluntary organization participation. Advantages for the individual include, but are not limited to, less criminal victimization, fewer accidents (at home, work, or in motor vehicles), lower tax rates, free services, and reduced costs for a variety of commodities. There are genuine detriments in biological and social-psychological life accompanying the aging process; however, a counterbalance needs to be made in the mind of judicious gerontologists so that we can better understand both the advantages and the disadvantages associated with longevity (Baltes, 1993). Better understanding of these countervailing forces should also help us in mitigating some of the negative effects and accentuating some of the positive ones. A respected gerontologist once remarked to me that, yes, there are numerous biological challenges and detriments associated with growing older but that from another perspective, our bodies are "overbuilt." We have more capacity for activity than we really need or choose to utilize throughout the life course. We will return to this topic later, but suffice it to say that aging is rife with change, but change can be positive or negative for the individual or society.

Aging as Multifaceted Change

Aging involves biological, psychological, social, and spiritual changes in individuals at varying rates. The transitions associated with the life course are not linearly related to chronological age, and the process of aging itself is also multidimensional in nature. As such, the approach to the study of aging must recognize the dynamics of aging and the multidimensionality of this dynamism. Any given discipline interested in the study of aging may base its approach on axioms such as "Humans are 'social creatures'" or "Humans are 'biological creatures.'" The study of gerontology does not preempt such fundamental approaches but must overlay them with the recognition that aging is multidimensional in nature (Marshall, 1994).

Featherman and Petersen (1986) note that there are special problems in attempting to mark or track individual aging. They note that, first, aging is a labile process—one that is liable to change or lapse. Aging entails changes, but not all of these changes are either progressive or detrimental. Second, "aging is a process that reflects duration in state" (p. 342). Thus, although aging is a lifelong process, from birth to death, the transitions identified throughout the life course are held for certain periods of time. In other words, we should be interested in the length of time that individuals occupy certain states or possess certain qualities. According to Featherman and Petersen, recognizing such duration dependence gives us a better sense of the pace of individual aging within the various spheres of human life, whether biological, psychological, social, or spiritual.

Featherman and Petersen (1986) state: "Aging is a process of imbedded dynamisms. Biological and psychosocial aging occur interactively, and the changing organism is involved by a societal and cultural context that also changes, develops, and ages. There are many clocks that time us" (p. 343). Finally, aging is a population process that encompasses interindividual commonalities and differences (p. 343). Or as other sociologists have noted, age stratification is but one of several systems of the stratification of society (Parsons, 1942; Riley, 1985). There are many things about aging that lead us to expect similarities of individuals of the same age, but aging is only one of several distinguishing characteristics of individuals. Gender, race, social class, and religious preference all shape the way in which aging occurs for individuals or groups.

Aging and Heterogeneity

Age is positively associated with heterogeneity in a population. In George Maddox's (1987) Kleemeier lecture, he considers the heterogeneity of older adults one of the fundamental axioms in his study of aging. It is convenient to utilize age as the categorizing variable for analyzing human life, but just because people are the same age does not necessarily mean that they have many things in common. This is especially the case as we consider the life course, because many scholars agree that people become less alike as they grow older. In statistical terms, means of traits may vary over the life course, but standard deviations on such traits will often be larger in the advanced years. Childhood and youth are extremely age-graded times of life. Whereas we all experience various normative life events, the *nonnormative events accumulate over time* and are often quite influential in shaping lives, creating more diversity between individuals.

The fact that older people are a diverse population has led one social scientist to caution investigators about the use of the mean, or average to describe older adults. As Quinn (1987) so aptly states, "The most important characteristic of the aged is their diversity. The average can be very deceptive, because it ignores the tremendous dispersion around it. Beware of the mean" (p. 64).

Empirical illustrations of this phenomenon abound. Maddox (1987) demonstrates this phenomenon in several ways in health research, most recently by studying trajectories of functional impairment in later life. Hayslip and Sterns (1979) examined a number of tests for age differences in crystallized and fluid intelligence and problem solving. Although some differences occurred across the ages, showing older adults with lower levels, the striking finding of their research was that the standard deviations on almost all of the measures examined were much greater for older adults than for younger ones. Methodologically, we should be sensitive to differences in the variance of scores across age groups as well as to differences in mean scores. Current cohorts of older adults are very diverse, and there is little reason to expect that such diversity will shrink in future years.

Aging and Individual Variation in Function

Although there is a tendency toward certain functional declines with aging, there are substantial individual differences in the rate of such declines. In addition, many functional abilities can be strengthened or maintained with intervention. One should not conclude that to age inevitably brings a decline in human structure and function. Willott, Jackson, and Hunter (1987) present evidence that aging does not always lead to a decline in the size of neurons, as is commonly believed. Instead, they found that (1) no inevitable change in neuronal size need occur, and (2) some neurons actually increase in size with aging (see chapter 4 of this volume for more details).

Although the concept of normal aging has gained considerable currency in gerontology, it also has its limitations. It is valuable for distinguishing normal aging from age-related changes that are really pathological in origin. Just as we noted that aging is a life process and that we must distinguish it from death processes, so also we must distinguish aging from disease processes. However, an insightful article by Rowe and Kahn (1987) indicates that "the emphasis on 'normal' aging focuses attention on learning what most older people do and do not do, what physiologic and psychologic states are typical. *It tends to create a gerontology of the usual*" (p. 143; emphasis added). Rowe and Kahn assert that we are ready for a new conceptual distinction to move the field of gerontology. Although they feel that the distinction between aging caused by pathological factors and normal aging is a useful one, they assert that the normal-aging concept is quite broad in and of itself.

Some of the weaknesses in the term "normal aging" include a neglect of (1) heterogeneity among older people undergoing normal aging, (2) the implication of risk or harm associated with normal aging, and (3) what is modifiable within the sphere of normal aging. Therefore, Rowe and Kahn (1987) recommend the division of normal aging into *successful aging* and *usual aging*. They note that there are certain tendencies toward functional declines with aging but that there are individuals who have grown older without such functional declines. They suggest that these individuals might be regarded as aging successfully with regard to the particular trait or characteristic under study. By contrast, people who show typical nonpathological, age-linked losses would be characterized as experiencing usual aging.

I think there are problems with this proposed conceptual distinction; chief among them is that the term *usual* is seen as describing the residual of successful aging. I see this as very problematic; it implies that usual is *not* successful. However, what Rowe and Kahn (1987) should be commended for is the emphasis on heterogeneity in later life, as well as the recognition that many traits can be modified through appropriate interventions. The concept of modifiability is directly linked to the heterogeneity of a population, as Maddox (1987) points out: "Heterogeneity constitutes prime evidence of the modifiability of aging processes and hence the potential for intentional modification of these processes" (p. 562).

Evidence now abounds from research on information processing that older adults can perform well on many intellectual tasks they were previously thought unable to do. Baltes (1993) concluded from an extensive review of research on the aging mind that for some types of cognitive function (i.e., cognitive pragmatics), "there is evidence for stability and positive change in persons who reach old age without specific brain pathology, and who live in favorable circumstances" (p. 580). Other research shows the value of intervention on cognitive functioning, such as in the case of being offered special instructions or coaching. Many of the specifics of such interventions are mentioned in chapter 5 of this volume on the psychology of aging. Suffice it to say that many of the assumptions we have had about performance decrements over the life course are neither pathologically induced nor necessarily "normal." If appropriate interventions can be modeled, many of the so-called declines in psychological and biological functioning can be abated (Baltes, 1993). By Willott's analogy, the gremlin can be slayed, tamed, or at least caged.

Aging and Ageism

There is a propensity toward ageism in modern societies; ageism may also exist among elderly people or those who work with or for elderly people. The paradigm of the gerontological imagination that I am developing here is readily recognized as being dependent on the current social and intellectual climate. Whereas Achenbaum (1987) claims that gerontology should be comparative in nature, it is important to note that societies and social structures have different images of and norms regarding growing older. Several scholars have noted, when comparing societies, a tendency toward ageism in modern societies (Dowd, 1975). Fry probes this question further in chapter 7 of this volume.

A stunning illustration of the problem of ageism in American society, as well as in other modern societies, was offered by Patricia Moore (1985) in a 3-year participant observation study. Moore, a young industrial designer, disguised herself as an older person to experience more fully what it means to be an older person in America. Perhaps the reader will recall the potent revelations of Griffin (1960) in the book *Black Like Me*, an account of a white man who underwent cosmetic changes to make himself look black and then experienced the cultural and social life of a member of a minority group. Just as Griffin staged a racial transition, Moore staged an age transition. With the help of a professional makeup artist, she disguised herself as an older person and traveled throughout the United States and Canada over several years in a variety of settings. She varied the "old" Pat Moore by portraying different levels of social standing: a poor old woman, a middle-class old woman, and a relatively wealthy old woman.

Moore's reflections regarding this experience, described in her book *Disguised* (1985), are most illuminating for understanding ageism in modern societies. She was both loved and hated, welcomed and spat on. Some individuals recognized her situation and in some cases her plight and offered assistance unconditionally. Others found her easy prey for mugging or did not extend common courtesies shown to others. In one situation, she purchased a typewriter ribbon from the same store on 2 consecutive days, but on one day she was the older (senior citizen) Pat and one the young (28-year-old) Pat. She acted identically on both days and even wore the same dress on the two occasions. Mouthing the same words one day and the next, appearing as the "old" Pat Moore and then as the "young" Pat Moore, she received incredibly different reactions from the same clerk. Unfortunately, the clerk was condescending and curt with the "old" Pat but affable and gracious with the "young" Pat.

Lest we think that businesspeople and teenage gangs are the only ones who have ageism in their veins, Pat Moore also visited conferences on aging, where other gerontologists, social scientists, and planners were in attendance. As an "older lady" in the midst of a gerontology conference, she frequently experienced exclusion and neglect! Ageism runs deep, and unfortunately, it reemerged in the late 1980s and 1990s.

People who contact or work on a daily basis with impaired older individuals or those suffering from various forms of disadvantage may be particularly likely to be ageist in their orientations. Such ageism may not turn into discriminatory actions but rather spur kindness and self-sacrifice for the older adult. Clinicians frequently see those with serious problems; thus, the clinical perspective in gerontology can be dangerous if it leads to a mind-set of majoring on the minors.

Older adults are a very diverse population. The majority of older adults in America are relatively healthy, relatively independent, vibrant, and alert. If all we do is work with older adults who do not commonly display these characteristics, we may fail to recognize such diversity within this population. The relatively healthy and independent older adults are the so-called invisible elderly. The ones who receive the most media attention are the more extreme cases, usually the extremely disadvantaged but also, occasionally, the exceptionally successful older adult.

One thing that sociologists have taught us regarding racism, sexism, and ageism is that they are institutionally based phenomena. In other words, social structures may exist that maintain or reinforce ideas and actions based on some form of prejudice or discrimination (Minkler, 1990). Because these phenomena are institutionally based, it is entirely conceivable that members of minority statuses will hold some of the same ideas and may in fact also engage in discriminatory behaviors. Women are often held captive to the vestiges of sexism in society. African and Hispanic Americans may similarly be victims of ideas and actions that devalue their status. It is most unfortunate when these phenomena are internalized by the individuals at whom they are directed so that they exhibit them as well. Ageism may be lodged most deeply in the minds of individuals who are approaching advanced ages. Self-effacing behavior—on the basis of age—by older adults is just one illustration of the depth of the problem.

We expect certain behaviors of individuals at certain ages, and these constrain opportunities in social life. Fortunately, there are some signs that as a society we are becoming more willing to accept asynchronization over the life course. Although age norms are still structured in the very early ages, we are growing more tolerant of people in middle and later life who engage in behaviors atypical for their age.

As I mentioned earlier, however, ageism is unfortunately reappearing in new forms. Gerontologists and activists for older adults often felt that they had made great strides in stemming the tide of ageism in American society through the late 1970s and 1980s. However, one must watch recent developments in social policy to see if ageism is lodged within certain perspectives on social issues. I will mention two examples of the reemergence of ageist ideas that I think deserve attention. I do not assume that ageism is the blatant motivation for these ideas, but I do feel that we should be aware of the possible ageist consequences of these ideas.

First, in the health care arena a rationing perspective is developing that views age as a relevant criterion for dispensing medical care. In his book *Setting Limits: Medical Goals in an Aging Society*, Daniel Callahan (1987) argues that age *should* be a relevant variable in rationing decisions about medical care for older adults. He argues that the federal government should refuse to pay for life-sustaining treatment for citizens past a certain age. He sees old age as time of decline and withdrawal, as well as of lessening "service to the future." The premise on which this perspective rests is that some human lives are more valuable than others and that those lives judged as having lesser value should receive lesser treatment. Although there are important differences in when life-sustaining and life-extending medical care is considered appropriate, why is age singled out as the relevant criterion for rationing medical care? Indeed, findings from the first systematic national survey of public opinion on age-based rationing show that the majority of Americans do not favor withholding life-prolonging medical care on the basis of age (Zweibel, Cassel, & Karrison, 1993). Also at issue is the meaning of advanced age. Are older people, as survivors (who were probably more likely to participate in health promotive behaviors), to be penalized for long life? Instead of viewing advanced age as a problem, entailing insurmountable economic difficulty, the gerontological imagination views the rise in human life expectancy as a tremendous public health success (Butler, 1989).

A second example of potentially ageist policy initiatives can be seen in the activities of Americans for Generational Equity (AGE). This group is attempting to reevaluate the degree of emphasis and the financial commitment toward services and policy supports for older adults (see Fairlie, 1988; Longman, 1987). The questions that Americans for Generational Equity and other like-minded individuals are asking focus on (1) mortgaging our future by entitlement programs to older adults and (2) making sure that each age group in society gets its fair share. They implicitly assert that older Americans are now receiving more than their fair share and explicitly assert that social benefits to older adults must be tempered in the future.

Again, I do not assert that these are purely ageist initiatives, but I do think that they demand our keenest discernment and dialogue. They may not be manifestly ageist, but their consequences probably would be. In some of my own research I find substantial cooperation between generations and beneficence by the younger generation toward their elders (Ferraro, 1989). It may be that a relatively small number of citizens are interested in lighting fires of intergenerational tension, but most American citizens do not desire to reduce spending for programs aimed at older adults (Yankelovich, 1987). Instead, it appears that there are common bonds of interest at stake that make most citizens feel that older adults are a special group deserving of public support (Kingson, Hirshorn, & Cornman, 1986).

A FLUID IMAGINATION

There is no claim to a reified gerontological imagination in this essay; rather, this chapter has attempted to articulate the major tenets of a gerontological imagination. Such an imagination will, of course, undergo change, and that is a healthy process. This book is intended to help shape a gerontological imagination and work toward the definition of a paradigm in the study of aging. I do not feel that a revolution is occurring, but I do think a substantial refocusing may be in order in the field of gerontology. To this end, I welcome challenges or additions to this definition of a gerontological imagination. The intellectual climate for this discussion is vibrant, and the policy issues before us vigorously demand attention. It is hoped that this chapter and this volume will serve to clarify our fundamental image of what aging is and what we can do to enhance the experience of those fortunate enough to grow older.

REFERENCES

Achenbaum, W. A. (1987). Can gerontology be a science? *Journal of Aging Studies*, *1*, 3–18.

Achenbaum, W. A. (1995). *Crossing frontiers: Gerontology emerges as a science.* Cambridge: Cambridge University Press.

Achenbaum, W. A., & Levin, J. S. (1989). What does *gerontology* mean? *Gerontologist*, *29*, 393–400.

Adelman, R. C. (1995). The Alzheimerization of aging. *Gerontologist*, *35*, 526–532.

Baltes, P. B. (1993). The aging mind: Potential and limits. *Gerontologist*, *33*, 580–594.

Botwinick, J. (1977). Intellectual abilities. In J. E. Birren & K. Warner Schaie (Eds.), *Handbook of the psychology of aging* (pp. 580–605). New York: Van Nostrand Reinhold.

Botwinick, J. (1978). *Aging and behavior.* New York: Springer Publishing.

Boyer, E. J. (1990). *Scholarship reconsidered: Priorities of the professoriate.* Princeton, NJ: Carnegie Foundation for the Advancement of Teaching.

Butler, R. N. (1989). Dispelling ageism: The cross-cutting intervention. *Annals of the American Academy of Political and Social Science*, *503*, 138–147.

Callahan, D. (1987). *Setting limits: Medical goals in an aging society.* New York: Simon & Schuster.

Cumming, E., & Henry, W. E. (1961). *Growing old: The process of disengagement.* New York: Basic Books.

Cunningham, W. R., & Brookbank, J. W. (1988). *Gerontology: The psychology, biology and sociology of aging.* New York: Harper & Row.

Dowd, J. (1975). Aging as exchange: A preface to theory. *Journal of Gerontology, 30,* 584–594.

Elder, G. H., Jr. (1994). Time, human agency, and social change: Perspectives on the life course. *Social Psychology Quarterly, 57,* 4–15.

Fairlie, H. (1988). Talkin' 'bout my generation. *New Republic, 198,* 19–22.

Featherman, D. L., & Petersen, T. (1986). Markers of aging: Modeling the clocks that time us. *Research on Aging, 8,* 339–365.

Ferraro, K. F. (1989). The ADEA amendment and public support for older workers. *Research on Aging, 11,* 53–81.

Griffin, J. H. (1960). *Black like me.* New York: Signet.

Hayflick, L. (1965). The limited in vitro lifetime of human diploid cell strains. *Experimental Cell Research, 37,* 614–636.

Hayslip, B., & Sterns, H. L. (1979). Age differences in relationships between crystallized and fluid intelligences and problem solving. *Journal of Gerontology, 34,* 404–414.

Jarvik, L. F. (1975). Thoughts on the psychobiology of aging. *American Psychologist, 30,* 576–583.

Kingson, E. R., Hirshorn, B. A., & Cornman, J. M. (1986). *Ties that bind: The interdependence of generations.* Cabin John, MD: Seven Locks Press.

Kleemeier, R. W. (1962). Intellectual change in the senium. In *Proceedings of the Social Statistics Section of the American Statistical Association* (pp. 290–295).

Kuhn, T. (1962). *The structure of scientific revolutions.* Chicago: University of Chicago Press.

Longman, P. (1987). *Born to pay: The new politics of aging in America.* Boston: Houghton Mifflin.

Maddox, G. L. (1987). Aging differently. *Gerontologist, 27,* 557–564.

Marshall, V. W. (1994). Sociology, psychology, and the theoretical legacy of the Kansas City studies. *Gerontologist, 34,* 768–774.

Mills, C. W. (1959). *The sociological imagination.* London: Oxford University Press.

Minkler, M. (1990). Aging and disability: Behind and beyond the stereotypes. *Journal of Aging Studies, 4,* 246–260.

Moore, P. (1985). *Disguised.* Waco, TX: Word Books.

Palmore, E. (1979). Advantages of aging. *Gerontologist, 19,* 220–223.

Parsons, T. (1942). Age and sex in the social structure of the United States. *American Sociological Review, 7,* 604–616.

Quinn, J. F. (1987). The economic status of the elderly: Beware of the mean. *Review of Income and Wealth, 33,* 63–82.

Riegel, K. F., & Riegel, R. M. (1972). Development, drop, and death. *Developmental Psychology, 6,* 306–319.

Riley, M. W. (1985). Age strata in social systems. In R. H. Binstock & E. Shanas (Eds.), *Handbook of aging and the social sciences* (pp. 369–411). New York: Van Nostrand Reinhold.

Ritzer, G. (1975). *Sociology: A multiple paradigm science.* Boston: Allyn & Bacon.

Rowe, J. W., & Kahn, R. L. (1987). Human aging: Usual and successful. *Science, 237,* 143–149.

White, N., & Cunningham, W. R. (1988). Is terminal drop pervasive or specific? *Journal of Gerontology: Psychological Sciences, 43,* 141–144.

Willott, J. F., Jackson, L. M., & Hunter, K. P. (1987). Morphometric study of the anteroventral cochlear nucleus of two mouse models of presbycusis. *Journal of Comparative Neurology*, *260*, 472–490.

Yankelovich Group, Inc. (1987). *Intergenerational tension in 1987: Real or imagined?* Washington, DC: American Association of Retired Persons.

Zweibel, N. R., Cassel, C. K., & Karrison, T. (1993). Public attitudes about the use of chronological age as a criterion for allocating health care resources. *Gerontologist*, *33*, 74–80.

CHAPTER 2

Demography of Aging in the United States

Judith Treas
Charles F. Longino Jr.

The prime directive of the demography of aging is to provide an understanding of the aging population. There are other mandates given this enterprise, such as answering questions that planners or marketers ask that would help them to accomplish their particular goals. Nonetheless, the questions most often asked of demographers of aging are how many older people are there, where do they live, and what are their characteristics? This task, to provide somehow a picture or image of a whole population, may seem straightforward, but in reality it is very difficult to accomplish. It is difficult because each element of the picture begs for an explanation, suggests a trend, or presupposes an impact on other factors. No simple picture floats to the surface.

HOW BIG IS THE OLDER POPULATION?

Why is it so important to know how big a population is? This knowledge is important because American society and all its social institutions are affected by the elderly population in one way or another. Older Americans are consumers. They are voters. They are homeowners, hospital patients, and family members. Considerable effort is devoted everyday to determining older people's needs, researching their preferences, and looking for new ways to make use of their resources or marshal their contributions. The number of older people is an important component of planning, program development, marketing, and other enterprises.

America's older population is growing and changing. These are demographic developments of tremendous importance in the 20th century. Older people were once a very small share of the U.S. population. Due to falling fertility and longer lives, they have become a major segment of America's population.

The Older Population Is Growing

Strictly speaking, the "age" of a population is defined in terms of the proportion of older people within that population. The definition of the elderly population in terms of chronological age is arbitrary. Everyone "knows" that old age begins in your parent's generation. Yet because full Social Security benefits and other entitlements, such as Medicare coverage, are pegged to age 65, this chronological age is widely used in the United States to identify "the elderly." A convenient way to track the aging of a population is to compare the relative numbers of those aged 65 and over during this century.

In 1995 almost 34 million Americans, having lived past their 65th birthday, accounted for one in eight Americans (Treas, 1995). Because there are so many older Americans, this population has become prominent in local elections, at the doctor's office, at the neighborhood supermarket, and in the family album.

In 1900 there were only 3 million older adults in the U.S.; they accounted for only 1 in 25 Americans (see Table 2.1). The older population's growth is *primarily* due to the surer survival of the increasingly big cohorts of Americans born during the first quarter of this century when birthrates were higher than they are now. The aging of the 19 million foreign-born persons who entered the United States between 1900 and 1930 added to this increase. Most of today's foreign-born elderly immigrated to America long ago as children or young people. Others, coming only recently to join younger family members in the United States, have also contributed to the number of older people in the United States.

The population aged 65 and older quadrupled during the first half of the 20th century. What is less well known is that the older population is not growing as quickly today. This is because a comparatively small generation born during the Great Depression of the 1930s is moving into old age. It is easy to imagine what will happen when the first baby boomers turn 65 in the year 2011. Then the numbers of older Americans will begin to balloon once more. After 2030, the older population's rate of increase will fall markedly, because the smaller baby-bust generation will start to turn 65. By the middle of the 21st century one in five Americans will be older Americans. There will be 80 million people age 65 or older.

The number of older Americans grew more quickly than the overall population between 1900 and 1950. As a consequence the elderly's share of total population went from 4% to 8%. By 1995 those age 65 and older stood at nearly 13% of the U.S. population. Although declining mortality and the aging of ever larger generations account for the numbers who are elderly, their share of the

TABLE 2.1 U.S. Population and Population Age 65 and Older, 1900–2050

	Population in thousands			% increase from preceding decade	
Year	Total	Age 65+	% Age 65+	Total	Age 65+
1900	75,994	3,099	4.1	—	—
1910	91,972	3,986	4.3	21.0	28.6
1920	105,711	4,929	4.7	14.9	23.7
1930	122,755	6,705	5.5	16.1	36.0
1940	131,669	9,031	6.9	7.3	34.7
1950	152,271	12,397	8.1	15.6	37.3
1960	180,671	16,675	9.2	18.7	34.5
1970	205,502	20,107	9.8	13.5	20.6
1980	227,225	25,707	11.3	10.6	27.9
1990	249,415	31,224	12.5	9.8	21.5
Projections					
1995	263,434	33,649	12.8	—	—
2000	276,241	35,322	12.8	10.8	13.1
2010	300,431	40,104	13.3	8.8	13.5
2020	325,942	53,348	16.4	8.5	33.0
2030	349,993	70,175	20.1	7.4	31.5
2040	371,505	77,014	20.7	6.1	9.7
2050	392,031	80,109	20.4	5.5	4.0

Source: U.S. Bureau of the Census, *Historical Statistics of the United States: Colonial Times to 1970* (Washington, DC: GPO, 1975); and *Current Population Reports* P25–1104 (Washington, DC: GPO, 1993), Table 2.

total U.S. population is due largely to fertility trends. Except for the time when the baby boomers were being born (1946–1964), U.S. birthrates have fallen throughout this century. On average, American women have had 2.1 births or less during the last quarter of the century. Such long-run fertility declines enlarge the share of the population in the older ages because there are fewer children born to populate the bottom of the age structure.

The demographic trends of the 20th century are reflected in the population pyramids shown in Figure 2.1. In 1900 the United States had a young population, with relatively few older people. Fertility was high, so each new generation was even bigger than the one before it. As fertility declined and more people lived to see old age, the elderly's share of total population increased. By 1970 a growing elderly population was to be found at the top of the population pyramid. Squeezed in the middle was the small generation born during the Great Depression of the 1930s. The baby boomers, who were between 6 and 24 years of age in 1970, were a bulge at the bottom of the pyramid.

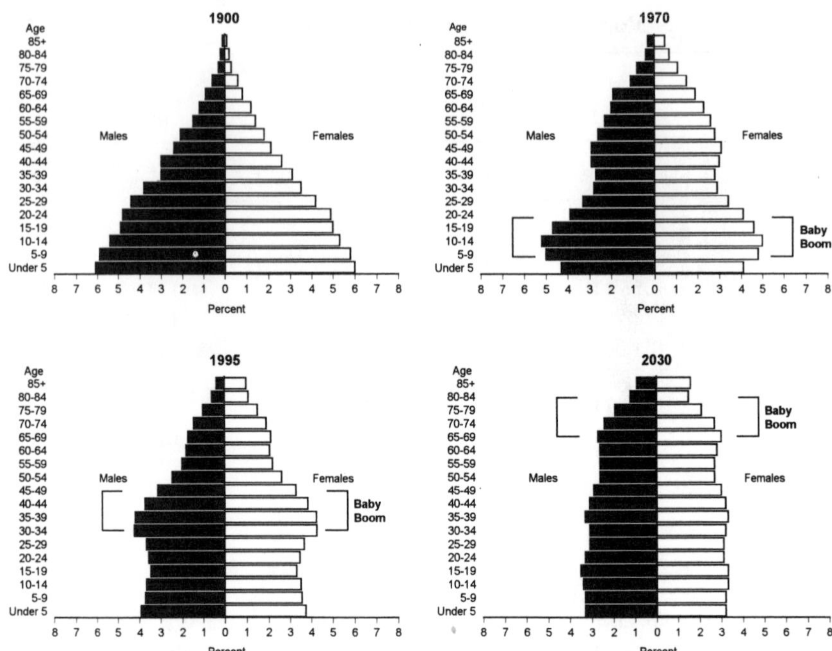

FIGURE 2.1 U.S. Population by age and sex, 1990, 1970, 1995 and 2030. U.S. Bureau of the Census, *Historical Statistics of the United States: Colonial Times to 1970* (Washington, DC: GPO, 1975); and *Current Population Reports* P25-1104 (Washington, DC: GPO, 1993), Table 2.

The baby boomers "younged" the U.S. population temporarily. During the 1970s, however, when falling fertility rates produced the smaller baby-bust cohort, population aging resumed. The median age of the population was 28. By 1995 the baby boomers were a bulge in the middle of the population pyramid, raising the median age of Americans to 34 years (U.S. Bureau of the Census, 1993b, 1994). By the third decade of the 21st century this entire baby-boom generation will have moved into the ranks of the elderly population. The median age of the U.S. population is projected to be almost 39 years by then.

Given the aging of the U.S. population, will our society be able to pay for pensions, finance health care for chronically ill elders, and offer the personal assistance that disabled older adults need in their daily lives? This capacity will depend in good measure on the performance of the economy over the long haul, and economic trends are much harder to forecast than the invariable aging of cohorts who have already been born. No demographer would argue that the ability to support our oldest population depends on the number of elderly people alone. More important is the number of older persons vis-à-vis the number of "working age" taxpayers, breadwinners, and caretakers. The number

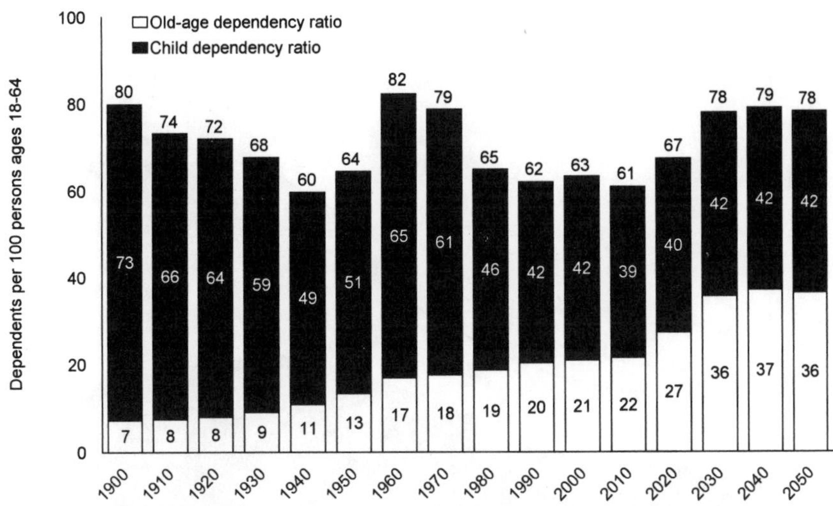

FIGURE 2.2 Child, old age, and total dependency ratios: United States, 1990–2050. Old-age dependency ratio is the number of persons age 65 and older per 100 persons of working age (ages 18–64). Child dependency ratio is the number of children under age 18 per 100 persons of working age (ages 18–64). U.S. Bureau of the Census, *Historical Statistics of the United States: Colonial Times to 1970* (Washington, DC: GPO, 1975); and *Current Population Reports* P25-1104 (Washington, DC: GPO, 1993), Table 2.

of dependent children is also important, as a measure of other needs that must be addressed. The old age dependency ratio—the number of persons age 65 and older per 100 adults ages 18 to 64—nearly tripled between 1900 and 1990, from 7 to 20. Meanwhile, the relative number of children declined (see Figure 2.2). Considering both children and older adults, overall dependency is lower now than it was in the early decades of the 20th century, when fertility was higher. It is lower than in the 1960s and 1970s, when the baby boom was young. Today there are nearly 60 million middle-age baby boomers to support both the young and the old. In the 21st century, when the relative number of elderly dependents starts to rise steeply, generational balance will become a more pressing issue.

The Older Population Is Aging

If the U.S. population is growing older, so too is the older population. In part because of gains in life expectancy at advanced ages, the number of American centenarians more than tripled, to 52,000, between 1980 and 1995; persons 100 years of age and older may reach 1 million by the middle of the 21st century. Because the oldest ages often bring with them chronic illness that interferes with the ability to care for oneself, the aging of the older population implies that the need for health care and supportive social services will increase.

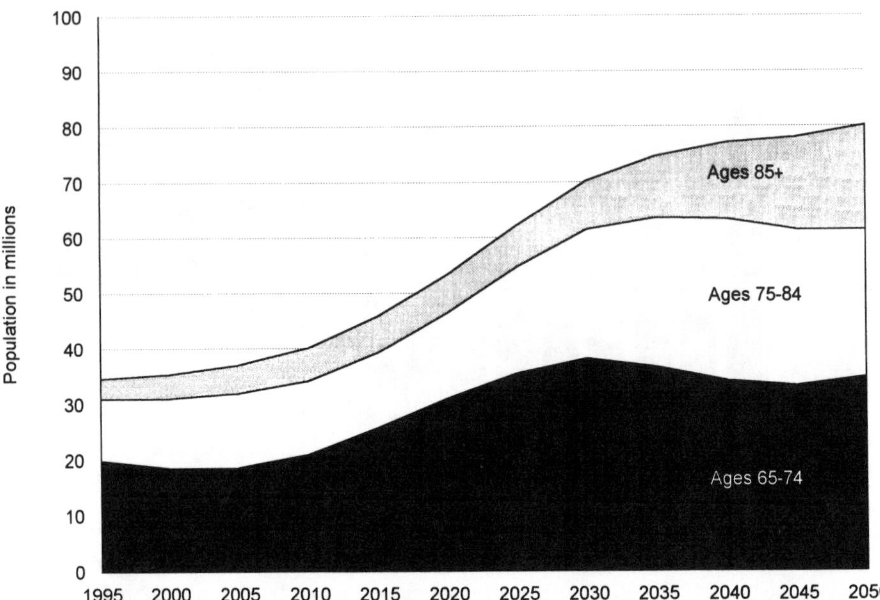

FIGURE 2.3 Projections of the 65+ population by age: United States, 1995–2050. U.S. Bureau of the Census, *Current Population Reports* P25-1104 (Washington, DC: GPO, 1993), Table 2.

It is tempting to assume that if there are twice as many older persons there will be twice as much demand for the things that older persons use. This is a risky assumption, however, because the characteristics of the elderly population are also changing over time. Effective planning, for example, needs to incorporate the very rapid growth of the oldest old, those 85 years of age and older. Already the fastest-growing age group within our entire population, these oldest Americans will pose special planning challenges because per capita hospital and nursing home costs peak at these ages. Indeed, the current influx of the oldest old has already saturated existing nursing home facilities, and the 85 and older population is projected to nearly triple by the year 2020 and nearly double again by 2040. By the middle of the 21st century most of the projected growth of older Americans will occur because of increases in the population aged 85 and older (see Figure 2.3). This boom in the number of oldest old can be explained both by the aging of the baby-boom generation into advanced old age and by the continuing mortality declines at extreme ages that are projected.

Because of the staggered impact of the aging of the baby boom, pressures for societal adaptation will shift quickly from one aspect of planning and policy-making to another. As these large cohorts reach 65, for example, they will have an immediate effect on income transfer programs such as Social Security and private pension funds. Within a few decades, concerns about financing retirement income programs will give way to a new focus on the ability of various health care programs and institutions to absorb an unprecedented number of very old and potentially frail elderly persons.

The Older Population Is Living Longer

When a large birth cohort, such as the baby boom, moves through old age, it can age the population dramatically. But the long-term, steady increase in life expectancy is also behind the aging of the older population. The life expectancy of Americans made extraordinary gains in this century. In 1900 a newborn could expect to live only 47.3 years. By 1993, U.S. life expectancy was 75.5 years—a gain of 28.2 years (see Table 2.2).

High infant and child mortality once depressed overall life expectancy. Eventually, better nutrition, improved sanitation, and medical developments curbed many acute and infectious diseases that once killed the young. The initial gains in life expectancy at birth were due largely to the improved odds of infants reaching adulthood rather than to a greater probability of adults living to see old age. Although infant mortality remains higher than the national average in some localities and among some minority groups, the U.S. rate is low by world standards—8.3 deaths to infants under age 1 per 1,000 births in 1993. Children's crude death rates are also very low—an estimated 30 deaths annually per 100,000 children ages 1 to 14 in 1993. Given so few deaths among infants and children,

TABLE 2.2 Life Expectancy at Birth and at Age 65 by Sex: 1900–1993

	Life expectancy in years					
	At birth			At age 65		
	Total	Male	Female	Total	Male	Female
1900[a]	47.3	46.3	48.3	11.9	11.5	12.2
1950	68.2	65.6	71.1	13.9	12.8	15.0
1960	69.7	66.6	73.1	14.3	12.8	15.8
1970	70.8	67.1	74.7	15.2	13.1	17.0
1980	73.7	70.0	77.4	16.4	14.1	18.3
1990	75.4	71.8	78.8	17.2	15.1	18.9
1993[b]	75.5	72.1	78.9	17.3	15.3	18.9

[a]Based on 10 states and the District of Columbia (Death Registration Area); age 65 data for 1900–1902 period.
[b]Provisional data.
Source: National Center for Health Statistics, *Vital Statistics of the United States, 1989: Volume II, Mortality, Part A* (Washington, DC: GPO, 1993), Table 6-4, and unpublished data.

only small improvements can be expected in the average mortality of U.S. children.

The situation for the elderly population is very different, because most deaths now occur in the older ages. In 1993, 73% of all deaths occurred in persons age 65 and older; 23% occurred in persons age 85 and older. Deaths prevented among the young add more years to remaining life than do older lives that are saved, but declining death rates among the population 65 and older have still become a major cause of the gains in overall life expectancy. Unfortunately, increases in mortality for young adults have worked to offset improvements for the elderly. With HIV now the third leading cause of death among young adults ages 25 to 44, provisional data for 1993 show life expectancy at birth down slightly from 1992.

By permitting Americans to live to older and older ages, long-run mortality declines added to the increase in the older population. The long lives older people enjoy are a surprisingly new development. Half of this century's gains in life expectancy after age 65 occurred since 1960. Just between 1980 and 1991 the population aged 65 and older gained an extra year of life! Further improvements may permit the elderly to reach even older ages. Although a 65-year-old in 1900 could expect to live another 11.9 years, life expectancy at age 65 had risen to 17.3 years by 1993. Even those who lived to age 85 and older averaged 6.0 years of remaining life in 1993.

Chronic Diseases of Old Age Are Now the Leading Killers

An "epidemiological transition" accompanied the increase in life expectancy. Causes of death shifted. Acute and infectious disease of infancy and childhood (e.g., measles or gastrointestinal illnesses) once dominated, but today's major killers are the chronic, degenerative illnesses of old age. The threat posed by infectious disease has been reduced by higher standards of living, improved public health, and medical advances such as antibiotics. In the 19th century, for instance, tuberculosis was the leading cause of death. In the 1990s heart disease, cancer, and strokes are the major killers of Americans; together they make up more than two-thirds of deaths among persons 65 and older (see Table 2.3). Because people often have numerous health problems by the end of life, the aging of the population has led to an increase in the percentage of all deaths attributed to multiple causes. About three-quarters of all deaths can be linked to more than one cause.

Despite the dominance of chronic illness, both new and old infectious diseases constitute a health risk, especially for older Americans whose immune systems are compromised by aging, chronic health problems, organ transplants, chemotherapy, or other factors. In recent decades newspaper headlines have documented the public health threat posed by new infectious diseases (such as AIDS), newly virulent forms of known bacteria (such as Legionnaire's disease), and newly drug-resistant strains of tuberculosis, pneumonia, and other diseases.

TABLE 2.3 Leading Causes of Death for Persons 65 and Older, 1992

Cause	Number of deaths	Percent
All Causes	1,575,214	100.0
Diseases of heart	595,314	37.8
Malignant neoplasms (cancer)	362,060	23.0
Cerebrovascular diseases (stroke)	125,392	8.0
Chronic lung diseases	78,182	5.0
Pneumonia and influenza	67,489	4.3
Diabetes mellitus	37,328	2.4
Unintentional injuries	26,633	1.7
Kidney diseases	18,711	1.2
Atherosclerosis	15,995	1.0
Septicemia	15,884	1.0

Source: National Center for Health Statistics, *Monthly Vital Statistics*, 43, no. 6, Supplement (Dec. 1994), Table 6.

Older people are vulnerable to various infections, not only because of impaired immunity but also because the close quarters of nursing homes and hospitals expose the frail elderly to communicable illnesses.

Women Live Longer than Men

In every region of the world, women live longer than men. In the United States, at every age women have a mortality advantage. In 1993 female life expectancy at birth was 78.9 years. Life expectancy for males was 72.1. Over time, but not recently, this gender gap widened because women's life expectancy rose more quickly than did men's. Only recently has this gender gap begun to show signs of narrowing.

In 1900 women's life expectancy at birth was 48.3 and exceeded men's by 2 years. The widest sex gap was in 1979, when women, on average, lived 7.8 years longer than men. In the 1980s men's life expectancy began to gain on that of women, probably because deaths from heart disease fell significantly for males but not for females (U.S. Bureau of the Census, 1992a). The sex differential was certainly higher in 1993 than it had been at the start of the century, but the gender gap in life expectancy—6.8 years in 1993—had narrowed by a whole year since 1979.

As gender differentials in mortality widened, the sex ratio—the number of men per 100 women—increased. In 1990 there were 67 men for every 100 women in the population 65 and older. With advancing age, death continues to claim more men, and the sex ratio for those 85 and older is only 39 men per 100 women.

The lopsided sex ratio that resulted from women's greater life expectancy affects the lives of the elderly in many ways. When the elderly gather, women predominate in most settings, and it is women who live to experience the problems of very old age. Women are especially vulnerable to widowhood, institutionalization, and late-life poverty. During the 1980s the sex ratio stabilized for older adults. A continued narrowing of the sex gap in mortality would help to equalize the number of men and women in the older population and to mitigate some of the ill effects of a shortfall of older men.

White Americans Live Longer than African Americans

Despite changes in sex differentials in mortality, little progress has been made in narrowing racial gaps in life expectancy. Given racial differences in AIDS and homicide deaths, the mortality differential may even increase in coming years.

Life expectancy has improved for both races, but African Americans continue to display a striking mortality disadvantage compared to Whites. African American men live 8.3 fewer years than White men, on average. African American women can expect to live 5.8 fewer years than White women. Mortality at the younger ages accounts for much of the racial difference in life expectancy. Whether we consider Black babies or young Black males, their death rates are twice those of their White counterparts. By age 65, however, White Americans' advantage has dwindled to about 2 years. In 1993, Black men aged 65 could expect to live another 13.4 years, whereas the figure was 15.4 years for White men of that age. Sixty-five-year-old Black women and White women had an estimated 17.0 and 19.0 remaining years of life, respectively.

At very advanced ages data show a surprising reversal that some demographers call the "Black-White crossover" in mortality. At the oldest ages, African Americans register lower mortality rates than do Whites. Some people have inferred that elderly African Americans, having been exposed to many health risks, must be uniquely fit to survive into their 80s. Other evidence, however, suggests the cause of the crossover is to be found in age misreporting (Elo & Preston, 1994); elderly African Americans appear to exaggerate their age more than do their White counterparts, who more often have official birth certificates to document their age.

Can We Live Longer and Healthier Lives?

Should we reasonably expect life expectancy to continue to rise? Are we apt to live longer than our parents? Will the quality of life in old age be better or worse in the future than it is today? These are big questions, with important implications for individuals who must plan for their futures and public agencies that must plan for the needs of tomorrow's elderly. There are several reasons to expect continued increases in life expectancy, especially at the older ages (Treas, 1995).

1. Compared with other wealthy countries like Japan, life expectancy in the United States falls short. Life expectancy would rise if the United States closed the gap with the several countries that have achieved life expectancies that surpass our own. In 1990 the United States tied for 23rd place in the world in life expectancy at birth for men and ranked 15th for women (National Center for Health Statistics, 1994a). At age 65, the United States ranked 10th for both men and women.

2. Average life expectancy is depressed by the higher mortality of disadvantaged Americans. If all Americans enjoyed the higher life expectancies achieved by advantaged groups in U.S. society, life expectancy would rise. If Blacks had the same mortality rates as Whites, for example, overall U.S. life expectancy would be higher.

3. We can all name many risk factors for life-threatening chronic disease, and we already know how to control them. Most Americans know that smoking, obesity, high blood pressure, and high cholesterol are bad for health. Just reducing these risks via healthier lifestyles and medical treatment would mean later onset of disease and more years of life, especially at older ages. Smoking is an example of a declining risk factor: 42% of Americans 18 and older smoked in 1965, but only 27% were smokers in 1992 (National Center for Health Statistics, 1994b).

Does a longer life expectancy mean more healthy years of life? Or does it mean more years of coping with increasingly serious disabilities? The answer to this question has important implications for public policy and future health costs.

Older Americans reported declines in their health in surveys taken in the 1970s and early 1980s, but factors other than worsening health might have produced increased reporting of health problems. For example, survey respondents may just have become more aware of their health problems because they saw doctors more often and because doctors acquired better tools for diagnosing illness.

Since the late 1980s, however, the health status of the elderly appears to have improved (Crimmins & Ingegneri, 1992; Manton, Corder, & Stallard, 1993). Perhaps expanded knowledge of the causes and treatment of many diseases delayed their onset or slowed their progress. For example, routine screening led to the earlier detection and treatment of cervical cancer, and screening for hypertension prevented many strokes.

The evidence that illness and disability are being delayed among the elderly is relevant to the "compression of morbidity" argument espoused by physician James Fries (1980). According to Fries, the onset of chronic illness will be delayed longer and longer. Fries believes that life expectancy can increase little because it is already close to the 85 years he sees as the biological maximum for the human species. If so, the years of life spent with a chronic health condition would be squeezed between the increasing age for the onset of illness and the fixed age of death. Illness and disability would be limited to a brief period before death. The idea of a biological limit points out that health deteriorates in old age because of two processes—age-related diseases and aging itself. Even in the absence of chronic disease, death is a certainty because immunity, organ function, and the body's adaptive capacity eventually falls to a level that cannot sustain life.

But what is the maximum number of years humans can live? What is the likely upper limit for average life expectancy in a population? Continuing gains in life expectancy have led many to question maximum life spans previously taken for granted. According to the Census Bureau, more than 50,000 Americans were 100 years or older in 1995. There have been documented cases of individuals living as long as 120 years, although such individuals may have extraordinary and unique genetic endowments not shared by the rest of us. Assuming the human species' life span is 110 or 120 years, our present life expectancy is not apt to run into a biological limit to life in the near future. It remains to be seen whether the process of aging itself can be slowed. Some scientific developments suggest that the "maximum" life span itself can be extended. Limiting calorie intake, for example, prolongs the life of laboratory mice, and long-lived fruit flies can be created with selective breeding. Given cumulating evidence about the mechanisms of aging at the systemic, cellular, and genetic levels, the middle of the 21st century may see markedly higher life expectancies as scientific advances lead to more complete understanding of complex aging processes (Rusting, 1992).

WHERE DO OLDER PEOPLE LIVE?

Although older Americans do not differ much from younger Americans in terms of where they live, some places develop reputations as havens for older people (see Figure 2.4). Florida, where 18% of the population was 65 or older in 1990, is a clear example of a state that has aged by virtue of attracting older retirees. Other states (e.g., Iowa) have relatively high shares of the older population because younger people have moved elsewhere, leaving behind the state's older residents. A few states are distinguished by the low percentage of elderly in their population. Only 4% of Alaska's population is elderly, for example, because so many of the state's residents are newcomers, who tend to be younger. Utah, where 9% are 65 or older, has not only young newcomers but also unusually high fertility rates.

During the 1980s the number of elderly increased in all 50 states despite the fact that some local areas saw a decline. These increases were to be expected given the large generation of adults who crossed the threshold of old age during the 1980s. After retirement, most adults remain in their own homes or communities, a pattern demographers call "aging in place." This pattern accounted for most of the increase in the elderly in state and local areas.

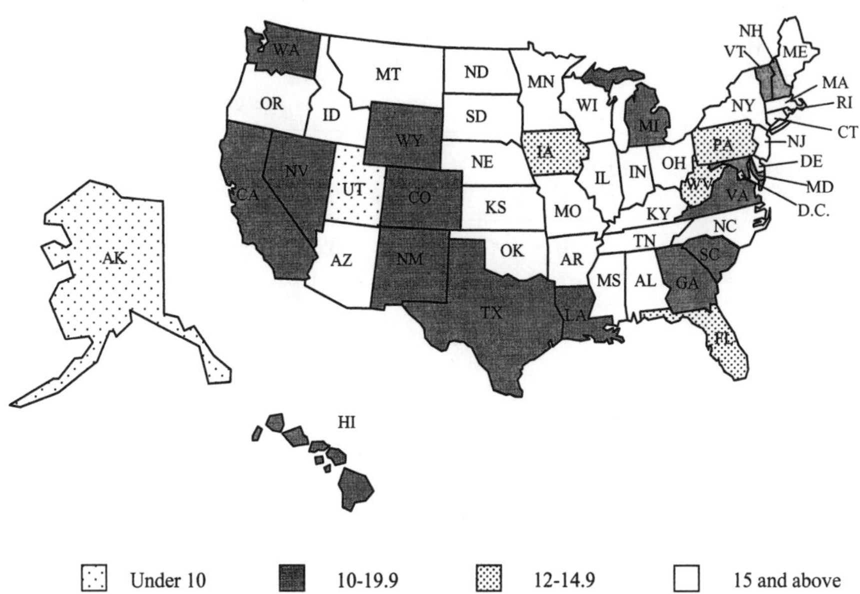

FIGURE 2.4 Percentage of population 65 and older, by state: 1990. U.S. Bureau of the Census, 1990 Census of Population, *General Population Characteristics, United States Summary* (Washington, DC: GPO, 1993), Table 251.

Compared to younger people, older people are less likely to move to a new home or community. In March 1994, 19% of Americans ages 20 to 64 reported moving in the past year, but only 6% of those age 65 and older had made such a move. The elderly have a strong commitment to their current neighborhood that means fewer want to move, and they are not likely to have to move on account of a job. Relocating involves physical, financial, and emotional demands that poor or frail elderly may not be able to meet.

Over half of the moves made by the elderly are within the same county (see Table 2.4). Age-related changes in housing needs often account for short-distance moves. Such movers seek out housing that is closer to family and services, more affordable, scaled to their smaller household size, and less trouble to maintain. Some moves are to nursing homes or into the homes of relatives.

When They Move Out, Where Do They Go?

Only a small minority of retirement-age persons move. The census asks where persons lived 5 years earlier. About three-quarters of older persons lived in the same house 5 years earlier. The proportion who moved long distances, indicating that they lived in a different state 5 years earlier, has held nearly steady at about 4% in the past four censuses. Having a stable trend that reaches back over four decades encourages one to expect the same in the future.

TABLE 2.4 Geographic Mobility of Elderly and Nonelderly Americans, March 1993 to March 1994

	Percentage of age group				
Type of move	Under age 65	Age 65+	Ages 65–74	Ages 75–84	Ages 85+
Total	100.0	100.0	100.0	100.0	100.0
Nonmovers	81.7	94.4	94.0	95.1	94.2
Movers	18.3	5.6	6.0	4.9	5.8
Same county	11.4	3.2	3.3	2.9	3.4
Different country, same state	3.5	1.1	1.2	0.9	1.0
Different state	2.8	1.2	1.3	1.0	1.2
From abroad	0.5	0.1	0.1	0.1	0.1

Source: Population Reference Bureau analysis of the March 1994 Current Population Survey.

Interstate migration may have been only half as common in the population over age 60 (4.5%) as in the general American population (9.4%) between 1985 and 1990, but retirement migration is much more channeled in the elderly. Retirees move in greater proportions to fewer states than do migrants of all ages; thus, metaphorically, they dig deeper channels. From 1985 to 1990, 58% of older migrants moved to only 10 states, 43% to only 5. Retirement migration is not of much consequence in most states, but in some it is a major industry (Longino, 1995).

When comparing the rankings of states over the four census decades, however, the underlying trend is one of a gradual dechanneling of retirement migration—that is, a gradual decrease in the share of migrants received by the major destination states, a gentle spreading out of the flows. Dechanneling is good news for all of those states that are not already on the top of the list of destinations if they are interested in attracting retirees. Planners seeking out migrant concentrations would not notice the changes at all because there were more than a quarter million more interstate migrants over age 60 in 1990 than in 1980.

The consolidation of the Sunbelt as a retirement region can be seen in these rankings. In 1960 there were 6 northern states and 4 sunbelt states among the top 10 receiving states. In the latest census there were two northern states, Pennsylvania and New Jersey, and seven Sunbelt states (see Table 2.5). But even though the Sunbelt is still the region of preference for migrants, within the region, the winds of change are blowing.

TABLE 2.5 Ten States Receiving Most In-Migrants Age 60+ in 5-Year Periods Ending in 1960, 1970, 1980, and 1990

	1960			1970			1980			1990		
Rank	State	No.	%	State	No.	%	State	No.	%	State	No.	%
1	FL	208,072	22.3	FL	263,200	24.4	FL	437,040	26.3	FL	451,709	23.8
2	CA	126,883	13.6	CA	107,000	9.9	CA	144,880	8.7	CA	131,514	6.9
3	NJ	36,019	3.9	AZ	47,600	4.4	AZ	94,600	5.7	AZ	98,756	5.2
4	NY	33,794	3.6	NJ	46,000	4.3	TX	78,480	4.7	TX	78,117	4.1
5	IL	30,355	3.3	TX	39,800	3.7	NJ	49,400	3.0	NC	64,530	3.4
6	AZ	29,571	3.2	NY	32,800	3.0	PA	39,520	2.4	PA	57,538	3.0
7	OH	27,759	3.0	OH	32,300	3.0	NC	39,400	2.4	NJ	49,176	2.6
8	TX	26,770	2.9	IL	28,800	2.7	WA	35,760	2.2	WA	47,484	2.5
9	PA	25,738	2.8	PA	28,600	2.7	IL	35,720	2.1	VA	46,554	2.4
10	MI	20,308	2.0	MO	25,300	2.3	NY	34,920	2.1	GA	44,475	2.3
Total interstate migrants		931,012			1,079,200[a]			1,622,120[b]			1,901,105	
% of total in top 10 states			60.7			60.4			59.5			56.3

[a]This figure was derived by extrapolating from a 1-in-100 sample. The actual census count was 1,094,014.
[b]This figure was derived by extrapolating from a 1-in-40 sample. The actual census count was 1,654,000.
Source: U.S. Bureau of the Census.

When They Move In, Where Do They Come From?

Each retiree who enters one state leaves another. The 1990 census data show a changing pattern of retiree out-migration as well. It is generally assumed that the major origin states are all in the "rust belt." That is not so. In fact, in 1990 fewer migrants were leaving New York, Illinois, and Ohio than in 1980. And surprisingly, some Sunbelt states were climbing rapidly to the top of the list of *sending* states. California increased its share of out-migrants to other states in 1990, and Florida moved from fourth rank in 1980 to third in 1990 (see Table 2.6).

When the counties of origin are considered, it turns out that retirement out-migration is primarily a metropolitan phenomenon. The leading origin counties nearly all contain cities or suburbs. City people may be less rooted than small town and rural people and therefore more capable of a major relocation in retirement. Further, many people move to large cities when they are young because economic opportunities are greater there, making retirement moves more affordable later.

TABLE 2.6 Ten States Sending Most Out-Migrants Age 60+ in 5-Year Periods Ending in 1970, 1980, and 1990

	1970			1980			1990		
Rank	State	No.	%	State	No.	%	State	No.	%
1	NY	154,300	14.3	NY	242,960	14.6	NY	222,781	11.7
2	IL	86,600	8.0	CA	141,440	8.5	CA	187,240	9.8
3	CA	74,400	6.9	IL	120,160	7.2	FL	128,561	6.8
4	(Tie) OH	53,400	4.9	FL	92,280	5.6	IL	107,136	5.6
5	(Tie) PA	53,400	4.9	NJ	86,880	5.2	NJ	106,556	5.6
6	MI	52,400	4.9	OH	85,760	5.2	PA	78,903	4.2
7	NJ	50,100	4.6	PA	81,280	4.9	MI	74,661	3.9
8	FL	46,000	4.3	MI	72,040	4.3	OH	74,271	3.9
9	TX	30,300	2.8	MA	47,000	2.8	TX	69,856	3.7
10	IN	29,200	2.7	IN	39,440	2.4	MA	56,737	3.0
Total interstate migrants		1,079,200			1,662,120			1,901,105	
% of total in top 10 states			58.4			60.7			58.2

Source: U.S. Bureau of the Census.

How Much Does Migration Affect the Size of the Older Population?

The percentage of older people increased in all 50 states during the 1980s. Where older people live and move is a factor determining older residents' share of a state's population, but the number of births and the geographic distribution and redistribution of younger Americans is also important. In the midwestern farming states, for example, the percentage of elderly residents increased during the 1980s, in part because many young people moved to other states that offered better employment prospects. The migration of working-age people affects age concentrations more than elderly migration does. There are, after all, more young people, and the young are much more likely to move than are the old. Between 1993 and 1994, nearly 1 in 5 working-age adults (20 to 64 years) moved to a new residence; only 1 in 18 elderly adults moved.

In the 1960s, 1970s, and 1980s both younger and older adults moved away from the older industrial cities of the North. Elderly persons were usually making a retirement move to smaller cities in the Sunbelt or nonmetropolitan areas in the West. The in-migration of seniors did not necessarily cause additional aging in their destination communities, because young adults also moved to these places during the 1970s. However, the young and old went their separate ways in the 1980s. The Sunbelt's larger metropolitan areas, where jobs were plentiful, attracted younger movers. In 1990 seniors were slightly less likely than younger people to live in a metropolitan area (74% vs. 78%).

CHARACTERISTICS OF THE OLDER POPULATION

Population processes are important for understanding the aging of America, but they offer only a skeletal vision of the future. This is because changes in numbers per se do not translate easily and directly into a forecast of total needs or resources. The characteristics of the population change over time, and their mix is constantly in flux. Only the very naive would infer an *x*% increase in units of long-term care service from a comparable percentage of increase in the number of very old persons. Diversity within the older population, both present and future, proves the undoing of such simple logic. Contrary to popular stereotypes, not all of the elderly population, not even the oldest part, are socially, physically, or economically dependent. Indeed, with increasing age, there is increasing variance within a "normal" range.

Keeping the high level of diversity in mind while creating a coherent image of the older population is not easy to do. General descriptions tend to paint a population profile that is essentially a caricature. In reality, there is no "typical" older person. The more populations age, the greater the characteristics of the members diverge. As discussed in chapter 1, there is more diversity in the older population than in a middle-aged or younger one. Subsequent chapters will highlight elements of this diversity; a brief overview of the characteristics of the older population is presented here.

Ethnic Diversity

One example of the diversity among the older population is seen in its racial and ethnic composition. Like the U.S. population as a whole, the older population is becoming more ethnically and racially diverse. Because of higher birthrates and immigration rates for ethnic and racial minority groups, Asian, African American, and Hispanic populations are increasing more rapidly than the non-Hispanic White population. In 1980 non-Hispanic Whites constituted about 80% of the total U.S. population, but this share dropped to 74% by 1995. The numbers of minority elderly are also growing more rapidly than those of non-Hispanic Whites. Between 1980 and 1995, non-Hispanic Whites' share of the older population slipped from 88% to 85%. The pace of diversification will speed up in coming decades. By 2050, only 67% of the elderly population is projected to be non-Hispanic White (see Figure 2.5).

The ethnic composition of the elderly minority population will change dramatically. Whereas African and Native Americans will gradually increase their

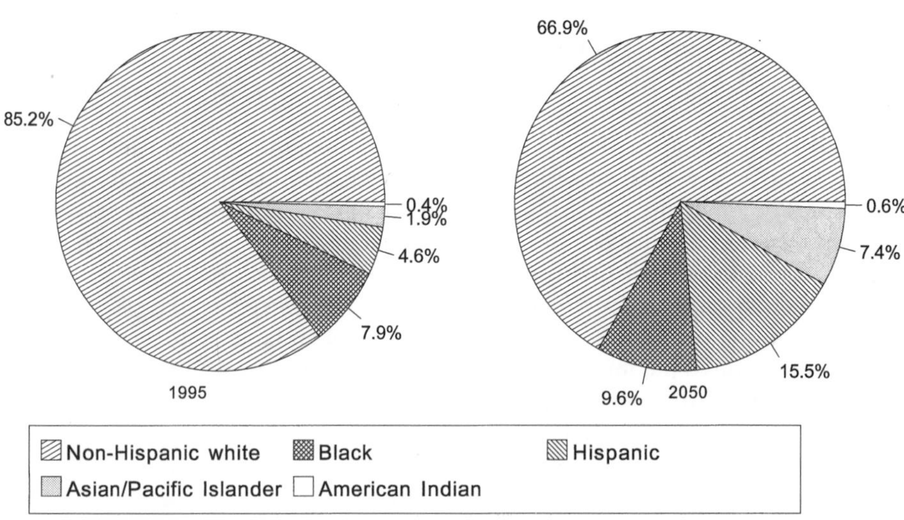

FIGURE 2.5 U.S. elderly population by race/ethnicity, 1995 and 2050. U.S. Bureau of the Census, *Current Population Reports* P25-1104 (Washington, DC: GPO, 1993), Table 2.

shares of population, Hispanics and Asians and Pacific Islanders are expected to see the most growth. In 1995 African Americans, who made up 8% of the 65-and-older population, were the largest minority group; however, there may be more Hispanic elderly than African American elderly before 2020. Assuming continued patterns of immigration and fertility, one in six Americans age 65 and older is expected to be Hispanic by the middle of the 21st century. Similarly, Asians and Pacific Islanders are expected to grow from 2% of older Americans in 1995 to 7% in 2050.

In keeping with this greater ethnic diversity, tacos lunches, tai chi exercise classes, and Vietnamese newspapers are the staple at more and more senior centers. Typically, minority seniors have relied more on family members and used fewer formal services and less nursing home care than have other older Americans. As the number of elderly minorities grow, however, programs and services for the elderly population will have to change even more to accommodate their needs, values, and preferences. Minority seniors tend to be less educated, they have lower incomes and fewer assets, and they are less likely to own their own homes. Elderly immigrants often speak little or no English. The diets and health practices of their cultures are strong influences. The health needs of minority seniors are also unique; for example, because African Americans are at risk for high blood pressure, they benefit more from medical screening to determine who needs medication or lifestyle changes to control the disease.

Because the younger population is more diverse than the elderly population, some people have voiced concerns that the increasingly diverse population of younger taxpayers may come to feel less responsibility for the support of pensioners who are mostly non-Hispanic Whites. In 1995, 72% of the population under age 65 was non-Hispanic White. By 2050, however, the under-65 population will be only 49% non-Hispanic White; nearly one-fourth will be Hispanic; 16%, African American; and 10%, Asian. These younger generations will eventually grow older. Their "aging in race" will have the same effect on ethnic groups that "aging in place" has on neighborhoods. Thus, the ethnic diversity of the young will eventually be reflected in the total elderly population.

International Migration Contributes to Diversity

To see how immigration is affecting the U.S. population, visit America's biggest cities—particularly port cities such as Greater New York City, Chicago, New Orleans, Los Angeles, and San Francisco—and the states that border Mexico. Immigration has been a cause of ethnic change. It adds to numbers and diversity through two processes. First and most important, there is the aging of immigrants who entered the United States long ago as children or working-age adults. Second, there is the more recent arrival of elderly immigrants.

Because people who immigrate are typically young, immigration adds to the middle of the population age structure and slows population aging. This "younging" effect is dampened by the loss of an estimated 150,000 to 200,000 persons who emigrate from the United States to other countries each year (Martin & Midgley, 1994). If immigration does not continue, the younging effect is only temporary. Immigrants eventually grow old and ultimately add to the ranks of the elderly population.

One-tenth of the U.S. population age 65 and older is foreign-born. The share is larger in states that have been leading destinations for immigrants. For example, the foreign-born constitute about one-fifth of the older populations of California, New York, and Hawaii. Most foreign-born elderly Americans are not recent arrivals but rather immigrated when they were young; more than half entered the United States before 1950. In 1990, however, 10% of foreign-born persons age 65 and older were newcomers who entered the United States during the 1980s. These newcomers are part of the reason that more than 1 million older people say they are unable to speak English very well.

Why do older people move to the United States at an age when most of their counterparts are content to "age in place"? Nearly one-fourth (23%) of legal immigrants age 65 or older who were admitted in 1993 were refugees fleeing war and persecution. However, most older people who immigrated came just to be closer to family members already living in the United States. Of older people admitted to permanent U.S. residence in 1991, more than two of three gained entry as the parents of U.S. citizens, an admission category that was not subject to direct numerical limitation under U.S. immigration law.

Elderly newcomers differ in many ways from the foreign-born individuals who have lived in the United States for many decades (Treas, 1995). They are younger. They are not as likely to speak English. They are more likely to come from Asia and Latin America than from Europe. Of the 40,000 persons age 65 and older who were granted permanent residency in 1993, more than half were born in Asia or the Pacific region. In fact, the only European birthplace reported by many older immigrants in 1993 was the Soviet Union (see Table 2.7). When the former Soviet Union eased immigration restrictions in the face of economic hardship and the end of communism, it stimulated a surge of refugees in the early 1990s, but this flow is likely to taper off.

When elderly immigrants enter the United States, they seldom have pensions or other regular income. They must either depend on their kin or seek public assistance. More than one-quarter of the elderly immigrants who entered the United States since 1980 received welfare in 1989, compared with about 7% of U.S.-born elderly (Fix & Passel, 1994). In 1992, more than 400,000 legal aliens age 65 and older received Supplemental Security Income (SSI), the federal assistance program for the aged, blind, and disabled (Scott, 1993). Most noncitizens except refugees are already prevented from receiving public assistance for 5 years after entering the United States, but the rapid increase in immigrant SSI recipients has prompted Congress to tighten up on SSI eligibility for aliens. Because most elderly legal aliens have no other income and very poor

TABLE 2.7 Countries of Birth for Elderly Immigrants Admitted in 1993

Country	Immigrants (in 1,000s)	%
All countries	39.8	100.0
Former Soviet Union	7.0	17.5
Philippines	4.7	11.9
China	4.3	10.7
India	2.2	5.6
Mexico	2.2	5.6
Vietnam	2.1	5.4
Iran	1.9	4.7
Cuba	1.5	3.9
Dominican Republic	1.0	2.6
South Korea	0.8	2.1
Other	12.1	30.0

Source: Immigration and Naturalization Service, *1993 Statistical Yearbook of the Immigration and Naturalization Service* (Washington, DC: GPO, 1994), Table 13.

employment prospects, eliminating federal benefits is likely to shift more responsibility for the support of destitute elderly newcomers to state and local agencies. The impact of greater local responsibility for older immigrants will weigh most heavily on the states with the most elderly immigrants, such as California, Hawaii, and Florida.

ROLES AND RESOURCES ARE DIVERSE

At one time, the popular stereotype of the elderly population was so benignly negative that it came as a surprise to most when the affluent, healthy, powerful, and productive received more media attention in the last decade. Today the diversity is much more visible and recognized. Large segments of the elderly population have very positive characteristics.

Most older Americans entered the 1990s in relatively fortunate circumstances. This generation of older adults can count on education, income, and assets unknown to earlier cohorts. Their well-being is due in part to 60 years of Social Security and 30 years of Medicare. Addressing their special needs are many public and private organizations, institutions, programs, and products inconceivable in their grandparents' day. Looking toward old age, most Americans can anticipate independence, leisure, opportunities for rewarding and productive activity, dignity, and a decent standard of living. Given the diversity of the older population, however, it is not surprising to learn that some older Americans confront loneliness, poverty, and poor health.

Economic Well-Being Has Risen

Today's older Americans enjoy a living standard that is unprecedented. The economic position of the most recent cohort of elderly persons reflects its historical advantages—employment when wage growth was strong, expansion of Social Security and private pensions, the introduction of Medicare, the spread of home ownership, and periods of inflation that swelled home equity. Contrast their situation to that of their grandparents, who had the benefit of neither government old-age programs nor the postwar prosperity that permitted today's seniors to buy their own homes and to put aside money for their old age.

A variety of income sources underpin the economic security of older people today. Social Security accounts for two of every five dollars older Americans receive (see Figure 2.6). Employer pensions and income from assets, savings, and investments make up another two dollars out of the five going, on average, to older individuals. Although only a minority of older people still collect paychecks, earnings are an important income source for those who are working.

The government's role in making up for income lost at retirement is crucial. If Social Security and other government payments were to vanish tomorrow, the

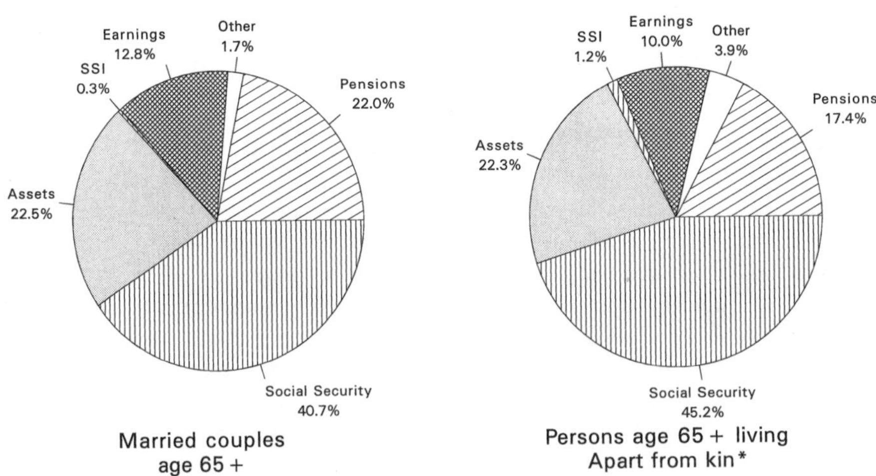

FIGURE 2.6 Sources of income for the U.S. elderly population, 1992. *Includes people living alone or with unrelated individuals. U.S. House of Representatives, Committee on Ways and Means, *1994 Green Book* (Washington, DC: GPO, 1994), 864–865.

poverty rate for the elderly population would be four times higher than its current rate (U.S. Bureau of the Census, 1993a). Half of all Americans age 65 and older would live in poverty. Government noncash benefits also improved the economic welfare of older people. About 5% of the elderly population resided in subsidized or public housing in 1993, and 5% lived in a household receiving food stamps (Treas, 1995). Virtually every older person gets significant health insurance from Medicare at little or no cost.

Special laws reduce the tax burden on older people. As a consequence, 46% of the elderly population owed no federal taxes in 1993 (U.S. House of Representatives, 1993). For example, Social Security income is exempt, in whole or part, from federal taxes. Persons age 65 and older (who do not itemize) get to claim an extra standard deduction. State taxes also favor the elderly population. Some programs allow elderly homeowners to defer property taxes until after they sell their homes or die.

Some Seniors Are Still Needy

Once again, one must be careful not to characterize the older population by only the positive trends. Despite various public provisions for seniors, not all Americans fare well in their later years. Most older people see their incomes reduced by one-third or one-half when they quit working. Retirees, who no longer have employment-related expenses, can usually get by on less income than during their working years, but a big drop in income at retirement leaves some people poor. For those who earned low wages throughout their working years, Social Security retirement income is no guarantee against poverty in old age because the amount of Social Security benefits depends on previous earnings.

Individuals who fail to qualify for adequate public and private retirement benefits typically wind up poor. Although some older people are eligible for public assistance, these benefits do not necessarily raise recipients' incomes above the poverty line. Because the federal Supplemental Security Income (SSI) benefit for the poorest elderly individuals is only 75% of the poverty line and SSI for older couples is only 90% of poverty (U.S. House of Representatives, 1994), state programs usually supplement federal payments to the low-income elderly.

Compared to younger Americans, older Americans fare reasonably well. The 1993 poverty rate for children under age 18 (23%) was much higher than that of the elderly population. The rate for working-age adults (ages 18–64) was the same as for seniors—12% (U.S. Bureau of the Census, 1995). The elderly population may not seem particularly disadvantaged compared with other adults, but younger people tend to move out of poverty as their job and family situations change. Older people may be less likely to become poor, but once poor, they are more apt to remain poor. There are few ways out of poverty in later life for people who are too old to get a job or establish new relations of economic support with others.

Older Americans should not be characterized as affluent, nor are they poor. They are both. An elderly poverty population exists, but so does a sizable segment of very affluent seniors and an even larger group that is comfortably middle-income. These well-off elderly are courted by those who sell financial services, luxury goods, and a host of other products. There is, however, even greater income inequality among the older population than among the young because advantages and disadvantages have accumulated over a lifetime, sometimes exacerbated by catastrophic contingencies of later life (Holden & Smeeding, 1990). (For additional information on the economic status of the older adult population, see chapter 14).

Educational Level Is Rising Among the Elderly

At one time, older people were at a real educational disadvantage compared to the young. Today, however, America's young-old—those aged 65 to 74—are the best-educated generation of seniors ever. Two-thirds finished high school, contrasted with just over half of those age 75 or older. Future generations of older Americans will fare even better (see Figure 2.7). Despite this upward trend in educational attainment, some older people did not receive the schooling that would enable them to cope readily with day-to-day situations that require literacy. Four percent had fewer than 5 years of schooling in 1994; this is less

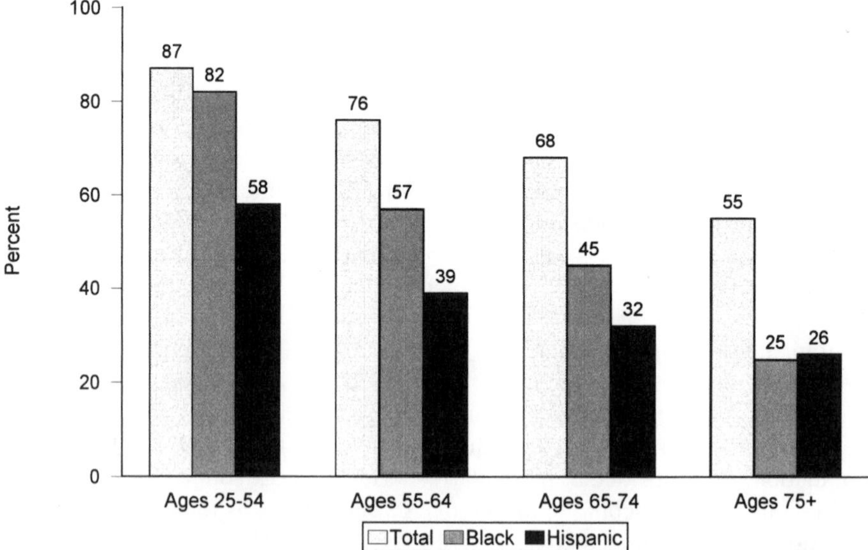

FIGURE 2.7 Percentage with 4 years of high school or more by age and race/ethnicity: United States, 1994. *Note*: Persons of Hispanic origin may be of any race. Population Reference Bureau analysis of the March 1994 Current Population Survey.

schooling than is generally necessary to read an insurance policy, a product-warning label, or the daily newspaper. Basic literacy is a particularly serious problem for the Hispanic elderly (27% of whom have fewer than 5 years of schooling) and for their African American counterparts (12% with less than 5 years of schooling).

The rising educational attainments of the elderly population have been a very positive development because people with more education are at an advantage in many different ways (Treas, 1995). Even taking account of their higher incomes, people with more education have fewer disabilities, avoid the early onset of chronic disease, and enjoy lower death rates. It is likely that better-educated seniors have greater access to information about how to promote health, how to recognize illness, and how to get treatment. Schooling shapes lifestyle preferences, too. Every year tens of thousands of well-educated seniors attend "Emeriti College" courses across the United States and have made some college towns, with their libraries and varied cultural activities, popular retirement communities.

Not All Older People Are Permanently Retired

Not all older Americans favor leisure activities over paid work. Over 3.8 million persons age 65 and older were either working or looking for work in 1994. These older working Americans represented 12% of all older noninstitutionalized Americans. Those most likely to be working are elderly men who are still relatively young: nearly 1 in 4 men aged 65 to 69 but only 1 in 18 men aged 75 or older were in the labor force in 1994. Elderly men were twice as likely as their female counterparts to be in the labor force. These figures underscore the fact that not all of the elderly population are retired from the labor force and that there is no one age at which to retire.

Although age 65 is often referred to as the "normal" retirement age, most people retire earlier. The average age to begin receiving Social Security retirement benefits has been about 63.7 for men and 63.5 for women for more than a decade (U.S. Social Security Administration, 1994).

Few people realize that widespread retirement—particularly early retirement—is a relatively recent invention. As recently as 1950, nearly half of all men aged 65 and older could be found in the labor force. Older men's labor force participation rate declined steadily until the mid-1980s (see Figure 2.8) and has since held steady at about 15%. Older women, too, have been retiring from the labor force. However, the greater propensity of each generation of women to work for pay has offset women's late-life labor force withdrawals. As a consequence, the trend for women's labor force participation has been flat, with a low of 7.3% and a high of 10.8% since World War II.

Although some older people will be forced by economic need to continue working, most will ease out of the work force as soon as they can afford to do so. Those who do want or need to work will do so, but they are likely to work off and

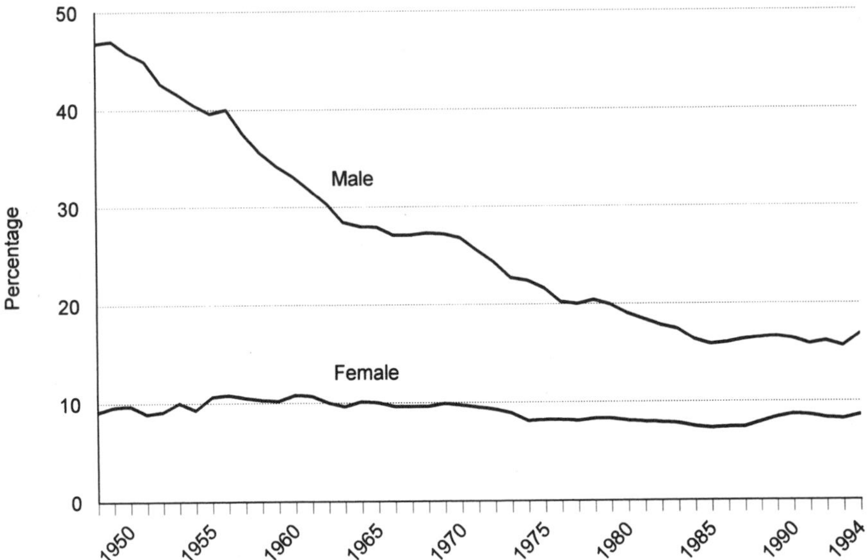

FIGURE 2.8 Percentage of population 65 and older in the civilian labor force, by sex: United States, 1948–1994. U.S. Department of Labor. Bureau of Labor Statistics, *Handbook on Labor Statistics*, Bulletin 2340 (Washington, DC: GPO, Aug. 1989), Table 5; and *Employment and Earnings*, vols. 37–42, Table 3.

on, at fewer hours per week and for fewer weeks per year than do younger adults (Quinn & Burkhauser, 1990; Weaver, 1994).

Family Ties and Living Arrangements Are Important in Older Ages

Family members are important in the lives of older people. Kin are thought about often, socialized with frequently, and helped out in various ways. Of course, older family members are also the beneficiaries of kin support. Spouses offer day-to-day companionship, siblings lend a hand in a crisis, and children pitch in to meet the needs of the seriously impaired. In 1984, fully 84% of noninstitutionalized persons age 65 and older who received help with activities such as bathing or housework were assisted by relatives (Hing & Bloom, 1990). Grown children are a particularly important source of intimacy and support for elderly women who have outlived their spouses.

The numbers and kinds of kin available to older people, however, are the product of demographic processes. Births and marriages add to the kinship network; deaths and marital dissolution (e.g., widowhood and divorce) subtract from it. Because fertility, mortality, and marriage patterns have changed over time, some cohorts of elderly have been more likely than others to have spouses and children to help out in old age.

Nearly all older people today have at least some kin. A substantial minority, however, have no surviving children. These proportions are expected to decline, however, as the parents of the baby boom generation enter this oldest age group. In the near term relatively few old people will be without children who could care for them should they become disabled and need help. By 2020 the proportion of women aged 85 and older who are childless is projected to be less than half of the 1990 figure.

Because the U.S. fertility rate has fallen, the baby-boom generation is virtually certain to arrive at old age with a higher childless proportion than that of their parents' generation. Nearly 16% of baby-boom women who were aged 40 to 44 in 1992 had never borne a child. Most will remain childless. Consequently, the 21st century's elderly population may need more formal services to substitute for the informal care so often provided by adult children.

Most Older Men Are Married, Most Older Women Widowed

The likelihood of an older person having a spouse has also changed over time—a trend of considerable importance because married people generally fare better than do the unmarried. Compared to single people, especially single women, couples have higher incomes. Husbands and wives offer day-to-day companionship to each other, and they often provide care when one partner needs assistance. As a consequence, older people who are married are less likely to be institutionalized than are those who are single. Because mortality has declined and the age at widowhood has increased, married couples approaching retirement age today expect more years of married life ahead.

Looking to the future, the Census Bureau projects that only 21% of American women aged 65 to 74 will be widowed in 2040, compared with 34% in 1994 and 44% in 1970 (U.S. Bureau of the Census, 1992b). The proportion who are divorced, however, will continue to rise for the foreseeable future. Since the 1960s, divorce has become more common, and remarriage has become less common among American adults. As these divorced people move into old age, the percentage of elderly who are divorced rises. Because increases in divorce offset declines in widowhood, the 1980s, unlike earlier decades, witnessed no increase in the proportion of 60- to 64-year-olds who were married as they moved into old age (Treas & Torrecilha, 1995). As divorce and the percentage who never marry increase, the elderly population of the 21st century will be no more likely to have a surviving spouse than today's generation of the elderly population.

The likelihood of being married varies by gender, age, and racial and ethnic group. Although older men are usually married, older women are usually widowed. Gender differences are marked, especially at the oldest ages. Most of the younger elderly are married: 78% of men and 52% of women aged 65 to 74 were married and living with their spouses in 1994. Among those age 85 and older, however, 57% of men but only 13% of women lived with a spouse. Wives usually

TABLE 2.8 Marital Status of the U.S. Population Aged 65 and Older, by Gender and Race/Ethnicity, 1994

	Men			Women		
	White	Black	Hispanic[b]	White	Black	Hispanic[b]
Total (1,000s)[a]	11,470	978	608	16,111	1,532	783
Percent of total	100	100	100	100	100	100
Never married	5	6	7	4	5	8
Married, spouse present	76	63	63	42	28	37
Married, spouse absent	2	6	5	2	4	5
Widowed	13	18	18	46	55	41
Divorced	5	7	8	6	9	3

[a] Noninstitutionalized population.
[b] Persons of Hispanic origin may be of any race.
Source: Population Reference Bureau analysis of the March 1994 Current Population Survey.

outlive their husbands because women are usually younger than their husbands and because women at every age have lower mortality rates than do men. Women are widowed at an earlier age than are men. The average age at widowhood was estimated to be 68.9 years for women and 72.3 years for men in 1988. As a consequence of their earlier age of widowhood, women spent an average of 15.3 years as widows, whereas men lived 8.4 years as widowers (Schoen & Weinick, 1993).

Racial and ethnic differences are also apparent. Although older Hispanic women are less likely than Whites to be married and living with a spouse, White and Hispanic women are quite similar in the proportion widowed. Elderly Hispanic women, however, are more likely than Whites or Blacks never to have married. Older African American women are less likely to be married than either older White or Hispanic women (see Table 2.8). However, the share of Black men who were married and living with wives was the same as for Hispanic men (63%), and below the 76% recorded for White men. Older African Americans are more likely than older Whites to be divorced or never to have married. Because Blacks, especially Black men, have higher mortality rates than do Whites, their spouses are more likely to be widowed.

Living Arrangements

Living independently in the community in their own homes is the goal of most older people. Only 5% live in nursing homes and other institutions. Among the community-dwelling elderly who make up the overwhelming majority of older Americans, about 90% of men and 80% of women maintain their own homes as either the householder or the householder's spouse. Some older people live in

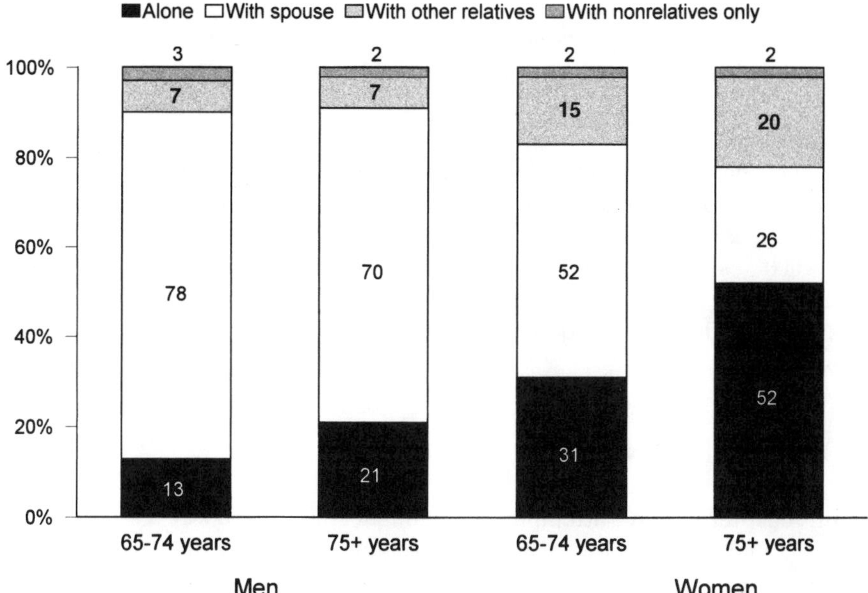

FIGURE 2.9 Living arrangements of elderly men and women, 1994. *Note*: Population aged 65 and older not living in a nursing home or other institution. Population Reference Bureau analysis of the March 1994 Current Population Survey.

the homes of family members or of unrelated individuals, but this residential arrangement has become increasingly uncommon as the older population has been better able to afford independent living.

Marital status as well as age-related needs and resources affect the choice of living arrangements. Because most older men and young-old women are married, it is not surprising that the majority live with spouses. Most women 75 or older live alone; they continue to maintain their own homes even after they are widowed (see Figure 2.9). But in general, adults 75 or older are more likely than the young-old to live with relatives other than their spouses. These living arrangements of the old-old reflect their greater need for support, as they are more likely to be poor, to be widowed, and to have difficulty caring for themselves. African American and White elders are more likely to live alone than the Hispanic elderly.

Recall that most people age in place. After retirement, people are still anchored to their communities by home ownership, by the comfort of familiar surroundings, by friends and family, and by meaningful past experiences (Longino, 1994). However inconvenient the neighborhood, these attractions usually loom large in the minds of older people. Older people, in fact, are more likely to hold favorable opinions of their housing and their neighborhood than are the younger residents (U.S. Bureau of the Census, 1993a).

Although a number of housing alternatives have been designed to address the special needs and tastes of older people, most seniors—like most younger people—prefer single-family houses or apartments in residential neighborhoods. Other options range from community board-and-care homes to congregate housing that offers a residential option for more independent elderly. Real estate developers have also created age-segregated apartment buildings, towns, subdivisions, and mobile home parks specifically for active seniors. These communities may be as small as a dozen or so residents or as big as Arizona's Sun City with its 45,000 residents. Retirement communities for the active elderly—many founded in the 1960s—have experienced their own aging in place and must now cope with residents who require more and more assistance with their everyday lives.

CONCLUSIONS

In this chapter we have attempted to highlight some of the key features of the demographic process known as population aging; at the same time, we have tried to convey a sense of the complexity encountered in integrating these dimensions into a rational policy framework. In reviewing both the size and the characteristics of the older population as they change over time, we have attempted to balance understanding of aging at the individual level with aging at the societal level. Although it is possible to generalize about the elderly population, their characteristics, needs, resources, and activities are far too diverse to justify stereotyping older people. Older people are rich *and* poor, blessed with family *and* bereft of kin, on the move *and* aging in place. Population aging will be a major force shaping our collective future. Despite its inevitability and importance, it does not yield easily or neatly to analysis. Appreciating the complexity of population aging and the diversity of older people, however, can inform our understanding of elderly Americans, who make up growing numbers of voters, readers, workers, shoppers, caregivers, homeowners, and taxpayers.

REFERENCES

Crimmins, E. M., & Ingegneri, D. G. (1992). Health trends in the American population. In A. M. Rappaport & S. J. Schieber (Eds.), *Demography and retirement: The 21st century* (pp. 259–278). Westport, CT: Greenwood.

Elo, I. T., & Preston, S. M. (1994). Estimating African-American mortality from inaccurate data. *Demography*, *31*, 427–458.

Fix, M., & Passel, J. S. (1994). *Immigration and immigrants: Setting the record straight.* Washington, DC: Urban Institute.

Fries, J. F. (1980). Aging, natural death and the compression of morbidity. *New England Journal of Medicine*, *303*, 130.

Hing, E., & Bloom, B. (1990). Long-term care for the functionally dependent elderly. In *Vital and health statistics*, Series 13, No. 104, 28. Washington, DC: National Center for Health Statistics.

Holden, K. C., & Smeeding, T. (1990). The poor, the rich, and the insecure elderly caught in between. *Milbank Quarterly*, *68*, 191–219.

Longino, C. F., Jr. (1994). Where retirees prefer to live: The geographical distribution and migratory patterns of retirees. In A. Monk (Ed.), *The Columbia retirement handbook* (pp. 405–416). New York: Columbia University Press.

Longino, C. F., Jr. (1995). *Retirement migration in America.* Houston, TX: Vacation Publications.

Manton, K. G., Corder, L. S., & Stallard, E. (1993). Estimates of change in chronic disability and institutional incidence and prevalence rates in the U.S. elderly population from the 1982, 1984, and 1986 National Long Term Care Surveys. *Journal of Gerontology: Social Sciences*, *48*, S153–166.

Martin, P., & Midgley, E. (1994). Immigration to the United States: Journey to an uncertain destination. *Population Bulletin*, *49*(2), 4–5.

National Center for Health Statistics. (1994a). *Health, United States, 1993*. Hyattsville, MD: Public Health Service.

National Center for Health Statistics. (1994b). *Health, United States, 1993*. Hyattsville, MD: Public Health Service.

Quinn, J. F., & Burkhauser, R. V. (1990). Work and retirement. In R. H. Binstock & L. K. George (Eds.), *Handbook on aging and the social sciences* (pp. 308–327). New York: Van Nostrand.

Rusting, R. L. (1992). Why do we age? *Scientific American*, *267*(6), 130–141.

Schoen, R., & Weinick, R. W. (1993). The slowing metabolism of marriage: Figures from 1988 marital status life tables. *Demography*, *30*, 740–741.

Scott, C. (1993). *SSI payments to lawfully resident aliens.* Washington, DC: Office of Supplemental Security Income.

Treas, J. (1995). Older Americans in the 1990s and beyond. *Population Bulletin*, *50*(2), 1–45.

Treas, J., & Torrecilha, R. (1995). The older population. In R. Farley (Ed.), *Social and economic trends in the 1980s* (pp. 47–92). New York: Russell Sage Foundation.

U.S. Bureau of the Census. (1992a). Population trends in the 1980s. In *Current population reports* (P23-175, No. 4). Washington, DC: U.S. Government Printing Office.

U.S. Bureau of the Census. (1992b). Sixty-five plus in America. In *Current population reports* (Special Studies P23-178, prepared by C. M. Taeuber). Washington, DC: U.S. Government Printing Office.

U.S. Bureau of the Census. (1993a). Our nation's housing in 1991. In *Current population reports* (H121/93-2, prepared by T. S. Grail). Washington, DC: U.S. Government Printing Office.

U.S. Bureau of the Census. (1993b). Population projections of the United States, by age, sex, race, and Hispanic origin: 1993 to 2050. In *Current population reports* (P25-1104). Washington, DC: U.S. Government Printing Office.

U.S. Bureau of the Census. (1993c). Voting and registration in the election of November 1992. In *Current population reports* (P20-466). Washington, DC: U.S. Government Printing Office.

U.S. Bureau of the Census. (1994). *Statistical abstract of the United States*, 114th ed. Washington, DC: U.S. Government Printing Office.

U.S. Bureau of the Census. (1995). Income, poverty, and valuation of cash benefits: 1993. *Current population reports* (P60, No. 188). Washington, DC: U.S. Government Printing Office.

U.S. House of Representatives, Committee on Ways and Means. (1993). *1993 green book.* Washington, DC: U.S. Government Printing Office.

U.S. House of Representatives, Committee on Ways and Means. (1994). *1994 green book.* Washington, DC: U.S. Government Printing Office.

U.S. Social Security Administration. (1994). *Annual statistical supplement to the Social Security Bulletin, 1994.* Washington, DC: U.S. Government Printing Office.

Weaver, D. A. (1994). The work and retirement decisions of older women: A literature review. *Social Security Bulletin, 57*(1), 3–24.

PART II

Salient Perspectives in Gerontology

In the development of gerontology, some disciplines have been central—dominant, if you will—in shaping the field. Although all disciplines, whether sciences or humanities, have some contribution to make to a better understanding of human aging, part I considers in detail some of the major disciplinary players in developing contemporary gerontology.

After sketching out a gerontological imagination and sensitizing ourselves to some of the population dynamics of an aging America in chapters 1 and 2, part II enhances our gerontological imagination by reviewing the major contributions of the disciplines that have greatly nurtured gerontology. Five disciplines are represented, ranging from the biological to the sociocultural. These certainly do not exhaust all perspectives on gerontology, but they do represent core areas as defined by many gerontological educators. Other important areas of inquiry are covered elsewhere in the book.

Griffiths helps the reader view aging from a biological perspective. In doing so he examines organic systems as well as cellular aging. Willott's chapter on neurogerontology links biological science with psychology by examining the aging brain. France and Alpher move the inquiry to the cognitive and social-psychological level in their discussion of the psychology of aging. Ferraro discusses the social context of aging, with special attention to the link between the microsociology and macrosociology of aging. Fry completes this section by inviting the reader to consider aging across various cultures. This final endeavor gleans insights from the anthropology of aging.

Whenever we want to learn more about an object, we benefit from taking several views of it. If we were interested in the Statue of Liberty, our understanding of it could be enhanced not only by seeing it from Staten Island but also by viewing it from the air and the harbor and by ascending the tower. Each view or perspective would give us a greater appreciation for and understanding of the whole. By analogy, we enhance our gerontological imagination by incorporating different views of the aging process, whether of cellular or societal processes.

CHAPTER 3

Biology of Aging

T. Daniel Griffiths

Aging is a complex process involving many factors. Numerous models for aging have been proposed, tested, and finally abandoned. If it is difficult to understand the mechanisms behind aging, it is also difficult to define aging. The definition that probably is most widely accepted by biologists today is that aging involves a "gradual deterioration in function and in the capacity of the body's homeostatic systems to respond to environmental stresses" (Vander, Sherman, & Luciano, 1990, p. 146). This definition has the advantage of allowing us to distinguish the aging process from degenerative changes that result from diseases. Although diseases such as cancer and atherosclerosis can interact and compound the aging process, they do not always accompany aging and therefore must be thought of as distinct processes.

This definition of aging also has a disadvantage in that it suggests that there is always a continuing and unrelenting age-associated decline in the ability of individuals to function in the environment. This is certainly not the case. First, as was mentioned in chapter 1, our bodies are "overbuilt." In other words, there is a large reserve capacity in most of our organs and systems. We will discuss this in relation to our respiratory system later. Second, there are cases in which there seems to be little change in the body's ability to adapt. For instance, Clarkson and Dedrick (1988) reported that when women over 60 were compared to college-age women, there was no difference in the ability of their muscles to repair and adapt to muscle damage. Thus, although there is certainly an age-associated decrease in muscle strength in individuals over the age of 35, this study suggests that the ability of muscles to respond to a particular type of stress is not diminished. Third, as was also mentioned in chapter 1, there is a great deal of heterogeneity in the extent and rate of decline of homeostatic responses in different individuals. Finally, non-age-related changes can accelerate this decline. We have already mentioned disease, but other factors such as an individual's lifestyle or work environment can accelerate the decline in homeostatic processes. For example, smoking or working in a polluted environment can accelerate age-related changes.

HOMEOSTASIS AND AGING

The term *homeostasis* was first coined by 19th-century French physiologist Claude Bernard. He noted that mammals had the ability to regulate their internal environment within very narrow limits. In fact, "constancy of the internal milieu," as Bernard (1957) put it, appears to be a nearly universal phenomenon in animals. From unicellular to multicellular animals, homeostasis is crucial for survival. For those unfamiliar with the term *homeostasis*, consideration of some everyday examples using man-made items should help. For example, consider how we maintain temperature within a house. If the temperature falls below a set point (e.g., 68°F), the thermostat may signal the furnace to turn on. As a result, the temperature in the house will rise. When the temperature reaches a certain set point, then the thermostat will signal the furnace to shut off. This is an example of negative feedback. In other words, in the system just described the initial change in the variable (in this case, decrease in temperature) brought about a change (turning on the furnace) that tended to push the variable (temperature) in the opposite direction of the initial change. Such a heating system alone, however, allows for fairly wide fluctuations in temperature. For example, when the furnace is shut off, heat that is still in the furnace is given off, resulting in the temperature of the house rising a degree or two above the set point.

To maintain a more constant temperature, one could add an air conditioner to the system so that when the furnace is shut off, the air conditioner comes on, thus reducing the overshoot in temperature. Equipment utilizing both heating and cooling cycles is frequently used in scientific or industrial research when it is essential to maintain temperatures within very narrow limits.

The human body has intricate mechanisms for maintaining the internal body temperature as close to 37°C (98.6°F) as possible. It is critical to maintain the internal organs (heart, lungs) and the brain at a consistently warm temperature because a rise or fall in core body temperature can result in injury or death (Lybarger & Kilbourne, 1985). A drop of more than 2°C signals the onset of hypothermia, which produces shivering, dulled mental awareness, and pallor in its early stages. If hypothermia persists or becomes more severe, the central nervous system loses its ability to regulate temperature, and the patient becomes unconscious; if preventive measures are not taken, the patient dies. It is well known that the death rate from hypothermia increases with age.

Several mechanisms have evolved to help maintain body temperature (Davis & Zenser, 1985). Of greatest importance is the ability to control or limit the amount of blood sent to the skin and peripheral organs. When the outside temperature decreases, blood vessels to the skin and peripheral organs constrict, thus reducing the amount of blood flow to the areas. This in turn reduces the amount of heat loss. Likewise, when outside temperature rises, more blood is sent to these areas, thus increasing heat loss. Another mechanism that maintains core body temperature when the outside temperature falls is shivering. The rapid muscular contractions that cause shivering produce large amounts of heat that can be picked up by the blood. Finally, numerous behavioral responses help maintain temperature; simply putting on a coat, turning the thermostat up, or going to a warmer room are examples.

This increased susceptibility of the elderly to hypothermia results from a number of factors (Davis & Zenser, 1985). First, because of sensory impairment, the elderly may be less able to detect and/or respond to a decrease in external temperatures. This could be due to defects in either the peripheral or central nervous system. Second, the ability of peripheral blood vessels to constrict is impaired in the elderly. This results in decreases in both the rate and extent of vasoconstriction in the vessels leading to the skin and a corresponding increase in heat loss through the skin (Collins, Easton, & Exton-Smith, 1981). Third, the shivering response may also be decreased in the elderly (Collins et al., 1981), resulting in decreased ability to generate heat to compensate for losses. Fourth, the basal metabolic rate (BMR) of elderly persons is decreased (BMR refers to the body's metabolic rate when a person is at mental and physical rest). The standard BMR for a 70-year-old man is 17% lower than that of a 10-year-old boy (Collins, 1983). Because metabolic processes produce heat, the elderly have a lower basic rate of heat production and therefore may be less able to withstand lower temperatures. Fifth, the endocrine system that helps the body maintain a constant internal temperature may not function as well in older persons as in younger persons. Finally, if an elderly person has a disease that inhibits or decreases locomotion (e.g., arthritis), muscular activity will be decreased. Because muscular activity produces heat (80% of the energy released during muscular contraction is released as heat, and only 20% is used for the actual contraction), a decrease in mobility correspondingly decreases one's ability to generate heat.

HUMAN AGING AND ORGANS

Through this discussion we have seen how several processes work together to maintain core body temperature at or near 37°C and how these processes may be altered in the elderly. If we look at the individual organs in the body, we also observe an age-related decrease in the ability to cope with changes in the environment. Indeed, "it is probably safe to state that the ability of *every* organ or organ system to function declines with age" (Kohn, 1978, p. 168). It is impossible in this chapter to discuss all organs and organ systems in the body, but the general trend can be observed by looking at the heart and the lungs.

One of the organs that has been studied extensively with relation to aging is the heart. The ability of the heart to pump blood to the rest of the body can be determined by measuring the cardiac output. Most frequently, cardiac output in humans refers to the amount of blood pumped out of the left ventricle per minute because the left ventricle pumps blood into the peripheral circulation. (We will restrict our discussion to the left ventricle.) Cardiac output varies with body size. For this reason cardiac output is frequently given in terms of the cardiac index: the cardiac output per square meter of surface area of the body. Cardiac index can be increased or decreased by altering either the heart rate or the amount of blood pumped into the aorta during each contraction (called the stroke volume). For many years it was thought that the cardiac index at rest decreased with age (Brandofonbrener, Landowne, & Shock, 1955). The Baltimore Longitudinal Study of Aging has questioned this conclusion, however (Shock et al., 1984). Specifically, it was noted that when individuals suffering from occult coronary artery disease (CAD) were excluded, there appeared to be no decrease in cardiac output at rest. Thus; the decline in cardiac output observed in earlier studies apparently was due to disease, not aging.

What is clear, however, is that under stress there are age-related changes in various heart functions in individuals free from CAD (Lakatta, 1990). Most interestingly, it has been reported that there is an age-associated increase in the amount of blood entering the left ventricle prior to contraction (end-diastolic filling volume). It has been suggested that this may be our bodies' attempt to help maintain cardiac output because there is an age-associated decrease in the heart rate under stress (Shock et al., 1984). In addition, it was pointed out that the increased filling pressure would have some disadvantages, such as increased cardiac work and energy production.

Besides observing an age-associated decrease in the heart rate, the Boston Longitudinal Study also showed a significant decrease in the fraction of blood ejected by the heart during each contraction. The age-associated changes observed in the human heart appear to be caused by several factors. For example, changes in the musculature of the ventricles or decreased distensibility of the peripheral blood vessels may play a role in the age-associated decrease ejection fraction. Alterations in the neural and hormonal factors appear to be responsible for the age-associated decrease in heart rate (Lakat, 1987; Narayaman & Tucker, 1986).

Age-related changes have also been observed in the lungs. When we breathe normally, we use only a portion of the volume of each lung available for breathing. During a normal breath an individual will inspire and expire around 500 ml of air, referred to as the tidal volume. Normal individuals can inspire an additional 3,000 ml of air on top of the tidal volume; this is referred to as the inspiratory reserve volume addition. During *forced* expirations an individual can typically force out an additional 1,100 ml of air, known as the expiratory reserve volume. The total amount of air that can be forced into or out of the lungs is the sum of these three volumes and is termed the vital capacity (Vander et al., 1990).

During exercise we not only breathe more rapidly but also use these reserve volumes. It is important to note that even during exercise a healthy person rarely uses more than 50% of his or her vital capacity. This is a prime example of the reserve capacity built into our organs and systems. However, diseases such as asthma and emphysema decrease capacity and can seriously affect an individual's health. This becomes even more serious in older adults because there is a progressive loss of vital capacity with age. For example, there is almost a 50% decline in vital capacity between ages 30 and 80 (Kohn, 1978). Thus, the elderly are less able to deal with stresses that increase the breathing rate or with diseases that decrease vital capacity.

Although there are many actions involved in the decline in vital capacity, the elasticity of the lungs appears to be a principal factor. Niewoehner, Kleinerman, and Liotta (1975) report that the elasticity of the lungs decreases by greater than 90% between the ages of 20 and 80. This decrease in elasticity (increase in rigidity) has another effect that further reduces the efficiency of breathing in the elderly: For oxygen from the air to get to the blood, it must pass through lung tissue. As the lung becomes more rigid, there appears to be a decrease in the capacity of oxygen to diffuse or pass through.

AGING AND STRESS

The age-related changes we have discussed in relation to hypothermia, cardiac output, and vital capacity all result in individuals' being less able to cope with stress. This can best be demonstrated by reviewing some experiments with animals. For example, as reported in Kohn (1978), when mice of varying ages were placed at 6° to 7°C for 14 days, the percentage surviving decreased linearly with age. At 8 months approximately 80% survived, but at 20 months less than 20% survived. Thus, in mice as in humans, the various processes that tend to protect the body from hypothermia become less efficient with increasing age, resulting in old mice being less able to respond to cold environments.

The loss of the ability among older people to adapt to stress was most tragically shown in July 1995. More than 500 individuals died in Chicago when the temperature peaked at over 100°F for three consecutive days. Soon after the deaths began to be reported, it became clear that (1) the vast majority of deaths from hyperthermia occurred in the elderly, and (2) in most of these cases, heat was not the primary cause of death. Defects in other homeostatic processes involving systems such as the respiratory or circulatory system were the primary cause of death, with the excessive heat contributing to the death by simply putting too much stress on these other homeostatic processes (Chicago Tribune, July 30, 1995).

Recently it has been suggested that it may be possible to alter that ability of individuals to respond to stress. Specifically, it has been known for over 60 years that animals fed a restricted diet that is nutritionally adequate yet reduced calorically (calorie-restricted [CR]), have a longer life span and reduced deaths from cancer than do animals that are allowed to eat freely (ad lib [AL]) (McCay, Crowell, & Maynard, 1935; Taylor et al., 1995). Although the extent of this effect and the cause(s) are currently being debated, recent studies have shown that CR animals produce more stress proteins (Aly et al., 1994). Such proteins are produced under specific stresses, such as heat, and appear to allow the organism to respond better to that particular stress.

Many other examples could be given of the various physiological changes that result in a decreased ability of aged animals to respond to stress. One point needs to be reemphasized. Although there is a general decrease in various physiological processes in all individuals, the extent of this decrease is quite variable. Some individuals may exhibit only modest changes; other individuals may exhibit more severe changes. Numerous factors, such as nutrition, lifestyle, and heredity, account for this variability.

CELLULAR AGING

In the preceding section we discussed a few of the age-related changes that occur in various organs and systems and how these result in a generally decreased ability to respond to stress. To understand better how these changes come about, it is necessary to consider how individual cells change with age.

The cellular and molecular biology of aging received a major boost in the early 1960s, when Hayflick and his co-workers were able to grow fibroblasts (taken from normal individuals) in petri dishes and synthetic media (in vitro). They also discovered that these fibroblasts grown in vitro had finite life spans (Hayflick, 1965). The cells *senesced*, or failed to replicate their DNA and divide, after reaching their *Hayflick limit* of 50 ± 10 divisions for human cells. If one removed cells from young and old humans and determined the number of divisions the cells made prior to senescing, one would find an age-dependent decrease, indicating that the Hayflick limit reflects the in vivo experience and is not merely an artifact of growth in vitro.

These findings spurred a great deal of research into the mechanism of cellular senescence, as it had been theorized that depletion or senescence of a key population of cells (e.g., stem cells) could account for some aspects of aging. Theories and research centered on this question have focused on two alternatives to account for senescence: senescence is (1) the result of the production or accumulation of a senescence factor or (2) the result of damage to DNA. In the following section we briefly examine the changes found in cells as they age or senesce, the models proposed for cellular aging, and finally, whether in vitro aging is an appropriate model for aging on the organismic level.

Listed below are the age-related changes that occur in a variety of molecules and structures in a given cell. They are broken down into groups of related compounds to facilitate seeing the changes as a package of alterations (adapted from Stanulis-Praeger, 1987).

Lipids and Membranes

Senescing cells may have increased membrane fluidity (although this is not certain) and an alteration in membrane composition. The alteration in membrane composition may be partially the result of free radical–mediated peroxidation of membrane lipids. There is a model (discussed below) that claims free radical metabolic intermediates are involved in age-related damage, particularly membrane damage (Spirduso, 1995). Another alteration is a decrease in the number of connections between cells, called gap junctions. These junctions are important in that they allow the exchange of low molecular weight materials and ions and may provide a means of cell-to-cell communication. Changes also have been found in the glycoproteins present on the outer face of the membrane, with a molecule unique to cells at the end of their replicative life spans.

Ribonucleic Acid (RNA)

There have been reports of an increase in the transcriptional activity of genes such as *ras*, a cellular oncogene that codes for a G-protein-like molecule (G-protein is a guanosine triphosphate protein that is important in the activation of adenyl cyclase after a cell surface receptor binds a hormone) (Srivastava, Norris, Shmookler-Reis, & Goldstein, 1985). For most other messenger RNAs and for transfer RNA and ribosomal RNA there appears to be an age-dependent decrease in the rate of RNA synthesis. The mechanism(s) responsible for these changes are not known, but the following findings are important:

1. The level of methylation of cytosine bases decreases with age (Wilson & Jones, 1983). Experiments using 5-azacytidine, a drug that inhibits methylation, have shown that hypomethylation may allow expression of repressed genes such as ras.
2. There is an increase in the level of positive supercoiling with increasing age. This effectively "tightens" the DNA and reduces the availability of single-stranded regions of DNA required for transcription (Hartwig & Koerner, 1987).

Protein

One model (discussed below) is based on the theory that as a cell ages, proteins are produced that contain more and more errors, until a "killer" protein is produced or the cell is filled with useless enzymes and proteins. Most studies have, however, found no changes in the amino acid sequences in proteins produced by senescing cells. This is not to say, however, that there are no changes. For a variety of the enzymes sampled, activity is reduced in cells from older individuals. The affinity of the enzymes for their substrate is not reduced, however. Covalent modifications (carbohydrates or phosphates) change with age and have been found to make enzymes from senescing cells less tolerant of heat (increased thermal sensitivity). The reason for this remains, for now, unknown.

Cellular protein content and turnover rate also change as cells age. The rate of protein degradation (turnover) decreases as a cell reaches senescence, and logically, there is a corresponding increase in total protein content with age. As noted above, however, this is not accompanied by an increase in defective proteins.

The proteins involved in the cytoskeleton (e.g., actin and tubulin) show degenerative changes in aging in that the cytoskeleton becomes more rigid and less organized in senescing cells, possibly due to cross-links formed between the protein molecules that make up the cytoskeleton.

Other Cellular Changes

The inner mitochondrial membrane is not as folded in senescing cells and may result in a decrease in the ability to generate the proton gradient required for the oxidative phosphorylation of adenosine triphosphate (ATP). There is an increase in the number of granulated vacuoles and lysosomes in cells nearing senescence, along with an increase in the amounts of lysosomal degradation enzymes. There is an accumulation of a lipid-based pigment called lipofuscin in the cell (Sohal & Buchan, 1981). The efficiency of old cells to attach in vitro is lower than that of younger cells, and the fibronectin secreted by senescing cells does not secure the old cell to the bottom of the dish as well.

Deoxyribonucleic Acid (DNA) and Chromosomes

Several of the changes found in DNA have already been alluded to: decreases in methylation and changes in supercoiling. The average length of the cell cycle increases as cells near senescence, whereas the role of DNA synthesis remains constant (Griffiths, 1984). Other DNA changes occur in the form of mutations (changes in the DNA sequence).

DNA is arranged in a double-stranded configuration in chromosomes. The two strands of DNA, however, are arranged in an antiparallel fashion, with one oriented in a 5′ to 3′ direction, and the other in a 3′ to 5′ orientation. This antiparallel orientation, the fact that replication occurs only in the 5′ to 3′ direction, and the fact that RNA primers are required for the initiation of DNA replication cause several problems. One of these is that the very ends of chromosomes lose a small portion of DNA during every round of DNA replication (Harley et al., 1995; Olovnikov, 1973). This could potentially result in the eventual loss of critical genetic information.

For certain cells, such as our germ cells (reproductive cells) and cancer cells, both ends of chromosomes contain large amounts of redundant DNA of specific repeated sequences, termed telomers, which can be constantly replaced by an RNA enzyme called telomerase. A promising model for cellular aging, discussed below, proposes that aging in normal or somatic cells is caused by or related to the loss of telomeric sequences at both ends of chromosomes.

MODELS OF CELLULAR AGING

There are two families of models that attempt to relate the damages listed above with cellular aging and senescence. One group, referred to as "extrinsic models," holds that stochastic damage or its imperfect repair is the key to aging. The other group, the "intrinsic models," holds that aging is determined by the cell itself and that cellular damage is irrelevant. A fuller treatment of the models mentioned below may be found in a variety of reviews, including Cristofalo (1988) and Spence (1989).

The extrinsic model, supported by the largest body of data, holds that the destruction of a key gene would cause a cell to stop dividing and senesce, so longevity could be a function of how well a cell could either shield its DNA from damage or repair the damage that does occur. In practice it is not possible to protect the DNA to a significant degree (the better the shielding, the more difficult the DNA would be to read or use). However, Hart and Setlow (1974) have found that there is a direct correlation between the extent to which DNA damage is removed from the cells of a given species and the life span of that species. For example, cells taken from Chinese hamsters (maximum life span, 3 years) remove less than one-third of the DNA damage induced by ultraviolet light in a 24-hour period, whereas human cells (maximum life span, 110 years) remove over 50% during the same period.

Research both supporting and contradicting the relationship of DNA repair and aging have been reported. For example, humans deficient in DNA repair, such as those suffering from xeroderma pigmentosum generally do not exhibit classical forms of premature aging, yet they generally die in their teens or 20s. Research with patients who exhibit classical premature aging (progeria) has produced conflicting results. Initial results suggested that such patients show only marginal, if any, defects in DNA repair (Regan & Setlow, 1974); however, a recent study reports that cells from progeria patients, in contrast to cells from normal patients, exhibit a striking age or cell-passage decline in DNA repair capacity (Sugita, Suzuki, Fujii, & Niimi, 1995). Future research is needed to address this controversy.

There is, moreover, evidence for the source of this extrinsic damage to DNA. Molecules that contain unpaired electrons, called free radicals, are known to be produced by exposure to ionizing radiation, and these free radicals are responsible for most of the DNA damage and cell killing. These molecules are also produced during normal energy metabolism. Organisms that contain high levels of enzymes such as copper/zinc superoxide dismutase, which degrades free radicals, have been shown to have significantly longer life spans than organisms with low levels of these enzymes. It has also been noticed that organisms that contain large amounts of materials that appear to protect cellular materials from being oxidized (antioxidants), such as alpha-tocopherol (vitamin E) and ascorbic acid (vitamin C), have longer life spans than organisms with low levels of these antioxidants (Cutler, 1985). Humans, with their approximately 110-year maximum life span, have significantly higher levels of all three materials than shorter-lived species, such as most types of rodents.

The observation that calorically restricted animals have a longer life span has been used to support the free radical model because such animals have a lower metabolic rate and consequently lower levels of free radical production. In addition, animals placed under conditions that reduce their metabolic rate, such as hibernation or reduced temperature for cold-blooded animals, show an increase in life span. It should be noted, however, that there is not always a correlation between the levels of antioxidants, enzymes that break down free radicals, and aging. For example, the levels of catalase, which degrades hydrogen peroxide, do not exhibit a consistent decrease with age and are not correlated with life span (Gsell et al., 1995; Durusoy, Diril, & Bozcuk, 1995).

Another model ignores the direct role DNA damage may play in senescence. This model, originally proposed by Leslie Orgel (1963), considers the cumulative effect that errors in translating messenger RNA into protein could have on a cell. It is theorized that if errors were made in proteins responsible for synthesizing other macromolecules (i.e., ribosomal proteins, RNA or DNA polymerases), then the fidelity of these macromolecules would be reduced (Cristofalo, 1988). These would then produce more defective proteins until the cell died from lethal DNA mutations or the burden of producing a large number of nonfunctional proteins. This "error catastrophe" model was directly tested by incubating cells in the presence of amino acid analogues. It was thought that incorporation of the analogues would mimic the spontaneous errors and provide a test of Orgel's theory. In only one organism, *Neurospora*, researchers did find a significant life span reduction in analogue-treated cells. When the amino acid sequences from proteins isolated from young and old cells were determined, as discussed above, no alteration in the amino acid sequence was noted, effectively refuting Orgel's theory. Although the data indicate that the model is incorrect in explaining the *primary reason* for senescence, it is not possible to ascertain whether it may play a secondary role in some cells or organisms.

One "intrinsic model" proposes that there is a *senescence factor* that accumulates in cells and inhibits DNA replication in senescent cells (Muggleton-Harris & Hayflick, 1976; Pereira-Smith & Smith, 1982). One can separate the cytoplasm (cytoplast) or nucleus (karyoplast) from young or old cells and fuse cells, cytoplasts, or karyoplasts with young or old cells and determine whether the resultant cell (or heterokaryon) acts as a young or an old cell. When old cells, nuclei, or cytoplasts were fused to young cells, the young cells were forced into premature senescence. The effect of old cytoplasts could be abolished if they were pretreated with chemicals that inhibit protein synthesis. Fusion of young cells or cytoplasts to intact senescent cells allow senescent cells to undergo a few (up to four) rounds of replication, but the heterokaryon quickly senesces. These experiments indicate that the senescence factor is a protein and that it acts in a dominant fashion (i.e., the presence of this factor is sufficient to force an otherwise young cell into senescence).

Mutants that have been generated by treating normal cells with mutagenic chemicals have further defined the senescence factor. These cells have lost the ability to senesce, although they will senesce when fused with an old cell. When several of these lines of cells were fused to one another, it was found more than one senescence factor was required (Smith & Lincoln, 1984). Three distinct complementation groups were found. If one fused cells from the same complementation group, the resultant cell would not senesce; but if one fused cells from the other two groups, the cells would complement each other's mutation, and the heterokaryon would senesce.

Unfortunately, we currently know little about these proteins. Their exact composition is unknown, as is the location of the genes they are transcribed from, how synthesis of the proteins is regulated, what precisely they regulate, and how the biological clock is "reset" in germ (egg and sperm) cells (Kanugu, 1994).

Recently, another intrinsic model has been proposed that does not involve the accumulation of an aging factor but instead involves the loss of DNA. Specifically, the fact that normal diploid cells lose a small portion at the ends of chromosomes during each division has led to a model proposing that cellular aging is due to the loss of this telomeric DNA. In mammalian cells telomeric DNA is composed of multiple copies of TTAGGG repeats. Germline cells contain around 15 to 20 kilobases of these telomeric repeats, whereas normal somatic cell lines constantly lose telomeric DNA as they divide. Work by Harley and his co-workers (Allsopp et al., 1992) showed a strong correlation between the loss of this telomeric DNA and the loss of replication potential (Hayflick phenomenon) in mammalian cells (Fig. 3.1). Figure 3.1A shows the cellular life span, as measured by remaining replicative capacity as a function of age of the human cells. Figure 3.1B shows the mean telomeric length of the same cells, and Figure 3.1C shows that these two endpoints appear to be correlated. In a recent review, Woodring and Shay (1995) propose that the loss of telomeric DNA may also be the cause of many other degenerative changes that accompany aging. Future research is being aimed at determining whether this loss of telomeric DNA is a cause of aging and/or other degenerative processes or that the loss simply accompanies aging.

We must, finally, consider whether what has been observed in vitro has a significant bearing on the in vivo experience. The answer, not surprisingly, is that what is observed on the cellular and molecular level is only partially re-

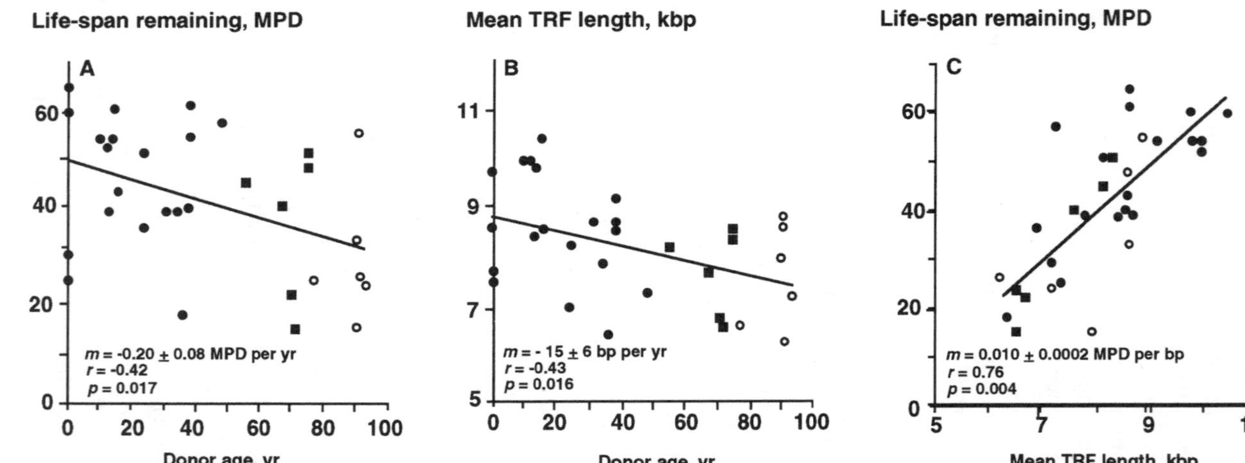

FIGURE 3.1 Replicative capacity is proportional to terminal restriction fragment (TRF) or telomeric length. TRF length (*B*) and remaining replicative capacity (mean population doubling [MPD]) after the initial 19 population doublings in culture (*A*) are shown as a function of donor age for a random subset of the strains tested. From these data, replicative capacity was plotted as a function of TRF length (*C*). Values for the slope (*m*), regression coefficient, and probability ($P{:}H_0{:}{:}\text{slope} = 0$) of the linear regression lines are shown.

Source: Allsopp, et al., 1992. Reproduced with permission of the authors.

flected on the organismic level. Although some aspects of aging, such as the lowered T cell response in older individuals, may reflect the reduced proliferative capacity of older immunological stem cells (primitive progenitor cells; a fraction of their progeny will differentiate into lymphocytes), other aspects, such as stamina, may not be solely the province of biology. Subsequent chapters will describe the nonbiological factors that play an important role in modifying the biology of aging.

REFERENCES

Allsopp, R. D., Vazier, H., Patterson, C., Goldstein, S., Young, E. V., Futcher, A. B., Greider, C. W., & Harley, C. B. (1992). Telomere length predicts replication capacity. *Proceedings of the National Academy of Sciences, USA*, *89*, 10114–10118.

Aly, K. B., Pipkin, J. L., Hinson, W. G., Feulls, R. J., Duffy, P. H., & Hart, R. W. (1994). Temporal and substrate-dependent patterns of stress protein expression in the hypothalamus of caloric restricted rats. *Mechanisms of Aging and Development*, *76*, 1–10.

Bernard, C. (1957). *An introduction to the study of experimental medicine.* New York: Dover.

Brandofonbrener, M., Landowne, M., & Shock, M. N. (1955). Changes in cardiac output with age. *Circulation*, *12*, 557–566.

Clarkson, P. M., & Dedrick, M. E. (1988). Exercise-induced muscle damage, repair and adaptation in old and young subjects. *Journal of Gerontology*, *43*, M91–96.

Collins, K. J. (1983). *Hyperthermia: The facts.* New York: Oxford University Press.

Collins, K. J., Easton, J. C., & Exton-Smith, A. N. (1981). Shivering thermogenesis and vasomotor responses with convective cooling in the elderly. *Journal of Physiology*, *320*, 76P.

Cristofalo, V. J. (1988). An overview of the theories of biological aging. In J. E. Birren & V. L. Bengtson (Eds.), *Emergent theories of aging* (pp. 119–127). New York: Springer Publishing.

Cutler, R. G. (1985). Antioxidants and longevity of mammalian species. In A. D. Woodhead, A. D. Blackett, & A. Hollaender (Eds.), *Molecular biology of aging* (pp. 15–74). New York: Plenum Press.

Davis, B. B., & Zenser, T. V. (1985). Biological changes in thermoregulation in the elderly. In B. B. Davis & W. Gilson (Eds.), *Aging: Vol. 30. Homeostaticfunction and aging* (pp. 157–166). New York: Raven Press.

Durusoy, M., Diril, N., & Bozcuk, A. N. (1995). Age-related activity of catalase in different genotypes of Drosophila-Melanogaster. *Experimental Gerontology*, *30*, 77–86.

Griffiths, T. D. (1984). DNA synthesis, cell progression and aging in human diploid fibroblasts. In A. K. Roy & G. Chaterjee (Eds.), *Molecular basis of aging* (pp. 95–118). New York: Academic Press.

Gsell, W., Conrad, R., Hickethier, M., Sofic, E., Frolich, L., Wichart, I., Jellinger, K., Moll, G., Ransmayr, G., Beckman, H., & Riederer, P. (1995). Decreased catalase activity but unchanged superoxide-dismutase activity in brains of patients with dementia of Alzheimer-type. *Journal of Neurochemistry*, *64*, 1216–1223.

Harley, C. B., Kim, N. W., Rowse, K. R., Winrich, S. L., Hirsch, K. S., West, M. D., Bachetti, S., Hirte, H. W., Counter, C. M., Greider, C. W., Pistyszer, M. A., Sright, W. E., & Shay, J. W. (1995). *Cold Spring Harbor Symposium*, *59*, 307–315.

Hart, R., & Setlow, R. B. (1974). Correlation between DNA excision repair and life span in a number of mammalian species. *Proceedings of the National Academy of Science, USA*, *71*, 2169–2173.

Hartwig, M., & Koerner, I. J. (1987). Age related changes of DNA winding and repair in human peripheral lymphocites. *Mechanisms of Ageing and Development*, *38*, 73–78.

Hayflick, L. (1965). The limited in vitro lifetime of human diploid cell strains. *Experimental Cell Research*, *37*, 614–636.

Kanugu, M. S. (1994). *Genes and aging*. Cambridge: Cambridge University Press.

Kohn, R. R. (1978). *Principles of mammalian aging*. Englewood Cliffs, NJ: Prentice-Hall.

Lakatta, E. G. (1990). Heart and circulation. In E. L. Schneider & J. W. Rowe (Eds.), *Handbook of the biology of aging* (pp. 181–216). San Diego, CA: Academic Press.

Lybarger, J. A., & Kilbourne, E. M. (1985). Hyperthermia and hypothermia in the elderly: An epidemiologic review. In B. B. Davis & W. Gilson (Eds.), *Aging: Vol. 30. Homeostatic function and aging* (pp. 149–156). New York: Raven Press.

McCay, C. M., Crowell, M. F., & Maynard, L. A. (1935). The effect of retarded growth upon the length of life span and upon the ultimate body size. *Journal of Nutrition*, *10*, 67–99.

Muggleton-Harris, A. L., & Hayflick, L. (1976). Cellular aging studied by the reconstruction of replicating cells from nuclei and cytoplasms isolated from normal diploid fibroblasts. *Experimental Cell Research*, *103*, 321–330.

Narayaman, N., & Tucker, L. (1986). Autonomic interactions in the aging heart: Age-associated decrease in the muscarinic cholinergic receptor mediated inhibition of β-adrenegic activation of adenylate cylase. *Mechanisms of Ageing and Development*, *34*, 249–259.

Niewoehner, D. E., Kleinerman, J. D., & Liotta, L. (1975). Elastic behavior of postmortem human lungs: Effects of aging and mild emphysema. *Journal of Applied Physiology*, *39*, 943–949.

Olovnikov, A. M. (1973). A theory of marginotomy: The incomplete copying of template margin in enzymic synthesis of poklynucleotides and biological significance of the phenomenon. *Journal of Theoretical Biology*, *41*, 181–190.

Orgel, L. E. (1963). The maintenance of accuracy of protein synthesis and its relevance to aging. *Proceedings of the National Academy of Science, USA*, *49*, 517–521.

Pereira-Smith, O. M., & Smith, J. R. (1982). Phenotype of low proliferative potential is dominant in hybrids of normal tissue fibroblasts. *Somatic Cell Genetics*, *8*, 731–742.

Regan, J. D., & Setlow, R. B. (1974). DNA repair in progeriod cells. *Biochemical and Biophysical Research Communications*, *59*, 858–864.

Shock, N. W., Greulich, R. C., Costa, P. T., Jr., Andres, R., Lakatta, E. G., Arenberg, D., & Tobin, J. D. (1984). *Normal human aging: The Baltimore longitudinal study of aging*. Washington, DC: U. S. Department of Health and Human Services.

Smith, J. R., & Lincoln, D. W. (1984). Aging of cells in culture. In G. H. Bourne, J. F. Danielli, & K. W. Jeon (Eds.), *International review of cytology* (Vol. 89, pp. 151–177). New York: Academic Press.

Sohal, R. S., & Buchan, P. B. (1981). Relationship between fluorescent age pigment and physiological and physical activity in the housefly, *Musca domestica*. *Mechanisms of Ageing and Development*, *15*, 243–249.

Spence, A. P. (1989). *Biology of human aging.* Englewood Cliffs, NJ: Prentice-Hall.

Spirduso, W. W. (1995). *Physical dimensions of aging.* Champaign, IL: Human Kinetics.

Srivastava, A., Norris, J. S., Shmookler-Reis, R. J., & Goldstein, S. (1985). c-Haras-l proto-oncogene amplification and overexpression during the limited replicative life-span of normal human fibroblasts. *Journal of Biological Chemistry, 260,* 6404–6409.

Stanulis-Praeger, B. M. (1987). Cellular senescence revisited: A review. *Mechanisms of Ageing and Development, 38,* 1–48.

Sugita, K., Suzuki, N., Fujii, K., & Niimi, H. (1995). Reduction of unscheduled DNA synthesis and plasminogen activator activity in Hutchinson-Gilford fibroblasts during passaging *in vitro*—partial correction by interferon-beta. *Mutation Research, 316,* 233–238.

Taylor, A., Lipman, R. D., Jahngen-Hodge, J., Palmer, V., Smith, D., Padhye, N., Dallal, G. E., Cyr, D. E., Laxman, E., Shepard, D., Morrow, F., Salomon, R., Perrone, G., Asmundsson, G., Meydani, M., Blumberg, J., Mune, M., Harrison, D. E., Archer, J. R., & Shigenaga, M. (1995). Dietary calorie restriction in the Emory mouse: Effects on lifespan, eye lens cataract prevalence and progression, levels of ascorbate, glutathione, glucose, and glycohemoglobin, tail collagen breaktime, DNA and RNA oxidation, skin integrity, fecundity, and cancer. *Mechanisms of Aging and Development, 79,* 33–57.

Vander, A. J., Sherman, J., & Luciano, D. (1990). Homeostatic mechanisms and cellular communication. *Human physiology: The mechanisms of body function.* New York: McGraw-Hill.

Wilson, V. L., & Jones, P. A. (1983). DNA methylation decreases in aging but not in immortal cells. *Science, 220,* 1054–1057.

Woodring, E. W., & Shay, J. W. (1995). Time, telomeric and tumors: Is cellular senescence more than an anticancer mechanism? *Current Topics in Cell Biology, 5,* 293–297.

CHAPTER 4

Neurogerontology: The Aging Nervous System

James F. Willott

The brain is the "organ" of behavior and cognition. Learning, perception, locomotion, language, and virtually every human endeavor are the outcomes of the brain's unceasing activity. If we are to begin to appreciate the aging process, we must have some understanding of how the nervous system fares. It is the goal of this chapter to impart an overview of our current knowledge in this regard.

The term *neurogerontology* is used in this chapter to identify the field that integrates neuroscience and gerontology. It is a challenging field because of the brain's baffling complexity and the diversity of arcane scientific disciplines that comprise modern neuroscience, not to mention the many biological and behavioral changes that accompany aging, described in the other chapters of this book. Because many readers will have little sophistication in neuroscience, the topic will be approached in as nontechnical a manner as possible.

The brain's work is performed by billions of neurons. As Figure 4.1 shows, these cells come in many shapes, often having elaborate arrays of branching dendrites. The dendrites make contact with the dendrites and axons of other neurons to form circuits and networks of remarkable sophistication. Interactions among vast communities of neurons provide the method by which the brain functions.

A good way to appreciate some basic principles of neurophysiology is to consider the neural circuits underlying a "simple" behavior, as shown in Figure 4.2. A person is tapped on the back. The peripheral somatosensory system detects the tap, and the central somatosensory system determines it to be a relatively light tap to the back. The association cortex determines that such a tap is not to be expected under the present conditions and initiates movement of the head via a motor system; at the same time, the autonomic nervous system is

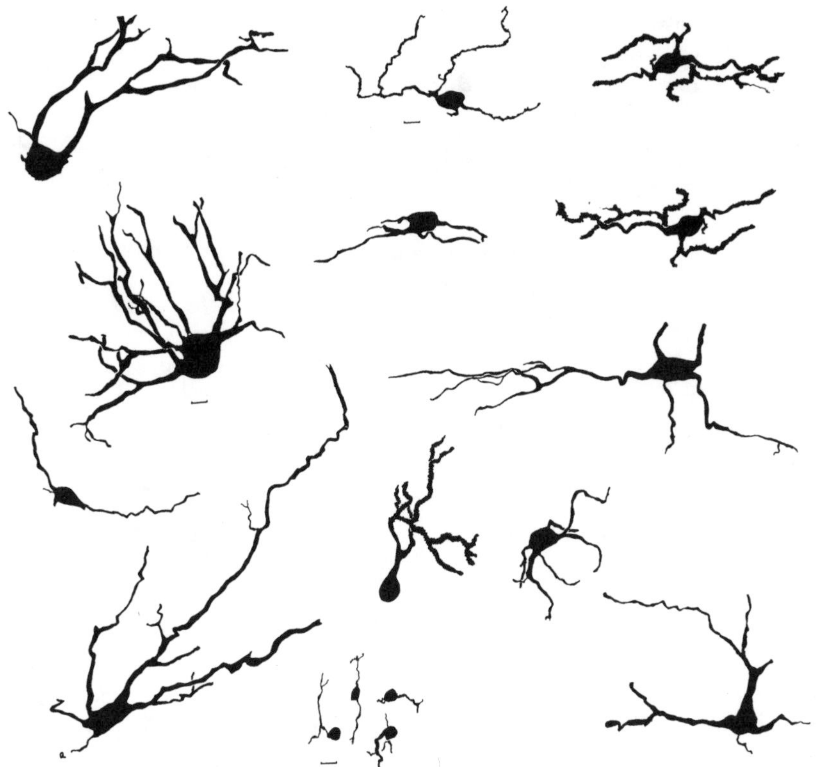

FIGURE 4.1 Examples of a variety of neurons in the anteroventral cochlear nucleus of a 33-month-old C57 mouse. These neurons were stained with the Golgi stain, which stains complete neurons, and then traced with a microscope drawing tube. All neurons were traced with the same magnification (scale bars = 10 microns). The differences in size among neurons can be striking, as shown by comparing the large "octopus cells" in the upper left with the cluster of four diminutive "granule cells" in the upper left with the cluster of four diminutive "granule cells" at the bottom center. Despite the fact that the mouse was extremely old (median life span is about 26 months), these neurons are, in general, similar in appearance to those found in young mice.

activated to help ready the body for action. The eyes sight the tapper and relay this information to the visual cortex, which deciphers the identity of the tapper as a friend. This information is sent back to the association cortex, where a decision is made to ask the tapper what he wants. Because that action is verbal, speech areas of the brain come into the picture, and the process continues.

If aging were a gremlin bent on interfering with behavior, its targets would be many, and it would have numerous strategies. It could short-circuit the behavior just described by attacking any one structure, or it could sever the lines of communication between structures. It could bring on a mild but generalized

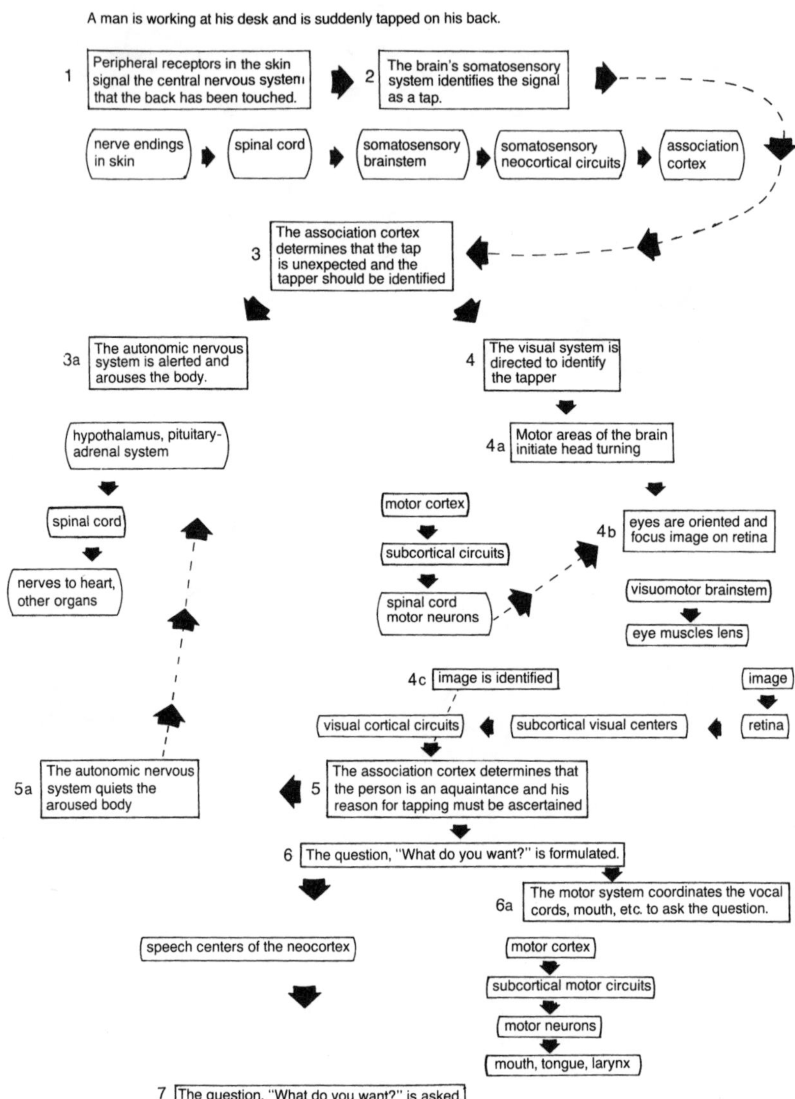

FIGURE 4.2 Diagram of possible circuitry underlying a simple behavioral sequence. Rectangles = a process; ovals = anatomical structure or region. See text for discussion.

decline of the whole system (e.g., by destroying or incapacitating some neurons). It could impair the ability of individual neurons to receive information (e.g., by eliminating some dendrites). It could slow the system down to the point where the behavior was useless. It could remove biochemicals the neurons require to function properly. It could impair the ability of the sensory receptors to respond to the tap, so the behaviors would not be initiated. It could impair the ability of the muscles to enact the behaviors. It could remove the "tone," or readiness of the nervous system to react.

The degree to which such gremlinesque activities accompany aging will be considered on the following pages. But first, some special problems arising in neurogerontological research must be addressed. A major problem in neuroscience research of any kind is the difficulty in working with the human brain for the following reasons:

1. Most anatomical procedures require excellent *fixation* of brain tissue. A fixative such as formaldehyde must be introduced into the circulatory system quickly, preferably following flushing out the blood while the heart is still beating. Such procedures are easily performed on deeply anesthetized animals but are not feasible with humans for obvious reasons. Without good fixation, brain tissue undergoes rapid postmortem change.
2. Most procedures that measure biological events in living organisms cannot be used with humans because they require surgery or other potentially harmful procedures. In short, it is difficult to obtain biological data from humans.
3. During aging, experimental and environmental variables interact with biological variables. The variance in the life histories of humans is great, and this is typically reflected in variant patterns of "biological aging," particularly where the brain is concerned. Thus, it is difficult to draw general conclusions from human data.

Given these problems, it is not surprising that much neurogerontological research has been performed with animal models. Proper fixation of tissue, the use of many technical procedures in vivo, and control over environmental variance can all be accomplished humanely with animals that are allowed to age in the laboratory colony. Thus, much of the data to be presented has been obtained from animals. However, a good deal of excellent research has also been done on the aging human nervous system despite these technical problems, and human data will be presented in this chapter whenever possible.

Now, back to the gremlin. The potential points of downfall mentioned above all have actual anatomical and/or physiological correlates. The nature of these correlates and their fates during the course of aging is reviewed below. The discussion begins with the neurobiological correlates of "healthy" aging, including basic neuroanatomical features, chemically mediated communication (synapses) among neurons, cerebral metabolism, sensory and motor systems, and the autonomic nervous system. We then turn to pathological conditions that are especially prevalent in the elderly, such as Alzheimer's disease and other dementias. We finish by addressing the ability of the aging brain to change in response to environmental influences, drugs, and other factors. An important caveat should be kept in mind: Discussions of aging, by nature, tend to focus on deficits, declines, and pathology; however, *no* aging person succumbs to all of the deleterious effects of aging, *few* are seriously afflicted by the pathological conditions described, and *many* are affected only minimally by the gremlins of aging.

THE AGING BRAIN IN THE ABSENCE OF AGE-RELATED DISEASE

The Number of Neurons in the Brain

The loss of neurons to aging could have consequences with regard to the integrity of various brain regions and their ability to communicate with one another. Thus, a number of researchers have measured the number of neurons as a function of age. Because merely counting neurons does not require excellent fixation, much of the data has been obtained from humans. This body of literature may be summed up succinctly in three conclusions:

1. In some parts of the brain, neurons are lost with age; in other parts they are not. For instance, Brody (1955) found a decrease in the number of neurons in some regions of the human neocortex but not in others. The neocortex forms the surface of the brain and is essential for most functions, from movement and perception to language, thinking, and other "higher" functions.
2. For a particular region of the brain, the relationship of aging to neuron number can vary between species (Flood & Coleman, 1988). Unlike the human, rodents typically do not appear to lose neurons in the neocortex (Duara, London, & Rapoport, 1985).
3. Within the same species, considering the same brain region, various factors can contribute to the age-related loss of neurons. Willott, Jackson, and Hunter (1987) estimated the number of neurons in a region of the mouse brainstem, the anterior ventral cochlear nucleus (AVCN), using two inbred strains. In one strain (the C57BL/6J strain) some AVCN neurons were lost in early adulthood but not thereafter. In another strain (the CBA/J) neurons were not lost until very late in life. Apparently, factors associated with each genotype determined the life course of neuron loss.

These and other studies indicate that aging is often accompanied by a loss of neurons. However, loss of neurons is not a universal concomitant of aging, nor is it a straightforward process. Rather, the loss or survival of neurons appears to depend on a number of variables, including species, specific brain region, and genetic makeup of the individual.

Neuron Size

Changes in the size of a neuron's soma (cell body) may indicate cellular pathology. A number of studies have measured cell size in the brains of young and old individuals (Flood & Coleman, 1988). All three possible outcomes have been reported—increased, decreased, or unchanged sizes as a function of aging (Hinds & McNelly, 1977; Kemper, 1984; Peters & Vaughan, 1981). Some of these discrepancies may be accounted for by technical problems of fixation, postmortem change, and the like, mentioned above. However, even when technical procedures seem not to confound experimental findings, changes in cell size are not necessarily uniform. In a study from the author's laboratory, cited above, Willott and colleagues (1987) measured the size of neurons in the AVCN brain region of aging C57BL/6J mice. One type of neuron *decreased* in size with aging, but another type of neuron in the same region *increased* in size. Although the functional implications of these different directions of size change are not clear, it seems that, like the loss of neurons with aging, changes in the size of neurons are not governed by a simple principle.

Neuronal Cytoskeleton

Each neuron has a "skeleton" made up of minute tubules and filaments. They give the neuron its shape, move vital substances within the cell body, and are important in the storage and release of chemical neurotransmitters (see below). As reviewed by Anderton et al. (1986), several age-related degenerative diseases seem to involve abnormalities in the neuronal cytoskeleton. One example, discussed below, is the neurofibrillary tangle of Alzheimer's disease. The extent to which more subtle age-related changes in neural function may involve the cytoskeleton remains to be determined, but it seems likely that the cytoskeleton may play an important role in a variety of age-related changes in neurons (Rao & Cohen, 1990).

Neuronal Nuclei

The nucleus is the functional center of a neuron, controlling the activities of the cell. As is the case for the cell soma, changes in the cell's nucleus may also indicate changes in cellular function. Work on the mouse AVCN brain region again demonstrates how the nucleus may change with age. Figure 4.3 shows electron micrographs of AVCN nuclei from an old mouse. The irregularities in the shape of the nucleus from the old mouse are obvious. Similar observations have been made on other neuronal nuclei (Mervis, 1981; Peters & Vaughan, 1981) and may be interpreted as indicative of some sort of change in the cell's functioning.

Dendritic Morphology

The size, shape, orientation, and complexity of the neuron's dendritic tree have a great deal to do with the number of functioning contacts that can be made with other neurons. A time-tested method to examine dendrites is the Golgi staining

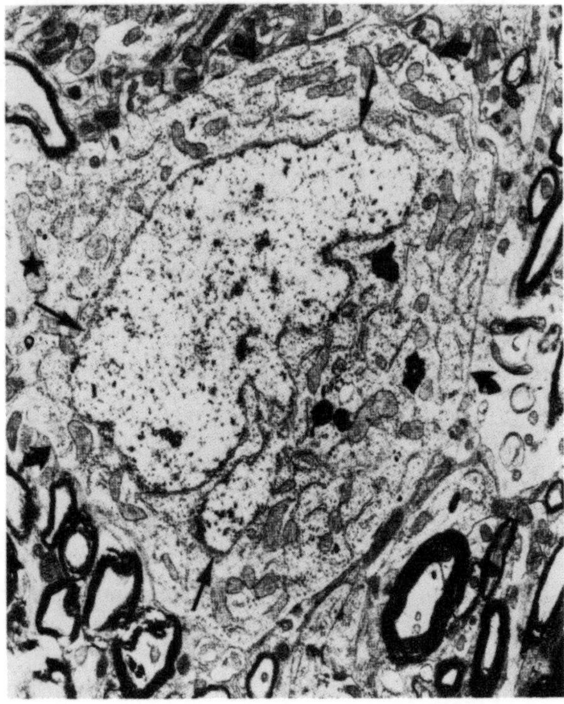

FIGURE 4.3 Example of a neuron from the cochlear nucleus of an old (2 years) C57 mouse. The nucleus is the light region in the center, delineated by the nuclear membrane (straight, narrow arrows); in young mice this type of neuron has a plump, round nucleus. The neuron's body (soma) is delineated by the thick, curved arrows. It contains numerous mitochondria (designated by black star), which are involved in energy production and other functions. Four deposits of lipofuscin are seen at the center left. Magnification; ×10,000. Micrograph courtesy of Dr. W. E. Briner.

technique, which permits visualization of even the minutest detail of neurons. Using this method, Peters and Vaughan (1981) studied one particular type of neuron in the rat, the cortical pyramidal cell. In young rats, cortical pyramidal cells have a characteristic form, with extensive dendritic "trees" that are covered with spines (sites of synaptic contact). In very old rats obvious changes occur in the dendrites, with reduction in dendritic lengths by up to 50% and a loss of one-third of the dendritic spines. Similar structural losses are observed in pyramidal cells from elderly humans (Scheibel, Lindsay, Tomiyasu, & Scheibel, 1975). However, completely normal-looking neurons are often seen right next to degenerating neurons. In addition, in some pyramidal cells there appears to be continuous dendritic *growth* from adulthood into old age (Buell & Coleman, 1979). Once again, degenerative processes most certainly occur but are not universal during aging.

FIGURE 4.4 Tracings of bushy neurons from a 33-month-old C57 mouse, stained with the Golgi technique. The neurons at the top and bottom have characteristic bushy dendritic trees; however, the three cells in the middle appear to have lost their trees. (These were not simply cut off when tissue sections were prepared.) Thus, both normal- and abnormal-looking neurons occur in the same old animal. Scale bar = 10 microns.

Observations from the author's laboratory suggest that similar age-related changes can occur in other neuron types. Figure 4.4 shows drawings of Golgi-impregnated "bushy" neurons in the auditory system (AVCN again) of a very old mouse. Some of the cells have the characteristic busy dendritic tree, whereas others appear to have lost the bushy portion (similar observations have been documented in another part of the mouse cochlear nucleus by Willott and Bross [1991]). As was the case with the cortical pyramidal cells of aging rats, both normal- and abnormal-appearing bushy neurons are found in the same aged animal.

Myelin

Myelin is the lipid substance that forms the insulating covering of many axons; myelination increases the speed and efficiency of the conduction of action potentials (nerve impulses) among neurons. Changes in the myelin content of the nervous system, therefore, have the potential to disrupt communication among neurons. Several studies have found age-related changes in myelin. For instance, Morell, Greenfield, Constantino-Cellarine, and Wisniewski (1972) and Sun and Samorajski (1972) found that myelin continued to be produced during adulthood in mice, but the composition of the myelin (and perhaps its effects on neural conduction) changed.

Glia

Glia are small cells that are actually more numerous than neurons. They serve several functions, including structural and physiological support for neurons, production of myelin, and elimination of nonfunctioning tissue (phagocytosis). The fate of glial cells during aging is difficult to assess. The death of neurons or other cells would likely be associated with the proliferation of the phagocytic microglia because they are involved with the cleanup of dead material. On the other hand, astrocytes (glial cells that perform a supportive function for neurons) or oligodendrocytes, which produce myelin for neuronal axons, may be lost to attrition. Aging-related loss of glial cells has been observed (Kemper, 1984) and could have serious consequences for the ability of neurons to function normally.

Gross Brain Weight and Morphology

All of the features thus far described probably contribute to the gross properties of the brain. Because gross measurements can be reliably obtained from postmortem material and from living humans by using computed tomography (CT) scans and other methods, a good deal of data on humans is available. Many researchers have reported a moderate (e.g., 6%–11%) loss of brain weight in humans older than 80 years. Corsellis (1976) estimated the volumes of the gray matter (brain regions heavily occupied by neuron cell bodies and dendrites) and the white matter (areas occupied by myelinated axons) and projected a 3.5% per decade decline in males and a 2% per decade decline in females.

Gross morphological changes are often observed in aged brains. These include atrophy of the ridges (gyri) and crevices (sulci) of the cerebral surface. Enlargement of the fluid-filled ventricles of the brain's interior is often seen as well (Duara et al., 1985; Kemper, 1984).

It would appear that loss of brain weight and/or gross morphological changes often accompanies aging. However, these findings are generally based on average measurements from a number of brains. If individuals are considered, such changes are by no means inevitable, as many elderly people show little sign of gross brain atrophy. The causes of the apparent individual differences in age-related change are unclear. However, data on the relationships among neuropathology, aging per se, and brain size, which are often not reported, might provide a better understanding of these differences.

Synapses

The synapse is the means by which most neuronal communication occurs. Most synapses involve the release of a chemical *neurotransmitter*, which crosses a narrow cleft to react with postsynaptic receptors on other neurons, muscles, or glands, and causes them to respond. Figure 4.5 summarizes various structures comprising one particular type of synapse, that of the neuromuscular junction.

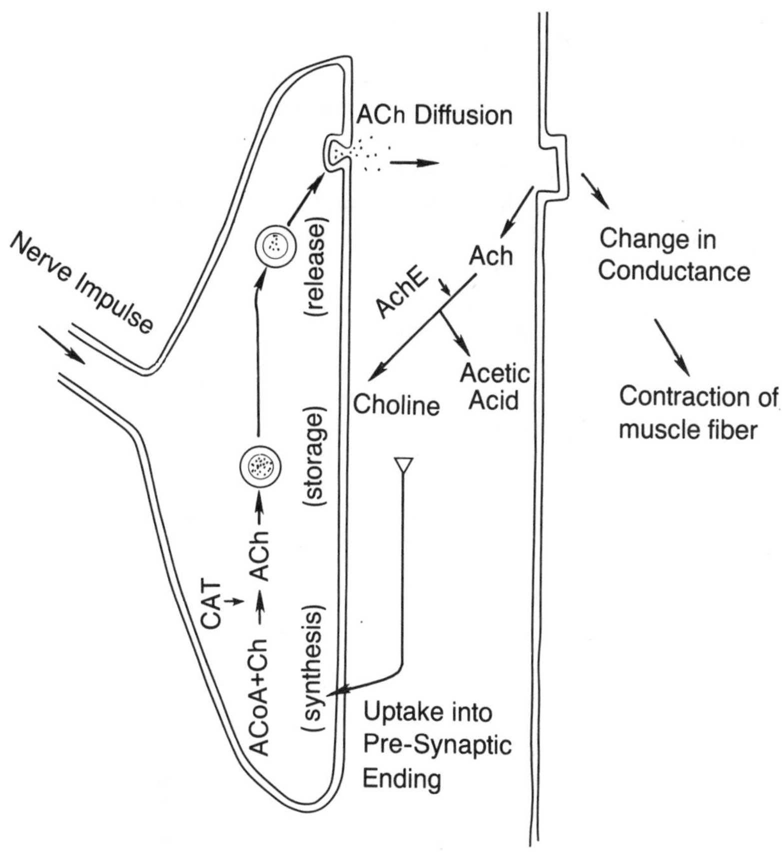

FIGURE 4.5 The neuromuscular junction. Acetylcholine (ACh) is synthesized in the presynaptic nerve terminal from choline (Ch) and acetyl coenzyme A (ACoA), with the catalyst choline acetyltransferase (CAT), and stored in presynaptic vesicles. The arrival of a nerve impulse (action potential) causes the vesicles, which have moved to the presynaptic membrane, to open, releasing Ach into the synaptic cleft. The ACh diffuses across the cleft, where it binds to a postsynaptic receptor on the muscle fiber. This alters certain properties of the muscle (e.g., conductance of certain ions), making it contract. After this, ACh is broken down by the enzyme acetylcholinesterase (AChE) into choline and acetic acid so that it will not continue to cause muscle contraction. The choline is reused by the presynaptic terminal to make more ACh. Even a simple, brief, coordinated movement involves thousands of such events on the correct muscle fibers used in the movement and in a precisely timed sequence. Similar events are constantly occurring in the many millions of synapses among neurons in the brain.

The neuromuscular junction is the synapse between peripheral motor nerves and skeletal muscles and is the most thoroughly studied of synapses because of its accessibility. It can serve as a model for synapses in the brain by demonstrating the key components of synaptic functioning. Figure 4.5 shows that the neurotransmitter, in this case acetylcholine (ACh), must be synthesized from precursor substances, stored, and released into the synaptic cleft; react with synaptic receptors after crossing the synaptic cleft; affect the postsynaptic membrane; and be inactivated. If any one of these synaptic events is disrupted by aging, the synapse could be affected.

Synapses in the brain can be much more complex than the neuromuscular junction, adding to the potential for a variety of age-related changes. For example, many synapses involve *dendritic spines*, tiny appendages on the dendrites of neurons that indicate a synapse, and these can decrease in number with age. But whereas most researchers who have estimated the number of synaptic sites in the aging brain have reported losses, absence of change and increases in synaptic sites have also been seen (Cotman, 1990). Unfortunately, little is known at present about the vulnerability of the various synaptic components during aging, and a great deal of work has yet to be done.

Neurotransmitter Systems

Further information on synaptic function is derived from the study of synaptic neurotransmitters. Whereas all neuromuscular junctions use ACh as their transmitter, a number of chemical neurotransmitters are used by the brain. Several factors make it difficult to understand how neurotransmitter systems vary with aging. First is the sheer number of chemicals that are believed to act as neurotransmitters in one part of the brain or another: dopamine, norepinephrine, serotonin, histamine, ACh, gamma aminobutyric acid (GABA), glutamate, glycine, taurine, beta endorphin, and many others. Second, neurotransmission is a dynamic process, as shown in Figure 4.5. The amount of a particular chemical may be less important than the balance among a number of substances (e.g., the neurotransmitters, enzymes that break down the transmitters, receptors for the transmitters, chemicals within the neuron that interact with the transmitters, etc.). An increase in the levels of a neurotransmitter might indicate an overactive system that is producing extra transmitter or a system that cannot use its transmitter because its receptors are impaired. Thus, it is often difficult to interpret experimental findings.

ACh is the neurotransmitter in several brain circuits (as well as at the neuromuscular junction, discussed above). As we are already familiar with ACh, let us briefly review some findings on aging and ACh in the brain, to impart a sense of the types of experiments that are performed and some of the problems in interpreting them. This discussion is derived from a detailed review of neurotransmitters and aging by Rogers and Bloom (1985).

Recall that ACh is synthesized from choline, which is taken into the neuron by presynaptic terminals, where it combines with coenzyme A, catalyzed by choline acetyltransferase (CAT). There is evidence that the uptake of choline is reduced in the aged rat brain, at least under certain conditions. However, this could be due to a loss of cholinergic neurons (i.e., neurons using ACh as their transmitter) rather than to biochemical changes. A reduction in brain CAT activity has also been reported in aged rodents and humans by some researchers. However, others have reported no age-related changes in CAT, and there appear to be individual differences in humans. For instance, dementia (see below) is correlated with significantly reduced CAT levels, and the degree to which reduced CAT varies with normal aging is unclear. Thus, it appears that the synthesis of ACh and therefore the amount available for use by the brain is reduced in some elderly individuals, although the cause(s) of this deficit may be difficult to interpret.

If it is established that ACh synthesis is diminished in the elderly, can it be assumed that there is less ACh available to neurons? Not necessarily. Reduced synthesis could be counterbalanced by decreased release of ACh from the neurons or reduced enzymatic breakdown of ACh after it is released. As we have seen (Fig. 4.5), the breakdown of ACh is accomplished by AChE; unfortunately, the effects of aging on AChE, if any, are not clear.

The actions of ACh can also be affected independently of synthesis or amounts of ACh if some postsynaptic receptors (Fig. 4.5) are lost with aging. There is good evidence that the amount of ACh that can be bound to receptors is reduced in old age, most probably because of a loss of active receptor sites. This view is supported by experiments using iontophoresis, a technique by which ACh is applied directly to neurons with fine-tipped glass micropipettes. The responses normally evoked by ACh are diminished in the neurons of old animals.

Finally, indirect evidence for the loss of efficacy of a transmitter system can be obtained from behavioral experiments. ACh is known to affect certain memory processes. For instance, pharmacologically blocking ACh in young animals can cause memory deficits. Thus, one interpretation of memory deficits that accompany aging (see chapter 5) is that ACh systems are affected.

It should be clear that dealing with even one neurotransmitter is a difficult task and that many problems can arise in interpreting experimental findings (see Morgan & May, 1990). Multiply this by the number of possible brain transmitters, and the challenge of this area of research is evident.

Intracellular Structures

The appearance of abnormal structures within neurons is often associated with aging.

Lipofuscin. Lipofuscin is a dark-pigmented fatty substance that builds up within neurons as aging occurs. The dark blotches in the old neuron shown in Figure 4.3 are lipofuscin. At present it is unclear whether lipofuscin interferes with the ability of neurons to function normally. For instance, in one brain structure in humans, the inferior olive, neurons can accumulate large amounts of lipofuscin yet survive (Monagle & Brody, 1974). Thus, accumulation of lipofuscin may be a marker of aging but may be without deleterious consequences.

It should also be noted that cells playing a supporting role in the activity of the nervous system may accumulate particles of lipofuscin or other pigment. This is demonstrated in Figure 4.6, which shows a nonneural stria vascularis cell from the inner ear of an old mouse. The stria vascularis is essential for the normal functioning of the inner ear. Although strial cells in young animals often contain melanin pigment, dense accumulations like those seen in Figure 4.6 are not found. Changes such as this and a general age-related thinning of the stria vascularis suggest functioning pathology that may impair the inner ear's physiological processes. Indeed, a major cause of age-related hearing loss is malfunctioning of the stria vascularis (Schuknecht, 1974).

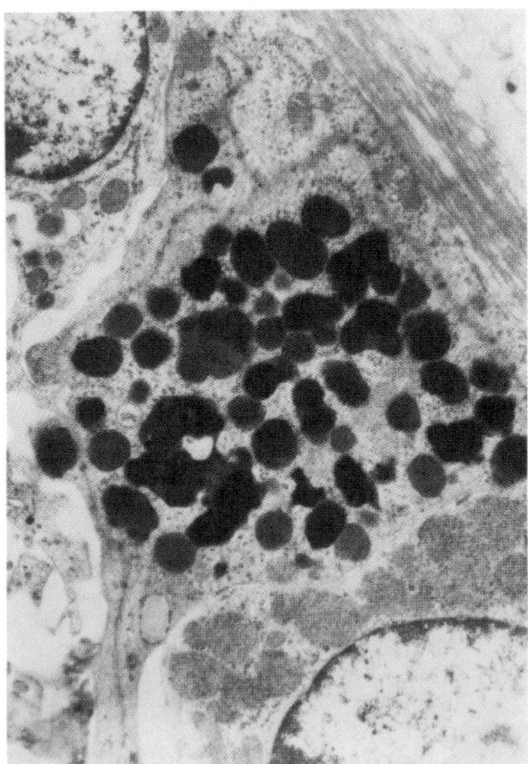

FIGURE 4.6 Electron micrograph of a cell in the stria vascularis of an old (2 years) C57 mouse. Note numerous pigment particles. Magnification, ×18,000. (This micrograph was produced in collaboration with Dr. Remy Pujol in Montpellier, France.)

Granulovascular Degeneration, Hirano Bodies, Lewy Bodies. These represent varieties of structures that are sometimes found in aged human brain cells and are not typically found in young neurons (Kemper, 1984). Intracellular bodies such as these appear to be more closely related to age-related pathology than lipofuscin because they are found in increased quantities in dementias such as Alzheimer's disease (see below).

Plaques, Tangles, and Amyloid. These features sometimes appear in the brain during the normal aging process but are also symptoms of aging-related pathologies such as Alzheimer's disease (Kemper, 1984). Neurofibrillary tangles are masses of paired helical filaments (components of the cytoskeleton) that occur within the neurons and are readily visualized microscopically with tissue stains employing silver as a staining element. Tangles are primarily a feature of the aging human brain but similar structures can be induced in other animals by, for example, injecting toxic aluminum salts into brain tissue. Neurofibrillary tangles are more common in some regions of the aged brain than in others, being rare in parts of the neocortex but more common in the hippocampus (a part of the brain involved in memory and certain emotional behaviors).

So-called senile and neuritic plaques are composed of degenerating neuronal processes, often with astrocyte glial cells surrounding a core of amyloid (a starchlike substance). Unlike tangles, they are most likely to occur in the neocortex of normal elderly people. Plaques are also associated with pathology, and plaquelike structures can be induced in animals by aluminum injections or scrapie virus. Amyloid (which is properly characterized as a glycoprotein) can also be found independent of neuritic plaques, infiltrating the blood vessels and surface membranes of the brain or the brain tissue itself, with damaging results.

Metabolism

Neurons rely almost exclusively on glucose and oxygen to fuel their activity. The metabolism of these and other substances has been evaluated in several neurogerontological studies. In both humans and other species the results of various studies are mixed. For instance, in humans some studies show a decrease in metabolism; some do not (Duara et al., 1985). The reasons for the discrepancies are unclear, but one probable source of confusion is the failure of some researchers to specify their subjects' medical histories (which could affect metabolism) or the state of their sensory systems. When sensory systems are active, the regions of the brain that interact with them increase their metabolic activity; if the sensory systems are not functioning properly, as sometimes occurs during aging (see below), then those brain regions may display reduced metabolic activity, which could be mistakenly attributed to aging. However, a study by Willott, Hunter, and Coleman (1988) suggests that age-related sensory deficits need not contribute to a decline in certain aspects of metabolism. These authors studied old CBA mice that had near-normal hearing sensitivity and C57 mice that had profound age-related hearing loss. They injected a radioactively labeled 2-deoxyglucose (a glucoselike substance) into the mice and used autoradiography to measure the relative amounts that were taken from the bloodstream into brain cells in the auditory system. Profound hearing loss did not appear to diminish the auditory system's ability to incorporate 2-deoxyglucose.

Sensory Systems

The link between the brain and the body or the outside world is made by the sensory systems. The peripheral sensory apparatuses (eyes, ears, etc.) change energy in the environment to nerve impulses, which are relayed to the brain for processing. Thus, in addition to impairment of the peripheral sensory structures, changes in the brain, discussed above, can also contribute to perceptual problems in the elderly.

Visual System. Patterns of light are focused on the retina after entering the eye via the cornea and lens. The retina is, embryologically, an extension of the brain and contains a complex network of neurons, in addition to the sensory cells that transduce light into neural responses. Nerve impulses in the optic nerves carry the information from the retina to the brain, where further information processing occurs. The end result is visual perception. The peripheral visual system is vulnerable to aging, as reviewed by Ordy and Brizzee (1979). Changes in the lens system's ability to focus the image, opacity of the transparent optical path, changes in pupil size, impaired functioning of the retina, and loss of myelin in the optic nerves can all contribute to a loss of acuity.

After age 60 loss of acuity is common, and by age 80 relatively few individuals have vision correctable to 20/20. Other aspects of vision can also suffer during the aging process, such as the ability to accurately see moving objects, the critical flicker frequency (the rate at which a flickering image, such as a motion picture, is seen not to flicker), and depth perception. Declines such as these cannot be attributed to optical changes and are presumably due to changes in the retina or central visual pathways (see Spear, 1993).

Auditory System. The term *presbycusis* refers to auditory dysfunction associated with aging. The most common form of presbycusis is sensorineural, involving degeneration of the sensory hair cells of the inner ear and the axons of the auditory nerve that provide neural input to the brain. However, other forms of presbycusis also may occur, including changes in the mechanical properties of the ear, metabolic dysfunctions in the inner ear, loss of blood flow in the capillaries serving the inner ear, or, of course, changes in the central nervous system (Schuknecht, 1974; Willott, 1991). Sensorineural presbycusis is typically most severe for the tissue that responds to high-pitched sounds; thus, presbycusic hearing loss is typically most severe for high-pitched sounds, and some loss of hearing sensitivity often begins well before age 50 (reviewed in Willott, 1991).

Another observation is that men tend to have more severe presbycusis than women. At first blush, this observation might suggest that men are biologically more vulnerable to presbycusis, as they appear to be for other medical conditions (as reflected by mortality data, discussed elsewhere in this volume). Although this may be true, men are typically exposed to more noise at work or play, and noise can also produce sensorineural impairment. The fact that some rural third world peoples show no gender differences in presbycusis (Kryter, 1983) suggests that the environment may actually be responsible for gender differences in industrialized societies. Here is an excellent example of how difficult it can be to differentiate biological and environmental contributions to age-related changes in perception and behavior.

Our work on the central auditory system of mice provides an example of why the brain must be studied in addition to the peripheral sensory structures. The ability of an auditory brain region, the inferior colliculus (IC), to respond to tones was assessed. In young animals, neurons in the upper half of the IC normally respond to low-pitched tones but not to high-pitched tones, whereas neurons in the lower half of the IC respond only to high-pitched tones. This organization is due to neural circuits that connect these regions to sensory cells of the inner ear responding to low- and high-pitched sounds. Aging C57 mice succumb to presbycusis; like many humans, the sensory cells of the inner ear degenerate and lose their ability to respond to high-pitched sounds. This, of course, prevents the lower half of the IC from responding to high-pitched sounds. However, the IC neurons that have lost their ability to respond to high-pitched sounds develop a new capacity—they now respond *better* to low-frequency sounds than they did during young adulthood (Willott, 1986). These findings are summarized in Figure 4.7.

This reorganization of the central auditory system may have its benefits: the animal may now have enhanced ability to deal with the low-frequency sounds its ears can still detect. On the other hand, problems may arise because the rules of the game by which IC neurons have learned to function are now changed, perhaps confusing the brain. Such changes might account for the problems many older people have in accurately perceiving sounds even when they can hear them.

Studies of the aging mouse auditory system demonstrate two different types of age-related effects on the brain: the central effects of biological aging (CEBA) and the central effects of peripheral pathology (CEPP). The type of neural plasticity occurring in the IC is an example of CEPP because aging affected the cochlea, which in turn affected the brain. CEBA refers to central changes that occur with aging irrespective of changes in the cochlea, the types of changes discussed earlier in this chapter. For many elderly people, the ability to hear accurately is challenged by both CEBA and CEPP. This underscores the necessity to understand the often complex interactions among different parts of the

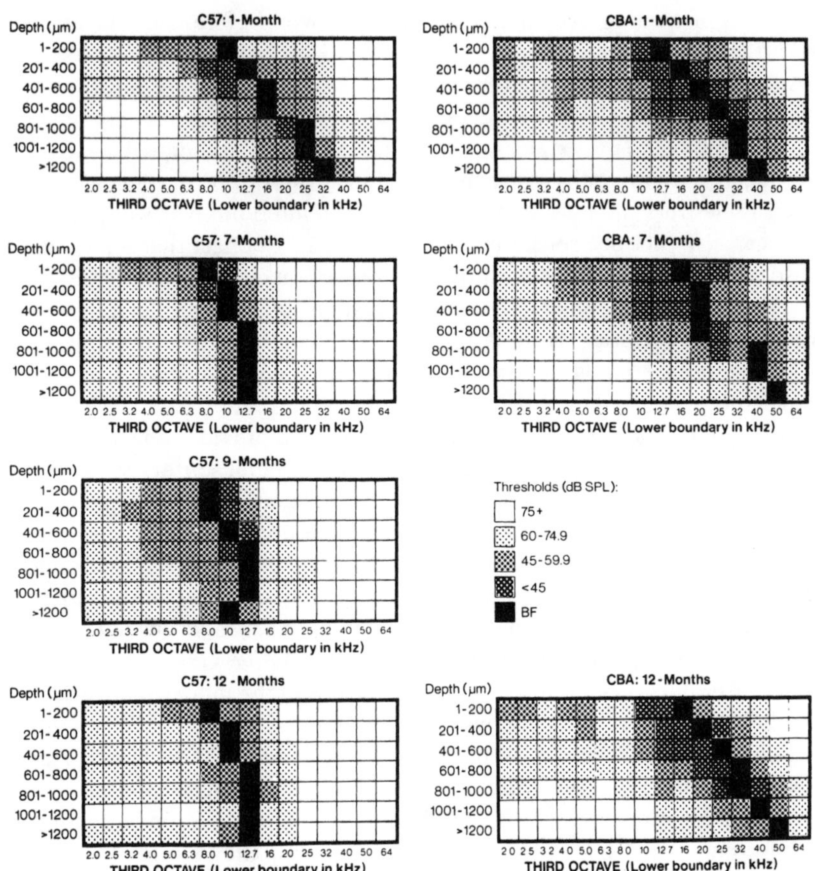

FIGURE 4.7 Reorganization of frequency representation in the inferior colliculus (IC) of mice with presbycusis. The frequency of tones used to test the sensitivity of the mouse's hearing are presented on the abscissa; the location of neurons tested (depth within the IC) is presented on the ordinate. The darker the shading in a box, the more sensitive are the neurons to a particular tone frequency. In young mice (top panel), the deeper IC neurons are sensitive to high frequencies but not to low frequencies. As the mice age and lose their hearing for high-frequency sounds, the "tonotopic" organization changes. The deep neurons no longer respond to high frequencies but are now more sensitive to low frequencies than younger deep neurons. From "Changes in Frequency Representation in the Auditory System of Mice with Age-Related Hearing Impairment" by James F. Willott, 1984, *Brain Research*, *309*, pp. 159–162, with kind permission from Elsevier Science-NL, 1055 KV Amsterdam, The Netherlands.

nervous system (both peripheral and central) and how they are affected during aging.

Other Sensory Systems. The other sensory systems include somatosensory systems (touch, pressure, pain, body position, movement, heat and cold, etc.), olfaction (smell), gustation (taste), and vestibular systems (balance, acceleration). Any of these systems can be affected by general changes in the central nervous system or by loss of sensory and/or nerve axons that transmit sensory information to the brain. The various body sensations can be dulled, or balance can be impaired. Losses or alterations in taste and smell can be particularly troublesome to many seniors. Changes in ability to detect and identify the four basic taste sensations (sweet, sour, salty, bitter) and a number of aromas often lead to changes in food preferences or difficulties in appreciating favorite meals (Schiffman, 1979).

Motor Systems

Movements require complex processing of information in the brain to send neural messages out through nerve fibers to the muscles of the body (Fig. 4.2). As we have seen, the neuromuscular junction accomplishes this nerve-muscle communication, using ACh as the transmitter. As is the case with sensory systems, therefore, age-related changes in brain function, peripheral nerve function, neurotransmitters, and the muscles themselves can all potentially affect movement in the elderly.

One type of brain neuron, the Betz cell, is found in the motor neocortex and has been studied in aged humans by Scheibel and Tomiyasu (1977). These are very large neurons, and only 35,000 to 40,000 are found in the human neocortex—a rather modest number. These cells are largely responsible for control of the large extensor muscles of the back and lower extremities, which maintain us in an upright stance. Animal research indicates that the neurons actually seem to cause the muscles to relax, creating a level of muscle tone that is conducive to smooth movement. In the brains of people who died during the 7th to 8th decades of life, it is not uncommon to find a 70% to 80% loss of Betz cells, with the surviving cells often showing signs of age: loss of dendritic spines, disintegration of dendritic shafts, loss of small dendritic branches, and shrinkage of the cell body. One might predict (from the basic animal research) that this loss of Betz cells in humans would create a situation of abnormal muscle tone, leading to stiffening and slowing of activity and muscle fatigue after work. This is precisely what happens in many elderly people. Thus, senescence of the motor cortex seems to contribute to the problems created by the aging of muscles and nerves. Here is an excellent example of how basic neurobiological research can provide insights into the human aging process.

When the central and peripheral problems reach severe degrees, say in the 8th to 9th decades, the "senile gait" may result (Adams, 1984). The step shortens to a shuffle, the base of the stance widens, and turning becomes difficult. The arms do not swing easily, running is impossible, and frequent falls may occur. Although this degree of motor disruption is by no means inevitable, a degree of motor decline is a common concomitant of aging. Fortunately, it is becoming clear that much of this decline can be prevented or reversed by proper exercise and fitness (see chapter 15).

Autonomic Nervous System

The sympathetic and parasympathetic divisions of the autonomic nervous system (ANS) influence numerous bodily functions, from heart rate and blood pressure to thermoregulation, gastrointestinal functions, sleep regulation, and penile erections. Components of the ANS reside in the brain and spinal cord, as well as in the peripheral nerves of the body that innervate the heart, smooth muscles, and glands. Obviously, age-related problems of the ANS would have the potential to affect a variety of important functions. This is particularly the case with the sympathetic division, which plays an important role in reactions to stress (e.g., increased heart rate and blood pressure).

As reviewed by Finch and Landfield (1985), levels of plasma norepinephrine, a hormone associated with sympathetic nervous system activity, increase in aging humans. Such increases could indicate a hyperactive sympathetic system or a reduction in clearance of norepinephrine after it is released, but it seems likely from several studies that enhanced responses to various stressful stimuli and longer periods of time to return to resting levels often occur in the elderly. On the other hand, "target" organs may become more or less responsive to norepinephrine, further complicating our understanding of the effects of aging on the ANS. Although the fate of the ANS with aging is not yet clear, alterations in the ANS do occur, and these could reduce control of neural and other physiological activities.

Biological Rhythms

Certain regions of the brain play the role of "biological clock" in establishing circadian (daily) rhythms that affect various behaviors, such as eating and sleeping. The neural mechanisms that control these rhythms may change with aging. For example, the period of the daily biological clock appears to shorten with age, and the magnitude of the day-night differences may decrease (Richardson, 1990). These changes could have subtle effects on a variety of psychological and biological functions.

NEUROPATHOLOGY ASSOCIATED WITH AGING

Up to this point we have been addressing age-related changes in the nervous system that vary greatly in their effects on individuals and are generally not associated with specific pathologies. It is clear from other chapters in this book that these changes have little deleterious effect on many older individuals; the notion that "senility" is an inevitable aspect of aging is demonstrably false. The effectiveness of the gremlin of aging varies greatly. There are, however, a number of conditions that can be devastating to the elderly—conditions that present the most serious obstacles to normal, healthy aging. These are briefly reviewed below.

Alzheimer's Disease

Alzheimer's disease (AD) is a term often used to include related syndromes: early onset ("presenile") AD and senile dementia of the Alzheimer type (occurring after age 65). For this discussion, the two forms will not be differentiated (they may or may not be variants of the same disease). In recent years, AD has been the subject of an intensive research effort. A summary of this work is well beyond the scope of this chapter, and it must suffice to describe the symptoms and some possible causes of AD (for a thorough, recent review, see the book edited by Terry, Katzman, & Bick, 1994).

Behavioral Symptomatology. The onset of AD is often subtle, being first manifested by mood changes, faulty judgment, memory impairment, disorientation, or depression. These can progress, possibly being joined by bouts of irritability or anxiety, loss of communication, disruption of sleep, and the need for institutionalization. The disease may progress to include severe neurological complications, apathy, loss of responsiveness to stimuli, and ultimately, death.

Pathology. Neuritic plaques and neurofibrillary tangles (described above) are typical of AD and remain the primary criteria for a diagnosis of AD, although they can be assessed only after death. Modern neuroimaging techniques (CT, MRI, and PET scans) can be used to assess other pathologic signs of AD in living patients, such as enhanced brain atrophy, particularly in the frontal and temporal lobes and in the "basal forebrain," a subcortical cholinergic brain region whose neurons send axons to the neocortex (see below).

Possible Causes. The reasons that certain abnormalities arise in AD patients are not yet clear, but both environmental and genetic factors are likely to play key roles (Terry et al., 1994). For example, people with close relatives suffering from AD are several times as likely to develop the disease as those without a familial history of AD, and several studies have identified genes associated with AD (Terry et al., 1994). A number of possible causes of AD that could be triggered by genetic and/or other factors have been proposed. In reviewing them, it is important to keep in mind that AD probably represents related disorders with differing etiologies.

Failure of cholinergic systems. A good deal of early evidence indicated that cholinergic neurotransmitter systems in the brain (those utilizing ACh), were impaired in AD patients; for example, cholinergic neurons of the basal forebrain degenerate in AD (Coyle, Price, & DeLong, 1983). Axons of neurons in this basal forebrain system project widely to the cerebral cortex and hippocampus, important regions for memory and other cognitive function. Since ACh has been implicated in cognitive functioning, impairment of this transmitter might be associated with some of the symptoms of AD. Unfortunately, a preeminent role of cholinergic mechanisms of AD has proved to be less compelling than was first believed. Many other pathologic changes also accompany AD, and alterations in ACh systems appear to provide only a partial explanation of AD (Terry et al., 1994).

Excitotoxicity. One of the major excitatory neurotransmitters in the brain is glutamate, and when such synapses are overactive, neurons can be damaged. Glutamate excitotoxicity has been implicated in neural damage caused by stroke and in various neurodegenerative diseases, perhaps including AD (Terry et al., 1994). If processes associated with AD were to enhance excitotoxic death of cortical and other neurons, the symptoms and pathology of the disease could result.

β-Amyloid. β-amyloid protein is a major components of the plaques that are characteristic of AD. Some research has suggested that the protein itself might be a cause of the pathology associated with AD (not just a result of AD) and that its occurrence can be associated with genetic abnormalities (Terry et al., 1994).

Aluminum and other trace elements. Aluminum salts can produce tanglelike structures in experimental animals, and there have been reports of increased aluminum content with the disease. Thus, AD could reflect aluminum toxicity of some sort. Research in this area has been somewhat controversial, but strong evidence for a causative role of aluminum or other elements has not been provided. Aluminum may, however, accumulate in degenerating neurons and might exacerbate degeneration, as might mercury and certain other elements (Terry et al., 1994).

Other possible causes of AD. This list of possible causes of AD is only partial. AD researchers have also evaluated the role of viral infections or "exaggerated aging" processes, but these have not received strong scientific support over the years. A number of other biochemical and structural changes in brain tissue have been considered more recently (Terry et al., 1994) and hold promise for understanding AD. Some of these occur at the molecular level, and techniques to study them are only now becoming available.

Other Dementias

Several other less common syndromes can impair mental functions in older people (Alexander & Geschwind, 1984). *Pick's disease* is most common between 40 and 60 years. It has clinical similarities to AD, but changes in personality, social behavior, and emotionality typically occur with only minimal cognitive dysfunction. Also, unlike AD, language deficits are often early symptoms. Pick's disease is associated with neuronal degeneration in different regions of the neocortex, and a subcortical area, the amygdala, may be seriously affected. Interestingly, the amygdala is known to be involved in emotional and social behaviors. *Huntington's disease* typically reveals itself during middle age. Subcortical motor areas of the brain (the caudate nucleus and putamen) are usually affected, probably accounting for the motor disturbances that are characteristic of this disease. Cognitive disturbances, particularly of nonverbal thought processes, and emotional problems also occur.

Parkinson's disease is most commonly first noticed during the mid-50s but often emerges after 65. Subcortical motor regions that utilize the neurotransmitter dopamine (the striatum and substantia nigra) degenerate, accounting for tremor, rigidity, and other motor dysfunctions that accompany the relatively moderate cognitive symptoms of Parkinson's disease. Treatment of Parkinson's disease may serve as a model for that of other dementias. A drug called L-dopa is administered to Parkinson's disease patients. L-dopa is changed to dopamine in the brain, restoring dopamine levels that were reduced by neuronal degeneration. Although undesirable side effects may result, this treatment can be very effective in reversing symptoms. *Multiinfarct dementias* are caused by small infarcts (lesions caused by the rupture of capillaries or blood vessels) that may occur at any age but are increasingly common after 65 or when the patient has a history of strokes. Multiinfarct dementias have a sudden onset, and the particular type of dementia that results depends on the region(s) of the brain that are involved.

The various types of dementias provide instructive, albeit unfortunate, examples of the power of basic animal neuroscientific research in understanding and ameliorating some of the psychological problems that accompany aging. Insights into the functions of the brain's neurons allowed hypotheses to be formulated concerning the possible neuropathological causes of psychological symptoms in humans. New therapeutic approaches (e.g., L-dopa) have been and continue to be developed as a result of those hypotheses.

Other Disorders

The elderly may be especially susceptible to a variety of other causes of dementia, including infections, neoplasms, trauma, hydrocephalus, metabolic disorders, and toxic disorders, including alcoholism (Alexander & Geschwind, 1984).

CHANGING THE AGING BRAIN

To this point we have discussed the types of changes that accompany aging, either as normal correlates of the aging process or as aspects of pathological states—the work of the gremlin. Can anything be done to counteract this? The answer is a qualified yes; the means are there, but we do not yet understand them well.

Synaptic Growth and Remodeling

Alteration in the pattern and number of synapses has long been recognized as an important aspect of neural development during maturation, and an implicit assumption has often been made that such changes cease during adulthood and aging. A growing body of evidence indicates that this is not the case (Kaas, 1991). The adult brain is capable of change (plasticity). An example of plasticity has already been provided (Fig. 4.7) in which the adult mouse auditory system changed the way it represented sound frequency.

Damage to axons or to the neurons on which they synapse often stimulates *sprouting* of axonal branches and formation of new synapses. This mechanism has the potential to reorganize or remodel local regions of the brain. Aging can slow the sprouting process and reduce its magnitude; however, ample sprouting continues to occur, and new connections are made in old brains (Cotman, 1990). If axonal sprouting is a mechanism for repair or recovery from minor damage, the implication is that the aged brain retains this capacity. It is also likely that plasticity can result from changing the strength of existing synapses, but less is known about the possible effects of aging on such mechanisms.

Environmental Influences

Evidence is also accruing to indicate that environmental factors can have potent influences on the aged brain's physiology and anatomy. For instance, Connor, Melone, Yuen, and Diamond (1981) examined the brains of aged rats that had spent their final 30 days in either environmentally enriched or normal housing. They found that certain dendrites were 86% longer in the enriched rats. Apparently, a more interesting environment may slow certain deleterious correlates of aging.

Finch (1987) discusses some intriguing possibilities with regard to environmental influences on the aging brain. Certain steroids (a class of hormones) have been found to be toxic to brain cells. Environmental stress elevates levels of some steroids (e.g., corticosterone), suggesting the possibility that stress, over a lifetime, may contribute to some of the age-related deficits discussed previously.

Dietary restriction has been shown to retard or ameliorate a variety of biological declines in aging rodents (Ausman & Russell, 1990). Maintaining rodents on a calorically restricted diet for long periods may retard some age-related changes in the brain, as well (Algeri, Biagini, Manfridi, & Pitsikas, 1991; Castiglioni, Legare, Busbee, & Tiffany-Castiglioni, 1991). However, such effects may vary greatly according to an animal's genotype (Willott, Erway, Archer, & Harrison, 1995), clouding the potential for general benefits for all individuals: it is possible that some people could benefit from altered dietary regimens, whereas others might not. Nevertheless, this area of research may provide important insights for slowing the effects of aging on the brain.

As this type of research progresses, we may learn how to slow or reverse age-related changes in the human brain. We may also find that some correlates of aging are actually the result of environmental variables.

Neural Transplantation

An emerging technology is the transplantation of brain tissue from one organism to another. The possibility of replacing brain tissue lost to aging, thereby restoring function, is an exciting future possibility, with some encouraging results being obtained from animal research. Several studies have shown that fetal brain tissue can be successfully transplanted into the brains of aged rodents. An interesting series of experiments attempted to reverse the symptoms of reproductive senescence in female rats (Matsumoto, Kobayashi, Maralsami, & Arai, 1984). Typically, by about 10 months of age (early middle age in rats), the female's estrus cycle becomes irregular and undergoes changes, and reproductive impairment results. The reproductive cycle in female mammals is controlled by neurons in the hypothalamus in the basal region of the brain, and declines in this region contribute greatly to the reproductive problems. When young hypothalamic tissue was transplanted into old rats, significant increases in the weight of the ovaries and uterus resulted, and the reproductive decline was halted or partially reversed (Matsumoto et al., 1984). A different group of researchers transplanted fetal tissue from the locus ceruleus, an area of the brain that uses norepinephrine as its neurotransmitter, into old rats (Gash, Collier, & Sladek, 1985). After 6 weeks, the aged animals showed improvement on a test measuring retention of a learning task.

Although the degree of innervation may be less than is found when tissue is transplanted into young animals, under certain conditions the aged brain may be a very good "host" for transplanted tissue (Cotman, 1990). Of course, a great deal of work must be done before the feasibility of applying this technology to humans can be assessed, and a number of practical and ethical problems must be addressed.

Drugs

The use of drugs to change the way the aging brain works presents both promise and problems. Drugs such as centrophenoxine may reduce the buildup of lipofuscin that occurs in brain and other tissues, suggesting a possible role in lessening age-related changes (Schneider & Reed, 1985). Administration of phosphatidylserine to rats has been shown to reduce the age-related loss of dendritic spines in hippocampus neurons (Nunzi, Milan, Guidolin, & Toffano, 1987). The ameliorating effects of L-dopa on Parkinson's disease are well documented, and drugs associated with ACh show promise in treating memory impairment in the elderly (Bartus, Dean, Beer, & Lippa, 1982). Numerous other drugs have been used with the elderly, with mixed results (Cohen, 1988; Schneider & Reed, 1985), and new ones will undoubtedly produce benefits in the years to come.

There are, however, concerns associated with the use of behavior-modifying drugs by the older population. The elderly are the heaviest users of prescription drugs on a per capita basis (Vestal & Cusack, 1990). Their heavy drug usage is cause for concern because of the complex interplay of bodily functions that are brought into play when drugs are taken (i.e., more opportunities for our gremlin). Drugs first need to be absorbed into the body, most typically in the digestive tract. Decreases in gastric output or gut motility might alter the absorption process. After absorption, drugs are distributed throughout various body tissues. Many psychoactive drugs are lipid-soluble, with an affinity for fatty tissue; many drugs can also become bound (hence less active) to plasma proteins. Thus, bodily changes in fat or blood protein content could alter the fate of drugs.

Drugs must ultimately be metabolized and eliminated from the body. Diminished functional capacity of the kidneys or liver has the potential to create problems in drug clearance (Braithwaite, 1982). Given these factors, it is not surprising that adverse drug effects are common in the elderly. As an example, one study found that 16% of patients admitted to a neuropsychiatric unit were experiencing adverse effects of psychotherapeutic drugs, such as confusion, excessive sedation, agitation, paranoia, or other problems (Learoyd, 1972). Difficulties also arise due to noncompliance with drug therapy; many elderly people fail to take medication as prescribed (Vestal & Dawson, 1985).

Even when drugs are taken as prescribed, their actions may not be totally predictable. The mode of action of most psychoactive drugs appears to involve neurotransmitter systems, directly or indirectly. It was shown above that the functioning of certain neurotransmitter systems is affected by aging. At present, the relationships among changes in transmitter systems and drug actions are unclear, and it is imperative that research address this issue.

CONCLUSIONS

This brief review has attempted to provide the reader with a glimpse of the formidable body of neurogerontological research—an introduction to the gremlin of aging and some strategies for understanding its mischief. Although neurogerontology is still a rather young field, a huge amount of information has already been produced, only a small fraction of which could be addressed here. The scientific literature reveals impressive progress in understanding both normal aging and pathological conditions that affect the aging nervous system.

Despite this progress, however, most of the major work to be done lies ahead. Fortunately, the future of neurogerontology is bright. As the field grows, several encouraging trends should be nurtured. First, enhanced interdisciplinary communication is beginning to promote greater understanding of the many physiological changes that accompany aging. These interactions often affect the functioning of neural systems in subtle or unsuspected ways. Interdisciplinary cooperation should lead to new avenues of research. Second, many neuroscientists working on gerontological problems have become more fully acquainted with the aging process per se. They are beginning to think of themselves as neurogerontologists rather than as neuroscientists seeing what happens if they use their techniques on some old animals. The field of neurogerontology is emerging. Third, neuroscience in general is making great technological strides. Application of the sophisticated new technologies to the problems of aging will lead to exciting new findings. Finally, research on how to alter the deleterious changes of aging is growing, with regard to both pathological and more moderate deficits. Techniques that were science fiction a few years ago (e.g., neural transplantation) are now a reality and may someday have widespread therapeutic applications.

The gremlin is getting nervous.

REFERENCES

Adams, R. D. (1984). Aging and human locomotion. In M. L. Albert (Ed.), *Clinical neurology of aging* (pp. 381–386). New York: Oxford University Press.

Alexander, M. P., & Geschwind, N. (1984). Dementia in the elderly. In M. L. Albert (Ed.), *Clinical neurology of aging* (pp. 254–276). New York: Oxford University Press.

Algeri, S., Biagini, L., Manfridi, A., & Pitsikas, N. (1991). Age-related ability of rats kept on a life-long hypocaloric diet in a spatial memory test: Longitudinal observations. *Neurobiology of Aging, 12*, 277–282.

Anderton, B. H., Brion, J.-P., Flament-Durand, J., Haugh, M., Kahn, J., Miller, C. C. J., Probst, A., & Ulrich, J. (1986). Changes in the neuronal cytoskeleton in aging and disease. In M. Bergener, M. Ermini, & H. B. Stahelin (Eds.), *Dimensions in aging* (pp. 69–90). New York: Academic Press.

Ausman, L. M., & Russell, R. M. (1990). Nutrition and aging. In E. L. Schneider & J. W. Rowe (Eds.), *Handbook of the biology of aging* (3rd ed., pp. 384–406). San Diego, CA: Academic Press.

Bartus, R. T., Dean, R. L., Beer, B., & Lippa, A. S. (1982). The cholinergic hypothesis of geriatric memory dysfunction. *Science, 217*, 408–417.

Braithwaite, R. (1982). Pharmacokinetics and age. In D. Wheatley (Ed.), *Psychopharmacology of old age* (pp. 46–54). Oxford: Oxford Medical Publications.

Brody, H. (1955). Organization of the cerebral cortex: 3. A study of aging in cerebral cortex. *Journal of Comparative Neurology, 102*, 511–556.

Buell, S. J., & Coleman, P. D. (1979). Dendritic growth in the aged human brain and failure of growth in senile dementia. *Science, 206*, 854–856.

Castiglioni, A. J., Legare, M. E., Busbee, D. L., & Tiffany-Castiglioni, E. (1991). Morphological changes in astrocytes of aging mice fed normal or caloric restricted diets. *Age, 14*, 102–106.

Cohen, G. D. (1988). *The brain in human aging.* New York: Springer Publishing.

Connor, J. R., Jr., Melone, J. H., Yuen, A. R., & Diamond, M. C. (1981). Dendritic length in aged rats' occipital cortex: An environmentally induced response. *Experimental Neurology, 73*, 827–830.

Corsellis, J. A. N. (1976). Some observations on the Purkinje cell population and on brain volume in human aging. In R. D. Terry & S. Gershon (Eds.), *Aging: Vol. 3. Neurobiology of aging* (pp. 205–210). New York: Raven Press.

Cotman, C. W. (1990). Synaptic plasticity, neurotrophic factors, and transplantation in the aged brain. In E. L. Schneider & J. W. Rowe (Eds.), *Handbook of the biology of aging* (3rd ed., pp. 255–274). San Diego, CA: Academic Press.

Coyle, J. T., Price, D. L., & DeLong, M. R. (1983). Alzheimer's disease: A disorder of cortical cholinergic innervation. *Science, 219*, 1184–1190.

Duara, R., London, E. D., & Rapoport, S. I. (1985). Changes in structure and energy metabolism of the aging brain. In C. E. Finch & E. L. Schneider (Eds.), *Handbook of the biology of aging* (pp. 595–616). New York: Van Nostrand Reinhold.

Finch, C. E. (1987). Environmental influences on the brain during aging. In M. W. Riley, J. D. Matarazzo, & A. Baum (Eds.) *Perspectives in behavioral medicine: The aging dimension* (pp. 77–92). Hillsdale, NJ: Erlbaum.

Finch, C. E., & Landfield, P. W. (1985). Neuroendocrine and autonomic functions in aging mammals. In C. E. Finch & E. L. Schneider (Eds.), *Handbook of the biology of aging* (pp. 567–594). New York: Van Nostrand Reinhold.

Flood, D. G., & Coleman, P. D. (1988). Neuron numbers and sizes in aging brain: Comparisons of human, monkey, and rodent data. *Neurobiology of Aging, 9*, 453–463.

Gash, D. M., Collier, T. J., & Sladek, J. R. (1985). Neural transplantation: A review of recent developments and potential applications to the aged brain. *Neurobiology of Aging, 6*, 131–150.

Hinds, J. W., & McNelly, N. A. (1977). Aging of the rat olfactory bulb: Growth and atrophy of constituent layers and changes in size and number of mitral cells. *Journal of Comparative Neurology, 171*, 345–368.

Kaas, J. H. (1991). Plasticity of sensory and motor maps in adult mammals. In W. M. Cowan, E. M. Shooter, C. F. Stevens, & R. F. Thompson (Eds.), *Annual review of neuroscience* (pp. 137–168). Palo Alto, CA: Annual Reviews.

Kemper, T. (1984). Neuroanatomical and neuropathological changes in normal aging and in dementia. In M. L. Albert (Ed.), *Clinical neurology of aging* (pp. 9–52). New York: Oxford University Press.

Kryter, K. D. (1983). Presbycusis, sociocusis and nosocusis. *Journal of the Acoustical Society of America, 73*, 1897–1916.

Learoyd, B. M. (1972). Psychotropic drugs and the elderly patient. *Medical Journal of Australia, 1*, 1131–1133.

Matsumoto, A., Kobayashi, S., Maralsami, S., & Arai, Y. (1984). Recovery of declined ovarian function in aged female rats by transplantation of newborn hypothalamic tissue. *Proceedings of the Japanese Academy, 60*, 73–76.

Mervis, R. (1981). Cytomorphological alterations in the aging animal brain with emphasis on Golgi studies. In J. E. Johnson (Ed.), *Aging and cell structure* (pp. 143–186). New York: Plenum Press.

Monagle, R. D., & Brody, H. (1974). The effects of age upon the main nucleus of the inferior olive in the human. *Journal of Comparative Neurology, 155*, 61–66.

Morell, P., Greenfield, S., Constantino-Cellarine, E., & Wisniewski, H. (1972). Changes in the protein composition of mouse brain myelin during development. *Journal of Neurochemistry, 19*, 2545–2554.

Morgan, D. G., & May, P. C. (1990). Age-related changes in synaptic neurochemistry. In E. L. Schneider & J. W. Rowe (Eds.), *Handbook of the biology of aging* (3rd ed., pp. 219–254). San Diego, CA: Academic Press.

Nunzi, M. G., Milan, F., Guidolin, D., & Toffano, G. (1987). Dendritic spine loss in hippocampus of aged rats: Effect of brain phosphatidylserine administration. *Neurobiology of Aging, 8*, 501–510.

Ordy, J. M., & Brizzee, K. R. (1979). Functional and structural age differences in the visual system of man and nonhuman primate models. In J. M. Ordy & K. R. Brizzee (Eds.), *Sensory systems and communication in the elderly* (pp. 13–50). New York: Raven Press.

Peters, A., & Vaughan, D. W. (1981). Central nervous system. In J. E. Johnson (Ed.), *Aging and cell structure* (Vol. 1, pp. 1–34). New York: Plenum Press.

Rao, K. M. K., & Cohen, H. J. (1990). The role of the cytoskeleton in aging. *Experimental Gerontology, 24*, 7–22.

Richardson, G. S. (1990). Circadian rhythms and aging. In E. L. Schneider & J. W. Rowe (Eds.), *Handbook of the biology of aging* (3rd ed., pp. 275–305). San Diego, CA: Academic Press.

Rogers, J., & Bloom, F. E. (1985). Neurotransmitter metabolism and function in the aging central nervous system. In C. E. Finch & E. L. Schneider (Eds.), *Handbook of the biology of aging* (pp. 645–691). New York: Van Nostrand Reinhold.

Scheibel, M. E., Lindsay, R. D., Tomiyasu, U., & Scheibel, A. B. (1975). Progressive changes in aging human cortex. *Experimental Neurology, 47*, 392–403.

Scheibel, M. E., & Tomiyasu, U. (1977). The aging human Betz cell. *Experimental Neurology, 56*, 598–609.

Schiffman, S. (1979). Changes in taste and smell with age: Psychophysical aspects. In J. M. Ordy & K. R. Brizzee (Eds.), *Sensory systems and communication in the elderly* (pp. 227–246). New York: Raven Press.

Schneider, E. L., & Reed, J. D. (1985). Modulations of aging processes. In C. E. Finch & E. L. Schneider (Eds.), *Handbook of the biology of aging* (2nd ed., pp. 45–76). New York: Van Nostrand Reinhold.

Schuknecht, H. (1974). *Pathology of the ear.* Cambridge, MA: Harvard University Press.

Spear, P. D. (1993). Neural bases of visual deficits during aging. *Vision Research, 33*, 2589–2609.

Sun, G. Y., & Samorajski, T. (1972). Age changes in the lipid composition of whole homogenates and isolated myelin fractions of mouse brain. *Journal of Gerontology, 27*, 10–17.

Terry, R. D., Katzman, R., & Bick, K. L. (Eds.). (1994). *Alzheimer disease.* New York: Raven Press.

Vestal, R. E., & Cusack, B. J. (1990). Pharmacology and aging. In E. L. Schneider & J. W. Rowe (Eds.), *Handbook of the biology of aging* (3rd ed., pp. 349–383). San Diego, CA: Academic Press.

Vestal, R. E., & Dawson, G. W. (1985). Pharmacology and aging. In E. L. Schneider & J. W. Rowe (Eds.), *Handbook of the biology of aging* (2nd ed., pp. 744–819). New York: Van Nostrand Reinhold.

Willott, J. F. (1986). Effects of aging, hearing loss, and anatomical location on thresholds of inferior colliculus neurons in C57BL/6 and CBA mice. *Journal of Neurophysiology*, *56*, 391–408.

Willott, J. F. (1991). *Aging and the auditory system: Anatomy, physiology, and psychophysics*. San Diego, CA: Singular.

Willott, J. F., & Bross, L. S. (1991). Morphology of the octopus cell area of the cochlear nucleus in young and aging C57BL/6J and CBA/J mice. *Journal of Comparative Neurology*, *300*, 61–81.

Willott, J. F., Erway, L. C., Archer, J. R., & Harrison, D. E. (1995). Genetics of age-related hearing loss in mice: 2. Strain differences and effects of caloric restriction on cochlear pathology and evoked response thresholds. *Hearing Research*, *88*, 143–155.

Willott, J. F., Hunter, K. P., & Coleman, J. R. (1988). Aging and presbycusis: Effects on 2-deoxy-D-glucose uptake in the mouse auditory brainstem in quiet. *Experimental Neurology*, *99*, 615–621.

Willott, J. F., Jackson, L. M., & Hunter, K. P. (1987). Morphometric study of the anteroventral cochlear nucleus of two mouse models of presbycusis. *Journal of Comparative Neurology*, *260*, 472–480.

CHAPTER 5

Psychology of Aging: Stability and Change in Intelligence and Personality

Anne-Claire I. France
Victor S. Alpher

Psychology is the systematic study of behavior and the factors that influence behavior. To understand behavior, psychologists study biological and environmental factors, and because these factors are continuously intertwined, psychologists study the relationships between these factor domains. The task of the psychology of adult development and aging is to explore and explain how behavior becomes organized and differentiated during the adult years of the life span. That is, investigators explore how behavior becomes organized (or disorganized) as we age.

The psychology of adult development and aging subscribes to several tenets of Ferraro's gerontological imagination as outlined in chapter 1. Some of those tenets are especially relevant to the study of intelligence and personality. Age is a relevant variable in any study with a developmental focus. However, it must be remembered that age is not a causal variable; rather, it is a descriptor variable that enables us to make interpretations about the organization of intelligence and personality at different points across the life span. Adult development and aging involves a series of lawful transitions from which we can make psychological interpretations about life processes. Although there are certainly controversies within the psychological domains of intelligence and personality, we feel that the field of adult development and aging can be advanced by interpreting diverse studies with reference to these broad core constructs.

The research literature related to the aging process is certainly burgeoning. Psychologists interested in this discipline have studied a wide variety of focal topics, including neuropsychological changes, motivation, memory, sensory behavior, and learning. Chapter 4, by Willott, covers the major issues in neuropsychological changes with age. The purpose of this chapter is to integrate approaches to the study of aging processes, using the psychological constructs of intelligence and personality as frames of reference. We believe this conceptual structure will allow the reader to organize future research findings in a concise and useful manner.

INTELLIGENCE: STABILITY AND CHANGE

In everyday conversation, we often equate intelligence with IQ, an abbreviation for the intelligence quotient derived from performance on intelligence tests. When asked what intelligence and IQ are, many people might respond, "That's how smart one is." But intelligence must be more than IQ, and although everyone has some idea of what intelligence is, not everyone defines it in the same way. Yet the way one defines and measures intelligence will have important implications for studying it across the life span.

Because most research conducted on intelligence has utilized intelligence, or IQ, tests to assess levels of intelligence, it is reasonable to raise the question of what a standard test of intelligence is measuring (i.e., test validity), especially across the life span. Conceptually, intelligence refers broadly to adaptive behavior (Wechsler, 1981; see also Sternberg, 1980). Historically, the IQ test was constructed to predict academic achievement of children and adolescents. Tests that were designed for and standardized on children and adolescents pose problems when used to assess adult intelligence. Although IQ tests predict academic achievement well, the test validity changes when applied to adults who have long been out of school. That is, the tests may not tap important aspects of adult adaptive behavior. Another question when interpreting research on intelligence is the type of research design used to collect the data. This question is addressed together with assessment of research on the development of general intelligence.

Aging and General Intelligence

To obtain data in relatively little time, most of the research on intellectual development in adulthood has utilized a cross-sectional design. In other words, the same measure of intelligence has been administered to various groups of people of different ages at the *same* point in time. For example, Matarazzo (1972) administered the Wechsler Adult Intelligence Scale (WAIS) to persons 16 to 75 years of age. The test scores revealed a peak in intelligence during young adulthood and a decline beginning about age 30 and continuing steadily thereafter. Studies by Matarazzo and others seem to indicate that there is a decline in mental power as people age.

The validity of the cross-sectional method as an appropriate tool to investigate intellectual development has been strongly criticized (e.g., Nesselroade &

Labouvie, 1985; Schaie, 1983; Schaie & Hertzog, 1985). Acceptance of cross-sectional findings includes the assumption that differences in intelligence between age groups are a function of physiological change. However, people who differ in age often differ in other domains as well. For example, different ages imply different generations, educational opportunities, and other life experiences; that is, people of different ages are members of different cohorts. As a result, valid conclusions regarding age *change* cannot be drawn on the basis of cross-sectional research; only conclusions regarding age *differences* can be drawn. Hence, one can conclude that 20-year-olds are different from 80-year-olds, but one cannot conclude that the 80-year-olds changed because of age.

An alternative to the cross-sectional design is the longitudinal design, in which the development of certain cohorts is followed as they age. Thus, cohort differences are not a problem; however, there are other interpretational difficulties. One problem is subject-selective survival. It has been argued that subjects who remain throughout a longitudinal study may not be representative of the population of concern. They may be more educated, cooperative, hardy, and so on. Another problem is unique maturation variables. Subjects may experience something in the environment that will affect their cohort in a way unrelated to what is being measured (e.g., the Great Depression).

Despite such difficulties, data from several well-designed long-term longitudinal studies have shed light on the stability of intellectual ability across the life span (e.g., Jarvik & Bank, 1983; Lachman & Leff, 1989; Schaie & Hertzog, 1983). These studies have not found substantial declines in intellectual ability until *after* 60 years of age. This is an important result, given the strength of these specific longitudinal studies and the fact that previous cross-sectional research had suggested decline beginning at earlier ages.

It is important to emphasize that the above conclusion pertains to *general* intelligence. That is, although most intelligence tests involve assessments of several specific skills (e.g., vocabulary and domain-specific knowledge and performance), the total score reflects a composite of such skills—what we may term general intelligence. However, in research concerning age changes in intelligence during adulthood, specific skills involved in intelligence assessment have been categorized in a number of ways. These categories include information processing, specific intellectual skills, learning, problem solving, creativity, cognitive structure, memory, attention, concept acquisition, adult education, and more. Our purpose here is to facilitate an initial understanding of aging and intelligence. Therefore, it should prove helpful to limit the presentation to four of these categories: specific intellectual skills, problem-solving ability, memory, and cognitive structure.

Aging and Specific Intellectual Skills. Many researchers distinguish between fluid and crystallized intelligence, as was proposed by Raymond Cattell (1963). Cattell and colleague John Horn have suggested that intelligence, as measured in usual ability tests, is a collection of skills and achievements, and these skills and achievements can be described as reflecting fluid or crystallized intelligence (Horn, 1982).

Fluid intelligence reflects performance on tasks for which level of education provides little advantage or disadvantage (creating ideas, maintaining a number of factors in immediate awareness, response speed). It has been argued that fluid intelligence is dependent on the efficient functioning of the central nervous system (Aronson & Vroonland, 1993; Bee, 1987). Crystallized intelligence, in contrast, is heavily dependent on education and experience. That is, it is reflected in tasks that are affected by education and acculturation (vocabulary, technical skills, remote associations).

It has been contended that fluid abilities begin to decline after the age of 14, with the sharpest decline occurring in the years of early adulthood (Horn, Donaldson, & Engstrom, 1981). However, it has also been suggested that fluid intelligence is related to memory, in that the processes that are involved are those that enable persons to organize information and concentrate intensely on the task at hand. Therefore, one cannot say that the decline represents a truly diminished capacity or that it represents a disinclination to attend to certain kinds of tedious tasks (many intelligence test tasks can be construed as tedious [e.g., Anstey, Stankov, & Lord, 1993; Christensen et al., 1994]).

On the other hand, crystallized intelligence has been found to increase *throughout* adulthood. Grasel (1994) demonstrated the positive influence of cognitive training on crystallized intelligence of elderly people without cognitive impairments. The increase is a function of formal, institutionalized learning and the accomplishment of tasks that are mandated by society (e.g., balancing a checkbook). Whereas fluid intelligence encompasses initial organization and storage of information, crystallized intelligence is defined by the restructuring of knowledge to make it more accessible. A decline in crystallized abilities is not apparent until age 70 or so (Horn, 1982).

A general model of age change in "unexercised" and "exercised" intellectual activities has been proposed by Denney (1982). Specifically, she describes the relationship between exercise and functioning, noting a pattern of rise and then fall, with age, in many skills and abilities. The basic curve holds whether an individual exercises an ability or not. But the level of the curve is higher for those skills that are well exercised. Denney believes that fluid intelligence is an unexercised ability and crystallized intelligence is an exercised ability (see also Morse, 1993; Perlmutter & Nyquist, 1990). Thus, the adage "use it or lose it" may be relevant to intellectual activity as well.

Another class of specific skills involved in intelligence assessment is the distinction between speeded tasks and unspeeded tasks (Lindenberger, Mayr, & Kliegl, 1993; Nettelbeck & Rabbit, 1992; Robbins et al., 1994). On most intelligence tests, there are subtests that require persons to perform a required task within a specific time (speeded tasks). There are also subtests that have no time limits (unspeeded tasks). The general finding is that there is more of a decline in speeded task performance earlier in the adult years than on unspeeded task performance.

Finally, there is an important distinction between performance tests and verbal tests. Performance tests are those that involve manipulating objects in a required fashion, and verbal tests involve manipulating words and ideas. It should be noted that most performance tests are timed, whereas verbal tests are untimed. Thus, considering the findings regarding speeded and unspeeded tasks, it is not surprising that there is an increase or stability in verbal abilities throughout the adult years but a noticeable decline in performance tasks earlier in adulthood (Cockburn & Smith 1991; Denney, 1982).

Given the above comments, it seems that specific intellectual skills are classified as either crystallized or fluid, exercised or unexercised, unspeeded or speeded, and verbal or performance. Furthermore, crystallized, exercised, unspeeded, and verbal intellectual skills are well maintained during adulthood, whereas fluid, unexercised, speeded, and performance intellectual skills show signs of early decline.

Aging and Problem-Solving Ability. There is a small but significant loss of problem-solving ability as one ages; a decrement often appears during the 60s or 70s. Problem solving refers to the complex processes one uses to arrive at a solution to a problem. For example, if one experiences a flat tire while out on a bicycle, the procedures one goes through to figure out how to repair the tire or to obtain some help are forms of problem solving. In general, problem solving involves having access to bits of information and then figuring out a solution. It has been found that older adults require more bits of information to solve problems (Denney, 1982).

The game of "20 Questions" has been used in the laboratory to study problem solving (e.g., see Denney, 1982; Siegler, 1977). Subjects are exposed to a matrix of numbers and asked to figure out which one of the numbers the experimenter is thinking of. In order to figure out the problem, a subject must think of appropriate questions (subjects may ask only questions that can be answered yes or no) and also evaluate the answers to the questions to arrive at a solution. The kinds of questions a person asks can be classified as one of two types, one type being more informative than the other (Mosher & Hornsby, 1966). The less informative type includes questions that are of a specific nature (e.g., "Is it 17?"); these are called hypothesis questions. The more informative type includes questions that cover several possibilities (e.g., "Is it in the top half of the matrix?"); these are called constraint questions.

Several cross-sectional studies of problem solving in adults have consistently found that middle-aged to older adults, beginning at around age 40, ask fewer constraint questions than do younger adults (Denney, 1982; Denney & Palmer, 1981). Thus, it takes older adults more questions to arrive at the solution. However, as discussed earlier, one must be cautious of results derived from cross-sectional methods. Older populations typically have less education than do younger populations, and education may have an effect on awareness of the strategies available for use in problem solving. Indeed, there is some evidence from longitudinal research that lends support to such a cautious interpretation (Arenberg, 1974; Arenberg & Robertson-Tchabo, 1977). Among subjects aged 24 to 87 who were tested twice, 6 years apart, declines in problem solving were found only among adults older than 70 years. The general finding of longitudinal research is similar to that of cross-sectional research, but the *early* onset of decline found in cross-sectional studies (e.g., age 40) may have been due to differences in educational level or some other cohort attribute.

At the outset of this chapter, it was noted that individuals have varying ideas regarding the definition of intelligence. Sternberg, Conway, Ketron, and Bernstein (1981) have reported that psychologists' concepts of intelligence involve behavioral characteristics such as verbal intelligence and problem-solving ability and that, in general, people believe *practical* problem-solving ability and social competence to be important components of intelligence. Social competence includes traits such as "has a social conscience" and "admits mistakes." Practical problem-solving abilities and social competence have received less attention than verbal and abstract problem-solving abilities in most developmental research on intelligence.

Another possible explanation for the striking differences between age groups in the cross-sectional research may be the kinds of test items used. Again, most experiments in problem solving involve using abstract problems such as the 20 Questions game. However, there is reason to believe that level of familiarity with problems influences the response time required to arrive at solutions. That is, practical problem solving may differ in response time from abstract problem solving. For example, if a person is given a problem with which he or she is familiar (e.g., the car will not start), the quality of solution finding may not differ dramatically among younger and older adults. In fact, Cornelius and Caspi (1987) created the Everyday Problem-Solving Inventory (EPSI) and found that people get better with age. (See Table 5.1 for sample situations/problems from the EPSI.) In addition, when adults are faced with solving problems that pertain to some aspect of their lives, no noticeable decline in problem solving skill is apparent until *after* 80 years of age (Denney & Palmer, 1981).

Thus, there does appear to be some decrement in problem-solving skills in old age. However, extant research indicates that experience and knowledge certainly have an impact on intellectual performance in older (and younger) adults. As will be seen, a similar conclusion may be drawn concerning research on adult memory.

Aging and Memory

Most people, young and old, have complained of not being able to remember something that they thought they would not have trouble remembering. How-

TABLE 5.1 Excerpts from the Everyday Problem-Solving Inventory

Domain	Situation and modes of response
Consumer	You have a landlord who refuses to make some expensive repairs you want done because he or she thinks they are too costly: A. Try to make the repairs yourself. B. Try to understand your landlord's view and decide whether they are necessary repairs. C. Try to get someone to settle the dispute between you and your landlord. D. Accept the situation and don't dwell on it.
Home	You would like to leave your home at night to attend a meeting or concert but are unsure whether it is safe to be out alone. A. Take precautions to insure your safety. B. Re-evaluate how important it is to attend. C. Ask someone to accompany you. D. Avoid worrying about it.

Note: Following each problem situation, the four modes of response are problem-focused action (A), cognitive problem analysis (B), passive-dependent behavior (C), and avoidant thinking and denial (D). From "Everyday problem-solving in adulthood and old age" by Steven W Cornelius and Avshalom Caspi, 1987. *Psychology and Aging*, 2, 144–153.

ever, in American culture, loss of systematic memory is assumed to be a manifestation of the aging process. A consequence of this assumption is an abundance of research concerned with issues such as the amount of memory loss during adulthood. Most investigators concerned with adult memory development apply a cognitive processing model of sorts to study aspects of memory. That is, a model is used to describe the sequence of steps persons take to encode, store, and retrieve information. It is these individual steps that are studied in order to assess where a decrement, if any, originates.

The model dominating most recent research is an information-processing model. According to such a model, information must first flow from the environment to the organism. A person must see or feel information relevant to the task at hand, so perceptual and attentional capabilities are involved. These capabilities are described as being a function of sensory memory. Once the information is in the system, it must be acted on. The person applies strategies and manipulations to the incoming information. These functions occur in the working, or short-term, memory, which can best be thought of as a work space of the mind. The strategies that are applied in this work space come from using long-term memory. Long-term memory can be thought of as the mind's encyclopedia, housing the person's memories of problems encountered, rules and techniques for problem solving, and more general knowledge about the world. Thus, long-term memory provides a knowledge base and strategies needed to deal with present tasks being confronted in short-term memory (Ericsson & Kintsch, 1995).

Consider the application of such a model to an adult solving an arithmetic problem. First, the adult must seek out the information to understand the problem. She perceives that there is a problem to solve and attends to this information; this is sensory memory. Thus, her perceptual attentional system has put the necessary problem information into her mental work space, or short-term memory. The adult now draws on relevant arithmetic strategies stored in long-term memory to solve the problem. Obviously, getting information into long-term memory requires the most effort. In other words, to be able to store information in the mind's encyclopedia, a good deal of processing is required. As will be seen, addressing the question of whether there is memory loss with age depends to a large extent on which of the steps of the information-processing sequence has been studied. We will address evidence concerning sensory memory, short-term memory, and long-term memory in turn.

Sensory Memory. Many people assume that sensory memory becomes less efficient as one gets older. This assumption most likely originates from the fact that most older adults have poorer vision, hearing, and other perceptual capabilities. Indeed, it has been shown that sensory functioning is a strong late-life predictor of individual differences in completion of visual and auditory tasks (Howieson, Holm, Kaye, Oken, & Howieson, 1993; Lindenberger & Baltes, 1994). However, sensory memory involves the ability to hold information for a fraction of a second, that is, to perceive and attend long enough to transfer the information to short-term memory. Thus, research on sensory memory assumes that the information (like the arithmetic problem) has been perceived. The concern is not with how long it takes for the information to be perceived. Given these considerations, the evidence shows that older adults have as good a sensory memory as younger adults (Baltes, Reese, & Lipsitt, 1980; Craik, 1977; Labouvie-Vief & Schnell, 1982).

Short-term Memory. Often, testing of short-term memory involves subjects' being exposed to words or digits one after the other in lists of 5 to 13 items and then being required to recall as many as possible (e.g., Horn et al., 1981). Findings differ depending on whether subjects are asked to simply repeat the lists or to manipulate the information in some fashion (e.g., recall it in an order different from the order in which it was given).

If subjects are repeating lists, younger subjects repeat longer lists than older subjects do. Interestingly, the difference in length of list repeated is on the order of one item fewer for persons in their 70s compared to persons in their 20s. Granted, the difference is quite small, but it is consistent. On the other hand, when subjects are required to manipulate the information, the age-dependent differences are more striking. So if people are asked to repeat items only of a certain type or to rearrange the items, older adults are at a greater disadvantage than if they are asked to simply repeat the items as given. Therefore, the influential factor in age-dependent differences in short-term memory seems to be a function of complexity of the memory task.

Long-term Memory. Transferring information to long-term memory requires more cognitive processing than encoding information in sensory or short-term memory. As a result, there are a number of ways to approach the issue of age changes in long-term memory capacity. For example, if there is a change over age, does the change occur at the level of encoding the information or at some level of retrieval? Extant research indicates that there is indeed an age difference in long-term memory, and the difference seems to operate during both encoding and retrieval (e.g., Craik, 1977; Rankin & Collins, 1985). Because most research addresses either encoding or retrieval, each will be discussed separately.

Most research concerning long-term memory involves subjects' learning (encoding) information by some method (e.g., making associations, varying length of time the information is available, rehearsing) and then being asked to recall (retrieval) the information immediately or at some later point in time. The magnitude of the encoding differences among younger and older adults depends to a large extent on whether subjects are (1) aware that they will be required to recall the information at some point and (2) provided with strategies that will aid learning. Older adults are at a disadvantage on both counts. To be specific, older adults do not spontaneously use as effective learning strategies as do younger adults. However, the discrepancy between the performance of older and younger subjects becomes smaller if older subjects are cued regarding what they will have to remember and/or are provided with efficient strategies for organizing the new material (Craik & Rabinowitz, 1985; Macht & Buschke, 1984; McFarland, Warren, & Crockard, 1985; Rankin & Collins, 1985).

Findings regarding older adults' retrieval capacities are determined by whether retrieval is a function of recognition or recall. Basically, recognition is easier than spontaneous recall. For example, if one is trying to remember the name of a movie seen the week before, it is highly likely that if shown a list of movie titles, the correct one will be recognized. In general, there are no important differences in performance on recognition tasks among young and old adults, although older adults are slightly slower (Cerella, 1985; Madden, 1985). However, the age-dependent difference becomes larger on tasks demanding recall (Craik, 1977; Labouvie-Vief & Schnell, 1982). Consequently, retrieval apparently becomes slower with age; however, if cued, information comes readily to the mind of an older adult.

In the section concerning age change in problem-solving skills it was noted that the level of familiarity with information domains influences the response time required to arrive at solutions. A similar argument can be made regarding memory ability. In other words, if older adults are tested for memory on familiar rather than unfamiliar information domains, will the decrements in memory be less apparent? Indeed, research has shown that prior knowledge and experience does have a positive impact on memory regardless of age (e.g., see Chi, 1978). The first author would fare much better at recalling a list of psychological terms than recalling a list of engine components.

The findings of research dealing with memory of familiar and unfamiliar information domains vary. There is some evidence revealing that younger and older adults remember information equally well from domains with which both groups are familiar; and when information is particularly familiar to one group, that group remembers better than groups who are unfamiliar with the information (e.g., see Hanley-Dunn & McIntosh, 1984; Perfect & Rabitt, 1993). On the other hand, other research has shown older adults doing less well with real-life material that is equally familiar to younger and older adults (e.g., see Evans, Brennan, Skorpanich, & Held, 1984; Kausler, Lichty, & Freund, 1985). Thus, in general, familiarity of material does not make age-dependent differences on memory capacity disappear entirely, but it does seem to lessen age differences in recall to some extent.

In closing this section, it is obvious that despite the abundance of research touching on the issue of age change in memory during adulthood, there is no definite answer. There does seem to be some change of memory ability as one reaches the later years. However, it should be noted again that the majority of research on this topic is cross-sectional in design. There may be individual differences in adult changes in memory. Some individuals may exhibit a great deal of change, whereas others may show little or no change. The nature of the encoding and retrieval tasks is an important influence on the observed effects. Consequently, further research is needed on individual differences in memory change during the adult years.

Aging and Cognitive Structure

The last issue regarding intellectual change that we would like to address is cognitive structure, which is somewhat different from the issues previously discussed. Changes in specific subsets of intelligence (e.g., quantitative ability), problem solving, and memory are assessed by levels of skill. In fact, most intelligence tests are designed to get a measure of performance or skill rather than intellectual capacity. On the other hand, cognitive structure is the focus of rational thought, the reason people come up with certain answers regardless of correctness.

The notion of cognitive structure originated from Jean Piaget's (1967, 1972) theory of cognitive development. Piaget was interested in the mental processes that children of different ages engage in during reasoning. More specifically, the interest was in the kind of logic children use to solve problems or to simply acknowledge their surroundings. According to Piagetian theory, children pass through four stages of cognitive development in an invariant sequence. The elements of each stage form a logical and necessary basis for the next stage. In essence, as children pass through the various stages, their reality changes because new skills and abilities become available. So each stage represents a pattern of thinking. For example, a child who can talk sees his environment differently from one who cannot talk. In order, the four major stages are sensorimotor (0–2 years), preoperations (2–6 years), concrete operations (6 or 7–11 or 12), and formal operations (11 or 12 through adulthood).

Inclusion of cognitive structure here is in part a response to the common notion that elderly adults "regress to a second childhood." This notion has come about in the scientific community as a result of adult researchers' utilizing Piagetian tasks designed to measure structure of thought. For example, consider a situation in which groups of objects that have one or more properties in common are presented randomly. Preoperational children and adults over 65 have been found to classify such objects on the basis of complementarity, for example, "The doll, the baby food, and the spoon go together because the doll will use the spoon to eat the baby food." However, older children and younger adults group objects on the basis of dimension similarity—spoon and fork, cookie and baby food, dress and shoes (see Denney, 1982, for a review of relevant research).

Accepting these findings as a manifestation of regression is, however, premature. If older adults are told that the classification should be made on the basis of similarity, they are able to do so, whereas preoperational children are not. The question then is, why do older adults choose the complementarity approach rather than the similarity approach when similarity is not specified? A possibility may be that there are thinking patterns that are more useful in later life than patterns of formal operations (Arbuckle et al., 1992; Labouvie-Vief, 1985).

Formal operational thought is quite useful during early adulthood because young adulthood is characterized by exploring all possible opportunities to establish identity. However, much of later adulthood is characterized by retaining continuity of established roles and relationships. Therefore, thought patterns serve to deal with problems involved with those established roles. This change in thought does not reflect a regression—especially as older adults demonstrate the formal operational analytical skills when asked—but an adaptive cognitive structural change. In general, the change is made to make sense of the world that the older adult experiences (Basseches, 1984; Jones et al., 1991; Pascual-Leone, 1983).

Conclusions Regarding Aging and Intelligence

It has been emphasized that the major part of research on adult intellectual development is cross-sectional in design and that certain limitations should be kept in mind when reviewing the findings. Some longitudinal findings have also been presented. Despite the differences in interpretation between cross-sectional and longitudinal findings, the results of both types of studies tend to indicate a decline in some intellectual abilities. At this point, it seems that the age at onset, extent, and nature of decline are sensitive to design features, as well as sample characteristics and methods of measurement.

Hence, extant research on intellectual functioning in adulthood provides the reader with quite a variety of findings. Some studies indicate declines in mental abilities as early as the 30s, 40s, or 50s, whereas others show little decline until well into the 80s. Certainly the processes of mental aging are explained not only by normative data but by individual differences as well. And as noted elsewhere in this volume, older adults are a very diverse group. In summary, there seems to be measurable loss in fluid and speeded tasks and in some aspects of the processes involved in problem solving and in memory. In general, well-practiced, familiar, and adaptive skills are retained well into old age, whereas less practiced skills and those that require responses within a fixed time interval decline earlier.

PERSONALITY: STABILITY AND CHANGE

As with the concept of intelligence, it is difficult to get agreement when raising the question, what is personality? Everyone has his or her own way of thinking, feeling, and reacting to the environment. Even though each person is unique in behaviors, these behaviors are not random but occur systematically (although some have suggested that the inference of personality in the subject is an artifact of observer bias). Individuals show some consistency in behavior patterns across situations, suggesting why various persons may behave quite differently when in the same situation (see Epstein, 1979b). This consistency is often designated as personality. Personality refers to stable, distinctive patterns of behavior, thought, and emotion that characterize each person's adaptation to the situations of his or her life (Mischel, 1981). Notably, this global conceptualization has been incorporated into current clinical nomenclature as well (American Psychiatric Association, 1994).

Given that the concept of personality involves stability and consistency in behavior over the life span, it is interesting that many people believe that aging affects personality in *predictable* ways. Stereotypical ideas have long been generated about the personalities of old people. For example, graduate students in the United States have described old people as being touchy, bossy, stubborn, and apt to complain excessively (Thomae, 1980). Most stereotypes are a result of overgeneralization from specific, isolated, and salient cases with which the stereotyping individual is familiar. We all know of specific incidents from our own personal experiences that tend to color our perceptions and beliefs about our social environment.

Therefore, it comes as a surprise to the neophyte that many studies indicate that most global personality characteristics are stable from young adulthood to old age among healthy adults who live in the community (Thomae, 1980). A person who is sociable in youth is sociable in old age; a person who is generous in youth is generous in old age, and so on. Of course, there is great individual variation that may contribute to the mistaken impression of overall instability.

Personality is not unidimensional. Literally hundreds of studies have accumulated in the past three decades to examine age-related differences in various dimensions of personality (Goldberg, 1993). Most researchers focus on particular bipolar traits such as introversion/extroversion (e.g., see Neugarten, Havighurst, & Tobin, 1968) and activity/passivity (e.g., see Botwinick, 1969).

More recent research has indicated that the domain of personality may be captured by five orthogonal (independent) factors or dimensions (Costa & McCrae, 1986; Goldberg, 1993; McCrae & Costa, 1984; McCrae & John, 1992). Researchers and clinicians alike refer to these factors as the Big Five. There are subtle differences in factor names, depending on the method of analysis and interpretation. Goldberg (1993) summarizes the factors of several competing Big-Five models as follows:

Factor I (Surgency or Extraversion): talkativeness, assertiveness, activity level contrasted with silence, passivity, and reserve.

Factor II (Agreeableness or Pleasantness): kindness, trust, warmth contrasted with hostility, selfishness, and distrust.

Factor III (Conscientiousness or Dependability): organization, thoroughness, and reliability contrasted with carelessness, negligence, and unreliability.

Factor IV (Emotional Stability vs. Neuroticism): nervousness, moodiness, and temperamentality.

Factor V (Intellect/Openness to Experience): imagination, curiosity, and creativity contrasted with shallowness and imperceptiveness.

Much of the research related to the Big-Five model has supported the notion of consistency and stability of personality across the life span (see also Block, 1995; Costa & McCrae, 1995).

Previous cross-sectional research has been subject to the criticism that changes in traits are the result of cohort effects, that is, generational differences in education, experience, values, and/or socioeconomic status (Reedy, 1983). However, more recent longitudinal studies have shown that personality tends to be stable, especially after young adulthood (e.g., Costa & McCrae, 1980; McCrae & Costa, 1984; Siegler, George, & Okun, 1979). For example, Costa and McCrae (1988) examined self-reports and spouse ratings using the NEO Personality Inventory. Utilizing both cross-sectional and longitudinal data, cross-lagged and cross-observer analyses, they concluded that "aging itself has little effect on personality" (p. 862). This is certainly remarkable, considering the accumulation of major life events across the life span, such as disease, loss, divorce, marriage, childbearing and child rearing, and socioeconomic changes.

There has been much debate over the nature of personality and methods by which its manifestations should be studied, from the nihilistic assertion that there is no such thing as personality (Mischel, 1968) to the more recent advances in taxonomic representation of the domain of personality structure. It seems likely that individual variability in behavior is mediated not only by the structure of traits within the individual but also by the level of analysis used to characterize one's response (Bengston, Reedy, & Gordon, 1985). For example, we could not expect an individual's response to an item in a neuropsychological testing battery to be well predicted by personality traits. For the interested reader, Epstein (1979a, 1979b) reviews the methodological issues in selecting prediction problems and chronicles the conceptual shift that led to the empirical resuscitation of personality trait psychology. Goldberg (1993) and others have provided some evidence that the Big-Five factors may indeed predict important behavioral outcomes in real-world situations such as personnel selection.

The findings of research efforts concerning personality development illustrate the important point of continuity in development. As people develop, they retain underlying psychological constructs (or motives), but the specific responses utilized to express a psychological construct may change. For example, a person will demonstrate that he or she is attached to another person in different ways, depending on age. Therefore, if smaller "units" of personality are investigated, the smaller units will be found to be less stable than if one classified the units as the expression of a global construct. If people examine smaller units of personality and notice that a unit has changed, they may incorrectly infer that the overall personality has changed. When pooled, cultural truisms and scientific findings regarding personality development seem to raise more questions than they conclusively answer.

Obviously, a great deal of attention has been dedicated to how personality should be conceptualized, as well as how it should be studied. In efforts to find the most enduring and stable human attributes, personality psychologists have generated theories about human nature and individuality and about the causes and meanings of important psychological differences among people. Theories have attempted to explain how people develop and change and how they achieve stability throughout the course of life.

Interestingly, most theories of personality development elaborate on experiences that take place during infancy, childhood, and adolescence (Cameron & Rychak, 1985). However, this final section of this chapter is devoted to the relatively few theories of personality that specifically address experiences during the years of *late* adulthood. These theories focus not on global changes in personality in later life but on individual adaptation to the challenges of this period of life in the context of stability of personality for most people. The theorists Erik Erikson, Robert Peck, and Daniel Levinson have made important contributions to the theory of adptation in later adulthood.

Erik Erikson's Theory of Personality Development

Erikson's (1963, 1982) life span developmental theory of personality emphasizes the influence of culture and society on an individual's destiny. The theory describes eight stages of development. Each stage centers around a salient and distinct emotional conflict stemming from biological pressures from within the individual (e.g., maturation) and sociocultural expectations from outside the individual (e.g., social institutions). Hence, these stages have a psychosocial foundation. The conflicts may be resolved in a positive and healthy manner or in a pessimistic and unhealthy manner.

In Erikson's theory, a different psychological issue constitutes the conflict for the ego at each developmental stage, but the same issue is always present in preceding and later stages. For example, the problem of trust and mistrust is predominant in infancy, and it is also present in childhood, adolescence, and adulthood. Resolution of conflict at each stage of ego development has implications for development and resolution at subsequent stages. An individual cannot successfully resolve issues such as generativity (middle adulthood), whether the solution is positive or negative, until issues pertaining to ego identity (adolescence) and intimacy (young adulthood) have been resolved. Erikson's theory of ego development is one of the few examples of a developmental theory of personality that encompasses late adulthood as well as infancy, childhood, adolescence, and young and middle adulthood.

The psychosocial conflict during late adulthood is ego integrity versus despair. This stage involves looking back at what one has done with one's life and developing either a sense of coherence and wholeness (ego integrity) or a sense of gloom and despair over the worth of one's life. Ego integrity involves accepting life, seeing meaning in it, and believing that one did the best one could under the circumstances. In essence, preceding psychosocial conflicts are resolved in a positive way. However, if retrospection of one's life reveals a picture of negative resolutions in preceding stages, then despair will dominate the later years of life. One who despairs over life fears death and wishes desperately for another chance.

It should be noted that Erikson does not believe that the proper solution to a psychosocial conflict should always be completely positive in nature. Some exposure to a negative resolution is often inevitable and sometimes helpful. For example, resolution of the conflict pertaining to basic trust versus mistrust (infancy) in a somewhat negative way may aid in survival. Persons who resolve in the direction of mistrust may benefit because of the unfortunate fact that not all people can be trusted.

Like all psychoanalytic theories, Erikson's theory is difficult to test through empirical research. Clear definitions of terms are not given, nor are the concepts clearly defined. This vagueness results in different investigators' developing different standards when designing a study. Experts in adult development recognize the importance of Erikson's theory, but there is very little empirical information that helps in evaluating the theory per se. Of the tests that are available, most have focused on college students; the number of attempts to study late adulthood is very small.

Butler (1963) has incorporated Erikson's concepts of integrity and despair. He examined the reasons that the elderly engage in retrospection and reminiscence.

The contention is that reminiscence, or the process of life review, produces candor, serenity, and wisdom in old age. Butler believes that constructive retrospection facilitates a creative, positive reorganization of personality (i.e., integrity). For a recent review and formulation see Simon, 1995.

Similarly to Erikson, Butler notes that integrity is not the only possible outcome of life review. Another possible outcome is despair, that is, the inability to accept one's fate. Those who despair cannot accept death and are victimized by the feeling that time is running out. Feelings of regret, frustration, discouragement, and meaninglessness accompany despair. In addition, there is speculation about how life might have been if different choices had been made, other events had occurred, or certain goals had been accomplished. In the end, death is viewed as the ultimate usurper and eliminates any hope of fulfilling one's lifetime ambitions.

Robert Peck's Psychological Developments in Later Life

Robert Peck (1968) has noted that Erikson conceived of the stages of early life by considering the conflicts of the ego that must be met and mastered at specific ages (developmental periods). He has argued that the first seven of the eight stages encompass the periods of life corresponding to infancy through the age of about 30. However, the eighth stage, ego integrity versus despair, seems to represent in a global, nonspecific way all of the psychological conflicts and resolutions of the adult years past 30. Given that persons live another 40 or 50 years past age 30, Peck has suggested that it might be useful to divide the second half of life into several quite different kinds of psychological "adjustments." Each adjustment takes place at different stages in the latter half of life. Peck has divided adult life into two broad chronological divisions, the middle-age period and the old-age period. Within each period, psychological adjustments (stages) occur. The primary psychological adjustments of the old-age period is discussed here.

Ego Differentiation versus Work Role Preoccupation. The central issue here is the impact of retirement from the labor force. Retirement results in a shift in individual value systems, so it is very important for retirees to establish a set of valued activities that extend beyond the previous work role. Many elderly people wonder if they are worthwhile citizens if they are not employed full-time. Can they be worthwhile in ways that are different from their vocational roles? Peck believes that ego differentiation is an important issue at the time of retirement. Retirees must derive self-worth from activities beyond their careers in order to establish a continuing vital interest in living rather than experiencing a loss of meaning in life. Consequently, establishing a variety of valued activities and self-attributes, so that any one of several alternatives can be pursued with satisfaction and a sense of worthfulness, may be a critical prerequisite for successful aging. (This adjustment is quite congruent with activity theory as described in chapter 6.)

Body Transcendence versus Body Preoccupation. Although many elderly people experience a marked decline in resistance to illness, a decline in recuperative powers, and an increase in general body aches and pains, those who focus their lives on human interaction and creativity seem to be able to enjoy life nonetheless. Peck maintains that older people who equate comfort and pleasure in life with physical well-being will perceive a decline in health as a grave insult. The perceived insult requires ever-increasing concern with the state of the body; this concern is referred to as body preoccupation. However, as already mentioned, there are many elderly people who enjoy life despite declines in physical health. These people, according to Peck, have learned to define happiness and comfort in terms of satisfactory relationships with others and/or creative mental activities. They have established a value system in which self-respect and social and mental pleasures go far beyond physical comfort alone.

Ego Transcendence versus Ego Preoccupation. A critical task for elderly people is realizing that death is inevitable and not likely to be too far away. Many philosophers have suggested that a constructive lifestyle includes a positive adaptation to the prospect of inevitable death. Peck (1968) elaborates this suggestion in a most eloquent manner:

> To live so generously and unselfishly that the prospect of personal death—the night of the ego, it might be called—looks and feels less important than the secure knowledge that one has built for a broader, longer future than any one ego ever could encompass. Through children, through contributions to the culture, through friendships—these are the ways in which human beings can achieve enduring significance for their actions which goes beyond the limit of their own skins and their own lives. It may, indeed, be the only knowable kind of self-perpetuation after death. (p. 91)

According to Peck, a positive adaptation to the unwelcome prospect of death requires a deep effort to make life meaningful for those who continue living after one dies. There is an active ego transcendence of the elderly person to enhance the possibility of making life good for descendants. Rather than being preoccupied with immediate self-gratification, ego transcendence focuses on gratification in experiencing a vital absorption with the future of others. In addition, religious interpretations of mortality may shape responses to growing older. (Chapter 10, by Moberg, examines this subject in greater detail.)

Peck emphasizes that there is far greater variability in the chronological age at which any particular psychological crisis arises in later life than is true of the crisis periods of early life. For example, a test of body transcendence occurs when one's health begins to decline. This may happen at an earlier age for one person than for another. If resolution of a later-life psychological crisis depends on how one deals with the critical experiences of that period, then older people in the same stage may differ widely in chronological age. As a result, stages in later life may have to be less related to chronological age per se than stages in childhood and adolescence.

Daniel Levinson's Seasons of Life

Levinson's (1978, 1980) theory is similar to Peck's in that he pays attention to the relationship of physical changes of the body to personality. Levinson emphasizes that a person does not suddenly become old, but changes in mental and physical capacities intensify one's awareness of aging and sense of mortality. He refers to this increasing awareness as the late adult transition.

Awareness of aging and sense of mortality are intensified by factors within the individual. Aches and pains serve as reminders of decreasing capacities, and there is a stronger likelihood that one will experience at least one major impairment. Externally, there is an increasing frequency of death and serious illness among the older person's friends and family age mates (e.g., siblings).

Persons experiencing the late adult transition also become very aware of the ways in which their generation is defined by society. More often they hear themselves being referred to by terms such as "elderly," "senior citizen," "old folks," and "golden years"; often such terms acquire negative connotations that serve to enhance anxiety about aging. Cultural definitions of later adulthood emphasize that the elderly must reduce their societal responsibilities, which in turn reduces recognition, power, and authority. In many cases, major responsibility and authority are relinquished to offspring.

Retirement should come about with dignity and should reflect a person's needs, capabilities, and life circumstances. If a person retires with dignity, then he or she can engage in some other valued activity that is separate from his or her vocation. These activities should be pleasing, make use of creative energies, and not be dictated by external pressure.

During the late adult transition, people must acknowledge the inevitability of death and prepare for the process of dying. This preparation includes attainment of a final sense of what one's life is about; this is quite similar to Erikson's sense of ego integrity versus despair. Hence, the final and ultimate task is to come to terms with the self, particularly viewing the self in a positive light and being ready to give it up.

The primary source of Levinson's theory was a series of in-depth interviews during the young adulthood and early midlives of 40 men. The theory may also describe women's personality development, but Levinson did not interview women and made no attempt to apply his findings to them. In addition to the descriptive studies of the 40 men, there is information on the lives of other men. The information was gathered by analyzing drama, biographies, poetry, and fiction. Therefore, the additional information was gleaned from the lives of both real and fictional men. The oldest of the "real" men studied by Levinson was nearly 50 years of age; hence, the theory begins to become somewhat uncertain after the midlife transition.

Conclusions Regarding Aging and Personality

Some readers may be wondering about the validity of personality theories that have minimal additional empirical support. However, investigators utilize the theories to interpret findings generated from formal empirical research to explore various domains of adult development, including personality development.

No one theory of personality development can completely explain why persons make successful or unsuccessful adjustments during their later years. As stated earlier, literally hundreds of studies have been done, most focusing on specific aspects of personality. Self-concept, attitudes, gender, and other factors are contributors to stability and change in personality and adaptation, which in turn influence the probability of "successful" aging. However, no single pattern of aging appears to guarantee satisfaction in later life. Generally, morale and adaptation seem to be highly related to an individual's lifelong personality style and to his or her way of handling stress and change (Vaillant, 1977).

REFERENCES

American Psychiatric Association. (1994). *Diagnostic and statistical manual of mental disorders* (4th ed., rev.). Washington, DC: Author.

Anstey, K., Stankov, L., & Lord, S. (1993). Primary aging, secondary aging, and intelligence. *Psychology and Aging, 8*, 562–570.

Arbuckle, T., Gold, D., Andres, D., Schwartzman, A., & Chaikelson, J. (1992). The role of psychosocial context, age, and intelligence in memory performance of older men. *Psychology and Aging*, 7, 25–36.

Arenberg, D. (1974). A longitudinal study of problem solving in adults. *Journal of Gerontology*, *29*, 650–658.

Arenberg, D., & Robertson-Tchabo, E. A. (1977). Learning and aging. In J. E. Birren & K. W. Schaie (Eds.), *Handbook of the psychology of aging* (pp. 421–449). New York: Van Nostrand Reinhold.

Aronson, H., & Vroonland, J. (1993). The residual cognitive competence of elderly females. *Journal of Clinical Psychology*, *49*, 724–731.

Baltes, P. B., Reese, H. W., & Lipsitt, L. P. (1980). Life-span developmental psychology. In M. R. Rosenzweig & L. W. Porter (Eds.), *Annual review of psychology* (pp. 65–110). Palo Alto, CA: Annual Reviews.

Basseches, M. (1984). *Dialectical thinking and adult development.* Norwood, NJ: Ablex.

Bee, H. L. (1987). *The journey of adulthood.* New York: Macmillan.

Bengtson, V. L., Reedy, M. N., & Gordon, C. (1985). Aging and self-conceptions: Personality processes and social contexts. In J. E. Birren & K. W. Schaie (Eds.), *The psychology of aging* (2nd ed., pp. 544–593). New York: Van Nostrand Reinhold.

Block, J. (1995). A contrarian view of the five-factor approach to personality description. *Psychological Bulletin, 117*, 187–215.

Botwinick, J. (1969). Cautiousness in advanced age. *Journal of Gerontology, 115*, 55–83.

Butler, R. N. (1963). The life review: An interpretation of reminiscence in the aged. *Psychiatry, 26*, 65–76.

Cameron, N., & Rychak, J .F. (1985). *Personality development and psychopathology: A dynamic approach*. Boston: Houghton-Mifflin.

Cattell, R. B. (1963). Theory of fluid and crystallized intelligence: A critical experiment. *Journal of Educational Psychology, 54*, 1–22.

Cerella, J. (1985). Information processing rates in the elderly. *Psychological Bulletin, 98*, 67–83.

Chi, M. T. (1978). Knowledge structure and memory development. In R. S. Siegler (Ed.), *Children's thinking: What develops?* (pp. 73–96). Hillsdale, NJ: Erlbaum.

Christensen, H., Mackinnon, A., Jorm, A., Henderson, A., Scott, L., & Korten, A. (1994). Age differences and interindividual variation in cognition in community-dwelling elderly. *Psychology and Aging, 9*, 381–390.

Cockburn, J., & Smith, P. (1991). The relative influence of intelligence and age on everyday memory. *Journals of Gerontology, 46*, P31–P36.

Cornelius, S. W., & Caspi, A. (1987). Everyday problem solving in adulthood and old age. *Psychology and Aging, 2*, 144–153.

Costa, P. T., Jr., & McCrae, R. R. (1980). Still stable after all these years: Personality as a key to some issues in aging. In P. B. Baltes & O. G. Brim (Eds.), *Life-span development and behavior* (Vol. 3, pp. 65–102). New York: Academic Press.

Costa, P. T., Jr., & McCrae, R. R. (1985). *The NEO Personality Inventory manual*. Odessa, FL: Psychological Assessment Resources.

Costa, P. T., Jr., & McCrae, R. R. (1986). Personality stability and its implications for clinical psychology. *Clinical Psychology Review, 6*, 407–423.

Costa, P. T., Jr., & McCrae, R. R. (1988). Personality in adulthood: A six-year longitudinal study of self-reports and spouse ratings on the NEO Personality Inventory. *Journal of Personality and Social Psychology, 54*, 853–863.

Costa, P. T., Jr., & McCrae, R. R. (1995). Solid ground in the wetlands of personality: A reply to Block. *Psychological Bulletin, 117*, 216–220.

Craik, F. I. M. (1977). Age differences in human memory. In J. E. Birren & K. W. Schaie (Eds.), *Handbook of the psychology of aging* (pp. 384–420). New York: Van Nostrand Reinhold.

Craik, F. I. M., & Rabinowitz, J. C. (1985). The effects of presentation rate and encoding task on age-related memory deficits. *Journal of Gerontology, 40*, 309–315.

Denney, N. W. (1982). Aging and cognitive changes. In B. B. Wolman (Ed.), *Handbook of developmental psychology* (pp. 807–827). Englewood Cliffs, NJ: Prentice-Hall.

Denney, N. W., & Palmer, A. M. (1981). Adult age differences in traditional and practical problem-solving measures. *Journal of Gerontology, 36*, 323–328.

Epstein, S. (1979a). Explorations in personality today and tomorrow: A tribute to Henry A. Murray. *American Psychologist, 34*, 649–653.

Epstein, S. (1979b). The stability of behavior: 1. On predicting most of the people much of the time. *Journal of Personality and Social Psychology, 37*, 1097–1126.

Ericsson, K. A., & Kintsch, W. (1995). Long-term working memory. *Psychological Review, 102*, 211–245.

Erikson, E. H. (1963). *Childhood and society* (2nd ed.). New York: W. W. Norton.

Erikson, E. H. (1982). *The life cycle completed: A review*. New York: W. W. Norton.

Evans, G. W., Brennan, P. L., Skorpanich, M. A., & Held, D. (1984). Cognitive mapping and elderly adults: Verbal and location memory for urban landmarks. *Journal of Gerontology, 39*, 452–457.

Goldberg, L. R., (1993). The structure of phenotypic personality traits. *American Psychologist, 48*, 26–34.

Grasel, E. (1993). Non-pharmacological intervention strategies on aging processes: Empirical data on mental training in "normal" older people and patients with mental impairment. *Archives of Gerontology and Geriatrics, 4* (Suppl.), 91–98.

Hanley-Dunn, P., & McIntosh, J. L. (1984). Meaningfulness and recall of names by young and old adults. *Journal of Gerontology, 39*, 583–585.

Horn, J. L. (1982). The aging of human abilities. In B. B. Wolman (Ed.). *Handbook of developmental psychology* (pp. 847–870). Englewood Cliffs, NJ: Prentice-Hall.

Horn, J. L., Donaldson, G., & Engstrom, R. (1981). Apprehension, memory and fluid intelligence decline in adulthood. *Research on Aging, 3*, 33–84.

Howieson, D., Holm, L., Kaye, J., Oken, B., & Howieson, J. (1993). Neurologic function in the optimally healthy oldest old: Neuropsychological evaluation. *Neurology, 43*, 1882–1886.

Jarvik, L. F., & Bank, L. (1983). Aging twins: Longitudinal psychometric data. In K. W. Schaie (Ed.), *Longitudinal studies of adult psychological development* (pp. 40–63). New York: Guilford Press.

Jones, K., Albert, M., Duffy, F., Hyde, M., Naeser, M., & Aldwin, C. (1991). Modeling age using cognitive, psychosocial and physiological variables: The Boston Normative Aging study. *Experimental Aging Research, 17*, 227–242.

Kausler, D. H., Lichty, W., & Freund, J. S. (1985). Adult age differences in recognition memory and frequency judgments for planned versus performed activities. *Developmental Psychology, 21*, 647–654.

Labouvie-Vief, G. (1985). Intelligence and cognition. In J. E. Birren & K. W. Schaie (Eds.), *The psychology of aging* (2nd ed., pp. 500–535). New York: Van Nostrand Reinhold.

Labouvie-Vief, G., & Schell, D. A. (1982). Learning and memory in later life. In B. B. Wolman (Ed.), *Handbook of developmental psychology* (pp. 828–846). Englewood Cliffs, NJ: Prentice-Hall.

Lachman, M., & Leff, R. (1989). Perceived control and intellectual functioning in the elderly: A 5-year longitudinal study. *Developmental Psychology, 25*, 722–728.

Levinson, D. (1978). *The seasons of a man's life*. New York: Ballantine.

Levinson, D. (1980). Toward a conception of the adult life course. In N. Smelser & Erikson (Eds.), *Themes of work and love in adulthood* (pp. 265–290). Cambridge, MA: Harvard University Press.

Lindenberger, U., & Baltes, P. (1994). Sensory functioning and intelligence in old men: A strong connection. *Psychology and Aging, 9*, 339–355.

Lindenberger, U., Mayr, U., & Kliegl, R. (1993). Speed and intelligence in old age. *Psychology and Aging, 8*, 207–220.

Macht, M. L., & Buschke, H. (1984). Speed of recall in aging. *Journal of Gerontology, 39*, 439–443.

Madden, D. J. (1985). Age-related slowing in retrieval of information from long-term memory. *Journal of Gerontology, 40*, 208–210.

Matarazzo, J. D. (1972). *Wechsler's measurement and appraisal of adult intelligence.* Baltimore: Williams & Wilkins.

McCrae, R. R., & Costa, P. T. (1984). *Emerging lives, enduring dispositions: Personality in adulthood.* Boston: Little, Brown.

McCrae, R. R., & John, O. P. (1992). An introduction to the five-factor model and its applications. *Journal of Personality, 60,* 175–215.

McFarland, C. E., Jr., Warren, L. R., & Crockard, J. (1985). Memory for self-generated stimuli in young and old adults. *Journal of Gerontology, 40,* 205–207.

Mischel, W. (1968). *Personality and assessment.* New York: Wiley.

Mischel, W. (1981). *Introduction to personality* (3rd ed.). New York: Holt, Rinehart, & Winston.

Morse, C. (1993). Does variability increase with age? An archival study of cognitive measures. *Psychology and Aging, 8,* 156–164.

Mosher, F. A., & Hornsby, J. R. (1966). On asking questions. In J. S. Bruner, R. R. Oliver, & P. M. Greenfield (Eds.), *Studies in cognitive growth* (pp. 86–102). New York: Wiley.

Nesselroade, J. R., & Labouvie, E. (1985). Experimental design in research on aging. In J. E. Birren & K. W. Schaie (Eds.), *The psychology of aging* (2nd ed., pp. 35–60). New York: Van Nostrand Reinhold.

Nettelbeck, T., & Rabitt, P. (1992). Aging, cognitive performance, and mental speed. *Intelligence, 16,* 189–205.

Neugarten, B. L., Havighurst, R. J., & Tobin, S. S. (1968). Personality and patterns of aging. In B. L. Neugarten (Ed.), *Middle age and aging* (pp. 173–177). Chicago: University of Chicago Press.

Pascual-Leone, J. (1983). Growing into human maturity: Toward a meta-subjective theory of adult stages. In P. B. Baltes & O. G. Brim Jr. (Eds.), *Life-span development and behavior* (Vol. 5, pp. 117–156). New York: Academic Press.

Peck, R. C. (1968). Psychological developments in the second half of life. In B. L. Neugarten (Ed.), *Middle age and aging* (pp. 88–92). Chicago: University of Chicago Press.

Perfect, T., & Rabitt, P. (1993). Age and the divided attention costs of category exemplar generation. *British Journal of Developmental Psychology, 11,* 131–142.

Perlmutter, M., & Nyquist, L. (1990). Relationships between self-reported physical and mental health and intelligence performance across adulthood. *Journal of Gerontology, 45,* P145–P155.

Piaget, J. (1967). *Six psychological studies.* New York: Vintage.

Piaget, J. (1972). Development and learning. In C. S. Lavetelli & F. Stendler (Eds.), *Readings in child behavior and development* (pp. 38–46). New York: Harcourt Brace Jovanovich.

Rankin, J. L., & Collins, M. (1985). Adult age differences in memory elaboration. *Journal of Gerontology, 40,* 451–458.

Reedy, M. N. (1983). Personality and aging. In D. S. Woodruff & J. E. Birren (Eds.), *Aging: Scientific perspectives and social issues* (2nd ed., pp. 112–136). Monterey, CA: Brooks/Cole.

Robbins, T., James, M., Owen, A., Sahakian, B., McInnes, L., & Rabbitt, P. (1994). Cambridge Neuropsychological Test Automated Battery (CANTAB): A factor analytic study of a large sample of normal elderly volunteers. *Dementia, 5,* 266–281.

Schaie, K. W. (1983). What can we learn from the longitudinal study of adult psychological development? In K. W. Schaie (Ed.), *Longitudinal studies of adult psychological development* (pp. 1–19). New York: Guilford Press.

Schaie, K. W., & Hertzog, C. (1983). Fourteen-year cohort-sequential analyses of adult intellectual development. *Developmental Psychology, 19*, 531–543.

Schaie, K. W., & Hertzog, C. (1985). Measurement in the psychology of adulthood and aging. In J. E. Birren & K. W. Schaie (Eds.), *The psychology of aging* (2nd ed., pp. 61–92). New York: Van Nostrand Reinhold.

Siegler, I. C., George, L. K., & Okun, M. (1979). Cross-sequential analysis of adult personality. *Developmental Psychology, 15*, 350–351.

Siegler, R. S. (1977). The 20-question game as a form of problem-solving. *Child Development, 48*, 395–403.

Simon, J. (1995). Satisfaction with retirement: Vocational script development. *Applied Preventive Psychology, 4*, 101–111.

Sternberg, R. J. (1980). Sketch of a componential subtheory of human intelligence. *Behavioral and Brain Sciences, 3*, 573–614.

Sternberg, R. J., Conway, B. E., Ketron, J. L., & Bernstein, M. (1981). People's conceptions of intelligence. *Journal of Personality and Social Psychology, 41*, 37–55.

Thomae, H. (1980). Personality and adjustment to aging. In J. E. Birren & R. B. Sloane (Eds.), *Handbook of mental health and aging* (pp. 285–309). Englewood Cliffs, NJ: Prentice-Hall.

Vaillant, G. (1977). *Adaptation to life.* Boston: Little, Brown.

Wechsler, D. (1981). *Wechsler Adult Intelligence Scale-Revised.* New York: The Psychological Corporation.

CHAPTER 6

Sociology of Aging: The Micro-Macro Link

Kenneth F. Ferraro

Sociology may be defined as the scientific study of social life, including interpersonal relationships, groups, institutions, and societies. At the heart of a sociological investigation, regardless of the scope of the social activity, is the examination of social processes and structures—reflections of change and stability, respectively. Unlike disciplines such as biology or psychology, sociology begins with the premise that humans are *social* creatures. In fact, humans would not be fully human without the social interaction that shapes biological and psychological development. In addition, because we are social creatures, our societies vary according to the environments, economic structures, and value systems within which human life occurs. Aging does not occur in a social vacuum but is greatly influenced by social structures and processes.

THE SOCIAL CONTEXT OF AGING

Thinking as sociologists interested in aging, we attempt to identify the social forces that influence beliefs, values, and behavior across the life course. Chief among these social forces is the normative order of society. Norms are widely understood as shared expectations of appropriate behavior, yet what people often fail to notice about norms is how many of them are linked to age.

The mass media is often drawn to spectacular human interest stories, such as a senior citizen who, when attacked by a mugger, took her umbrella and began to hit the man while calling for help. We marvel at her courage and strong will precisely because we generally do not *expect* people to fight off muggers. Thus, when an *older person* and a *woman* does so, we think that is pretty special.

Or consider the older man who wanted to bungee-jump on his 80th birthday. We may think, "He shouldn't do that at his age." The point is not whether bungee-jumping or fighting off a mugger are the best or most rational actions to undertake; rather, the key thought here is that our expectations of what people should and can do are strongly colored by their age. Some age norms are linked to particular ages such as 16, 21, or 65, but most often they are tied to stages or periods of the life course. Age norms may be codified in law or they may be quite informal, as in the case of appropriate dress. Most age norms are passed on through tradition, but many are being challenged by social movements and legal action (e.g., federal aviation regulations for mandatory retirement at age 60 for commercial pilots). When considering society as a whole, we can envision a conglomeration of age norms functioning with other norms, exerting pushes and pulls on what people think they should do. Sometimes these pushes and pulls are quite subtle; at other times they are quite explicit. Whatever the case, there is ample evidence that age remains a potent influence on daily activities (Verbrugge, Gruber-Baldini, & Fozard, 1996).

The existence of age norms also reflects another fundamental fact about social life: the dialectical nature of society. Society is greater than the sum of all the persons composing it; indeed, society reflects the synergy that results from the activities of all its members. Society is not some reified external force that "makes" people of certain ages do things, although some people try to use society as a scapegoat. Society certainly limits human choices and shapes human activity. In actuality, however, society is an emergent phenomenon resulting from human activity. Society shapes us, but we also shape society. We are influenced by norms of what is considered appropriate behavior, but we also help to define and modify such norms. As Berger (1969) summarizes, "Society is a dialectic phenomenon in that it is a human product, and nothing but a human product, that yet continuously acts back upon its producer" (p. 3). To genuinely grasp this dialectic, we need two levels of sociological analysis commonly referred to as microsociology and macrosociology. Further, we need a perspective that entertains this dialectic and leaves room for the contributions of both "sociologies" (Alexander, Giesen, Munch, & Smelser, 1987).

Although this dialectical challenge within sociology is larger than our present concerns, the sociology of aging is reflective of the problem and, I believe, offers an opportunity to redress some of the larger disciplinary problems (see also Riley, 1987). However, before attempting to demonstrate how this sensitivity to the dialectical nature of society is growing in the sociology of aging, it may be useful to briefly review theoretical developments and research contributions within the two levels of analysis.

SOCIOLOGICAL THEORIES AND RESEARCH IN GERONTOLOGY

The bulk of sociological research on aging over the past three decades has focused on either micro- or macro-level structures and process. Microsociology of aging focuses on the lives of aging individuals at certain points within or throughout the life course. Research here also examines roles and adaptation to life events and is described by Treas and Passuth (1988) as the "sociology of aging," emphasizing life-course processes and adaptation. Microsociology of aging has cross-pollinated with the psychology of aging in a number of circumstances, though the relative emphases are different (Baltes & Nesselroade, 1984, Dannefer; 1984; Featherman & Lerner, 1985).

Macrosociology of aging, what Treas and Passuth (1988) call the "sociology of age," focuses on social organization and change. Instead of individual or small-group structures and processes, this approach is primarily macrostructural, emphasizing the analysis of age in relation to social institutions, population, social organization, and structural change. Macrosociological research on aging has occurred on a diverse set of subjects, such as demographic change, the political economy of aging, generational conflict, and government policy on old age (e.g., see Myles, 1984; Pampel, 1981; Treas, 1977; Uhlenberg, 1988).

Table 6.1 summarizes the features of the micro and macro levels of sociological analysis related to aging. Exemplary research topics are identified, as well as salient theoretical perspectives. As Passuth and Bengtson (1988) point out, there are at least nine different theories of aging derived from the four major schools of thought in sociology (i.e., conflict, exchange, interactionism, and structural functionalism) and the fledgling perspective of phenomenology. Most of the major sociological theories of aging have been applied at either the micro or macro level of analysis. This is not to say that they cannot be applied to both

TABLE 6.1 Research Topics and Theoretical Perspectives in the Sociology of Aging

	Exemplary topics	Salient theories or perspectives
Microsociology of aging	Disability Life events Personal autonomy and dependency Role adjustments (retirement, widowhood) Social interaction	Activity Age stratification Disengagement Exchange Life course Phenomenology Social breakdown/competence Subcultural
Macrosociology of aging	Cross-national comparisons Demographic change Generational relations Organization analysis (health, labor) Government policy	Age stratification Conflict Modernization Political economy of aging

levels, only that such applications have not been widely undertaken. There are examples of both quantitative and qualitative research at each level of analysis. Now that the two general frameworks for analysis have been identified, it may be useful to consider the development of sociological theories and contributions from research within each framework over recent decades.

Development of Microsociological Theories

Early sociological theories of aging were almost exclusively articulated at the microsociological level. The first "implicit" sociological theory became known as activity theory and grew out of the Chicago school of symbolic interactionism (Cavan, Burgess, Havighurst, & Goldhamer, 1949; Havighurst & Albrecht, 1953). In its simplest form, this theory posits that the more active older adults are also more satisfied with life. Because growing older involves the loss of roles (e.g., retirement and widowhood), older adults who desire to maintain a positive sense of self need to find satisfaction in other, often newly substituted roles. Further explication and empirical tests of activity theory have continued the microsociological analysis of self, roles, and interaction (Lemon, Bengtson, & Peterson, 1972; Longino & Kart, 1982; Reitzes, Mutran, & Verrill, 1995). The evidence of research attempting to test this theory shows some support, especially on the impact of informal activity, although the general premise of the theory is always limited in some way.

The provocative disengagement theory emerged in the early 1960s as an explicit attempt to understand interaction and life satisfaction across the life course. Cumming and Henry (1961), in their book *Growing Old*, expressed disdain toward the "implicit" activity theory for its emphasis on keeping busy in advanced age. It may be argued, as Passuth and Bengtson (1988) do, that disengagement theory grew out of structural functionalism (Talcott Parsons, the noted functionalist, wrote the preface to *Growing Old* for Elaine Cumming, one of his former students). However, if that is the case, disengagement continued the emphasis on microsociological analysis (Marshall, 1994). Only occasional references to macrosociology exist in the theory, which viewed disengagement as withdrawal of both individuals and society. For example, Cumming and Henry (1961) asserted that "disengagement can be viewed as a phenomenon that functions to soften the rivalry between generations" (p. 219). Yet the bulk of the theory hinges on microsociological concerns (see also Cumming, Dean, Newell, & McCaffrey, 1960).

From this theoretical perspective, social withdrawal (i.e., decreased interaction) is a natural response to the (1) expectation of death, (2) perception of a decreasing life space, and (3) decreasing ego energy experienced by aging individuals. The problems with this theory are numerous, in light of both empirical evidence and soundness in the theory-building process (Achenbaum & Bengtson, 1994; Hochschild, 1975; Maddox, 1964). It is perhaps because sociologists interested in aging were so inflamed by the tone and conclusions of disengagement theory that researchers in the field spent enormous effort to debunk and refute the underlying principles of disengagement. It could be argued that disengagement was an ageist theory of social aging, which sociologists and social psychologists attacked in the broad enterprise of making gerontology the study of normal aging. Yet this effort by sociologists drove the subfield almost exclusively to microsociology for more than a decade.

In the process of burying disengagement theory a variety of alternative theoretical approaches were offered, but only a few have taken serious root in the field. As noted earlier, activity theory was further explicated and tested, yielding some limited empirical support. Other theoretical approaches that emerged during this period are noted in Table 6.1 (see Passuth & Bengtson, 1988, for details both bibliographic and substantive). These approaches, together with the bulk of the empirical research conducted by sociologists at this time, set an agenda for the microsociological research of aging that continues to this day.

Contributions from Microsociological Research

One area of sociological research that has received considerable attention is role loss and its accompanying life adjustments (Hagestad, 1990). Sociologists have long been interested in the effect of various role transitions on adults. Much of the early writing on this subject painted a pejorative view of the salient role losses associated with advanced age. Role loss was typically seen as creating social isolation and decrements in morale and even physical health. In short, most role losses were viewed as life crises accompanied by decrements in individual and social functioning. Rosow (1973) summarizes the social dimension of this view:

> The most crucial single rule by far involves the progressive loss of roles and functions of the aged, for this change represents a critical introduction of stress. Role loss generates the pressures and sets the conditions for the emerging crisis, and taken together, these delineate the social context of the aging self. What does this involve? First, the loss of roles *excludes the aged from significant social participation and devalues them*. (p. 82; emphasis added)

Consider retirement as an example. Some have characterized retirement as a "crisis"; however, doing so often distorts the reality of the experience in America and disconnects quality of life after retirement from quality of life before it (Calasanti, 1996; Quinn & Burkhauser, 1990). Whereas many people may consider retirement hazardous to health, the evidence has become quite compelling that this is not true (Ekerdt, 1987; Ekerdt, Baden, Bosse, & Dibbs, 1983; Streib & Schneider, 1971). When people die shortly after retirement, it is almost always their failing health *before* retirement that both prompted the retirement and led to death. There is even evidence that retirement may *improve* health in some cases (Ekerdt, Bosse, & LoCastro, 1983; Midanik, Soghikian, Ransom, & Tekawa, 1995).

There is no sound empirical evidence that retirement leads to social isolation and depression, either. Although this may occur for some people, the majority of retirees find new avenues for social life and seem to adjust fairly well (Atchley, 1982). It is a realignment of role relationships, rather than sheer loss, although the outcomes of the adjustment are contingent on several characteristics, most notably social class standing (Mutran & Reitzes, 1981).

Widowhood is another common role transition for older adults, especially women. Over half of all persons 65 years of age or older have lost a spouse, compared to less than 10% of those under 65 years of age. In terms of the degree of life change expected, this event has been characterized as one of the most stressful (Holmes & Rahe, 1967). Certainly, by comparison to retirement, widowhood is a more existentially challenging event, in part because of the lack of control over its happening. There is, in fact, considerable evidence to show that widowhood spurs decrements in physical and mental health, at least for the time immediately following the event (Feld & George, 1994; Ferraro, 1989b; Ferraro, Mutran, & Barresi, 1984). Yet the bulk of the research shows that most widows do emotionally recover from the event after about 1 year of grief work (Arbuckle & de Vries, 1995). Even more revealing is that social participation does not generally decline. Loss of one's spouse does not necessarily generate social isolation. Instead, it appears from longitudinal research that widows, even in advanced old age, are fairly active in social life relative to their level of activity before the event. It has also been shown that some types of social participation actually increase 2 or 3 years after the death of a spouse, indicating a compensatory effect. Like retirement, widowhood spurs a realignment in social life, often fostering high levels of social activity with friends who have also experienced the event (Ferraro et al., 1984; Lopata, 1979; Wan & Odell, 1983).

There are several sociological contributions from these findings. It may be useful to highlight four. First, although role losses may indeed involve considerable stress for the individual, most older adults effectively cope with the process. In this sense, most adults 50 years of age and older are more resilient than the decremental models imply. Second, rather than unilateral declines in health and effective functioning, role loss spurs a process in which older adults may realign their lives or compensate for the loss in new ways (Elder, 1994). There is a much wider range of outcomes to these experiences than was often believed. Third, there are notable individual differences due to the wide diversity among older people in comparison to younger people (see chapter 1 of this volume or Dannefer, 1987). Fourth, in the studies of both retirement and widowhood, it was apparent that a number of modifying factors, such as social class and gender, are involved in assessing the outcomes. Differences in various traits related to social class and gender were also observed *before* the role loss. As such, models of the stress process or role transitions need to incorporate the basic variables that differentiate us as people in a system of social stratification (George, 1980; O'Rand, 1990). This point will be mentioned again, but first it may be useful to consider some sociological contributions at the macro level of analysis concerning age and aging.

Development of Macrosociological Theories

What relatively little research and sociological theorizing were taking place at the macro level of analysis during the 1960s and 1970s tended to focus on the role that modernization played in defining the status of the older population (Cowgill, 1974; Cowgill & Holmes, 1972, Palmore & Manton, 1974). As Passuth and Bengtson (1988) assert, modernization theory can also be seen as being derived from structural functionalism, with emphasis on the macrostructural conditions that generate status rankings by age groups. In simple terms, modernization theory holds that the process of modernization in a society has negative effects on the status of its elders. Changes in health and economic technology, urbanization, and education purportedly lead to lower status for older adults (Cowgill, 1974).

Subsequent research to assess the utility of modernization theory, most of it based on historical analysis, again points to limited and qualified support (see also chapter 7). Laslett (1976) asserts that in the study of societal development and aging, we too commonly encounter the "world we have lost" syndrome—a bias that the world was better in times past and that social and moral entropy are inevitable. There are some indications that older age categories have lost status in the process of industrialization and modernization; however, the loss of status is not omnibus and unilateral. The decline in status appears to hit the nadir in industrial societies and may be reversed in postindustrial societies (Cox, 1990; Haber & Gratton, 1994).

Macrosociology of aging has recently been encouraged by an infusion of conflict theory to examine the status of older adults by considering institutional and macrostructural arrangements. The political economy theory of aging focuses attention on how the state affects the economy and the status of older people (Bonanno & Calasanti, 1988; Estes, 1979, 1993). Social programs for certain populations, such as older adults or the poor, often have limited effects on their target populations because the machinery of service delivery consumes such a large amount of resources. For instance, would poor older people be better off by just being given money instead of "using" a multibillion-dollar service network? Related to the political economy approach, theories based on internal colonialism in the dual economy and world systems are being considered for further study of the status of older people within a given society and among various societies, respectively (Hendricks, 1982).

Contributions from Macrosociological Research

Although macrosociological research on aging has been far less frequent over the past three decades than microsociological research, this type of research has nonetheless made some important contributions. In an era that is deeply concerned about the fair share of entitlement programs due to various generations, consider the contributions of macrosociological research to the relationship between older people and the state—most frequently referred to as the welfare state. Many modern nations have government policies that assign income and other entitlements, including health and social services, to various categories of its members. Some of these entitlements are earned, either in part or in whole; others are simply government policies based on compassion. Macrosociological research on aging has sought to understand the structural properties that determine how people adapt to old age, especially in light of these government policies.

This type of research has often been referred to as either the political sociology of aging (Myles, 1984) or the political economy of aging (Estes, 1979, 1993; Estes, Gerard, Zones, & Swan, 1984). Central to such analyses is the recognition that social and economic policies, largely shaped by social conflict, are the key determinants of the daily life of older adults. Even such basic policies as mandatory retirement and old age pensions grew out of political conflict (Guillemard, 1983; Marmor, 1995; Quadagno, 1988; Treas, 1986). These policies not only benefit older adults in many ways but also the social and economic system. In fact, it is conceivable that the development of a service network for older adults might consume so many resources that it would be impotent or grossly limited in the tangible benefits actually dispensed to older adults. At the same time that older adults may receive meager returns from these social policies, government programs often enhance the economy and benefit those holding the numerous service-oriented jobs. For instance, Bonanno and Calasanti (1988) show that entitlement programs for older adults and other recipients play an important role in capitalist development.

One of the major contributions of the macrosociological perspective on aging is to provide a sound background for understanding the achievement of "successful aging." Much of psychological, biological, and microsociological research on aging is oriented toward successful aging and how to best cope with the challenges presented by growing older. Many of these challenges can be referred to as "private troubles," as articulated by C. Wright Mills (1959). However, growing older is also a social and political process that both influences and is influenced by the political economy of a society. One of the lessons we have learned from this orientation to research on aging is that both the economy and the social institutions of a nation will shape and in some ways define the process of aging for individuals.

In the 1970s and early 1980s in America ageism was attacked and refuted as immoral. Judgments about an individual's behavior, entitlements, or life chances based purely on age were recognized as another form of discrimination. However, America and other modern societies are facing a substantial demand for services, spurring the development of new definitions of old age as well as new assessments of the entitlements and privileges generally accorded to it. An example of this is the proposed use of age as a criterion for rationing medical care (e.g., Callahan, 1987). Considering some of the major contributions of the political sociology of aging, we should not be surprised that such developments may occur in an era characterized by demand for services and limited or restrained public expenditures for meeting them.

THE MICRO-MACRO LINK

Current macrosociological theoretical approaches seem to share the indifference to the dialectic of social life common to many microsociological approaches (Marshall, 1994). For instance, neither political economy of aging theory nor activity theory seems to give priority to understanding the other side of social life. Each may be useful for explaining phenomena at one level of analysis; however, few theoretical perspectives in the sociology of aging—or within the discipline of sociology as a whole—seem concerned about and capable of giving serious attention to both the micro and macro level of analysis. Instead of ignoring the other level of analysis, there are actually several approaches to integrating theories and research from both levels of analysis. Whatever approach is taken, it is essential "to theoretically postulate, and then examine, interactionist or dialectical mechanisms linking the individual and society" (Marshall, 1994, p. 772). There is at least one theoretical perspective that has been developed to do this adequately. That theoretical perspective is known as age stratification (Riley, 1987). The emerging life course perspective also holds such promise for integrating the two levels of analysis (Elder, 1994), but age stratification is more developed. As we shall see, other theoretical perspectives, such as exchange, activity, and political economy of aging, can also be readily integrated into the age stratification perspective.

Before turning to a systematic consideration of age stratification theory, however, brief mention of the value of a link between the micro and macro levels of analysis is in order (Alexander et al., 1987; Marshall, 1994). First, it should not be assumed that sound empirical research within either level of analysis is somehow deficient or irrelevant. A given research project is always limited in its scope, both by what is of interest and what is realistically possible. *Sound research within each level is needed* and can advance the cumulative development of knowledge in this social science. The micro-macro link is, after all, an epistemological issue, not an ontological one. Empirical research spanning both levels of analysis, however, will almost by definition be costly and therefore rare. Yet such undertakings are probably worth the cost, as judged by the scientific potential of accumulating knowledge.

Second, the link between the micro and macro levels is indispensable to fully interpreting the landscape of research conducted at both levels. It is useful to understand social structures and processes at each level but even more enlightening to be able to discern how the dialectic of social life operates. We know the dialectic operates; specifying the mechanisms through which it operates is a substantial contribution.

If a theoretical perspective is capable of application at both the macro and micro levels of sociological analysis, then it should be useful for guiding research within each of those domains, as well as for enhancing our interpretation of the dialectic of social life. Of these two functions—guiding future research and interpreting research findings—I consider the latter to be more needed (what Boyer [1990] refers to as the scholarship of integration). Empirical research on aging has mushroomed in the past three decades, and an interpretive framework is needed to make sense of the morass of findings. By analogy, we need a theoretical road map.

AGE STRATIFICATION THEORY

Age stratification theory asserts that age is one focal point for understanding social organization, social change, and the location of individuals in society. Societies develop in such a way that age inequalities emerge. This occurs principally because social roles are differentially rewarded and because age is used as a criterion for allocating these roles (Foner, 1988). The theory is not so intellectually imperialistic as to assert that age is *the* focal point of social structure and process. That may be the case in some circumstances, but age stratification is seen as one of several overlapping systems of stratification. This thought was probably best pioneered by Parsons (1942): "In our society age grading does not to any great extent, except for the educational system, involve formal age categorization, but is interwoven with other structural elements" (p. 604). The actual development of a model of age stratification was and is primarily the contribution of Matilda Riley and Anne Foner. (See Riley, 1985, 1987, or Riley, Foner, & Waring, 1988, for extensive bibliographies.)

In the first major treatise on the subject, Riley, Johnson, and Foner (1972) sought to articulate a perspective that could span the scope of sociology from micro to macro levels of analysis while emphasizing the perspective of age strata: "Age also serves as an important link, on the one hand, between the individual and his biological life cycle and, on the other hand, between society and its history" (p. 4). The theoretical model of age stratification has three foci: (1) individual aging; (2) changing age structures, or societal aging; and (3) cohort flow (Riley et al., 1988). These are seen as three interdependent parts of age stratification, and it may be useful to consider them separately.

Individual Aging

Unlike Cumming and Henry (1961), who developed the disengagement theory by focusing on growing old, age stratification concerns *growing older*. Individual aging is seen as "a life-course process of growing up and growing *older* from birth to death, not simply growing *old* beyond some arbitrary point in the life course" (Riley et al., 1988, p. 246). Thus, on the micro level, age stratification theory examines individual aging as a multifaceted process involving biological, psychological, and social activities across the life course. Fundamental to aging in the social context is the activation of certain roles. There are normative expectations for individuals of various ages to adopt specific roles. We have certain expectations about the appropriate age to be a spouse, a president, or a student. Aging, therefore, is constantly judged by the adoption or relinquishment of certain roles.

Changing Age Structures

In terms of structure, age is a crucial ingredient, not only of social groups and institutions but also of people (individuals as well as populations). Roles, with their age-related criteria for occupancy or performance, are organized within families, schools, firms, and other social institutions. Moreover, at any given time the people in a society may be roughly divided by age into several categories—what may be termed age strata, ranging from the youngest to the oldest. Just as with stratification by social class, the number of age strata designated is arbitrary and typically determined by the purpose of the analysis. Often comparisons are made by simply dividing the adult population at ages 18 to 64 and 65 and over. Although this is certainly a useful division, we have already seen how diverse the older adult population is, let alone the age range of 18- to 64-year-olds. If the age strata are not simply demarcated by equal age intervals—of, say, 10 years—then the differences in the object under study should be minimal *within* a given stratum but hypothetically substantial *between* age strata. What one readily learns when considering various characteristics of individuals, whether biological, psychological, or social, is that many are related to age strata, sometimes linearly and sometimes in curvilinear fashion.

The focus of studying changing age structures is usually on the age strata, not on the process of individual aging. Recent changes in the population as a whole are sometimes referred to as societal aging, but populations not only grow older, such as many modern nations are now doing, but can also grow younger. For instance, America became a younger nation from 1940 to 1960 with the advent of the baby boom. Thus, there is value in examining changing age structures to understand how and why societies change or remain relatively stable. The meaning attributed to such changes may include discussions of age differences, age inequality, age deprivation, and age opportunity.

Cohort Flow

Cohort flow (or succession) is the concept that links individual aging and changing age structures. In short, individuals inevitably age, but they do so as members of a cohort—a set of people born at the same time.

Imagine for a moment, for heuristic purposes, an escalator analogy (as suggested in Riley et al., 1972). Consider a building with 10 floors and 9 operating escalators. All people currently riding the escalators can be considered the population, and the nine sets of people on the respective escalators can be considered cohorts. The settings on the respective floors, which are periodically rearranged, symbolize the surrounding social and institutional environments. We begin our journey at about the same time as those with whom we are riding. Those ahead of us experienced many of the same events we now encounter but some time ago. Thus, we all experienced youth, but the experience is different for the various cohorts because of social and environmental change. Our cohorts vary in size and other characteristics as we enter the first escalator, and the cohort continues to change through the progression; most notably, each cohort shrinks. War, technological accidents, and natural disasters are only a few of the many events that may alter cohort size and composition. Those who ride to the top of the building are, by analogy, the survivors—those who protected their lives and/or were fortunate enough to avoid catastrophes. A cohort succeeds to subsequent floors, but its composition is changed in the process; it shrinks but not randomly. Major world or national events affect us all, but differently depending on the cohort to which we belong.

The recognition of cohort flow is indispensable to the gerontological imagination as well as the sociological analysis of aging. An awareness of cohort flow helps one to have a healthy skepticism about supposed "aging effects" observed in cross-sectional studies. We have numerous examples of research on cohort flow that have shown that what was once thought to be an aging effect has actually been demonstrated to be a cohort effect or perhaps a period effect (social change indexed by time of measurement). As Riley et al. (1988) stated so well,

> studies of cohort flow . . . have been the source of some of the most crucial contributions to sociological understanding of age. They have been instrumental in undermining the biological and psychological determinism that characterized so much of the opinion on aging. They have challenged efforts at stereotyping age-related behaviors. They have shown how age-graded institutions operate in the society, and have illuminated the processes of social change. (p. 255)

Exemplars of this type of research include the work of Conger and Elder (1994), Easterlin (1987), Elder (1974), and Hayward, Friedman, and Chen (1996).

THE THEORETICAL POWER OF AGE STRATIFICATION

The utility of age stratification theory for the sociology of aging can be judged by the degree to which it can accommodate micro and macro levels of analysis and the insights of existing theories in sociology. With regard to the first of these concerns, it is apparent that the theory is capable of addressing both levels of analysis via its threefold focus: aging, changing age structures, and cohort flow. Although it is a slight oversimplification, these three foci correspond to the micro and macro levels and the link between the two. Some scholars have characterized age stratification as a macrosociological approach (Elder, 1994; p. 5; Estes et al., 1984, p. 9), but it is not *only* a macrosociological approach. It can be usefully applied to macrosociological issues, but considerable attention given to social roles and the interaction between the individual and age roles implies that the approach is suitable for microsociology as well. In the early articulation of the theory, Riley et al. (1972) defined aging as involving "the accumulation of experience through participation in a *succession of social roles*, and through psychological change and development . . . over the life course, individuals enter certain roles but relinquish others, acquire certain capacities and motivations but lose others" (p. 10; emphasis added). In sum, age stratification theory seems suitable for analyzing social life at either the micro or macro level of analysis (Dannefer, 1987). In addition, studies that shed light on the link between the two levels of analysis continue to appear (Ferraro, 1989a, 1992; Wolinsky, 1990).

Age stratification theory can also benefit from and extend the insights of the major schools of sociological theory. Congruence with structural functionalism is obvious (Dowd, 1980). The influence of Parsons (1968) is seen in system properties and multiple levels of analysis. Yet current versions of age stratification theory appear to have benefited from Merton's (1948) criticism of Parsons's too abstract "philosophical system" and instead try to make the theory, or at least parts of the theory, readily testable.

There is nothing in age stratification theory to preclude the application of conflict theory within its analytic framework. Age stratification theory does not assume consensus or conflict. Rather, it seeks to explicate the effects or emergence of either consensus or conflict on age structures and processes (Foner, 1974, 1986). Because age stratification incorporates both micro and macro levels of analysis, it can also be linked with conflict theory at both levels (e.g., Dahrendorf, 1958; Simmel [quoted in Wolff, 1950]). Dowd (1980) argues that the early articulation of age stratification theory did not adequately incorporate social conflict. Although there may be some merit in this criticism, it does not seem insurmountable in theory building.

As previously noted, the emphasis of age stratification theory on social roles makes the link with interaction or role theory logically strong (Blumer, 1969). Because considerable groundwork has already been laid on the convergence of interactionism and exchange theory (Singelmann, 1972), it should come as no surprise that there is ample room for conceptual integration between exchange theory and age stratification theory as well. The work remains to be done, but the *potential* for explicating exchange relationships in the context of age stratification is clear (Dowd, 1975). Mutran and Reitzes launch such an endeavor by considering intergenerational exchange relationships in the family (see chapter 8).

One should not conclude from this brief review that age stratification theory is the panacea for what ails the sociology of aging. The logical integration of it with some schools of sociological thought will require considerable dialogue and revision. However, my purpose has been to show how the potential exists for age stratification to advance research and interpretation of the sociological analysis of age and aging while keeping the dialectic of social life alive.

CONCLUSION

The sociology of aging has contributed much to our understanding of human aging. Yet social thought about aging has tended to focus on either the micro or macro levels of analysis, with little discussion of the link between the two. Research continues to mushroom within each level of analysis, and a "theoretical map" is needed to interpret and appreciate the landscape of findings.

As cartographers have long known, maps key in on certain information but obviously omit other interesting information. Moreover, maps vary by coverage and scale of presentation. By analogy, each theory for studying aging gives only part of the reality, but age stratification theory offers a number of advantages. It is applicable within either the micro or macro level of analysis and can be integrated with other maps—that is, sociological theories. It can readily accommodate many of the findings of recent research, whether the issue is the role of social class in moderating stress processes or the influence of social institutions and changing age structures on each other. Age stratification is certainly not the only theory that discusses the societal dialectic, but it does provide considerable insight into this critical issue. Society shapes the aging experience, but the aging experience also shapes society.

REFERENCES

Achenbaum, W. A., & Bengtson, V. L. (1994). Re-engaging the disengagement theory of aging: On the history and assessment of theory development in gerontology. *Gerontologist*, *34*, 756–763.

Alexander, J. C., Giesen, B., Munch, R., & Smelser, N. J. (1987). *The micro-macro link.* Berkeley: University of California Press.

Arbuckle, N. W., & de Vries, B. (1995). The long-term effects of later life spousal and parental bereavement on personal functioning. *Gerontologist*, *35*, 637–647.

Atchley, R. C. (1982). The process of retirement: Comparing women and men. In M. Szinovacz (Ed.), *Women's retirement* (pp. 153–168). Beverly Hills, CA: Sage.

Baltes, P. B., & Nesselroade, J. R. (1984). Paradigm lost and paradigm regained: Critique of Dannefer's portrayal of life span developmental psychology. *American Sociological Review*, *49*, 841–847.

Berger, P. L. (1969). *The sacred canopy.* Garden City, NY: Doubleday.

Blumer, H. (1969). *Symbolic interactionism: Perspective and method.* Englewood Cliffs, NJ: Prentice-Hall .

Bonanno, A., & Calasanti, T. M. (1988). Laissez-faire strategies and the crisis of the welfare state: A comparative analysis of the status of the elderly in Italy and in the United States. *Sociological Focus, 21*, 245–263.

Boyer, E. J. (1990). *Scholarship reconsidered: Priorities of the professoriate.* Princeton, NJ: Carnegie Foundation for the Advancement of Teaching.

Calasanti, T. M. (1996). Gender and life satisfaction in retirement: An assessment of the male model. *Journal of Gerontology: Social Sciences, 51B*, S18–S29.

Callahan, D. (1987). *Setting limits: Medical goals in an aging society.* New York: Simon & Schuster.

Cavan, R. S., Burgess, E. W., Havighurst, R. J., & Goldhamer, H. (1949). *Personal adjustment in old age.* Chicago: University of Chicago Press.

Conger, R. D., & Elder, G. H., Jr. (1994). *Families in troubled times: Adapting to change in rural America.* Hawthorne, NY: Aldine de Gruyter.

Cowgill, D. O. (1974). Aging and modernization: A revision of the theory. In J. F. Gubrium (Ed.), *Late life* (pp. 123–46). Springfield, IL: Charles C Thomas.

Cowgill, D. O., & Holmes, L. D. (Eds.). (1972). *Aging and modernization.* New York: Appleton-Century-Crofts.

Cox, H. G. (1990). Roles for aged individuals in post-industrial societies. *International Journal of Aging and Human Development, 30*, 55–62.

Cumming, E., Dean, L., Newell, D., & McCaffrey, I. (1960). Disengagement—a tentative theory of aging. *Sociometry, 73*, 23–35.

Cumming, E., & Henry, W. E. (1961). *Growing old: The process of disengagement.* New York: Basic Books.

Dahrendorf, R. (1958). Toward a theory of social conflict. *Journal of Conflict Resolution, 7*, 170–183.

Dannefer, D. (1984). Adult development and social theory: A paradigmatic reappraisal. *American Sociological Review, 49*, 100–116.

Dannefer, D. (1987). Aging as intracohort differentiation: Accentuation, the Matthew effect, and the life course. *Sociological Forum, 2*, 211–236.

Dowd, J. J. (1975). Aging as exchange: A preface to theory. *Journal of Gerontology, 30*, 584–594.

Dowd, J. J. (1980). *Stratification among the aged.* Monterey, CA: Brooks/Cole.

Easterlin, R. A. (1987). *Birth and fortune: The impact of numbers on personal welfare* (2nd ed.). Chicago: University of Chicago Press.

Ekerdt, D. J. (1987). Why the notion persists that retirement harms health. *Gerontologist, 77*, 454–457.

Ekerdt, D. J., Baden, L., Bosse, R., & Dibbs, E. (1983). The effect of retirement on physical health. *American Journal of Public Health, 73*, 779–783.

Ekerdt, D. J., Bosse, R., & LoCastro, J. S. (1983). Claims that retirement improves health. *Journal of Gerontology, 38*, 231–236.

Elder, G. H., Jr. (1974). *Children of the Great Depression.* Chicago: University of Chicago Press.

Elder, G. H., Jr. (1994). Time, human agency, and social change: Perspectives on the life course. *Social Psychology Quarterly, 57*, 4–15.

Estes, C. L. (1979). *The aging enterprise.* San Francisco: Jossey-Bass.

Estes, C. L. (1993). *The aging enterprise revisited. Gerontologist, 33*, 292–298.

Estes, C. L., Gerard, L. E., Zones, J. S., & Swan, J. H. (1984). *Political economy, health, and aging.* Boston: Little, Brown.

Featherman, D. L., & Lerner, R. M. (1985). Ontogenesis and sociogenesis: Problematics for theory and research about development and socialization across the lifespan. *American Sociological Review, 50*, 659–676.

Feld, S., & George, L. K. (1994). Moderating effects of prior social resources on the hospitalizations of elders who become widowed. *Journal of Aging and Health, 6*, 275–295.

Ferraro, K. F. (1989a). The ADEA Amendment and public support for older workers. *Research on Aging, 11*, 53–81.

Ferraro, K. F. (1989b). Widowhood and health. In K. Markides & C. L. Cooper (Eds.), *Aging, stress, social support and health* (pp. 69–89). New York: Wiley.

Ferraro, K. F. (1992). Self and older-people referents in evaluating life problems. *Journal of Gerontology: Social Sciences, 47*, S105–S114.

Ferraro, K. F., Mutran, E., & Barresi, C. M. (1984). Widowhood, health, and friendship support in later life. *Journal of Health and Social Behavior, 25*, 245–259.

Foner, A. (1974). Age stratification and age conflict in political life. *American Sociological Review, 39*, 187–196.

Foner, A. (1986). *Aging and old age: New perspectives.* Englewood Cliffs, NJ: Prentice-Hall.

Foner, A. (1988). Age inequalities: Are they epiphenomena of the class system? In M. W. Riley (Ed.), *Social structures and human lives* (pp. 176–191). Newbury Park, CA: Sage.

George, L. K. (1980). *Role transitions in later life.* Monterey, CA: Brooks/Cole.

Guillemard, A. M. (1983). The making of old age policy in France: Points of debate, issues at stake, underlying social relations. In A. M. Guillemard (Ed.), *Old age and the welfare state* (pp. 75–99). Beverly Hills, CA: Sage.

Haber, C., & Gratton, B. (1994). *Old age and the search for security: An American social history.* Bloomington, IN: Indiana University Press.

Hagestad, G. O. (1990). Social perspectives on the life course. In R. H. Binstock & L. K. George (Eds.), *Handbook of aging and the social sciences* (pp. 151–168). San Diego, CA: Academic Press.

Havighurst, R. J., & Albrecht, R. (1953). *Older people.* New York: Longmans, Green.

Hayward, M. D., Friedman, S., & Chen, H. (1996). Race inequities in men's retirement. *Journal of Gerontology: Social Sciences, 51B*, S1–S10.

Hendricks, J. (1982). The elderly in society: Beyond modernization. *Social Science History, 6*, 321–345.

Hochschild, A. (1975). Disengagement theory: A critique and proposal. *American Sociological Review, 40*, 553–569.

Holmes, T. H., & Rahe, R. H. (1967). The social readjustment rating scale. *Journal of Psychosomatic Research, 11*, 213–218.

Laslett, P. (1976). Societal development and aging. In R. H. Binstock & E. Shanas (Eds.), *Handbook of aging and the social sciences* (pp. 87–116). New York: Van Nostrand Reinhold.

Lemon, B. W., Bengtson, V. L., & Peterson, J. A. (1972). An exploration of the activity theory of aging: Activity types and life satisfaction among in-movers to a retirement community. *Journal of Gerontology, 27*, 511–523.

Longino, C. F., & Kart, C. S. (1982). Explicating activity theory: A formal replication. *Journal of Gerontology, 37*, 713–722.

Lopata, H. Z. (1979). *Women as widows*. New York: Elsevier.

Maddox, G. (1964). Disengagement theory: A critical evaluation. *Gerontologist*, *4*, 80–82.

Marmor, T. R. (1995). *The politics of Medicare*. Hawthorne, NY: Aldine de Gruyter.

Marshall, V. W. (1994). Sociology, psychology, and the theoretical legacy of the Kansas City studies. *Gerontologist*, *34*, 768–774.

Merton, R. (1948). Discussion of Parsons' "The position of sociological theory." *American Sociological Review*, *13*, 164–168.

Midanik, L. T., Soghikian, K., Ransom, L. J., & Tekawa, I. S. (1995). The effect of retirement on mental health and health behaviors: The Kaiser Permanente retirement study. *Journal of Gerontology: Social Sciences*, *50B*, S59–S61.

Mills, C. W. (1959). *The sociological imagination*. London: Oxford University Press.

Mutran, E., & Reitzes, D. C. (1981). Retirement, identity and well-being: Realignment of role relationships. *Journal of Gerontology*, *36*, 733–740.

Myles, J. (1984). *Old age in the welfare state: The political economy of public pensions*. Boston: Little, Brown.

O'Rand, A. M. (1990). Stratification and the life course. In R. H. Binstock & L. K. George (Eds.), *Handbook of aging and the social sciences* (pp. 130–148). San Diego, CA: Academic Press.

Palmore, E. B., & Manton, K. (1974). Modernization and status of the aged: International correlations. *Journal of Gerontology*, *29*, 205–210.

Pampel, F. C. (1981). *Social change and the aged*. Lexington, MA: Lexington.

Parsons, T. (1942). Age and sex in the social structure of the United States. *American Sociological Review*, *7*, 604–616.

Parsons, T. (1968). *The structure of social action*. New York: Free Press.

Passuth, P. M., & Bengtson, V. L. (1988). Sociological theories of aging: Current perspectives and future directions. In J. E. Birren & V. L. Bengtson (Eds.), *Emergent theories of aging* (pp. 333–355). New York: Springer Publishing.

Quadagno, J. S. (1988). *The transformation of old age security: Class and politics in the American welfare state*. Chicago: University of Chicago Press.

Quinn, J. F., & Burkhauser, R. V. (1990). Work and retirement. In R. H. Binstock & L. K. George (Eds.), *Handbook of aging and the social sciences* (pp. 308–327). San Diego, CA: Academic Press.

Reitzes, D. C., Mutran, E. J., & Verrill, L. A. (1995). Activities and self-esteem: Continuing the development of activity theory. *Research on Aging*, *17*, 260–277.

Riley, M. W. (1985). Age strata in social systems. In R. H. Binstock & E. Shanas (Eds.), *Handbook of aging and the social sciences* (pp. 369–411). New York: Van Nostrand Reinhold.

Riley, M. W. (1987). On the significance of age in sociology. *American Sociological Review*, *52*, 1–14.

Riley, M. W., Foner, A., & Waring, J. (1988). Sociology of age. In N. J. Smelser (Ed.), *Handbook of sociology* (pp. 243–290). Newbury Park, CA: Sage.

Riley, M. W., Johnson, M., & Foner, A. (1972). *Aging and society: Vol. 3. A sociology of age stratification*. New York: Russell Sage Foundation.

Rosow, L. (1973). The social context of the aging self. *Gerontologist*, *13*, 82–87.

Singelmann, P. (1972). Exchange as symbolic interaction: Convergences between theoretical perspectives. *American Sociological Review*, *37*, 414–424.

Streib, G. F., & Schneider, C. J. (1971). *Retirement in American society*. Ithaca, NY: Cornell University Press.

Treas, J. (1977). Family support systems for the aged: Some social and demographic considerations. *Gerontologist, 17*, 486–491.

Treas, J. (1986). The historical decline in late life labor force participation in the U.S. In J. Birren, P. Robinson, & J. Livingston (Eds.), *Age, health, and employment* (pp. 158–173). Englewood Cliffs, NJ: Prentice-Hall.

Treas, J., & Passuth, P. M. (1988). Age, aging, and the aged: The three sociologies. In E. F. Borgatta & K. Cook (Eds.), *The future of sociology* (pp. 394–417). Newbury Park, CA: Sage.

Uhlenberg, P. (1988). Aging and the societal significance of cohorts. In J. E. Birren & V. L. Bengtson (Eds.), *Emergent theories of aging* (pp. 405–425). New York: Springer Publishing.

Verbrugge, L. M., Gruber-Baldini, A. L., & Fozard, J. L. (1996). Age differences and age changes in activities: Baltimore longitudinal study of aging. *Journal of Gerontology: Social Sciences, 51B*, S30–S41.

Wan, T. T. H., & Odell, B. G. (1983). Major role losses and social participation of older males. *Research on Aging, 5*, 173–196.

Wolff, K. H. (Ed.). (1950). *The sociology of Georg Simmel.* New York: Free Press.

Wolinsky, F. D. (1990). *Health behavior among elderly Americans: An age-stratification perspective.* New York: Springer Publishing.

CHAPTER 7

Cross-Cultural Perspectives on Aging

Christine L. Fry

A gerontological imagination that maintains heterogeneity as a major tenant, invites a comparative perspective. In fact, if we are to understand diversity at any level (cellular, individual, or societal), comparison is imperative. Because age is a temporal phenomenon, occurring in many dimensions simultaneously, the potential for diversification is tremendous. Culturally, we find order in classification. Unfortunately, time or age have proved to be oversimplified in the study of life processes. The "aged," as a distinct social category, dissolves once we peer beyond the stereotype and discover the heterogeneity of life experiences.

At the same time, this heterogeneity does not defy understanding; it only challenges our scientific imagination. One path we have followed in this pursuit is to investigate the contexts in which people grow older and come to experience old age. Social and cultural factors shape the way people make a living, the social units in which they live and work, and the meanings they assign to their lives. These factors are not nearly as diverse as the people whose lives they structure, but at the same time, we must be careful not to oversimplify these as well by looking primarily at racial and ethnic boundaries (e.g., *the* Black aged or *the* Navajo aged).

One strategy of comparative research is to actually increase the diversity in sociocultural factors and look beyond the boundaries of any one cultural system. The distinct advantage in doing this is that we transcend what seems natural and obvious within one society to discover that what we thought was a natural law is only a phenomenon conditioned by local circumstances. The gerontological imagination can only benefit from this strategy. Most of our scientific knowledge about aging is based on research from contemporary North American and European industrialized societies. Here, science as a way of knowing developed. These societies have the resources and the need to know about their older people. Also, in spite of political boundaries and ideological differences, these social contexts are remarkably similar. They all are based on industrial modes of production, are state-level societies, and have increasingly individuated their members in linkages to the state and production.

In this chapter we consider what we have learned about aging in other societies. We first examine the comparative method and then evaluate age as a comparative unit for such analysis. Lessons from comparative research are considered next, with application to our understanding of aging in America.

USES OF THE COMPARATIVE METHOD

Comparison is one of the foundations of science. Linguists would also argue that it is the basis for human thought. In making sense of and ordering the world of experience, humans use language to code it; to think about it; and to talk about it. Everything has its name, and when it doesn't, we make up one. Names reflect a more abstract order based on differences, similarities, and comparisons. A name tells us what something is and what it is not. For instance, to say people are "old" means they *are* old and also that they *are not* young or middle aged. A name not only points to similarities with other things, actions, or qualities. It also highlights the differences with things, actions, or qualities not included within the category. Comparisons, then, are the cornerstones of the way we understand experience. The comparative method builds on this substructure of human thought processes.

The comparative method is basic to all sciences embracing a range of phenomena, from the geology of the earth to biological evolution to studies of human behavior and culture. Three features distinguish the scientific use of the comparative method: (1) the units to be compared are explicitly defined, (2) these units are selected for specific reasons, and (3) the features under study are also made explicit. For studies of aging, the units may be nations, societies, ethnic groups, communities, or even groups. The reasons for selection of units may range from a probability sample of the 3,000-plus societies of the world to selection of a few cases because they represent a theoretically interesting range of variation (e.g., level of economic development). Our third element, the features studied, is even more variable because each research project has its own focus.

Researchers have generally used three broad strategies in their application of the comparative method. The first involves secondary analysis of data from published reports (e.g., Albert & Cattell, 1994; Foner & Kertzer, 1978; Simmons, 1945, 1960). The second uses primary data collected by individual research projects. The third also uses primary data but involves a team of researchers working in collaboration. Cross-cultural research examples include Project A.G.E. (Keith et al., 1994), and cross-national examples include research on elders in the Western Pacific (Andrews, 1986) and industrialized societies (Shanas et al. 1968).

AGE AS A COMPARATIVE UNIT

As we take this comparative method to other cultural contexts, using age as our window, we must ask the question, how useful is age as a comparative unit? The answer is, it is very problematic. Initially, it would appear to be an ideal unit for comparative analysis because it is easily measured, and its measurement is exact and refined. We can measure age in years, months, or even days. However, when we push our investigations beyond the bounds of industrial societies, we find that age as chronology vanishes. Many cultures do not organize and calibrate lives in years. Birth dates are not always known or even considered important. Years may be named, but it is the name of the year, not the time elapsed, that is important. Time is not always important in organizing life. In these contexts age is something that is functional, based on capacities and capabilities.

Why did the first gerontologists focus on age as a defining feature of the old? Gerontology emerged in societies that emphasize chronological age. Age and the way it organizes life courses is an integral part of industrialized, bureaucratized societies. Records of vital statistics (births and deaths) are kept. A periodic census is taken to monitor the characteristics of the labor force. With the individuation of people, age becomes an important marker in ordering lives: an age for school; an age for driving, drinking, military service, voting; and an age for receiving a pension. Age has become a proxy for other things, a shortcut in placing people and granting or removing privileges. Even in these societies there is a concern for the reliance on chronological age. The main issue is that we don't know what it means. In its precision it is divorced from social events. In its arbitrariness it masks variation and produces confounds. When asked, even Americans are likely to use a functional definition of age in defining old age (National Council on the Aging, 1976).

If chronology presents us with problems, then what do we use? A major conceptual breakthrough in gerontology is the twofold recognition that (1) age is not what we are studying, and (2) we cannot divorce old age from earlier life stages. With this advance the "life course" replaced age as our unit. As a cultural unit it is potentially better suited for the comparative method (Fry, 1988; Fry & Keith, 1982). However, even the way we have conceptualized the life course has largely been defined by the need to rationalize the labor force in industrialized societies (Fry, 1994).

Lives are lived through time. In viewing aging as a series of transitions, the life course encompasses the duration and unfolding of lives from birth to death. Time, however, is subject to local circumstance and is far more complicated than simple linear progression, which is the metaphor used in European and North American industrialized societies. Time is conceived much as the three-sided mechanical drawing ruler. It is calibrated in at least three different ways: life time, social time, and historical time (Neugarten & Datan, 1973). Life time is chronological time roughly indexing the sequence from infancy to old age and the biological sequence of change. Social time is the cultural definition of the age grading that occurs in every society and is specific for that society. Historical time refers to major processes of change and historical events that shape a society and its definition of the life course. What makes the life course an attractive comparative unit is that it demands that we look for and document variation in the way these three dimensions of time are defined. It invites us to look for variation.

Some of this variation is just beginning to be understood. For openers, the life course has become institutionalized in industrial states. Childhood was differentiated as a life stage (Aires, 1962). Then came the rationalization and structuring of the life course (Meyer, 1986). The industrial political economy rationalized its labor force by individuating its citizens, not seeing them as members of greater collectivities such as tribes, communities, or families. Chronological references increased, and states have structured the life course through child labor laws, graded and mandatory education, rules concerning seniority and career sequencing, and formalized retirement and entitlement programs (Kohli, 1986; Mayer & Muller, 1986). Where the state has not penetrated the lives of individuals, we find less institutionalization and standardization in life courses and the way they are perceived. Lives are not easily divisible into stages with age norms.

Social clocks, calibrated by social time, reflect local conditions. To discover the calibrations we have to ask, "What ages people?" or "What do people need to know to judge someone's age?" Answers to these questions reveal that people use a combination of social statuses, functionality, and psychological attributes. In urban industrial societies a core of career lines and family cycles serve as markers of age, followed by other themes (Fry, 1980, 1988, 1994). These themes reflect stratification, community identity, and specific community issues that include such things as paying off mortgages, community organizations, and the status of one's parents. In nonurban contexts, functionality and physical capacity loomed larger. Even family cycles and the maturity of children are not as salient here because of higher fertility and limited participation in universal education.

Regardless of the life course supplanting age as our unit, we still are interested in the later stages of that life course. Who are the older people? Every society has an answer to this question. The life course is divided into age grades from infancy to old age. What moves individuals into the older or oldest age grades is society-specific. Only rarely is it a chronological event. In industrialized societies it is retirement from or withdrawal from the labor force, complemented by changes in the domestic cycle such as grandparenthood or great-grandparenthood. In nonindustrialized societies it may be marked by declining abilities to participate in production and a gradual shift in work activities, again complemented by changes in the family cycle. Health status also contributes to definitions of old age. Two issues are of importance here. The first is that the meaning of old age is defined by each society and is a cultural construct. Second, there may well be more than one age grade of older people. In the United States we now differentiate between the "young old" and the "old old," with probably more refinements on the way.

CROSS-CULTURAL RESEARCH AND AGING

Age and the Comparative Method

One way of looking at other societies is as an experiment in accommodating to a natural and social environment, arranging social linkages between its members and giving meaning to life. We often group these societies into industrial/nonindustrial or modern/traditional. Such dichotomies oversimplify the diversity of these collective experiments. Even for the simpler societies we often label as traditional, there are major differences in such features as stratification, societal scale, energy utilization, subsistence strategies, and population size (Halperin, 1984, 1987). Gathering and hunting bands (e.g., Eskimos, !Kung San Bushmen) that subsist by foraging are noted as low energy, low population, egalitarian, and small scale. Tribal societies (e.g., Iroquois, Pueblos, Yanomamo, Nuer) that subsist by horticulture or pastoralism utilize more energy and have slightly higher populations but are still egalitarian and small-scale. Chiefdoms are more complex (e.g., Tikopia, Trobriands), making a shift from low-energy subsistence to more intensive agriculture, the advent of stratification (unequal access to resources), and an increase in population and scale. Kingdoms and empires represent further political centralization, with their increases in stratification, intensification in agriculture, and increases in scale and population size. This evolutionary typology reflects some of the diversity and is a reminder that we cannot treat the nonindustrial or traditional world as uniform. This variation also stimulates us to exploit this diversity in answering our research questions.

In answering these questions we are partially limited by what has been asked about older people because that shapes what is known. For gerontology a major question has been "How are they doing?" This certainly was the theme of the first comparative work on aging, Leo Simmons's (1945) *The Role of the Aged in Primitive Society*. Indeed, well-being or life satisfaction has been a major dependent variable in gerontological research as investigators study adjustment in old age. However, for the comparative method, well-being presents some problems because most strategies to measure it are psychometric. A battery of questions probes evaluation of well-being on several dimensions to arrive at a score. For non-Euro-Americans, well-being is not necessarily a meaningful construct and may not necessarily be something that can be monitored like an emotional pulse. Consequently, alternatives to well-being have included such variables as treatment, status, esteem, and prestige, as well as strategies for asking about life satisfaction and evaluation of well-being. These variables are quite distinct in their measurement and meaning but do reflect a common theme. What factors promote the security of older people (i.e., increase their status, esteem, prestige, and well-being as well as promote good treatment)? Contrarily, what factors leave older adults vulnerable to bad treatment and decreased status, esteem, prestige, and lowered well-being?

Results indicate that health and wealth are major factors in promoting security and enhanced well-being. However, as our comparative laboratory and the issue of comparability warns us, these factors are shaped by society-specific circumstances and are given cultural meaning. In examining our question of what promotes security or increases vulnerability for older people in our natural laboratory we will focus on five issues: (1) the material basis of social life, which includes control of resources and the effects of subsistence requirements; (2) health and functionality; (3) social linkages in both the domestic and public domain; (4) cultural values, especially those of independence; and (5) the forces of change that affect the security of the old.

Material Factors

A generalization that has withstood the test of time is that control of significant resources improves the lot of older people. Simmons's (1945) now classic study documents that older people who own property or other resources have higher status and receive better treatment. Control over resources is not a simple matter of older people hoarding the wealth and younger people being nice to them in hopes of receiving a share. In fact, hoarding of wealth brings contempt (Maxwell & Maxwell, 1980). The broader sociological principle at work seems to be rooted in exchange and reciprocity (Dowd, 1975). With something to give in the negotiation of everyday life, older people can take from others and continue exchanging. Without resources to exchange, social relations become more susceptible to termination, withdrawal, or compliance with the wishes of others in what becomes increasingly asymmetrical interactions. Control of family or community property, social resources, supernatural resources, or information enable older people to exchange and to secure deference, better treatment, prestige and/or status (Maxwell & Silverman, 1970; Silverman, 1987; Silverman & Maxwell, 1983).

Economies vary, differentially favoring resource control by elders or the young and middle-aged. Control of wealth is favored when the extended family is a viable residential or economic unit (Fry, 1996), especially if it is a land- or animal (cattle)-owning unit. In these "family corporations," seniority and survivorship count for a lot, as decision making is often in the hands of the elders or senior males (Fry, 1996). Some economies, however, do not favor resource accumulation. Quite striking are the Inuit Eskimos (hunters of the Arctic) whose environment and technology eliminate surplus and storage. Hunters are bonded in an ethos of sharing to even out the effects of bad luck. An aged hunter compensates for declining endurance by outproducing younger hunters during less harsh seasons and may even renew the productivity of his household by marrying a young wife (Guemple, 1980). Ultimately, however, he cannot accumulate material resources. Likewise, other economies require the wealth of parents be dispersed on the marriage of their children, the youngest one depleting the family coffers. Among the pastoral Fulani, older men and women exist on the periphery of their eldest son's homestead. The aging father is marginal because he has no cattle, and similarly, his wife has no calabashes with which to milk the cows. They sleep, almost over their own graves, because they are already "socially dead" (Stenning, 1971).

Other economies devalue the significance of the resources older people may have. For instance, economies that open new opportunities in urban areas erode the resource foundations older people may have built. Knowledge of the "right way" becomes supplanted with new information from the city, leaving the testimony of older people no longer valued. Whatever respect, prestige, or power an older person had in making decisions, advising, arbitrating conflict, instructing, or even telling entertaining stories is diminished. Because their knowledge is no longer seen as significant, there is less reason for social exchange, which brings increased negative consequences for older people.

Health Factors

Health factors are a major dimension promoting the security of all people, including older adults. As bodies age, they become increasingly vulnerable to health problems and frequently to decreasing functional capabilities. It should come as no surprise that health and functionality have culturally specific definitions. The World Health Organization (1946) defines health as "a state of complete physical, mental and social well-being, and not merely the absence of disease of infirmity." The very vagueness of this definition reflects the diversity of contexts to which it must be applied. Well-being has no universal definition. Similarly, functionality, or the physical abilities to do the tasks of adults, takes on different meanings depending upon context (Beall & Eckert, 1986). For instance stairs become a major barrier with advanced age, often necessitating retreating to the first floor or moving when stairs can no longer be negotiated. Where stairs are not an environmental feature, however, the ability to go up and down them makes no difference. Where interior plumbing and central heating are nonexistent, the abilities to get water and firewood are critical. Socially defined skills like driving, dealing with bureaucracies (banks, post offices, government), or reading and writing are subject to even more variability.

In spite of variable definitions there are generalizations to be made. The first is, there is no Shangri-la, the paradise where people do not age. The closest we have come are a few cultures tucked away in the high mountains of Pakistan (Humzakut in the Karakoran Mountains), Ecuador (Vilcabamba in the Andes), and Russia (Abkhasia in the Caucasus Mountains). Mountain environments free of many pollutants and pathogens, combined with founder effects (good genes in the ancestors of these populations), were thought to account for long-lives of 119 or even 130 years. Research into these populations has revealed they are not extraordinarily long-lived. The oldest old, as elsewhere in the world, attain maximum ages in the 80- or 90-year range and rarely exceed 100.

Once existing records of life events were cross-checked, researchers discovered that superlongevity was a product of age escalation, which systematically increased as age increased (Fries & Crapo, 1981; Mazess & Foreman, 1979). Why increase your age? For individuals imputed to be extremely old, the rewards were prestige and authority. Claiming to be older, looking older, or acting older in many circumstances can have its advantages. On the other hand, denial of age is also encouraged. The availability of face creams, hair color, antiwrinkle lotions, and plastic surgery lets those so inclined mask their advancing years. The point is that because age changes the body so gradually, the process is subject to interpretation and negotiation.

One change is next to impossible to manipulate: the deterioration of functional capabilities. As functionality declines, compensations can and are made. Humans use culture to resolve problems as body systems weaken. Cultural contexts, especially technological capabilities, have profound consequences for people with disabilities. Where technology is limited, the compensation is primarily in the form of people. Someone else gets the water; a grandchild is on loan to bring firewood. On the other hand, where technology is abundant and laborsaving devices abound, the consequences of a disability are not as devastating. First, such conveniences as indoor plumbing, central heating, electricity, or even an automobile place less of a premium on physical strength. Second, when a specific body part fails, medical technology can often "fix it." Eyes with cataracts receive new plastic lenses. Irregular hearts get pacemakers. Broken hips are replaced with artificial joints. Consequently, people can live fairly normal lives with multiple disabilities for a fairly long time.

Severe disability or extreme frailty can trigger death hastening. In many societies, older age grades are differentiated into at least two groupings: the intact old and the decrepit old (Glascock 1990). Labels given to the latter group include "overaged," the "useless stage," the "sleeping period," the "age grade of the dying," or the "already dead" (Simmons, 1960). The consequence of shifting from intact to decrepit can mean the difference between life and death. Abandonment, suicide, or even the killing of older people are not rare events. Deaths are hastened, but they are the deaths of those who are defined as decrepit (Glascock, 1982; Glascock & Feinman, 1981, 1986) or as between the world of the alive and the ghosts (Barker 1990). In most societies, support is given to those who have deteriorated. Harsh environments (tundras, deserts, savannas), combined with low-energy subsistence strategies (foraging) and egalitarian social structures, promote withdrawal of support. On the other hand, there is some evidence that harshness of the environment does not appear to be a statistically significant factor in the prevalence of gerontocide (Maxwell, Silverman, & Maxwell, 1982). A possible trigger for gerontocide is stress placed on social units when seasonal variation exceeds normal ranges (very bad years) or when warfare shifts group priorities.

Social Linkages

Society is the arena in which the drama of aging unfolds. Connections with other humans create networks of reciprocal rights and duties. People collect and discharge social capital all of their lives. The structure of social arrangements conditions the strategies available in mobilizing support or elevating security and position by aging individuals. For older people, family constitutes a very important web of social relationships. We learned this lesson for industrialized nations when Ethel Shanas (Shanas et al., 1968) discovered that families in Denmark, England, and the United States were not neglecting their older members. Yet families are highly variable, ranging from small nuclear units (two adults and children) to large extended units (many adults and children) linked by lineage and clan affiliation. Extended families are favorable contexts for older people. In societies where the nuclear family predominates, respect for the old came from valued activities in which they were also engaged (McArdle & Yeracaris, 1981). The first line of defense and the institution that protects its senior members against negative treatment is the family (Maxwell et al., 1982; Silverman & Maxwell, 1978). Loss of family support, especially from children, is by far a more important factor in precipitating contempt and withdrawal of support than is declining physical strength.

Transitions through age grades take place in the social arena and alters positions, rights, and duties. How these are defined can differentially favor young or old (Fry, 1996). When role sequences reflect greater continuity, older adults will benefit. When transitions are gradual, less traumatic, and individuals are prepared for the passage, the distinction between age grades, especially young and old, will be less distinct. Without the official retirement party, older people do not become postmature because they are not that much different from socially mature adults. Also, role sequences can entail progressive advances in authority, responsibility, or influence. If these continue into the older age grades, then older people, especially older males, have the advantage. The ethnographic literature is full of examples of gerontocratic organization. Religious cargo systems in Mesoamerica are hierarchies that men ascend across their lives, reaching the apex only in old age (Cancian, 1965; Nash, 1970). Among the Tiwi, in Australia, successful marital careers place men as heads of a work force of women. Freed from hunting and gathering, these older men tend to local politics and rituals, becoming ever more influential (Hart, Pilling & Goodale, 1988). Where rank and prestige are themes across the life course, not everyone can be a winner. A few will be of high rank, but the majority will share lesser prestige.

Values

Culture gives meaning to life. Values define what is good and what is bad. Aging has its valences. Old age is not always a positive category, but then youth has its problems too. For Americans a singular issue that renders old age as negative is being a burden or being dependent on others. Independence is a dominant value orientation in American culture. Interdependence, the midground between the extremes of dependence and independence, is rooted in reciprocity and exchange, a universal feature of all human societies. Giving and taking links humans and reinforces the continuity of social life. Giving enables one to maintain a balance in a relationship in which one is taking. To be dependent is to take nonreciprocally. Nonreciprocity is tolerated in certain roles such as illness, rites of passage, or infancy and childhood (Clark, 1972; Fry, 1996). These roles also have temporal limitations. Chronic dependence exceeds the limitations of these norms and threatens the basic reciprocal framework of exchange of every society.

Americans emphasize rugged individualism and self-reliance (Simic, 1990). As an ideal, it reflects an economic organization that emphasizes immediacy of reciprocity and sees participants as mobile unconnected entities. Individuals are responsible for themselves. Also, affluence has made it possible for many individuals to achieve most of the ideal by maintaining separate households. Once problems necessitate dependency, it becomes obvious and painful, as the asymmetrical exchanges flow between residential units or redefinition of those units occur. The value of independence is by no means universal. Dependency in nonindustrial economies takes on a different meaning (Fry, 1996). Households are usually not as differentiated, with exchanges following a norm of generalized reciprocity where temporal limits are lifelong. Where social units are more cohesive and life more collective, the value of interdependence, not independence, is accentuated

Cultural Change

One truism about culture is that it is dynamic. Evolutionary forces transform social and cultural organization and alter available opportunities. Life chances are modified as the arena in which people live is revised. Life-stage conditions how the change is experienced as well as the consequences of change for individuals. Older people may benefit or they may not. Before we can examine how older people fare in the tide of change, we first have to briefly consider what has changed.

Modernization has emerged as a dominant process as researchers have sought to understand the great transformations that rocked Europe and North America during the industrial revolution. The shock waves of this change have been felt the world around as diverse societies have been linked into a world economic system. One of the first things to happen was a marked increase in stratification, both domestic and international. A first world and a third world appeared as wealth became concentrated in the developed world. Another consequence of this revolution was rapid population growth and a dramatic alteration of age structures (Myers, 1985). Populations became young in spite of absolute increases in the numbers of older people. Then, following the demographic transition, populations began to age, first in the nations that were first industrialized. Projections estimate that nearly 20% of the population will be older adults before the effects of modernization on population structures subside. In the third world, where the demographic transition has not yet occurred, populations are still young, although the absolute numbers of older adults are rapidly increasing.

Has modernization benefited older people, or has it increased their vulnerability? Our earliest data gave a negative answer. As modernization proceeds, the status and treatment of older people declines (Cowgill & Holmes, 1972). The factors associated with modernization are medical improvements and population changes, economic transformations, urbanization and associated mobility, and social organizational change, plus increased education (Cowgill, 1974, 1986). The net effect is negative for older people.

Additional lessons have been learned as modernization theory faced further evidence and scientific refinement. Modernization theory argues that societies can be ordered from low (no modernization) to high (postindustrial) and that societies can be ranked by this scale in a linear fashion. When we try to do this, however, we discover that the negative effects on older people are not linear. A useful metaphor to describe the pattern is that of a wave or a cycle (Finley, 1982). In the shift from foraging to horticulture there is an increase in the status of the aged. Then there is a decline in the early phases of modernization (Lee & Kezis, 1981; Sheehan, 1976). This is followed by improvement in the later stages, with the effects of pension and health plans improving the security of older adults (Palmore, 1976; Palmore & Manton, 1974).

Data may revise or substantiate a theory or may lead to abandonment of its major variables. In the case of modernization, data have increasingly called it into question. Comparative data on attitudes toward older people by modernity of society and individuals within the society have produced contradictory results (Arnhoff, Leon, & Lorge, 1964; Bengtson, Dowd, Smith, & Inkles, 1975). Historical data giving us before/after pictures are not consistent with the predictions of modernization theory. The situation of the elderly has not declined as predicted, and paradise has not been lost (Achenbaum, 1978; Achenbaum & Stearns 1978; Fischer, 1977; Quadagno, 1982).

Any theory is declared obsolete without scientific substantiation. Modernization is virtually the only theory that has had to endure the test of the comparative method, because in examining societal development, societal comparisons were necessary. Early modernization theory's main shortcoming is that it oversimplified the transformation that has changed the world. Although societies can be ranked according to modernity, this masks the specific processes that are at work in those societies and that affect the lives of people in specific communities in those societies. Consequently, modernization is increasingly being seen in a framework that considers asymmetry in power between core and peripheral areas in the world economic system and as a process that involves multiple and distinct forces of change (Hendricks, 1982).

Opportunity structures are changed as requirements for labor force participation demand certain skills like the ability to read and write or type or operate a computer. Industrialized societies have rationalized their labor forces through universal education to develop minimal skills. Which age group is most likely to be able to take advantage of new opportunities? It is ususally younger persons. This is dramatically illustrated in New Guinea, where former Asmat headhunters find themselves in a void (Van Arsdale, 1981). Indonesian rule favors those who can speak Indonesian. Younger men who are bilingual have thus assumed leadership roles, leaving the formerly powerful elders without influence. Lack of requisite skills is a barrier to full participation.

Changing opportunity also changes who is available in the social arena. Young people are pulled to cities and opportunity. With out-migration, rural populations become increasingly old and female as men move to jobs, leaving wives and parents at home. Consequently, there is a lack of younger personnel. Reduction in family network can increase risks for older people. In Nepal otherwise healthy, vigorous elders experience an unsatisfactory old age. Emigration of youngest sons has removed the family member who is supposed to help them as they age (Goldstein & Beall, 1981, 1982). On the other hand, rising prosperity in an area can keep young people there, resulting in a more satisfactory old age. This is the case in rural Malay (Strange, 1987).

Culture also changes in an ideological dimension: the realm of ideas, spiritual life, and cultural identity. Transformation here can open opportunities for older people. When younger people want to discover their roots and the details of their traditions, they turn to the experts, elders. Older people had the most direct experience with the previous ways. Among the Coast Salish on the Northwest Coast of the United States, elders have become culturally central in revitalizing the rituals and knowledge that have almost vanished (Amoss, 1981). Likewise in Paris, elderly Corsicans benefit from participation in an ethnic organization and community (Cool, 1981). They are the legitimizers of an ethnic identity. They were there in the old village and were chronologically closer to the real thing.

Who benefits and who doesn't is always a question we have to ask with respect to change. Age and cohort are important variables determining who can take advantage of change and who will be adversely affected by the change. Our lesson here is that change is not uniformly bad for older people. Certain processes will increase vulnerability. These generally are more material in nature, involving barriers to entering the labor market and to participation in the political process or disruptions to social networks. Other processes can bring benefits. Improvement in health care is certainly a major benefit (Foster, 1981), although its availability and quality is shaped by stratification. Change that calls for things older people have to give only increases the value of what they have to exchange.

CONCLUSIONS

What has our excursion into the natural laboratory of other cultures taught us about aging and growing older? First, there are many different ways of growing older. These differences are not the differences in race, class, or ethnic affiliation we see within the United States. Certainly race and ethnicity are profound issues because they are based on a system of stratification and differential opportunity that has lifelong consequences. However, the differences we see in other cultures are major differences in productive organization, family structures, political centralization, stratification, and worldviews. It is these differences that make this laboratory of cultural diversity a gold mine in searching for factors promoting a good or a precarious old age.

Second, the experience of growing older is not uniformly good or uniformly bad in the diversity of cultures we call "traditional." It is neither life in Shangri-la nor abandonment to the wolves and animals of prey. With old age defined as a problem here at home, we have looked at other cultures and past times in search of paradise or the golden age. The more we learn, the more we realize that such stereotypes do not exist. Also, as we discover more, we learn that exotic customs have more than shock value. Ethnographic differences can tell us something about the universal human experience of aging. They can tell us what is indeed universal about it, but only after we have ascertained what is conditioned by local circumstance and culture.

Finally, and most important, older people are people. The best use of the comparative method is for discovering principles that shape behavior. Older people are people who have been here longer than others. They are experiencing the senior age grades and aging bodies. These life stages and bodies cannot be divorced from earlier stages, younger bodies, and historical circumstances. Because life is lived as a whole, the principles governing social action are not of a different order (Keith, 1982). Our goal is not to study only the end of life and its uniqueness. Instead, it is to understand this life stage through theories of human behavior that include age as a variable. Age, of course, is more than chronology. It broadly embraces lives and the way societies shape and use the lives of its members, from birth to senescence. Herein lies the promise of the gerontological imagination in a comparative perspective.

REFERENCES

Achenbaum, W. (1978). *Old age in the new land: The American experience since 1790.* Baltimore: Johns Hopkins University Press.

Achenbaum, W., & Stearns, P. (1978). Essay: Old age and modernization. *Gerontologist, 18*, 307–312.

Aires. M. (1962). *Centuries of childhood.* New York: Random House.

Albert, S. M., & Cattell, M. G. (1994). *Old age in global perspective: Cross-cultural and cross-national views.* New York: Maxwell Macmillan International.

Amoss, P. T. (1981). Cultural centrality and prestige for the elders: The Coast Salish case. In C. L. Fry (Ed.), *Dimensions: Aging, culture and health* (pp. 47–64). New York: Praeger.

Andrews, G. R. (1986). *Aging in the Western Pacific.* Manila: World Health Organization, Regional Office for the Western Pacific.

Arnhoff, F. N., Leon, H. V., & Lorge, I. (1964). Cross-cultural acceptance of stereotypes toward aging. *Journal of Social Psychology, 63*, 41–58.

Barker, J. (1990). Between humans and ghosts: The decrepit elderly in a Polynesian society. In J. Sokolovsky (Ed.), *The cultural contexts of aging: World wide perspectives* (pp. 295–313). New York: Bergin & Garvey.

Beall, C. M., & Eckert, J. K. (1986). Measuring functional capacity cross-culturally. In C. L. Fry & J. Keith (Eds.), *New methods for old age research* (pp. 21–56). South Hadley, MA: Bergin & Garvey.

Bengtson, V. L., Dowd, J. J., Smith, D. H., & Inkles, A. (1975). Modernization, modernity and perceptions of aging: A cross-cultural study. *Journal of Gerontology, 30*, 688–695.

Cancian, F. (1965). *Economics and prestige in a Mayan community.* Palo Alto, CA: Stanford University Press.

Clark, M. M. (1972). Cultural values and dependency in later life. In D. O. Cowgill & L. D. Holmes (Eds.), *Aging and modernization* (pp. 263–274) New York: Appleton-Century-Crofts.

Cool, L. E. (1981). Ethnic identity: A source of community esteem for the elderly. *Anthropological Quarterly, 54*, 179–189.

Cowgill, D. O. (1974). Aging and modernization: A revision of the theory. In J. Gubrium (Ed.), *Late life: Communities and environmental policy* (pp. 123–146). Springfield, IL: Charles C Thomas.

Cowgill, D. O. (1986). *Aging around the world.* Belmont, CA: Wadsworth.

Cowgill, D. O., & Holmes, L. D. (Eds.). (1972). *Aging and modernization.* New York: Appleton-Century-Crofts.

Dowd, J. J. (1975). Aging as exchange: A preface to theory. *Journal of Gerontology, 30*, 584–594.

Finley, G. E. (1982). Modernization and aging. In T. Field, A. Huston-Stein, H. Quay, L. Troll, & G. E. Finley (Eds.), *Review of human development* (pp. 511–523). New York: Wiley.

Fisher, D. H. (1977). *Growing old in America.* New York: Oxford University Press.

Foner, A., & Kertzer, D. (1978). Transitions over the life course. *American Journal of Sociology, 83*, 1081–1104.

Foster, G. M. (1981). Old age in Tzintzuntzan, Mexico. In J. L. McGaugh & S. B. Kiseler (Eds.), *Aging, biology and behavior* (pp. 115–137). New York: Academic.

Fries, J. F., & Crapo, L. M. (1981). *Vitality and aging.* San Francisco: Freeman.

Fry, C. L. (1980). Cultural dimensions of age. In C. L. Fry (Ed.), *Aging in culture and society: Comparative perspectives and strategies* (pp. 42–64). New York: Praeger.

Fry, C. L. (1988). Theories of age and culture. In J. E. Birren & V. L. Bengtson (Eds.), *Emergent theories of aging* (pp. 447–481). New York: Springer Publishing.

Fry, C. L. (1994). Age and the life course. In J. Keith, C. L. Fry, A. P. Glascock, C. Ikels, J. Dickerson-Putman, H. C. Harpending, & P. Draper (Eds.), *The aging experience: Diversity and commonality across cultures* (pp. 144–197). Thousand Oaks, CA: Sage.

Fry, C. L. (1996). Age, aging, and culture. In R. H. Binstock & L. K. George (Eds.), *Handbook of aging and the social sciences* (pp. 117–136). San Diego, CA: Academic Press.

Fry, C. L., & Keith, J. (1982). The life course as a cultural unit. In M. W. Riley, R. Ables, & M. Teitelbaum (Eds.), *Aging from birth to death: Sociotemporal perspectives* (pp. 51–70). Boulder, CO: Westview.

Glascock, A. P. (1982). Decrepitude and death-hastening: The nature of old age in third world societies. In J. Sokolovsky (Ed.), *Aging and the aged in the third world: Part 1* (pp. 43–66) "Studies in Third World Societies" (Pub. No. 22). Williamsburg, VA: Department of Anthropology, College of William and Mary.

Glascock, A. P. (1990). By any other name it is still killing: A comparison of the treatment of the elderly in America and other societies. In J. Sokolovsky (Ed.), *The cultural context of aging: World wide perspectives* (pp. 43–56). New York: Bergin & Garvey.

Glascock, A. P., & Feinman, S. (1981). Social asset or social burden: Treatment of the aged in non-industrial societies. In C. L. Fry (Ed.), *Dimensions: Aging, culture and health* (pp. 13–32). New York: Praeger.

Glascock, A. P., & Feinman, S. (1986). Toward a comparative framework: Propositions concerning the treatment of the aged in non-industrial societies. In C. L. Fry & J. Keith (Eds.), *New methods for old age research: Strategies for studying diversity* (pp. 281–292). South Hadley, MA: Bergin & Garvey.

Goldstein, M., & Beall, C. (1981). Modernization and aging in the third and fourth world: Views from the rural hinterland in Nepal. *Human Organization*, *40*, 48–55.

Goldstein, M., & Beall, C. (1982). Brief note on demographic aspects of aging in the less developed countries. *Association for Anthropology and Gerontology Newsletter*, *3*, 2.

Guemple, D. L. (1980). Growing old in Inuit society. In V. W. Marshall (Ed.), *Aging in Canada: Social perspectives* (pp. 95–102). Don Mills, Ontario: Fitzhenry & Witeside.

Halperin, R. (1984). Age in cultural economics: An evolutionary approach. In D. I. Kertzer & J. Keith (Eds.), *Age and anthropological theory* (pp. 159–194). Ithaca, NY: Cornell University.

Halperin, R. (1987). Age in cross-cultural perspective: An evolutionary approach. In P. Silverman (Ed.), *The elderly as modern pioneers* (pp. 283–311). Bloomington: Indiana University Press.

Hart, C. W. M., Pilling, A. R., & Goodale, J. C. (1988). *The Tiwi of north Australia*. New York: Holt, Rinehart & Winston.

Hendricks, J. (1982). The elderly in society: Beyond modernization. *Social Science History*, *6*, 321–345.

Keith, J. (1982). *Old people as people: Social and cultural influences on aging and old age*. Boston: Little, Brown.

Keith, J., Fry, C. L., Glascock, A. P., Ikels, C., Dickerson-Putman, J., Harpending, H. C., & Draper, P. (1994). *The aging experience: Diversity and commonality across cultures*. Thousand Oaks, CA: Sage.

Kohli, M. (1986). The world we forgot: A historical review of the life course. In V. W. Marshall. *Later life: The social psychology of aging* (pp. 271–303). Beverly Hills, CA: Sage.

Lee, G. R., & Kezis, M. (1981). Societal literacy and the aged. *International Journal of Aging and Human Development*, *12*, 221–234.

Maxwell, E. K., & Maxwell, R. J. (1980). Contempt for the elderly: A cross-cultural analysis. *Current Anthropology, 21*, 569–570.

Maxwell, R. J., & Silverman, P. (1970). Information and esteem. *Aging and Human Development, 1*, 127–146.

Maxwell, R. J., Silverman, P., & Maxwell, E. K. (1982). The motive for gerontocide. In J. Sokolovsky (Ed.), *Aging and the aged in the third world: Part 1* (pp. 67–84) "Studies in Third World Societies" (Pub. No. 22). Williamsburg, VA: Department of Anthropology, College of William and Mary.

Mayer, K. U., & Muller, W. (1986). The state and the structure of the life course. In A. B. Sorensen, F. W. Weinert, & L. R. Sherrod (Eds.), *Human development and the life course: Multidisciplinary perspectives* (pp. 217–246). Hillsdale, NJ: Erlbaum.

Mazess, R. B., & Foreman, S. H. (1979). Longevity and age exaggeration in Vilcabamba, Ecuador. *Journal of Gerontology, 34*, 94–98.

McArdle, J. L., & Yeracaris, C. (1981). Respect for the elderly in preindustrial societies as related to their activity. *Behavioral Science Research, 16*, 307–339.

Meyer, J. W. (1986). The self and the life course: Institutionalization and its effects. In A. B. Sorensen, F. W. Weinert, & L. R. Sherrod (Eds.), *Human development and the life course: Multidisciplinary perspectives* (pp. 199–216). Hillsdale, NJ: Erlbaum.

Myers, G. C. (1985). Aging and worldwide population change. In R. H. Binstock & E. Shanas (Eds.), *Handbook of aging and the social sciences* (pp. 173–198). New York: Von Nostrand Reinhold.

Nash, J. (1970). *In the eyes of the ancestors*. New Haven, CT: Yale University Press.

National Council on Aging. (1976). *The myth and reality of aging in America*. Washington, DC: Author.

Neugarten, B. L., & Datan, N. (1973). Sociological perspectives on the life cycle. In P. B. Baltes & K. W. Schaie (Eds.), *Life-span developmental psychology: Personality and socialization* (pp. 53–69). New York: Academic.

Palmore, E. (1976). The future status of the aged. *Gerontologist, 16*, 297–302.

Palmore, E., & Manton, K. (1974). Modernization and status of the aged. *Journal of Gerontology, 29*, 205–210.

Quadagno, J. (1982). *Aging in early industrial society: Work, family, and social policy in nineteenth century England*. New York: Academic.

Shanas, E., Townsend, P., Wedderburn, D., Friis, H., Nilhoj, P., & Stehouwer, J. (1968). *Old people in three industrial societies*. New York: Atherton.

Sheehan, T. (1976). Senior esteem as a factor in socioeconomic complexity. *Gerontologist, 5*, 2–23.

Silverman, P. (1987). Comparative studies. In P. Silverman (Ed.), *The elderly as modern pioneers* (pp. 312–344). Bloomington: Indiana University Press.

Silverman, P., & Maxwell, R. J. (1978). How do I respect thee? Let me count the ways: Deference towards elderly men and women. *Behavioral Science Research, 13*, 91–108.

Silverman, P., & Maxwell, R. J. (1983). The significance of information and power in the comparative study of the aged. In J. Sokolovsky (Ed.), *Growing old in different societies: Cross-cultural perspectives* (pp. 43–55). Belmont, CA: Wadsworth.

Simic, A. (1990). Aging, world view, and intergenerational relations. In J. Sokolovsky (Ed.), *The cultural context of aging: Worldwide perspectives* (pp. 89–108). South Hadley, MA: Bergin & Garvey.

Simmons, L. W. (1945). *The role of the aged in primitive society.* New Haven, CT: Yale University Press.

Simmons, L. W. (1960). Aging in preindustrial societies. In C. Tibbits (Ed.), *Handbook of social gerontology* (pp. 62–91). Chicago: University of Chicago Press.

Stenning, D. J. (1971). Household viability among the pastoral Fulani. In J. Goody (Ed.), *The developmental cycle in domestic groups* (pp. 92–119). London: Cambridge University Press.

Strange, H. (1987). Rural Malay aged in contrasting developmental contexts. In H. Strange & M. Teitelbaum (Eds.), *Aging and cultural diversity* (pp. 14–38). South Hadley, MA: Bergin & Garvey.

Van Arsdale, P. W. (1981). Disintegration of the ritual support network among aged Asmat hunter-gatherers of New Guinea. In C. L. Fry (Ed.), *Dimensions: Aging, culture and health* (pp. 33–46). New York: Praeger.

World Health Organization. (1946). *Charter.* Geneva: Author.

PART III

Aging in the Institutional Context

Parts I and II were designed to articulate and embellish a gerontological imagination. For the remainder of this book, the objective is to apply that gerontological imagination. Part III examines the major social institutions that influence and are influenced by older adults. The five institutions analyzed obviously do not exhaust the institutional context, but they are central to understanding aging in modern societies.

A social institution may be described as an organized pattern of beliefs, behaviors, and norms that enables a society to function. When one considers such functions as the preservation of order, socialization, medical care, production and distribution of goods and services, and identity formation, it should become apparent why these five merit detailed consideration.

Mutran and Reitzes help us to understand intergenerational family relations by considering exchange processes. Sterns, Matheson, and Park analyze work by considering both older adults at work and the transition from work to retirement. Religion is one of those social institutions that plays an important role in the daily life of most older people, yet it gets only scant attention from social gerontologists. Moberg, one of the foremost authorities on religion and aging, attempts to redress this problem by demonstrating the salience of religion in the lives of older adults. Dunkle and Kart discuss the range of long-term care services in considering how modern societies provide medical care for the chronically ill elderly. Finally, Bass and Noelker extend ideas raised in chapters 8 and 11 by reviewing the burgeoning literature on caregiving by family members. They summarize what we know about family caregiving and identify what types of research will better enable us to understand the structure and process of caregiving.

CHAPTER 8

Reciprocity Between Family Generations

Elizabeth Mutran
Donald C. Reitzes

The family has experienced numerous changes within the past several decades, and the aging of our society is propelling even more changes within kinship systems. The relationship between elderly parents and their adult children is changing rapidly because of the demographic trends noted in chapter 2. Family members experience a greater variety of intergenerational roles now than in previous years, and the time demands and the duration of the roles are increasing. Today over one half of adult children live within an hour's drive of their parents. In addition, 69% of adult children report at least weekly contact with their mothers (56% report weekly contact with their fathers) (Lawton, Silverstein, & Bengtson, 1994).

The relationship between elderly parents and adult children involves some of the most challenging family roles. On one hand, these are among the least clearly defined roles, for neither parents nor adult children may be well prepared for the opportunities and demands of the relationship. American society has never before faced a situation in which large numbers of *older* adults have one or more parents living. Thus, adult children and their elderly parents do not have examples from past generations that can serve as models for managing these relationships (Gove, Ortega, & Style, 1989).

On the other hand, these roles are dynamic and require adjustments and changes in expectations. Aging and poor health may require elderly persons to make compromises in their activities or living arrangements in order to maintain independent living for as long as possible, even as adult offspring are called on to increase their involvement or contribution, personal or otherwise, in the lives of their parents. This is not just the reversal of the teenage years, where the young adult strives for independence and tests his or her relationship with parents; teenagers struggle to balance their desires and fantasies with realistic assessments of their identity and the real world (Erikson, 1963). The adjustments made between adult offspring and their parents have some of the same components—tension between generations, establishment of boundaries and lines of authority—but the outcome is not a new life but the end of life. Instead of the emergence of adolescence into independence, aging often involves what Rossi and Rossi (1990) describe as a "bittersweet pathos" (p. 84) associated with waning energy, declining health, the loss of a partner of long standing, and all too often a sharp decline in income.

One of the most interesting theoretical issues in the study of the aging family deals with the exchange processes between elderly parents and adult children. From an exchange theory perspective, social life can be analyzed as a series of transfers between individuals or groups, and these transfers may be described in economic terms. Early theoretical formulations generally assumed that individuals try to maximize their outcomes, that is, receive rewards greater than costs (Blau, 1964; Homans, 1961; Thibaut & Kelley, 1959). However, maximizing outcomes (i.e., profits or benefits) may lie counter to norms of proper behavior and intimacy in family relations. For example, benefits accruing to the older parent (i.e., the parent receives more than he or she provides) may be interpreted as dependency, which appears counter to normal expectations of parents remaining in charge of the familial relationship (Dowd, 1975). Because equity theory holds that people who receive more than they "should" from an exchange are likely to feel guilty because of their favored position and those who receive less than they "should" may feel anger and resentment (Walster, Walster, & Berscheid, 1978), the effects of perceived reciprocity or equity in exchanges on social functioning is key to understanding these intergenerational relationships.

As an example of how these processes may operate, consider the many decisions an older retired couple may confront in regard to the husband's widowed mother in her 80s. Faced with the mother's increasing physical impairments, how do exchange processes affect family functioning and outcomes? Does the couple evaluate the mother as deserving of unlimited personal sacrifices? Would they be willing to restructure the household to facilitate caring for the elderly mother? Are there circumstances in which the couple would solicit help from the husband's siblings to care for their mother? Are economic exchanges, such as deeding property to the couple (or son), important to continue aid? Which member of the couple will give more tangible aid to the husband's mother? The questions families are now facing are numerous and have mammoth implications for society and the older population.

In this chapter we focus on the exchanges that characterize the dynamic relationship between aging parents and their adult children and that may influence the well-being of older persons. The inquiry is divided into three sections. First, a symbolic interaction perspective is used to establish our underlying assumptions and theoretical orientation to the elderly parent–adult child role relationship. Second, there is a review of research that has investigated the equity of exchanges between elderly parents and adult children. Third, we offer new directions for future research, research we believe will be most helpful in furthering our understanding of exchange processes in the aging family.

THEORETICAL ISSUES

Symbolic interaction theory provides a rich frame of reference for pursuing our investigation of intergenerational family roles. One can trace the intellectual ancestry of the symbolic interaction approach from David Hume and the Scottish moral philosophers to William James and the American pragmatists. It culminates in the work of George Herbert Mead (1934), who argued that meaning emerges from social interaction and common discourse and does not exclusively reside in either the perceiving subject or perceived object. Symbolic interactionists have focused attention on two especially important symbols: self and roles. A person's self or self-concept is a special symbol. On the one hand, it contains shared social meanings about self as an "object." On the other hand, because a person is capable of reflective thought and symbol manipulation, self is also a "subject" capable of understanding, reflection, and action. A role reflects shared expectations about people occupying a social position or social category. However, roles are not entirely defined or "scripted'; there is also some room for variation or novelty in the way an individual fills a role (Turner, 1962). Behavior is motivated by an active person's interacting with others to work out the definitions of a situation and the desired outcomes of action (Stryker, 1981). A symbolic interaction approach suggests three issues in the investigation of the intergenerational family role: (1) the impact of social structure on family interaction, (2) the importance of subjective factors and self-motives in behaviors, and (3) the impact of past events and expectations of future events on the construction of the parental and adult child roles.

Recent developments in symbolic interaction theory have emphasized *the impact of social structure on self-conceptions and behaviors*. Symbolic interaction recognizes that individuals are influenced by social structure and processes, not just in the passive manner of spectators but as active participants whose behaviors and beliefs are directly and indirectly influenced by the wealth, status, and power associated with social positions (Stryker & Serpe, 1994). Higher education and greater income may reduce the economic dependence of elderly parents on their adult children, and children with greater financial resources are better able to provide more extensive material benefits to their parents. The gender of the parent may change the intergenerational dynamics, with surviving older fathers having greater financial resources than older mothers, and the gender of the adult child may be associated with differences in caregiving practices. The loss of a valued spouse by an older parent may create the willingness and need for more giving and receiving of aid from adult children. Thus, education, income, age, poor health, gender, and marital status are some of the structural factors that create opportunities for or limit the interactions of elderly parents.

One of the strengths of symbolic interaction theory is its recognition of *the importance of subjective meanings and self-motives in influencing behavior.* A basic symbolic interaction tenet is that the naming and the assignment of both shared and subjective meanings to self, others, and situations structure interactions and motivate action (Cooley, 1902; Stryker, 1981). One of the factors that may affect the receptiveness of an older parent to either giving or receiving aid is the subjective importance that he or she assigned to the adult child (Mutran & Reitzes, 1984). In addition, symbolic interactionists note that role playing requires not just learning the shared expectation of a position but also the appropriate motives and actions for a role (Stryker, 1981). Both the parent and child roles contain the self-responses of (1) identity, which refers to the cognitive content of self-descriptions in a role; (2) commitment, which entails the individual's investments in a role; (3) satisfaction, tapping a person's affective responses to a role; (4) centrality, which addresses the prominence or relative importance of a role to a person; and (5) self-esteem, which covers a person's assessment of self (La Rossa & Reitzes, 1993).

Symbolic interaction theory also recognizes that *roles exist over time and that temporal factors influence the way in which individuals create self-conceptions and construct definitions of the situation.* Roles are not fully formed, prepackaged, "instant" sets of expectations but develop their form and texture over time (Burke, 1980; Turner & Shosid, 1976). The notion of the career (Goffman, 1959; Gove, Ortega & Style, 1989; McCall & Simmons, 1966) reflects the temporal dimensions of a role and suggests two interesting features of parent and child roles. First, there is a dialectical relationship in which the past and future influence the present (Mead, 1934). Past experience and events as well as future goals and expectations give shape and form to the present. The positive and negative features of past parent–child encounters as well as any sense of sacrifice or "goodwill" may influence the current definitions of obligation and credit attached to the roles. Similarly, expectations of the future, including perceptions of imminent death and dying, may give shape and form to the present (Maines, Sugrue, & Katovich, 1983). As current events change, the present may serve as a new reference point to reinterpret and reformulate the past and future. Thus, recent positive (or negative) experiences in the parent-child relationship may lead to a revision of the recollected past or a reconstruction of the anticipated future (Wheaton, 1990). Second, individuals gradually move from external to internal references in the process of role acquisition (Reitzes & Mutran, 1994). For example, a newly widowed parent may be very influenced in the construction of his or her new role by anticipatory socialization or perceptions of the expectation of others, but with time the development of self-standards provides another set of expectations and motives for behavior. Time in a role influences the nature of role portrayals and may influence features of the manner in which parent and child respond to each other.

FINDINGS OF PREVIOUS RESEARCH

Previous research regarding the relationship between adult children and their parents is reviewed in this section. Ten major findings are articulated.

First, it is important to begin by clarifying the nature and extent of intergenerational family exchanges. The National Survey of Families and Households (NSFH) was a national representative survey conducted in 1987–88. Four kinds of intergenerational support were measured: (1) monetary and material, (2) household assistance, (3) child care or care during illness, and (4) emotional support or advice. In general, the findings suggest that there are only modest levels of assistance. Over half of all adult children are uninvolved in exchanges with their parents; 17% received money from their parents, and only 4% gave money; 13% received child care assistance from their parents in the month before the interviews; 17% received household assistance from their parents, whereas 32% of adult children gave household assistance to their parents; and finally, 27% received advice and emotional support from their parents, and 25% report giving such support. Parents report slightly higher levels of assistance given and received from their adult children than the adult children report. However, at any given point, more than one third of the elderly are not involved in giving, and over 60% have not received anything from any of their children (Eggebeen, 1992). (Similarly, Silverstein, Lawton, and Bengtson [1994] found that no more than 35% of children or parents report giving or getting hands-on assistance such as running errands, helping with repairs, or babysitting.) This general summary belies the diversity of exchange patterns. Researchers found four distinct patterns of assistance: 53% of the U.S. population are not involved in any intergenerational exchanges; 19% are "receivers only" of assistance, 17% are advice givers, and only 11% are enmeshed in strong exchange networks (Eggebeen, 1992).

Second, in an attempt to put the rather low level of intergenerational exchange into perspective, two important points have been raised. First, Uhlenberg and Cooney (1990) note that, even though well under half of adult children receive support from their parents, more than half of these adult children, 45 and younger, named parents as *potential* sources of help in times of need. Thus, although older parents may not assume active, regular supportive roles in their children's lives, they are viewed by their children as valued and dependable sources of support should the need for help arise. We suspect that the same is true for the way older parents view their adult children. Indeed, Hogan, Eggebeen, and Clogg (1993) suggest that family support can provide an important security net for family members (both old and young) during periods of high need. Second, several studies have expanded the scope of family ties to go beyond the exchange of assistance and to cover dimensions such as affective closeness, frequency of contact, and value similarity (Bengtson & Harootyan, 1994; Rossi & Rossi, 1990). When these dimensions are also considered, the intergenerational family emerges as an important source of symbolic and emotional support for both older parents and their adult children. Thus, 72% of adult children report feeling very close to their mothers, 55% feel very close to their fathers, and 81% of elderly parents report feeling very close to their eldest adult child (Harootyan & Bengtson, 1994).

Turning now to the impact of intergenerational family exchanges, the third set of findings deals with the importance of the parental role. The parental role may provide an older person with an important source of meaning, value, and fulfillment. In support of this position, Mutran and Reitzes (1984) found that elderly persons who have children have a higher level of positive well-being than do childless older people; and Mancini and Blieszner (1989) reported that among older parents, feeling competent in the parenting role was positively related to well-being. In a historical study of elderly women in 18th- and 19th-century Japan, Cornell (1992) noted that the presence of adult children and grandchildren, especially for widows, reduced mortality. Conversely, Umberson and Chen (1994) argued that one indicator of the symbolic importance of parents to adult children was the finding that adult children whose mothers had died in a 3-year period experienced greater psychological distress and reduced physical health, whereas those who lost a father consumed more alcohol than did adult children who did not experience the loss of a parent.

Fourth, the distinctive character of the elderly parent–adult child role relationship must also be considered. To begin, the exchanges between elderly women and their friends are more likely to be reciprocal than are exchanges with adult children (Rook, 1987). Further, reciprocal exchanges with friends are strongly associated with satisfaction in friendship, but reciprocity in exchanges with adult children is not nearly as important to older mothers' satisfaction with their children. These findings highlight two interesting temporal features of the parent-child relationship. First, the family roles are long-term careers, where present interaction may be tempered by past experiences and future expectations. Parents or children may give more than they receive at any one point in time because they expect to reestablish the balance in the future. Family roles may show low levels of reciprocity at any one point in time, and the imbalance still may not negatively influence satisfaction with the relationship. Second, friendship ties may be bound in the present (or present and past) but not contain firm and clear expectations for the future. So satisfying friendship ties may require more immediate efforts to reciprocate supports than ties between family members.

These findings suggest that because friendship is defined as voluntary and friendship ties can easily be dissolved, equity would be important in the maintenance of the relationship. However, family relationships are based on nonvoluntary ties and expectations, which adds the motive of obligation to exchanges. If a friend does something or gives something, the elderly person can more clearly make the attribution that the friend cares for him or her. If a family member makes the same contribution, its meaning is less clear. In the first instance, the attribution may be of concern and affection; in the latter instance, the attribution includes concern and affection but also duty. It may take being overbenefited to make the attribution of love (the adult son or daughter went above and beyond the call of duty), whereas underbenefiting is more clearly a sign of not being loved (they did not even live up to their obligations).

A fifth major finding is that the quality of contact with children is an important factor that influences parents' well-being. Mancini and Blieszner (1989) reviewed the literature and suggest that relationship quality, measured in terms of communication patterns and amount of affection and interpersonal conflict, are relatively more important for well-being of older parents than contact variables. Umberson (1992) found that although frequency of contact with children and extent of social support from children did not influence parents' psychological distress, both relationship strain with children and parental dissatisfaction increased their psychological distress. Similarly, relationship strain with parents increased psychological distress for adult children.

Sixth, there are major differences in how exchange processes operate for married and nonmarried people and the effect these processes have on the well-being of older parents. The loss of a spouse generates a major realignment in the parent-child relationship and increases the influence of exchanges with children on the well-being of the widowed parents. Mutran and Reitzes (1984) explored this distinction and found that for elderly widows (but not for older married persons), receiving help from children *decreases* negative well-being, whereas giving aid to their children *increases* negative well-being. Widowhood appears to increase awareness of the costs and benefits of personal interactions, and widowed parents are more willing than married parents to place importance on satisfying their own psychological or physical needs in dealing with their children. Further, negative self-feelings among widowed parents increased the aid they received from their adult children. The finding suggests that widows use their affective state as a "signal" when their lives need "input" or help from their children.

Seventh, research findings have also included factors that influence the extent and consequences of intergenerational exchanges. When adult children are perceived as valued significant others by their parents, changes occur in the nature of the role ties. The use of an adult child as a confidant encourages elderly parents to give aid and be less afraid of interfering in the lives of their children (Mutran & Reitzes, 1984). Being a confidant also appears to increase the willingness of adult children to aid their parents. The demands and expectations of the elderly parent–adult child role relationship are unclear and open to negotiation. When the ties are affectively positive, the role relationship appears to be defined as reciprocally active and involves the increased likelihood of both giving and receiving assistance (Talbott, 1990).

Eighth, it is important to separate emotional exchanges from instrumental exchanges when studying intergenerational exchange relationships in the aging family. Emotional exchanges include activities such as confiding or grief work; instrumental exchanges include household chores or providing care for a person while he or she is sick. It now appears that reciprocity is especially prevalent in the instrumental exchanges (Ingersoll-Dayton & Antonucci, 1988). In addition, parents who report that they confide in their children less than their children confide in them perceive their networks as more demanding than parents who report greater balance in their emotional exchanges. Similarly, parents who expect to provide more sick care to their children than they expect to receive are more likely to feel their networks are too demanding than are parents who report greater balance in their instrumental exchanges with their children.

These findings show clearly that role relationships differ in their attendant expectations and the subjective meanings assigned to exchanges. Therefore, the implications of equity or imbalance in exchanges are not always the same between various roles. As we have seen before, elderly parents in underbenefited exchanges with adult children are less comfortable with their networks or themselves, but the implication of imbalance for an older adult is not the same for exchanges between spouses and friends as for exchanges with adult children.

Ninth, previous research indicates that women are more involved than men in intergenerational family roles. Ties among women have been found to be stronger, more frequent, more reciprocal, and less contingent on circumstances than those of men. Women, as adult daughters or as older mothers, provide important social and emotional links connecting family members (Rossi & Rossi, 1990). Daughters are more likely than sons to provide care to both parents, and parents of either gender are more likely to be cared for by daughters than by sons; although when fathers receive care, the predominance of daughters is less (Lee, Dwyer, & Coward, 1993). In the example raised earlier in the chapter regarding exchanges between a retired couple and the husband's mother, it is not rare to find the older woman giving considerable aid to her mother-in-law while simultaneously giving to other relationships—with her parents, her children, and her grandchildren. It would not be inappropriate to argue that the modern euphemism of "caregiver" in today's vocabulary really means an older woman in most cases (Spitze & Logan, 1992).

Tenth, and finally, exchanges are influenced by geographic, social, and economic factors, as well as by the age and health of family members. Several studies have found that proximity, measured in terms of how close a child lives to the parent, influences frequencies of contact and helping behaviors (Atkinson, Kivett, & Campbell, 1986; Hoyert, 1991; Rossi & Rossi, 1990). The social and economic resources of parents and children influence their need and ability to give assistance. Education increases the likelihood that adult children will reciprocate assistance by parents (Hogan et al., 1993), and parents' income was positively correlated to the level of help given to adult children (Hoyert, 1991; Rossi & Rossi, 1990). African Americans are consistently less likely than Whites or Mexican Americans to be involved in any sort of intergenerational assistance, which may reflect the negative impact of financial and human capital resources on intergenerational exchanges (Eggebeen, 1992; Mutran, 1985;

Silverstein et al., 1994). Further, the age of a parent has a negative effect on both the amount of help received from adult children and, even more dramatically, the amount of help offered by the parent (Morgan, Schuster, & Butler, 1991); similarly, poor health, reflected in restricted mobility and increasing physical limitations, increases the need of elderly parents for assistance from their children (Eggebeen, 1992).

NEW DIRECTIONS FOR FUTURE RESEARCH

Current demographic trends, especially the increase in life expectancy, highlight the increasing importance of intergenerational family roles. As elderly parents live longer, more adult children will experience intergenerational family roles and for a longer duration than in any earlier period of our history. The nature of exchange processes between elderly parents and their adult children needs to be better understood, as well as the implications of exchanges on the well-being of family members. In this final section of the chapter, we will use symbolic interaction theory as a frame of reference to pursue the implications of social background and social structure, self and subjective meanings, and time (expectations and memories) and temporal duration for exchange processes in the aging family. Our goal is to extend our current knowledge by suggesting new directions for future research.

First, *the effect of gender on intergenerational family roles definitely warrants further study*. On the one hand, Ingersoll-Dayton and Antonucci (1988) found that the literature suggests that older women report receiving more support than do men, but there appear to be no differences by gender in the extent of the reciprocal relationships. On the other hand, Hogan, Eggebeen, and Clogg (1993) found that the gender of the parent made no difference in exchanges among intact parental couples but that, among surviving parents, mothers were more likely than fathers to both give and receive assistance from their adult children. The lower economic resources of widowed women and sex role expectations that women be less independent and more nurturing than men suggests that gender differences need to be studied more in the future. Similarly, intergenerational caregiving is influenced when the offspring and parent are of the same sex. Adult daughters are more likely than adult sons to provide care to both parents, and parents of either gender are more likely to be cared for by daughters than sons, but the predominance of daughters as caregivers is much greater when the parent receiving care is the mother. When fathers receive care, the predominance of daughters is slight (Lee et al., 1993). Clearly, it would be empirically and theoretically worthwhile to investigate the influence of the gender of both older parents and adult children on exchanges and well-being.

Second, because elderly parents and adult children are not just passive occupants of social positions but actively infuse family roles with subjective meanings and self-motives, we need to know more about how *the quality of intergenerational ties influences the nature and consequences of exchanges.* The greater the affective closeness, feelings of closeness and intimacy, that adult children feel toward their parents, the more contact they have with those parents; and affective closeness increases the help offered from adult children to parents and from elderly parents to adult children (Rossi & Rossi, 1990). Further, subjective assessments of the quality of contact with children increases the impact of intergenerational roles on the well-being of parents (Mancini & Blieszner, 1989). As Stryker and Serpe (1994) assert, individuals order roles that they perform into a salience hierarchy; therefore, future research should explore the salience an individual assigns to family roles. The three initial hypotheses would be that (1) the greater the salience of the parental (or adult child) role, the greater the impact of satisfactory interactions on well-being; (2) the greater the salience of the parental (or adult child) role, the more frequent the contacts and the more extensive the intergenerational exchanges; and (3) the greater the salience of the intergenerational role to both parents and adult children, the greater the giving and receiving of help and the stronger the impact of exchanges on well-being.

Third, *the reciprocal relationship between well-being and exchanges needs to be more systematically pursued in the future.* Previous research has tended to focus on the impact of exchanges on well-being. However, parents' well-being may also influence exchanges with children; recall that Mutran and Reitzes (1984) found that negative well-being increased the receiving of help by widowed parents. Further, it should be noted that self-concept is more extensive than summary measures of self-evaluation such as well-being and self-esteem (Rosenberg, 1979). Indeed, there are also interesting and important measures of cognitive and affective dimensions of self. Identity refers to self-meanings in a role, the way that a person views himself or herself in a social position (La Rossa & Reitzes, 1993). Mortimer, Finch, and Kumka (1982) suggest three identity dimensions: (1) sociability, (2) competence, and (3) unconventionality. Parents who view themselves as more sociable may more readily engage in emotional exchanges with their children, whereas parents who perceive themselves as very competent may resist receiving instrumental aid from their children. Commitment refers to a sense of belonging or affective attachment to a role. Older people who are more committed to the role of parent may be engaged in more exchanges with their children and less concerned about maintaining equity in exchanges. Clearly, what is important in future research is to *broaden the scope of self-concept to include identity, commitment, salience, and well-being.* In addition, future research should consider the impact of the self-conceptions of both parents and children, and the congruity of those self-conceptions, on the nature and consequences of family exchanges.

A recurrent theme in the work of Beckman (1981), Rook (1987), and Ingersoll-Dayton and Antonucci (1988) is that the implications of reciprocal or nonreciprocal exchanges are not constant or universal. *Equity appears to be more important in friendship roles than in family roles*, but a better understanding of exchanges requires a gradual move away from a simplistic comparison of role relationships. The next step is to recognize that *expectations of others and exchanges vary across roles*. Older parents may have higher expectations for exchanges with their children than they do for exchanges with their friends. So the quantity and quality of intergenerational exchanges must be assessed relative to the expectations that parents have for their children (and children have for their parents). Similarly, recent research on social support suggests that it is the subjective meanings and assessments of interactions, such as whether they are sufficient, satisfactory, and supportive, that influence well-being (Cohen & Syme, 1985; Thoits, 1985). Thus, expectations and subjective meanings are crucial to understanding the implications and consequences of intergenerational exchanges. Future research needs to link more directly the investigation of the family with the burgeoning social support literature.

Symbolic interaction theory also recognizes that roles exist over time and so contain a temporal dimension. Beckman (1981) found that parents who perceive that they have given more aid to their children in the past than they received are more willing to accept a positive imbalance in current exchanges with their children than are those who perceive past reciprocity. She described the process as parents' perceiving that they had accrued "psychological credit." Ingersoll-Dayton and Antonucci (1988) used the phrase "support bank" to note that individuals might build up their accounts by providing support over time and only later in life begin to draw on their savings. Future research needs to probe more directly and explicitly the long-term pattern of exchanges, especially between family members. However, the objective history of exchanges is probably not sufficient. Individuals actively interpret the past, and it is the symbolic meanings assigned to the past that often influence current definitions of the situation. Of critical importance is the subjective assessment of the quality as well as the quantity of past exchanges. The most important factor may be the extent to which parents and children agree that present overbenefits are "due" to parents, that is to say, reflect a just and fair reward for past support.

Not only does the past influence the definition of the present, but the past also influences the future. Another research initiative would be to include measures of the future nature of the role relationship, especially to get indicators of the perceived duration of ties as well as the frequency and intensity of support. Friendship roles typically have only vague and poorly defined expectations for future ties. However, adult children may recognize a greater responsibility for the care and well-being of their parents in the future as age and poor health limit parental independence and deplete the resources of older adults. The subjective responses of both parents and adult children to their anticipated future may powerfully influence the nature of current exchanges.

Finally, it is important to consider suggestions that may improve the quality of future research on the aging family. First, our discussion of social structure factors that may influence intergenerational family exchanges highlights the need for research with a nationally representative database. (Witness the importance of the findings from national surveys presented by Bengtson & Harootyan,

1994; Eggebeen, 1992; Umberson, 1992). A sample that includes both older fathers and mothers is necessary, to explore the effect of gender on family ties. Similarly, a more representative sample would allow the investigation of socio-economic, ethnic, and cultural factors on the character and consequences of intergenerational family exchanges. Further, a broader set of social status and economic indicators is needed to probe the opportunities and constraints placed on elderly parents and adult children. Second, our discussion of self and subjective meanings suggests the need for qualitative as well as quantitative measures of exchanges. Direct measures of the expectations of exchanges and the subjective assessments of role relationships can enable researchers to understand better the motives for the behaviors of parents and children. There is a major need to broaden the measurement of self-concept if we are to improve our understanding of the ways in which family members infuse their roles with purpose and direction. Third, our discussion of the temporal dimension of roles suggests the need for measures of past and anticipated future exchanges, as well as subjective assessments of the quality and meaning of past, present, and future family exchanges. However, the most serious problem with current research is the absence of data on both elderly parents and their adult children. It is vital that we explore the structural resources, subjective meanings, and interpretations of time for both parents and children if we are to understand better the dynamics of the intergenerational family relationships.

REFERENCES

Atkinson, M. P., Kirvett, V. R., & Campbell, R. T. (1986). Intergenerational solidarity: An examination of a theoretical model. *Journal of Gerontology*, *41*, 408–416.

Beckman, L. J. (1981). Effects of social interaction and children's relative inputs on older women's psychological well-being. *Journal of Personality and Social Psychology*, *41*, 1075–1086.

Bengtson, V. L., & Harootyan, R. A. (1994). *Intergenerational linkages: Hidden connections in American society*. New York: Springer Publishing.

Blau, P. (1964). *Exchange in power in social life*. New York: Wiley.

Burke, P. J. (1980). The self: Measurement implications from a symbolic interactionist perspective. *Social Psychology Quarterly*, *43*, 18–29.

Cohen, S., & Syme, S. L. (1985). *Social support and health*. New York: Springer Publishing.

Cooley, C. H. (1902). *Human nature and the social order*. New York: Scribner's.

Cornell, L. L. (1992). Intergenerational relationships, social support, and mortality. *Social Forces*, *71*, 53–62.

Dowd, J. J. (1975). Aging as exchange: A preface to theory. *Journal of Gerontology*, *30*, 584–594.

Eggebeen, D. J. (1992). From generation unto generation: Parent-child support in aging American families. *Generations*, *17*, 45–49.

Erikson, E. H. (1963). *Childhood and society*. New York: W. W. Norton.

Goffman, E. (1959). The moral career of the mental patient. *Psychiatry: Journal for the Study of Interpersonal Processes*, *22*, 123–142.

Gove, W. R., Ortega, S. T., & Style, C. B. (1989). The maturational and role perspectives on aging and self through the adult years: An empirical evaluation. *American Journal of Sociology*, *94*, 1117–1145.

Harootyan, R. A., & Bengtson, V. L. (1994). Intergenerational linkages: The context of the study. In V. L. Bengtson & R. A. Harootyan (Eds.), *Intergenerational linkages: Hidden connections in American society* (pp. 1–18). New York: Springer Publishing.

Hogan, D. P., Eggebeen, D. J., & Clogg, C. C. (1993). The structure of intergenerational exchanges in American families. *American Journal of Sociology*, *98*, 1428–1458.

Homans, G. C. (1961). *Social behavior: Its elementary forms*. New York: Harcourt, Brace & World.

Hoyert, D. L. (1991). Financial and household exchanges between generations. *Research on Aging*, *13*, 205–225.

Ingersoll-Dayton, B., & Antonucci, T. C. (1988). Reciprocal and nonreciprocal social support: Contrasting sides of intimate relations. *Journal of Gerontology*, *43*, S65–S73.

La Rossa, R., & Reitzes, D. C. (1993). Symbolic interactionism and family studies. In P. Boss, W. Doherty, R. LaRossa, W. Schumm, & S. Steinmetz (Eds.), *Sourcebook of family theories and methods: A contextual approach* (pp. 135–163). New York: Plenum.

Lawton, L., Silverstein, M., & Bengtson, V. L. (1994). Solidarity between generations in families. In V. L. Bengtson & R. A. Harootyan (Eds.), *Intergenerational linkages: Hidden connections in American society* (pp. 19–42). New York: Springer Publishing.

Lee, G. R., Dwyer, J. W., & Coward, R. T. (1993). Gender differences in parent care: Demographic factors and same-gender preferences. *Journal of Gerontology: Social Sciences*, *48*, S9–S16.

Lowenthal, M. F., & Haven, C. (1968). Interaction and adaptation: Intimacy as a critical variable. *American Sociological Review*, *33*, 20–30.

Maines, D. R., Sugrue, N. M., & Katovich, M. A. (1983). The sociological import of G. H. Mead's theory of the past. *American Sociological Review*, *48*, 161–173.

Mancini, J. A., & Blieszner, R. (1989). Aging parents and adult children: Research themes in intergenerational relations. *Journal of Marriage and the Family*, *51*, 275–290.

McCall, G. J., & Simmons, J. L. (1966). *Identities and interactions*. New York: Macmillan.

Mead, G. H. (1934). *Mind, self, and society*. Chicago: University of Chicago Press.

Morgan, D. L., Schuster, T. L., & Butler, E. W. (1991). Role reversals in the exchange of social support. *Journal of Gerontology: Social Sciences*, *46*, S278–S287.

Mortimer, J. T., Finch, M. D., & Kumka, D. (1982). Persistence and change in development: The multidimensional self-concept. *Life-Span Development and Behavior*, *4*, 263–313.

Mutran, E. (1985). Intergenerational family support among blacks and whites: Response to culture or socioeconomic differences. *Journal of Gerontology*, *40*, 382–389.

Mutran, E., & Reitzes, D. C. (1984). Intergenerational support activities and well-being among the elderly: A convergence of exchange and symbolic interaction perspectives. *American Sociological Review*, *49*, 117–130.

Reitzes, D. C., & Mutran, E. (1994). Multiple roles and identities: factors influencing self-esteem among middle-aged working men and women. *Social Psychology Quarterly*, *57*, 313–325.

Rook, K. (1987). Reciprocity of social exchange and social satisfaction among older women. *Journal of Personality and Social Psychology*, *52*, 1097–1108.

Rosenberg, M. (1979). *Conceiving the self*. New York: Basic Books.

Rossi, A. S., & Rossi, P. H. (1990). *Of human bonding: Parent-child relations across the life course*. New York: Aldine de Gruyter.

Silverstein, M., Lawton, L., & Bengtson, V. L. (1994). Types of relationships between parents and adult children. In V. L. Bengtson & R. A. Harootyan (Eds.), *Intergenerational linkages: Hidden connections in American society* (pp. 43–76). New York: Springer Publishing.

Spitze, G., & Logan, J. R. (1992). Helping as a component of parent-adult child relations. *Research on Aging, 14*, 291–312.

Stryker, S. (1981). Symbolic interactionism: Themes and variations. In M. Rosenberg & R. H. Turner (Eds.), *Social psychology: Sociological perspectives* (pp. 3–29). New York: Basic Books.

Stryker, S., & Serpe, R. T. (1994). Identity salience and psychological centrality: Equivalent, overlapping, or complementary concepts? *Social Psychology Quarterly, 57*, 16–35.

Talbott, M. M. (1990). The negative side of the relationship between older widows and their adult children: The mother's perspective. *Gerontologist, 30*, 595–603.

Thibault, J. W., & Kelley, H. (1959). *The social psychology of groups.* New York: Wiley.

Thoits, P. A. (1985). Social support and psychological well-being: Theoretical possibilities. In I. G. Sarason & B. R. Sarason (Eds.), *Social support: Theory, research, and applications* (pp. 51–72). Dordrecht, The Netherlands: Martinus Nijhoff.

Turner, R. H. (1956). Role-taking, role standpoint, and reference-group behavior. *American Journal of Sociology, 61*, 316–328.

Turner, R. H. (1962). Role-taking: Process versus conformity. In A. M. Rose (Ed.), *Human behavior and social processes.* Boston: Houghton Mifflin.

Turner, R. H., & Shosid, N. (1976). Ambiguity and interchangeability in role attribution. *American Sociological Review, 41*, 993–1006.

Uhlenberg, P., & Cooney, T. M. (1990). Family size, and mother-child relations in later life. *Gerontologist, 30*, 618–625.

Umberson, D. (1992). Relationships between adult children and their parents: Psychological consequences for both generations. *Journal of Marriage and the Family, 54*, 664–674.

Umberson, D., & Chen, M. D. (1994). Effects of a parent's death on adult children: Relationship salience and reaction to loss. *American Sociological Review, 59*, 152–168.

Walster, E., Walster, G. W., & Berscheid, E. (1978). *Equity: Theory and research.* Boston: Allyn and Bacon.

Wheaton, B. (1990). Life transitions, role histories, and mental health. *American Sociological Review, 55*, 209–223.

CHAPTER 9

Work and Retirement

Harvey L. Sterns
Nancy Kubitz Matheson
Lisa Schwartz Park

Work plays a major role in society. Not only does it provide an organizing force in our activities, but it also helps to form our self-concept. Who we are and how we see ourselves is determined, in part, by our work. The ability to continue to work is based on capability in terms of knowledge, skills, and ability. Self-management of career, maintaining competence, and updating skills have become major issues. In the past, the career search was often thought of as culminating in discovery of that one special career with which one would stay until retirement. However, the workplace is dramatically changing in response to economic, societal, and technical forces (Forteza & Prieto, 1994; Warr, 1994).

Today there is uncertainty about how long someone will be able to work for a particular organization. We continue to be in the throes of downsizing. Thirteen million people reported losing jobs at some point from 1991 to 1993. Figures on job status in 1994 of workers displaced between 1991 and 1993 were 36% still unemployed, 27% employed with income equal or higher than old job, 18% employed at less than 50% income of old job, 10% employed at 75%–100% of the income of old job, and 8% employed at 50%–75% of the income of old job (St. George, 1996). In 1994, 460,063 jobs were lost, and in 1995 slightly fewer jobs were projected to be lost.

The Laborforce 2,000 study found that proportionately more older workers lost their jobs via corporate cutbacks over the 5-year study period. Often, firms that made the greatest reductions-in-force were mature companies and those in heavy industry. Both had a large share of workers over age 55 (Mirvis & Hall, 1995), 440,000.

The conception of the life span is also changing. No longer can we view adulthood as a time of career stability, when people find that special job and stick with it. Today, middle age can be a time to explore new work alternatives and consider retirement options.

Many people today assume that most older workers retire before or around their sixty-fifth birthday. They expect that they themselves will retire at about the same age. But retirement as we know it has been experienced by large numbers of people only in the past two generations (Sonnenfeld, 1988). A major theme of the 1971 White House Conference on Aging was the normality of retirement and why it was a positive goal for most older people. Only in the 1980s did gerontologists begin to realize that perhaps too much focus was being placed on preparing and encouraging people to retire. Today, later-life planning involves considering second or third careers and choices regarding the point at which one might stop working. A major consideration is how capable older people will be able to continue to work (Sterns & Sterns, 1995).

This chapter applies a life-span orientation to the issues involved in the areas of work and retirement. After briefly reviewing various definitions of the older worker, the possibility of age bias in the workplace is considered. Finally, both the antecedents and the consequences of retirement are examined.

OLDER ADULTS AT WORK

The Commonwealth Fund published in 1993 a major report, *The Untapped Resource*, a study of Americans over 55 at work. They found that over 14 million people, or 27% of individuals 55 and over, are employed and consistently receive high ratings on key performance attributes. Case studies and research have shown that older workers can be as flexible, trainable, and cost-effective as younger employees. For example, in a case study conducted at Days Inn, older workers were easy to train, flexible about assignments, and more likely to stay with the job (McNaught & Barth, 1992). In fact, three-fourths of the older adults (55+) in the United States are actively engaged in contributions to society either through work, volunteer activities, or caregiving (Bass, 1995).

Despite the productivity of older adults, there are still approximately 5.4 million (10%) older adults who would prefer to work and are unable to find suitable jobs. Of individuals age 55 and over who do not work, the majority (51%) are retired and prefer not to work. Another 12% would like to work but are unable to due to health or disability. This large number of individuals includes 2 million people 55–64 years old, 2.3 million people 65–74 years old, and 1.1 million adults 75 and older (Commonwealth Fund, 1993).

Over the past 30 years or so there have been significant changes in the work force participation of older adults. In 1950, 87% of males and 27% of females 55–64 were in the work force. For individuals 65 and over, 46% of males and 10% of females were still working. In 1990, 65% of males and 42% of females between the ages of 55 and 64 were in the work force. For individuals 65 and over, 14%

of the males and 7% of the females were still working. The percentage of these individuals in the work force has decreased, although the absolute number has increased (Kutcher & Fullerton, 1990). The expanding population of older workers may experience diminished opportunities.

A new field has emerged to address the issues and challenges faced by older workers. The study of aging and work focusing on the employment and retirement issues of middle-aged and older workers is called industrial gerontology. "Work-life extension" is a term referring to increasing the labor force participation rate of older adults through delayed retirement or labor force reentry by retirees.

The aging of the U.S. population has created an aging work force. As the baby boom moves into adulthood and older adulthood, it will constitute one-third of our population (Pifer & Bronte, 1986). The present and future aging work forces bring unique issues to corporations and society: early retirement options; staffing shortages; career problems, including mid- and later life career change; and training and retraining issues due to plant closings and technological innovations.

Older workers have a great deal to offer organizations. Older workers are able to compensate for productivity declines by taking advantage of improved skills and knowledge gained through experience (Schwab & Heneman, 1978). Consistency of output tends to increase with age. Older workers perform at steadier rates and have less job turnover, fewer accidents, and less absenteeism than younger workers (Rosen & Jerdee, 1985; Sterns & McDaniel, 1994).

Despite these findings, inaccurate negative stereotypes exist regarding the older worker. It is believed that they are more difficult to train, resistant to change, more likely to have accidents, and less motivated (Sterns & Alexander, 1987). A growing literature exists regarding the prevalence and the effects of age bias and discrimination in the workplace. Age discrimination includes such practices as discrimination against the older worker in the employment interview (Arvey, 1979; Britton & Thomas, 1973; Haefner, 1977), with regard to promotion and in performance appraisal (Schwab & Heneman, 1978; Sterns & Alexander, 1988), and in making managerial decisions. An overview of the numerous definitions of "older worker" is a useful starting point in understanding and eliminating age discrimination.

DEFINITIONS OF "OLDER WORKER"

A continuing dilemma for industrial gerontology is to agree on definitions for adult and older adult workers. Much of the confusion may stem from selecting the approach based on the issue to be studied. This leads to situationally based definitions with limited generalizability. Aging is a multidimensional process that is difficult to reflect adequately in a single definition.

There are different levels of analysis related to different aspects of aging. One can choose to study individuals, organizations, or society. Five approaches to defining older workers have been proposed by Sterns and Doverspike (1989) and are included in the following section. These definitions provide discrete but related ways to conceptualize various aspects of aging, addressing several important levels of analyses and providing an organizing framework to discuss issues of aging and work.

Chronological/Legal

The distinction between older and younger workers rests most frequently on a definition based on chronological age. Although little theoretical justification is offered for the age ranges, there is an implicit justification based on a legal definition of age. The Age Discrimination in Employment Act (ADEA) of 1967, amended in 1978 and 1986, protects workers over the age of 40. In recommending such a law, President Johnson stated that approximately half of all private job openings were barred to applicants over 55 and a quarter were closed to applicants over 45 (Edelman & Siegler, 1978). Another commonly used cut-off point comes from the Job Training Partnership Act and the Older Americans Act. Both acts recognize people aged 55 and older as older workers. Thus, for federal programs, people aged 55 and older have been included in the older worker category. Set ages are convenient, but do not contribute theoretically to a gerontology that must consider both environmental and individual factors of aging and work.

Functional

The second approach to defining older workers is a functional approach (Sterns & Doverspike, 1989). This is a performance-based definition of age and recognizes that there is great individual variation in abilities and functioning at all ages. As chronological age increases, individuals go through various biological and psychological changes, including declines as well as increased experience, wisdom, and judgment. The concept of functional age refers to a performance-based definition of age. Individuals can be identified as "younger" or "older" than their chronological age, based on objective measures. The concept of functional age has been criticized from a number of perspectives, including the definitional, research design, and statistical points of view (Avolio, Barrett, & Sterns, 1984; Salthouse, 1986). Major problems are the use of a single index and the assumption of decline. Despite these criticisms of the concept, different approaches and definitions of functional age continue to exert their influence on the field. Alternative approaches propose a more traditional methodology drawn from industrial psychology that emphasizes appropriate assessment strategies and the design of measures that assess attributes directly related to job performance (Avolio et al., 1984).

Psychosocial

Psychosocial definitions of older workers are the third approach studied and are based on social perceptions, including age-typing of occupations, perceptions of the older worker, and the aging of knowledge, skill, and ability sets. The individual's self-perception is also considered. How individuals perceive themselves and their careers at a given age may be congruent or incongruent with societal image. Relatively little research has addressed the quite basic question of how we know when workers will perceive themselves to be perceived by others as old.

A significant amount of research has investigated the perceived attributes of older workers. Older workers may be perceived as harder to train, less able to keep up with technological change, more accident-prone, and less motivated (Rosen & Jerdee, 1976; Stagner, 1985). They are also seen as dependable, cooperative, conscientious, consistent, and knowledgeable (Rosen & Jerdee, 1976; Schwab & Heneman, 1978).

Organizational

The fourth approach, an organizational view of older workers, recognizes that the effects of age and tenure are necessarily related and that individuals age in both jobs and organizations (Sterns & Doverspike, 1989). An older worker has often spent a substantial amount of time in a job and substantially more time in an organization. A definition of older workers based on the aging of individuals in organizational roles is more commonly discussed under the topics of seniority and tenure. The effects of aging may often be confounded by the effects of tenure and vice versa. Organizations, too, age (Schrank & Waring, 1981). Indeed, an organization may be perceived as old because of the average age of its members. As the average age of its members increases, new demands are placed on the organizational subsystems such as human resources.

Life-Span Approach

The life-span approach borrows from a number of the previous approaches but adds its own unique emphasis (Sterns & Doverspike, 1989). It advances the possibility for behavioral change at any point in the life cycle. Substantial individual differences in aging are recognized as critical in examining adult career patterns.

Three sets of factors are seen as affecting behavioral change during the life cycle. The first set includes normative, age-graded, biological and/or environmental determinants. These bear a strong relationship to chronological age. The second set of factors is normative, history-graded influences that affect most members of a cohort in similar ways. The third set of events is nonnormative. This includes unique career and life changes, as well as individual health and stress-inducing events. The unique status of the individual is the result of the joint impact of these factors. According to this approach, there are more individual differences as people grow older (Baltes, Reese, & Lipsitt, 1980).

These differences create difficulty in developing theories that adequately address the broad range of differences. Late careers are often more difficult to study than early careers because there is less consistency in the developmental tasks. For example, in early career, individuals must chose a career. In late career, a person may continue a career, start a new career, modify a career, or retire.

AGE BIAS AT WORK?

Although the perspective for studying older workers varies, the issues of interest to industrial gerontologists tend to focus on age bias in selection, interviewing, and performance appraisal, training and retraining, and mid- and later-life career changes. A brief summary of each of these areas follows.

Age bias, often in the form of age-related stereotyping, has been reviewed by many authors (Doering, Rhodes, & Schuster, 1983; Forteza & Prieto, 1994; Rosen & Jerdee, 1985; Warr, 1994). The belief that older persons are at a disadvantage in the workplace has played an important role in social and legal efforts to eliminate such perceived discrimination.

Rosen and Jerdee (1976) in their classic study using vignettes mailed to *Harvard Business Review* subscribers found that older employees were at a disadvantage when decisions involved employee development or promotion. Older employees were reviewed as less flexible and more resistant to change than younger workers. When it came to recommendations for solving the various problems, older employees were less likely than younger workers to receive organizational support such as training, career development, or supervisor feedback.

In 1995 a follow-up revised survey by Rosen and Jerdee (1995) was carried out with the support of AARP's Women's Initiative and Public Policy Institute. The revised survey had some of the original vignettes and several new ones to capture current personnel issues. The results indicated that managerial bias against older workers in general and against older women in particular, whether intentional or not, often puts older female workers at a disadvantage.

The Age Discrimination in Employment Act (ADEA) of 1986 specified the protection of workers from age discrimination from the age of 40 and older. Employers cannot discharge, refuse to hire, or discriminate in other ways against an individual because of age. Workers cannot be limited, segregated, or classified in a way that might deprive any individual of employment opportunities or adversely affect the employee's status. In other words, individuals have the opportunity to work as long as they are able.

However, under certain conditions, the ADEA has allowed employers to consider an individual's age in employment decisions. Such exceptions in employment decisions are justified and legally acceptable when the employer can show that age is a bona fide occupational qualification reasonably necessary to the normal operations of a business. The establishment of this exception is difficult. Organizational practices, such as setting maximum age limits on hiring, must be substantiated with proof that age requirements are essential for the protection of the public or allowed on the basis of some reasonable factors other than age, such as physical fitness.

The act does not prohibit the discharge or discipline of an older worker for good cause. The issues involved in the establishment of a bona fide occupational qualification concern the question of whether certain age-related changes would impair performance on the job. A chronological definition of age is used instead of individual evaluation (Bessey & Ananda, 1991; Borgatta, 1991).

Selection

According to the U.S. General Accounting Office (1994), ADEA charges increased about 25% between 1989 and 1992. In fiscal year 1993 the total number of charges that the Equal Employment Opportunity Commission (EEOC) handled increased 25% over 1992. The number of unresolved antidiscrimination charges that the EEOC carried forward from one year to another is approximately 2,000 to 30,000, and a typical charging party must wait 20 months or more for the EEOC to make a determination under the ADEA (Gamse, 1995).

A major personnel issue is the selection and hiring of workers. Today middle-aged and older workers are being considered for hire. When testing an individual for possible selection and hire, the important concern is whether or not the selection battery predicts job performance for older workers as well as it does for younger workers. When ability or aptitude tests are used, the possibility exists that such selection procedures may be biased against older applicants. In addition, many tests have been scored and normed on the basis of the young population. Studies showing that older adults scored, on the average, lower than younger workers on selection tests, with no average age differences in performance, are often cited as evidence for potential age bias in selection testing (Doering et al., 1983).

When predicting older worker performance, selection testing should consider the occupation and the job requirements. The focus should be on the nature of the job demands and whether an individual older worker has the ability, background, and experience to be hired for the job (Sterns & Miklos, 1995).

Interviewing

Similar issues pertain to the use of the interview. The interview has become the most widely used selection device. There has been a relative lack of research regarding the existence of age bias in the interview process, and what has been done has been conducted in the laboratory rather than in organizational settings. A paper by Avolio and Barrett (1987) has argued that past laboratory research has been confounded, thus making it difficult to draw conclusions. When these confounds were controlled, it was found that interview bias tends to favor younger applicants rather than be negative toward older applicants. The bias, however, accounted for only a small percentage of the variance in hiring recommendations. This means that other factors besides age had an influence on whether or not an applicant was hired. The potential for bias can be reduced by training the selection interviewer and designing the interview to gather only information relevant to the applicant's future job performance (Avolio et al., 1984).

Performance Appraisal

The accurate evaluation of each employee's job performance is of paramount importance to the individual worker and to the organization. Accurate appraisals of job performance help to ensure a better match between the position held by the employee, the wages awarded to the employee, and the employee's value to the organization (Cascio, 1991). When evaluating the performance of the older worker, the manager must use *actual* job performance. The appraisal system cannot be based on popular beliefs that performance declines with age. Sterns and Alexander (1988) remind us that performance appraisals must be reasonable, relevant, and reliable. Decisions based on performance appraisal information should consider only relevant job performance data, regardless of age. For instance, when the older worker is being evaluated for a promotion, the information to consider is the worker's ability to perform the job. In a layoff decision the question is how well the worker performs the job relative to other workers; in a termination decision the question is whether or not the worker performs the job at the minimally acceptable level. Whether these ideals are followed, however, is a topic of considerable debate.

Training and Retraining

Older workers have much to offer the modern organization and should be considered for training opportunities. Any training program should be based on a careful task analysis to determine the sequence of training (Sterns, 1986; Wexley, 1984). The individual will benefit from training that breaks the task into its component parts and trains each to a criterion level, with mastery of basic skills preceding the more difficult ones (Gagne & Briggs, 1974; Willis, 1985).

According to Sterns (1986) and Sterns and Doverspike (1989), training should be relevant, should provide positive feedback in an attempt to encourage the self-confidence of the trainee, and should target the development of new knowledge and skills for successful job performance. Further, training is facilitated when material is organized to enhance learning. Finally, the training program should allow the older worker to take the time necessary to learn the new tasks. Well-designed training programs will give individuals at all ages an equal opportunity to complete the program successfully (Belbin & Belbin, 1972).

Career Development

Early models of career development were linear models that assumed that individuals moved through predictable career stages. For older adults, maintaining skills for a period of time and then declining was the predicted pattern. This notion that career stages are linked to age will lead practitioners to incorrectly choose career development opportunities that are congruent with the age and stage of various cohorts. These models ignore individual differences and the contributions that older workers make.

The conventional conception of career has been limited to a single career. The individual is to decide early in adulthood on the career goals that will be pursued. The individual then moves through establishing himself and moving up in the organization, through a period of stability, and then into retirement (Super, 1980). Most vocational counseling and literature has been conceived under this or similar assumptions. At present, career theorists and counselors must grapple with the fact that many individuals will not be able to follow such a simple trajectory. Technological changes and massive layoffs in some employment sectors have forced large numbers of individuals out of preordained career paths. Despite these realities, large numbers of individuals still manage to survive under the one life, one career model. Industrial gerontologists are challenged to build models that are flexible yet substantive enough to be useful to individuals and organizations.

CAREER DEVELOPMENT FROM A LIFE-SPAN PERSPECTIVE

Continuing growth, moving to other jobs or to entirely new careers are realistic ventures at any age. A life-span approach emphasizes individual differences and an ability to make a change at any point. Super (1980) emphasizes that career choices are a series of mini-decisions that are inseparable from other aspects of the life cycle. For example, a woman who has stayed home to raise a family may at an older age complete her formal education and be eager to pursue a career with full commitment. Many people will not follow a traditional path. In fact, there is little support for an age-linked notion of career changes (Sterns & Miklos, 1995).

A non-age-specific model of adult career development has been proposed by Sterns (1986). The model assumes that transitions in work life may occur many times throughout a career (see Figure 9.1). According to this model, the decision

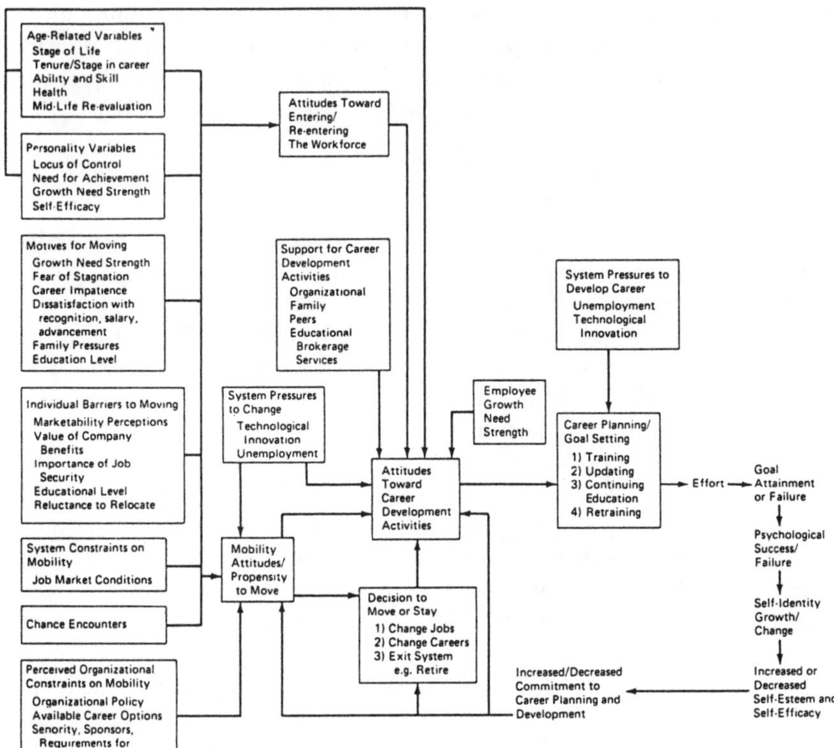

FIGURE 9.1 Career progression in middle and later adulthood. From "Training and Retraining Adult and Older Adult Workers" by H. L. Sterns, 1986, in J. E. Birren and P. K. Robinson, eds., *Age, Health, and Employment*, pp. 93–113, Englewood Cliffs, NJ: Prentice-Hall.

to change jobs or to exit the system is directly influenced by attitudes toward mobility and success or failure in previous career activities. The model incorporates Hall's (1971) model of career growth, which conceptualizes career planning from a goal-setting perspective. When a career-goal decision is made, the resulting outcome can lead to identity growth and enhanced self-esteem. The enhancement of self-esteem may in turn lead to greater commitment to future career development goals.

The decision to change jobs or careers is directly influenced by attitudes toward mobility and success or failure in previous life situations. Once the individual perceives a need for change, he or she must consider the various life roles that are possible at this particular time in life. Self-concept becomes of prime importance, as the individual must assess the salience of the worker role in addition to the life roles of spouse, citizen, "leisurite," and provider (Super, 1983). At different stages of life some roles may be more important or more appropriate than others. A person may also play more than one role at a time. These roles carry with them certain expectations for behavior and may influence an individual's needs. The roles interact to form a self-concept that is influenced by personal and environmental conditions. For those older adults who are no longer satisfied with their jobs, this fit between personal and environmental variables no longer exists. Super emphasizes that self-concept is an integral influence in the vocational development of the individual.

Lydia Bronte (1993) interviewed individuals who had long careers into their 80s and 90s. The participants are proof that it is possible to continue being creative and productive past age 65. They present a positive view of what can be accomplished late in one's career or even early in a career started late in life. Although it is not a rigorously designed study, it provides portraits of individuals who break the stereotypes of older adult careers.

Although Bronte (1993) found a great deal of variety in careers, she identified three basic career patterns. The homesteaders are individuals who stay in the same job or profession for their entire careers. Many of these individuals are in artistic or scientific fields. They are still deeply engaged in their careers and feel that they have more potential for growth.

The second group, the transformers, change jobs once. Early transformers change careers shortly after starting an occupation. This change seems to be part of the trial-and-error process. In contrast, late transformers tended to be well-established financially and personally, giving them the freedom to pursue another interest later in life.

The third group, the explorers, changed careers from as few as 3 to as many as 10 times. The reasons for the shifts were varied, as were the career paths. Bronte's (1993) book illustrates the variability in career pattern and ages of career peaks and contributions.

Mid- and later-life readjustment calls for a redefinition of work and life roles. Some people may choose to change careers; in many circumstances, hobbies may become second careers. Another option is retirement.

People not only may wish to work longer; they may have to. A recent survey of 12,600 Americans, undertaken by F. Thomas Juster with support from the National Institute on Aging, the University of Michigan, and the Alliance for Aging Research (Rich, 1993), showed that a significant proportion of the next generation of potential retirees had few resources on which to retire. The results indicated that, in the 1990s, 40% of working Americans aged 51 to 60 would have no pension income other than Social Security were they to retire. Twenty percent of all respondents had no assets (house, investments, or savings), 14% had no health insurance, and 20% were disabled. All of these individuals, regardless of their health and disability status, will feel the financial pressure to continue working.

The Juster study also reported some positive trends. Most people in their 50s were healthy, and many were in good shape economically. The median household income was $37,500, and median net assets, including home and cars, totaled $80,000. But substantial numbers of people in their 50s were not well off, especially among minority groups (see chapter 14 for additional information.) Although most people were better off financially than their counterparts of a few decades ago, they might not have been ready to face retirement. A logical conclusion from the survey findings is that many older people will continue to work because they will not have the resources to retire (Rich, 1993).

Sterns and Sterns (1995) have emphasized that until the late 1980s, most adult and older adult workers felt that they would have a choice about working after the normal retirement age. This belief was based on the expectation of an expanding economy and a strong economic climate. Many middle-aged and older workers are now surprised by the prevalence of early buyouts, layoffs, and downsizing, even by successful companies. This has resulted in fewer attractive full- or part-time employment opportunities.

This places middle-aged and older workers in the position of having to be responsible for their own careers, maximizing the employment opportunities presented to them and competing with people of all ages in finding new employment. People will have to fight harder to remain in the work force longer. The present 50- and 60-year-olds were hired at a time when they could choose among jobs. They were a part of the work force when there was accelerated growth and numerous promotions. They had to deal with the slower promotions and salary increases of the 1980s but still expected that they would have control over how long they worked and when they exited the work force.

Employment benefits, especially retirement benefits, will also change in the future. Individuals may have to pay or co-pay into pension and health benefit programs both before and after retirement. This will leave fewer discretionary resources in retirement than past retirees have experienced.

DECISION TO RETIRE

Researchers have attempted to describe the retirement decision as well as the impact of retirement, the result being a wide range of opinion (Quinn & Burkhauser, 1990). Atchley (1988) emphasizes the importance of an individual's felt need to continue employment as an influencing factor in the consideration of retirement. This need can be either internal or stem from external or system pressures. He suggests that two comparisons are vital when considering retirement. First, expected financial needs in retirement are compared with expected financial resources. Second, the individual compares his or her social situation in retirement with what it was while working. It is noted that access to information, availability of and accuracy of information, and personality variables will have an impact on these comparisons. The actual timing of retirement is proposed to be dependent on the expected income comparison. According to this discussion, an individual whose perceived financial resources in retirement are less than his or her perceived economic needs is expected to continue working if physically able to do so.

RETIREMENT FROM A LIFE-SPAN PERSPECTIVE

Life-span researchers may view retirement as a continuation of the career development process. Atchley (1976, 1988) has identified various phases through which one may approach the retirement role.

1. *Preretirement.* The first phase one may encounter is the preretirement phase. It is at this time that an individual orients himself or herself toward the notion of retirement. Fantasies of what retirement will be like are common.
2. *Retirement.* Retirement may be followed by one of three possible phases: (I) the honeymoon phase, (2) immediate retirement routine, or (3) rest and relaxation. When people enter the honeymoon phase, they may attempt to do all the things that they were unable to do before retirement, including travel. Not all individuals experience the euphoric honeymoon period. Some individuals, especially those who have cultivated a satisfying off-the-job routine, may easily settle into a retirement routine. The people who follow the path of the "immediate retirement routine" already have stable groups and activities and need only alter the time perspective of these activities. Finally, some individuals may enter a rest-and-relaxation phase following retirement. This phase is characterized by a temporary reduction in activity, opposite to that of the honeymoon phase.
3. *Disenchantment.* A period of disenchantment or depression may result if, for example, an individual's fantasies concerning retirement are not met.
4. *Reorientation.* A period of reorientation often occurs among disenchanted retired individuals. At this time depressed individuals go through a process of reassessment and develop more realistic perceptions of their retirement experience.
5. *Routine.* People may develop a means of dealing routinely with change. Stable retirement lifestyles are accompanied by well-developed criteria for making life choices. According to Atchley (1988), people with a satisfying retirement routine are aware of their capabilities and limitations, know what is expected of them, and have mastered the retirement role.
6. *Termination.* For some people, the retirement role becomes irrelevant, whether because of a return to employment or, more likely, illness or disability. In the case of illness or disability, the retirement role is exchanged for the sick and disabled role.

Retirement can be defined in many ways. Whether or not an individual is perceived as retired will depend on which definition of retirement is adopted

(Beehr, 1986; Fields & Mitchell, 1984). Fields and Mitchell (1984) describe six often-used definitions of retirement: (1) absence of participation in the labor force, (2) acceptance of Social Security benefits, (3) reception of a private pension, (4) reductions in hours of work or pay per hour, (5) subjective evaluation by the individual as retired, and (6) permanent withdrawal from long-term job or career.

Beehr (1986), in his review of the process of retirement, summarizes the common dichotomies pertaining to retirement: voluntary versus involuntary, early versus on-time, and partial versus complete. Voluntary versus involuntary retirement is most often assessed through an individual's perception of choice in the retirement process. Early versus on-time retirement is often gauged by using age. Finally, number of hours worked is used to quantify the partial versus complete retirement distinction.

Although the effect of mandatory retirement policies has been minimized in most occupations, pension plans can also be used as incentives to regulate the timing of an employee's retirement (Kingson, 1982). Employers may offer complete pension coverage prior to age 65 and may therefore influence the structure of the work force, with many older workers removing themselves from the labor force.

Some organizations now offer varying degrees of retirement education to their workers, ranging from financial planning to individual counseling. The federal government has encouraged people to plan and develop retirement income by using formal approaches such as Individual Retirement Accounts (IRAs), Social Security, investment, or private pension income. Concomitant with the use of IRAs and other pension funds is the trend toward long-term retirement financial planning, often beginning when the individual enters the labor force.

Finally, the acceptance rates for Social Security reflect a societal change in retirement age. The Social Security Act of 1935 regards age 65 as the normal age for retirement, with eventual changes to 66 and 67 by 2010. It is then that an individual may collect full Social Security benefits. Despite the advantage of waiting until 65, a growing proportion of workers have been choosing to retire earlier and receive reduced benefits, since they were first made available to women in 1956 and to men in 1961 (Fix, 1990).

Retirement creates many life changes for older adults. For the vast majority of people, with retirement comes an increase in free time as well as a decrease in income. These are not the only changes that occur as the result of retirement, but they are those likely to be the most dramatic.

Do the changes that result from the retirement process lead to negative consequences for retirees? Research studies examining this question have reached inconsistent conclusions. Some research has found that retirement does create problems for retirees. For example, Bosse, Aldwin, Levenson, and Ekerdt (1987) discovered that retired men (mean age, 66.35 years) reported a greater number of psychological symptoms than did working males (mean age, 56 years). Retirees scored significantly higher on depression, anxiety, somatization, phobic anxiety, and obsessive/compulsive scales. These differences, with the exception of the anxiety scale, held up even when health was taken into consideration. Men who were still working after age 65 reported the fewest symptoms. The authors proposed that three stresses created by retirement—loss of income, loss of friends, and marital difficulties—could lead to the psychological difficulties found. The stress of retirement does not always lead to adverse effects on the functioning or well-being of retirees. For example, George, Fillenbaum, and Palmore (1984) found no adverse effects of retirement on life satisfaction. Additionally, Beehr (1986) discovered that the mental health of retirees was similar to their mental health prior to retirement. This finding was moderated by the amount of planning, occupational goal attainment, retirement expectations, and propensity to work. Therefore, even if retirement does promote negative effects, these effects are influenced by characteristics of the individual.

FACTORS INFLUENCING THE RETIREMENT EXPERIENCE

It is clear that the effects of retirement are largely determined by an individual's specific retirement experience. An aspect of this experience that influences one's retirement adjustment is whether or not the decision to retire is voluntary. In addition to the nature of the retirement decision, four personal characteristics have been linked to retirement satisfaction: health, income, attitudes, and preparedness for retirement. Each of these can influence the ease with which a person adjusts to retirement.

Voluntary Versus Nonvoluntary Retirement

The negative effects of retirement may be more pronounced for those who do not choose to retire. Voluntary retirees have reported higher life satisfaction, income, health, and occupational status than involuntary retirees. Involuntary retirees, in contrast, have shown signs of poor adaptation (Sterns, Laier, & Dorsett, 1994).

In 1986 amendments to the ADEA eliminated mandatory retirement policies in most occupations. Because older adults will no longer be forced to retire, does this mean that retirees in the future will have greater satisfaction in retirement? Unfortunately, the adjustment difficulties resulting from involuntary retirement are not so easily eliminated.

Mandatory retirement legislation is only one cause of involuntary retirement; another cause is poor health (Sterns & Sterns, 1995). Research has shown that those who are forced to retire because of poor health are more likely to suffer negative consequences than those who retire as a consequence of mandatory retirement laws. Palmore et al. (Palmore, Burchett, Fillenbaum, George, & Wallman, 1985) analyzed data from three longitudinal studies (the Retirement

History Study, the National Longitudinal Surveys, and the Duke Second Longitudinal Study) and discovered that retiring for compulsory reasons other than health had no significant effects on life satisfaction, whereas health-related retirement was associated with lower living standards, poorer health, and lower satisfaction (with life, leisure, activity, and retirement). This suggests that the poor health of many involuntary retirees, not the involuntary nature of the retirement decision, leads to problems seen in this group.

Therefore, the elimination of mandatory retirement may not greatly improve retirement satisfaction. Rather, it may be the factors that influence the retirement decision, such as health, income, and preretirement attitudes, that will determine adjustment. In fact, these factors, as well as preparation for retirement, have been associated with retirement adjustment (Sterns et al., 1994).

Health

Retirement is one of the experiences that is significantly influenced by health. Although health may not be the primary factor in the decision to retire, poor health is probably the most salient reason for poor adjustment to retirement. Healthier retirees have higher life satisfaction and an easier retirement transition than do unhealthy persons. The robustness of the relationship between health and satisfaction is maintained even when other factors, such as the nature of the retirement decision, are controlled (Quinn & Burkhauser, 1990).

Income

Another personal variable that influences adjustment to retirement is income level. Income is a significant predictor of retirement satisfaction. Researchers have investigated the importance of income for the retirement experience in two different ways. The *loss* of money in retirement has been regarded as a primary stressor in retirement. On the other hand, Maxwell (1985) found that life satisfaction was related to the *absolute level* of retirement income, as opposed to the level of income relative to preretirement income. Although the loss of money may be a stressor in retirement, what may be more important is the adequacy of the older person's present income. To adapt successfully to retirement, individuals need adequate financial resources in addition to the other factors discussed.

Attitudes

Attitudes toward retirement influence the retirement decision as well as satisfaction with retirement. Having a positive attitude toward retirement does not guarantee successful adaptation to retirement, however. For example, attitudes do not predict retirement satisfaction for women (Belgrave, 1988) or for Blacks

(Behling & Merves, 1985). Additionally, people with positive attitudes toward retirement are not always prepared for the changes that will occur with retirement. Behling and Merves (1985) found that White professionals were better prepared financially for retirement than were Black or Puerto Ricans professionals, in spite of similar attitudes toward retirement. What may be more important than a positive attitude is a realistic appraisal of the retirement situation (Beehr, 1986), coupled with adequate preparation.

Preparation for Retirement

People who plan for major life changes tend to be more successful in dealing with them. Because retirement is a major life change, it follows that those who are prepared for retirement will be better able to adapt to the retirement process. In fact, research has substantiated this proposition.

There are personal characteristics that influence the degree to which an individual is prepared for retirement. For example, research has indicated that persons with higher income levels are better prepared and have a greater number of resources to utilize in retirement. Regardless of whether or not an individual has assets such as a high income, active planning for retirement can be undertaken to ease the transition. Some of the potential benefits of planning for retirement are more financial equity, the possibility of a healthier lifestyle, the opportunity to explore new leisure activities, and the possibility of exploring alternative housing (Sterns et al., 1994).

CONSEQUENCES OF RETIREMENT

Another area of study important to researchers concerns the effects of retirement on postretirement activities and satisfaction. Theories include those proposing a large effect of retirement on subsequent life satisfaction, those that posit little effect, and those that propose that the effect is influenced by moderating factors (Beehr, 1986). Continuity theory proposes that attitudes and activities undergo a minimal amount of change after retirement (Atchley, 1976). Disengagement theory, on the other hand, posits that retirement is accompanied by an individual's withdrawal from his or her roles in society and society's withdrawal from the individual (Atchley, 1979). Finally, consistency theory states that the link between retirement and satisfaction is moderated by the degree to which a retiree's expectations concerning retirement are met.

The research findings concerning the effects of the retirement decision on postretirement satisfaction are mixed. Gratton and Haug (1983) state that, in general, research reveals no substantive evidence that women experience difficulty adjusting to retirement. Further, no consistent gender differences exist with regard to adjustment. A small proportion of retired women do experience dissatisfaction with retirement, often focusing on health, financial, and social resources (George & Maddox, 1977; Szinovacz, 1983).

George et al. (1984) found no evidence that a retiree's subjective well-being was influenced by retirement except in one sample of married men. In this sample, however, life satisfaction increased significantly after retirement, which counters the frequently held belief that retirement adversely effects the individual.

Some factors have emerged, however, that moderate the effect of retirement on postretirement life satisfaction. Consistent with the predictors of retirement, both subjective health and financial indicators often emerge as significant predictors of retirement satisfaction (Barfield & Morgan, 1978; Bengtson, Kasschau, & Ragan, 1977; Riddick, 1985).

POSTRETIREMENT EMPLOYMENT

The assumption often held by employers and workers is that retirement marks the end of paid employment. This is not always the case, however (Bass, 1995). Research on labor force participation rates of retirees indicates that work during retirement is more common than had been previously assumed (Beck, 1985; Parnes & Sommers, 1994). As a relatively new area of study, students and professionals interested in gerontology will find many avenues of research into the causes and consequences of postretirement employment.

A compilation of existing evidence results in the profile that retirees who work tend to be well educated, white-collar rather than blue-collar workers, self-employed, and have a positive attitude toward work (Duggan, 1984; Parnes & Less, 1983; Skoglund, 1979). Most of the existing research reveals a strong influence of financial variables (Beck, 1985; Duggan, 1984; Parnes & Less, 1983) and health (Beck, 1985; Hayward, Friedman, & Chan, 1996; Parnes & Less, 1983) on postretirement employment decisions.

There are a number of federally funded programs designed to deal with the employment issues of individuals aged 55 and up. Title V of the Older Americans Act of 1965 is one such policy, offering postretirement employment opportunities to eligible individuals. The Older Americans Act authorizes the Senior Community Service Employment Program (SCSEP), a federally funded employment program for individuals 55 and up. Eligibility for this program is limited to individuals whose annual family income does not exceed 125% of the federal poverty income guidelines. The actual dollar value is a function of the number of family members in the prospective applicant's household. Eight national contractors administer the SCSEP. These include (1) Green Thumb, Inc., (2) National Council of Senior Citizens, (3) American Association of Retired Persons, (4) National Council on Aging, (5) U.S. Department of Agriculture Forest Service, (6) National Urban League, (7) National Center on Black Aged, and (8) National Association of Pro Spanish Speaking Elderly.

CONCLUSION

The term "older worker" has taken on new meaning in the workplace. There is greater fluidity to the definitions of work and retirement than previously believed. Full-time work and retirement are not the only two options available. Although not yet fully embraced by organizations, work options such as part-time employment, job sharing, job redesign, and phased retirement are gradually being implemented. Early buyouts may be based on the mistaken belief that older workers may no longer be able to perform on the job. However, the buyouts may offer the older adult new work and retirement opportunities. All of these alternatives are useful to both the organization and the individual. Older individuals are able to expand their skills and grow beyond the period of traditional retirement age. Organizations are afforded the benefit of the older, experienced worker. At the same time, older adults have the option of continuing work or engaging in traditional and nontraditional retirement.

REFERENCES

Age Discrimination in Employment Act of 1967, 29 U.S.C. Sec. 621 et seq. (1976 & Supp V.1978 & 1986).

Arvey, R. A. (1979). *Fairness in selecting employees.* Reading, MA: Addison-Wesley.

Atchley, R. (1976). *The sociology of retirement.* Cambridge, MA: Schenkman.

Atchley, R. (1979). Issues in retirement research. *Gerontologist, 9*, 44–54.

Atchley, R. (1988). *Social forces and aging: An introduction to social gerontology.* Belmont, CA: Wadsworth.

Avolio, B. J., & Barrett, G. V. (1987). The effect of age stereotyping in a simulated interview. *Psychology and Aging, 2*, 56–63.

Avolio, B. J., Barrett, G. V., & Sterns, H. L. (1984). Alternatives to age for assessing occupational performance capacity. *Experimental Aging Research, 10*, 101–105.

Baltes, P. B., Reese, H. W., & Lipsitt, L. P. (1980). Lifespan developmental psychology. *Annual Review of Psychology, 31*, 65–110.

Barfield, R. E., & Morgan, J. N. (1978). Trends in planned early retirement. *Gerontologist, 18*, 13–18.

Bass, S. A. (1995). *Older and active: How Americans over 55 are contributing to society.* New Haven, CT: Yale University Press.

Beck, S. (1985). Determinants of labor force activity among retired men. *Research on Aging, 7*, 251–280.

Beehr, T. A. (1986). The process of retirement: A review and recommendations for future investigation. *Personnel Psychology, 39*, 31–55.

Behling, J. H., & Merves, E. S. (1985). Pre-retirement attitudes and financial preparedness: A cross-cultural and gender analysis. *Journal of Sociology and Social Welfare, 12*, 113–126.

Belbin, E., & Belbin, R. M. (1972). *Problems in adult retraining.* London: Heinemann.

Belgrave, L. L. (1988). The effects of race differences in work history, work attitudes, economic resources, and health or women's retirement. *Research on Aging, 10*, 383–398.

Bengtson, V. L., Kasschau, P. L., & Ragan, P. K. (1977). The impact of social structure on aging individuals. In J. E. Birren & K. W. Schaie (Eds.), *Handbook of the psychology of aging* (pp. 327–353). New York: Van Nostrand Reinhold.

Bessey, B., & Ananda, S. (1991). Age discrimination in employment: An interdisciplinary review of ADEA. *Research on Aging, 13*, 413–457.

Borgatta, E., (1991). Age discrimination issues. *Research on Aging, 13*, 476–484.

Bosse, R., Aldwin, C. M., Levenson, M. R., & Ekerdt, D. J. (1987). Mental health differences among retirees and workers: Findings from the Normative Aging Study. *Psychology and Aging, 2*, 383.

Britton, J. O., & Thomas, K. R. (1973). Age and sex as employment variables: Views of employment service interviewers. *Journal of Employment Counseling, 10*, 180–186.

Bronte, L. (1993). *The longevity factor*. New York: Harper-Collins.

Commonwealth Fund. (1993). *The untapped resource: The final report of the Americans over 55 at work program*. New York: Author.

Doering, M., Rhodes, S. R., & Schuster, M. (1983). *The aging worker*. Beverly Hills, CA: Sage.

Duggan, J. E. (1984). The labor force participation of older workers. *Industrial Labor Relations Review, 37*, 416–430

EEOC's expanding workload: Increases in age discrimination and other changes call for new approach. Washington, DC: U.S. General Accounting Office, February, 1994.

Edelman, C. D., & Siegler, I. C. (1978). *Federal age discrimination in employment law: Slowing down the gold watch*. Charlottesville, VA: Michie Co.

Fields, G. S., & Mitchell, O. S. (1984). *Retirement, pensions, and Social Security*. Cambridge, MA: MIT Press.

Fix, S. E. (1990). *Older workers*. Santa Barbara, CA: ABC-CLIO, Inc.

Forteza, J. A., & Prieto, J. M. (1994). Aging and work behavior. In M. Dunnette, L. Hough, & H. Triandis (Eds.), *Handbook of industrial and organization psychology* (Vol. 4, pp. 447–483). Palo Alto, CA: Consulting Psychologists Press.

Gagne, R. M., & Briggs, L. (1974). *Principles of instructional design*. New York: Holt, Rinehart, & Winston.

Gamse, D. N. (1994). Age equity in the American workforce. In *Mini White House Conference on Aging on Expanding Employment Opportunities for Older Americans*. February 7–8, 1995 (pp. 1–30). Washington, DC: Commonwealth Fund, ICF, Inc.

George, L. K., Fillenbaum, G. G., & Palmore, E. (1984). Sex differences in the antecedents and consequences of retirement. *Journal of Gerontology, 39*, 364–371.

George, L. K., & Maddox, G. L. (1977). Subjective adaptation to loss of the work role: A longitudinal study. *Journal of Gerontology, 32*, 456–462.

Gratton, B., & Haug, M. (1983). Decision and adaptation: Research on female retirement. *Research on Aging, 5*, 59–76.

Haefner, J. R. (1977). Race, age, sex, and competence as factors in employer selection of the disadvantaged. *Journal of Applied Psychology, 62*, 199–202.

Hall, D. T. (1971). Potential for career growth. *Personnel Administration, 34*, 18–30.

Hayward, M. D., Friedman, S., & Chen, H. (1996). Race inequities in men's retirement. *Journal of Gerontology: Social Sciences, 51B*, S1–S10.

Kingson, E. (1982). Current retirement trends. In M. Morrison (Ed.), *Economics of aging: The future of retirement* (pp. 98–135). New York: Van Nostrand Reinhold.

Kutscher, R. E., & Fullerton, H. N. (1990). The aging labor force. In I. Bluestone, R. J. V. Montgomery, & J. D. Owen (Eds.), *The aging of the American work force* (pp. 37–54). Detroit: Wayne State University Press.

Maxwell, N. (1985). The retirement experience: Psychological and financial linkages to the labor market. *Social Science Quarterly, 66*, 22–33.

McNaught, W., & Barth, M. C. (1992). Are older workers good buys? *Sloan Management Review, 33*, 53–63.

Mirvis, P., & Hall, D. (1995). Increasing the value of older workers: Flexible employment and lifelong learning. In *Mini-White House Conference on Aging and Expanding Employment Opportunities for Older Americans* (pp. 1–40). Washington, DC: Commonwealth Fund, ICF, Inc.

Palmore, E. B., Burchett, B. M., Fillenbaum, G. G., George, L. K., & Wallman, L. M. (1985). *Retirement: Causes and consequences.* New York: Springer Publishing.

Parnes, H. S., & Less, L. (1983). *From work to retirement: The experience of a national sample of men* Columbus, OH: Ohio State University, Center for Human Resource Research.

Parnes, H., & Sommers, D. (1994). Shunning retirement: Work experience of men in their seventies and early eighties. *Journal of Gerontology: Social Sciences, 49*, S117–S124.

Pifer, A., & Bronte, L. (1986). *Our aging society: Paradox and promise.* New York: W. W. Norton.

Quinn, J. F., & Burkhauser, R. V. (1990). Work and retirement. In R. H. Binstock & L. K. George (Eds.), *Aging and the social sciences* (pp. 308–327). San Diego, CA: Academic Press.

Rich, S. (1993, June 13). A grim outlook for retirement. *Akron Beacon Journal*, p. A12.

Riddick, C. C. (1985). Life satisfaction for older female homemakers, retirees, and workers. *Research on Aging*, 7, 383–393.

Rosen, B. L., & Jerdee, T. H. (1976). The nature of job-related stereotypes. *Journal of Applied Psychology, 61*, 180–183.

Rosen, B. L., & Jerdee, T. H. (1985). *Older employees: New roles for valued resources.* Homewood, IL: Dow-Jones-Irvin.

Rosen, B. L., & Jerdee, T. H. (1995). The persistence of age and sex stereotypes in the 1990s: The influence of age and gender in management decision making (Issue Brief No. 22). Washington, DC: Public Policy Institute.

St. George, D. (1996, January 28). Downsizing: The American nightmare. *Akron Beacon Journal*, p. A1.

Salthouse, T. A. (1986). Functional age: Examination of a concept. In J. E. Birren, P. K. Robinson, & J. E. Livingston (Eds.), *Age, health and employment* (pp. 78–91). Englewood Cliffs, NJ: Prentice-Hall.

Schrank, H. T., & Waring, J. M. (1981). Aging and work organization. In B. B. Hess & K. Bond (Eds.), *Leading edges: Recent research on psychosocial aging* (pp. 91–118). Washington, DC: U.S. Department of Health and Human Services, National Institute on Aging.

Schwab, D. P., & Heneman, H. G., III. (1978). Age stereotyping in performance appraisal. *Journal of Applied Psychology, 63*, 573–578.

Skoglund, J. (1979). Work after retirement. *Aging and Work, 2*, 103–112.

Sonnefeld, J. (1988). Continued work contributions in late career. In H. Dennis (Ed.), *Fourteen steps in managing and aging workforce* (pp. 191–214). Lexington, MA: Lexington Books.

Stagner, R. (1985). Aging in industry. In J. E. Birren & K. W. Schaie (Eds.), *Handbook of the psychology of aging* (pp. 789–817). New York: Van Nostrand Reinhold.

Sterns, H. L. (1986). Training and retraining adult and older adult workers. In J. E. Birren, P. K. Robinson, & J. E. Livingston (Eds.), *Age, health, and employment* (pp. 93–113). Englewood Cliffs, NJ: Prentice-Hall.

Sterns, H. L., & Alexander, R. A. (1987). Industrial gerontology: The aging individual and work. In K. W. Schaie (Ed.), *Annual review of gerontology and geriatrics* (pp. 243–264). New York: Springer Publishing.

Sterns, H. L., & Alexander, R. A. (1988). Step 6: Use objective performance appraisals. In H. Dennis (Ed.), *Fourteen steps to managing an aging workforce* (pp. 171–190). Lexington, MA: D. C. Heath.

Sterns, H. L., & Doverspike, D. (1989). Step 7: Offer well-designed retraining programs and encourage older workers to participate. In H. Dennis (Ed.), *Fourteen steps in managing an aging workforce* (pp. 97–110). Lexington, MA: D. C. Heath.

Sterns, H., Laier, M., & Dorsett, J. (1994). Work and retirement. In B. Bonder & M. Wagner, (Eds.). *Functional performance in older adults*. Philadelphia: F. A. Davis.

Sterns, H. L., & McDaniel, M. A. (1994). Job performance and the older worker. In S. E. Rix (Ed.), *Older workers: How do they measure up?* Washington, DC: American Association of Retired Persons, Public Policy Institute.

Sterns, H., & Miklos, S. (1995). The aging worker in a changing environment: Organizational and individual issues. *Journal of Vocational Behavior, 47*, 248–268.

Sterns, H., & Sterns, A. (1995). Health and employment capability of older Americans. In S. A. Bass (Ed.), *Older and active: How Americans over 55 are contributing to society*. New Haven, CT: Yale University Press.

Super, D. E. (1980). A life-span, life-space approach to career development. *Journal of Vocational Behavior, 16*, 282–298.

Super, D. E. (1983). Assessment in career guidance: Toward truly developmental counseling. *Personnel and Guidance Journal, 61*, 555–562.

Szinovacz, M. E. (1983). Beyond the hearth: Older women and retirement. In E. W. Markson (Ed.), *Older women: Issues and prospects* (pp. 93–120). Lexington, MA: D. C. Heath.

Warr, P. (1994). Age and employment. In M. Dunnette, L. Hough, & H. Triandis (Eds.), *Handbook of industrial and organization psychology* (Vol. 4, pp. 485–550). Palo Alto, CA: Consulting Psychologists Press.

Wexley, K. N. (1984). Personnel training. *Annual Review of Psychology, 35*, 519–551.

Willis, S. L. (1985). Towards an educational psychology of the older adult learner: Intellectual and cognitive bases. In J. E. Birren & K. W. Schaie (Eds.), *Handbook of the psychology of aging* (pp. 818–847). New York: Van Nostrand Reinhold.

CHAPTER 10

Religion and Aging

David O. Moberg

A substantial and growing body of reliable information demonstrates that religion is very important in the lives of the majority of older adults. This chapter summarizes and interprets research on the subject; it examines the important role and functions of religion in the lives of older people, benefits received from and problems faced in organized religion, theoretical applications, and intimations of needs for future research.

AGE DIFFERENCES IN RELIGION

The Gallup Poll has included questions about religion for over half a century, enabling comparisons over time as well as between subsamples of the population. One question it has asked since 1939 is "Did you, yourself, happen to attend church or synagogue in the last 7 days?" In February 1939, 41% of all adults answered affirmatively. The lowest figure, 37%, was in 1940. It then rose to the highest levels on record—49% in 1955 and 1958—and remained in the upper 40s until 1964 (45%). Then a gradual decline to 40% in 1971 is explained mainly by the reduced attendance by Catholics after the Second Vatican Council, and the national figure has fluctuated between 38% and 42% ever since.

There are large differences by age. In the typical year of 1993, for instance, only 32% of the adults under age 30 attended church or synagogue in a typical week, compared to 52% of those aged 65 and older (Princeton Religion Research Center, 1982, 1993–94). Most early Gallup polls used "50 and older" for the highest age grouping, but the same pattern of highest weekly attendance by the highest age group has consistently emerged.

Examples of findings from recent polls are given in Table 10.1, which shows that people aged 65 and older are the most likely to be church or synagogue

TABLE 10.1 Age Differences in Religious Variables

	Under 30	30–49	50–64	65 and older
Is a church/synagogue member (1993)	59%	68%	73%	80%
Attended church/synagogue in last 7 days (1993)	32	38	44	52
How often do you attend church or synagogue? (Dec. 1994)				
Weekly	23	26	38	40
Almost weekly	15	11	11	10
Monthly	16	16	16	16
Seldom	33	36	25	22
Never	13	11	8	11
How important is religion in your own life? (Dec. 1994)				
Very important	48	58	67	73
Fairly important	38	29	26	18
Not very important	14	13	7	7
Describes oneself as a "born again" or evangelical Christian (1993)	36	40	46	46
Which of these are you involved in? (1990)			Ages 50 and older	
Bible study groups	21	29	33	
Prayer and meditation groups	22	28	31	
Religious education classes	17	33	28	

Adapted from Gallup polls reported in *Religion in America 1992–1993* and its 1994 supplement, Princeton Religion Research Center, Princeton, NJ; Gallup Poll, 1993–1994; George Gallup Jr., *The Gallup Poll: Public Opinion 1994*, Wilmington, DE: Scholarly Resources, Inc., 1995; and David W. Moore, Most Americans say religion is important to them, *The Gallup Poll Monthly*, No. 353, pp. 16–21, February 1995.

members, have the highest religious attendance rates, are involved heavily in other religious groups, believe religion is very important in their lives, and have high proportions that call themselves "born again" or evangelical.

The most complete Gallup survey on religion with comparisons by age (Princeton Religion Research Center, 1982) shows that, compared to younger adults, people past 65 are more likely

- to believe that God loves them even though they may not always please him (94%).
- to try hard to put their religious beliefs into practice in relationships with all people (89%).

- to receive a great deal of comfort and support from their religious beliefs (87%).
- to wish their religious faith were stronger (84%).
- to welcome social changes that make religious beliefs play a greater role in people's lives (88%).
- to watch religious television (44% in the past 7 days).
- to rate themselves high for living a very Christian life (41% in the two highest of 11 categories).
- to have high levels of spiritual commitment (66%).
- to say that it is completely or mostly true that they "constantly seek God's will through prayer" (84%).

Older Americans believe (73% completely, 21% mostly) that God loves them even though they may not always please him, and 89% say they try hard to put their religious beliefs into practice in their relations with all people, including those of different races, religions, nationalities, and backgrounds. Over a third (36%) are involved in charitable or social service activities. They receive a great deal of comfort and support from their religious beliefs (58% completely and 29% mostly true). A strong majority believe in the divinity of Jesus Christ (75% completely, 18% mostly). Their self-ratings for "living a very Christian or a very un-Christian life" place 41% in the two most highly Christian ratings in the 11-point scale and 44% in the next three highest, higher than any other age category. They also have the largest percentage (23%) ranked as highly committed and the fewest highly uncommitted (5%) on Gallup's multidimensional Spiritual Commitment Scale. In spite of these high levels of religious faith, over half (52%) say it is completely true that they wish their religious faith were stronger, and another third (32%) say that it is mostly true (Princeton Religion Research Center, 1982).

The general pattern of highest religiosity among the elderly on almost all measures has remained the same year after year when similar questions are asked. They are confirmed by parallel findings from other national polls. For example, the 1993 and 1994 surveys of the Barna Research Group (Barna, 1994) showed that respondents aged 67-plus were more likely than young and middle-aged Americans to believe that the Christian faith is relevant to the way they live today (89%), that the Christian churches in their area also are relevant (77%), that they are absolutely certain they can count on God to take care of them in times of personal crisis (84%), that religion is very important in their lives (85%), that a person who is active in a church will have an easier time getting ahead financially in our society than one who is inactive (53%), and that local churches serve the needs of people very well (37%) or pretty well (31%), to mention but a few of dozens of its findings about religion.

Many research projects also have revealed the importance of religion among older people. Although limited by sampling problems, cross-sectional rather than longitudinal design, and other deficiencies, most have found that prayer,

Bible reading, strength of faith, religious beliefs, use of mass media religious programs, and other measures of commitment are higher in older than in younger age groups (see Agostino, 1987; Koenig, 1995; Payne, 1982). Stronger religious commitment helps to explain the large number of older people in many churches. In 315 United Methodist churches in Kansas, for example, 30.4% of members were past age 65 (Oliver & Carey, 1988).

Age-Period-Cohort Explanations

Any attempt to explain why senior citizens are more religious than middle-aged and young adults must consider the age-period-cohort issue. As discussed in chapter 1, differences by age are not necessarily evidence that aging in and of itself is the reason for the variations, so we must also take into account potential period and cohort explanations. One possibility is that the elderly generation experienced more religious training during early socialization (a cohort effect), but evidence on this subject is not clear. In the Duke longitudinal studies of aging, church activities increased in late middle age, then leveled off in the 70s, with a decline beginning at an average age of about 80 (Palmore, 1981). Despite the decrease in church attendance among the old-old that is associated with increased physical limitations and transportation problems, polls have persistently found the highest levels among those past 60 for over half a century. If higher levels of religiousness were strictly a cohort phenomenon, one would expect the pattern to change over time, each successive (younger) generation being less religious in old age.

The differences between generations could be a consequence of the period effects of having different kinds of experiences during the life cycle. World War I, the deadly flu epidemic of 1919–1920, the Great Depression of the 1930s, and World War II produced countless disruptions that strongly affected most older Americans. Events on the religious scene also influenced their beliefs, attitudes, affiliations, and activities. Not least among these were the revivalism of Dwight L. Moody, Billy Sunday, and thousands of lesser-known evangelists; the Pentecostal movement; the fundamentalist-modernist controversies; the Scopes trial; and the immigration of millions of European Catholics (see Moberg, 1984a). Yet younger generations have had analogous experiences, such as the changes associated with World War II, the wars in Korea and Vietnam, the assassinations of John and Robert Kennedy and Martin Luther King Jr., the Billy Graham crusades, the Charismatic Renewal movement, and the tensions related to such controversial public policy issues as the legalizing of abortion and religion in public schools.

Many sociologists have claimed that secularization (social change toward a nonreligious worldview, activities, and behavior) is advancing under the impact of modernization and technology. If it prevails, each generation attaining old age will have a successively lower level of religiousness. But secularization theory, best epitomized by the title of Barnes's (1929) book, *The Twilight of Christianity*, has fallen on hard ground, as evidence mounts against it (see Bruce, 1984; Finke & Stark, 1992; Hammond, 1985). Decade after decade, the age patterns revealed by research and public opinion surveys are very similar, failing to confirm the predicted trend. To date there is no evidence that the baby boom generation is an exception (Harley & Firebaugh, 1993; Princeton Religion Research Center, 1995).

Surprisingly, theologically conservative religious groups, which the secularization thesis considers the most obsolete, generally are growing, whereas most of those that have made the greatest concessions to the rationality and relativity of modernity are declining (Moberg, 1987). However distorted and deviant some of its forms may be, religion plays a prominent role in current events in America, Lebanon, Israel, India, South Africa, Iran, and elsewhere around the earth. Its expanding influence is strongly evident in the quiet spread of Islam and Christianity into new territories and in the creation and spread of countless new religious movements.

Secularization is intertwined with sacralization (increasing religiousness) in complex patterns of interaction and reaction. It is a useful sensitizing concept, but it should not be treated as the best way to understand religion in the modern world, least of all that of old people. It is less an explanation than something that needs to be explained in the context of cultural analysis of all symbols, landmarks, and boundaries of social life (Lyon, 1985). The web of period effects is so tangled that it is impossible to identify any specific pattern of events that could have made the oldest generation "more religious" than the others.

Therefore, the explanation that stands up best is that the aging process itself contributes to a deepening of religious concern in the later years, especially on the private, nonorganizational level. Yet to acknowledge that is not necessarily to have a firm grasp on the causal processes that are involved. Is disengagement from other responsibilities the cause? (Perhaps people have more time to devote to religion during retirement.) Are the elderly so obviously near the end of earthly life that they devote increased time to "preparing for their finals"? (Is there an existential fear of death and, as that inevitable event approaches, an enhanced desire to prepare to face one's Creator and ultimate destiny?) Have we been socialized or "programmed" by our culture to be busy activists until deteriorating bodies force us to slow down? (Does society teach us that religion is chiefly a compensation for those who are deprived and a comfort for those who cannot be "useful"—the deprivation hypothesis?) Is there within each person a longing for reconciliation with Deity or a desire for unity with God that is squelched by the pressures of life during youth and middle age but released by freedom from social constraints in late life? (Many Christians believe that this is a universal human desire, suppressed only when people allow "the world" to squeeze them into its mold.) Obviously, there is a need for careful research to test these and other plausible hypotheses, as well as for learning from personal reflection, conversations with mature adults, and interdisciplinary sharing of perspectives from various scriptural, theological, and philosophical worldviews.

Differential Survival

Another possible explanation of the higher levels of religiosity among the oldest generation is the variation in average longevity of population subgroups. As knowledge increases about such matters as psychosomatic illness and the ways in which stress and mental attitudes affect physical health, it is increasingly clear that wholesome lifestyles and mental orientations contribute to longevity. The 1981 Gallup Poll showed that people who had high levels of religious involvement and spiritual commitment were far more likely than others to say that they were very happy and extremely satisfied with the way things were in their personal lives, marriage and family life, housing, free time, standard of living, work, and community (Princeton Religion Research Center, 1982). People who adhere most strongly to conventional religious values are also the least likely to indulge in several kinds of behavior that increase mortality rates, including the use of tobacco and recreational drugs, alcohol abuse, sexual intercourse outside of marriage with its guilt feelings and dangers of an unwelcome pregnancy or a venereal disease, and the stress of divorce. They are more likely to have personal habits conducive to physical and mental health.

All who work in the field of aging "know older individuals who have a sense of serenity and peace that goes beyond the positive life review and may be related to a resolution of the existential problems we all must face, perhaps even a coming to terms with their Creator" (Thorson, 1983, p. 10). Frankl's (1963) reflections on his observations in and study of Nazi concentration camps concluded that those who were able to survive had an inner spiritual strength and will to live. Spiritual well-being thus seems to be an important source of both long length and high quality of life (see Moberg, 1979, 1986b).

This suggests the possibility that less religious people die earlier in life, on average, than those who are strongly religious. If that is the case, the higher proportion of religiously committed people in the oldest generation may result mainly from their outliving others. Research in epidemiology and other fields of medicine indeed suggests that less religious people are more likely to die before old age. For example, among White men aged 45 to 64 in Washington County, Maryland, the risk of dying from arteriosclerotic heart disease was 60% lower among those with weekly or more church attendance than in a control group of infrequent attenders who were matched for race, sex, and age. Among women, the relative risk of dying from arteriosclerotic heart disease was more than twice as great among the infrequent than the frequent church attenders. Infrequent attenders in the general population were 2.3 times as likely to die from pulmonary emphysema, 3.9 times as likely to die from cirrhosis, and 2.1 times likelier to die from suicide than the frequent attenders (Comstock & Partridge, 1972).

Berkman and Syme (1979) discovered that both men and women who belong to a church or temple have lower mortality rates than nonmembers, although social contacts with a spouse, relatives, and friends had a greater effect on mortality. Religious organizations benefit people as social networks giving support to their members. Yet in a study of 400 elderly residents of New Haven, Connecticut, church attendance frequency, self-assessed religiousness, and, most of all, the extent to which religion was a source of strength were all inversely related to mortality, especially among those who were medically ill. It therefore is not likely that the longevity benefits associated with religiousness are due exclusively to social contacts made through church attendance (Zuckerman, Kasl, & Ostfeld, 1984). They emerge from shalom—the serenity and well-being of being at peace with oneself, other people, and God.

Numerous other health-related conditions are associated with religious activity and commitment (Koenig, Smiley, & Gonzales, 1988). When ill, those who are religiously committed require less medication to control pain than do the uncommitted. They recover from acute ailments more quickly, have higher levels of subjective well-being, and more often benefit from prayer and other religious devotions that speed up the natural recuperative forces of the body (MacNutt, 1977). It therefore is possible that the lower age-specific mortality rates during youth and adulthood among people with a high levels of religiousness may explain much of the higher rates of religious observance found among elderly than among younger adults.

DIVERSITY IN RELIGION AND AGING

There are vast variations among older people from one social and cultural setting to another. Simmons's (1945) survey of primitive societies revealed that older men and women generally have been "regarded as depositories of knowledge and imparters of valuable information, as specialists in dealing with the uncertain aleatory element, and as mediators between their fellows and the fearful supernatural powers" (p. 175). At least five kinds of religious roles have been assigned to the elders of various societies (Cowgill, 1986): (1) magicians, including sorcerers, necromancers and witches; (2) prophets and fortune-tellers; (3) medicine men and healers using or alleging supernatural forces; (4) priests and other clergy; and (5) the roles assigned lay people who participate in religious rites and ceremonies as followers, celebrants, or supplicants in events like midwifery, christenings, infant purification, circumcision, initiation into adulthood, weddings, funerals, burials, cremations, arts and crafts, sickness, accidents, and natural or technological disasters.

There also is great diversity in religious beliefs and behavior by ethnicity, social class, denomination, and other characteristics. In America women rather consistently have higher levels of religiosity than men have, and Blacks consistently measure higher than Whites (Levin, Taylor, & Chatters, 1994). Churches are an even more significant source of social support and center of social life among African Americans than among Caucasians. They play a prominent role in the lives of older Black adults, who nevertheless display considerable heterogeneity in religious participation and attitudes. Multidimensional perspectives on religion therefore are at least as important for the minority as for the majority group. Both the private or personal emotional support, which helps to reduce stress, enhance self-esteem, and maintain positive mental health, and the public corporate role of churches, which positively influences the development of Black communities, are outcomes of Black religion (Smith, 1993; Taylor, 1993).

Because religious and secular concerns generally are less differentiated from each other in the Black than in the White community, its churches and religious traditions are integrated more fully with political and social concerns of the community at large (Chatters & Taylor, 1994). The national data on elderly Blacks show no decline in church attendance with increasing age despite increased health disability. Their subjective religiosity is significantly higher than that of younger respondents. The church is very important in their lives, but no evidence supports the deprivation-compensation theory that claims religious participation is merely a form of alternate gratification for people of low socioeconomic status (Taylor, 1986). Distinguishing between organizational, nonorganizational, and subjective religiousness also helps to correct the erroneous view that African American religion is homogeneously oriented, with little variation in the form, intensity, and pattern of religious involvement (Levin, Taylor, & Chatters, 1995).

Gitelman (1976) found that most older urban poor Blacks emphasize the importance of religion in their daily lives. Over three-fourths said they belonged to a church. Almost as many said religion was extremely important, and another one-fifth said it was important. Nearly three-fourths said they pray a lot. In contrast, more than three-fourths of urban poor Jews were not synagogue members; most noted that religion was not very important in daily life, and they had difficulty naming specific activities to serve, worship, or express their faith. Yet 85% of the Blacks and 76% of the Jews said that they either were more religious now than in their youth or that they had always been religious. Gitelman attributed the low level of Jewish religious practice to the removal of resources like kosher butcher shops, spiritual leaders, and synagogues from their neighborhoods. A midwestern study of Jews found that older men were much more likely than others to belong to five or more Jewish organizations and that elderly women had stronger religious commitment than younger women (Kart, Palmer, & Flaschner, 1987).

It is easy to overlook the wide variations in interests, abilities, backgrounds, and subcultural values among older people even within any given community. The 20-year gap between persons aged 65 and 85 years adds cohort and period differences besides almost a generation of age. The highest church participation rates in most American groups occur among the young-old (ages 65 to 75); attendance declines among the old-old as infirmities bring problems of mobility, hearing, eyesight, incontinence, and the like. Such findings seem to support disengagement theory. However, discontinued attendance at religious services seldom means that people have become less "religious," nor even that they are uninvolved in their religious organizations. Mindel and Vaughan's (1978) study of elders aged 62 to 98 (median, 77 years) in central Missouri found that about

55% did not attend religious services regularly. Yet despite those low levels of "organizational religiosity" (if 45% regularity is "low"), they had high levels of "nonorganizational religiosity"—listening to religious services on radio and television, praying, listening to religious music, and gaining help from religion to understand their own lives. Although they appeared nonreligious or "withdrawn from religion" by measures of participation in religious organizations, religion continued to be salient in their lives.

The Multidimensionality of Religion

To base generalizations about the place of religion in the lives of people on only a single indicator or "measure" of it is a common but serious error. As we have seen, the fact that attendance rates often decline among the old-old does not prove that religion has lost its importance to them.

Ever since Glock's (1962) seminal work, sociologists of religion often refer to "5-D religiosity," that is, five dimensions of religiousness: the *ritualistic* (what people do when they are being religious, like praying, attending church activities, genuflecting, tithing, singing, etc.), the *ideological* (religious beliefs), the *intellectual* (knowledge of one's own religion's history, scriptures, creeds, etc.), the *experiential* (feelings, sensations, and emotions involved with religion), and the *consequential* (effects of the other four dimensions on daily life). There are still more dimensions, such as the *communal*, which pertains to the association and fellowship of people with one another in religious gatherings (Fichter, 1969). Psychologists emphasize the contrast between *intrinsic* religiousness—that which is lived as the master motive of one's life—and *extrinsic* religiousness, used for selfish ends (Donahue, 1985). There also is a *spiritual* component that cuts across and infuses all of the dimensions (Moberg, 1967).

In addition to aspects of religion conventionally explored in social research, Williams (1994) suggests the importance of also studying variables like religion as a social support, religious rituals and symbols, the organizational climate of religious institutions, church architecture, and subjective religiosity, including motivations, tolerance of ambiguity, and spiritual well-being. Each of these poses problems of which indicators to use and how to measure their effects.

All of the dimensions and variables associated with religion overlap with one another in significant but complex combinations, permutations, and interactions that make it very misleading to classify people simply as "religious" or "nonreligious." (Indeed, if one defines religion as a person's ultimate concern [Tillich, 1959] or as one's relationship to God, everybody is either positively or negatively religious.)

Personal Variety among Older People

Denominational, theological, ethical, and behavioral differences provide thousands of possible combinations of religious traits and measures within and among religious groups. Variations in personal religious behavior, beliefs, attitudes, and ideologies reflect the cultural and religious backgrounds from which people have come. Not only are there important differences in the ways in which aging and elderly people are viewed between the Christian, Jewish, Muslim, Hindu, and Buddhist religions (Payne, 1994), but there also are significant variations within each of the various sects or denominations, and there typically are wide differences in the specific programs and activities oriented to older adults within their local congregations or branches. Some of these are related to social class, ethnicity, or race.

There also is great personal diversity in individuals' experiences of both aging and religion. To understand "the interior drama of human aging," one must get beyond the reductionistic delusion that examines only exterior phenomena that are reducible to statistical or scientific analysis and look also at the interior values and commitments of people that provide more complete knowledge and wisdom about the guiding forces in their lives. Intuitive introspection, insights from self-experiences, and the meanings in them that older people share provide some of the best resources for understanding the interior life experiences accompanying the aging process. Thus, "the vast . . . implacable unfolding of time into an irreversible never-again-to-be-recovered momentum of time [is] a kind of silent Signal of the pathos of aging" (Sittler, 1985, p. 167) to which we ought to be sensitive.

> Time involves relentless forward-leaning movement. The past is rememberable but not reversible. . . . Aging without a sense of infinite and implacable diminishments is not possible. . . . We should shape research models to the sobriety of the material. Let us try to fashion models that have the exquisite inwardness of the thing we are dealing with. . . . Old age for the reflective is a time of "coming to ripeness," with a kind of wry and godly sense of humor. Old age is beholding the truth about oneself, of the ambiguous actualities that underlie one's public reputation. (Sittler, 1985, pp. 168, 171–172)

Aging has been described as a spiritualizing process. In many cultures "the aging process is seen as *the* informing pilgrimage producing spirituality or wisdom" (Jones, 1984, p. 3). Even in the United States, "inner religion" (more than ritualistic activity) has increasing importance among older people. It leads to a "new" or deepened spirituality when people cope with such issues as (1) the anamnesis of remembering and discovering meaning in their past; (2) the sacramental evocation of sense from contemplation on minutiae of life; (3) the enfleshment and realization of the unity of all experience; (4) the contingency of death and the daily gift of life; (5) the ironic paradoxes and truth in apparent contradictions of meaning and experiences; (6) the instrumental and expressive importance of being, not only of doing; (7) the inner dialogical self-consciousness of conversations between the "I" and the "me"; (8) the trust of relationship in both prayer and silence; (9) the attainment of faith-filled (rather than fatalistic) trust through the resignation and detachment of "letting go"; and (10) other aspects of spiritual growth toward increased maturity (Jones, 1984).

The living histories, life reviews, case studies, and personal documents of aged people, along with many resources in literature, religious studies, philosophy, art, and the other humanities, can aid our quest to understand the multiple dimensions of religion and aging. As we recognize the rich cultural, religious, philosophical, economic, experiential, social, and other diversities in old age and apply the insights, knowledge, and wisdom gleaned from them, we will be immeasurably enriched.

ORGANIZED RELIGION AND OLDER PEOPLE

The champions of any given religion tend to notice and publicize its positive contributions to humanity and society and to ignore any negative effects. Meanwhile, its critics and antagonists do the opposite. In reality the actual picture is often mixed, and the impact on persons varies considerably from one specific instance to another.

Benefits from Organized Religion

The significant contributions people receive from their religious institutions are evident from much of the discussion above. Churches and synagogues have stimulated the personal faith on which spiritual well-being, with its accompanying benefits and satisfactions, rests. Religious ethics and the Bible are foundations for humane treatment of elderly people (Dulin, 1988), the historical source of many human services (Tobriner, 1985), and the ultimate moral base for many public policies related to their health, welfare, and social security (Moberg, 1980). Programs to provide food, shelter, clothing, medical care, emergency help, social opportunities, friendships, counseling, and other needs besides spiritual enrichment have been sustained by Christians ever since the diaconate was established in the apostolic church (Acts 6:1–7). Many churches help homebound members remain integrated in the congregation through regular visits by staff persons or lay volunteers. Some impart an uplifting sense of usefulness by engaging them in ministries of prayer, telephone reassurance, weekly bulletin folding, and other forms of serving.

A statewide Connecticut survey (Sheehan, Wilson, & Marella, 1988) found that the most common service programs for older adults were visitation of homebound, nursing home, and hospitalized constituents; transportation services; telephone reassurance; social/recreational activities; food distribution; education/discussion groups; support groups for caregivers; and self-help groups. However, 79% of the churches and synagogues contacted did not respond, and most clergy who did were not interested in educational programs on aging issues.

The clergy and other representatives of religion often are among the first to bring comfort to the bereaved, counsel to the distressed, and material aid during emergencies. Most people first turn to their pastor, priest, or rabbi when they have a social service need (Veroff, Kulka, & Douvan, 1981).

Many churches and synagogues provide information, referral, and recreational programs; transportation; home health care; cultural enrichment; opportunities for paid or voluntary part-time work; and other services, mostly distributed informally in the role of family surrogate (Koenig, 1995). Some are service-delivery channels for public welfare or health care (e.g., see Hendrickson, 1985–1986; Steinitz, 1981). The ways in which they can work with secular agencies to meet the human needs of older people are almost limitless (Tobin, Ellor, & Anderson-Ray, 1986).

People who frequently attend church or other religious meetings have larger non-kinship social networks than those who attend only infrequently. They also have a wider variety of emotional and social supports, more frequent face-to-face and telephone contacts with other people, and greater satisfaction with their social relationships (Ellison & George, 1994). The aged are more likely to find friendships and other resources that reduce loneliness through churches than through any other institution outside their immediate families (Kivett, 1979).

Older people gain numerous benefits through their churches. Research in two Chicago congregations shows that these include alleviation of the fear of death, companionship and friendships, a welcome into many social and religious activities, help in adjusting to bereavement, support during discouragements and crises, supportive reaching out when they are ill or have other problems, and satisfaction of the social and psychological needs to belong, to be valued, and to be understood (Gray & Moberg, 1977). The main contributions of churches to well-being in late life are a belief system centered around the Christian gospel, active roles that develop personalities, provision of social relationships, cultivation of positive attitudes and emotions, compensations to release tensions and anxieties, and a wholesome social environment. Those who are "closest" to the church (i.e., most strongly integrated into it) are the most likely to reap its benefits. Hence, "it is better for a person to become active in the church in his early years than to turn to the church and religion only upon meeting the problems of old age" (Gray & Moberg, 1977, p. 97).

The satisfactions and services older people receive help to explain why more are members of churches and synagogues than of all other voluntary associations (clubs, lodges, etc.) together. Even when church membership itself is omitted, older people's religiously based memberships exceed all other categories. In the 1974–1975 National Opinion Research Center (NORC) General Social Surveys, 49% were members of church-affiliated groups; 18%, fraternal groups; 10%, labor unions; 9%, veterans' groups; and 9%, hobby or garden clubs, to mention only the five most frequent types (Cutler, 1976). Belonging to church-affiliated groups was significantly correlated with overall happiness and life satisfaction; none of the other memberships were, nor even all collectively. Analysis of data for 17 types of voluntary associations from the 1972 American National Election

Study reached the same conclusion: only membership in a church or religious group was significantly related to life satisfaction (Cutler, 1976).

Problems Experienced in Churches and Synagogues

Sometimes religious organizations unwittingly erect barriers that make it difficult for many elderly people to participate in their activities (Moberg, 1982). These vary greatly from one congregation to another, but they include such problems as steep stairways, heavy doors, inconvenient toilet facilities, slippery or sloping floors, echoing or dull acoustics, small print in hymnals and lectionaries, dimly lit corridors, and difficult access to public transportation.

In addition to physical barriers to participation, the sermons, adult education programs, and special activities of many congregations are oriented mainly toward personal or family needs that are typical of young and middle-aged adults, not senior citizens. Except for the main worship service (usually on Sunday morning in Christian churches), most group activities and midweek meetings are held after dark, when many older people are reluctant to venture forth because of diminishing eyesight or fear of becoming victims of crime. Challenges to live out their faith often are applicable only in the context of social, work, or family roles they no longer play or of political and civic actions they feel incapable of accomplishing. They seek comfort from their faith more than the challenge that often is emphasized.

Participant observations, case studies, and interviews with senior members of two large Chicago churches of different denominations revealed many negative reactions to conditions within them (Gray & Moberg, 1977). Some felt that they had been pushed aside from meaningful jobs within the church, that they could no longer attend because of reduced ability to make financial contributions, that they were unable to dress well enough to fit into the congregation, that they were ignored or slighted, that changes in the church were detrimental to its ministries or to themselves, and that their wisdom and experience were spurned. Physical illness and transportation problems also kept some away from church activities. A similar negative impact of physical, economic, or social impairment on church participation is apparent also among many rural elderly people (Adams & Brittain, 1987).

Many older people are delighted with changes like innovations in worship styles, rituals, music, modes of serving Communion, dialogic sermons, and opening up to alternative interpretations of their faith. Others, however, resent such modifications, feeling deprived of the opportunity for "genuine worship" or believing that the changes contradict sacred traditions, dilute "true religion," or open the door to heresy. Theological deviations and moral compromises also irk those who "stand firm in the faith."

Youth-valuing stereotypes and myths about aging that demean old people sometimes are disseminated by the clergy and congregation leaders. Some of these become a part of the cultural baggage, self-fulfilling expectations, and self-images of the elders themselves. Fiscal policies and inflationary needs of religious institutions that lead to strong pleas for contributions embarrass members who are forced to reduce, rather than increase, their level of giving. The assumption that only younger adults are qualified for elective leadership positions demeans capable retired persons who have more discretionary time available to serve their religious organizations than they have ever had before. An emphasis on "family ministries" and youth as "the future of the church" similarly makes elderly singles, "empty nest" married couples, and widowed persons feel that they no longer truly belong and are being treated merely as "has-beens" awaiting their departure from this life.

Clergy Deficiencies

Elderly people who are shut-ins at home or in nursing homes often are neglected by their pastors, priests, and rabbis, who tend to devote more of their limited time for pastoral care to young and middle-aged persons who need counseling or are ill and hospitalized than to elderly members. An Indiana survey (Pieper & Garrison, 1992) showed that pastors have very low levels of knowledge about the social aspects of aging. Over half of their congregations had one-third or more of their membership aged 65 and over, but less than one-fourth had assistance programs to provide concrete help for elderly members. (Informal channels of help undoubtedly were present, but these tend to be haphazard, missing many people in need of support.) In addition, a tendency to concentrate on material, physical, and social needs in ministries for the aging easily leads to neglect of the spiritual ministries that ought to be a central focus of religious institutions (Moberg, 1986a).

Many clergy not only fail to understand the aging process but also are unaware of the contributions that even shut-in elders can make to their church or synagogue. Even though pastors have a higher level of gerontological knowledge than comparable reference groups (Gulledge, 1991), their ministries with and for older people are hampered by mistaken ideas about their needs, by ignorance, myths, and stereotypes about aging, by psychological barriers between the generations, and by accepting social values that identify youth, innovation, and newness with goodness, worth, and beauty. All of these negatively affect their ministry among older adults (Gray & Moberg, 1977; Gulledge, 1992). Most clergy do not realize that their effectiveness for ministry can be greatly improved by a gerontological strategy that satisfies both the expressive-emotional and the instrumental-pragmatic needs of elderly people in the context of their environmental settings, theological values, opportunities, and available resources. Besides, pastors can learn much to enrich all of their ministry through mutual interchange with older people (Cooley, 1989).

Some clergy, like those in other helping professions, are afflicted by gerontophobia, an irrational fear of one's own aging that leads to an unconscious avoidance of anything that might remind one of its inevitability (Bunzel, 1972). This desire to avoid thinking about one's possible future disability and distress contributes to the neglect of ministries with and for the elderly. It tends to become part of a vicious cycle, for pastors often are required to deal with older persons, their families, and their caretakers when their members have problems associated with Alzheimer's disease, mental illness, sickness, disability, housing, institutionalization, death, dying, or bereavement. As a result, most of the time they do spend with older people is devoted to those who are in the poorest mental condition, physical health, or social circumstances. That experientially biased sample reinforces the myth that all old people are disabled, dependent, or in other trouble. This impresses fear of their own aging process even more strongly into their unconscious minds and aggravates their gerontophobia.

Although sensitivity to older people and sensibility in meeting their needs are increasing among religious leaders, theological education, like that for other professions, has been slow to include gerontology. Many seminaries have added courses of study under the impact of Project GIST (Gerontology in Seminary Training) and other National Interfaith Coalition on Aging activities, the Interreligious Liaison Office of the American Association of Retired Persons (AARP), and the materials, conferences, and workshops of denominational and interdenominational agencies, but these typically are only elective, with small enrollments (see Carlson, 1985; Lewis, 1991; Payne & Brewer, 1989; Ziegler, 1980).

RELIGION AND WELL-BEING

Relationships between religion and various aspects of health have been explored in hundreds of social, clinical, epidemiological, and other empirical research projects. One of the first behavioral scientists to work on this was psychologist George Lawton (1943). On the basis of extensive counseling with older people, he listed trust in God or "health of the spirit" as second only to good physical health as a source of contentment in late life; it was more important than a cheerful state of mind, money, friends, a gainful occupation, pleasant relationships with family members, the satisfaction of doing things for others, and ordinary kindness and consideration from others.

Many studies from the late 1940s through the 1960s (summarized in Gray & Moberg, 1977) found positive correlations between religion and personal adjustment in old age. Church membership was correlated with good adjustment, but more focused research showed that this relationship was spurious. It was not a consequence of membership per se but of the intervening variables of religious beliefs and activities that are associated with membership (Moberg, 1951, 1995).

In the Duke longitudinal study on aging a lack of fear of death was associated with frequent Bible reading, belief in a future life, and religious conceptions of death. People who were widowed adapted with emotional stability supported by deep religious faith, and "religious activity and attitudes are correlated with happiness, feeling useful, and personal adjustment" (Palmore, Busse, Maddox, Nowlin, & Siegler, 1985, p. 457).

Most Hispanics in a San Antonio, Texas, survey of elderly persons were "quite religious," and 78% said their religious faith was "very helpful" in old age. Compared to other periods in their lives, 59% were the closest ever to God, 20% closer, and 17% just as close as in earlier periods of their lives (Maldonado, 1994). But a study of older Mexican-American men found that the main effect of church attendance on their positive life satisfaction was eliminated by removing the effect of health indicators, whereas for women attendance remained a strong predictor of life satisfaction even after taking the effects of health into account (Levin & Markides, 1988).

The predominant finding in all of the research is a positive relationship between various measures of religiosity and high levels of morale, life satisfaction, successful aging, health, and wellness during mature adulthood. Here are some examples:

- Data from a large National Institute on Aging study "strongly support the hypothesis that religious involvement [is] associated with better health" (Idler, 1994, p. xv).
- The intercessory prayers of Christian believers have significant therapeutic effects on the progress of hospitalized coronary care patients (Byrd, 1988).
- Faith in God and Christian living are among the leading "secrets" to health and a long life among people past age 85 (Hogstel & Kashka, 1989).
- The positive relationship between religion and subjective well-being is stronger among older than among younger samples in 28 studies on the subject (Witter, Stock, Okun, & Haring, 1985).
- Persons with stronger religious faith have higher life satisfaction and happiness than others (Ellison, 1991).
- A spiritual outlook helps elders to cope constructively with the vicissitudes of life (Marcoen, 1994).
- Religion is a bulwark of continuity that serves at least seven positive functions in the normal aging process of elderly Black Americans (Nye, 1992–93).
- Elderly Blacks have higher life satisfaction scores than elderly Whites, an association due mainly to friendships made through their churches (Ortega, Crutchfield, & Rushing, 1983).
- Church participation significantly relates to life satisfaction among African American seniors, and self-rated religiosity is a stronger predictor of life satisfaction than any of the other variables in the research by Coke (1991).
- Religious faith contributes to long and successful marriages (Robinson, 1994).
- Religion is an important resource for improving the quality of life of older people (Holt & Dellmann-Jenkins, 1992; Morrison, 1991).

- Among those past age 75, only health accounts for more of the explained variance in morale than religious behaviors and attitudes (Koenig, Kvale, & Ferrel, 1988).
- Elderly people with high levels of religious activities and beliefs are psychologically healthier than those with low levels (Morse & Wisocki, 1987).
- The use of familiar religious rituals, symbols, and worship patterns among mentally ill or impaired people has significant therapeutic results among Jewish, Catholic, and Protestant patients who were religiously active in the past (Ellor, Stettner, & Spath, 1987).
- Prayer in a daily program for mentally impaired Jewish elders has significant therapeutic value (Abramowitz, 1993).
- Religious coping is inversely related to depression (Koenig et al., 1992).
- High religiosity is associated with low death anxiety (Thorson, 1991).

The predominant findings of all the research "point consistently, though not unanimously, to a positive, health promotive role for religion" (Levin, 1994, p. xvi; see also Koenig, 1994; Koenig, Smiley, & Gonzales, 1988).

Spiritual Well-Being

Any attempt to develop a complete understanding of aging must include attention to the human spirit. Sturzo (1947), an Italian social scientist, emphasized that humanity is engulfed by the supernatural, the "true life" that surrounds the natural outward life, much as the atmosphere surrounds the earth. Hence, even those who deny the reality of the supernatural live within it and are spiritual beings. There are many evidences that human nature either is basically spiritual or has a very important spiritual component (Moberg, 1967). Because few of them are empirically observable according to positivistic criteria, skeptics rightly argue that one cannot prove this by "the scientific method." By the same token, neither can they disprove it by that method.

The National Interfaith Coalition on Aging (NICA) concluded that spiritual well-being is central to all concerns of "the religious sector." However, its members had a wide variety of implicit definitions, so a NICA workshop developed a working definition: "Spiritual well-being is the affirmation of life in a relationship with God, self, community and environment that nurtures and celebrates wholeness" (Thorson & Cook, 1980, pp. xiii–xiv). That definition and related research support the hypothesis that health of the human spirit is central to the well-being of the whole person. All valid indicators of spiritual wellness correlate positively with independent measures of mental, physical, and social wellness.

The most widely used research instrument to study spirituality empirically is the Spiritual Well-Being Scale developed by Paloutzian and Ellison (1982). Its results correlate highly with those from other measures and strongly indicate the benefits of spiritual wellness for physical and mental health (Bufford, Paloutzian, & Ellison, 1991; Ellison, 1988; Moberg, 1984b, 1986b).

The nursing profession has added "spiritual distress" to its diagnostic classifications (Kim, McFarland, & McLane, 1984) and conducted research on the subject. It has found, for example, that religious and spiritual resources help patients cope with cancer (Sodestrom & Martinson, 1987), chronic illness (Miller, 1983), hemodialysis (Baldree, Murphy, & Powers, 1982), and other diseases and treatments. The grounded theory research of Hungelmann, Kenkel-Rossi, Klassen, and Stollenwerk (1985) concluded that spiritual well-being involves a harmonious interconnectedness between self, others, nature, and Ultimate Other (God or Life Principle). It exists throughout and beyond past, present, and future time and space and "is achieved through a dynamic and integrative growth process which leads to a realization of the ultimate purpose and meaning of life" (p. 152). Spirituality is an important resource for the mental health care of older adults (Reed, 1991). Contributions nurses make to the spiritual health of patients are increasingly recognized within their profession (see Carson, 1989; Fish & Shelly, 1988).

THEORETICAL PERSPECTIVES

Relatively little attention has been given to major gerontological theories in the study of religion and aging. As already intimated, there is mixed evidence as to whether or not *social disengagement*, a progressive withdrawal from associations, responsibilities, and activities, occurs in the context of religion. Organizational participation tends to decrease among the old-old, but the religious memberships and faith of most people remain basically the same in old age, although many hold their beliefs and engage in private devotions with deeper faith. The Duke longitudinal study, for instance, found that the religious attitudes and satisfactions of aging subjects tended to remain much the same as they were 17 years earlier. Yet the correlations of religious attitudes and activities with happiness, feelings of usefulness, and personal adjustment tended to increase over time (Blazer & Palmore, 1976). This supports the hypothesis, consistent with sociopsychological functionalism, that the importance of religion for personal adjustment increases or is reinforced in the later years.

Activity theory is implicitly advocated by most religious leaders who work with the elderly. Denominational materials to aid their ministries generally aim to keep older people actively involved in congregational and community life through volunteer services, participation in social groups, and spiritual ministries of prayer, counsel, welcoming visitors, encouragement, and extending "the listening ear." There is no question but that this is wholesome for most older people. Yet to insist or imply that activism is the only appropriate mode of life for elderly members contributes to the "new ageism" (Kalish, 1979). It can be a form of tyranny, trying to squeeze everyone into the same mold instead of allowing indulgence in personal preferences for "merely passive" behavior like watching television, reading, meditating, or praying. If "nonactive" conduct is considered a symptom of maladjustment, or if "successful aging" is interpreted as requiring activity patterns more suitable to young or middle-aged people, feelings of disappointment and failure may be projected onto older people. As a result, activity theory may become little more than a subtle form of youth glorification (Bianchi, 1984).

The various *stage theories* of aging and the life course provide helpful descriptions of typical aging patterns. Differences between the age groups, some of which were reported earlier in this chapter, help to anticipate normal changes in religious interests and activities during the life cycle, but if these are built into rigid patterns of expectation that are normatively imposed on everyone as the way one ought to act, they also can become dehumanizing.

Many older people in effect operate on the basis of *exchange theory*, feeling that they must compensate tangibly for every service they receive from others. They are reluctant to accept the home maintenance services, personal care, transportation, and other aid offered by volunteers or friends in their congregations, feeling that they can give nothing in return. In fact, however, they can recompense such favors with nonmaterial gifts, such as their counsel, prayers, thankfulness, cheer, and willingness to listen to others and to share their personal life stories. When they recognize that they can give spiritual benefits to others long after their material giving has ceased, their self-esteem and sense of usefulness increases.

In many respects *continuity theory* is the best basis for predicting the religious life of people in their later years. What they already are, they increasingly become. Yet significant religious changes do occur and are most often toward intensified faith, almost never in the direction of diminished religious commitment. Most, if not all, of those very few elderly persons who are atheists and agnostics formed that philosophy of life much earlier, and some of them convert to religious faith during late life. (I know of no "scientific" work on this topic, but most mature pastors of Christian churches know such converts.)

The retrospective questions asked by Brennan and Missinne (1980) of 92 independently living participants at three congregate meal sites and a retirement village found no differences between current and "Have you always?" responses about belief in God (99%), the afterlife (93%, 91% always), and regular church or temple attendance (67%, 68% always), but there were significant differences on several other items:

	Now	*Always*
Do you consider yourself a religious person?	91%	72%
Do you pray or meditate regularly?	83	68
Do you feel accepted by the members of your church?	93	83
Do you belong to one or more church-related organizations?	59	72

These findings support continuity theory, but they also indicate a shift toward increased religious self-concepts, feelings of acceptance by church members, and more regular prayer or meditation, alongside diminished participation in church-related organizations. Yet the hypothesis that religious commitment tends to increase more than to decrease during old age needs to be tested through longitudinal research. There may be considerable differences between various religious subcultures.

Conflict theory is reflected in the intergenerational tensions (also associated with the alleged "generation gap" of *age stratification theory*) that occasionally emerge in religious circles. Sometimes elderly church members feel that youth receive too much attention, whereas youths think that old people control all decisions made in the church or synagogue without considering their interests. Half or more of the members of many congregations in old-line denominations are aged 50 and over; when that is the case, worship service attendance tends to be dominated by older people. In such a situation, youths often feel uncomfortable and drop out or go elsewhere. Young and growing congregations, on the other hand, tend to have high proportions of youths and young adults. The mature members sprinkled among them sometimes feel deprived of peer companionship in the congregation. Wise leadership is needed to deal with the power struggles that sometimes emerge in such situations.

Social support or integration (sometimes referred to as *social cohesiveness* and *networking*) is an important aspect of participation in religious groups. It is positively associated with physical and mental health, but the relationships between them are so complex that the crude measures used in much research cannot adequately explain the connections (Idler, 1994; Williams, 1994). Analysis of nationwide survey data shows that religious practice has a salutary effect on health above and beyond its role of social support among African American subjects but not among Whites (Ferraro & Koch, 1994).

Religion operates as a coping mechanism more strongly among Blacks than Whites. This supports the *consolation* or *comfort theory* that religion is a resource for handling structural, health, or other disadvantages or for dealing with real or imagined deficiencies and deprivations (Ferraro & Koch, 1994). Yet although religiosity tends to counterbalance or offset the deleterious effects of physical and mental health problems and of bereavement, there is no evidence that older Blacks turn to religion or increase their levels of religious involvement only when they confront stress. Their faith is a coping resource in its own right, not merely a result of seeking the social support it provides (Krause, 1992). This is consistent with Koenig's (1994) *theory of religious faith development*, which emphasizes that

> If the decision is to place God at the center of ultimate concern, then religious faith takes on a personal meaning that is vastly different from the meaning of faith associated with an imitation of others or a conformation to expectations of family or society.... Mature faith, then, is born out of adversity and involves action.... This type of faith is generally stable and may act as a source of strength, peace, and hope for persons in later life as they face the trials of aging. (p. 133)

Closely related to such findings is the *social deprivation* or *deprivation compensation theory* that people turn to religion mainly because of deficiencies like poverty, disabilities, health problems, discrimination, low self-esteem, and the like. A study of AARP chapter participants in El Paso, Texas, does not support it. Young and Dowling (1987) tested the extent to which nine variables influenced differences in both organized religious activities and private religious behavior. Poor health, low income, reduced activity, and living alone did not predict higher levels of nonorganized religious behavior among these mobile elders, as deprivation theory might imply. Strong kinship and friendship networks were related to high levels of private devotion, but firm religious conviction, rather than conventional sociological variables, was the best predictor of both private and organized religious behavior.

Obviously, all of these and other theories of aging have both merits and deficiencies. Theoretical development in the context of religion must move beyond limitations like those of the biological theories that generally are "tautological or empty formulations, tending merely to restate observations, or else insist on a partisan, unproved view" (Yates, 1985, p. 47).

CONCLUSIONS

We have seen that religion plays a significant role in the lives of older people. With only rare exceptions, it is highly beneficial, giving them many services and enhancing their life satisfaction and spiritual well-being. In an open society like America all who remain active in a church, mosque, or synagogue, as well as all who retain a religious faith, do so as a matter of choice, so questions remain. Have those who are outside religious organizations been harmed or "burned" by negative personal experiences or by the real or imagined hypocrisy found in them? Have those who remain had similar experiences, merely responding differently? Is a spiritual orientation to life the basic distinction that lies behind the contrasting reactions?

Although we have briefly summarized much of the research and theory related to religion and aging, we have hardly scratched the surface. The literature is already substantial and is growing in scope and quality (Kimble et al., 1995; Koenig, 1995; LeFevre & LeFevre, 1985). Yet it is difficult to locate because it is so widely scattered in the publications of numerous disciplines and professions. As a result, gerontologists who do not explicitly seek the reports of research on religion tend to perpetuate the error of ignoring the subject (see Thomas & Eisenhandler, 1994; Payne, 1986). The exclusion of spiritual well-being from the 1981 and 1995 White House conferences on aging, in spite of its importance to most older people and its significant role in the 1971 conference (Delloff, 1983), reinforces that neglect. Koenig's (1995) excellent annotated bibliography on 291 research studies from 1980 to 1995 helps to remove a prominent excuse for ignoring religion in gerontology and geriatrics.

Analysis of the reciprocal and interactive relationships of each gerontological theory to spiritual well-being during late life may become one of the most important developments in both qualitative and quantitative research on the role of religion in health. Accumulating evidence suggests that spiritual well-being is a significant source, if not the central core, of life satisfaction, psychological health, and holistic well-being (Moberg, 1986b; Seeber, 1990). It has therapeutic effects on physical health, ameliorates the suffering connected with sickness, hastens recovery from illness, and provides many other benefits (see Koenig, 1994, 1995; Koenig, Smiley, & Gonzales, 1988; McSherry, 1983).

"We know what's best for them" has long been an oppressive technique used to manipulate minorities, including many dependent older people. As we have seen, the religious interests and activities of senior adults tend to differ from those of most students, young adults, and professional people who study or work with them. The personal inclinations, preconceptions, and precedents of those who make and implement policy decisions unfortunately often are based more on their personal interests and concerns than on those of the people who are the objects of their actions. It is far better to consider first the religious (and other) interests, needs, and potentialities of older people and then to work *with* them, not merely *for* them, in all activities aiming to meet their needs (Ellor, Muncie, & Seicol, 1993; O'Connell, 1994; Sullivan, 1993). Religion and spirituality infuse all domains of human life, so they should be recognized appropriately in all areas of theoretical and applied gerontology.

There are important differences of opinion about the best ways to identify, define, investigate, and serve people's spiritual needs. Those needs overlap with and are served by religion yet are not limited to nor identical with it. Most religious leaders agree that spiritual health and thus holistic well-being is the ultimate goal that their faiths seek for people, however many and diverse the means used to attain it. Everyone who is aging and, most of all, those who work with elderly people in any professional or volunteer capacity should be aware of the central importance of religion and spirituality in their lives.

REFERENCES

Abramowitz, L. (1993). Prayer as therapy among the frail Jewish elderly. *Journal of Gerontological Social Work, 19*(3/4), 69–73.

Adams R. G., & Brittain, J. L. (1987). Functional status and church participation of the elderly: Theoretical and practical implications. *Journal of Religion and Aging, 3*(3/4), 35–48.

Agostino, J. N. (1987). Religiosity and religious participation in the later years: A reflection of the spiritual needs of the elderly. *Journal of Religion and Aging, 4*(2), 75–82.

Baldree, K. S., Murphy, S. R., & Powers, M. J. (1982). Stress identification and coping patterns in patients on hemodialysis. *Nursing Research, 31*, 109–111.

Barna, G. (1994). *Virtual America: What every church leader needs to know about ministering in an age of spiritual and technological revolution.* Ventura, CA: Regal Books.

Barnes, H. E. (1929). *The twilight of Christianity.* New York: Vanguard Press.

Berkman, L. F., & Syme, S. L. (1979). Social networks, host resistance and mortality: A nine-year follow-up study of Alameda County residents. *American Journal of Epidemiology*, *109*, 186–204.

Bianchi, E. C. (1984). *Aging as a spiritual journey*. New York: Crossroad.

Blazer, D., & Palmore, E. (1976). Religion and aging in a longitudinal panel. *Gerontologist*, *16*, 82–85.

Brennan, C. L., & Missinne, L. E. (1980). Personal and institutionalized religiosity of the elderly. In J. A. Thorson & T. C. Cook Jr. (Eds.), *Spiritual well-being of the elderly* (pp. 92–99). Springfield, IL: Charles C Thomas.

Bruce, S. (1984). *Firm in the faith*. Brookfield, VT: Gower.

Bufford, R. K., Paloutzian, R. F., & Ellison, C. W. (1991). Norms for the spiritual well-being scale. *Journal of Psychology and Theology*, *19*, 56–70.

Bunzel, J. H. (1972). Gerontophobia pervades U.S. life, sociologist says. *Geriatrics*, *27*(3), 41–49.

Byrd, R. C. (1988). Positive therapeutic effects of intercessory prayer in a coronary care unit population. *Southern Medical Journal*, *81*, 826–829.

Carlson, R. W. (1985). The Episcopal seminaries and aging: A survey of Episcopal seminaries and schools of theology as to teaching and training in the field of ministry to the aged. *Journal of Religion and Aging*, *1*(4), 1–11.

Carson, V. B. (1989). *Spiritual dimensions of nursing practice*. Philadelphia: W. B. Saunders.

Chatters, L. M., & Taylor, R. J. (1994). Religious involvement among older African-Americans. In J. S. Levin (Ed.), *Religion in aging and health* (pp. 196–230). Thousand Oaks, CA: Sage Publications.

Coke, M. M. (1991). *Correlates of life satisfaction among the African-American elderly*. New York: Garland Publishing.

Comstock, G. W., & Partridge, K. B. (1972). Church attendance and health. *Journal of Chronic Diseases*, *25*, 665–672.

Cooley, R. N. (1989). Learning from our elders: Education in a geriatric environment. *Journal of Pastoral Care*, *43*(3), 260–267.

Cowgill, D. O. (1986). *Aging around the world*. Belmont, CA: Wadsworth.

Cutler, S. J. (1976). Membership in different types of voluntary associations and psychological well-being. *Gerontologist*, *16*, 335–339.

Delloff, L.-M. (1983). The WHCoA and WAA: Spiritual well-being gets lost. *Generations*, *8*(1), 8–10.

Donahue, M. J. (1985). Intrinsic and extrinsic religiousness: Review and metaanalysis. *Journal of Personality and Social Psychology*, *48*, 400–419.

Dulin, R. Z. (1988). *A crown of glory: A biblical view of aging*. Mahwah, NJ: Paulist Press.

Ellison, C. G. (1991). Religious involvement and subjective well-being. *Journal of Health and Social Behavior*, *32*, 80–99.

Ellison, C. G., & George, L. K. (1994). Religious involvement, social ties, and social support in a southeastern community. *Journal for the Scientific Study of Religion*, *33*(1), 46–61.

Ellison, C. W. (1988). *Spirituality: Theory, research and application*. Unpublished manuscript, Alliance Theological Seminary, Nyack, NY.

Ellor, J. W., Muncie, M., & Seicol, S. (1993). *The development of spiritual awareness programs in long-term care settings*. San Francisco: American Society on Aging.

Ellor, J. W., Stettner, J., & Spath, H. (1987). Ministry with the confused elderly. *Journal of Religion and Aging*, *4*(2), 21–33.

Ferraro, K. F., & Koch, J. R. (1994). Religion and health among black and white adults: Examining social support and consolation. *Journal for the Scientific Study of Religion, 33*(4), 362–375.

Fichter, J. H. (1969). Sociological measurement of religiosity. *Review of Religious Research, 10*, 69–177.

Finke, R., & Stark, R. (1992). *The churching of America, 1776–1990: Winners and losers in our religious economy.* New Brunswick, NJ: Rutgers University Press.

Fish, S., & Shelly, J. A. (1988). *Spiritual care: The nurse's role* (3rd ed.). Downers Grove, IL: InterVarsity Press.

Frankl, V. (1963). *Man's search for meaning.* New York: Washington Square Press.

Gallup, G., Jr. (1995). *The Gallup Poll: Public opinion 1994.* Wilmington, DE: Scholarly Resources.

Gitelman, P. J. (1976). *Morale, self-concept and social integration: A comparative study of black and Jewish aged, urban poor.* Unpublished doctoral dissertation, Rutgers University, New Brunswick, NJ.

Glock, C. Y. (1962). On the study of religious commitment. *Religious Education, 57* (Research Supplement), S98–S110.

Gray, R. M., & Moberg, D. O. (1977). *The church and the older person* (rev. ed.). Grand Rapids, MI: Eerdmans.

Gulledge, J. K. (1991). Influences on clergy attitudes toward aging. *Journal of Religious Gerontology, 8*(2), 63–77.

Gulledge, J. K. (1992). Gerontological knowledge among clergy: Implications for seminary training. *Educational Gerontology, 18*, 637–644.

Hammond, P. E. (Ed.). (1985). *The sacred in a secular age: Toward revision in the scientific study of religion.* Berkeley, CA: University of California Press.

Harley, B., & Firebaugh, G. (1993). Americans' belief in an afterlife: Trends over the past two decades. *Journal for the Scientific Study of Religion, 32*, 269–278.

Hendrickson, M. C. (Ed.). (1985–1986). The role of the church in aging. *Journal of Religion and Aging, 2*(1–4).

Hogstel, M. O., & Kashka, M. (1989). Staying healthy after age 85. *Geriatric Nursing, 10*(1), 16–18.

Holt, M. K., & Dellmann-Jenkins, M. (1992). Research and implications for practice: Religion, well-being/morale, and coping behavior in later life. *Journal of Applied Gerontology, 11*(1), 101–110.

Hungelmann, J., Kenkel-Rossi, E., Klassen, L., & Stollenwerk, R. M. (1985). Spiritual well-being in older adults: Harmonious interconnectedness. *Journal of Religion and Health, 24*, 147–153.

Idler, E. L. (1994). *Cohesiveness and coherence: Religion and the health of the elderly.* New York: Garland Publishing.

Jones, W. P. (1984). Aging as a spiritualizing process. *Journal of Religion and Aging, 1*(1), 3–16.

Kalish, R. A. (1979). The new ageism and failure models: A polemic. *Gerontologist, 19*, 398–402.

Kart, C. S., Palmer, N. M., & Flaschner, A. B. (1987). Aging and religious commitment in a midwestern Jewish community. *Journal of Religion and Aging, 3*(3/4), 49–60.

Kim, M. J., McFarland, G. K., & McLane, A. M. (1984). *Classification of nursing diagnoses.* St. Louis: C. V. Mosby.

Kimble, M. A., McFadden, S. H., Ellor, J. W., & Seeber, J. J. (Eds.). (1995). *Aging, spirituality, and religion: A handbook.* Minneapolis: Fortress Press.

Kivett, V. R. (1979). Discriminators of loneliness among the rural elderly. *Gerontologist, 19*, 108–115.

Koenig, H. G. (1994). *Aging and God: Spiritual pathways to mental health in midlife and later years.* New York: Haworth Pastoral Press.

Koenig, H. G. (1995). *Research on religion and aging: An annotated bibliography.* Westport, CT: Greenwood Press.

Koenig, H. G., Cohen, H. J., Blazer, D. G., Pieper, C., Meador, K. G., Shelp, F., Goli, V., & DiPasquale, R. (1992). Religious coping and depression among elderly, hospitalized medically ill men. *American Journal of Psychiatry, 149*, 1693–1700.

Koenig, H. G., Kvale, J. N., & Ferrel, C. (1988). Religion and well-being in later life. *Gerontologist, 28*, 18–28.

Koenig, H. G., Smiley, M., & Gonzales, J. P. (1988). *Religion, health, and aging: A review and theoretical integration.* Westport, CT: Greenwood Press.

Krause, N. (1992). Stress, religiosity, and psychological well-being among older blacks. *Journal of Aging and Health, 4*, 412–439.

Lawton, G. (1943). Happiness in old age. *Mental Hygiene, 27*, 231–237.

LeFevre, C., & LeFevre, P. (Eds.). (1985). *Aging and the human spirit: A reader in religion and gerontology* (2nd ed.). Chicago: Exploration Press.

Levin, J. S. (Ed.). (1994). *Religion in aging and health: Theoretical foundations and methodological frontiers.* Thousand Oaks, CA: Sage Publications.

Levin, J. S., & Markides, K. S. (1988). Religious attendance and psychological well-being in middle-aged and older Mexican Americans. *Sociological Analysis, 49*, 66–72.

Levin, J. S., Taylor, R. J., & Chatters, L. M. (1994). Race and gender differences in religiosity among older adults: Findings from four national surveys. *Journal of Gerontology, 49*, S137–S145.

Levin, J. S., Taylor, R. J., & Chatters, L. M. (1995). A multidimensional measure of religious involvement for African adults. *Sociological Quarterly, 36*(1), 157–173.

Lewis, A. M. (1991). The middle-aging of America: Spiritual and educational dilemmas for clergy education. *Journal of Religious Gerontology*, 7(4), 47–53.

Lyon, D. (1985). *The steeple's shadow: On the myths and realities of secularization.* Grand Rapids, MI: Eerdmans.

MacNutt, F. (1977). *The power to heal.* Notre Dame, IN: Ave Maria Press.

Maldonado, D., Jr. (1994). Religiosity and religious participation among Hispanic elderly. *Journal of Religious Gerontology, 9*(1), 41–61.

Marcoen, A. (1994). Spirituality and personal well-being in old age. *Ageing and Society, 14*, 521–536.

McSherry, E. (1983). The spiritual dimension of elder health care. *Generations, 8*(1), 18–21 .

Miller, J. F. (1983). *Coping with chronic illness: Overcoming powerlessness.* Philadelphia: F. A. Davis.

Mindel, C. H., & Vaughan, C. E. (1978). A multidimensional approach to religiosity and disengagement. *Journal of Gerontology, 33*, 103–108.

Moberg, D. O. (1951). *Religion and personal adjustment in old age.* Unpublished doctoral dissertation, University of Minnesota, Minneapolis.

Moberg, D. O. (1967). The encounter of scientific and religious values pertinent to man's spiritual nature. *Sociological Analysis, 28*, 22–33.

Moberg, D. O. (Ed.). (1979). *Spiritual well-being: Sociological perspectives*. Washington, DC: University Press of America.

Moberg, D. O. (1980). Sociology of the aging and Christian responsibility. In C. P. DeSanto, C. Redekop, & W. L. Smith-Hinds (Eds.), *Sociology: Christian perspectives* (pp. 335–351). Scottdale, PA: Herald Press.

Moberg, D. O. (1982). Is your church an honest ally or a friendly foe of the aged? *Journal of Christian Education, 3*, 51–64.

Moberg, D. O. (1984a). *The church as a social institution* (2nd ed.). Grand Rapids, MI: Baker Book House.

Moberg, D. O. (1984b). Subjective measures of spiritual well-being. *Review of Religious Research, 25*, 351–364.

Moberg, D. O. (1986a). Spirituality, aging, and spiritual care. In G. G. Magan & E. L. Haught (Eds.), *Well-being and the elderly: An holistic view* (pp. 11–21). Washington, DC: American Association of Homes for the Aging.

Moberg, D. O. (1986b). Spirituality and science: The progress, problems, and promise of scientific research on spiritual well-being. *Journal of the American Scientific Affiliation, 38*, 186–194.

Moberg, D. O. (1987). The paradox of modern evangelical Christianity: The United States and Sweden. In R. F. Tomasson (Ed.), *Comparative social research: Vol. 10. Religion and belief systems* (pp. 47–99). Greenwich, CT: JAI Press.

Moberg, D. O. (1995). Applications of research methods. In M. A. Kimble, S. H. McFadden, J. W. Ellor, & J. J. Seeber (Eds.), *Aging, spirituality, and religion: A handbook* (chap. 37, pp. 541–557). Minneapolis: Fortress Press.

Moore, D. W. (1995). Most Americans say religion is important to them. *Gallup Poll Monthly*, No. 353, 16–21.

Morrison, J. D. (1991). The Black church as a support system for Black elderly. *Journal of Gerontological Social Work, 17*(1/2), 105–120.

Morse, C. K., & Wisocki, P. A. (1987). Importance of religiosity to elderly adjustment. *Journal of Religion and Aging, 4*(1), 15–26.

Nye, W. P. (1992–93). Amazing grace: Religion and identity among elderly black individuals. *International Journal of Aging and Human Development, 36*(2), 103–114.

O'Connell, L. J. (1994). The role of religion in health-related decision making for elderly patients. *Generations, 18*(4), 27–30.

Oliver, D. B., & Carey, L. (1988). A survey of aging and aging-related programs in Kansas area United Methodist churches. *Quarterly Papers on Religion and Aging, 4*(4),1–8.

Ortega, S. T., Crutchfield, R. D., & Rushing, W. A. (1983). Race differences in elderly personal well-being: Friendship, family, and church. *Research on Aging, 5*(1), 101–118.

Palmore, E. B. (1981). *Social patterns in normal aging*. Durham, NC: Duke University Press.

Palmore, E. B., Busse, E. W., Maddox, G. L., Nowlin, J. B., & Siegler, I. C. (Eds.). (1985). *Normal aging: 3. Reports from the Duke longitudinal studies, 1975–1984*. Durham, NC: Duke University Press.

Paloutzian, R. F., & Ellison, C. W. (1982). Loneliness, spiritual well-being, and the quality of life. In A. Peplau & D. Perlman (Eds.), *Loneliness: A sourcebook of current theory, research and therapy* (pp. 224–237). New York: Wiley InterScience.

Payne, B. (1982). Religiosity. In D. J. Mangen & W. A. Peterson (Eds.), *Research instruments in social gerontology: Vol. 2. Social roles and social participation* (pp. 343–387). Minneapolis, MN: University of Minnesota Press.

Payne, B. (1986). Religion in gerontological research, training, and practice. *Quarterly Papers on Religion and Aging, 2*(2), 1–8.

Payne, B. (1994). Spirituality and religious affiliation. In R. J. Manheimer (Ed.), *Older Americans almanac* (pp. 701–721). Detroit: Gale Research.

Payne, B., & Brewer, E. D. C. (Eds.). (1989). *Gerontology in theological education: Local program development.* New York: Haworth Press.

Pieper, H. G., & Garrison, T. (1992). Knowledge of social aspects of aging among pastors. *Journal of Religious Gerontology, 8*(4), 89–105.

Princeton Religion Research Center. (1982). *Religion in America.* Princeton, NJ: Gallup Poll.

Princeton Religion Research Center. (1993–1994). *Religion in America 1992–93 and 1994 Supplement.* Princeton, NJ: Gallup Poll.

Princeton Religion Research Center. (1995). The importance of religion intensifies as people grow older. *Emerging Trends, 17*(3), 4–5.

Reed, P. G. (1991). Spirituality and mental health in older adults: Extant knowledge for nursing. *Family and Community Health, 14*(2), 14–25.

Robinson, L. C. (1994). Religious orientation in enduring marriage: An exploratory study. *Review of Religious Research, 35*, 207–218.

Seeber, J. J. (Ed.). (1990). *Spiritual maturity in the later years.* New York: Haworth Press.

Sheehan, N. W., Wilson, R., & Marella, L. M. (1988). The role of the church in providing servicers for the aging. *Journal of Applied Gerontology, 7*, 231–241.

Simmons, L. (1945). *The role of the aged in primitive society.* London: Oxford University Press.

Sittler, J. A. (1985). Epilogue: Exploring the multiple dimensions of aging. *Journal of Religion and Aging, 2*(1/2), 165–172.

Smith, J. M. (1993). Function and supportive roles of church and religion. In J. S. Jackson, L. M. Chatters, & R. J. Taylor (Eds.), *Aging in Black America* (pp. 124–147). Newbury Park, CA: Sage Publications.

Sodestrom, K. E., & Martinson, I. M. (1987). Patients' spiritual coping strategies: A study of nurse and patient perspectives. *Oncology Nursing Forum, 14*, 41–46.

Steinitz, L. Y. (1981). The local church as support for the elderly. *Journal of Gerontological Social Work, 4*(2), 43–53.

Sturzo, L. (1947). *The true life: Sociology of the supernatural* (B. B. Carter, Trans.). London: Geoffrey Bles.

Sullivan, E. M. (1993). The importance of the human spirit in self-care for older adults. *Generations, 17*(3), 33–36.

Taylor, R. J. (1986). Religious participation among elderly blacks. *Gerontologist, 26*, 630–636.

Taylor, R. J. (1993). Religion and religious observances. In J. S. Jackson, L. M. Chatters, & R. J. Taylor (Eds.), *Aging in Black America* (pp. 101–123). Newbury Park, CA: Sage Publications.

Thomas, L. E., & Eisenhandler, S. A. (Eds.). (1994). *Aging and the religious dimension.* Westport, CT: Auburn House.

Thorson, J. A. (1983). Spiritual well-being in the secular society. *Generations, 8*(1), 10–11.

Thorson, J. A. (1991). Afterlife constructs, death anxiety, and life reviewing: The importance of religion as a moderating variable. *Journal of Psychology and Theology, 19*(3), 278–284.

Thorson, J. A., & Cook, T. C. (Eds.). (1980). *Spiritual well-being of the elderly.* Springfield, IL: Charles C Thomas.

Tillich, P. (1959). *Theology of culture.* New York: Oxford University Press.

Tobin, S. S., Ellor, J. W., & Anderson-Ray, S. M. (1986). *Enabling the elderly: Religious institutions within the community service system.* Albany: State University of New York.

Tobriner, A. (1985). Almshouses in sixteenth-century England: Housing for the poor elderly. *Journal of Religion and Aging, 1*(4), 13–41.

Veroff, J., Kulka, R. A., & Douvan, E. (1981). *Mental health in America.* New York: Basic Books.

Williams, D. R. (1994). The measurement of religion in epidemiologic studies: Problems and prospects. In J. S. Levin (Ed.), *Religion and aging in health* (pp. 125–148). Thousand Oaks, CA: Sage Publications.

Witter, R. A., Stock, W. A., Okun, M. A., & Haring, M. J. (1985). Religion and subjective well-being in adulthood: A quantitative synthesis. *Review of Religious Research, 26*, 332–342.

Yates, F. E. (1985). Knowing your age. *Journal of Religion and Aging, 2*(1/2), 41–53.

Young, G., & Dowling, W. (1987). Dimensions of religiosity in old age: Accounting for variation in types of participation. *Journal of Gerontology, 42*, 376–380.

Ziegler, J. H. (Ed.). (1980). Education for ministry in aging: Gerontology in seminary training. *Theological Education, 16*, 267–415.

Zuckerman, D. M., Kasl, S. V., & Ostfeld, A. M. (1984). Psychosocial predictors of mortality among the elderly poor. *American Journal of Epidemiology, 119*, 410–442.

CHAPTER 11

Long-Term Care

Ruth E. Dunkle
Cary S. Kart

Long-term care involves the provision of "one or more services . . . on a sustained basis to enable individuals whose functional capacities are chronically impaired to be maintained at their maximum levels of psychological, physical and social well-being" (Brody, 1984). Individuals can receive such services at home, in community-based agencies, or within an institutional setting. Typically, long-term care is evoked when an individual is functionally disabled enough to require assistance in two or more activities of daily living. Long-term care services may provide diagnostic, preventive, therapeutic, rehabilitative, supportive, and/or maintenance care. The goals of long-term care involve a three-pronged strategy: (1) to delay the onset of preventable disease in healthy adults, (2) to lengthen the period of functional independence in those elderly with chronic disease, and (3) to improve the quality of later life.

Long-term care is actually a hybrid, part health care and part social service, in which individual functioning is the key (Kane & Kane, 1987). Services can be continuous or intermittent and delivered over an extended period. It is impossible to consider all aspects of long-term care in a short chapter such as this. Of necessity, the presentation will be limited in several ways. First, we discuss service needs and their assessment, as well as patterns of service utilization in the elderly population. Second, we describe selected types of noninstitutional services. Third, we discuss briefly the actual risks of an older person's being institutionalized, the decision to institutionalize, and the effects institutionalization may have on the aged individual. Finally, selected policy issues related to long-term care are briefly examined.

ASSESSING SERVICE NEEDS AND PATTERNS OF SERVICE UTILIZATION

The U.S. National Center for Health Statistics estimates 1.7 million elderly in nursing homes at any given time (U.S. Bureau of the Census, 1994). This represents approximately 5.3% of the elderly population. It is generally believed that some additional number of elderly living in the community are homebound with functional deficits comparable to those seen in institutions, although estimates vary widely. Kemper, Applebaum, and Harrigan (1987) estimate this number at an additional 10%. Liu and Manton (1987) argue that for every one elderly person in a nursing home, four more are in the community, bedfast or homebound, and as functionally impaired as those in institutions. Although the help needed by older people living in the community varies greatly, anywhere from 12% to 40% may require some kind of supportive services (Manton, 1989). The Pepper Commission (1990) estimates that between 9 and 11 million additional Americans of all ages are at risk for needing long-term care services.

Functional ability is a key to defining the need for long-term care (Kane & Kane, 1987). Emphasis on functioning shifts the focus away from a disease or chronic condition itself and toward the behavioral consequences of that condition. Deficient functional capacities are viewed as relating directly to the need for assistance, usually from another person, in basic activities of daily living (Katz, 1983). Currently, about 7 million elderly are limited in activities of daily living (ADLs, e.g., eating, dressing, and bathing) or instrumental activities of daily living (IADLs, e.g., preparing meals, shopping, and doing light housework). A little more than 3 million of these older people are severely disabled (in need of assistance in three or more ADLs), with approximately 4 million suffering from significant mental health problems as well (Pepper Commission, 1990).

Data from National Health Interview Surveys, including the 1984 Supplement on Aging (SOA) covering 16,000 respondents 55 years of age and older, demonstrate the high functional dependency rates of the oldest old. Almost three times as many people aged 85 and over as those in the 65 to 74 group report needing help with IADLs (59.7% vs. 20.5%) and ADLs (49.5% vs. 17.2%). Also, women, those with family incomes under $15,000, non-Whites, and those residing in central city or rural areas report needing the greatest assistance with both IADLs and ADLs.

Does every individual who needs assistance with IADLs and ADLs receive it? Unfortunately not. Translating needs into services can be a complex issue. Models of long-term care service delivery to the aged are relatively scarce. The bulk of evidence on efforts to evaluate systems of long-term care is derived from approximately 20 demonstration projects conducted since 1970 (Kane & Kane, 1987). Generally, these projects support the importance of a careful targeting of services to those most in need, the importance of maintaining informal support during the delivery of formal support services, and the potential use of case management.

Simply creating services and making them available is not enough to ensure that they are utilized, however. People must perceive a need and feel that the service is worth pursuing. How older people choose the long-term care services they will use is determined by a complex set of interacting personal and environmental factors (McAuley & Blieszner, 1985). Personal factors include demographic, psychological, economic, and health-related characteristics. Environmental issues relate to the availability of informal support and community and institutional services (Deimling & Poulshock, 1985; Murtaugh & Frieman, 1995).

Although researchers have identified predictors of institutional versus home-based long-term care, few have examined how older people might select among various types of long-term care services. Stoller (1982) asked elderly persons living in the community what they would do if they were ill and needed constant care. Most frequently mentioned was the nursing home; 30% could offer no strategy for obtaining care. Dunkle, Coulton, Mackintosh, and Goode (1982) found that a majority of hospitalized elderly with long-term care needs had no idea what services were available in their own communities. Lack of knowledge about resources and services reduces the search for knowledge about what services exist (Silverstein, 1984). In addition, knowledge about services does not mean that people are able to see the connection to their own needs. Older people may simply not know how to negotiate receiving services from agencies.

A body of research suggests that presence of family may be an important factor in delaying, if not preventing, the institutionalization of a chronically ill elderly person (Morrow-Howell, Proctor, & Berg-Werner, 1993). Still, we really do not know enough about the views toward various long-term care arrangements held by family members of the elderly who are prospective consumers of such services. We do not know if the views of the elderly and their family members differ with regard to the perceived efficacy of these various arrangements (Neu, 1982) or even if congruence of view is related in any way to successful outcomes for the elderly person. However, we suspect that such congruence would contribute to a successful outcome in any long-term care arrangement.

THE DUALITY OF INFORMAL AND FORMAL SUPPORTS

Families provide the main support to their elders in the community who are in need of care, but these family members do not provide this care in isolation. Many formal service organizations as well as numerous informal supports are called into play to help. The help may be for the care receiver, and at times it is for the caregiver as well. Litwak (1985) argues that the needs of the frail and vulnerable elderly are best met if there is a proper balance between formal and informal support, with each system performing the tasks for which it is best suited. Four predisposing factors affect the likelihood of a mixed helper network: advanced age, living alone, being non-White, and poor functional capacity (Bass & Noelker, 1987; Soldo, Wolf, & Agree, 1986). It appears to be not just level of need but the nature of the need that affects the structure and composition of the care network (Soldo, Agree, & Wolf, 1989).

Barbara Silverstone (1985) describes the informal support system as "a rich fabric of informal relationships which envelopes the majority of elders in our society along a number of dimensions. This fabric is bonded most strongly by marriage, and adjacent generational and peer relationships and for racial minorities, by expanded kin as well" (p. 156). Various family members are involved in caregiving, depending on the type of help required. For instance, the main source of support for the bedfast and homebound is the husband or wife of the invalid. When children are available, they provide a second important source of help. Childless elders rely on other sources of informal support. It needs to be acknowledged that caregiving research has not explored caregiving with other types of family members to any great degree.

Informal helpers are instrumental in community care arrangements but are also active in formal settings as well. They participate in the decision to institutionalize their relative (Townsend & Poulshock, 1986) and provide food, clothes, and toiletries for the elder after institutionalization (Dobrof & Litwak, 1981). The balance of the formal and informal involvement may shift over time (Moroney, 1986), but to date, with the use of cross-sectional data, we do not know.

It has been shown that African Americans more readily rely on informal services (Chatters, Taylor, & Jackson, 1986; Gibson & Jackson, 1989). This group has a range of choices for informal helpers, such as siblings, relatives, friends, and neighbors (Chatters et al., 1986). Even with these sources of aid, questions have been raised about the adequacy of family and friends to meet the needs of elders who are chronically ill (Chadiha, Proctor, Morrow-Howell, Darkwa, & Dore, 1994).

Several researchers have noted that health, function, and care conditions of the caregiver influence use of formal services. Noelker and Bass (1989) note that it is the caregiver's needs measured by restriction in activity, own health, and perceived burden that predict the probability of formal care augmentation. Soldo and Myllyluoma (1983) and Brody and Schoonover (1986) found that the work status of adult offspring also affects the likelihood of formal service use by informal helpers.

Although the continuum that defines long-term care is skewed toward formal institutional services, the trend in the United States is to bolster formal community at-home services through regulation of the institutional services. The Omnibus Reconciliation Act regulations (Eichmann, Griffin, Lyons, Larson, & Finkel, 1992) exemplify this trend as they mandate the placement of dependent and disabled individuals of all ages in the least restrictive environments possible. There is no doubt that there is a growing demand for deinsitutionalization. However, as with the deinstitutionalization movement of the 1960s, the needed community-based support services are slow to develop, delivery is fragmented, financing is complicated, and outcomes remain unmeasured (Dunkle & Stone, 1995).

Community-Based Care

Most impaired elders live in the community and receive care there (Doty, 1986). It is generally recognized that family and other informal supports frequently have difficulty providing help on a long-term basis to elders who are impaired and disabled. Emotional, physical, and financial strains appear to be associated with personal and situational characteristics of the caregiver, with emotional strain seemingly the hardest to bear. Isolation of a caregiver, as well as a decrease in emotional resilience and morale, may provoke many elderly persons and their families to turn to formal service providers for help.

The array of services that are available to older people outside institutions covers a broad range, including health, housing, and nutrition. Services have been designed to aid the informal caregiving structure. How these services are organized and delivered is the result of a complex web of policy and financial issues. Below, some existing formal services are identified to help define the range of services available. Many communities have a substantial number of these services; however, only a limited number of communities are able to provide a complete set of services. By no means is the list all-inclusive. Community-based services are presented in order of most to least restrictive.

Adult Day Care

The term *day care* applies to any service provided during the day. Such services range from social to health-related care, home care to hospital care, and include rehabilitation as well as physical and mental health care (Harder, Gornick, & Burt, 1986). Day care is a unique service modality because it meets the long-term care needs of people while allowing for individual differences. These tailor-made services can have a therapeutic objective of prevention, rehabilitation, or maintenance. Day care can be used to provide respite for caregivers as well.

A study by Weissert, Wan, Livieratos, and Katz (1980) is the major experiment in adult day care done in the United States. Clients met Medicare requirements for skilled care before being randomly assigned to day care coverage or a control group. The results were disappointing. While it appeared that day care participants used fewer inpatient hospital services than controls and had fewer nursing home admissions and days spent in such care, the differences were not significant after controlling for baseline characteristics.

Home Health Care

Home health care is service provided to individuals and their families in their home for the purpose of promoting, maintaining, or restoring health or for maximizing the level of independence (Strahan, 1993). Guidelines for these services were developed around the Medicare regulations, a major third-party payer for these services (Fairchild, Knebl, & Burgos, 1995). Patients receiving home health care "must be homebound, need intermittent care, be able to show evidence of recovery, and need either skilled nursing or physical therapy" (Estes, Swan, & Associates, 1993, p. 147).

Services range from a physician's care at one end of the continuum to volunteer or low-wage companions in the home at the other end. Much home health care consists of services to compensate for functional impairments. The provision of home care may aid the elderly person in the performance of ADLs that are essential for maintaining independence. The most frequently provided services are nursing, personal care, and infusion therapy (Marion Merrel Dow, 1993).

Research findings on the effectiveness of home health care services are mixed. Some studies support the fact that home health care reduces the need for institutional care and is less costly (Harrow, Tennstedt, & McKinlay, 1995). Hughes, Cordray, and Spiker (1984) found no difference in mortality and hospitalization rates when 122 experimental subjects served by a hospital-based program of coordinated home health services were compared with a control group of 123 clients of an Administration on Aging Title III program. Interestingly, home care was also associated in this study with increased subjective perception of good health, decreased ADL capacity, and increased use of other community services. The authors report costs for the experimental group to be 20% higher than for the controls, although this figure is skewed by a few high-cost users.

Foster Care

Foster family care approximates the normal living environment with the added dimension of supervision. Relatively new in its application to adults, foster care allows the older person an element of privacy as well as freedom not possible in the larger protected environment of the nursing home. Adult foster care is considered among the least restrictive housing options available to help older persons remain in the community. It utilizes private residences for the care of a nonrelated elderly person who is in need of supervision and/or assistance with ADLs. Definitions of foster care vary from state to state.

Certain problems are inherent in the provision of adult foster care. For example, unlike foster care for children, where the child moves toward independence and gains the capacity to contribute to the foster family, the elderly person is often viewed as moving only toward greater dependence. As a result, many potential care providers are reluctant to offer their foster homes to the elderly.

The adequacy of the match between the individual and the environment is important to foster care outcomes. In a national survey of residential care homes

(RCHs) and a five-state survey of RCHs and their elderly residents, Mor, Sherwood, and Gutkin (1986) found the adequacy of the match to be strongly related to residents' reported satisfaction and negatively related to functional impairment, incontinence, or high personal care needs.

Board and Care Homes

The likelihood of being able to live independently decreases with age. One service on the long-term care continuum that has received more attention of late is the board-and-care home, a facility that provides shelter, food, and protection to frail and disabled individuals (Subcommittee on Health and Long Term Care, 1989). Sixty-eight thousand Americans currently reside in licensed and unlicensed board-and-care homes. The majority of residents are female and old. Although more than half of the residents had been discharged from state mental hospitals, 78% were found to be suffering from a mental illness (Subcommittee on Health and Long Term Care, 1989).

Hospice

Hospice is a concept of care for the terminally ill that is gaining popularity in the United States. More than a program of medical health care for the terminally ill, it is a model of care that can be delivered in several forms. Typically, these services are directed by a physician, who oversees an interdisciplinary team providing psychological, social, and spiritual services when needed by the patient and/or family members on a 24-hour, 7-day-a-week basis. Services can continue for family and friends after the patient's death. The average patient is 74 years old, White, and a cancer victim. About 10% of hospice patients suffer from other life-threatening illness (Dunkle & Stone, 1995).

The National Hospice Study used a quasi-experimental design to compare hospital-based and home-based hospice care with conventional care in 40 sites across the country (Greer et al., 1986). Basically, no differences were found between experimental and control groups on variables such as pain control, affect, or symptoms. Where significant differences did occur, they tended to be in levels of satisfaction expressed by the family caregivers.

Protective Services

The primary functions of protective services include receiving and investigating reports or referrals; coordinating or providing services to prevent, correct, or alleviate injury or harm; and seeking legal intervention in the form of surrogate decision making for the incapacitated adult or criminal penalty for the abused (Anetzberger, 1995). Protective or surrogate services consist of visits by a social worker, along with supplemental community services provided by visiting nurses, homemakers, clinical services, meals, telephone checks, and transportation. A myriad of needs are addressed under protective services, including daily living, physical health, psychosocial problems, household management, housing, economic management, and legal protection. These services are similar to those delivered through the social service delivery system, although their effects may vary due to the potential for legal intervention in the form of guardianship, conservatorship, placement, and/or commitment and emergency services.

Adult protective services may be particularly useful in cases of elder abuse because the population needing long-term care is vulnerable to abuse, neglect, and exploitation (Wolf & Pillemer, 1989). The needs of abuse victims are similar to elders needing long-term care, but there are major differences in the areas of physical and emotional abuse, which are more likely to happen to functionally independent but emotionally distraught older people (Wolf, Godkin, & Pillemer, 1986). Victims of caregiver neglect as well as self-neglect are more likely to be physically and emotionally impaired (Fabian & Rathbone-McCuan, 1992). Seventy percent of protective services situations concern elderly people (National Aging Resource Center on Elder Abuse, 1990), with self-neglect being the most common form of abuse, followed by caregiver neglect.

Respite Care

Respite care offers support to family caregivers so that they can continue to provide care for the frail elderly (Pepper Commission, 1990). The characteristic feature is that the care enables family members to get relief from caregiving responsibilities. There is clear evidence that families express a need for respite care and that it may prevent or delay institutionalization (Kane & Kane, 1987). Even with these noted advantages, respite care is not widely available to families caring for disabled elders, and according to Kane and Kane, evaluative research must be considered preliminary at best.

There are four models of respite care: (1) home-based, (2) group day care, (3) group residential care, and (4) residential programs providing respite care as an adjunct service (Upshur, 1983). Home-based respite care uses trained sitters who provide the service in the client's home and who are matched with the appropriate family. Residential care involves a residential facility that is established to provide respite care to small groups of disabled persons (Upshur, 1983). More intensive care can be given in this setting to medically and behaviorally difficult clients. These services, while offered in a facility designed and staffed for short stays, can also be given on an adjunct basis.

THE LOGIC OF INSTITUTIONAL CARE

It is in the hospital setting that many older people make decisions about long-term care services. When the hospitalization is associated with physical or mental impairment, plans must often be made for some other type of long-term care.

A sense of urgency typically accompanies discharge from the hospital, and this may interfere with usual patterns of problem solving. Moreover, the extent to which the elderly patient participates in arriving at a decision may be limited by the circumstances under which the plans are made (Brody, 1984).

Hospitals serve more elderly persons than any other community agency. About 20% of all older people use inpatient facilities at least once a year. Based on discharge data for 1992, hospital stays are 126% higher for patients 65 years of age and older than they are for people of all ages and average 44% longer, consuming a total of 33% of total hospital bed days in the U.S. health care system (U.S. Bureau of the Census, 1994).

Although most Americans fear and resist living in a nursing home; the reality is that most will not live in one. Only about 5% of the old find themselves in institutions on any given day (U.S. Bureau of the Census, 1991); two thirds of aged Americans will never reside in a long-term care facility (Gratton, 1986).

Nursing homes provide long-term institutional care, but this arrangement is not the only one. With changes in the way health care for the aged is financed, developments in medical technology as well as the delivery of care and the recent prominence of issues of bioethics and aging, nursing homes are now viewed as just one point on a continuum of long-term care service options in the community (Evans & Welge, 1991).

The Risk of Institutionalization

Of the 9–11 million Americans at risk for needing long-term care, services (Pepper Commission, 1990), two thirds are old. Functional health status is an important predictor of nursing home placement (Wolinsky, Callahan, Fitzgerald, & Johnson, 1992), with an almost linear relationship between number of dependencies in ADLs and risk of institutionalization (Hing & Bloom, 1991).

Five percent of the elderly reside in an institution on any day (U.S. Bureau of the Census, 1991); an additional 10% live in the community but are as functionally impaired as those in institutions (Kemper et al., 1987). The probability of nursing home use increases sharply with age at death: "17% for age 65–74, 36% for age 75–84, and 60% for age 85–94" (Kemper & Murtaugh, 1991, p. 595).

McConnel (1984) has estimated that the risk of being institutionalized in a lifetime is 48.2% at birth and 63% at age 65, but these estimates have been criticized on methodological grounds (Liang & Tu, 1986). The consensus among researchers seems to be that the total chance of institutionalization before death among normal elderly persons living in the community would be about 1 in 3 for males and 1 in 2 for females who turned 65 in 1990 (Kemper & Murtaugh, 1991).

These figures increase with age. For example, people 85 years of age or older represent 11% of the aged population but about 45% of the populations of nursing home residents. Estimates predict that 3 million elderly (7% of those 65 years and over) will be in nursing homes by the year 2010 (Zedlewski, Barnes,

Burt, McBride, & Meyer, 1990). This figure makes it easy to understand the potentially high financial and human costs of institutionalization and the tremendous strain it may place on public and private resources in our society.

Medicare and Medicaid

Approximately 56% of the bill for care in nursing homes is paid out of public funds (U.S. Bureau of the Census, 1994). The principal programs involved are Medicare and Medicaid, both of which began in 1965. One estimate is that these programs spent some $42 billion on nursing home bills for 1.4 million elderly in 1993 (Nursing homes, 1995).

Medicare (health insurance for older people) is a federal insurance program that finances a portion of the health care costs of persons aged 65 and over. Part A, the hospital insurance portion of Medicare, is financed through Social Security, and nearly all elderly persons are automatically covered without paying premiums. Part A benefits for nursing home care are extremely limited. Only persons in Medicare-certified homes are eligible, and benefits cover the first 100 days of care for those with conditions certified as requiring skilled nursing care. For the elderly patient who enters the skilled care nursing home directly from a hospital stay of at least 3 consecutive days, Medicare Part A covers the cost for the first 20 days with no deductible or coinsurance. After that, there is a daily coinsurance of $89.50 (1995 rate) for days 21 through 100 for basic services. This coinsurance amount changes annually and is computed at 1/8 of the inpatient hospital deductible rate. Medicare also covers an increasing number of skilled nursing services, including intravenous and tube feedings, insulin injections, and speech, occupational, and physical therapy. On average, beneficiaries use about 57 days of skilled nursing care in any calendar year (Nursing homes, 1995). When these benefits run out (after 100 days), typically patients move to private-pay status or onto Medicaid.

No nursing home benefits are provided under Medicare for so-called intermediate nursing care or for custodial care. Medicare does not pay for the kind of care many infirm people need to bathe, dress, or go to the toilet, if that's the only type of care they require. Part B of Medicare pays for such things as physicians' services, diagnostic tests, and some drugs. Elderly persons must enroll for Part B and pay a monthly premium that increases annually ($46.10 in 1995). Many Social Security recipients elect to have their Part B premiums withheld from their monthly benefit. Part B includes no coverage for nursing home care.

Medicaid is a joint federal-state program established to pay for medical care for low-income Americans. States set their own eligibility requirements. In general, persons who are eligible for state public assistance or for Supplemental Security Income (SSI) under the federal program for the aged, blind, or disabled poor automatically are eligible for Medicaid. Others must "spend down" all assets, with the exception of a home, household furnishings, a car, a burial plot, and $2,000 to a limit of $75,000, before becoming eligible for Medicaid. Spouses may similarly retain up to $75,000 in assets. If they have no income of their own, they also may keep a monthly amount (which varies by state) of the nursing home patient's income.

Medicaid provides long-term, unlimited nursing home care without requiring previous hospitalization. Not surprisingly, Medicaid has become the principal public mechanism for funding nursing home care. Medicaid accounts for about 90% of government expenditures for nursing home care and 45% of all costs for nursing homes in the United States; approximately 6 in 10 nursing home patients receive Medicaid payments.

According to the National Center for Health Statistics, there were 33,000 nursing and related care facilities in the United States in 1991. This is a 43% increase from 1980. Approximately 45% of these facilities are nursing homes; the rest are board-and-care homes. The great majority of nursing homes are run for profit (71.4%). Although nonprofit and government nursing homes make up only about 28% of the facilities, their greater capacity (an average of 112 beds vs. 103 beds for proprietary facilities) enables them to serve about 30% of all nursing home residents.

Over the past three decades medical care prices rose much faster than prices in general. Nursing home costs have been no exception. Through the 1980s to date, nursing home charges have continued to rise at a faster pace than the Consumer Price Index (CPI). According to a 1986 publication of the American Association of Retired Persons (AARP), daily nursing home costs ranged from a low of about $37 for custodial care to a high of about $140 for skilled nursing care. These rates pale in comparison to those of the mid-1990s. *Consumer Reports* (Nursing homes, 1995) compared monthly charges for private-pay patients, including different services such as incontinence care and hand-feeding, at seven Maryland nursing homes and found that they ranged from $3,500 to $5,500. They identified facilities in other parts of the United States where rates for "special care units" (e.g., for patients with Alzheimer's disease and/or other cognitive deficits) are even higher than $5,500 per month.

The Decision to Institutionalize an Older Person

Old-age institutions have been described as dehumanizing and depersonalizing. Despite the unfavorable reputation of old-age institutions and the negative attitudes of elderly citizens toward them, many elderly individuals need and seek out institutional care. Usually, this need is apparent to family members and/or is based on a physician's recommendation. In cases involving physical illness and/or debility, the need may be apparent to the elderly patient as well.

The availability of adequate and applicable home care and community services can prevent the institutionalization of many elderly patients. Family members are often very much involved in decisions concerning the institutionalization of an elderly person. When an aged family member is placed in a nursing home, many of the responsibilities for caring for that individual shift from the family to the institution. Some literature suggests that when families remain involved with their relative in a nursing home, the quality of nursing home care appears to improve (Shuttlesworth, Rubin, & Duffy, 1982). Unfortunately, some nursing home administrators fail to recognize the importance of family involvement in the care process, and the willingness of families to continue to be responsible for nontechnical tasks. Lack of congruence of view between relatives of the institutionalized individual and nursing home staff may result in aggressive behavior directed at nursing home personnel by residents' family members (Vinton & Mazza, 1994).

INSTITUTIONAL EFFECTS: REAL OR IMAGINARY?

The gerontological literature is filled with descriptions of the institutionalized elderly as disorganized, disoriented, and depressed. Tobin and Lieberman (1976) review three explanations for this portrait: relocation and environmental change, readmission effects, and the "totality" of institutions.

Relocation and Environmental Change

The relationship of environmental change to mortality and morbidity has been investigated in mental hospitals, nursing homes, and homes for the aged. Much controversy exists regarding the effect of relocation on mortality and other health status outcomes (Horowitz & Schulz, 1983; Mirotznik & Lombardi, 1995). However, researchers generally agree that moving the older person from a familiar setting into an institution leads to psychological disorganization and distress. This may be especially the case when the move is involuntary.

Some investigators argue that the disruption of life caused by relocating an elderly individual to new surroundings may create many of the effects attributed to living in that new setting (Lieberman & Tobin, 1983). Others argue that it is not simply the stress of relocation but rather *environmental discontinuity*, the degree of change between a new and an old environment, that may explain the effects observed after institutionalization (Lawton, 1974). Interestingly, some evidence suggests that environmental change can elicit desirable behavior and increase the competence of the older individual.

Readmission Effects

Anticipating and preparing for the actuality of moving into an institution can be very stressful. The effects of this stress on the older person before admission are often very similar to what are described as institutional effects. Tobin and Lieberman (1976) found old people who were awaiting institutionalization to be markedly different from those living in the community, in cognitive functioning, affective response, emotional state, and self-perceptions. What is even more interesting is that the psychological status of the study sample awaiting institutionalization was not unlike the psychological status generally descriptive of aged persons in institutions: slight cognitive disorganization, constriction in affective response, less than optimal feelings of well-being, diminished self-esteem, and depression (Tobin & Lieberman, 1976).

The Total Institution

According to Goffman (1961), a basic social arrangement in contemporary society is that the individual tends to sleep, play, and work in different settings with different coparticipants. A central feature of the "total" institution is the breakdown of these barriers so that all three activities take place in the same setting with the same people. One category of total institution includes those places that care for persons who are perceived to be generally incapable of caring for themselves and harmless to themselves and others. Included in this category are nursing homes, homes for the aged, and homes for the poor and indigent.

Common to all total institutions is the fact that individuals in such institutions undergo a process of mortification of the self. This process, which involves interacting with others in the institutional setting, strips the resident of his or her identify and reduces the control individuals perceive they have over events of daily life (Diamond, 1992). The features of an institutional environment that contribute to mortification of the self include admission procedures that detach individuals from the social system at large, barriers that separate people from their social roles outside the institution, and the humiliation and loss of self-esteem that results from forced relationships with others and lack of privacy.

Whereas mortification of self is characteristic of all total institutions (no matter how therapeutic the environment), it makes intuitive sense that some institutional settings are less mortifying than others and provide higher-quality care. How such evaluations are made is often difficult to determine. Health care practitioners and researchers find the issue of evaluating institutional care to be extraordinarily complex (Lemke & Moos, 1986). What is a good nursing home? Should quality be measured in terms of resident satisfaction or professional nursing care? Given limited resources, is it more important to spend money on gardeners, interior design, janitorial services, and food quality, or on an abundance of aides, orderlies, and health professionals?

A number of researchers have looked to the relationship between institutional characteristics and quality of care. Characteristics of institutions thought to be related to quality of care include ownership status, size, socioeconomic status, social integration, and staff professionalism (Kart & Manard, 1981). Higher-quality care has been found in institutions that are nonproprietary, relatively small in size, wealthy in resources, sociable, and staffed with persons who have positive attitudes toward the residents. But institutions with all these characteristics are scarce (Lemke & Moos, 1986; Kart & Manard, 1981).

Can high-quality care in nursing homes be ensured? In recent years government efforts to control abuse have been aimed primarily at reducing costs rather than improving quality of care. Still, cost-containment efforts by the federal government could force better compatibility of patient needs and long-term care services. One approach involves some efficient substitution of long-term care services for acute services (Vladeck, 1985). Another is the single or channeling agency, an organizational reform intended to provide opportunities for better matching resources in the community with the needs of the area's elderly population (Breecher & Knickman, 1985).

Little is known about the best ways to deliver long-term care services. For the most part, the lack of homogeneity within the nursing home population requires flexibility in service delivery. For example, the needs of the short-stay rehabilitation patient differs from those of the short-stay terminally ill person or the long-term cognitively ill patient. And many times the patient's needs are not primarily medical. The interdisciplinary nature of service-delivery personnel allows for these diverse needs to be potentially met within one setting. Still, variability in the course of long-term care makes it problematic to determine which long-term care services can be delivered most effectively to which patients and where.

Within the long-term care service delivery system, measures such as mortality, morbidity, functional deficits of residents, overall health condition, appropriateness of use of health facilities such as emergency rooms and acute care hospitals, and resident complaints are commonly identified as appropriate criteria to study service efficacy (Mezey & Knapp, 1993).

The lack of firm consensus on an outcome measure for long-term care has resulted in staffing being used as a measure of quality of care in nursing facilities (Mezey & Scanlon, 1988). Staffing personnel characteristics alone do not ensure high quality of care, but without good professional and paraprofessional staff, the quality of care provided to residents does suffer (Institute of Medicine, 1986; Mohler & Lessard, 1991).

One complex aspect of viewing staffing as an indicator of quality of care is that organizational, managerial, and professional staffing characteristics that may influence quality of care in nursing homes are mediated through nursing aides and assistants, the staff members who provide the greatest amount of direct care to residents (Bowers & Becker, 1992).

Nursing aides and assistants are often described as poorly trained, with high turnover and low job satisfaction (Chartock, Nevins, Rzetelny, & Gilberto, 1988). This is particularly problematic in the case of mentally ill elders. Estimates of mental illness among residents of nursing homes run in excess of 50%, yet nursing aides and assistants constitute about 63% of the primary caregivers for mentally ill elderly. Because nursing assistants have become de facto mental health technicians, additional training in mental health and aging is clearly required to maintain some semblance of quality of care (Spore, Smyer, & Cohn, 1991). Almost by definition, without such training, most nursing home residents could be defined as inappropriately placed relative to the resources available in that nursing home.

LONG-TERM CARE POLICY ISSUES

Services that are delivered across the continuum of long-term care are fragmented. Community based long-term care programs, including those described above, comprise a heterogeneous collection of agencies, institutions, and programs dominated by public funding. In particular, Medicaid, which accounts for about one-third (34%) of all long-term care expenditures for the elderly in the United States, attempts to meet the acute and long-term care needs of the elderly poor (Davis & Rowland, 1986).

In addition to home health care and nursing home care, Medicaid now covers chore services, homemaker aid, and other types of social services under a waiver provision if a state can demonstrate that total expenditures are not increased by the use of this type of service. States vary widely in their approaches to determining eligibility for long-term care services. Even with the appearance of such expanded service benefits, public spending has, for the most part, reinforced the use of institutions for providing long-term care (Davis & Rowland, 1986).

Medicare accounted for about 18% of all nursing home and home care expenditures in the United States in 1993. Home health care benefits under Medicare have been liberalized to cover some part-time health care or therapy on an intermittent basis if the beneficiary is housebound and under a physician's care. Recent amendments to Medicare have shown increased sensitivity to connecting acute care services to long-term care services. It is not unusual for long-term care patients to be frequently moved back and forth between hospital and nursing home. In fact, Kane and Kane (1989) suggest that "hospitalization might be more accurately viewed as phases of acute care within the long-term care episode" (p. 235).

Anticipating relationships between acute care and long-term care service use should help meet needs and control costs. Improved patient assessment should help to identify high-risk cases, reduce subsequent long-term care utilization and mortality, and improve function (Wan & Ferraro, 1991). Providing postacute care is an area of service need that requires greater recognition.

"Short-term" long-term care is considered care that is offered for a period of less than 90 days. "Step-down" services, which range from outpatient rehabilitation to community outreach services, can be used. Brody and Magel (1986) recommend the use of step-down services to cross traditional service lines where settings are organized to respond to a hierarchy of patient care needs. When short-term care is used, case management is frequently called into play. It relies on an agent to coordinate and supervise the provision and delivery of appropriate services.

Posthospital care is often provided by long-term care service agencies. Although Medicare usually pays for these services, there has been discussion to explore ways to tie these costs to the prospective payment system now used in reimbursement hospitals (Kane & Kane, 1989). A total capitation system may be a device for recognizing episodes of care in payment policies. Within such a system a single payment would cover all care, including long-term care (Kane & Kane, 1989).

Medicaid and Medicare are not the only public payers for long-term care for the elderly. At the federal level the Social Services Block Grant, Title III of the Older Americans Act, and the Veterans Administration (VA) accounted for about 3% of all long-term funding for the elderly in the United States in 1993 (Wiener, Illston, & Hanley, 1994). The largest of these public programs is that of the VA, which maintains nursing homes, domiciliary care facilities, and hospital-based home health care programs for low-income veterans.

According to the Health Insurance Association of America, about 2.9 million private long-term care insurance policies were sold in 1992, many to nonelderly persons (Coronel, 1994). Thus, whereas approximately 97% of those 65 years and older had Medicare coverage and over 60% had supplementary insurance in addition to Medicare, about 5% of the aged had private insurance to cover the catastrophic costs of long-term care.

In addition to the public programs and private insurance, long-term care recipients have considerable out-of-pocket costs, perhaps as much as 44% of all expenditures in the United States in 1993. Still, Hanley, Wiener, and Harris (1994) estimate that fewer than 10% of elderly nursing home users could afford to pay for a year of nursing home care out of income. Average out-of-pocket costs for nursing home care in 1993 were over $28,000, and one estimate is that about 36% of all nursing home patients spent more than 40% of their income and assets for long-term care in 1993.

Policy proposals and initiatives for reforming the system abound. Until relatively recently, these proposals were for expanded or additional services, including additional homemaking and other community-based services to reduce the rate of institutionalization, providing transportation to or centralizing the location of needed services, or even providing direct payment or tax incentive to family caregivers for their services (Doty, 1986; Hudson, 1996).

Some policy suggestions contain latent functions that may be difficult to anticipate. One special concern involves the possibility that the new program or a program change might act as a disincentive to continuation of family care or that a newly developed service would simply act as a substitute for family care. Although there is no research to support this concern, no family policy for older people has been developed in the United States. The future trend in family support of older people is somewhat unpredictable as a result of uncertain family rates. Changes in family composition and/or dependency ratios may cause changes in the quantity and types of care that families can offer their elders. Nevertheless, commitment to the American ideal of individuals taking responsibility for themselves and their family members is likely to remain strong.

Most people agree that reform is needed in the current system for financing health and long-term care services for the elderly, as this current system appears to satisfy no one. Clearly, there is some conflict between the need for acute and chronic health services, long-term care, and budgetary constraints. Other flaws include a lack of public and private insurance, having catastrophic out-of-pocket costs, an institutional bias, lack of services in many communities, and a finance system oriented toward welfare rather than the assumption that the need and use of long-term care services is a normal life risk (Wiener & Illston, 1996).

Tapping home equity and employing private insurance are two private-sector approaches to financing long-term care. Money accumulated in home equity could be related to older people through reverse annuity mortgages and other sale-leaseback arrangements. According to *Consumer Reports* (Nursing homes, 1995), however, by mid-1992 only about 3,000 individuals nationwide had taken advantage of an FHA program to promote reverse annuity mortgages.

Private insurance is being marketed to enable people who can afford to pay for services to have access to some sort of saving insurance mechanism (Brody & Magel, 1986). Tax-deductible or tax-deferred medical or long-term care retirement accounts and medical or long-term care versions of IRAs are also being promoted, especially for those upper-middle- and upper-income individuals with discretionary incomes. This assumes that working-age adults will prepare for the risk of needing long-term care. Many have competing demands, deny the risk, or mistakenly believe that Medicare will cover these costs (Wiener & Illston, 1996). Even if private insurance and/or long-term care IRAs are available and grow in the near future, they are unlikely to have an impact on Medicaid spending (Wiener et al., 1994).

Unfortunately, in the current political environment, reform is often simply a euphemism for reducing costs. As of this writing, Democratic and Republican leaders in Congress, together with President Clinton, are recommending cuts in the federal matching funds for Medicaid and reductions in the growth of Medicare spending. As a result, there will likely be an increase in efforts to move elderly individuals into managed care arrangements. Such options would be widely available under both Medicare and Medicaid. About 25% of Medicaid beneficiaries are currently enrolled in managed care, although most are mothers and children (Riley, 1995); only 18 states are currently enrolling non-institutionalized people in risk-based managed care. About 2.3 million Medicare beneficiaries (7%) were enrolled in managed care programs in 1994, and most of these were living in California, Oregon, Arizona, New Mexico, Nevada, or Florida.

Arizona may have the longest experience in enrolling older people in managed care. According to Riley (1995), over the past 9 years, Arizona found that costs increased at a slower pace in their managed care program than was the case in the fee-for-service Medicaid program. Minnesota has recently received the first waiver to operate a managed care demonstration for elders dually enrolled in Medicare and Medicaid. Conflicts in the rules that govern the two programs remain. Also, as other states proceed with applications for the waiver, it is not clear whether they will be held accountable for providing certain mandatory services and if so, which critical services are most likely to be jeopardized by cost controls.

REFERENCES

Anetzberger, G. (1995). Protective services and long-term care. In Z. Harel & R. E. Dunkle (Eds.), *Matching people with services in long-term care* (pp. 261–282). New York: Springer Publishing.

Bass, D., & Noelker, L. (1987). The influence of family caregivers on elder's use of in home services: An expanded conceptual model. *Journal of Health and Social Behavior, 28*, 184–196.

Bowers, B., & Becker, M. (1992). Nurse's aides in nursing homes: The relationship between organization and quality. *Gerontologist, 32*, 360–366.

Breecher, C., & Knickman, J. (1985). A reconsideration of *long*-term care. *Journal of Health Politics, Policy and Law, 10*, 245–273.

Brody, S. J. (1984). Goals of geriatric care. In S. Brody & N. Persily (Eds.), *Hospitals and the aged: The new old market* (pp. 51–62). Rockville, MD: Aspen.

Brody, S. J., & Magel, J. (1986). Long term care: The long and short of it. In C. Eisdorfer (Ed.), *Reforming health care for the elderly: Recommendations for national policy*. Baltimore: Johns Hopkins University Press.

Brody, E., & Schoonover, B. (1986). Patterns of parent care when adult daughters work and when they do not. *Gerontologist, 26*, 372–381.

Chadiha, L., Proctor, E., Morrow-Howell, N., Darkwa, O., & Dore, P. (1994). Posthospital home care for African-American and white elderly. *Gerontologist, 35*, 233–239.

Chartock, P., Nevins, A., Rzetelny, H., & Gilberto, P. (1988). A mental health training program in nursing homes. *Gerontologist, 28*, 503–507.

Chatters, L., Taylor, R., & Jackson, J. (1986). Aged Blacks' choices for an informal helper network. *Journal of Gerontology, 41*, 94–100.

Coronel, S. (1994). *Long-term care insurance in 1992.* Washington, DC: Health Insurance Association of America.

Davis, K., & Rowland, D. (1986). *Medicare policy*. Baltimore: Johns Hopkins University Press.

Deimling, G. T., & Poulshock, S. W. (1985). The transition from family in-home care to institutional care. *Research on Aging*, 7, 563–576.

Diamond, T. (1992). *Making gray gold: Narratives of nursing home care.* Chicago: University of Chicago Press.

Dobrof, R., & Litwak, E. (1981). *Maintenance of family ties of long term care patients: Theory and guide to practice* (DHHS Publication No. ADM 81-400). Washington, DC: U.S. Government Printing Office.

Doty, P. (1986). Family care of the elderly: The role of public policy. *Milbank Quarterly, 64*, 34–75.

Dunkle, R., Coulton, C., Mackintosh, J., & Goode, R. (1982). The decision making process among the hospitalized elderly. *Journal of Gerontological Social Work, 4*(3), 95–106.

Dunkle, R., & Stone, M. (1995). Long-term care services: Processes and outcomes. In Z. Harel & R. Dunkle (Eds.), *Matching people with services in long-term care* (pp. 137–159). New York: Springer Publishing.

Eichmann, M., Griffin, B., Lyons, J., Larson, D., & Finkel, S. (1992). An estimation of the impact of OBRA-87 on nursing home care in the United States. *Hospital and Community Psychiatry, 43*, 781–789.

Estes, C., Swan, J., & Associates (Eds.). (1993). *The long term care crisis: Elders trapped in the no-care zone.* Newbury Park, CA: Sage.

Evans, M., & Welge, C. (1991). Trends in the spatial dimensions of the long-term care delivery system. *Social Science and Medicine, 33*, 477–487.

Fabian, D., & Rathbone-McCuan, E. (1992). *Self-neglecting elders: A clinical dilemma.* New York: Auburn House.

Fairchild, T., Knebl, J., & Burgos, D. (1995). The complex long-term care service system. In Z. Harel & R. E. Dunkle (Eds.), *Matching people with services in long-term care* (pp. 73–88). New York: Springer Publishing.

Gibson, R., & Jackson, J. (1989). The health, physical functioning, and informal supports of the Black elderly. In D. P. Willis (Ed.), *Health policies and Black Americans* (pp. 421–454). New Brunswick, NJ: Transaction Publishers.

Goffman, E. (1961). *Asylums.* Garden City, NY: Doubleday.

Gratton, B. (1986). *Urban elders.* Philadelphia: Temple University Press.

Greer, D. S., Mor, V., Morris, J. N., Sherwood, S., Kidder, D., & Birnbaum, H. (1986). An alternative in terminal care: Results of the National Hospice Study. *Journal of Chronic Diseases, 39*, 9–26.

Hanley, R. J., Wiener, J. M., & Harris, K. M. (1994). *The economic status of nursing home users.* Washington, DC: Brookings Institute.

Harder, W. P., Gornick, J. C., & Burt, M. R. (1986). Adult day care: Substitute or supplement? *Milbank Quarterly, 64*, 414–441.

Harrow, B. S., Tennstedt, S. L., & McKinlay, J. B. (1995). How costly is it to care for disabled elders in a community setting? *Gerontologist, 35*, 803–813.

Hing, E., & Bloom, B. (1991). Long-term care for the functionally dependent elderly. *American Journal of Public Health, 81*(2), 223–225.

Horowitz, M. J., & Schulz, R. (1983). The relocation controversy: Criticism and commentary in five recent studies. *Gerontologist, 23*, 229–234.

Hudson, R. B. (1996). Social protection and services. In R. H. Binstock & L. K. George (Eds.), *Handbook of aging and the social sciences* (pp. 446–466). San Diego, CA: Academic Press.

Hughes, S. L., Cordray, D. S., & Spiker, V. A. (1984). Evaluation of a long-term home care program. *Medical Care, 22*, 460–475.

Institute of Medicine. (1986). *Improving the quality of care in nursing homes.* Washington, DC: National Academy Press.

Kane, R. L., & Kane, R. A. (1987). *Long-term care: Principles, programs, and policies.* New York: Springer Publishing.

Kane, R., & Kane, R. (1989). Transitions in long-term care. In M. Ory & K. Bond (Eds.), *Aging and health care: Social science and policy perspectives* (pp. 217–243). New York: Routledge.

Kart, C., & Manard, B. (1981). Quality of care in old-age institutions. In C. Kart & B. Manard (Eds.), *Aging in America: Readings in social gerontology* (2nd ed., pp. 441–453). Sherman Oaks, CA: Alfred Publishing.

Katz, S. (1983). Assessing self-maintenance: Activities of daily living, mobility and instrumental activities of daily living. *Journal of American Geriatrics Society, 31*, 721–727.

Kemper, P., Applebaum, R., & Harrigan, M. (1987). Community care demonstration: What have we learned? *Health Care Financing Review, 8*(4), 87–100.

Kemper, P., & Murtaugh, C. M. (1991). Lifetime use of nursing home care. *New England Journal of Medicine, 324*, 595–600.

Lawton, M. P. (1974). Social ecology and the health of older people. *American Journal of Public Health, 64*, 257–260.

Lemke, S., & Moos, R. H. (1986). Quality of residential settings for elderly adults. *Journal of Gerontology, 41*, 268–276.

Liang, J., & Tu, E. J-C. (1986). Estimating lifetime risk of nursing home residency: A further note. *Gerontologist, 26*, 560–563.

Lieberman, M., & Tobin, S. S. (1983). *The experience of old age: Stress, coping, and survival.* New York: Basic Books.

Litwak, E. (1985). *Helping the elderly*. New York: Guilford Press.

Liu, W., & Manton, K. (1987). *Department of Health and Human Services Task Force on Long Term Care Policies: Report to Congress and the Secretary*. Washington, DC: U.S. Government Printing Office.

Manton, K. G. (1989). Epidemiological, demographic, and social correlates of disability among the elderly. *Milbank Quarterly, 67*, 13–58.

Marion Merrell Dow, Inc. (1993). *Managed care digest: Long term care edition*. Kansas City, MO: Author.

McAuley, W., & Blieszner, R. (1985). Selection of long-term care arrangements by older community residents. *Gerontologist, 25*, 188–193.

McConnel, C. E. (1984). A note on the lifetime risk of nursing home residence. *Gerontologist, 24*, 193–198.

Mezey, M., & Knapp, M. (1993). Nursing staffing in nursing facilities: Implications for achieving quality of care. In P. R. Kane, R. L. Kane, & M. D. Mezey (Eds.), *Advances in long term care* (Vol. 2, pp. 130–151). New York: Springer Publishing.

Mezey, M., & Scanlon, W. (1988). *Registered nurses in nursing homes: Secretary's commission on nursing*. Washington, DC: Department of Health and Human Services.

Mirotznik, J., & Lombardi, T. G. (1995). The impact of intrainstitutional relocation on morbidity in an acute care setting. *Gerontologist, 35*, 217–224.

Mohler, M., & Lessard, W. (1991). *Nursing staff in nursing homes: Additional staff needed and cost to meet requirements and intent of OBRA'87*. Washington, DC: National Committee to Preserve Social Security and Medicare.

Mor, V., Sherwood, S., & Gutkin, C. (1986). A national study of residential care for the aged. *Gerontologist, 26*, 405–417.

Moroney, R. M. (1986). *Shared responsibility: Families and social policy*. Hawthorne, NY: Aldine.

Morrow-Howell, N., Proctor, E. K., & Berg-Werner, M. (1993). Adequacy of informal care for elderly patients going home from the hospital: Discharge planner perspectives. *Journal of Applied Gerontology, 12*, 188–205.

Murtaugh, C. M., & Freiman, M. P. (1995). Nursing home residents at risk of hospitalization and the characteristics of their hospital stays. *Gerontologist, 35*, 35–43.

National Aging Resource Center on Elder Abuse. (1990). *Summaries of national elder abuse data: An exploratory study of state statistics based on a survey of state adult protective service and aging agencies*. Washington, DC: Author.

Neu, C. R. (1982). Individual preferences for life and health: Misuses and possible uses. In R. L. Kane & R. A. Kane (Eds.), *Values and long-term care* (pp. 261–275). Lexington, MA: Lexington.

Noelker, L., & Bass, D. (1989). Home care for elderly persons: Linkages between formal and informal caregivers. *Journals of Gerontology, 44*, 63–70.

Nursing homes: Covering the cost. (1995, September). *Consumer Reports*, pp. 591–597.

Pepper Commission Hearing. (1990). Washington, DC: U.S. Government Printing Office.

Riley, P. (1995). Long-term care: The silent target of the federal and state budget debate. *Public Policy and Aging Report, 7*(1), 4–5, 7.

Shuttlesworth, G. E., Rubin, A., & Duffy, M. (1982). Families versus institutions: Incongruent role expectations in the nursing home. *Gerontologist, 22*, 200–208.

Silverstein, N. (1984). Informing the elderly about public services: The relationship between sources of knowledge and service utilization. *Gerontologist, 24*, 37–40.

Silverstone, B. (1985). Informal social support systems for the frail elderly. In Institute of Medicine/National Research Council (Eds.), *America's aging: Health in an older society* (pp. 153–181). Washington, DC: National Academic Press.

Soldo, B., Agree, E., & Wolf, D. (1989). The balance between formal and informal care. In M. Ory, K. Bond, & T. F. Williams (Eds.), *Aging and health care* (pp. 193–216). New York: Routledge.

Soldo, B., & Myllyluoma, J. (1983). Caregivers who live with dependent elderly. *Gerontologist, 23*, 605–611.

Soldo, B., Wolf, D., & Agree, E. (1986). *Family, household, and care arrangements of disabled older women: A structural analysis.* Paper presented at the annual meeting of the Gerontological Society of America, Chicago.

Spore, D. L., Smyer, M. A., & Cohn, M. D. (1991). Assessing nursing assistants' knowledge of behavioral approaches to mental health problems. *Gerontologist, 31*, 309–317.

Stoller, E. P. (1982). Sources of support for the elderly during illness. *Health and Social Work, 7*, 111–122.

Strahan, G. (1993). *Overview of home health and hospice care patients: Preliminary data from the 1992 National Home and Hospice Care Survey* (Advance Data from Vital and Health Statitistics, No. 235). Hyattsville, MD: National Center for Health Statistics.

Subcommittee on Health and Long-term Care, Select Committee on Aging, United States House of Representatives. (1989). *Board and care homes in America: A national tragedy*. Washington, DC: U.S. Government Printing Office.

Tobin, S., & Lieberman, M. (1976). *The last home for the aged.* San Francisco: Jossey Bass.

Townsend, A., & Poulshock, S. (1986). Intergenerational perspectives on impaired elders' support networks. *Journal of Gerontology, 41*, 101–109.

Upshur, C. (1983). Developing respite care: A support service for families with disabled members. *Family Relations, 31*, 13–20.

U.S. Bureau of the Census. (1991). *Statistical abstract of the United States: 1991.* Washington, DC: U.S. Government Printing Office.

U.S. Bureau of the Census. (1994). *Statistical abstract of the United States: 1994.* Washington, DC: U.S. Government Printing Office.

Vinton, L., & Mazza, N. (1994). Aggressive behavior directed at nursing home personnel by residents' family members. *Gerontologist, 34*, 528–533.

Vladeck, B. (1985). Reforming Medicare provider payment. *Journal of Health Politics, Policy and Law, 10*, 513–532.

Wan, T. T. H., & Ferraro, K. F. (1991). Assessing the impacts of community-based health care policies and programs for older adults. *Journal of Applied Gerontology*, *10*, 35–52.

Weissert, W. G., Wan, T., Livieratos, B., & Katz, S. (1980). Effects and costs of daycare services for the chronically ill. *Medical Care*, *18*, 567–584.

Wiener, J. M., & Illston, L. H. (1996). The financing and organization of health care for older Americans. In R. H. Binstock & L. K. George (Eds.), *Handbook of aging and the social sciences* (pp. 427–445). San Diego, CA: Academic Press.

Wiener, J. M., Illston, L. H., & Hanley, R. J. (1994). *Sharing the burden: Strategies for public and private long-term care insurance*. Washington, DC: Brookings Institute.

Wolf, R., Godkin, M., & Pillemer, K. (1986). Maltreatment of the elderly: A comparative analysis. *Pride Institute Journal of Long Term Home Health Care*, *5*(4), 10–17.

Wolf, R., & Pillemer, K. (1989). *Helping elderly victims: The reality of elder abuse*. New York: Columbia University Press.

Wolinsky, F., Callahan, C., Fitzgerald, J., & Johnson, R. (1992). The risk of nursing home placement and subsequent death among older adults. *Journal of Gerontology*, *47*, 173–182.

Zedlewski, S. R., Barnes, R. O., Burt, M. R., McBride, T. D., & Meyer, J. A. (1990). *The needs of the elderly in the 21st century*. Washington, DC: Urban Institute Press.

CHAPTER 12

Family Caregiving: A Focus for Aging Research and Intervention

David M. Bass
Linda S. Noelker

As discussed in the preceding chapter, families provide a substantial amount of long-term care to their older members. The purpose of this chapter is to review the burgeoning literature on family care by examining the characteristics of caregivers and effects of caregiving on family relations and the well-being of those involved.

Family caregiving for impaired elderly reemerged as an important topic for empirical investigation in gerontology during the 1970s. This reemergence followed two earlier conceptual approaches to the elderly person's involvement with kin. In the 1930s and 1940s, social scientists generally held pessimistic views of family structure and functioning, positing continued disintegration of the extended family due to industrialization, geographic mobility, and isolation of the nuclear unit (Parsons, 1964; Sorokin, 1937). Correspondingly, older persons were seen as having little involvement or role in family life and in some instances were characterized as "abandoned" by their families.

Subsequent behavioral and social science research in the 1960s demonstrated the prominence of family members in the lives of the elderly and adult children's filial responsibilities for aged parents (Blenkner, 1965; Shanas et al., 1968). In 1977, the results of a community survey of older persons and their use of assistance showed that 80% of the ongoing help received by chronically ill and disabled elderly came from informal caregivers, predominantly family members (Comptroller General, 1977). Soon thereafter, Shanas (1979a, 1979b) published her definitive articles on "social myth as hypothesis" and the centrality of older persons' family support systems, thereby dispelling previously held negative conceptions about the relationship between the elderly and their families.

In the 1980s, the concepts of family caregiving and a "primary kin caregiver," namely, a spouse or adult child, were widely investigated, with federal research support targeted to this topic and the growth of national associations advocating on behalf of family caregivers, such as the National Alzheimer's Disease Association. Findings from current research, however, underscore the fact that family caregiving is not a phenomenon separate from ongoing family life but is a part of the full range of experiences of the family unit. The focal attention given to family caregiving when it reemerged as a major theme in gerontological research may have been necessary to sensitize society to the important role families play in the care of the aged; however, family caregiving is best understood in context of lifelong family relationships (Antonucci, 1990).

The research attention given to family caregiving, like gerontological research generally, can be explained by sociodemographic changes in the size of the aged population, family structure, and women's roles. The disproportionate growth in the aged population, particularly in the group 85 years and older, pointed to a growing need for long-term care services for later-life chronic illnesses such as arthritis, heart problems, diabetes, and dementia. With the increased likelihood that older family members would live into their 80s, when chronic health problems and associated care needs are most prevalent (Himes, 1992), the issue of who would care for the escalating number of impaired elderly came to the forefront.

Although chronic conditions have periodic flare-ups that necessitate hospitalization or nursing home placement, most long-term care has traditionally been given at home and has focused on symptom management and maintenance of routine functioning. This daily care was given by family members because the need for long-term care far outstrips formal service resources and public support (Litwak, 1985).

Changes in family structure raised serious doubts about the capacity of the family to meet the care needs of the elderly. Most of these concerns related to changes in women's roles and their ability and willingness to continue to serve as the primary caregivers for dependent family members (Brody, 1985). In the 1960s, women began entering the labor force in record numbers, thereby decreasing their availability for caregiving (Stoller & Pugliesi, 1989). Higher divorce rates produced more single-headed female households in which women had sole child care responsibility and presumably less time and energy for elder care (Cicirelli, 1983). Geographic mobility resulted in more residentially dispersed families and elders without proximate kin (Himes, 1992). And decreased family size, due to the growing number of couples who were childless by choice or who limited the number of their offspring, reduced the potential pool of family caregivers (Noelker, 1984). Together, these social trends presaged the need for alternative approaches to caring for the growing population of frail and impaired older persons.

Family caregiving research also was fueled by concerns about escalating health care costs (Doty, 1986). One strategy for reducing these costs was to shorten or eliminate acute care hospital and nursing home stays, as evidenced by federal reimbursement changes in the implementation of diagnostic related groups (DRGs) and the growth of outpatient surgical units and managed care systems (Estes, Swan, & Associates, 1993). By reducing acute care and institutional stays, impaired elderly returned home "sicker and quicker." Their greater care needs were left to family members and home care services paid out-of-pocket because public support for community-based health and social services was not proportionately increased. However, the lessened reliance on inpatient care settings was consistent with the preferences of both the elderly and their families for autonomy, independence, and continued residence in private homes. As a result of these trends, there are three times as many older persons living at home, compared to those in nursing homes with comparable levels of impairment (Brody, 1985).

The focus on family caregiving in gerontological research over recent decades can be linked to the belief that changes in families and health care systems could produce a crisis in health care should families no longer continue as the major caregivers for older relatives. It also was assumed that family members who did accept the caregiving role would suffer serious negative consequences because of competing demands, lack of support, and more intense responsibilities related to the greater care needs of a larger number of older relatives.

We now know that the assumed negative consequences for family members and associated social costs for society that stimulated the development of the field of family caregiving represent a narrow vision of the caregiving experience. Family members, as well as friends and neighbors, form a close network within which most elderly are embedded (Kovar, 1986). Moreover, most elderly are part of an ongoing pattern of exchanges among family members, which continues even when failing health necessitates caregiving (Cantor, 1975). Older care receivers report reciprocating for the assistance they receive by providing material aid, help with care of grandchildren, and emotional support (Dunkle, 1983). Other research based on caregivers' reports, however, indicates that care receivers' activities are mostly passive and unstimulating (Lawton, Moss, & Duhamel, 1995).

Family caregiving has been shown to assume diverse forms that change over time, with variable effects on family members (Kahana, Biegel, & Wykle, 1994). This does not mean that caregiving is a totally unique and individualized experience from person to person. Rather, there are various regularly recurring patterns in caregiving, the forms reflecting the history and characteristics of the family and its members in contrast to the characteristics of the older person's illness.

Caregiving also involves major transitions (Aneshensel, Pearlin, Mullan, Zarit, & Whitlatch, 1995), such as when a chronic illness is first diagnosed, when the care receiver is admitted to a hospital or nursing home, when a shared household is established for caregiving, or when the care receiver dies (Pearlin, 1992). Moreover, the intensity of caregiving does not necessarily follow a linear pattern. Similar to the course of chronic illnesses, caregiving demands wax and wane with periods of improvement and unexpected changes for the worse

(Aneshensel et al., 1995; Bass, Noelker, Townsend, & Deimling, 1990). The changing nature of caregiving is reflected in the concept of the "caregiving career," which implies that it is a process made up of a series of related but distinct stages (Aneshensel et al., 1995; Pearlin, 1992). As the field of research develops further, caregiving may come to be defined as part of the larger career of the family and viewed as one of many activities that comprise a family history.

DEFINITIONS AND PREVALENCE OF FAMILY CAREGIVING

Family caregiving refers to continuing assistance provided by a relative to an older family member because of limitations caused by chronic illness, accident, disability, or physical or mental frailty. Caregiving is distinct from other helping behaviors because it is linked to deteriorating health and functioning and is long-term in nature. However, this definition is problematic to operationalize for three reasons: the ambiguous meaning of the concept of "assistance," determining when caregiving begins, and identifying who is the major caregiver (Barer & Johnson, 1990).

There is no accepted standard or threshold for determining when the type or amount of assistance provided is sufficient to constitute a caregiving situation. Most frequently, the phenomenon of caregiving is determined by the provision of help with activities of daily living (ADL) that typically include assistance with bathing, dressing, grooming, toileting, eating, and mobility (Horowitz, 1985). These tasks are essential in daily life and are usually performed without help from another person unless physical or mental incapacity limits self-care abilities (Lawton & Brody, 1969).

Sometimes a broader array of tasks is used to identify family care situations; these are referred to as instrumental activities of daily living (IADL) and include tasks such as laundry, shopping, finances, or household chores, along with ADL tasks. In the case of Alzheimer's disease and other forms or irreversible dementia, the need for supervision or cueing in the performance of ADL and IADL tasks, in contrast to direct help, is defined as caregiving.

Identifying when caregiving begins is another complication related to the difficulty separating usual patterns of family assistance from those specifically due to an ongoing physical or mental health problem. In cases of acute onset, such as a major stroke or heart attack, the beginning of caregiving is more obvious (Noelker & Shaffer, 1986). But when disability due to chronic illness and advanced age occurs over a number of years, the point at which interdependence between family members becomes caregiving may be unclear. This is particularly true for elderly husbands and wives. Furthermore, when both marital patners experience chronic illness and disability, it is difficult to identify who is the caregiver and who is the care receiver because the roles shift over time in relation to changes in each one's health and functioning.

A variety of approaches, apart from help with specific tasks, have been used to define and identify caregiving families. These include the presence of a specific medical diagnosis such as Alzheimer's disease or certain symptoms such as cognitive incapacity; families' use of care-related health or social services; and self-identification, that is, caregivers' or care receivers' assertion that they need or give significant amounts of help because of chronic illness or disability. The diversity of methods for defining caregiving results in wide variation in estimates, with the number of family caregivers ranging from 2.2 million to 13.3 million (Noelker & Whitlatch, 1995). Smaller estimates reflect confinement of the definition to a *primary* kin caregiver (usually a spouse or adult child), households in which the caregiver and receiver live together, and certain types of assistance (e.g., personal care). Broader definitions that yield larger prevalence estimates give consideration to a wider array of tasks, non-kin and extended-kin caregivers, caregivers who live apart from care receivers, caregivers who supply supplemental or intermittent assistance, and families who assist the 1.7 million elderly in nursing homes.

CHARACTERISTICS OF FAMILY CAREGIVERS

Earlier research and caregiving interventions focused on a single family member who served as the primary caregiver. The notion of primary caregiver reflects the fact that there often is one person who provides most of the care and directs the care of other informal and/or formal helpers (Archbold, 1982; Brody, 1981; Stone, Cafferata, & Sangl, 1987). One study showed that about one-third of the primary caregiver respondents stated that no one else in the family could substitute for them if they could not continue in their role (Guberman, Maheu, & Maille, 1992). Some researchers, however, have argued that too much attention is placed on the primary caregiver (Barer & Johnson, 1990), and this emphasis may be a methodological convenience to reduce complex caregiving networks to single subjects for investigation.

Recent studies show that 60% of older care receivers have at least one secondary caregiver and the number ranges from one to four (Penrod, Kane, Kane, & Finch, 1995). Unpublished findings from one of our recent studies suggests that the primacy of informal caregivers shifts in relation to the type of assistance (e.g., household help, personal care) given to the care receiver. Other researchers, however, report that secondary caregivers assist with tasks similar to those of primary caregivers but provide less frequent and predictable help (Tennstedt, McKinlay, & Sullivan, 1989). Moreover, assistance from secondary caregivers does not affect the type or amount of help given by primary caregivers (Penrod et al., 1995).

One of the most comprehensive descriptions of the demographic characteristics of kin primary caregivers in the United States is based on data from the Informal Caregivers Survey, which was a component of the 1982 National Long

Term Care Survey (Stone et al., 1987). Results show that most (72%) caregivers are women; 29% of all caregivers are adult daughters and 23% are wives. Husbands comprise 13% of caregivers, and approximately 9% are sons. Also, sons are considerably less likely to be primary caregivers and more likely to be secondary caregivers. The average age of caregivers in this study was 57.3 years. Husband caregivers were the oldest, with an average age of 73. Data from this study also show that most primary caregivers have been providing care for 1 to 4 years and, on average, spend about 4 hours per day on extra activities related to caregiving.

Our research studies of primary kin caregiver indicate that caregivers often help with a wide array of tasks well beyond ADL and IADL activities (Noelker & Bass, 1994). Examples of other task areas include health care tasks such as wound care and administering medications; care management tasks such as finding, arranging, and monitoring services; supervision tasks such as stopping by or telephoning to check on the relative; and emotional support such as talking with the relative about feelings related to needing help and discussing ways to improve care.

The range of tasks performed by caregivers also varies in relation to the nature of the care receiver's illness and disability. A broader range of help is typically provided to more impaired elderly, particularly those with mental impairment related to Alzheimer's disease (McClendon, Bass, & Noelker, 1994). In general, the ADL tasks with which assistance is more commonly given are dressing and bathing. However, two-thirds of the care receivers with Alzheimer's disease, compared to one-half of the care receivers with other mental disorders and one-fourth of the mentally intact care receivers, have help with these ADL tasks. Assistance with meal preparation, shopping, banking, and keeping appointments are the most common IADL tasks for primary caregivers. Similarly, findings show that 80% to 90% of mentally impaired care receivers, compared to 50% to 80% of the mentally intact care receivers, have these types of help.

Two factors consistently have important effects on the nature and course of caregiving: living arrangement, meaning whether the caregiver and care receiver live together or apart, and how the caregiver and care receiver are related. Moreover, these two characteristics are inherently intertwined. Virtually all spouse caregivers and receivers live together, and the majority tend to be not only the primary caregiver but the *sole* caregiver (Deimling, Bass, Townsend, & Noelker, 1989; Stone et al., 1987). In situations where the spouse caregiver does have help from others, the network of secondary caregivers tends to include adult children, grandchildren, and sisters and brothers of the care receiver (Penrod et al., 1995). As will be discussed below, the advanced age of spouse caregivers, along with their greater health vulnerabilities and strong commitment to keeping their impaired husband or wife at home, make them more susceptible to negative caregiving consequences.

Another common caregiving situation involves an adult child, most often a daughter, as the primary caregiver; approximately 60% live with the care receiver (Stone et al., 1987). Following are some reasons shared households are established: the older parent, usually a widow, is no longer able to live alone due to severe impairment; ongoing supervision is needed because of memory loss or other cognitive impairment; and caregiving tasks can be managed more easily in a shared household. Other shared households reflect lifelong patterns, where parents and children shared a residence prior to the onset of caregiving (Noelker & Wallace, 1985). When an adult child is the primary caregiver, the caregiving network tends to include the caregiver's spouse, children, and siblings (Penrod et al., 1995).

As implied in the above discussion, the relative who assumes the role of primary caregiver typically follows a hierarchical pattern based on the closeness of the kin relationship, a phenomenon influenced by societal values and norms (Cantor, 1980; Pratt, Schmall, Wright, & Hare, 1987; Shanas et al., 1968). Thus, spouses are most likely to become primary caregivers, followed by adult children (daughters or daughters-in-law), extended kin such as grandchildren or nieces, and, least frequently, friends and neighbors. In situations involving multiple daughters, the daughter's marital status and living arrangement affect the likelihood of being the primary helper (Stoller, 1983). Daughters who are unmarried and unemployed and those who live with the care receiver prior to caregiving more frequently are primary caregivers.

Other structural factors that influence who becomes the primary caregiver relate to availability and accessibility. Geographic distance can make it impossible for certain family members to be primary helpers (Robinson & Thurnher, 1979). Similarly, other filial obligations, such as caregiving for other dependent family members and job responsibilities, limit the availability of certain family members (Brody, 1985).

Although structural characteristics have an important influence on who becomes the primary caregiver, motivation to serve in that role also is important. Early research on filial expectations and obligation indicated that there was limited endorsement of norms about family members' duty to care for and protect older parents. Moreover, race and age differences in endorsement were found, with White and younger cohorts expressing greater endorsement. More recent studies indicate that parents' filial expectations have less influence on adult-child caregiving than the amount of help the parent gave to the child, the desire to reciprocate, and the love and affection in the parent-child relationship (Finley, Roberts, & Banahan, 1988; Guberman et al., 1992).

CHARACTERISTICS OF CARE RECEIVERS

The National Long-Term Care (LTC) Survey provides comprehensive descriptive information on noninstitutionalized persons aged 65 and over who have one or more ADL limitations and receive unpaid help from an informal caregiver (Stone et al., 1987). Findings indicate that the average age of care receivers is

77.7 years, and one-fifth are 85 or older. Most are female (60%), 51% are married, and 41% are widowed. Only about 11% of care receivers live alone, which is substantially lower than the 30% reported in other research studies of impaired older persons (Kovar, 1986; Stephens & Christianson, 1986). This difference suggests that the LTC survey sample overrepresents more disabled elderly who need regular assistance with personal care, which is more easily provided when caregiver and receiver live together.

Caregiving research has shown that the type and level of the care receiver's disability are important determinants of the nature of caregiving. This focus is on limitations in the older persons' self-care abilities rather than on the presence of disease. The presence of disease or a diagnosed illness is less important for understanding family caregiving than the symptoms of the disease and associated disabilities.

The focus on symptoms and impairment, however, must be qualified because the type of diagnosed disease does have an impact on perceptions and help-seeking behaviors of care receivers and caregivers. Different diseases vary in terms of progression and prognosis, anticipated responsiveness to treatment, expected symptoms, and stigma or embarrassment. For example, diagnoses associated with progressive mental deterioration, such as Alzheimer's disease, have important adverse effects on emotional and social well-being of care receivers and caregivers as distinct from objective observable symptoms (Bass, McClendon, Deimling, & Mukherjee, 1994).

The nature and extent of impairment in care receivers have been a major focus of investigation and have been conceptualized in multidimensional ways. Five dimensions are widely researched, including physical disability, cognitive incapacity, negative behaviors, social functioning, and functional dependencies (Bass, Noelker, & Rechlin, 1996; Deimling & Bass, 1986; Gurland, 1980; Nagi, 1976; Reisberg et al., 1984; Zarit, Reever, & Bach-Peterson, 1980).

Physical disability represents the older person's inability to perform routine movements such as bending, reaching, or lifting. Cognitive incapacity is one dimension of mental impairment and reflects impairments in short- and long-term memory, forgetfulness, and confusion. Negative behavior includes actions such as being disruptive, yelling or swearing, physical aggression, inappropriate sexual activities, wandering, and, in the extreme, catastrophic reactions. Social functioning represents positive interactions such as being friendly, enjoyable to be with, and cooperative with others. The absence of these positive characteristics is considered a symptom of mental impairment. Functional dependencies reflect the need for help with ADLs, and these dependencies may result from either mental or physical impairment. Large national studies of caregivers and care receivers have not included detailed multidimensional measures of these concepts, making it difficult to assess how common they are in care receivers.

Few studies have obtained information directly from care receivers; most investigations rely on caregiver reports about care receivers' status and functioning. Those that exist provide different perspectives on the daily lives of elderly care receivers. One cross-sectional caregiving survey that involved a nonprobability sample of 647 spouse and adult child caregivers also conducted in-person interviews with 390 elderly care receivers who were capable of participating (Noelker & Poulshock, 1982). Although these care receivers were among the less impaired, 70% still had two or more ADL limitations. Data on the care receivers' personal well-being showed that approximately 60% rated their mental health as excellent or good, half defined their lives as "routine" and 25% as "exciting," and half reported that they hardly ever worried. Care receivers with spouse caregivers, compared to those with adult-child caregivers, were more critical of their husbands or wives and their life together. The most common complaints care receivers voiced about their caregivers were that they were impatient and did not listen to them.

Another study that used the same sample investigated the relationship between care receivers' reports of contributions made to the household and depression (Dunkle, 1983). The contributions care receivers were asked about included remembering birthdays or other special occasions, giving gifts and helpful advice, visiting with or entertaining others, providing companionship, baby-sitting, and helping with household tasks (cooking, housework). Data showed that, on average, care receivers said they made at least four types of contributions to the household. Findings suggested that care receivers benefited by making contributions to the household in terms of lower depression scores, although the causal order of the relationship between helpfulness and depression could not be determined.

A more recent study provides a quite different view of elderly care receivers' quality of life; however, it was based on caregivers' reports of care receivers' time use. The study sample was obtained from a larger study of 239 primary caregivers recruited through Pennsylvania's Medicaid nursing home assessment service and from four nursing home waiting lists. Only caregivers who lived with the care receiver or spent at least 4 hours a day in the care receiver's home were asked to keep time budgets for the care receivers' time. For the 116 caregivers who kept the time budgets, findings showed that most time was spent in passive activities such as resting, listening to the radio, or watching television. Very small portions of the care receivers' days were spent in activities involving relatives or friends apart from the primary caregiver. Very little time was spent away from home, and most time in the house was spent in the bedroom or living room. The authors conclude that elderly care receivers live unstimulating lives in constricted environments, based on observations of time use recorded by their primary caregivers. They note, however, that the care receivers were extremely impaired and were candidates for nursing home entry.

CAREGIVING CONSEQUENCES

In the field of family caregiving the topic that has received most attention is caregiving consequences; this refers to the stress, burden, and strain of caregiving and, more recently, to its positive aspects, such as mastery and satisfaction. Hundreds of studies and several excellent review articles have been published on this topic (Barer & Johnson, 1990; Schulz, Visintainer, & Williamson, 1990; Wright, Clipp, & George, 1993). Nearly all investigations focus exclusively on caregiving's consequences for primary caregivers while neglecting caregiving's effects on secondary and non-kin helpers and, more important, on care receivers.

Caregiving consequences have been conceptualized in two ways (Deimling, 1994; Stull, Kosloski, & Kercher, 1994). The first approach focuses on the caregiver's general state of well-being concurrent with or subsequent to taking on caregiving responsibilities. Caregiving's effects on general well-being are detected by observing changes in well-being over time or by comparing the levels of well-being observed in caregiver samples with similar samples of noncaregivers. The most common indicators for assessing general well-being are self-rated or clinically observed physical and mental health, functional status, depression, life satisfaction, mastery or control, and negative changes in the cardiovascular and immunologic systems.

A second approach conceptualizes caregiving consequences as the effects perceived by caregivers and attributed specifically to caregiving. These consequences are represented by reports of negative care-related changes in personal or leisure time; physical or mental health; relationships between caregivers, care receivers, and other family members; financial status and income; social and recreational activities; work or employment; performance of other roles; mastery; and satisfaction with caregiving (Cantor, 1983; Deimling, 1994; Kinney & Stephens, 1989; Lawton, Kleban, Moss, Rovine, & Glicksman, 1989; Stull et al., 1994).

It has been argued that general well-being measures are superior to measures of caregiving-specific strain or burden because they can be used with comparison groups of noncaregiving populations and are less biased than caregivers' perceptions about caregiving's effects (George & Gwyther, 1986). Others contend that perceived caregiving consequences are important in their own right because subjective evaluations directly represent family members' feelings and are more likely to influence caregiving behaviors and outcomes (Deimling & Bass, 1986). At present the most common approach is to examine both general well-being and caregiving-specific consequences (Stull et al., 1994).

Existing studies generally indicate modest levels of negative care-related consequences, with negative consequences greater for caregivers with certain characteristics, in certain caregiving situations, and at different points in the caregiving process (Wright et al., 1993). Generally, 20% to 30% of caregivers report high levels of adverse caregiving effects or have clinically significant symptomatology (Bass et al., 1996; Neundorfer, 1991). Research comparing caregivers with age-matched controls does indicate that the risk of poorer well-being is greater among caregivers (Anthony-Bergstone, Zarit, & Gatz, 1988; Kiecolt-Glaser et al., 1987; Neundorfer, 1991; Pruchno & Potashnik, 1989; Whitlatch & Noelker, 1995). Over the long term, declines occur in mental and physical health, immunologic functioning, and use of prescription drugs for emotional disorders and insomnia.

Investigations of caregiving's positive consequences are relatively limited, which may reflect implicit conceptual biases in caregiving research. More recent studies, however, have begun to explore benefits derived from caregiving, including satisfaction, mastery, uplifts, coping skills, and social support (Deimling, 1994; Kahana et al., 1994; Lawton et al., 1989). Findings show that these measures are moderately correlated with caregiver strain and burden, with general well-being, and with not institutionalizing the care receiver. From a clinical and intervention standpoint, further conceptual and measurement attention to positive consequences are warranted in order to capitalize on caregiver strengths and maximize potential benefits that caregiving affords.

Although a substantial body of research has accumulated on caregiving consequences, gaps in knowledge remain, including how these outcomes change over the course of caregiving (Pruchno, Kleban, Michaels, & Dempsey, 1990), the nature and extent of differences between caregivers and equivalent groups of noncaregivers (Wright et al., 1993), the full range of potential positive and negative consequences (Lawton et al., 1989), and the factors that attenuate and exacerbate caregiving consequences (Thompson, Futterman, Gallagher-Thompson, Rose, & Lovett, 1993; Wright et al., 1993).

PREDICTORS OF CAREGIVING CONSEQUENCES

Caregiver gender, kin relationship, and living arrangement are consistently found to influence caregiving consequences. Findings show that women, including wives, daughters, and daughters-in-law experience more negative caregiving consequences than do male caregivers (Barusch & Spaid, 1989; Horowitz, 1985; Schulz, Tompkins, & Rau, 1988; Tennstedt, Cafferata, & Sullivan, 1992). Several explanations for these differences have been advanced, including the following: female caregivers bear the brunt of caring for dependent persons, are more likely to provide hands-on-assistance with personal care tasks, provide a larger volume of help, and are less likely to use formal services to supplement their efforts (Abel & Nelson, 1990; Brody, Litvin, Hoffman, & Kleban, 1992; Miller & Cafasso, 1992). It should be noted, however, that studies of well-being in a variety of populations consistently report lower levels among women.

Caregiving wives are especially vulnerable to adverse effects because their more advanced age and related chronic health conditions make physically demanding tasks more taxing and because they are less likely to have assistance from others (Wright et al., 1993). Both wife and husband caregivers are more critical of their responsibilities and their care receiver. Studies of abusive spouse caregiving relationships indicate both genders are equally abusive; however, wives experience more severe injuries from the abuse. Negative effects on daughters and daughters-in-law have been attributed to role overload and gender inequities in carrying out filial responsibilities (Abel, 1990; Brody, 1981; Horowitz, 1985; Robinson & Thurnher, 1979).

Among the structural factors affecting caregiving consequences, living arrangement may be the most powerful determinant (Deimling et al., 1989). Caregivers who reside in the same household with care receivers report more negative physical, emotional, and social consequences, regardless of relationship and controlling for a variety of other factors, including the severity of care receiver symptoms. One explanation is that caregivers in shared households provide more intensive care and constant supervision, resulting in less time away from their responsibilities. Furthermore, in parent-child caregiving situations, the shared household is often initiated because the care receiver can no longer live independently. The new living arrangement can disrupt established family and household routines, generating additional stress.

There is one exception to the negative effects of a shared household. In contrast to other negative consequences, strain in the relationship between caregiver and care receiver appears greater when primary caregivers live in separate households (Deimling et al., 1989). Possible explanations for this phenomenon include long-standing problems in the care receiver–caregiver relationship keep shared households from being formed; children in separate households are perceived by impaired parents as not fulfilling their filial obligations; and children and parents in separate households have opposing perceptions about appropriate living and care arrangements.

Another set of factors commonly investigated as predictors of caregiving consequences are symptoms of care receivers' illness or disability. Results show that most symptoms, such as cognitive deterioration, physical disability, and functional impairment, have inconsistent or no relationship to negative caregiving consequences (Wright et al., 1993). However, behavioral problems, such as acting out, yelling, and being disruptive, are consistently associated with more negative consequences (Bass et al., 1994; Deimling & Bass, 1986).

Caring for persons with Alzheimer's disease or other forms of dementia is more stressful because of the range and intensity of symptoms and associated care needs, particularly in the latter stages of the disease, and the loss of care receivers' personality and capacity for social interaction (Cohen & Eisdorfer, 1986; Mace & Rabins, 1981). For example, the need for constant supervision is more common in dementia caregiving, as is the occurrence of distressing behaviors such as wandering and associated risks to the elder . Care receivers with dementia also are less able to participate in their care and often resist care (Bass, Tausig, & Noelker, 1989). Despite these differences observed in dementia-related caregiving, few studies have systematically compared caregivers for persons with dementia and those helping relatives with other illnesses.

Another characteristic being given more attention as a predictor of caregiving consequences is the caregiver's employment status. Issues of employment and caregiving are particularly relevant for adult daughters and, to a lesser extent, sons but less relevant to spouse caregivers, who typically are retired. As many as one-third of primary caregivers are employed (Scharlach & Boyd, 1989; Stone & Short, 1990). Comparisons between employed and unemployed caregivers show that employed caregivers less often assist with personal care, provide fewer hours of help, more often live in separate households, and tend to have other family members more involved in care (Brody, Kleban, Johnsen, Hoffman, & Schoonover, 1987; Neal, Chapman, Ingersoll-Dayton, & Emlen, 1993). A small but significant portion of employed caregivers stop working or take leaves from work to provide care, and labor force attrition is more common among women and when the care receiver is behaviorally disruptive or needs constant supervision (Neal et al., 1993; Noelker, Bowman, & Schur, 1991).

Early investigations of employed caregivers found a variety of negative consequences related to maintaining work and family care roles. In terms of work performance, caregiving is associated with more time and days off, reduced productivity, more frequent tardiness, and less energy (Brody et al., 1987; Creedon, 1987; Scharlach & Boyd, 1989; Select Committee on Aging, 1987). Other negative consequences include increased depression, anxiety, somatic symptoms, and strain in the relationship with care receivers (Neal et al., 1993; Wagner, 1987). These investigations assumed that combining work and caregiving exhausted the resources of caregivers and increased vulnerability to a variety of negative effects.

An alternative theoretical model posits that individuals benefit from maintaining multiple and diverse roles (Thoits, 1983). Multiple roles enable the development of a broader range of skills, enhance self-esteem, increase the informal social network, and provide access to more information. Investigations that examined the possibility of employment's positive effects on caregivers found improved feelings of self-worth and greater care-related satisfaction among employed caregivers (Orodenker, 1990; Scharlach, 1994; Stoller & Pugliesi, 1989). Caregivers who are employed also may experience less financial strain and use work as a source of respite, especially when they have higher-status jobs that offer more compensation and flexibility. As a result, these caregivers are more likely to use formal services to help offset caregiving demands and to function as "care managers" (Archbold, 1983). Work obligations also may negate social attitudes that incline kin to feel they should independently care for impaired relatives without help from outside sources (Collins, Stommel, King, & Given, 1991).

SOCIAL SUPPORT AS A MEDIATOR OF CAREGIVING CONSEQUENCES

Social support includes assistance from both informal and formal sources and is the most widely investigated characteristic that may offset or accentuate caregiving consequences. Informal support refers to assistance to care receivers or primary caregivers from family members, friends, and neighbors. Formal support refers to paid assistance and services provided by hired helpers or professionals such as nurses, social workers, home aides, physicians, and therapists. Services may be provided in the home, community setting, hospital, or nursing home. Social support also may include assistance from persons who can be classified as either formal or informal helpers, such as church members and persons from a volunteer program.

Thirty years of research has documented the important role that social support can have for dealing with all types of stressors, including family caregiving. This research has evolved a rich conceptual framework that is useful for guiding family care research (Folkman & Lazarus, 1980; House, Landis, & Umberson, 1988; Lin, 1986). In this framework social support is considered to be one type of coping mechanism that can alter the effects of a stressor through a variety of independent, mediating, or mobilizing effects (Lin, 1986). The social support framework highlights the interrelationship among different stressors and coping mechanisms (Pearlin, 1989). The social support concept is conceived as multidimensional and may include, for example, assistance with instrumental tasks, emotional support, providing information, material or monetary aid, and social integration. A distinction is made between support actually received and a person's feelings that help is available if needed. Distinction also is made between structural characteristics of a support network (i.e., size, density, and composition) and the type, quantity, and quality of help provided.

There are three weaknesses of the social support framework as it is applied to the study of family caregiving. First, formal sources of help generally have been overlooked as a potential source of aid; most studies concentrate on informal support, with immediate kin most prominent (Adelman, Parks, & Albrecht, 1987; Bass et al., 1996; Krause, 1990). Second, few studies have specified the causal relationships between social support and caregiving consequences (Clipp & George, 1990). Thus, it is unclear whether support or lack thereof responds to or causes caregiving consequences. Third, the reasons that support influences caregiving consequences seldom are measured directly but are only inferred from statistical relationships. Examples of suggested reasons for support's effects include reducing the direct care responsibilities of the primary caregiver because of supplemental task assistance (Clipp & George, 1990), reassuring caregivers that they have backup help, and showing appreciation for their efforts (Morycz, 1985), and reducing social isolation of the caregiver and maintaining other relationships that caregivers find rewarding (Stoller & Pugliesi, 1989).

Despite these limitations, there is consistent evidence that informal social support is associated with reduced negative caregiving consequences, although some types are more beneficial than others, and a few studies suggest that more support can have negative effects in certain situations. Initial research in this area used global support measures and found fewer negative caregiving consequences when caregivers perceived that there was a support network available to them (George & Gwyther, 1986; Zarit et al., 1980). The presence of an informal helper living in the household with the caregiver, such as a spouse, may be especially beneficial (Cantor, 1983).

More recent research has begun to clarify the types of situations and informal support that are most important. Two studies suggest that caregivers who lack informal support also have other vulnerabilities or disadvantages that exacerbate the negative effects of caregiving (Clipp & George, 1990; Vitaliano, Russo, Young, Teri, & Maiuro, 1991). Additionally, the perceived quality of support may be more important than quantity or structural features (Drum & Bass, 1994). The importance of quality rather than quantity is accentuated by suggestions that larger numbers of helpers may obscure each individual's care responsibilities and create tension among network members, particularly when care receivers are cognitively intact, participate in their own care, and desire to maintain usual patterns of family relationships (Bass et al., 1989; Wright et al., 1993).

Future trends in research on informal support are illustrated by one recent study that made very specific comparisons among several types of support and caregiving consequences. Findings showed that support in the form of social integration, or interaction with family members and friends, was most central to reducing a variety of negative caregiving effects (Thompson et al., 1993). Social integration was more important than emotional, tangible, esteem, or informational support. One explanation offered for the powerful effect of social integration was that the pleasures of other social relationships helped balance and distract caregivers from the demands and frustrations of caregiving. Like most studies, however, this research could not determine whether integrative support reduced negative caregiving consequences or less distressed caregivers interacted more with others.

The extensive literature on informal social support contrasts with the limited research on formal support or services. An important dichotomy in formal support research is between services for care receivers and services for caregivers, both of which have the potential to offset negative caregiving consequences.

Research on services for care receivers has rarely tested the effects on kin caregivers. A meta-analysis of 150 experimental studies on use of community services by the elderly identified only eight investigations that included outcomes for caregivers (Weissert, Cready, & Pawelak, 1988). The best-known existing study is the national Channeling Demonstration Project (Stephens & Christianson, 1986). Some promising results from that study suggested that formal support for care receivers was related to caregivers' having higher life satisfaction, less restricted social activities, and greater satisfaction with care arrangements. Caregivers' emotional strain, physical health deterioration, and financial strain, however, were uncorrelated with formal support for care receivers.

Results from our recent research also offer promising evidence of the benefits that care receiver formal support may have for caregivers (Bass et al., 1996). This research applied principles from the social support framework previously used only on studies of informal support. It found that health and personal care services for care receivers was associated with less negative consequences for caregivers in terms of depression, health deterioration, and social isolation. Results highlighted the importance of formal helpers for care receivers concurrently attending to the needs of caregivers. Service providers for care receivers have direct experience with care situations and thus may be in an ideal position to provide caregivers with an empathetic source of emotional support and reinforcement, relief from direct care tasks, respite, and instruction and information about how to perform tasks. Moreover, caregivers who are reluctant to seek help for themselves may be more accepting of services when provided in the context of attending to the needs of care receivers (Noelker & Bass, 1995).

The second body of literature on formal support focuses on the effects of services designed for caregivers, such as respite, health education and training, support groups, computer support networks, case management, and assistance with other household and child care responsibilities. Most survey and observational studies find caregivers quite satisfied with these services and perceive them to be very helpful (Toseland & Rossiter, 1989). Results of experimental research that compares caregivers who use and do not use services are less consistent, with no service effect as frequently observed as positive effects (Zarit & Teri, 1991). This has led some to conclude that caregiver services are not effective enough to justify their cost (Callahan, 1989).

Any overall conclusion about the viability of caregiver services is premature. For example, some experimental studies of support groups or counseling programs find that caregivers who use services, compared to equivalent controls, have reduced levels of depression and strain (Greene & Monahan, 1987), lower rates of nursing home placement (Mittelman et al., 1993), improved relationships with care receivers (Scharlach, 1987), and higher morale (Toseland & Smith, 1990). At the same time, a number of other well-designed experimental studies fail to show significant service effects in terms of caregiver strain, nursing home placement, and caregiver well-being (Haley, Brown, & Levine, 1987; Lawton, Brody, & Saperstein, 1991; Montgomery & Borgatta, 1989).

Despite their methodological strengths, existing experimental research on caregiver services has a number of shortcomings (for reviews, see Toseland & Rossiter, 1989; Zarit & Teri, 1991). One important limitation is that many caregivers in experimental service groups are exposed to limited amounts of the intervention. Further, control group caregivers often find alternative sources of support because research protocols ethically cannot limit assistance from other formal and informal sources. A second limitation is that the exact content of an experimental caregiver service often is not well controlled nor monitored. Thus, variation in service effects may be more evident in caregivers exposed to varying amounts and types of the experimental service than between experimental and control group caregivers (Kosloski & Montgomery, 1995). Another limitation is that there often is a mismatch between the difficulties encountered by the caregiver, the type of help offered by the service, and caregiving consequence selected as the desired outcome. The result of this mismatch is that effects are diminished because services are delivered to caregivers not experiencing the problem the service is intended to help, and beneficial changes go undetected because the outcomes are not sensitive to service effects.

A final limitation is in the interpretation of findings and translation of research results into policy. It is not clear how much effect is needed to justify the cost of caregiver services. The result is that the same scientific research finding can be used to support the need for more services for family caregivers or to argue that services for caregivers are ineffective. Whatever the case, family caregiving is substantial in the United States, and further research is needed to better understand and facilitate the caregiving process.

REFERENCES

Abel, E. K. (1990). Informal care for the disabled elderly: A critique of recent literature. *Research on Aging, 12*, 139–157.

Abel, E. K., & Nelson, M. K. (1990). *Circles of care: Work and identity in women's lives*. Albany: State University of New York Press.

Adelman, M., Parks, M., & Albrecht, T. (1987). Beyond close relationships: Support in weak ties. In T. Albrecht & M. Adelman (Eds.), *Communicating social support*. Beverly Hills, CA: Sage.

Aneshensel, C. S., Pearlin, L. I., Mullan, J. T., Zarit, S. H., & Whitlatch, C. J. (1995). *Profiles in caregiving: The unexpected career*. New York: Academic.

Anthony-Bergstone, C. R., Zarit, S. H., & Gatz, M. (1988). Symptoms of psychological distress among caregivers of dementia patients. *Psychology and Aging, 3*, 245–248.

Antonucci, T. C. (1990). Social supports and social relationships. In R. J. Binstock & E. Shanas (Eds.), *Handbook of aging and the social sciences* (3rd ed., pp. 205–227). San Diego, CA: Academic.

Archbold, P. G. (1982). All-consuming activity: The family as caregiver. *Generations, 7*, 12–13.

Archbold, P. G. (1983). Impact of parent-caring on women. *Family Relations, 32*, 39–45.

Barer, B. M., & Johnson, C. L. (1990). A critique of the caregiving literature. *Gerontologist, 30*, 26–29.

Barusch, A. S., & Spaid, W. M. (1989). Gender differences in caregiving: Why do wives report greater burden? *Gerontologist, 19*, 667–676.

Bass, D. M., McClendon, M. J., Deimling, G. T., & Mukherjee, S. (1994). The influence of diagnosed mental impairment on family caregiver strain. *Journals of Gerontology, 49*, S146–S155.

Bass, D. M., Noelker, L. S., & Rechlin, L. R. (1996). The moderating influence of services on negative caregiving consequences. *Journals of Gerontology, 51B*, S121–S131.

Bass, D. M., Noelker, L. S., Townsend, A. L., & Deimling, G. T. (1990). Losing an aged relative: Perceptual differences between spouses and adult children. *Omega: Journal of Death and Dying, 21*, 21–40.

Bass, D. M., Tausig, M. B., & Noelker, L. S. (1989). Elder impairment, social support and caregiver strain: A framework for understanding support's effects. *Journal of Applied Social Sciences, 13*, 80–117.

Blenkner, M. (1965). Social work and family relationships in later life with some thoughts on filial maturity. In E. Shanas & G. F. Streib (Eds.), *Social structure of the family: Generational relations*. Englewood Cliffs, NJ: Prentice-Hall.

Brody, E. (1981). Women in the middle and family help to older people. *Gerontologist, 21*, 471–480.

Brody, E. (1985). *Mental and physical health practices of older people.* New York: Springer Publishing.

Brody, E. M., Kleban, M. H., Johnsen, P. T., Hoffman, C., & Schoonover, C. B. (1987). Work status and parent care: A comparison of four groups of women. *Gerontologist, 27*, 201–208.

Brody, E. M., Litvin, S. J., Hoffman, C., & Kleban, M. H. (1992). Differential effects of daughters' marital status on their parent care experiences. *Gerontologist, 32*, 58–67.

Callahan, J. J., Jr. (1989). Play it again Sam—there is no impact. *Gerontologist, 29*, 5–6.

Cantor, M. (1975). Life space and social support system of the inner city elderly of New York. *Gerontologist, 15*, 23–34.

Cantor, M. H. (1980, November). *Caring for the frail elderly: Impact on family, friends, and neighbors*. Paper presented at the annual meeting of the Gerontological Society, Washington, DC.

Cantor, M. H. (1983). Strain among caregivers: A study of experience in the United States. *Gerontologist, 23*, 597–604.

Cicirelli, V. G. (1983). A comparison of helping behavior to elderly parents of adult children with intact and disrupted marriages. *Gerontologist, 23*, 619–625.

Clipp, E. C., & George, L. K. (1990). Caregiver needs and patterns of social support. *Journals of Gerontology, 45*, S102–S111.

Cohen, D., & Eisdorfer, C. (1986). *The loss of self: A family resource for the care of Alzheimer's disease and related disorders*. New York: W. W. Norton.

Collins, C., Stommel, M., King, S., & Given, C. W. (1991). Assessment of the attitudes of family caregivers toward community services. *Gerontologist, 31*, 756–761.

Comptroller General of the United States. (1977). *The well-being of older people in Cleveland, Ohio: A report to Congress*. Washington, DC: General Accounting Office.

Creedon, M. A. (1987). Introduction: Employment and eldercare. In M. Creedon (Ed.), *Issues for an aging America: Employees and eldercare: A briefing book*. Bridgeport, CT: University of Bridgeport, Center for the Study of Aging.

Deimling, G. T. (1994). Caregiver functioning. In M. P. Lawton & J. A. Teresi (Eds.), *Annual review of gerontology and geriatrics: Focus on assessment techniques* (Vol. 14, pp. 257–280).

Deimling, G. T., & Bass, D. M. (1986). Symptoms of mental impairment among elderly adults and their effects on family caregivers. *Journal of Gerontology, 41*, 778–784.

Deimling, G. T., Bass, D. M., Townsend, A. L., & Noelker, L. S. (1989). Care-related stress: A comparison of spouse and adult-child caregivers in shared and separate households. *Journal of Aging and Health, 1*, 67–82.

Doty, P. (1986). Family care of the elderly: The role of public policy. *Milbank Quarterly, 64*, 34–75.

Drum, M., & Bass, D. M. (1994, November). *The influence of structural network characteristics on caregiver distress*. Poster presented at the annual meeting of the Gerontological Society of America, Atlanta.

Dunkle, R. (1983). The effect of elders' household contribution on their depression. *Journal of Gerontology, 38*, 732–737.

Estes, C. L., Swan, J. H., & Associates. (1993). *The long term care crisis: Elders trapped in the no-care zone.* Newbury Park, CA: Sage.

Finley, N. J., Roberts, M. D., & Banahan, B. F. (1988). Motivators and inhibitors of attitudes of filial obligation toward aging parents. *Gerontologist, 28*, 73–78.

Folkman, S., & Lazarus, R. S. (1980). An analysis of coping in a middle-aged community sample. *Journal of Health and Social Behavior, 21*, 219–239.

George, L. K., & Gwyther, L. (1986). Caregiver well-being: A multidimensional examination of family caregivers of demented adults. *Gerontologist, 26*, 253–259.

Greene, V. L., & Monahan, D. J. (1987). The effect of a professionally guided caregiver support and education group on institutionalization of care receivers. *Gerontologist, 27*, 716–721.

Guberman, N., Maheu, P., & Maille, C. (1992). Women as family caregivers: Why do they care? *Gerontologist, 32*, 607–617.

Gurland, B. J. (1980). The assessment of the mental health status of older adults. In J. E. Birren & R. B. Sloane (Eds.), *Handbook of mental health and aging* (pp. 671–700). Englewood Cliffs, NJ: Prentice-Hall.

Haley, W. E., Brown, S. L., & Levine, E. G. (1987). Experimental evaluation of the effectiveness of group intervention for dementia caregivers. *Gerontologist, 27*, 376–382.

Himes, C. L. (1992). Future caregivers: Projected family structures of older persons. *Journals of Gerontology, 47*, S17–S26.

Horowitz, A. (1985). Family caregiving to the frail elderly. In C. Eisdorfer, M. P. Lawton, & G. L. Maddox (Eds.), *Annual review of gerontology and geriatrics* (Vol. 5, pp. 194–246). New York: Springer Publishing.

House, J. S., Landis, K. R., & Umberson, D. (1988). Social relationships and health. *Science, 241*, 540–545.

Kahana, E., Biegel, D. E., & Wykle, M. L. (1994). *Family caregiving across the lifespan.* Thousand Oaks, CA: Sage.

Kiecolt-Glaser, J. K., Glaser, R., Shuttleworth, E. E., Dyer, C. S., Ogrocki, P., & Speicher, C. E. (1987). Chronic stress and immunity in family caregivers of Alzheimer's disease patients. *Psychosomatic Medicine, 49*, 523–535.

Kinney, J. M., & Stephens, M. A. P. (1989). Hassles and uplifts of giving care to a family member with dementia. *Psychology and Aging, 4*, 402–408.

Kosloski, K., & Montgomery, R. J. (1995). The impact of respite use on nursing home placement. *Gerontologist, 35*, 67–74.

Kovar, M. (1986). Aging in the eighties: Preliminary data from the supplement on aging to the national health interview survey, United States, January–June 1984. In *Advance data from vital and health statistics* (DHHS Publication No. PHS 86-1250). Hyattsville, MD: Public Health Service.

Krause, N. (1990). Perceived health problems, formal/informal support, and life satisfaction among older adults. *Journals of Gerontology, 45*, S193–S205.

Lawton, M. P., & Brody, E. (1969). Assessment of older people: Self-maintaining and instrumental activities of daily living. *Gerontologist, 9*, 179–186.

Lawton, M. P., Brody, E. M., & Saperstein, A. R. (1991). *Respite for caregivers of Alzheimer patients: Research and practice.* New York: Springer Publishing.

Lawton, M. P., Kleban, M. H., Moss, M., Rovine, M., & Glicksman, A. (1989). Measuring caregiving appraisal. *Journals of Gerontology, 44*, P61–P71.

Lawton, M. P., Moss, M., & Duhamel, L. M. (1995). The quality of daily life among elderly care receivers. *Journal of Applied Gerontology, 14*, 150–171.

Lin, N. (1986). Modeling the effects of social support. In N. Lin, A. Dean, & W. Ensel (Eds.), *Social support, life events and depression* (pp. 173–209). Orlando, FL: Academic.

Litwak, E. (1985). *Helping the elderly: The complementary roles of informal networks and formal systems.* New York: Guilford.

Mace, N. L., & Rabins, P. V. (1981). *The 36-hour day.* Baltimore: Johns Hopkins University Press.

McClendon, M., Bass, D. M. , & Noelker, L. S. (1994, November). *Contrasting assistance use by persons with Alzheimer's disease and other illnesses.* Paper presented at the annual meeting of the Gerontological Society of America, Atlanta.

Miller, B., & Cafasso, L. (1992). Gender differences in caregiving: Fact or artifact? *Gerontologist, 32*, 498–507.

Mittelman, M. S., Ferris, S. H., Steinberg, G., Shulman, E., Mackell, J. A., Ambinder, A., & Cohen, J. (1993). An intervention that delays institutionalization of Alzheimer's disease patients: Treatment of spouse-caregivers. *Gerontologist, 33*, 730–740.

Montgomery, R. J. V., & Borgatta, E. F. (1989). The effects of alternative support strategies on family caregiving. *Gerontologist, 29*, 457–464.

Morycz, R. K. (1985). Caregiving strain and the desire to institutionalize family members with Alzheimer's disease. *Research on Aging, 7*, 329–361.

Nagi, S. (1976). An epidemiology of disability among adults in the United States. *Milbank Memorial Fund Quarterly, 54*, 439–467.

Neal, M. B., Chapman, N. J., Ingersoll-Dayton, B., & Emlen, A. C. (1993). *Balancing work and caregiving for children, adults, and elders.* Newbury Park, CA: Sage.

Neundorfer, M. M. (1991). Coping and health outcomes in spouse caregivers of persons with dementia. *Nursing Research, 40*, 260–265.

Noelker, L. S. (1984). Family care of elder relatives: The impact of policy and programs. In A. Kethley (Ed.), *Conference proceedings on family support and long term care* (pp. 52–85). Excelsior, MN: Inter Study.

Noelker, L. S. (1995). Service use by caregivers of elderly receiving case management. *Journal of Case Management, 4*, 142–149.

Noelker, L. S., & Bass, D. M. (1994). Conceptual approaches to linking informal and formal caregiving in late life. In E. Kahana, D. Biegel, & M. Wykle (Eds.), *Family caregiving across the lifespan* (pp. 356–381). Newbury Park, CA: Sage.

Noelker, L., Bowman, K., & Schur, D. (1991, November). *Factors related to employment status of caregiving daughters.* Paper presented at the annual meeting of the Gerontological Society of America, San Francisco.

Noelker, L. S., & Poulshock, S. W. (1982). *The effects on families of caring for impaired elderly in residents: Final report to the Administration on Aging.* Cleveland, OH: Benjamin Rose Institute.

Noelker, L. S., & Shaffer, G. (1986). Care networks: How they form and change. *Generations, 10*(4), 62–64.

Noelker, L. S., & Wallace, R. (1985). The organization of family care for impaired elderly. *Journal of Family Issues, 6*, 23–44.

Noelker, L. S., & Whitlatch, C. J. (1995). Service use by caregivers of elderly receiving case management. In G. Maddox (Ed.), *Encyclopedia of aging.* New York: Springer Publishing.

Orodenker, S. Z. (1990). Family caregiving in a changing society: The effects of employment on caregiver stress. *Family and Community Health, 12*, 58–70.

Parsons, T. (1964). The kinship system of the contemporary United States, 1943. In *Essays in sociological theory* (pp. 194–195). New York: Free Press of Glencoe.

Pearlin, L. I. (1989). The sociological study of stress. *Journal of Health and Social Behavior, 30*, 241–256.

Pearlin, L. I. (1992). The careers of caregivers. *Gerontologist, 32*, 647.

Penrod, J. D., Kane, R. A., Kane, R. L., & Finch, M. D. (1995). Who cares? The size, scope, and composition of the caregiver support system. *Gerontologist, 35*, 489–498.

Pratt, C., Schmall, V., Wright, S., & Hare, J. (1987). The forgotten client: Family caregivers to institutionalized dementia patients. In T. Brubaker (Ed.), *Aging, health, and family: Long-term care* (pp. 197–215). Newbury Park, CA: Sage.

Pruchno, R. A., Kleban, M. H., Michaels, J. E., & Dempsey, N. P. (1990). Mental and physical health of caregiving spouses: Development of a causal model. *Journals of Gerontology, 45*, P192–P199.

Pruchno, R. A., & Potashnik, S. L. (1989). Caregiving spouses: Physical and mental health in perspective. *Journal of the American Geriatric Society, 37*, 697–705.

Reisberg, B., Ferris, S., Anand, R., Buttinger, C., Bornstein, J., Sinaiko, E., & de Leon, M. (1984). Clinical assessments of cognition in the aged. In C. A. Shamonia (Ed.), *Biology and treatment of dementia in the elderly*. Washington, DC: American Psychiatric Press.

Robinson, B., & Thurnher, M. (1979). Taking care of aged parents: A family cycle transition. *Gerontologist, 19*, 586–593.

Scharlach, A. E. (1987). Relieving feelings of strain among women with elderly mothers. *Psychology and Aging, 2*, 9–13.

Scharlach, A. E. (1994). Caregiving and employment: Competing or complementary roles? *Gerontologist, 34*, 378–385.

Scharlach, A. E., & Boyd, S. L. (1989). Caregiving and employment: Results of an employee survey. *Gerontologist, 29*, 382–387.

Schulz, R., Tompkins, C. A., & Rau, M. T. (1988). A longitudinal study of the psychosocial impact of stroke on primary support persons. *Psychology of Aging, 3*, 131–141.

Schulz, R., Visintainer, P., & Williamson, G. (1990). Psychiatric and physical morbidity effects of caregiving. *Journals of Gerontology, 45*, P181–P191.

Select Committee on Aging. (1987). *Exploding the myths: Caregiving in America* (Comm. Pub. No. 99–611). Washington, DC: U.S. Government Printing Office.

Shanas, E. (1979a). The family as a social support system in old age. *Gerontologist, 19*, 169–174.

Shanas, E. (1979b). Social myth as hypothesis: The case of the family relations of old people. *Gerontologist, 19*, 3–9

Shanas, E., Townsend, P., Wedderburn, D., Fries, H., Milhj, P., & Stehouwer, J. (1968). *Old people in three industrial societies*. New York: Atherton.

Sorokin, P. A. (1937). *Social and cultural dynamics*. New York: American Book Co.

Stephens, S. A., & Christianson, J. B. (1986). *Informal care of the elderly*. Lexington, MA: D. C. Heath.

Stoller, E. P. (1983). Parental caregiving by adult children. *Journal of Marriage and the Family, 45*, 851–858.

Stoller, E. P., & Pugliesi, K. L. (1989). Other roles of caregivers: Competing responsibilities or supportive resources. *Journals of Gerontology*, *44*, S231–S238.

Stone, R., Cafferata, G., & Sangl, J. (1987). Caregivers of the frail elderly: A national profile. *Gerontologist*, *27*, 616–626.

Stone, R. I., & Short, P. F. (1990). The competing demands of employment and informal caregiving to disabled elders. *Medical Care*, *28*, 513–526.

Stull, D. E., Kosloski, K, & Kercher, K. (1994). Caregiver burden and generic well-being: Opposite sides of the same coin? *Gerontologist*, *34*, 88–94.

Tennstedt, S., Cafferata, G. L., & Sullivan, L. (1992). Depression among caregivers of impaired elders. *Journal of Aging and Health*, *4*, 58–76.

Tennstedt, S. L., McKinlay, J. B., & Sullivan, L. M. (1989). Informal care for frail elders: The role of secondary caregivers. *Gerontologist*, *29*, 677–683.

Thoits, P. A. (1983). Dimensions of life events that influence psychological stress: An evaluation and synthesis of the literature. In H. B. Haplan (Ed.), *Psychosocial stress: Trends in theory and research* (pp. 33–87). New York: Academic.

Thompson, E. H., Jr., Futterman, A. M., Gallagher-Thompson, D., Rose, J. M., & Lovett, S. B. (1993). Social support and caregiving burden in family caregivers of frail elders. *Journals of Gerontology*, *48*, S245–S254.

Toseland, R. W., & Rossiter, C. M. (1989). Group interventions to support family caregivers: A review and analysis. *Gerontologist*, *29*, 438–448.

Toseland, R. W., & Smith, C. G. (1990). Effectiveness of individual counseling by professional and peer helpers for family caregivers of the elderly. *Psychology and Aging*, *5*, 256–263.

Vitaliano, P. P., Russo, J., Young, H. M., Teri, L., & Maiuro, R. D. (1991). Predictors of burden in spouse caregivers of individuals with Alzheimer's disease. *Psychology and Aging*, *6*, 392–402.

Wagner, D. L. (1987). Corporate eldercare project: Findings. In M. A. Creedon (Ed.), *Issues for an aging America: Employees and eldercare: A briefing book* (pp. 25–29). Bridgeport, CT: University of Bridgeport, Center for the Study of Aging.

Weissert, W. G., Cready, C. M., & Pawelak, J. E. (1988). The past and future of home- and community-based long-term care. *Milbank Quarterly*, *66*, 309–388.

Whitlatch, C. J., & Noelker, L. S. (1996). Caregiving and caring. In J. E. Birren (Ed.), *Encyclopedia of gerontology* (pp. 253–268). New York: Academic.

Wright, L., Clipp, E., & George, L. (1993). Health consequences of caregiver stress. *Medicine, Exercise, Nutrition and Health*, *2*, 181–195.

Zarit, S., Reever, K., & Bach-Peterson, J. (1980). Relatives of the impaired elderly: Correlates of feelings of burden. *Gerontologist*, *20*, 649–655.

Zarit, S. H., & Teri, L. (1991). Interventions and services for family caregivers. *Annual Review of Gerontology and Geriatrics*, *11*, 287–310.

PART IV

Contemporary Issues in an Aging Society

This section of the book further applies the gerontological imagination to salient scientific and policy issues in contemporary society. Although the universe of policy issues related to aging is quite large, only a few have been selected for detailed analysis. Each chapter diagnoses the problem and offers some suggestions for improving the human condition, especially among older adults.

Barresi probes the area of ethnogerontology. He crystallizes some themes raised earlier (e.g., heterogeneity among older adults) and offers insight into the unique needs and lifestyles of ethnic and racial groups. The economic status of the older population is considered in detail in chapter 14, by DeVaney. She provides a concise analysis of the heterogeneity in income and wealth among older people and poses some probing policy questions for consideration. Walker discusses the need for health promotion among older adults in America and current policies and activities to promote healthy aging. This is a vital topic if we hope to see further gains in compressing morbidity and enhancing life.

The focus of the next two chapters is on aging and forms of deviant behavior. Milner reviews the types and prevalence of elder abuse and neglect in America and offers suggestions for improving both research and intervention. Doyle systematically examines the two faces of aging and crime: older person as victim and older person as offender. It is a most reasoned analysis of a subject area that evokes strong emotions.

Finally, Ferraro considers our orientation to death in modern societies and how this all too often leads to a myth devaluing older people, especially the disabled elderly population. He briefly reviews historical changes in death and dying and shows that many of the social movements surrounding death seek to enable the person to have more control over the dying process.

Whether we examine biological, psychological, or social phenomena, aging involves a variety of outcomes both positive and negative. Part IV is an attempt to soundly analyze some of the problems confronted by older people, without permitting our gerontological imagination to be swallowed up by a "problem orientation." No effort is made to deny the common problems of growing older. However, we must recall that these problems are not universal among older adults and that most of the elderly are more resilient in confronting the challenges of growing older than is commonly acknowledged. The objective of part IV is to foster sensitivity to the capacities and needs of this diverse population of older adults, without confusing "usual aging" with human potential. The analyses presented provide a strong foundation for shaping policy to maximize the quality of human lives across the life span.

CHAPTER 13

Current Issues in Ethnogerontology

Charles M. Barresi

Since the publication of the first edition of this book interest in ethnogerontology, the study of social aging in national, racial, and cultural groups, has progressed with a steady growth. This is evident in the number of publications that have appeared, the richness of the topics they contain, and the wealth of information presented. These publications represent a variety of sources, including both books and articles as well as book chapters, monographs, dissertations, and government publications. They range from general texts or readers that cover a wide range of topics in ethnogerontology (Harper, 1990; Stanford & Torres-Gil, 1992; Stoller & Gibson, 1994), to books that focus on a specific area of concern regarding ethnic elderly (Barresi & Stull, 1993; Gelfand, 1994). Other works include those that deal with a single group of elderly such as Black Americans (Harel, McKinney, & Williams, 1990; Jackson, Chatters, & Taylor, 1993), Hispanic Americans (Brink, 1992), Native Americans (Kunitz & Levy, 1991), and Asian Americans (Furuto, Biswas, Chung, Murase, & Ross-Sheriff, 1992).

With the proliferation of works in this area has come an increased recognition of the importance of understanding the impact of ethnicity on aging. There is a growing need for information that will address the process of aging in ethnic groups with solid knowledge rather than myths and stereotypes. The purpose of this chapter is to identify and examine the current issues in ethnogerontology.

DEFINITION AND SCOPE

Ethnogerontology is constrained by the definition of ethnicity that researchers employ. The definition of ethnicity that one uses influences the outcome of the logic and design as well as the results of a study. For example, a broad definition, one that is based strictly on race, religion, or national origin, is too inclusive and tends to disregard the diversity in such groups. When ethnicity is all-inclusive it tends to overlook the fact that not all persons who fall into similar categories of race, religion, or even national origin make up a single group. The variations found within these groups create differences that are often difficult for individuals to accept in identifying with one another. For example, not all Jews are orthodox in their belief, and the differences between Irish Americans or Italian Americans with origins in the northern or southern parts of their respective countries makes for little sense of closeness between them. There are similar differences in the regional origins of most ethnic Americans.

Even the current use of the term *African Americans* to refer to Black persons in our society is an exclusionary term that ignores the variety of origins among Blacks in the United States. Black Americans who trace their ancestry to Caribbean countries such as Haiti or Jamaica are culturally different from those who have African origins. Researchers who would ignore these distinctions invite overly broad and erroneous conclusions.

Although problems arise through the utilization of a definition of ethnicity that is too broad, employing one that is too narrow can also lead to conceptual difficulties. This is typically the case in studies that associate ethnic identity with minority status. Much of the recent research on "ethnic" elderly is more often research conducted on deprived "minorities" (i.e., Black Americans, Hispanics, Native Americans, and Asians/Pacific Islanders) (Barresi, in press). Investigators have failed to make a distinction between the effects of cultural factors and the results of discrimination because of the complicating influence of race and social class. By ignoring these cultural distinctions, researchers have focused on discriminatory practices and have not shed sufficient light on the social and cultural dynamics of aging in ethnic groups.

It therefore seems that a definition of ethnicity that will be useful to both researchers and policymakers alike is one that emphasizes those characteristics that are socially and culturally transmitted. These characteristics set a group apart while at the same time allowing it to preserve its uniqueness. Language, belief patterns, values, and a shared sense of history and place of origin are all aspects that should be included in a definition of ethnicity. These elements direct attention to the salient concepts of group identification and self-concept that are central to ethnic group membership. In addition, to allow for the dynamic aspects of ethnicity, the definition should incorporate the notions of growth and change.

Therefore, for the purposes of this chapter, ethnicity is defined as a large group whose members internalize and share a heritage of and a commitment to unique social characteristics, cultural symbols, and behavior patterns that are not fully understood by outsiders. This definition leans in the preferable direction of the broad approach, but it emphasizes both the individual commitment and socially shared aspects of ethnic group membership. It goes beyond nominal identification with the group solely by ancestry and stresses the existence of a common bond between group members. Moreover, it places the central emphasis on the cultural and social aspects of the concept and identifies ethnicity as a group phenomenon rather than simply a biological or geographic event.

ETHNOGERONTOLOGY COMES OF AGE

Ethnogerontology emerged in the late 1960s in a number of unpublished theses and dissertations. The first of these studies mainly involved research on Black Americans in the South. The 1970s saw the further development of these studies with the emergence of research on Hispanic elderly, mainly Mexican Americans (Markides, Liang, & Jackson, 1990). Later, interest in the general topic of ethnicity began to spill over into gerontology and resulted in increased interest in the aging process as it occurs among various ethnic, racial, and cultural groups. By the 1980s studies included Asian Americans, Native Americans, and White Americans of various national origins (Gelfand & Barresi, 1987b).

Interest in ethnicity as a variable in the aging process was given a further boost with the establishment of the Task Force on Minority Issues by the Gerontological Society of America. This was followed by the publication of editorials encouraging research on aging in minority populations in the official journals of the society (Gibson, 1988; Jackson, 1989b). As the literature in this area has increased, a number of issues have been debated. There are those who believe that ethnicity is no longer a salient issue because of the demise of those persons who came to this country in the great waves of immigration around the turn of the century. This, however, fails to take into consideration the steady flow of immigration that has taken place since the quota system was dropped in 1965, especially the recent large influx of immigrants and refugees from Southeast Asia and Latin America (Gelfand & Barresi, 1987a). It also overlooks the fact that many persons in ethnic communities, although native-born Americans, identify more with their ethnic group customs, language, and beliefs than they do with those of the wider society.

The increase of these ethnic populations along with the movement back to ethnicity among many native-born Americans has made the issue of aging in ethnic groups a very salient one indeed (Stanford & Torres-Gil, 1992). In the midst of such controversies as the proposals to make Spanish an official second language of the United States and the growing need for social services in ethnic groups, it behooves gerontologists to provide more scholarly research in this area. Before addressing the theoretical and methodological issues unique to this research, it may be useful to consider briefly some of the major ethnic differences in aging based on our current knowledge. Only selected demographic and social factors are considered here (see Gelfand & Barresi, 1987b; Markides & Mindel, 1987; or Stoller & Gibson, 1994, for a more comprehensive review).

ETHNIC DIFFERENTIATION

Ancestry Identification

In the 1990 census of the population, persons were surveyed regarding their ancestry. Respondents were allowed to select either single or multiple ancestry groups. Because persons who reported a multiple ancestry group were included in more than one category, the group sizes are not completely accurate, but they do afford an insight into the composition of the ethnic population of the United States. The German ancestry group is the largest, consisting of 23% of those reporting. Irish and English are next with 16% and 13%, respectively. Italians are next with 6%, followed by those who identified themselves as American, 5%. Next are French and Polish at 4% each; Dutch, 2.5%; Scotch-Irish and Scottish, 2% each; and last, Norwegian, 1.6%, and Russian, 1.2%. The remaining 36 ethnic groups were all less than 1% each (U.S. Bureau of the Census, 1992).

Elderly Minorities

Within these ethnic groups, some are regarded as minority groups and are typically dealt with in the literature as minority elderly. At present the majority of studies among ethnic elderly have been conducted on these groups. The typical identification of these groups is by racial characteristics. The largest of these racial groups is the Black American elderly. The second most studied group of ethnic elderly is the Spanish-speaking, or Hispanics. According to the 1990 census, of the 31 million elderly population of the United States (65 years or older), approximately 8% are Black Americans, 1.5% are of Asian origins, and 0.5% are Native Americans. The remaining 89% are classified as White, although this includes a variety of White ethnic groups. Hispanic elderly can be of any race, and they make up about 4% of the present elderly population (U.S. Bureau of the Census, 1992). Again, it should be pointed out that there is great diversity among Hispanic Americans, including persons with origins mainly in Mexico, Puerto Rico, and Cuba. There are, however, a number of Hispanics who trace their backgrounds to other Spanish-speaking countries.

The elderly population in the ethnic groups named above totaled a little over 3½ million in 1995 (excluding the Hispanic Americans, who can be of any race) (Table 13.1). This made up about 11% of the elderly population in the United States, a proportion has been steadily growing. Currently, the aged segment of ethnic groups has been growing at a faster rate than the elderly White population. In Table 13.1 we see that whereas the percentage of increase of both White and Black American elderly from 1980 to 1995 is close to the increase for all elderly, the increase for other groups ranges from three to five times the norm. For example, in the decade and a half since 1980 the American Indian, Eskimo, and Aleut group has increased 84%. The percentages of increase for Asians and

TABLE 13.1 Number and Percentage of Persons 65 Years and Older by Race and Hispanic Origin, 1980, 1990, and 1995, and Percent Increase in Number of Persons 65 Years ans Older between 1980 and 1995 (Numbers in Thousands)

		1980			1990			1995		
All Ages		No. 65+	% 65+	All Ages	No. 65+	% 65+	All Ages	No. 65+	% 65+	% Increase 65+ 1980–95
Total	226,546	25,549	11.3	248.710	31,242	12.6	263,434	33,649	12.8	31.7
White	188,372	22,948	12.2	199,686	27,852	13.9	218,334	30,129	13.8	31.3
Black	26,495	2,087	07.9	29,986	2,509	08.4	33,117	2,732	08.2	31.0
AIEA[a]	1,420	75	05.3	1,959	114	05.8	2,226	138	06.2	84.0
API[b]	3,501	212	06.1	7,274	454	06.2	9,756	650	06.7	206.6
Other	6,758	301	04.5	9,805	312	03.2	NA	NA	NA	NA[c]
Hispanic[d]	14,609	709	04.9	22,354	1,161	05.2	26,798	1,532	05.7	116.1

[a] American Indian, Eskimo, and Aleut.

[b] Asian and Pacific Islander.

[c] The "other" category is not comparable because different racial groups were included in 1980 and 1990. Also, the "other" category was not calculated for the 1995 figures.

[d] Persons of Hispanic origin may be of any race.

Sources: U.S. Bureau of the Census (1983), *1980 Census of population, general population characteristics, United States summary*, Vol. 1 (PC 80-1-B1). U.S. Government Printing Office, Washington, DC.; U.S. Bureau of the Census (1991), Selected tables provided by the Age and Sex Statistics Branch of the Population Division, U.S. Department of Commerce, Washington, DC. The 1995 figures are from Day, J. C. (1993), *Projection of the population, by age, sex, race and Hispanic origin, for the United Sates: 1993–2050*, U.S. Bureau of the Census, Current Population Reports (P25-1104), Washington, DC.

Pacific Islanders and for Hispanics are 207% and 116%, respectively. This rapid growth among ethnic elderly is projected to continue well into the next century.

Along with a growth in numbers, the ethnic elderly population also shows signs of aging. An example is provided by the increase in the number of persons 85 years old and older, a group commonly referred to as the oldest old. For instance, this segment of the Black American elderly population numbered 67,000 in 1960 and increased to 251,000 in 1990 and is expected to reach 500,000 by 2010 and 1.8 million by 2050 (Angel & Hogan, 1991). This will place a continued burden on health and social services because of increased use of such services.

Life Expectancy

Beyond demographic characteristics, ethnic differentiation also occurs in a number of health and social factors. None is more revealing of basic social differences than average life expectancy. Comparable life expectancy statistics are generally not available for all the above ethnic groups except for Whites and Blacks. The most recent census data indicates that expectation of life at birth in 1993 for Whites is 76.3 years; for Blacks, 69.3 years; and for Blacks and others together, 71.5 years (U.S. Bureau of the Census, 1995). Specific data for the other groups are older and are not comparable because of the variety of sources. However, a recent population report from the Bureau of the Census used certain demographic assumptions regarding mortality estimates for the Asian and American Indian groups in order to construct life tables. Using these assumptions, life expectancy projections were made, based on the 1990 census data figures (Day, 1993).

Table 13.2 shows the life expectancy for the middle series projections for the major racial and ethnic groups by sex, for 1995, 2005, and 2020. The table includes life expectancy at birth and at age 65. As expected, the projections indicate that for a child born in 1995 into the various groups mentioned above, the average life expectancy will be higher than in previous years. This increase will continue for both the 2005 and 2020 cohorts. What is more interesting, however, is that the order of ranking among the groups will change dramatically. Close examination of the table reveals that the ranking for various ethnic groups is consistent for both males and females except for Whites and Native Americans at birth. In these two groups males and females hold different positions in the rank order, with Native American women displaying higher life expectancies than White women. However, for convenience in ranking the entire group, the life expectancies for both males and females can be combined. The higher figures for White males thus offset the differences between Native American and White females. The resulting ranking of the projections of life expectancies at birth for 1995 shows that Asian and Pacific Islanders have the longest life expectancies, with Hispanics in second place. Native Americans have narrowly edged into third place ahead of Whites, and Blacks are last among these groups.

TABLE 13.2 Projection for Life Expectancy at Birth and at Age 65, by Race, Hispanic Origin, and Sex: 1995, 2005, and 2020 (Middle Assumption)

Projections for Year	Total		White		Black		American Indian, Eskimo, Aleut		Asian, Pacific Islander		Hispanic Origin	
	Male	Female	Male	Female	Male	Female	Male	Female	Male	Female	Male	Female
At Birth												
1995	72.8	79.7	73.7	80.3	65.8	74.8	72.5	82.1	80.2	86.2	75.2	83.0
2005	73.8	80.7	74.9	81.4	65.9	75.5	74.0	83.5	81.5	87.3	75.9	83.9
2020	75.7	82.3	76.9	83.1	67.6	76.9	75.4	84.9	82.8	88.4	77.5	85.0
At 65												
1995	15.9	19.6	16.0	19.7	14.2	18.2	19.4	24.0	20.4	24.7	18.8	22.3
2005	16.8	20.4	16.9	20.5	14.6	18.7	20.4	25.2	21.4	25.5	19.6	22.9
2020	18.0	21.5	18.2	21.6	15.3	19.3	21.4	26.1	22.3	26.4	20.5	23.7

Source: Day, J. C. (1993), *Population projections of the United States, by age, sex, race, and Hispanic origin: 1993–2050.* U.S. Bureau of the Census, Current Population Reports (P25-1104). U.S. Government Printing Office, Washington, DC.

The projections for 2005 and 2020 contain the same rank order although the gap between Native and White Americans closes somewhat.

As previously mentioned, the rank order of projections for life expectancies at age 65 for males and females is consistent within groups. These projections reveal much the same pattern as those at birth, with Asians in first place (Table 13.2). The exception is that Native Americans exhibit the second greatest number of years remaining, and Hispanics are in third place. Whites and Blacks are a distant fourth and fifth place, respectively. Beyond age 65 the differences between White and Black Americans tend to level out.

The diminishing differences between average life expectancy of older White and Black Americans is called racial mortality crossover. Crossover effect, as it is commonly called, is the phenomenon that is observed in comparing average years of life remaining for the two groups. At all ages up to approximately 65, Whites have a longer life expectancy. At that point the figures begin to come closer together, and at around age 75 Black Americans are observed to have a longer life expectancy (Manton, 1980). This is explained mainly by the higher infant mortality among Blacks and the superior medical treatment and nutrition experienced by Whites. The net effect is that more Whites who would have died at earlier ages survive to become "young old." However, the survivor effect culls out those persons who are more hardy and likely to endure. Hence, at the older ages Black Americans are more resistant to mortality causes and display longer life expectancy than do their White counterparts.

Mortality, Health, and Illness

Mortality rates reveal that elderly Black Americans die at a greater rate than do other groups. They experience a death rate of 5,585 deaths per 100,000 persons 65 years of age or older. Older Whites are next, with a rate of 4,958, followed by aged Hispanics at 3,517 and Native Americans at 3,471. Asian and Pacific Islander elders display the lowest rates of death: 2,379 per 100,000 persons (National Center for Health Statistics, 1992).

The two leading causes of death for elderly persons in the United States are diseases of the heart and cancer. It is interesting to note that the occurrence of these two diseases in the ethnic and racial groups mentioned above follow the same pattern as the distribution of the mortality rates. Black elderly rank first in terms of mortality from these two diseases; White elderly are next, followed by Hispanics, Native Americans, and Asian and Pacific Islanders. Whereas the death rates from these two diseases for Black and White elderly are quite close, Hispanic and Native American rates are a little more than half those of Blacks and Whites. Asian and Pacific Islander elderly display rates that are a little less than half of the Black and White rates (National Center for Health Statistics, 1992).

Just as we know there are important ethnic differences in mortality, research also has shown that morbidity and various health/illness reports vary significantly by ethnic groups. Elderly ethnic groups display different patterns of health and illness, which are mainly associated with lifelong deficiencies in nutrition and health care. These conditions are as much associated with poverty and substandard living conditions as they are with racial and cultural factors. Nevertheless, it is important to note that Black elders experience higher rates of hypertension and diabetes than do Whites. They also have a high incidence of breast, uterine, and cervical cancers, as well as glaucoma and alcoholism. Hispanics display the most varied set of health issues of all the groups. Puerto Ricans have a high stroke rate, whereas that for Mexican Americans is low. Hispanic elderly suffer from cancers of the cervix, uterus, and lungs, as well as diabetes, infectious and parasitic diseases, and drug addictions.

The health status of older Native Americans is complicated and attributed to excessive poverty. They have high rates of liver and gallbladder disease, rheumatoid arthritis, diabetes, and tuberculosis. Functional impairment, such as alcoholism and depression, is common and is related to high rates of cirrhosis, homicide, suicide, pneumonia, and complications of diabetes. Elderly Asian and Pacific Islanders experience hypertension, cardiovascular disease, and coronary heart disease. Other typical conditions are oral-pharyngeal cancers, diabetes, and suicide. However, this group generally displays the most positive health conditions of all the above groups (Barresi & Skinner, 1994). A further complication in the health of ethnic elders is the lack of adequate health care and the relatively few health care providers in some ethnic groups. This situation is further exacerbated by both poverty and ignorance about "ethnic medicine."

Long-Term Care and Caregiving

Among the factors contributing to the growth of the ethnic elderly population is a decrease in the non-Hispanic White population. In 1990 three-quarters of the total population was non-Hispanic White; however, this segment is projected to contribute only 35% of the population growth during the decade. After 2030 this group is projected to decline in size, therefore contributing nothing to the nation's population growth. In fact, projections envision the non-Hispanic White share of the U.S. population decreasing from 76% in 1990 to 53% in 2050 (Day, 1993). Further, the age group that will grow most rapidly during this period is that 85 years and over. It will double in size by 2020 and increase by sixfold by 2050 (Day, 1993). It is this oldest of the old that have the greatest need for long-term care (LTC) and the highest risk of institutionalization before death. Given this apparent need, it is important to examine the topic of LTC and family caregiving among ethnic elderly.

LTC includes a wide variety of health, social, and personal care services. These can be provided by both formal (private and public institutions) and informal (family friends and neighbors) sources. Usually, LTC is thought of as nursing home care, but it can also include a number of other services, such as hospitals, mental institutions, adult day care, community care, in-home care, homemaker services, and even self-care (Barresi & Stull, 1993). Given these distinctions and the variety of LTC services for ethnic elderly, it is helpful to visualize a cross-tabulation of the types and sources of service (Table 13.3). In addition, Table 13.3 reveals an interesting but neglected area—that of informal services provided in an institutional or formal setting. This type of service might consist of, for example, family and friends who come into the institutional setting and provide supplemental services and care for the resident. This could consist of both basic activities of daily living such as toileting, feeding, and grooming as well as instrumental activities such as personal business affairs. It might even include, when practical, preparation of ethnic foods, either brought in or prepared on site.

Although this author recognizes that this type of care is occasionally offered by family members, a unique aspect of this suggestion is that such services could be provided on a regular basis, with the family receiving credits applied against the cost of care. Thus, the motivation would be present not only for those relatives who are already supplying services but also for others who are less altruistic. This proposal would no doubt be difficult to implement, but it would have some very positive benefits for everyone involved. Ethnic elderly residents usually complain about the lack of ethnic food and familiar cultural practices, as well as a lack of understanding regarding their ethnic practices by other residents and staff. This would not only provide them with familiar food and frequent visitors but would also allow them to share these experiences with other residents, thus creating a more accepting environment.

Caregiving by family, friends, and neighbors accounts for 80% to 90% of LTC provided to elderly persons (Barresi & Stull, 1993). This is especially true for ethnic elderly. Black, Hispanic, and Asian elderly are dependent on informal networks for the majority of their LTC (Barresi & Menon, 1990; Lubben & Becerra, 1987; Mui & Burnette, 1994). Citing a number of studies, Barresi and Menon (1990) conclude that the frequency and size of support networks for elderly Black Americans are influenced by factors such as residential proximity of family members, presence of children in the household, being female, age,

TABLE 13.3 Long-Term Care Services by Location and Type of Service

Type of Service	Location of Service	
	Institutional	Community
Formal	Hospital, mental institution, nursing home, continuing care retirement center	Visiting nurses, home care, day care, foster care, hospice, respite care
Informal	Supplement to institutional care (a neglected area)	Family care, friends, neighbors, self-care

marital status (widowed, never married), and health status. In general, giving help in these families is influenced by levels of income, education, marital status, and health of the caregivers.

Among the four groups in Lubben and Becerra's (1987) study, Chinese and Mexican elderly were more likely to share housing and receive informal support than either Black or White elderly. In fact, little difference was found between the latter two groups. The authors conjecture that the greater support for Chinese and Mexican Americans is a result of cultural values and economic need. The inability to speak or understand English is a known barrier to formal service utilization and places a burden on the informal network.

Although the services provided to these ethnic elderly by their support networks is generally greater than that for most White groups, it does not mean, ipso facto, that they do not need or desire formal services. High social density, a large family, or informal support networks are not in themselves enough to assure adequate social support (Lockery, 1991). The assumptions that these groups "take care of their own" and have a "cultural aversion" to reception of formal LTC services is one of the reasons they have been systematically short-changed in policy, planning, and provision by both private and public agencies (Morrison, 1982). A recent study of Whites, Blacks, and Hispanics found that Whites utilized more LTC than the other two groups, but they also had fewer informal caregivers, higher incomes, and more positive attitudes toward LTC (Mui & Burnette, 1994).

Family Structures

Whereas ethnicity is frequently transmitted through ancestry, ethnic differences in family structure have strong implications for human aging. Because of the differences in mortality noted earlier, family structure in later life has some interesting patterns. When taken as a whole, more elderly men are married and more women are widowed. However, when one looks at the breakdown of these figures by ethnic group, we see that elderly Black Americans and Native Americans have more widows of both sexes than do Whites. In comparison, Hispanic groups have more widowers and fewer widows than do Whites, whereas the figures for Asian/Pacific Islanders are reversed.

Whites have approximately 6% of males and females 65 or over who are divorced or separated; each of the other ethnic groups mentioned above has almost double that amount for both sexes. Whites, Blacks, and Hispanics have about 6% never-married among both men and women. Native American and Asian/Pacific Islander men show about the same rate, but never-married women in these two groups amount to only about 3% (Barresi & Hunt, 1990).

In addition to these demographic patterns, ethnic differences permeate family functioning and values. Whereas most minority ethnic groups considered thus far experience disadvantages in employment, income, and housing, the opposite is true in regard to social contacts with their family members. Older Black

Americans and Hispanics manifest equal or greater levels of family contact compared to their White counterparts (Barresi & Menon, 1990). Although African American families have been fractured by considerable marital dissolution, intergenerational ties remain firm. In addition, there are notable differences among various White ethnic groups with regard to family structure and function (Gelfand & Barresi, 1987b).

Social Class

Any student of American society understands that ethnicity is related to social class, which in turn is related to a number of quality of life indicators. Indeed, the debate continues on how much of the ethnic differentiation in mortality and morbidity is due to the effect of ethnicity per se versus social class. Beyond health matters, income and wealth vary considerably by ethnicity. Thus, it should not be surprising that some ethnic groups such as Black Americans and Hispanics are more likely to be poor in later life than is the case with Jews, Germans, or Asian Americans. However, it is well to remember the heterogeneity found in ethnic groups. Although many members of ethnic groups are in the lower and working classes, there are also others whose education, occupation, income, and lifestyle place them in higher social class brackets. Unfortunately, as in all of social science, little research has been done on ethnic groups in higher socioeconomic statuses.

THEORETICAL ISSUES

At present there is no specific theoretical perspective in social gerontology that applies directly to ethnicity. There is the double jeopardy hypothesis, but that falls far short of providing a fully developed series of interrelated propositions to explain the aging process in ethnic groups. The traditional sociological theories of functionalism, conflict, interactionism, and exchange have been adapted to gerontology but have been found wanting when it comes to understanding the social process of ethnic aging. Detailed consideration of how each of the existing theoretical explanations in gerontology can contribute to our understanding of ethnic aging is beyond the scope of this chapter. However, the life course perspective is one that holds substantial promise for advancing this inquiry, and it merits further examination.

Life Course

The life course perspective in sociology was first developed by John Clausen (1972, 1986). The life course can be defined as the personal biographical record as one progresses through time. The timing of events over an individual's lifetime in such areas as education, work, and family affect the overall life course whether they are "on-time" or "off-time." For example, marriage at 18 may lead to early parenthood and grandparenthood or to greater chance for divorce and multiple marriages. In contrast, the person who marries at 38 or 48 will experience similar family roles at a later age. Both the "too early" and the "too late" experience of role changes will create difficulties for individuals who are off-time according to the norms of their social group. They may remain off-time for the remainder of their life course in that particular area, or they may accelerate the next stage in order to catch up.

Clausen (1972) states that individuals are affected in their life course by sociological, psychological, and biological determinants. These are identified as (1) personal resources, (2) sources of support, (3) availability of opportunities, and (4) investments of individual effort. Thus, we see that one's characteristics, group memberships, socialization, and motivation can all affect the life course. This is especially true for such major social identifications as social class, ethnic group, and religion. The norms of these groups will provide the individual with different prescriptions relative to the entrance and exit timing of role transitions. It is also important to keep in mind the effect of social approval and disapproval on the self-concept of the individual.

In a modification of the basic Clausen framework, Barresi (1987) applies the life course perspective to aging in the context of an ethnic group. He notes that even those factors that are biological and psychological in nature are carried out in a group context and are thus affected by the structure and cultural aspects of the group. With an emphasis on the interplay of the basic characteristics mentioned above, the life course perspective holds promise in its ability to explain ethnic aging.

For example, attitudes and behavior shaped at an early age are more than likely to carry over into the adult years and influence how individuals view such important areas as work and family values in later years. These essential values tend to vary by ethnic group and are manifested through statements and actions that are identifiable as associated with one or another ethnic group. Moreover, they tend to vary by generation within the group, depending on the amount of contact with the wider or host culture. This variation by generation may lead to difficulties in intergenerational relations and ultimately help to explain the differences in levels of assimilation and contact with the host culture among ethnic elderly. Ethnic elders find rejection of the "old ways" by younger persons difficult to understand. In their minds these are more than a set of rules for living, they constitute a way of life that is "right" and has helped them cope with a strange and sometimes hostile world.

The life course perspective holds much promise as a theoretical framework for research in ethnogerontology (Gibson, 1988; Jackson, 1989b; Markides et al., 1990). Burton, Dilworth-Anderson, and Bengtson (1991) describe the life course perspective as one that demonstrates promise in the study of ethnic minority elderly because of its interdisciplinary nature and its dynamic approach, which allows for conceptual flexibility and diversity. They believe that this theoretical approach, is especially suited to the study of ethnic minority elderly, particularly as related to family development in culturally diverse contexts. Further support is provided to this approach by the third edition of the *Handbook on Social Aging* (Binstock & George, 1990), which devotes a separate section and a third of the chapters to topics related to the life course.

METHODOLOGICAL ISSUES

Sampling issues are foremost in conducting research on ethnic groups. The accessibility of ethnic groups is often limited, making random and representative samples difficult if not impossible to obtain in many instances (Cox, 1987). More often researchers are limited to convenience samples, as in the case of a group at an ethnic-oriented senior center or a church group. All too often gerontologists find themselves limited to the study of available rather than randomly selected groups. However, a recent study found that data sources supported by U.S. federal agencies are generally adequate to conduct research on White and Black elders, but other ethnic groups are rarely included in sufficient numbers (LaVeist, 1995). The development of screening procedures for large geographical areas hold promise for the selection of samples of racial and ethnic groups (Jackson, 1989a; Markides et al., 1990).

Identifying ethnic background from available data is usually unreliable, and even when it has been carefully identified, the resulting numbers in respective ethnic groups are too small to make valid comparisons. In collecting original data, questions must be very carefully worded, for when respondents are requested to identify their ethnicity, one is more likely to wind up with vague or general responses that do not make a clear identification of the ethnic group.

Other issues concern the problem of data collection, the comparability of measures, and the discrepancy that can enter into questions (Markides et al., 1990). In dealing with subcultural groups it is important to understand that persons may attach different meanings to words than those assigned by investigators. It is important to pretest instruments in the group being studied. Too often investigators either fail to pretest or use instruments that have been pretested on other populations.

Further methodological concerns in ethnic aging research deal with the context of the investigation and the stereotypes the researcher may possess (Cox, 1987; Jackson, 1989a; Markides et al., 1990). Utilizing a "deviant" or "minority" perspective can create a predetermined but often unwitting direction to research because of the contextual orientation of the researcher. Of even more importance is the position of the researcher vis-à-vis his or her relationship to the community being studied. Different issues and different results will be found if one takes the position of either insider or outsider, advocate or intruder. The age, sex, and race of interviewers have been found to be relevant to the validity of responses (Markides et al., 1990).

In conjunction with the above issues, researchers must also be accountable to the ethnic community regarding the outcome of their findings (Cox, 1987). Even though it may be costly in terms of time and energy it is necessary to involve and gain support of the community. It may even become necessary to engage in "politics" in order to accomplish some research goals. Although these are not new issues, they point out that when studying ethnicity a number of factors can further complicate the differences between the group being studied and the wider society or other ethnic groups.

THE FUTURE OF ETHNOGERONTOLOGY

Existing research in ethnogerontology consists for the most part of studies that concentrate too much on minority status and not enough on sociocultural differences both within and between groups. What is needed are studies that deal with the broad differences that exist not only in membership status but also in the important distinctions of gender, education, marital status, and other cogent variables.

In particular, the issue of socioeconomic status (SES) and ethnic group membership should be addressed. The confounding effects of social class need to be separated from those of ethnic group membership. Much of what is currently known in ethnogerontology is based on limited samples that are usually drawn from the most accessible segments of ethnic groups. Generalizations based on these studies fail to account for the variation in attitudes, preferences, and lifestyles of different levels of social class within the respective ethnic groups. Not only is it necessary to distinguish between socioeconomic levels in ethnic groups, but it is imperative that such differences be identified and correlated with behavior patterns.

Along with SES effects, the issue of generational effects also needs to be addressed. Present studies of ethnic groups generally fail to deal with the intergenerational differences within ethnic groups. Generalizations are made regardless of birth or migration order. Very often wide distinctions in education, health, language abilities, and a host of other variables exist between two or more generations within the ethnic group. Attention to these differences could also shed light on the effects of assimilation pressures on respective cohorts.

There is a pressing need to engage in more research into the broad range of ethnic groups that are found in our society. The common belief of a declining base of ethnic elderly is refuted by the evidence of continuing immigration and the aging of second and third generations that have continued to identify with their ethnic heritage (Gelfand & Barresi, 1987a). Of particular need is research that focuses on non-Hispanic White ethnics, Native Americans, and Asian/Pacific Islanders. It is also necessary to separate out the various ethnic groups that so frequently become blurred under the general rubric of Hispanic.

The future of ethnogerontology appears to be a bright one. However, if it is to make positive contributions to the wider field of gerontology, then the concerns expressed here regarding theoretical and methodological shortcomings must be addressed. Ethnogerontology is emerging as a multifaceted and exciting specialty area in the study of aging, one that will provide greater overall understanding of the process of aging in social groups.

REFERENCES

Angel, J. L., & Hogan, D. P. (1991). The demography of minority aging populations. In *Minority elders: Longevity, economics, and health* (pp. 1–13). Washington, DC: Gerontological Society of America.

Barresi, C. M. (1987). Ethnic aging and the life course. In D. E. Gelfand & C. M. Barresi (Eds.), *Ethnic dimensions of aging* (pp. 18–34). New York: Springer Publishing.

Barresi, C. M. (In press). The impact of ethnicity on aging: A review of theory, research, and issues. *Journal of Ethnogerontology, 17*, (Formerly the *Journal of Minority Aging*)

Barresi, C. M., & Hunt, K. (1990). The unmarried elderly: Age, sex, and ethnicity. In T. H. Brubaker (Ed.), *Family relationships in later life* (2nd ed., pp. 169–190). Beverly Hills, CA: Sage Publications.

Barresi, C. M., & Menon, G. (1990). Diversity in Black family caregiving. In Z. Harel, E. A. McKinney, & M. Williams (Eds.), *Black aged: Understanding diversity and service needs* (pp. 221–235). Newbury Park, CA: Sage Publications.

Barresi, C. M., & Skinner, J. E. (1994). Overview of health and minority elders: Implications for practice, management, policy and research. In *Health and minority elders: An analysis of applied literature, 1980-1990* (pp. 3–21). Washington, DC: American Association of Retired Persons, Minority Affairs.

Barresi, C. M., & Stull, D. E. (Eds.). (1993). *Ethnic elderly and long-term care*. New York: Springer Publishing.

Binstock, R., & George, L. K. (Eds.). (1990). *Handbook of aging and the social sciences* (3rd ed.). San Diego, CA: Academic Press.

Burton, L. M., Dilworth-Anderson, P., & Bengtson, V. L. (1991). Creating culturally relevant ways of thinking about diversity and aging: Theoretical challenges for the twenty-first century. *Generations, 15*, 67–72.

Brink, T. L. (1992). *Hispanic aged mental health*. Binghamton, NY: Haworth Press.

Clausen, J. (1972). The life course of individuals. In M. Riley, M. Johnson, & A. Foner (Eds.), *Aging and society: A sociology of age stratification* (Vol. 3, pp. 475–514). New York: Russell Sage Foundation.

Clausen, J. (1986). *The life course: A sociological perspective*. Englewood Cliffs, NJ: Prentice-Hall.

Cox, C. (1987). Overcoming access problems in ethnic communities. In D. E. Gelfand & C. M. Barresi (Eds.), *Ethnic dimensions of aging* (pp. 165–178). New York: Springer Publishing.

Day, J. C. (1993). *Population projections of the United States, by age, sex, race, and Hispanic origin: 1993–2050* (U.S. Bureau of the Census, Current Population Reports, P25-1104). Washington, DC: U.S. Government Printing Office.

Furuto, S. M., Biswas, R., Chung, D. K., Murase, K., & Ross-Sheriff, F. (Eds.). (1992). *Social work practice with Asian Americans.* Newbury Park, CA: Sage Publications.

Gelfand, D. E. (1994). *Aging and ethnicity: Knowledge and services.* New York: Springer Publishing.

Gelfand, D. E., & Barresi, C. M. (Eds.). (1987b). *Ethnic dimensions of aging.* New York: Springer Publishing.

Gelfand, D. E., & Barresi, C. M. (1987a). Current perspectives in ethnicity and aging. In D. E. Gelfand & C. M. Barresi (Eds.), *Ethnic dimensions of aging* (pp. 5–17). New York: Springer Publishing.

Gibson, R. C. (1988). Minority aging research: Opportunity and challenge. *Gerontologist, 28,* 559–560.

Harel, Z., McKinney, E. A., & Williams, M. (1990). *Black aged: Understanding diversity and service needs.* Newbury Park, CA: Sage.

Harper, M. S. (Ed.). (1990). *Minority aging: Essential curricula content for selected health and allied health professions* (DHHS Publication No. HRS [P-DV-90-4]). Washington, DC: Department of Health and Human Services, Health Resources and Services Administration.

Jackson, J. S. (1989b). Race, ethnicity, and psychological theory and research. *Journal of Gerontology: Psychological Sciences, 44,* P1–P2.

Jackson, J. S. (1989a). Methodological issues in survey research on older minority adults. In M. P. Lawton & A. R. Herzog (Eds.), *Special research methods for gerontology* (pp. 137–161). Farmingdale, NY: Baywood.

Jackson, J. S., Chatters, L. M., & Taylor, R. J. (1993). *Aging in black America.* Newbury Park, CA: Sage.

Kunitz, S. J., & Levy, J. E. (1991). *Navajo aging.* Tucson: University of Arizona Press.

LaVeist, T. (1995). Data sources for aging research on racial and ethnic groups. *Gerontologist, 35,* 328–339.

Lockery, S. A. (1991). Family and Social Supports: Caregiving Among Racial and Ethnic Minority Elders. *Generations, 15,* 58–62.

Lubben, J. E., & Becerra, R. A. (1987). Social support among Black, Mexican, and Chinese elderly. In D. E. Gelfand & C. M. Barresi (Eds.), *Ethnic dimensions of aging* (pp. 130–144). New York: Springer Publishing.

Manton, K. G. (1980). Sex and race specific mortality differential, in multiple cause of death rates. *Gerontologist, 20,* 480–493.

Markides, K. S., Liang, J., & Jackson, J. S. (1990). Race, ethnicity, and aging: Conceptual and methodological issues. In R. Binstock & L. K. George (Eds.), *Handbook of aging and the social sciences* (3rd ed., pp. 112–129). San Diego, CA: Academic Press.

Markides, K. S., & Mindel, C. H. (1987). *Aging and ethnicity.* Beverly Hills, CA: Sage.

Morrison, B. J. (1982). Sociocultural dimensions: Nursing homes and the minority aged. *Journal of Gerontological Social Work, 5,* 127–145.

Mui, A. C., & Burnette, D. (1994). Long-term care service use by frail elders: Is ethnicity a factor? *Gerontologist, 34,* 190–198.

National Center for Health Statistics. (1992). *Health, United States, 1991* (DHHS Pub. No. (PHS) 92-1232). Washington, DC: U.S. Government Printing Office.

Stanford, P. E., & Torres-Gil, F. (Eds.). (1992). *Diversity: New approaches to ethnic minority aging.* Amityville, NY: Baywood Publishing. (Originally published in *Generations, 25,* [4])

Stoller, E. P., & Gibson, R. C. (1994). *Worlds of difference: Inequality in the aging experience.* Thousand Oaks, CA: Pine Forge Press.

U.S. Bureau of the Census. (1992). *Statistical abstract of the United States: 1992.* Washington, DC: U.S. Government Printing Office.

U.S. Bureau of the Census. (1995). *Statistical abstract of the United States: 1995.* Washington, DC: U.S. Government Printing Office.

CHAPTER 14

Economic Status of Older Adults in the United States: Diversity, Women's Disadvantage, and Policy Implications

Sharon A. DeVaney

In this chapter the economic status of older adults is described, showing the economic diversity of this population. Subgroups of the elderly population, especially women, are identified as being especially disadvantaged, and the underlying issues that tend to explain economic disadvantage are examined. Finally, the issue of older adults as an economic burden in an era of federal debt is briefly addressed.

Often when the economic status of older adults is presented, only one measure, that of income, is discussed. Because of annual cost-of-living increases in Social Security, the income of older adults has improved over time. Whether older adults have reserves to increase their standard of living and meet emergencies is another aspect of their economic well-being. Although there is general agreement that the economic status of elders has improved in the past 20 years, experts are quick to note that elders are economically diverse. Careful examination reveals that income, assets, and net worth of older adults vary by demographic group and by age group and within each of those groups. Thus, the economic diversity of older adults as a population subgroup supports Ferraro's thesis that heterogeneity is a tenet of the gerontological imagination (see chapter 1). As you will observe, several measures of economic status—income, poverty level, net worth, and economic uncertainty and vulnerability—are examined in this chapter to provide a comprehensive perspective on the economic resources and needs of older adults.

ECONOMIC STATUS OF OLDER ADULTS

Income

In describing income among the older population, the median value (50% of the population have more, and 50% have less) is preferable to the average value because the median is less sensitive to extreme values in the distribution. Median household income when a householder was 65 years and over was $17,751 in 1993, but there was a wide range of incomes around that median. At the extremes of the distribution, 24.8% of all aged households had incomes below $10,000, whereas 4.6% had incomes of $75,000 and over in 1993 (U.S. Bureau of the Census, 1995). Table 14.1 provides a comparison of median income and the distribution at upper and lower income levels for older adults with other age groups.

Within each age group, income varies substantially among ethnic groups (U.S. Bureau of the Census, 1995). Average income for White, Black, and Hispanic households is shown in Table 14.2. (Median income and the distribution of income was not available.) At all age levels, White households have higher levels of income, on average. Compared to Hispanic households, Black households had lower average levels of income at each age except for midlife (45–54 and 55–64); at these ages, Blacks had slightly higher average incomes than Hispanics.

As might be expected, income levels disaggregated by marital status and the combination of marital status and race further highlight the economic diversity (Grad, 1992). In 1990 the median income of aged married couples ($23,352) was twice as much as the median income of nonmarried men ($10,893) and more than 2.5 times that of nonmarried women ($8,746). The median income for aged White married couples and nonmarried persons ($14,542) was twice the median income of aged Black households ($6,987) and that of aged Hispanic households

TABLE 14.1 Money Income of Households in 1993 by Age of Householder

	% Distribution		
Age	<$10,000	⩾$75,000	Median Income
15–24 years	26.0	2.1	$19,333
25–34 years	12.2	7.8	$31,281
35–44 years	8.9	16.7	$40,862
45–54 years	8.1	23.6	$46,207
55–64 years	13.1	14.6	$33,474
65 years and over	24.8	4.6	$17,751

Source: U.S. Bureau of the Census, Current Population Reports, P60-188; and unpublished data (U.S. Bureau of the Census, 1995, No. 725, p. 470).

TABLE 14.2 Money Income of Households in 1993 by Race and Hispanic Origin

	Average Income		
Age	White	Black	Hispanic
15–24 years	$24,298	$16,009	$21,423
25–34 years	$40,020	$23,455	$28,666
35–44 years	$52,205	$31,666	$34,520
45–54 years	$60,106	$38,156	#38,042
55–64 years	$46,650	$29,450	$29,316
⩾65 years	$26,761	$17,782	$20,459

Source: U.S. Bureau of the Census, Current Population Reports, P60-188; and unpublished data (U.S. Bureau of the Census, 1995, p. 471).

($7,879). When comparing age groups among the older population, median levels of income tend to decline. The median income for couples and persons in the 65–69 age group ($18,352) was twice that of the median for the 85-or-older group ($8,668) (Grad, 1992). In summary, examination of median income across all age groups reveals that both younger persons (age 15–24) and older persons (age 65 or older) were disadvantaged relative to persons in the middle ages. Among older adults the subgroups consisting of minorities, the oldest old, and nonmarried women were the least well off.

Poverty Level

Another way to judge the economic status of a population is the percentage of persons in poverty. Poverty thresholds were developed in 1963–64 by Mollie Orshansky, an economist working for the Social Security Administration. Although the original purpose was to develop a measure to assess the relative risks of low economic status among different demographic groups of families with children and not to introduce a new general measure of poverty, the Orshansky measure is still widely used. The poverty thresholds are issued annually by the Bureau of the Census and are used to estimate the number of people in poverty and tabulate them by race and other characteristics. The poverty estimates are criticized because they are based solely on money income before taxes and do not include the value of noncash benefits such as food stamps, Medicare, Medicaid, public housing, and employer-provided fringe benefits (Development and history, 1993).

Data from the Current Population Survey (shown in Table 14.3) indicate that White and Black persons under the age of 35 are more likely to be in poverty

TABLE 14.3 Persons below Poverty Level in 1993 by Race and Hispanic Origin

	% below Poverty Level			
Age	All	White	Black	Hispanic
<18 years	22.7	17.8	46.1	40.9
18–24 years	19.1	16.0	34.4	31.0
25–34 years	13.8	11.3	28.4	25.4
35–44 years	10.6	8.7	23.0	23.8
45–54 years	8.5	7.0	19.2	20.2
55–59 years	9.9	8.0	23.6	20.6
60–64 years	11.3	9.7	24.4	24.4
65 years and over	12.2	10.7	28.0	21.4

Source: Based on Current Population Survey (U.S. Bureau of the Census, 1995, p. 481).

than persons aged 65 and over. For Hispanic Americans, persons under the age of 45 are more likely to be in poverty than persons aged 65 and over.

Poor and near-poor older households have great difficulty in meeting housing expenses (Public Policy Institute G8, 1995). Near-poor households refer to households with incomes between 100% and 124% of the poverty level. Seventy-one percent of poor and 55% of near-poor older households have excessive housing cost burdens, defined by the federal government as exceeding 30% of income. About 40% of poor older households spend half or more of their incomes on housing. Excessive housing costs are particularly high among households headed by persons aged 75 and older and by older women living alone.

It is important to note that the poverty rate for people 65 years or older dropped from 24.6% in 1970 to 12.2% in 1993 (U.S. Bureau of the Census, 1995). This improvement in the economic status of older adults is attributed to increased employer-sponsored pension benefits and Social Security benefits, which have been indexed for inflation since 1972 (Schwenk, 1993).

One reason that poverty rates among older adults are not higher is that the government uses a poverty standard for older adults that is 8% to 10% lower than that used for all other age groups (Public Policy Institute G1, 1995). In 1993 the Bureau of the Census poverty threshold for a two-person household at age 65 or older was $8,740; for a similar household under age 65, the threshold was $9,728 (Poverty thresholds, 1994; U.S. Bureau of the Census, 1995). The different standard is based on the assumption that food consumption cost, which is lower among older adults, is a good measure of the overall cost of living. Because the poverty threshold is lower, some scholars assert that poverty statistics typically underestimate the true prevalence of poverty among older adults.

Lifetime Asset Accumulation

Net worth is a third indicator of economic status and represents the accumulation of wealth over a lifetime (i.e., work history, salaries, investments, family size, household needs, and patterns of spending and saving) (Schwenk, 1995). When households have low levels of assets, they are limited in their ability to handle crises related to health, housing, and other issues. Net worth, a more comprehensive measure of economic status than income, is the sum of assets minus the sum of liabilities. Mean and median values of net worth from the 1992 Survey of Consumer Finances (Kennickell & Starr-McCluer, 1994) offer further evidence of the diversity of economic well-being by age level. Kennickell and Starr-McCluer (1994) of the Federal Reserve Board observe that net worth, like income, rises with age of the household, peaks in late middle age, and then declines (see Table 14.4). As shown, the median level of net worth of the oldest families (heads aged 75 and over) falls between households in the age 35–44 and 45–54 categories.

Mean and median net worth increase as income and formal education increase (Kennickell & Starr-McCluer, 1994). Although findings from the 1992 Survey of Consumer Finances disaggregated by age and education are not available, the comparison of median net worth by educational attainment for heads of households over 65 in the 1989 Survey of Consumer Finances showed striking differences as shown in Table 14.5 (Schwenk, 1995). Median net worth is only slightly less than median assets in most instances because people in this age group have paid off their mortgage and tend to incur debt only for a car or a major medical bill. At the median level of assets and net worth, older household heads with a college degree were three times as well off as those with a high school diploma and seven times as well off as those with an eighth-grade education or less (see

TABLE 14.4 Family Net Worth in 1992 by Age of Household Head and Percentage of Families in Each Category

Age	Mean	Median	Percentage
<35 years	$60,200	$10,400	25.9
35–44 years	$157,000	$46,300	22.7
45–54 years	$304,500	$97,100	16.2
55–64 years	$371,000	$133,300	13.1
65–74 years	$369,800	$103,600	12.7
≥75 years	$257,600	$87,000	9.4

Note: The term *family* includes both married couples and single individuals. The term is close to the U.S. Bureau of the Census definition of "household."

Source: Kennickell & Starr-McCluer, 1994, p. 865.

TABLE 14.5 Median Assets and Net Worth in 1989 with a Household Head 65 and Over

Education attained	Assets	Net Worth
8th grade or less	$35,000	$35,000
Some high school	$69,000	$69,000
High school diploma	$82,000	$80,000
Some college	$231,000	$184,000
College degree	$249,000	$230,000

Source: Schwenk, 1995, p. 14.

Table 14.5). In short, research shows that households with low levels of assets were likely to be composed of persons with the following characteristics: single women, eighth-grade education or less, non-White or Hispanic, renters, and incomes of $10,000 or less. Further, the characteristics that identified low assets and low net worth were interrelated; households with low assets often possessed several of these characteristics (Schwenk, 1995).

Homeownership among older adults is extremely common, and it tends to represent the largest asset for many older adults. Although homeownership rates vary by data source and time period, about 65% of older adults are homeowners (Weinrobe, 1995). At about age 70, homeownership falls off, at first gradually and then more rapidly due to changes in health, marital status, and economic factors. Single women are less likely to own their homes than are couples or single men, and as women enter widowhood, frequency of homeownership is reduced.

The equity in a home is often viewed as an important financial backstop for older adults. But as Weinrobe (1995) observes: "A very important question is whether the fall in homeownership is tied to a tapping of home equity. . . . It is reasonable to surmise, however, that the home equity would be used in some instances to finance the expenses associated with advanced age" (p. 258). As an example of the use of home equity, DeVaney, Bechman, and Williams (1995) found that 30% of respondents would consider the use of a reverse mortgage to finance long-term care but only "when other assets were depleted."

The lack of agreement among economists on the savings behavior of older adults is a factor that complicates understanding of economic well-being and prediction of future economic well-being. Whether older adults will use assets that have been accumulated to meet immediate needs has not been clearly demonstrated. The life-cycle hypothesis of savings assumes that "dissaving"—spending down assets to meet needs—will occur as persons age (Ando & Modigliani, 1963). However, Schulz (1995a) points out that some studies (Danziger, Van Der Gaag, Smolensky, & Taussig, 1982–83; Menchik & David, 1983; Torrey & Taeuber, 1986) have shown that older adults continue to save, but other studies (Hurd, 1990) have shown that dissaving occurs.

Finally, a comprehensive understanding of economic well-being is complicated by errors in reporting income and assets. Respondents of household surveys sometimes do not know, do not remember correctly, refuse to answer, or give false information. Data are relatively reliable for low-income persons but may not be for those with extensive property, farm, or other self-employment income (Schulz, 1995a). Radner (1982) found very large errors, especially for older adults. A new questioning technique known as "bracketing" (asking if the amount is between an upper and lower level) has been found to be effective in reducing nonresponse and producing a reasonable estimate of amounts (Hurd, personal communication, November 18, 1995). If bracketing is adopted, it may be possible in the future to assume a higher level of accuracy with income and asset data, particularly for wealthy households that are reluctant to share information.

Living Arrangements

Older adults who live alone are one of the most vulnerable segments of society (Kassner, 1991). Data from the Current Population Survey shows that older women are much more likely than older men to live alone (see chapter 2, Figure 2.9). In general, older single women have lower levels of income and fewer assets than do older men and older couples. Kassner (1991) found that the proportion of older White and Black persons (32% and 31%, respectively) who lived alone was similar, but only 22% of older Hispanic Americans live alone. About one-fourth of elderly persons living alone have incomes below the poverty threshold, compared to 14% of older adults who live with others.

Economic Uncertainty and Vulnerability

Income is often compared with "average needs," but relatively few younger persons have very large expenses that differ from average needs. In contrast, older adults, because of expenses for acute health care and long-term care, are subject to substantial economic risks (Radner, 1992). Several studies have examined the question of economic risk among older adults and have found similar causes of economic uncertainty among older adults (Del Bene & Vaughan, 1992; Holden & Smeeding, 1990; Hurd & Shoven, 1983, 1985).

Hurd and Shoven (1983, 1985) identified three sources of economic uncertainty for older adults: (1) risk of large medical bills, as measured by reliance on Medicare as the only subsidized health insurance; (2) risk of unexpected housing cost increases, as measured by lack of in-kind housing income; and (3) risk of adverse changes in Social Security benefits, as measured by reliance on Old Age and Survivors Insurance as the primary source of money income. Holden and Smeeding (1990) identified five sources of risk: (1) lack of satisfactory insurance for acute health care, (2) lack of assets to pay for long-term care, (3) Social Security benefits as a constraint of Medicare eligibility, (4) high housing costs relative to income, and (5) chronic disabilities. These studies highlight the problems faced by older adults in regard to long-term care, housing, and chronic disabilities and the vulnerability felt by older adults with limited resources (Del Bene & Vaughan, 1992).

ECONOMIC DISADVANTAGE AMONG OLDER WOMEN

Underlying Causes of Economic Disadvantage among Older Adults

One of the main conclusions from this brief review of the economic status of older adults is that older women are particularly disadvantaged. Indeed, the expression "feminization of poverty" was first used by Diana Pearce (1978), who observed that poverty was rapidly becoming a female problem (Northrop, 1990). Almost two-thirds of the poor over 16 years of age were women, more than 70% of the elderly poor were female, and almost half of all poor families were headed by women (Pearce, 1976). Each measure had been growing over time, indicating that "it is women who account for an increasingly large proportion of the economically disadvantaged" (pp. 29–30). A decade later Minkler and Stone (1985) pointed out that the "feminization of poverty" had received growing attention, but the concept was focused disproportionately on single mothers and young women. They directed attention to poverty in older women, noting that women enter old age poorer than men and, as a consequence of widowhood, higher health care expenditures, and pay and pension inequities, tend to become poorer with age.

Meyer (1990) observes that elderly women enter old age poorer than elderly men. She argues that the primary sources of *retirement income*, such as Social Security and private pensions, are structured in ways that intentionally or accidentally favor men. Meyer believes that the incidence of poverty among older women is directly linked to their greater likelihood of being widowed or divorced. To understand the differences in retirement income, it is necessary to consider women's labor force participation and women's role as family caregivers.

Labor Force Patterns and Caregiving Role

Retirement income is based on preretirement income and length of time on the job. Compared to men, women's labor force participation tends to be shorter and less continuous. Women's work patterns are related to changing family roles over the family life cycle (Hogan & Astone, 1986; Moen, 1985; Moen & Smith, 1986; Pienta, Burr, & Mutchler, 1994). Women are more likely to be caregivers for younger and older family members, and they will often adjust their employment status accordingly (Brody, Kleban, Johnsen, Hoffman, & Schoonover, 1987; Hatch & Thompson, 1992; O'Rand, Henretta, & Krecker, 1992; Pienta et al., 1994).

Income in jobs typically held by women is, on average, lower than for jobs held by men. Women are less likely to be employed in jobs offering retirement benefits. Women who retire earlier are less likely to have lengthy work histories and less likely to work at jobs from which they will receive pension benefits. Although the work histories of African American women are longer than those for White women, they exhibit a similar pattern of interruptions. Among current cohorts of older women, married women have been the least likely to participate continuously in the labor force; thus, they have low levels of individual income, if any. In the same cohort, never-married women have been more likely to participate continuously in the labor force and have greater resources than do women who marry and later become single (Hatch, 1990; Patterson, 1993).

Women's traditional role as the primary caregiver to infants and children is expanding to caregiver to parents and other elderly family members. The dramatic increase in the survival of aging parents over time has created an increased need for caregiving to older adults. Because women are the primary caregivers and because so many women are employed, this need for elder care is creating problems that may hit workers harder than child care. Increased absences, stress, distraction, and quit rates are observed as a result of providing care to elders. A recent study concludes that each personal caregiver costs the company $3,142 a year in absences, work interruptions, added supervisor workload, medical and employee-assistance costs, and replacing those who quit (Shellenbarger, 1995). A conservative estimate is that 2% of employees are providing personal care (help with basic needs of eating, bathing, and dressing) to an elder. Shellenbarger (1995) indicates that this focus on only personal caregiving may exclude as many as 75% of those providing elder care. Although the study did not indicate what proportion of personal caregivers are women, older women workers are far more likely than older male workers to leave paid employment to care for an ill spouse or relative. In addition to possible adverse effects on their health when providing care, older women often lose credit for earnings for Social Security and pensions (if covered by a pension plan).

Social Security Benefits as Retirement Income

Eligibility for Social Security is based on 40 quarters or 10 years in the paid labor force. The quarter years need not be continuous. Social Security benefits are based on earnings averaged over 35 years, excluding the 5 years of lowest earnings. A substantial length of time without earnings, whether due to part-time employment or unemployment, illness or family responsibilities, reduces benefits considerably. Of all adults receiving monthly Social Security benefits at the end of 1993, 42% were men and 58% were women. More than 80% of the

TABLE 14.6 Amount of Old-Age, Survivors, and Disability Insurance (OASDI) Benefits in 1993 by Sex

Beneficiary Type	Men	Women
Total benefit	$743	$548
Retired workers	759	581
Spouses	212	349
Disabled workers	715	516
Spouses	109	157
Survivors		
Nondisabled widow/er	461	632
Disabled widow/er	286	437
Mothers and fathers	315	456

Source: U.S. Department of Health and Human Services, 1994, p. 20.

men and 50% of the women received retired-worker benefits. About a fourth of the women received survivor benefits (U.S. Department of Health and Human Services, 1994).

When women receive Social Security benefits based on their own earnings, usually the amount is considerably lower than men receive because of the differential in working wages. As shown in Table 14.6, average monthly benefits in 1993 for men were $743, compared to $548 for women (U.S. Department of Health and Human Services, 1994).

Eligibility for Social Security retirement benefits may be based on a person's own earnings record or that of the spouse. Spousal benefits are based on marriages of at least 10 years and are equal to half of the worker's benefit. Social Security benefits are more advantageous to the spouse if the marriage ends in death rather than divorce. When a spouse dies, the surviving spouse receives two-thirds of the couple's combined Social Security benefit. After a divorce each spouse retains his or her portion of the combined Social Security benefit. The wife typically receives one-third of the couple's combined benefit, and the husband receives two-thirds. If a spouse enters a nursing home, Social Security income is divided as under divorce (Meyer, 1990).

Although Social Security affords couples an adequate level of protection, even widows are vulnerable. Burkhauser (1994) points out that due to the expansion of Social Security in the early 1970s, replacement rates (the amount of wages replaced by Social Security benefits in the first year of retirement) were substantially increased. "Thanks in large part to those increases, the poverty rate of older married couples plummeted and is now extremely low" (p. 148). Although benefits are reduced by 20% for workers accepting benefits at 62, over the past two decades the average age for men to receive benefits has declined from 65 to 62. Apparently, men have been able to retire earlier and avoid poverty.

Private Pensions

In 1994, 48% of retirees ages 55 and older reported employer-provided pension benefits either in the form of a lifetime annuity or a lump sum distribution taken in 1994 or earlier and used for retirement. Pension benefits were received by 57% of all male and 38% of all female retirees aged 55 and over (U.S. Department of Labor, 1995). Among retirees 65 and over, 42% receive pension benefits, 25% receive health coverage, 96% receive Social Security benefits, and only 2% receive no benefits (U.S. Department of Labor, 1995). Table 14.7 shows pension receipt status by sex, race, and education level of retired private-sector workers ages 55 and over.

As might be expected, persons who are more likely to receive pension benefits are men, Whites, and those with higher levels of education. There is also a direct association between income level and firm size and receipt of pension benefit. Only 12% of retirees who had earnings of less than $10,000 per year received a pension, whereas 68% of those who earned more than $40,000 in their last year of work received pension benefits. Only 11% of retirees formerly employed in firms with fewer than 25 workers received pensions, compared to 68% of former employees of firms with 1,000 or more workers (U.S. Department of Labor, 1995).

Meyer (1990) contends that women are less well off than men in regard to private pensions. In fact, the structure of private pensions is based on industries,

TABLE 14.7 Pension Receipt Status of Retired Private Sector Workers Ages 55 and Older in 1994

	% Distribution	
	Recipients	No Benefits
Gender		
Men	55	45
Women	32	68
Race		
White	44	56
Black	31	69
All other	35	65
Education level		
Less than 12 years	33	67
High school diploma	45	55
Some college	49	51
Bachelor's degree	59	41
Master's degree or higher	62	38

Source: U.S. Department of Labor, 1995, p. 51.

specific jobs, length of service, and continuity of service that are more typical of men's labor force participation. Private pensions are more likely to be offered by large unionized firms, where women are less likely to be employed; women are more likely to be employed in retail and service industries, which tend to have the lowest pension coverage. Private pensions favor lengthy and continuous employment, which is more compatible with men's labor force participation. Pension plans may pay a spousal benefit after the death of the wage-earner. This amount is frequently one-half of the couple's pension benefit (Leimberg & McFadden, 1995). And as Meyer (1990) notes, women do not receive private pensions for unpaid labor such as child rearing, caregiving, and housework.

Individual Retirement Accounts: An Example of Private Savings

Private pensions such as an Individual Retirement Account (IRA) are another opportunity for financial preparation for retirement. Since the passage of the Employee Retirement Income Security Act (ERISA) in 1974, it has been possible for individuals and couples to contribute to IRAs to provide a tax-deferred means of saving for retirement as a supplement to Social Security benefits (Congressional Budget Office, 1987; Meyer, 1990). At first, the IRA could be used only if wage and salary earners were not covered by qualified pension plan. In 1981 legislation allowed every worker to invest up to $2,000 annually even if they were covered by a group plan. However, the Tax Reform Act of 1986 changed the liberal legislation of 1981. Since 1986 those covered by private pensions may invest in an IRA, but the extent to which the investment is tax-free depends on annual income. If only one member of a dual-earner couple is covered by a private pension plan, the other member loses his or her right to tax-free status if their combined income exceeds the limit.

Beginning in 1997 legislation attached to the minimum-wage bill will allow nonworking spouses to set aside $2,000 a year in a tax-sheltered IRA in addition to the $2,000 set aside by the spouse who qualifies for a tax-sheltered IRA (Lewis, 1996). That is a major change from the 1986 tax law which limited the contribution of a wage-earner with a nonworking spouse to a total of $2,250. Longtime sponsor of the proposal, Senator William Roth, a Republican from Delaware, said, "With this bill we end discrimination against homemakers, putting them on equal footing with their spouses" (Lewis, 1996, p. 3).

The arguments presented by Meyer (1990) provide some support for the thesis that retirement income is based on gender. If nonemployed spouses do not qualify for their own Social Security benefits, they are dependent on spousal benefits, which are more generous if they remain married. Private pensions are geared to the types of positions usually held by men and to long and uninterrupted work histories. Tax-deferred status of an IRA depends on whether an earner is covered by a private pension plan and by level of income. From a more optimistic perspective, changes have occurred in women's work histories, and one wonders whether women will continue to be economically disadvantaged in the future.

Factors Influencing Retirement Income and Asset Accumulation

There is some encouraging evidence that the gender gap in pay is shrinking (O'Neill, 1994). During the 1960s and 1970s, women's wages hovered around 60% of men's despite the fact that an increasing proportion of women entered the labor force. During the 1980s the gender gap in wages began to decline noticeably; estimates put the ratio of women's to men's wages between 70% and 80%. In 1992, when ages 25 to 64 were considered, the hourly earnings of women were 74% of men's earnings, compared to 62% in 1979. At ages 25 to 34, where women's skills have increased the most, the ratio was 87% (O'Neill, 1994). In addition, women have acquired more years of continuous work experience than in the past as a result of delayed marriage, low fertility, and an increasing tendency for mothers of young children to work. Almost 60% of married women with children under 6 are in the labor force, compared to 19% in 1960.

The increase in women's work experience is also related to changing expectations about preparation for employment. In 1960 women received 35% of all bachelor's degrees in the United States, compared to about half of all bachelor's degrees in the 1980s. Over the years women's comparative advantage in the labor market has increased as the service sector has expanded, providing jobs that required mental acuity and skills rather than physical strength (O'Neill, 1994).

Although older men are continuing to drop out of the labor force at earlier ages, older women are increasingly staying in longer. In 1978, 41% of women aged 55 to 64 were in the work force, compared to 47% in 1993. For men, comparable proportions were 73% and 66.5% in 1978 and 1993, respectively. The shift from manufacturing to service jobs has meant that there are fewer traditional jobs available for men but more jobs available for women. Corporate downsizing has displaced more older male workers than older females because men were more numerous in middle management and manufacturing where cuts have been most likely to occur. Once older men are out of the work force, there aren't many similar jobs waiting for them (Bennett, 1994).

Women now in their late 50s and early 60s were part of the big wave of women entering or reentering the work force in the late 1960s and early 1970s. O'Neill (1994) speculates that these women got used to working and that it is natural that they continue to work now. However, the National Longitudinal Survey (NLS) indicates that need is a major determinant of older women's employment. The survey showed that fewer than half of older working women were married, compared to nonworking older women, two-thirds of whom were married. The survey indicated that working women had less access to Social Security and pension payments than nonworking women.

Financial Management: Key to Economic Well-Being?

Previous research suggests that women need to become more involved in preparing for retirement or at least become as involved in retirement preparation as men are. The annual Merrill Lynch Retirement Planning Survey (1995) concludes that a gender gap in retirement preparation persists. The survey, which included responses from 809 Americans employed full-time, found that more Americans have realized the importance of saving but many are saving only a fraction of what will be needed. Over half (58%) of women, compared to 49% of men, are concerned about outliving the money they have put away for retirement. Men were more likely than women (70% vs. 62%) to participate in any type of retirement or pension plan through their employer. Men were more likely than women (74% vs. 56%) to choose to invest in options made available through 401(k) plans, which offer the opportunity to achieve greater investment performance in exchange for greater risk. Forty-one percent of women and 28% of men said they had not clearly identified long-term financial goals, and women were less likely (57% vs. 67%) to consider investment strategies when creating a financial plan (Merrill Lynch, 1995).

A survey of 4,200 women by the National Center for Women and Retirement Research (NCWRR) offers another perspective on women's preparation for retirement (Willis, 1995). Findings from the NCWRR survey showed that personality factors were more critical in women's financial decisions than were income, age, or marital or career status. Women who were assertive, open to change, and optimistic were more likely than others to set specific financial goals, save and invest regularly, make retirement planning a priority, and educate themselves about money management. Over half (58%) of the NCWRR survey respondents believed that they had control over the direction their lives were taking, whereas 42% regarded themselves as victims of circumstance. Of all who regarded themselves as victims, only 39% made regular monthly contributions to savings and investment accounts, and just 17% made saving for retirement a priority.

A study to determine factors that predicted *confidence* in having or preparing for a financially secure retirement compared nonretirees and retirees (DeVaney, 1995). Three factors—having a satisfactory pension plan, good health, and the belief that they had enough money for basic expenses—were common to both retirees and nonretirees who expressed confidence about financial preparation for retirement (DeVaney, 1995). Also, three additional factors predicted confidence for nonretirees. They were having started saving, the belief that their job was secure, and contributing to a supplemental retirement annuity (in addition to an employer-sponsored pension plan).

These findings support Patterson (1993), who urges women to plan early and aggressively for retirement. She states that "Social Security will provide a subsistence, retirement benefits earned while working will add no more than a third of necessary retirement income, and the remaining 40 to 70% must come from individual savings" (p. 337). Bianchi (1995) describes the economic progress made by women since the 1960s as a gradual process of cohort replacement. She states that cohorts moving toward retirement by the end of the 1990s will be less distinct in terms of lifetime work experience than were the baby boom cohorts and their mothers. As women assume a role of lifetime work experience similar to that of men, the question remains whether or not they will acquire the knowledge, attitudes, and behavior needed to prepare similarly for retirement.

OLDER ADULTS AS AN ECONOMIC BURDEN IN AN ERA OF FEDERAL DEBT?

This review of the economic status of older adults has shown diversity in income, net worth, and poverty status among older adults. Groups such as the very old, women, minorities, and those who live alone were shown to be least well off. Problems faced by older adults include increasing costs for medical care; possible need for long-term care, whether institutional or at home; and for some, limited resources with which to meet these needs. Meeting the economic burden of an aging population is complicated further by the concern that the "dependency ratio" is increasing. This ratio is expressed as the size of the retired population relative to the working population (Atkins, 1992). Due to the increase in the population over 80, Torrey (1992) estimates that federal benefits provided to this subgroup will increase by 66% from 1984 to 2000. This and other projections on population change, as well as increasing costs for health care and possible use of long-term care, raise the issue of how the cost of future benefits will be paid (Bengtson & Achenbaum, 1993; Binstock, 1990, 1992; Duff, 1995; Torres-Gil, 1992).

Today public resources are perceived as scarce, and it is argued by many politicians that the need to reduce the federal deficit is more important than continuing or increasing funding for social assistance programs. "Among policy elites and in the media there has been an erosion of the notion that older people, generally, are deserving of governmental benefits" (National Academy on Aging, 1994, p. 2). The compassionate stereotype of older persons of the 1960s when the Older Americans Act (OAA) was enacted has undergone a reversal since the late 1970s (Binstock, 1983). During the 1980s and into the 1990s, older persons are often depicted as prosperous, hedonistic, selfish, and politically powerful. Robert B. Hudson (1995a), professor of social welfare policy at the School of Social Work of Boston University, summarized the change in aging policy over the past 20 years: "The most striking change over that period of time is in the imagery of aging—from one of abject need to excessive affluence" (p. 4).

Two prominent factors have contributed to this change. One is the very large improvement in the aggregate economic status of older adults, largely due to the impact of federal programs. The second factor is the "graying of the federal

TABLE 14.8 Federal Outlays by Detailed Function in Millions of Dollars

Function	1980	1990	1995, estimated
Total	$590,947	$1,252,705	$1,538,920
National defense	133,995	229,331	271,600
Medicare	32,090	98,102	157,288
Social Security	118,547	248,623	336,149

Source: U.S. Office of Management and Budget, Budget of the United States Government (U.S. Bureau of the Census, 1995, p. 337).

budget" (Hudson, 1995a, p. 4). Table 14.8 shows the federal outlay for national defense, Medicare, and Social Security, as well as the total outlay for 1980, 1990, and 1995 (U.S. Bureau of the Census, 1995). In making comparisons, it is necessary to remember that Social Security includes disability benefits and survivor benefits that could be paid to younger persons as well as retirement benefits. Also, the expenditure on national defense, which is often cited as a basis for comparison, has been reduced as a result of lessening of international tension.

The possible ways of managing the economic burden to support programs that benefit older adults include increasing the share that older adults pay through coinsurance and deductibles for Medicare, decreasing benefits by raising the age for eligibility to Social Security and Medicare, and exploring new ways of financing the deficit. In the political climate that encompassed the 1994 congressional elections, the Contract with America, and the platforms of Republican presidential hopefuls, Hudson (1995b) observes the forces of decentralization, informalization, and privatization at work. Treas and Torrecilha (1995) ask, "Will the federal deficit be plugged with means-tests, caps, and taxes on entitlements?" (p. 90). The more difficult question may be what will happen to those older adults who are most at risk—the oldest old, those in poverty, women, and minorities? If social assistance programs for elders are reduced, how will the needs of *at-risk* older adults be met?

Finally, there is a need for additional scientific knowledge to help policymakers with decisions about economic aspects of aging because "economic policy decisions related to aging are still driven more by stereotypical notions than by scientific knowledge" (Schulz, 1995b, p. S271). Schulz points out that although we have data to differentiate the economic circumstances of various elderly subgroups, there are several specialized areas that need research. These include older women, ethnic minorities, social assistance programs, pensions, and the baby boom cohort.

Research on the special economic problems of older women and ethnic minorities is still dominated by descriptive analysis. There is a need for research on the operation and impact of social assistance programs (the safety net) for those who "fall through the cracks." There is a need for research to determine the levels, adequacy, and distribution of employer-sponsored pensions and the impact of pension trends on future benefits. There is a need for research on the economics of the retirement of the baby boom cohort. Collection and analysis of data and simulation projections on these topics should contribute to a better understanding of the economics of older adults and improved decision making about economic status and welfare.

REFERENCES

Ando, A., & Modigliani, F. (1963). The "life cycle" hypothesis of savings: Aggregate implications and tests. *American Economic Review*, *53*, 55–84.

Atkins, G. L. (1992). Making it last: Economic resources of the oldest old. In R. M. Suzman, D. P. Willis, & K. G. Manton (Eds.), *The oldest old* (pp. 359–380). New York: Oxford University Press.

Bengtson, V. L., & Achenbaum, W. A. (1993). *The changing contract across generations*. New York: Aldine DeGruyter.

Bennett, A. (1994, July 20). More and more women are staying on the job later in life than men. *Wall Street Journal*, pp. B1, B2.

Bianchi, S. (1995). Changing economic roles of men and women. In Reynolds Farley (Ed.), *State of the union: America in the 1990s* (pp. 107–154). New York: Russell Sage Foundation.

Binstock, R. H. (1983). The aged as scapegoat. *Gerontologist*, *23*, 136–143.

Binstock, R. H. (1990). The politics and economics of aging and diversity. In S. A. Bass, E. A. Kutza, & F. M. Torres-Gil (Eds.), *Diversity in aging* (pp. 129–149). Glenview, IL: Scott, Foresman.

Binstock, R. H. (1992). The oldest old and "intergenerational equity." In R. M. Suzman, D. P. Willis, & K. G. Manton (Eds.), *The oldest old* (pp. 394–417). New York: Oxford University Press.

Brody, E., Kleban, M., Johnsen, P., Hoffman, C., & Schoonover, C. (1987). Work status and parent care: A comparison of four groups of women. *Gerontologist*, *27*, 201–208.

Burkhauser, R. V. (1994). Protecting the most vulnerable: A proposal to improve social security insurance for older women. *Gerontologist*, *34*(2), 148–149.

Congressional Budget Office. (1987). *Tax policy for pensions and other retirement saving.* Washington, DC: U.S. Government Printing Office.

Danziger, S., Van Der Gaag, J., Smolensky, E., & Taussig, M. K. (1982–83). The life-cycle hypothesis and the consumption behavior of the elderly. *Journal of Post Keynesian Economics*, *5*(winter), 208–227.

Del Bene, L., & Vaughan, D. R. (1992). Income, assets, and health insurance: Economic resources for meeting the acute health care needs of the aged. *Social Security Bulletin*, *55*(1), 3–25.

DeVaney, S. A. (1995). Confidence in a financially secure retirement: Differences between non-retirees and retirees. *Consumer Interests Annual*, *41*, 42–48.

DeVaney, S. A., Bechman, J. C., & Williams, F. L. (1995). Consumers' knowledge and awareness of alternatives for financing long-term care. In C. Y. Kratzer (Ed.),

Proceedings of the Association of Financial Counseling and Planning Education (Vol. 13, pp. 118–132). Blackburg, VA: Virginia Polytechnic Institute and State University.

The development and history of the poverty thresholds. (1993). *Family Economics Review, 6*(4), 21.

Duff, C. (1995, September 28). Profiling the aged: Fat cats or hungry victims? *Wall Street Journal*, pp. B1, B8.

Grad, S. (1992). *Income of the population 55 or older, 1990.* Washington, DC: Social Security Administration, Office of Research and Statistics.

Hatch, L. R. (1990). Effects of work and family on women's later-life resources. *Research on Aging, 12*, 311–338.

Hatch, L. R., & Thompson, A. (1992). Family responsibilities and women's retirement. In M. Szinovacz, D. Ekerdt, & B. Vinick (Eds.), *Families and retirement.* Newbury Park, CA: Sage.

Hogan, D., & Astone, N. M. (1986). The transition to adulthood. *Annual Review of Sociology, 12*, 109–130.

Holden, K. C., & Smeeding, T. M. (1990). The poor, the rich, and the insecure elderly caught in between. *Milbank Memorial Fund Quarterly, 68*, 191–219.

Hudson, R. B. (1995a). Our guest editor. *Generations, 19*(3), 4.

Hudson, R. B. (1995b). The history and place of age-based policy. *Generations, 19*(3), 5–10.

Hurd, M. D. (1990). Research on the elderly: Economic status, retirement, and consumption and saving. *Journal of Economic Literature, 28*, 565–637.

Hurd, M. D., & Shoven, J. B. (1983). The economic status of the elderly. In Zvi Bodie & John B. Shoven (Eds.), *Financial aspects of the United States pension system* (pp. 359–397). Washington, DC: National Bureau of Economic Research.

Hurd, M. D., & Shoven, J. B. (1985). Inflation vulnerability, income, and wealth of the elderly, 1969–1979. In M. David & T. Smeeding (Eds.), *Horizontal equity, uncertainty, and economic well-being* (pp. 125–172). Chicago: University of Chicago Press.

Kassner, E. (1991). *Elderly people who live alone.* Washington, DC: AARP Public Policy Institute.

Kennickell, A. B., & Starr-McCluer, M. (1994, October). Changes in family finances from 1989 to 1992: Evidence from the Survey of Consumer Finances. *Federal Reserve Bulletin*, pp. 861–882.

Leimberg, S. R., & McFadden, J. J. (1995). *The tools and techniques of employee benefit and retirement planning.* Cincinnati, OH: National Underwriter Co.

Lewis, Robert. (1996). Critics give mixed reviews to new law overhauling pensions. *AARP Bulletin, 38*(8), p. 3.

Menchik, P. L., & David, M. (1983). Income distribution, lifetime savings, and bequests. *American Economic Review, 73*, 672–690.

Merrill Lynch, Pierce, Fenner & Smith Inc. (1995). *The seventh annual retirement savings survey in America: Confronting the savings crisis.* Princeton, NJ: Author.

Meyer, M. H. (1990). Family status and poverty among older women: The gendered distribution of retirement income in the United States. *Social Problems, 37*, 551–563.

Minkler, M., & Stone, R. (1985). The feminization of poverty and older women. *Gerontologist, 25*, 351–357.

Moen, P. (1985). Continuities and discontinuities in women's labor force activity. In G. H. Elder Jr. (Ed.), *Life course dynamics.* Ithaca, NY: Cornell University Press.

Moen, P., & Smith, K. R. (1986). Women at work: Commitment and behavior over the life course. *Sociological Forum*, *1*, 450–475.

National Academy on Aging. (1994). *Old age in the 21st century*. Syracuse, NY: Syracuse University, Maxwell School, & Greenberg House, Washington, DC.

Northrop, E. M. (1990). The feminization of poverty: The demographic factor and the composition of economic growth. *Journal of Economic Issues*, *24*(1), 145–160.

O'Neill, J. E. (1994, October). The shrinking pay gap. *Wall Street Journal*, p. A10.

O'Rand, A., Henretta, J., & Krecker, M. (1992). Family pathways to retirement. In M. Szinovacz, D. Ekerdt, & B. Vinick (Eds.), *Families and retirement*. Newbury Park, CA: Sage.

Patterson, M. P. (1993). *The working woman's guide to retirement planning: Saving and investing now for a secure future*. Englewood Cliffs, NJ: Prentice-Hall.

Pearce, D. (1978). The feminization of poverty: Women, work, and welfare. *Urban and Social Change Review*, *11*, 28–36.

Pienta, A. M., Burr, J. A., & Mutchler, J. E. (1984). Women's labor force participation in later life: The effects of early work and family experiences. *Journals of Gerontology*, *49*, S231–S239.

Public Policy Institute G1. (1995). *Income, poverty and wealth among the elderly*. Washington, DC: AARP.

Public Policy Institute G8. (1995). *The housing assistance needs of older Americans*. Washington, DC: AARP.

Poverty thresholds. (1994). *Family Economics Review*, 7(3), 49.

Radner, D. B. (1982). Distribution of family income: Improved estimates. *Social Security Bulletin*, *45*, 13–21.

Radner, D. B. (1992). The economic status of the aged. *Social Security Bulletin*, *55*(3).

Schulz, J. H. (1995a). *The economics of aging* (6th ed.). Westport, CT: Auburn House.

Schulz, J. H. (1995b). What we have learned about the economics of aging: "Ratings" for past years of research. *Journal of Gerontology: Social Sciences*, *50B*, S271–S273.

Schwenk, F. N. (1993). Changes in the economic status of America's elderly population during the last 50 years. *Family Economics Review*, *6*(1), 18–25.

Schwenk, F. N. (1995). Assets of elderly households. *Family Economics Review*, *8*(1), 13–19.

Shellenbarger, S. (1995, July 19). Study tries to lift fog on cost employers pay for elder care. *Wall Street Journal*, p. C1.

Torres-Gil. F. M. (1992). *The new aging: Politics and change in America*. Westport, CT: Auburn House.

Torrey, B. B. (1992). Sharing increasing costs on declining income: The visible dilemma of the invisible aged. In R. M. Suzman, D. P. Willis, & K. G. Manton (Eds.), *The oldest old* (pp. 381–393). New York: Oxford University Press.

Torrey, B. B., & Taeuber, C. M. (1986). The importance of asset income among the elderly. *Review of Income and Wealth*, *32*, 443–449.

Treas, J., & Torrecilha, R. (1995). The older population. In Reynolds Farley (Ed.), *Social and Economic Trends in the 1980s* (pp. 47–92). New York: Russell Sage Foundation.

U.S. Bureau of the Census. (1995). *Statistical abstract of the United States* (115th ed.). Washington, DC: U.S. Department of Commerce.

U.S. Department of Health and Human Services. (1994). *Fast facts and figures about Social Security* (SSA Pub. No. 13–11785). Washington, DC: U.S. Government Printing Office.

U.S. Department of Labor. (1995). *Retirement benefits of American workers: New findings from the September 1994 Current Population Survey*. Washington, DC: Pension and Welfare Benefits Administration.

Weinrobe, M. (1995). Homeownership's impact on the economic security of older persons. In *Expanding housing choices for older people: AARP WHCoA Mini-Conference* (pp. 249–270). Washington, DC: AARP Public Policy Institute.

Willis, C. (1995, February). Mind over money. *Working Woman*, pp. 30–37.

CHAPTER 15

Promoting Healthy Aging

Susan Noble Walker

A review of the gerontological and health care literature using the descriptors "health" and "aging" is most likely to yield an abundance of information about the incidence of various illnesses, signs and symptoms of disease, reasons for visits to physicians and for hospitalization, and causes of death for older adults—in actuality, the absence of health in old age. Although extensive research has been reported on the disease processes and chronic illnesses associated with aging, much less is known about *health* and health promotion in old age.

It is encouraging that the attention of gerontologists and health care professionals has been focused increasingly on health promotion among older adults during the past decade (see, e.g., Preventive healthcare, 1994). The somewhat fatalistic view of aging that held that heredity was the dominant determinant of longevity and the quality of life during one's later years has been superseded by the more balanced view that one's own behavior interacts with one's heredity and environment to determine both health and length of life. While recognizing the importance of each of these determinants of health, this chapter will focus particularly on individual lifestyles as they influence health and the potential for high level wellness of older adults.

This chapter examines the various meanings health may have for older adults, reviews current knowledge about the prevalence and determinants of health-promoting lifestyle patterns among older adults, and suggests conceptual frameworks for further study of such patterns. In addition, it describes some programmatic approaches to promoting healthy aging as one vital component of an effective national health policy.

AGING AND HEALTH

As described in chapter 2, ours is indeed an aging society. Life expectancy has been increasing in the United States; men at age 65 may now expect to live 15.1 more years, and women may expect to live 18.6 more years (Schick & Schick, 1994). What will those added years be like? Some (Fries & Crapo, 1981; Fries, Green, & Levine, 1989) interpret trends in mortality to mean that the survival curve will eventually become rectangular, with a compression of morbidity at the end of life; that is, that nearly everyone will survive to an advanced age and that significant infirmity and disability will not occur until shortly before death. Their optimistic view is countered by others who suggest that increasing life expectancy will result in more prolonged periods of chronic illness, disability, and dependency, with greater need for institutional and community-based health care services, especially among the group aged 85 years and older (Guralnik, 1991; Havighurst & Sacher, 1981). A recent analysis of data from the 1982, 1984, and 1989 National Long Term Care surveys revealed that the percentage of those over 65 reporting no disabilities rose, whereas the percentage of those with chronic disabilities grew at a much slower rate than forecast (Manton, Stallard, & Liu, 1993). One of three overarching goals of national public health objectives for the year 2000 is to increase the years of healthy disability-free life (U.S. Department of Health and Human Services, 1991).

If the quality of life is to be maximized and the health care needs of an aging society are to be met adequately, it is essential that health care providers and political decision makers, as well as society in general, have an accurate picture of the relationship between aging and health. All too often, aging is viewed as a period of inevitable decline associated with illness, senility, dependence, poverty, and powerlessness. Unfortunately, aging may mean some or all of these things for some individuals—but not for most. As demonstrated in earlier chapters, people age in diverse ways.

Negative stereotypes and myths about aging are detrimental in numerous ways. One characteristic of stereotypes is their potential for making their victims believe they are true, thus adversely affecting older adults' views of themselves and their expectations for health and effective functioning. If illness and disability are seen as inevitable accompaniments of aging, individuals may not seek treatment for correctable problems. The acceptance of myths may also influence the interactions of families and health care providers with older adults, such that they may inadvertently encourage unnecessary dependence and loss of decision-making power.

John Heinz, former chairman of the U.S. Senate Special Committee on Aging (1986), provided this succinct perspective on the relationship between aging and health:

> Growing old, while an inevitable process for all of us, has no common denominator when it comes to health. The image of a grayed and crippled, frail older American is

just as much a stereotype as that of a robust and active one: Neither captures the range of health status found in this segment of our Nation's population.

Age alone is a poor indicator of health status. As we age, our bodies change, yet aging itself is not a disease. Persons aged 65 to 74 have been found to have health profiles more like those persons aged 48 to 64 than of persons aged 75 and over. Only when the elderly reach their 80s do functional impairments occur more as a consequence of aging than of pathology.

One of the central challenges in meeting the health care needs of an aging society is to gain a better understanding of the relationship between age and health. Research now shows, for example, that lifestyle and health care patterns are better predictors of health status than age. Given advances in medical technology, coupled with the attention being placed today on preventive health care and healthier lifestyles, we can expect the health status portrait of tomorrow's elderly to look different than today's. (p. iii)

THE MEANING OF HEALTH FOR OLDER ADULTS

To promote healthy aging effectively, it is important to have some understanding of the meaning of health for older adults. Health is widely understood to be the variable most influential on measures of subjective well-being, life satisfaction, or morale. Within those studies, health was measured in a variety of different ways, which can be broadly classified as objective (physician's or other health professional's clinical examination findings) and subjective (subject's own report of specific health problems and/or evaluation of perceived general health). Although objective assessments are necessary and valuable for clinical diagnostic purposes, subjective ratings of health status are more readily obtained and may actually be more meaningful for a variety of research purposes. In interpreting self-ratings of health, however, it becomes essential to have some understanding of what "health" means to the older person who is reporting the evaluation.

Although 80% of older adults have at least one chronic health condition and 20% have some degree of disability, almost 1 in 4 assess their health as good or excellent (Schick & Schick, 1994). Objective health status as measured by clinical examination and perceived health status as measured by self-report often yield different results on the same subjects. Obviously, that finding is one of great interest. It may be that each evaluation is based on a different understanding of what health is, for health conception appears to have more than one dimension. The objective findings of a clinical examination may provide information about only a single dimension of health, health as the absence of illness. The individual's self-evaluation of health status may consider only that dimension as well, or it may include other aspects of health such as feeling good, being able to do things that are important, coping with life's demands, and achieving one's potential. Much of the gerontological literature pertaining to perceived health status does not discuss the definition of health, thereby assuming a shared or common meaning of health that may be fallacious.

A useful categorization of various definitions of health into four models was provided by Smith (1983). In the *clinical model*, health is viewed as the absence of disease or disability and is characterized by the absence of signs and symptoms. This view of health is reflected in traditional as well as much contemporary medical practice and literature. In the *functional model*, health is viewed as maximal performance of socially defined roles such as worker or parent and is defined with reference to the individual's participation in the social system. In the *adaptive model*, health is viewed as flexible adjustment to changing circumstances and is characterized by the ability to adapt both biologically and socially to varying environmental circumstances. In the *eudaimonistic model*, health is viewed as exuberant well-being or high-level wellness and reflects the realization of the individual's intrinsic potential for fulfillment and complete development.

Walker and Volkan (1987) studied these four definitions or dimensions of health conception among adults aged 55 to 91 living in the community. They found that older adults subscribed in descending order to the functional, eudaimonistic, adaptive, and clinical definitions of health and that there were two higher order dimensions underlying the four. Analyses revealed that eudaimonistic, adaptive, and functional definitions were related to one underlying dimension and that the clinical definition alone was related to a second underlying dimension of health conception.

Based on these findings, health as defined by older adults may be depicted as comprising intersecting continua representing the absence of illness and the presence of wellness, with various definitions of health subsumed on each. Within the model in Figure 15.1, the clinical conception of health, with health defined as freedom from illness, lies along a horizontal continuum, and the other three conceptions of health, with high level wellness as a positive goal, lie along a vertical continuum. Such a conceptualization of health allows for the possibility of experiencing high level wellness despite the presence of chronic or even terminal illness (such an individual would be placed in the upper left quadrant of the circle).

Such a multidimensional conceptualization was reflected in a broad definition of health suggested as appropriate for older adults in a background paper prepared for the 1981 White House Conference on Aging. Health was defined there as "the ability to live and function effectively in society, to exercise self-reliance and autonomy to the maximum extent feasible—but not necessarily total freedom from disease" (Minkler & Fullarton, 1980, p. 4). The traditional clinical definition of health as simply the absence of illness is clearly inappropriate for the majority of older adults for whom chronic illness is a fact of life. The three more positive, growth-oriented alternatives to the clinical definition of health—those described as functional, adaptive, and eudaimonistic—may have greater relevance for older adults because they allow for movement toward health

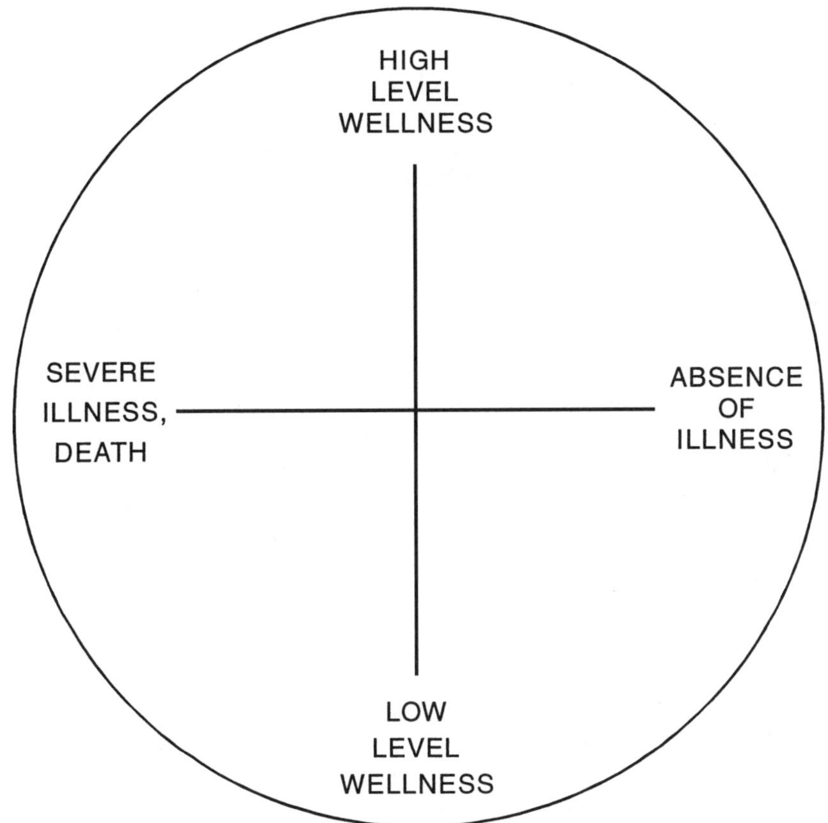

FIGURE 15.1 A multidimensional model of health conception among older adults.

despite the presence of disease. Subsequent studies have confirmed that older adults retain such varied positive images of health into advanced years (Butler, 1993; Perry & Woods, 1995; Strain, 1993; Viverais-Dresler & Richardson, 1991; Wondolowski & Davis, 1991).

HEALTH PROMOTION AS A COMPONENT OF NATIONAL HEALTH POLICY

Health and quality of life throughout the later years of adulthood is of enormous concern, not only to individuals and their families but also to society. Three complementary components of an effective national health strategy for people of all ages have been described as medical care, illness prevention, and health promotion. The health care system for older adults has been heavily weighted toward medical care, with some attention being paid to illness prevention. Older adults have only recently been viewed as appropriate targets of health promotion efforts.

The U.S. Department of Health and Human Services (1980) launched a major initiative to improve the health status and reduce the health risks of Americans with the publication of *Healthy People: The Surgeon General's Report on Health Promotion and Disease Prevention* (1979) and *Promoting Health/Preventing Disease: Objectives for the Nation*. In these documents the stated goal for older adults was to improve health and quality of life, but it was to be measured narrowly by reduction in the average number of days of restricted activity. Concern was expressed that these documents did not adequately address the needs and health priorities of the elderly (Green, 1985) and that many of the strategic target areas were not applicable to the elderly while many of the issues essential to their well-being did not fit in the established categories (Minkler & Fullarton, 1980).

These reports did, however, provide the impetus and organizational framework for a number of health promotion initiatives with older adults throughout the nation (Heckler, 1985). *Objectives for the Nation* also stimulated the collection of data relative to health promotion and disease prevention. Items about individual health behaviors and knowledge of health practices were included in the 1985 and 1991 National Health Interview Surveys. Responses broken down by four age groups now make it possible to compare knowledge and behavior of adults over 65 with those of younger groups.

The Surgeon General convened a panel of experts to assess what was known about health promotion for older adults and to make recommendations regarding policy, education, service, and research needs (Abdellah & Moore, 1988). The U.S. Preventive Services Task Force, a multidisciplinary panel of prevention experts, published recommendations in 1989 for a core set of clinical preventive services—screening for early detection of disease or risk factors, immunizations, and counseling about lifestyle modification—specific to age, gender, and risk status of individuals and including guidelines for services to be delivered to adults aged 65 and older. Subsequently, the Institute of Medicine (IOM), emphasizing that growing old does not necessarily mean growing frail, recommended that primary care providers not dismiss all functional limitations as the natural consequence of aging and that they encourage older individuals "to adopt healthier lifestyles and avail themselves of preventive services" (Berg & Cassells, 1990, p. 4). These sets of recommendations are reflected in the goals for older adults included in *Healthy People 2000: National Health Promotion and Disease Prevention Objectives* (U.S. Department of Health and Human Services, 1991).

Healthy People 2000 sets an agenda for the nation for the current decade in the areas of health promotion, health protection, preventive services, and surveillance and data systems (U.S. Department of Health and Human Services, 1991). Health promotion strategies are "those related to individual lifestyle—personal choices made in a social context—that can have a powerful influence over one's health prospects" (p. 6). A section of objectives for older adults identifies the maintenance of health and functional independence as the most important aspect of health promotion for older people. Key health status, risk reduction, and services and protection objectives targeting older adults are elaborated there. Objectives for older adults also are included in priority areas concerned with lifestyle behavior change throughout the document. Baseline data for many of the health promotion and preventive services objectives for older adults were obtained from the 1991 Health Promotion and Disease Prevention Supplement of the National Health Interview Survey conducted by the National Center for Health Statistics. The Public Health Service will monitor progress toward the objectives throughout the decade, publishing the *Healthy People 2000 Review* at regular intervals (e.g., National Center for Health Statistics, 1993) and summaries of progress reviews periodically (e.g., *Healthy People 2000: Mid-Course Review and 1995 Revisions* [U.S. Department of Health and Human Services, 1995]). These reports indicate that, although life expectancy continues to increase and progress has been made toward some objectives, many of the national health promotion and preventive services goals for older adults remain to be achieved.

Despite these promising initiatives, current health policy in the United States remains consistent with a medical model focused on combatting disease. Only 2.9% of all health care dollars are expended for public health activities (Wolinsky, 1990). A restructuring of the American health care system will be required if the goals of health, functional independence, and quality of life for older adults are to be widely achieved.

HEALTHY LIFESTYLES

We now know that many deaths in the United States each year are premature and are due to unhealthy lifestyles (U.S. Department of Health and Human Services, 1991). This knowledge is stimulating interest in lifestyle modification as a major strategy for the enhancement of health and prevention of illness throughout the life span. If that strategy is to be successful, a clear definition of the components of a healthy lifestyle is essential. A healthy lifestyle is described in varying ways in the literature, sometimes narrowly as simply the avoidance of "bad health habits" such as smoking or excessive drinking and sometimes more broadly as all behaviors that can have an impact on health status. If health is accepted as a multidimensional construct encompassing both the absence or control of disease and the potential for high level wellness, then the broader conceptualization of a healthy lifestyle seems most useful in designing interventions and planning programs to enable older adults to realize their full potential for health.

Pender (1987) suggests that illness-preventing or health-protecting behavior and health-promoting behavior should be viewed as complementary components of a healthy lifestyle and that their integration is critical to health enhancement throughout the life span. Recognition of the important contribution that each category of behavior makes within a healthy lifestyle is often blurred by the way in which the terms "prevention" and "health promotion" are used in the literature—sometimes interchangeably and sometimes so that one subsumes the other.

Illness-preventing behavior is directed toward decreasing the individual's probability of encountering illness or injury. It is "avoidance" behavior that is fear-motivated and disease-specific and may involve both the adoption of desirable health practices and the avoidance of deleterious health practices, such as beginning to exercise and stopping smoking to reduce the threat of a heart attack. It also may include adherence to self-care regimens to minimize the likelihood of complications of chronic illness, a component of particular relevance for older adults.

The health-promoting component of lifestyle is "a multidimensional pattern of self-initiated actions and perceptions that serve to maintain or enhance the level of wellness, self-actualization and fulfillment of the individual" (Walker, Sechrist, & Pender, 1987, p. 77). It is "approach" behavior that is not health problem–specific. It is a positive approach to living that leads individuals toward realization of their highest potential for well-being. Ardell (1979) emphasizes that the health-promoting component of lifestyle is pursued because it is satisfying and enjoyable, not because of a wish to avoid disease. Examples would include meditating for the sense of peace that is experienced, exercising for the exhilaration that occurs, or confiding in and embracing close friends for the support and affirmation of self that is provided.

Both the illness-preventing and the health-promoting components of a healthy lifestyle rather than either alone must be addressed in programs of health promotion for older adults. Unless clearly indicated otherwise, "health promotion" as used throughout most of this chapter refers broadly to the encouragement of both behavioral components of a healthy lifestyle.

The Value of Healthy Lifestyle Practices

As early as 1961, Dunn wrote of the value of lifestyle in promoting not only longevity but also wellness. Much of the early evidence that lifestyle is related to health outcomes came from studies in the Human Population Laboratory of Alameda County, California, begun in 1965 with a probability sample of nearly 7,000 adults drawn from a general population. A series of cross-sectional and longitudinal studies there has provided support for the association between lifestyle and current health status (Berkman & Breslow, 1983; LaCroix, Guralnik, Berkman, Wallace, & Satterfield, 1993), future health status (Wiley & Camacho, 1980), and mortality (Duffy & MacDonald, 1990; Kaplan, Seeman, Cohen, Knudsen, & Guralnik, 1987). Particular attention is paid to the value of physical activity and exercise in maintaining health and functioning into older adulthood (Emery, Burker, & Blumenthal, 1991; Rakowski & Mor, 1992; Wolinsky, Stump, & Clark, 1995). The findings of these studies suggest that lifestyle can indeed influence the quality of life for older adults.

Healthy Lifestyle Patterns of Older Adults

To what extent are adults accepting the responsibility to protect and promote their own health as they age? A number of studies have shown that the prevalence of healthy lifestyle behaviors is greater among older people. In the Alameda County, California, study, more than twice as many people over age 75 reported practicing all seven of the "good health habits" concerned with patterns of eating, sleeping, physical activity, alcohol use, and smoking, as contrasted with those under age 45, and follow-up studies confirm the importance of these practices over 9 years (Guralnik & Kaplan, 1989; Wiley & Camacho, 1980). Other studies also have found that older individuals report significantly higher frequencies of a variety of preventive and promotive behaviors than do middle-aged or young individuals (Bausell, 1986; Prohaska, Leventhal, Leventhal, & Keller, 1985; Walker, Volkan, Sechrist, & Pender, 1988). One notable exception to this pattern is in exercise behavior, with older adults reporting less in two of the studies and no difference found between age groups in the third. The greater prevalence of healthy behaviors among older people may be explained by the fact that those members of the cohort who followed deleterious lifestyles died at earlier ages as well as by the survivors' behavior change in response to an increasing sense of vulnerability and/or acceptance of self-responsibility that occurs with maturity.

Older adults have been directly asked in several studies what they do to protect, maintain, or improve their health. Brown and McCreedy (1986) reported that many mentioned a variety of lifestyle activities contributing to physical, mental, psychological, spiritual, and social well-being, whereas only a few cited activities involving contact with the health care system. Brody (1985) found that types of activities were varied and included walking or other exercise (reported by 84%), watching their diets (48%), keeping busy (25%), socializing (23%), avoiding worry (18%), and visits to health professionals (9%). When asked why they did these activities, older adults' responses reflected both specific illness-preventive and more general health-promotive reasons. Maloney, Fallon, and Wittenberg (1984) reported that the most prominent theme among responses was the need to stay active (referring to keeping busy and involved with people) and to maintain a positive outlook on life.

Most investigations of healthy lifestyle in older adults have examined only a few behaviors, and little is known about how their full range of healthy lifestyle behaviors relate to one another. Calnan (1985) examined the extent to which 2,084 Englishwomen aged 45 to 64 carried out seven different types of preventive behavior (breast screening, cervical screening, dental checkup, dietary practice, exercise, smoking avoidance, and use of seat belts) and found that all the interrelationships showed significant but modest (<0.20) positive correlations. The most impressive finding was that there was a group of women who carried out no preventive behaviors; they were older women who were not working, who left school before the age of 15, and who tended to be socially isolated. Rakowski, Julius, Hickey, and Halter (1987) derived four groupings of preventive health behaviors from a set of 37 individual health practices reported by a sample of 172 community-residing adults aged 64 to 96. Modest associations were found among individual behaviors and among the four health practice groups (information seeking, regular health routines, medical and self-examination, and risk avoidance). Walker et al. (1988) employed cluster analysis to group 97 adults aged 55 to 88 across six dimensions of health-promoting lifestyle behaviors and identified five distinct patterns of behavior within the sample. These findings suggest that older adults are a heterogeneous group: although many are following healthy lifestyles, many are not.

Determinants of Healthy Lifestyles: Who Participates?

Given the substantial differences in healthy lifestyle behavior within the older adult population, it is essential to know which factors may facilitate or impede desirable and effective lifestyle practices among older adults and why some individuals follow health-enhancing lifestyles while others follow damaging and debilitating patterns of behavior. Such knowledge will provide direction for individually tailored health promotion program interventions to enhance health and quality of life for a heterogeneous population in the later years.

Illness-preventing and health-promoting components of a healthy lifestyle appear to have different underlying motivational mechanisms and to be influenced by different, albeit sometimes overlapping, constellations of factors. Since the late 1950s the Health Belief Model has been the dominant paradigm for explaining behavior directed toward protecting the individual from the threat of a specific acute or chronic illness (Rosenstock, 1974). The Health Promotion Model (Fig. 15.2) was proposed to guide research in the area of health-promoting behavior, where a specific threat of disease is not relevant (Pender, 1987). The theoretical underpinnings of both models are provided by social learning theory, which emphasizes the importance of cognitive mediating processes in the regulation of behavior (Bandura, 1982). Cognitive/perceptual factors are seen as the primary motivational mechanisms that directly influence preventive and promotive behaviors, and modifying factors are proposed as variables that indirectly influence behaviors through their impact on cognitive/perceptual processes. Cues to action are internal or environmental stimuli that can "trigger" health-seeking behavior in a given situation. Within healthy lifestyles, specific behaviors (such as exercise) may indeed serve both preventive and promotive functions; thus motivation for performance of those behaviors may be mixed and/or fluctuating, requiring careful consideration of the circumstances under which each model is most appropriately applied.

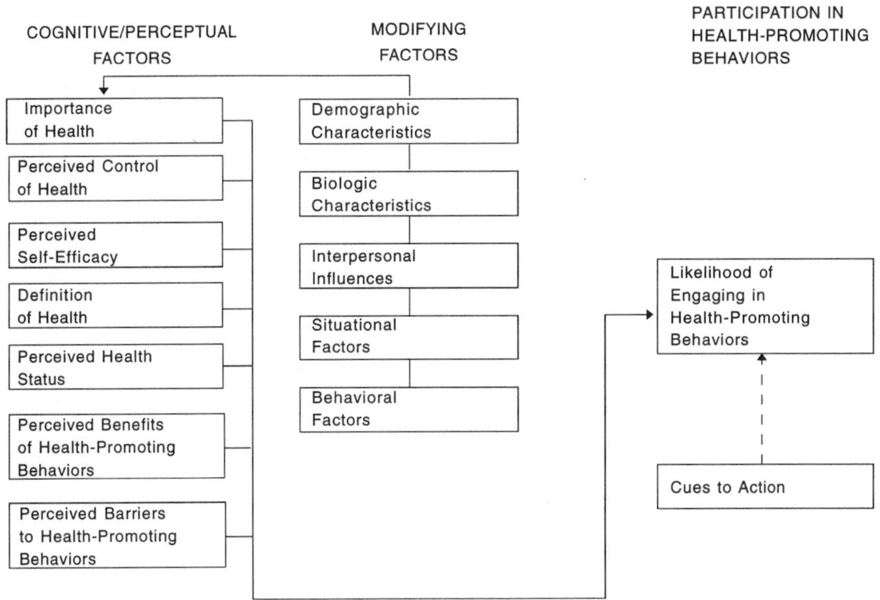

FIGURE 15.2 The health promotion model. From *Health Promotion in Nursing Practice*, 2nd ed., p. 58, by N. J. Pender, 1987, Norwalk, CT: Appleton & Lange. Reprinted by permission.

Relatively few studies of the correlates of healthy lifestyle patterns and behaviors among adult populations have included older adults in the samples, and even fewer have investigated samples of older adults exclusively. Findings from these studies have begun to suggest the possible usefulness of variables in each model for explaining healthy lifestyle behavior. Preventive health behaviors may be related to perceived seriousness and susceptibility, which combine to determine the threat posed by disease within the Health Belief Model (Prohaska et al., 1985; Wheeler & Rundall, 1980). Perceived benefits of action, barriers to action, and self-efficacy are proposed as influencing both illness-preventing and health-promoting behaviors within the Health Belief and Health Promotion Models, respectively. One or more of these variables have been found to influence nutritional and exercise behaviors among older adults (Ali & Bennett, 1992; Neuberger, Kasal, Smith, Hassanein, & DeViney, 1994; Sharpe & Connell, 1992). Some evidence supports the influence of health locus of control, definition of health, and perceived health status on health-promoting behavior (Duffy, 1993; Pender, Walker, Frank-Stromborg, & Sechrist, 1990; Speake, Cowart, & Pellet, 1989), as suggested by the Health Promotion Model. Older adults with high internal and low external (chance) locus of control were more likely to engage in health-promoting behaviors. Interestingly, powerful others locus of control was sometimes positively and sometimes negatively associated with behavior. Those who perceived themselves to be in better health and who defined health more as the presence of wellness and less as the absence of illness also were more likely to engage in health-promoting behaviors.

HEALTH PROMOTION PROGRAMS FOR OLDER ADULTS

While the knowledge base about the benefits, patterns, and determinants of healthy lifestyle behaviors among older adults has been expanding, there has been a simultaneous increase in interest in providing health promotion programming for the older segment of the population (Berg & Cassells, 1990; Fallcreek, Muchow, & Mockenhaupt, 1994; Haber, 1994). For many years, major research on the effectiveness of health promotion and disease prevention activities excluded persons over 60 years of age. In reviewing the limited literature available, Carter, Elward, Malmgren, Martin, and Larson (1991) found that participation rates in health promotion surveys, clinical research and programs for adults up to age 74 were fairly comparable to younger age groups and that lower participation rates for those over 85 often were associated with episodes of ill health rather than lack of interest. Recent intervention studies have confirmed the experience of gerontological health care practitioners that older adults can accomplish and benefit from health behavior modification (e.g., Benson et al., 1989; Mayer et al., 1994; Schmidt, 1993).

Some Model Programs

For a variety of reasons, older adults were overlooked earlier by the health promotion movement in the United States. Nevertheless, pioneering program designers have recognized that traditional health promotion–illness prevention program topics and approaches can be modified effectively for use with older adults and that programs can be made most relevant and appealing to older adults when additional areas of unique interest to them are included. A variety of single-purpose programs, in both the preventive and the promotive modes, have been offered by a range of sponsoring agencies and organizations throughout the country. Examples are blood pressure screening clinics at local health departments, nutrition education classes at senior centers, and walking, swimming, or aerobic exercise programs at YMCAs. Most notable, however, have been efforts to develop more comprehensive health promotion programs for older adults, such as those highlighted below.

The Senior Actualization and Growth Explorations (SAGE) Project, established in 1974, was among the first of the wellness-oriented programs for older people. It focused on both the individual and broader community dimensions of health promotion, as it provided individuals with information and skills to achieve physical and psychological health and also provided community education to create more positive attitudes toward aging (Minkler & Fullarton, 1980).

The Wallingford Wellness Project is a 15-week, comprehensive, community-based, intergenerational, lifestyle-change program that focuses on nutrition, physical fitness, stress management, and personal and community self-help as the pillars or necessities of health promotion for older people. One of the products of the program was a sourcebook that provides extensive information about program development and evaluation, curriculum content, and teaching materials, which should be valuable to professionals in developing such programs elsewhere (Fallcreek & Mettler, 1984).

The Healthy Lifestyle for Seniors model program meets for $3\frac{1}{2}$ hours twice a week for 6 months and includes four major program components: health monitoring, nutrition, exercise, and stress management. The individual's primary responsibility for lifestyle change is emphasized throughout. Information about program design, administration, curriculum, and evaluation is contained in a program development manual designed to help others adapt the model for use with their own populations (Warner-Reitz & Grothe, 1981).

The Dartmouth Institute for Better Health developed the Self-Care for Senior Citizens program, a comprehensive self-care program with more of a preventive focus than the others described here, that included 13 sessions concerned with medical self-care, lifestyle modification, and the appropriate use of health and human services. After evaluation and revision it provided the core curriculum for Staying Healthy After Fifty (SHAF), a program implemented nationwide in collaboration with the American Association of Retired Persons (AARP) and the American Red Cross (Simmons et al., 1989). It uses the *Medical and Health Guide for People Over Fifty* (Nelson, Roberts, Simmons, & Tisdale, 1986).

Healthwise, Inc.'s GROWING YOUNGER is a briefer, community-based, positive health–oriented program for adults aged 60 and over that is composed of four 2-hour workshops integrating the topics of physical fitness, nutrition, stress management, and medical self-care in each session (Kemper, 1986). Healthwise has also developed the GROWING WISER program, an additional series of sessions that focus on mental health and the development of personal potential among older adults. It has published handbooks for each of these programs (Kemper, Deneen, & Giuffre, 1989; Kemper, Mettler, Giuffre, & Matzek, 1986) and has workshops and training available to support them. More recently, it developed *Healthwise for Life* (Mettler & Kemper, 1992) to enhance older adults' self-care skills.

The W. K. Kellogg Foundation funded the development of Project H.E.A.L.T.H. (Helping Elders Adjust Lifestyles Toward Health), a comprehensive health promotion program designed to help older persons modify lifestyle behaviors, at the North Woods Health Careers Consortium in Wausau, Wisconsin. The curriculum includes 2- to 4-hour sessions weekly over 10 weeks and can be delivered on-site or over interactive television to reach more remote rural areas. Both a handbook for participants and an instructor's guide have been published (*Project H.E.A.L.T.H.*, 1991; Wroblewski, 1991).

There are, then, a number of resources available to those wishing to implement health promotion programs for older adults in their own communities. In addition to those cited above, Fallcreek and Franks (1984) developed a guide for state and local agencies that includes information about how to build coalitions within the aging and health networks in order to accomplish health promotion goals. AARP, through the National Eldercare Institute on Health Promotion, has distributed guidelines for developing health promotion programs for minority elders (Dorfman, 1993) and has produced a video, *Healthy Aging: Model Health Promotion Programs for Minority Elders*. AARP also publishes a quarterly newsletter, *Perspectives in Health Promotion and Aging*, that examines effective approaches to promoting healthful behaviors.

Target Areas for Health Promotion with Older Adults

Only the most comprehensive of health promotion programs is likely to address all of the promotive and preventive behaviors that comprise healthy lifestyles among older adults. In defining program objectives and choosing program content, the following areas are suggested by the research and program implementation literature as appropriate for consideration:

1. Self-responsibility for health
2. Nutrition
3. Exercise
4. Stress management
5. Interpersonal relationships and support
6. Spiritual growth, fulfillment of potential, self-actualization
7. Accident prevention
8. Safe use of medications and alcohol
9. Smoking cessation
10. Self-care regimens for chronic illness and common health concerns
11. Accessing preventive health services

Because many older adults have one or more chronic illnesses, this listing of health promotion program target areas is more extensive than for other population groups. All have relevance for individual behaviors older adults may undertake to enhance their health and functional status and the quality of their lives. Achieving health/wellness *despite* the presence of chronic illness is an achievable goal for most older adults in institutional as well as community settings.

Whether a broad or a limited focus is selected for a health promotion program, there are some guidelines to be kept in mind as the program is designed. First, it is desirable to involve older adults who are potential participants in the planning and conduct of the program. Planning the program *with* them rather than *for* them not only will increase their self-esteem and sense of program "ownership" but also will intensify their commitment to participating and ensuring the success of the effort. Second, a comprehensive integrated program is preferable to a piecemeal one for accomplishing lifestyle modification. A continuing program that incorporates several aspects of wellness in a holistic manner will be more effective than a single session with no follow-up, such as is often provided at health fairs. Finally, time and support are needed to integrate new learning into one's lifestyle. Programs should allow the opportunity to use new knowledge and skills within the context of the daily life situation, rather than simply dispensing information without opportunity for trial.

The Broader Context of Health Promotion

This chapter has intentionally addressed health promotion with older adults only in the context of facilitating individual behavior change and the adoption of healthy lifestyles. Minkler (1983) appropriately cautioned that such a focus on individual responsibility for health ignores the social context within which health-related decisions are made and "may inadvertently blame the victim by operating as though the individual is responsible for health problems which in reality often are caused . . . by forces over which the individual may have little control" (p. 13). She called for a broader, system-centered approach to health promotion for the elderly that includes interventions to achieve both individual and environmental change. As discussed more fully elsewhere (Walker, 1994), individuals, health care providers, and society must share the responsibility for achieving the goals of preventive health care and health promotion for older adults.

Certainly, health promotion in the broadest context must address social and environmental influences, such as the availability of housing and transportation, community health and social support services, and leisuretime activities and the opportunity for education and employment for older adults. Several of these areas are addressed in other chapters of this book, and they are indeed essential components of comprehensive health promotion programming for older people.

REFERENCES

Abdellah, F. G., & Moore, S. R. (Eds). (1988). *Surgeon general's workshop on health promotion and aging: Proceedings.* Washington, DC: U.S. Department of Health and Human Services, Public Health Service.

Ali, N. S., & Bennett, S. J. (1992). Postmenopausal women: Factors in osteoporosis preventive behaviors. *Journal of Gerontological Nursing, 18*(12), 23–32.

Ardell, D. B. (1979). The nature and implications of high level wellness, or why "normal health" is a rather sorry state of existence. *Health Values: Achieving High Level Wellness, 3*(1), 17–24.

Bandura, A. (1982). Self-efficacy mechanism in human agency. *American Psychologist, 37,* 122–147.

Bausell, R. B. (1986). Health-seeking behavior among the elderly. *Gerontologist, 26*, 556–559.

Benson, L., Nelson, E. C., Napps, S. E., Roberts, E., Kane-Williams, E., & Salisbury, Z. T. (1989). Evaluation of the Staying Healthy After Fifty educational program: Impact on course participants. *Health Education Quarterly, 16*, 485–508.

Berg, R. L., & Cassells, J. S. (Eds). (1990). *The second fifty years: Promoting health and preventing disability.* Washington, DC: National Academy Press.

Berkman, L., & Breslow, L. (1983). *Health and ways of living.* New York: Oxford University Press.

Brody, E. M. (1985). *Mental and physical health practices of older people.* New York: Springer Publishing.

Brown, J. S., & McCreedy, M. (1986). The hale elderly: Health behavior and its correlates. *Research in Nursing and Health, 9*, 317–329.

Butler, S. S. (1993). Older rural women: Understanding their conceptions of health and illness. *Topics in Geriatric Rehabilitation, 9*(1), 56–68.

Calnan, M. (1985). Patterns in preventive behavior: A study of women in middle age. *Social Science and Medicine, 20*, 263-268.

Carter, W. B., Elward, K., Malmgren, J., Martin, M. L., & Larson, E. (1991). Participation of older adults in health programs and research: A critical review of the literature. *Gerontologist, 31*, 584–592.

Dorfman, S. L. (1993). *A guide to the development of health promotion programs for minority elders.* Washington, DC: AARP, National Eldercare Institute on Health Promotion.

Duffy, M. E. (1993). Determinants of health-promoting lifestyles in older persons. *Image, 25*(1), 23–28.

Duffy, M. E., & MacDonald, E. (1990). Determinants of functional health of older persons. *Gerontologist, 30*, 503–509.

Dunn, H. L. (1961). *High level wellness.* Arlington, VA: R. W. Beatty.

Emery, C. F., Burker, E. J., & Blumenthal, J. A. (1991). Psychological and physiological effects of exercise among older adults. *Annual Review of Gerontology and Geriatrics, 11*, 218–238. New York: Springer Publishing.

Fallcreek, S., & Franks, P. (1984). *Health promotion and aging: Strategies for action* (DHHS Pub. No. [OHDS] 84-20818). Washington, DC: U.S. Government Printing Office.

Fallcreek, S., & Mettler, M. (1984). *A healthy old age.* New York: Haworth.

Fallcreek, S., Muchow, J., & Mockenhaupt, R. E. (1994). Health promotion with rural elders. In R. T. Coward, C. N. Bull, G. Kukulka, & J. M. Galliher (Eds.), *Health services for rural elders* (pp. 182–202). New York: Springer Publishing.

Fries, J. F., & Crapo, L. M. (1981). *Vitality and aging.* San Francisco: W. H. Freeman.

Fries, J. F., Green, L. W., & Levine, S. (1989). Health promotion and the compression of morbidity. *Lancet, 1*(8636), 481–483.

Green, L. W. (1985). Some challenges to health services research on children and the elderly. *Health Services Research, 19*, 793–815.

Guralnik, J. M. (1991). Prospects for the compression of morbidity: The challenge posed by increasing disability in the years prior to death. *Journal of Aging and Health, 3*, 138–154.

Guralnik, J. M., & Kaplan, G. A. (1989). Predictors of aging: Prospective evidence from the Alameda County Study. *American Journal of Public Health, 79*, 703–708.

Haber, D. (1994). *Health promotion and aging.* New York: Springer Publishing.

Havighurst, R., & Sacher, G. (1981). Prospects of lengthening life and vigor. In H. Wershow (Ed.), *Controversial issues in gerontology* (pp. 54–57). New York: Springer Publishing.

Heckler, M. M. (1985). Health promotion for older Americans. *Public Health Reports, 100*, 225–230.

Kaplan, G A., Seeman, T. E., Cohen, R. D., Knudsen, L. P., & Guralinik, J. (1987). Mortality among the elderly in the Alameda County study: Behavioral and demographic risk factors. *American Journal of Public Health*, 77, 307–312.

Kemper, D. (1986). The Healthwise program: GROWING YOUNGER. In K. Dychtwald (Ed.), *Wellness and health promotion for the elderly* (pp. 263–274). Rockville, MD: Aspen.

Kemper, D. W., Deneen, E. J., & Giuffre, J. V. (1989). *GROWING YOUNGER handbook* (3rd ed., rev.). Boise, ID: Healthwise.

Kemper, D. W., Mettler, M., Giuffre, J., & Matzek, B. (1986). *GROWING WISER: The older person's guide to mental wellness.* Boise, ID: Healthwise.

LaCroix, A. Z., Guralnik, J. M., Berkman, L. F., Wallace, R. B., & Satterfield, S. (1993). Maintaining mobility in late life. II. Smoking, alcohol consumption, physical activity, and body mass index. *American Journal of Epidemiology, 137*, 858–869.

Maloney, S. K., Fallon, F., & Wittenberg, C. K. (1984). *Aging and health promotion: Market research for public education.* Washington, DC: U.S. Public Health Service, Office of Disease Prevention and Health Promotion.

Manton, K. G., Stallard, E., & Liu, K. (1993). Forecasts of active life expectancy: Policy and fiscal implications. *Journal of Gerontology, 48* [Special issue], 11–26.

Mayer, J. A., Jermanovich, A., Wright, B. L., Elder, J. P., Drew, J. A., & Williams, S. J. (1994). Changes in health behaviors of older adults: The San Diego Medicare Preventive Health Project. *Preventive Medicine, 23*, 127–133.

Mettler, M., & Kemper, D. (1992). *Healthwise for life: Medical self-care for healthy aging.* Boise, ID: Healthwise.

Minkler, M. (1983). Health promotion and elders: A critique. *Generations*, 7(3), 13–15, 67.

Minkler, M., & Fullarton, J. (1980). *Health promotion, health maintenance and disease prevention for the elderly.* Unpublished background paper for the 1981 White House Conference on Aging, prepared for the Office of Health Information Health Promotion, Physical Fitness and Sports Medicine (USPHS), Washington, DC.

National Center for Health Statistics. (1993). *Health United States 1992 and healthy people 2000 review.* Hyattsville, MD: Public Health Service.

Nelson, E., Roberts, E., Simmons, J., & Tisdale, W. (1986). *Medical and health guide for people over fifty.* Glenview, IL: Scott Foresman.

Neuberger, G. B., Kasal, S., Smith, K. V., Hassanein, R., & DeViney, S. (1994). Determinants of exercise and aerobic fitness in outpatients with arthritis. *Nursing Research, 43*(1), 11–17.

Pender, N. J. (1987). *Health promotion in nursing practice* (2nd ed.). Norwalk, CT: Appleton & Lange.

Pender, N.J., Walker, S.N., Frank-Stromborg, M., & Sechrist, K.R. (1990). *The health promotion model: Refinement and validation: A final report to the National Center for Nursing Research.* DeKalb, IL: Northern Illinois University.

Perry, J., & Woods, N. F. (1995). Older women and their images of health: A replication study. *Advances in Nursing Science, 18*(1), 51–61.

Preventive healthcare and health promotion for older adults. (1994). *Generations, 18*(1).

Prohaska, T. R., Leventhal, E. A., Leventhal, H., & Keller, M. L. (1985). Health practices and illness cognition in young, middle aged, and elderly adults. *Journal of Gerontology, 40*, 569–578.

Project H.E.A.L.T.H.: A handbook for health and wellness for those 55 and better. Wausau, WI: North Woods Health Careers Consortium, Northcentral Technical College.

Rakowski, W., Julius, M., Hickey, T., & Halter, J. B. (1987). Correlates of preventive health behavior in late life. *Research on Aging, 9*(3), 331–355.

Rakowski, W., & Mor, V. (1992). The association of physical activity with mortality among older adults in the Longitudinal Study of Aging. *Journal of Gerontology, 47*, M122–M129.

Rosenstock, I. M. (1974). Historical origins of the health belief model. In M. H. Becker (Ed.), *The health belief model and personal health behavior* (pp. 4–16). Thorofare, NJ: Charles B. Slack.

Schick, F. L., & Schick, R. (Eds.). (1994). *Statistical handbook on aging Americans.* Phoenix, AZ: Oryx Press.

Schmidt, R. M. (1993). HEALTH WATCH: Health promotion and disease prevention in primary care. *Methods of Information in Medicine, 32*, 245–248.

Sharpe, P. A., & Connell, C. M. (1992). Exercise beliefs and behaviors among older employees: A health promotion trial. *Gerontologist, 32*, 444–449.

Simmons, J. J., Nelson, E. C., Roberts, E., Salisbury, Z. T., Kane-Williams, E., & Benson, L. (1989). A health promotion program: Staying Healthy After Fifty. *Health Education Quarterly, 16*, 461–472.

Smith, J. A. (1983). *The idea of health.* New York: Teachers College.

Speake, D. L., Cowart, M. E., & Pellet, K. (1989). Health perceptions and lifestyles of the elderly. *Research in Nursing and Health, 12*, 93–100.

Strain, L. A. (1993). Good health: What does it mean in later life? *Journal of Aging and Health, 5*, 338–364.

U.S. Department of Health and Human Services. (1980). *Promoting health/preventing disease: Objectives for the nation.* Washington, DC: U.S. Government Printing Office.

U.S. Department of Health and Human Services. (1991). *Healthy people 2000: National health promotion and disease prevention objectives.* Washington, D.C.: U.S. Government Printing Office.

U.S. Department of Health and Human Services. (1995). *Healthy people 2,000: Mid-course review and 1995 revisions.* Washington, DC: U.S. Government Printing Office.

U.S. Preventive Services Task Force. (1989). *Guide to clinical preventive services.* Baltimore: Williams & Wilkins.

U.S. Senate Special Committee on Aging. (1986). *The health status and health care needs of older Americans* (Senate Committee Pub. No. 87-6635). Washington, DC: U.S. Government Printing Office.

Viverais-Dresler, G., & Richardson, H. (1991). Well elderly perceptions of the meaning of health and their health promotion practices. *Canadian Journal of Nursing Research, 23*(4), 55–71.

Walker, S. N. (1994). Health promotion and prevention of disease and disability among older adults: Who is responsible? *Generations, 18*(1), 45–50.

Walker, S. N., Sechrist, K. R., & Pender, N. J. (1987). The Health-Promoting Lifestyle Profile: Development and psychometric characteristics. *Nursing Research, 36*, 76–81.

Walker, S. N., & Volkan, K. (1987, September). *A model of health conception among older adults.* Paper presented at the Fourth National Forum on Research in Aging, Lincoln, NE.

Walker, S. N., Volkan, K., Sechrist, K. R., & Pender, N. J. (1988). Health-promoting lifestyles of older adults: Comparisons with young and middle-aged adults, correlates and patterns. *Advances in Nursing Science, 11*(1), 76–90.

Warner-Reitz, A., & Grothe, C. (1981). *Healthy lifestyle for seniors.* New York: Meals for Millions, Freedom from Hunger Foundation.

Wheeler, J., & Rundall, T. (1980). Secondary preventive health behavior. *Health Education Quarterly, 7*, 243–262.

Wiley, J. A., & Camacho, T. C. (1980). Life-style and future health: Evidence from the Alameda County study. *Preventive Medicine, 9*, 1–21.

Wolinsky, F. D. (1990). *Health and health behavior among elderly Americans.* New York: Springer Publishing.

Wolinsky, F. D., Stump, T. E., & Clark, D. O. (1995). Antecedents and consequences of physical activity and exercise among older adults. *Gerontologist, 35*, 451–462.

Wondolowski, C., & Davis, D. K. (1991). The lived experience of health in the oldest old: A phenomenological study. *Nursing Science Quarterly, 4*(3), 113–118.

Wroblewski, R. (Ed.). (1991). *An instructor's guide to Project H.E.A.L.T.H.* Wausau, WI: North Woods Health Careers Consortium, Northcentral Technical College.

CHAPTER 16

Elder Maltreatment

Joel S. Milner

Prior to the 1980s, elder maltreatment (i.e., other- or self-inflicted suffering that is unnecessary to maintaining the older person's quality of life [Johnson, 1986]) was not widely recognized as a societal problem in the United States. This occurred, in part, because American culture was insensitive to the plight of some older adults and was reluctant to intervene in "domestic problems." Although elder maltreatment has been viewed as an American problem or at least a problem associated with the values of Western industrialized nations, recent evidence suggests that elder maltreatment is a worldwide phenomenon (e.g., Kosberg & Garcia, 1995). It is important to note, however, that even when elder maltreatment is recognized as a problem, intervention is complicated by the fact that older people are adults and, unlike abused and neglected children, can usually make decisions for themselves. If older people are maltreated, they are viewed as having the option of initiating legal action against the perpetrator. Thus, older people generally have been expected to be responsible for their own welfare.

In the past two decades there has been a modest but steady increase in professional interest in the problems of older people. Likewise, the general public has developed some awareness that senior citizens are easily victimized by criminals and that elderly persons who are placed in residential care facilities may receive less than ideal custodial care. In response to past problems of elder maltreatment in institutions, states have passed legislation mandating minimal standards of care for older adults. States have also developed inspection systems to monitor the level of care provided. However, when it comes to elder abuse and neglect within the family, most elder maltreatment remains unrecognized (Tatara, 1993). As we enter the 21st century, additional efforts will be needed to increase the public's awareness of domestic elder abuse and neglect, as a precursor to the mobilization of the resources necessary to deal meaningfully with the problem.

In attempting to understand elder abuse and neglect, a gerontological imagination, which has been proposed as an analytic framework for understanding aging (chapter 1), contains components that can be used to facilitate analyses of the elder maltreatment literature. An analytic approach, such as the gerontological imagination, that can be applied across paradigms and disciplines is needed because attempts to define and explain elder maltreatment come from diverse fields, such as social work, sociology, anthropology, psychology, medicine, and law. Elements of the gerontological imagination that are particularly useful in understanding the elder maltreatment literature include the view that age (time) is not a causal variable but a variable marker for age-related phenomena (e.g., loss of a specific function) that may be associated with elder maltreatment; that an individual's development is marked by transitions (e.g., role changes), especially within the family, that may affect the likelihood of elder maltreatment; and that models of elder maltreatment must include an understanding of the heterogeneity of older adults and the variety of situations in which they live.

THE RECENT HISTORICAL CONTEXT OF ELDER MALTREATMENT

Current interest in the etiology, treatment, and prevention of elder maltreatment is the result, in part, of earlier developments in the family violence field. Many authors mark the beginning of professional and public interest in family violence with the coining of the term "the battered child" by Kempe in a 1961 address to the American Academy of Pediatrics (Helfer, 1987). In the following year the concept of the battered child was expanded into "the battered child syndrome" (Kempe, Silverman, Steele, Droegemueller, & Silver, 1962), which described an array of child-battering activities and outcomes.

In the 1960s and 1970s, family violence researchers expanded their focus to include the long-term effects of child abuse and neglect. In the 1970s, support grew for the view that abuse was transmitted across generations. This intergenerational transmission hypothesis resulted from the observation that in families where child abuse existed there was an increased likelihood that the abusing parent had been abused as a child. During the late 1970s researchers began to recognize the existence of violent *families*. As violent families were studied, it was found that adolescents who had been abused in childhood or were exposed to spouse abuse were more likely to abuse their siblings and their parents, as well as to grow up and abuse their own children (e.g., Straus, Gelles, & Steinmetz, 1980). The observation that the abused adolescent might abuse his or her parents increased our interest in parent abuse (e.g., Cornell & Gelles, 1982). Finally, it was recognized that abused children were more likely, as adults, to maltreat their elder parents. However, many factors in addition to a childhood history of abuse contribute to elder maltreatment, and not all perpetrators of elder maltreatment are previous victims of familial violence. Further, not all studies have found an intergenerational link (e.g., Pillemer, 1986).

Although a focus on violent families has led researchers to study elder maltreatment, a problem is that most of the research on elder abuse and neglect consists of survey and correlational studies. Controlled experimental studies are relatively rare. Further, the elder maltreatment literature is plagued by methodological problems. For example, studies use different terms and definitions of elder maltreatment, sample sizes are often limited, sample demographic characteristics are often not representative, and samples are usually taken from social services populations. More detailed criticisms of the elder maltreatment literature are available elsewhere (e.g., Hudson & Carlson, 1994).

Despite limitations in the research, studies in the elder maltreatment field helped increase public interest in the elder abuse problem. Quinn and Tomita (1986) noted that major public hearings on elder abuse held by the Select Committee on Aging of the U.S. House of Representatives were a direct response to early research endeavors. These congressional hearings resulted in the publication of an important report titled *Elder Abuse: An Examination of a Hidden Problem* (U.S. House of Representatives, 1981). In this report, elder abuse was identified as a national problem. Since the House hearings on elder abuse in 1981, hearings on elder maltreatment have continued, resulting in additional congressional publications describing the importance of various aspects of the elder maltreatment problem, including incidence rates, detection problems, intervention/treatment issues, prevention problems, and policy issues.

DEFINITION AND PREVALENCE OF ELDER MALTREATMENT

As interest in the elder abuse problem began to grow, a number of different labels were introduced to describe it. Perhaps influenced by Kempe et al. (1962), Block and Sinnott (1979) coined the term "the battered elder syndrome" to describe elder abuse. Other terms used initially to describe elder abuse ranged from "battered parents" (Harbin & Madden, 1979) and "abused elders" (Sengstock, Barrett, & Graham, 1984), to "granny-battering" (Burston, 1975) and "granny-bashing" (Illing, 1977). Although a variety of labels, including some catchy but nonspecific gender-related terms like "granny-battering," have been coined, today most authors use the terms elder abuse and elder neglect to describe the major types of elder maltreatment. It should be noted, however, that the common use of these terms has not precluded the development of new terms to describe subtypes of elder maltreatment, such as rights violation (e.g., financial exploitation) and self-neglect.

The development and use of a common set of descriptive terms does not mean that uniform definitions of these terms exist. The elder maltreatment field continues to be plagued by a lack of uniform operational definitions. Numerous authors (e.g., Hudson & Carlson, 1994; Pillemer & Finkelhor, 1988; Utech & Garrett, 1992) have noted the disparities in elder abuse and neglect definitions used in research studies. Similarly, important variations in the definitions of elder abuse and neglect exist among state reporting statutes (Hudson & Carlson, 1994). Some of these definitional problems involve very basic issues, including the minimum age used to define elder maltreatment (60 or 65 years).

In part because of the existing definitional problems, it is difficult to determine the prevalence of elder maltreatment. In fact, few efforts have been made to determine the national rates of elder maltreatment. No national registry of elder abuse and neglect reports exists. Likewise, many states do not maintain a state registry. Thus, complete descriptive data at the state level typically are not available (Tatara, 1993). Surprisingly, even at the local level, many departments of social services do not maintain annual summary data on elder abuse and neglect cases, and some departments maintain case records for only limited periods (e.g., in one North Carolina county department of social services, elder maltreatment case records are kept for only 3 years). As a result of these problems, complete historical data will never be available.

The earliest estimates of the extent of elder abuse ranged from 1.5% of all persons over 65 years of age (Gioglio & Blakemore, 1983) to 4.1% (U.S. House of Representatives, 1981). Estimates have varied in the past decade, but most fall within this range. For instance, Pillemer and Finkelhor (1988) conducted a large random sample survey study of 2,020 elders and found that 3.2% (confidence interval, 2.5%–3.9%) of the sample reported some form of elder maltreatment.

Using a different approach to determine the incidence rate, Tatara (1993) first estimated a national reporting rate of 52,502, based on 1991 social service data obtained from a majority of the states. Then, using an estimate by Pillemer and Finkelhor (1988) that only about 1 of 14 elder abuse victims (excluding self-neglecting elders) are reported, Tatara (1993) multiplied the estimated national reporting rate (52,502) by 14 to produce a national incidence rate of 735,000 cases of elder maltreatment (excluding self-neglect) in 1991. A separate computation generated an estimate of 842,000 cases of self-neglect in 1991, suggesting a combined rate of more than 1 million cases, or about 3% of all older adults. This rate is similar to a 1991 rate reported by the U.S. House of Representatives Select Committee on Aging (1991), which indicated that there are between 1 and 2 million cases of elder maltreatment each year.

Although the annual estimates of the number of reported cases has continued to increase (Tatara, 1993), it is unclear if elder maltreatment is actually on the increase or if it is simply less hidden today. It may be that increased public awareness combined with the passage of state reporting laws for elder maltreatment have resulted in an increase in the *reporting* of a problem that has always existed. Another issue is that, across time, the number of conditions that describe elder maltreatment have increased and the definitions of elder maltreatment have broadened. These factors, combined with an increase in the number of individuals in the elderly population of the United States, suggest that additional annual increases in reported cases of elder maltreatment might be expected.

Until recently, estimates of the rates of elder abuse and neglect have been for maltreatment in general, and only a few estimates have been provided for various subtypes. Except for one large-scale survey study (Pillemer & Finkelhor, 1988), the best available estimates of the relative incidence rates of maltreatment types appeared in studies of departments of social services records (e.g., Giordano, 1982; Hall, 1986; Milner, Gold, Curtiss, & Hawkins, 1989; Tatara, 1993). The problems with these studies are that they include only reported cases and are based on state reporting laws that have different definitions for elder maltreatment subtypes. In addition, because social service agencies do not record the same data in their case files, the survey data are not always comparable. Recognizing these limitations, definitions and estimates of the incidence of different types of elder maltreatment are presented.

Elder Physical Abuse

Elder physical abuse generally refers to intentional (nonaccidental) physical assault on an elderly person that produces injury and in extreme cases results in disfigurement and/or death. It is less clear among professionals whether observable sequelae (i.e., physical injury such as bruises, cuts, etc.) must occur, but it can be argued that physical assault without observable sequelae that results in mental and/or emotional distress should be included as a form of physical abuse.

The rates of elder physical abuse as a percentage of the total elder maltreatment cases are highly variable. For example, based on social service data, Milner et al. (1989) reported that elder physical abuse comprised 10% of all confirmed cases, and Tatara (1993) indicated rates around 20%. In contrast, based on survey data, Pillemer and Finkelhor (1988) reported that elder physical abuse comprised 64% of all elder maltreatment cases. In these studies, the variation in elder physical abuse rates appears to be due to differences in the populations studied and the definitions used. Milner et al. (1989) studied all elder maltreatment cases ($N = 208$) reported to four departments of social services in North Carolina for a continuous 6-year period (1982 to 1987). A study limitation was that the North Carolina reporting law restricts department of social services' involvement to disabled elder adult maltreatment cases. Tatara (1993) reported data from a survey of state agencies that receive reports of domestic elder abuse from social services agencies. Pillemer and Finkelhor (1988) surveyed a sample ($n = 2,020$) of elderly persons in the Boston area and found 63 cases of elder maltreatment, with 40 (64%) of the cases involving physical abuse. Although the rate reported by Pillemer and Finkelhor is much higher than the rates reported by Milner et al. and Tatara, the rate is based on a different definition of physical abuse. Milner et al. and Tatara included as physical abuse only those cases that involved actual physical trauma (e.g., bruises), whereas Pillemer and Finkelhor defined physical abuse as including a range of violent behaviors, from pushing and shoving to being assaulted with a knife or gun.

Elder Sexual Abuse

Elder sexual abuse refers to the commission of a sex act on an elderly person without that person's freely given consent. For the purposes of this discussion, sexual abuse is considered a category separate from elder physical abuse.

In contrast to other elder maltreatment types, more consistency is found in the estimated rates of elder sexual abuse. The frequency of elder sexual abuse appears to be quite low (Ramsey-Klawsnik, 1991; Tatara, 1993), with reported rates often below 1% of the total maltreatment cases. A major problem, however, is that studies often do not list elder sexual abuse as a separate category. In those studies it is not known if elder sexual abuse was overlooked, if no elder sexual abuse was reported, or if elder sexual abuse was combined with physical abuse.

Elder Psychological Abuse

Elder psychological abuse, which is sometimes called emotional abuse, refers to the intentional promotion of conditions that produce mental and/or emotional distress in the elderly person. Psychological elder abuse includes verbal assaults, threats, intimidation, harassment, humiliation, ridicule, and other degrading tactics and often occurs in conjunction with other forms of elder maltreatment.

The prevalence rates for elder psychological abuse range from about 12% (e.g., Tatara, 1993) to 72% (e.g., Wolf, Godkin, & Pillemer, 1984) of all elder maltreatment cases reported to departments of social services. In a general population survey study of elder maltreatment, approximately 41% of the reported cases indicated the presence of psychological abuse (Pillemer & Finkelhor, 1988). However, in this general population survey study, psychological abuse was listed even when it co-occurred with other forms of maltreatment.

Elder Rights Violation

Elder rights violation refers to conditions that include unwarranted confinement or other interference with personal liberty, as well as exploitation of the elderly person's financial or other material resources. Elder rights violation is most often viewed as an intentional rights violation that is to the disadvantage of the physical, mental, and/or emotional health and well-being of the elderly person. Material exploitation may be accomplished directly by threat and force or indirectly through misrepresentation and deceit.

The relative prevalence rate for the violation of elder rights, which includes all forms of inappropriate confinement and material exploitation, is difficult to determine from the literature. A variety of terms and definitions have been used to indicate elder rights violations. Further, some authors have included rights violations as a form of elder neglect. Data, however, are available on specific types of rights violations. For example, in studies using the files of departments of social services, financial exploitation rates are typically in a range from 17% (Tatara, 1993) or 18% (Milner et al., 1989) to 36% (Giordano, 1982) of all cases. For a second form of rights violation, inappropriate confinement, Milner et al. reported a rate of 12%.

Elder Neglect

Elder neglect is defined as a condition in which the caretaker intentionally or carelessly (nondeliberately) does not provide the elderly person with proper care or supervision, exposing the elder to the risk of physical, mental, and/or emotional harm. The careless type of elder neglect may be due to factors such as inadequate knowledge, lack of ability, lack of resources, or lack of motivation. Subtypes of elder neglect include lack of supervision, dangerous living conditions, inadequate nutrition, inadequate hygiene, and inadequate medical care.

In a general population survey, Pillemer and Finkelhor (1988) found that elder neglect occurred in only 11% of the elder maltreatment reports. Most research, however, indicates that elder neglect is the most prevalent form of elder maltreatment (Giordano, 1982; Milner et al., 1989, Tatara, 1993). Giordano (1982) and Tatara (1993) reported rates in the 45% to 47% range, and Milner et al. (1989) reported that a majority of their cases involved some form of elder neglect, with rates exceeding 90% for some types of neglect (e.g., medical neglect). Milner et al. also indicated that most cases involved multiple forms of neglect. In addition, elder neglect victims are more likely to be the older members of the elderly population and are more likely to have mental and/or physical impairment (Wolf et al., 1984).

Elder Self-Neglect (Elder Self-Abuse)

A relatively new category of elder maltreatment (i.e., self-neglect and self-abuse) that has not been used in the description of other forms of family violence has been identified. Self-neglect or self-abuse refers to the condition in which the elder, who is often living alone, does not maintain adequate living conditions and/or does not maintain adequate personal mental and physical health. The use of this new category is controversial, especially in situations where a nondependent elder adult is deliberately or unintentionally allowing self-neglect or self-abuse. The controversy exists because it is often a subjective judgment as to what is an adequate standard of self-care for an individual. In some cases, to insist that the elder is engaging in self-neglect or self-abuse because he or she does not meet an arbitrary standard of care may be to perpetrate another form of elder maltreatment, rights violation. A more complete discussion of the conceptual and clinical issues related to self-neglect and self-abuse is available elsewhere (e.g., Rathbone-McCuan & Fabian, 1992).

Although the literature has begun to discuss self-neglect and/or self-abuse as important forms of elder maltreatment, historically, these were not studied as separate categories. Recently, Milner et al. (1989) investigated self-neglect as a separate category and found a rate of 94%. This high rate, however, may be an artifact of the type of population studied, as Milner et al. studied only disabled elder maltreatment cases. Mentally and/or physically disabled elders by definition might be expected, as a consequence of their limitations, to engage in relatively high rates of self-neglect.

In conclusion, it should be evident that additional studies of the incidence and prevalence rates for elder maltreatment in general and for specific elder maltreatment types are needed. In regard to prevalence rates, a number of important questions need to be addressed. For example, social services studies (e.g., Milner et al., 1989; Tatara, 1993) indicate that the number of reported elder abuse and neglect cases are increasing each year. Does this increase mean that the absolute level of elder maltreatment is increasing, or are we merely more aware of elder maltreatment? Likewise, to what extent are increases in elder maltreatment reports due to expanded definitions of elder maltreatment and/or to increases in the elderly population?

ETIOLOGY OF ELDER MALTREATMENT

Given the variety of elder maltreatment types, it should be apparent that the different types of elder abuse and neglect probably cannot be explained by a single model or theory. In addition, explanatory models may need to vary, based on perpetrator and victim characteristics (e.g., gender, age, relationship) and whether the maltreatment is situational or chronic. Further, explanatory models of elder maltreatment cannot be developed with any precision until basic types of maltreatment, with associated operational definitions of each type of elder maltreatment, are agreed on and variables related to each specific type are experimentally evaluated for their relevance to etiology. As this occurs, new, competing models likely will be developed to explain each type of elder maltreatment. Eventually, resolution should occur as a result of the experimental testing of the different models.

Descriptive Characteristics of Elder Maltreatment

At present there is limited information on the descriptive characteristics or variables related to the different types of elder maltreatment. However, based on confirmed social services cases, some general characteristics of the elder maltreatment situation are relatively well documented in the descriptive literature. First, it appears that the older the elderly person, the greater the risk for maltreatment (both from others and from self-neglect [Tatara, 1993]). Women more often appear to be victims. Elderly individuals with mental and physical limitations and who are isolated are at greater risk. Elderly persons who live with relatives also appear to be at greater risk. Finally, many elderly persons report experiencing more than one type of maltreatment (which may or may not be from the same person) and report that maltreatment occurs on more than one occasion. Recent evidence also suggests that the type of elder maltreatment may vary as a function of race (e.g., Griffin & Williams, 1992; Longres, 1992).

The perpetrators of elder maltreatment are typically between 40 and 60 years of age. They often have caretaker responsibilities for a disabled elderly person. However, some authors recently have indicated that the dependency (e.g., financial dependence) of the offender may be important in cases of physical abuse (Anetzberger, Korbin, & Austin, 1994). In a national study of social services cases, Tatara (1993) found that adult children were the most frequent offenders (32%), followed by the spouse (15%). Historically, it was thought that the offender was more often a female; however, among reported social services cases, Tatara found that males were more often the offenders. Some studies suggest the offender is more likely to have mental health and alcohol problems. The offender may have an inadequate knowledge of the special needs of the elderly person. The perpetrator may have experienced stress just prior to or at the time of the maltreatment and may be socially isolated. Frequently, the perpetrator appears to be in need of respite care (i.e., needs a break from the caretaker role). However, somewhat surprising is the finding that frequently both the victim and the perpetrator deny the maltreatment (Tomita, 1990) and refuse services (Milner et al., 1989).

Although the aforementioned list of victim and perpetrator characteristics was obtained from studies using social services records, different results were obtained from a general population study conducted by Pillemer and Finkelhor (1988). These authors found that the spouse, instead of a younger family member such as a son or daughter, was the most frequent perpetrator of elder maltreatment. Pillemer and Finkelhor did not find that the older person was abused more often, and they found that elderly men were as likely as women to be maltreated. The authors note that their general population findings appear to be at odds with the general literature.

Regardless of the characteristics that are determined to be descriptive of elder maltreatment, it should be noted that a descriptive list of correlated variables does not tell us anything about which variables actually contribute to the etiology of elder maltreatment. A specific variable may appear to be related to elder maltreatment because of a relationship to some third or common variable. Thus, women may be at greater risk for maltreatment because they live longer. The older person may be at greater risk for maltreatment because with extreme age the likelihood of mental and physical limitations increases and with these limitations comes increased dependency on others. Longitudinal studies are needed to determine which of the descriptive variables are relevant to the etiology of elder maltreatment and which variables account for the largest portions of the variance in explaining elder maltreatment. These studies would involve the evaluation of personal, interactional, and environmental variables at different points in time. High-risk and comparison families with elder members would be followed across time, and study variables would be related to observed elder maltreatment. Such research would assist in model development and is needed for each type of elder maltreatment.

Models of Elder Maltreatment

A number of conceptual frameworks and theoretical perspectives have appeared in the family violence literature, describing conditions thought to contribute to the etiology of family violence. Although not complete explanatory models, the conceptual frameworks describe variable domains, including characteristics that appear to be descriptive of elder maltreatment. The putative domains include physical characteristics; psychological characteristics, including the cognitive schema of the perpetrator; and sociological conditions, including the nature of the present family member interaction, the amount of distress experienced by family members, the social isolation of the family, and the intergenerational or historical aspects of violence in the family. It should be noted that these domains are not independent of one another. Overlap clearly exists. For example, intergenerational variables may be correlated with perpetrator characteristics, and perpetrator characteristics may produce social isolation and other interactional problems.

The psychiatric model, which emphasizes perpetrator characteristics, was the first family violence model, appearing in the 1960s. Next, the sociological model, which emphasizes societal values and the social organization of the culture, gained favor during the 1970s. More recently, family violence researchers have attempted to develop broad explanatory models that include factors from the psychiatric and sociological models, as well as social interaction factors. These integrative models have a variety of names, such as "social psychological" (Burgess & Conger, 1978) and "ecological integration" (Belsky, 1980) but can be collectively referred to as social interactional models. Although these models were developed to explain child maltreatment, it can be expected that the popularity of the social interactional perspective in the family violence field will continue to influence the formation of explanatory models in the elder maltreatment field.

Generally, social interactional models emphasize the importance of the social interactions preceding maltreatment, as well as the consequences that may serve to maintain the maltreatment. Thus, social interactional models emphasize the importance of family interactions preceding an abusive act, as well as the consequences that may serve to maintain the act. The frequency and intensity of aversive interactions within the family of origin and the present family are also viewed as factors that contribute to maltreatment.

Although revised psychiatric (Tomita, 1990) and sociological (Anetzberger, 1990) models have been proposed, the social situational model, a type of social interactional model, appears to be the most widely accepted explanatory model of elder maltreatment. This model, as summarized by Phillips (1986) and Tomita (1990), includes perpetrator characteristics, structural factors, and situational factors that increase the likelihood of maltreatment of a vulnerable elderly person. In this model the elderly person typically is seen as a source of stress. The elder may have special health care needs, impaired mental and/or physical abilities, emotional dependency, and/or a "difficult" personality. The perpetrator characteristics include factors such as a history of family violence, substance abuse, social isolation, and exhaustion from caregiving. Structural variables include economic and environmental factors. If a combination of victim, perpetrator, and structural factors are present in a situation that includes increased levels of stress, it is believed that there is an increased likelihood of elder maltreatment.

Other interactional theories that have been developed to explain one or more forms of elder maltreatment include social learning theory (Nadien, 1995; Tomita, 1990), social exchange theory (Nadien, 1995; Phillips, 1986; Tomita, 1990), attachment theory (Cicirelli, 1983), symbolic interactionism (Nadien, 1995; Phillips, 1986; Tomita, 1990), and role theory (Nadien, 1995). Although one author (Steinmetz, 1988) has used path analysis to test an interactional elder abuse model, the development and testing of explanatory models for the different forms of elder maltreatment remain in the embryonic stage. There is a need for additional model development and model evaluation.

As may be apparent, many of the present models and theoretical perspectives attempt to explain different types of elder maltreatment within a single framework, and as previously discussed, this may be inappropriate. Different models appear to be needed to explain different types of elder maltreatment. However, as previously noted, to explain the different types of elder maltreatment we first need uniform operational definitions of them. Put simply, we need to have a concise definition of the behaviors and conditions that we are trying to explain.

Finally, competing models will have to consider the relationship of elder maltreatment to other forms of family violence. For example, some authors suggest that a major form of elder abuse is maltreatment by the spouse (e.g., Pillemer & Finkelhor, 1988). To the extent that this is true, some cases of elder abuse may simply be spouse abuse in its aged form. In contrast, some forms of elder neglect may not be related to family violence. For example, the failure of a caregiver to adequately provide medical care may be related to the lack of knowledge and/or the lack of economic resources. In the latter case, the failure of the caretaker to provide needed medical care may be influenced primarily by socioeconomic factors beyond the control of the caretaker. In this instance we have to ask what is the responsibility of society in the provision of appropriate resources to ensure that its members, including disadvantaged caretakers, have access to the resources that permit the elderly to receive adequate care. This appears to be a major issue, because research based on social services cases indicates that the majority of reported elder maltreatment cases involve caretaker neglect and that most of these cases involve socioeconomic factors rather than a broad array of family violence factors (e.g., Milner et al., 1989). Other important issues include the special needs of older adults, which in some cases are different from the needs of other victims, and the role the elderly victim may play in the maltreatment event.

ASSESSMENT

A variety of assessment protocols and instruments for assessing elder maltreatment have been described in the literature (e.g., Bennett, 1990; Lachs & Pillemer, 1995; Matlaw & Spence, 1994; Neale, Hwalek, Scott, Sengstock, & Stahl, 1991; Quinn & Tomita, 1986; Steinmetz, 1988), and increasingly, state agencies are using risk assessment protocols for elder maltreatment (Johnson, 1989). Assessment protocols are also beginning to appear that focus on special populations, such as incapacitated (Blunt, 1993; Fins, 1994) or sexually abused elders (Ramsey-Klawsnik, 1993). Unfortunately, only a few of the assessment devices have associated psychometric data on their reliability and validity.

An example of an existing protocol is the comprehensive two-step procedure for elder abuse assessment called the Elder Abuse Diagnosis and Intervention (EADI) model (Quinn & Tomita, 1986). Step 1 entails preparation for the assessment, and step 2 describes the actual assessment. The general EADI model also includes three different intervention strategies. Although not mentioned by the authors of the EADI model, prior to the use of the structured assessment model, elder maltreatment investigators should have a knowledge of general elder adult interviewing procedures (e.g., Patterson & Dupree, 1994).

The first step of EADI assessment of elder maltreatment involves preparation for the assessment by considering issues such as referral source, access and other first-contact issues, and conflict versus treatment approaches. The second step, which describes the actual assessment, includes a rationale, a methodology, a description of suspicious signs and symptoms, an interview outline for the reported victim, information on assessing injuries (including an interview sketch sheet that is used to document physical injuries), an interview outline for the caregiver, and instructions for obtaining information from collateral sources.

INTERVENTIONS

Three general types of prevention are possible: primary, secondary, and tertiary. Primary prevention assumes that all elderly persons are at risk and attempts to provide prevention services to older adults and to all individuals involved with the elderly person. Secondary prevention involves the determination of those at risk for elder maltreatment and the provision of prevention programs for the identified high-risk individuals and their families. Tertiary prevention refers to prevention that occurs after the fact, which includes legal intervention.

Although primary prevention programs exist (e.g., Blakely & Dolon, 1991; Harshbarger, 1993), they are rare. A few special programs have been developed for selected subgroups of older adults and their families, such as those with Alzheimer's disease. However, even though support programs may be offered to all Alzheimer's disease clients, the programs might be considered secondary prevention programs because Alzheimer's disease patients are thought to be an at-risk group. A few states (e.g., North Carolina) have implemented important secondary-prevention elder maltreatment programs that include support groups, education programs, and limited respite care for the caretakers.

Unfortunately, most prevention is still tertiary. A significant portion of tertiary prevention simply involves case management. Less frequently, family education programs, family therapy, and family support services developed specifically for elder maltreatment problems are provided. Although legal action is always possible (see Eisenberg, 1991, for a discussion of formal and informal legal interventions), as in other forms of family violence, it usually does not occur. Innovative intervention programs for all types of prevention still need to be developed, but new tertiary prevention models for elder maltreatment are starting to appear. For example, as noted earlier, the EADI model describes three tertiary intervention approaches (Quinn & Tomita, 1986). The intervention includes crisis intervention, short-term treatment, and long-term treatment. In the model an attempt is made to tailor the selected intervention strategy to the needs of each case. The EADI model also describes important termination issues related to each type of intervention.

Other intervention approaches have been described in the literature. For example, Braun, Lenxer, Schumacher-Mukai, and Snyder (1993) have provided a decision tree for managing cases of elder abuse and neglect. Hwalek, Williamson, and Stahl (1991) have summarized multidisciplinary team approaches (hospital-based, family practice, consortium, and community-based) that deal with elder maltreatment. Wasylkewycz (1993) has described a coordinated community program for intervening in elder maltreatment cases. Filinson (1993) has described the use of volunteer advocates for elder abuse victims. Njeri and Nerenberg (1993) have described interventions tailored to African-American families.

SUMMARY OF RESEARCH AND PRACTICE ISSUES

To effectively treat and prevent cases of elder maltreatment, professionals must know the who, what, when, where, and why of elder abuse and neglect cases and then tailor their programs and services accordingly. As an initial step in understanding the scope and etiology of elder maltreatment in the United States, policymakers, program managers, service supervisors, and direct services providers need accurate epidemiologic data that describe the prevalence of the different types of elder abuse and neglect. Additional data on victim and offender demographic characteristics across the different types of elder maltreatment and on the factors that contribute to elder maltreatment are especially needed. As more accurate and complete descriptive data become available, additional hypotheses about the etiology of elder maltreatment can be formulated and tested in longitudinal field studies.

Increasing the knowledge base for elder maltreatment will allow for more efficient management of tertiary prevention efforts in adult protective services and will give direction to primary and secondary prevention efforts. Without such a knowledge base for elder maltreatment, prevention programs must be developed based on best guesses as to the types and extent of existing problems, and intervention programs must be designed based on adult protective services providers' clinical intuition as to the related etiological factors. Without representative descriptive data and empirical studies, there is a greater likelihood that prevention and treatment efforts will be inadequate, with relevant etiological variables overlooked. An accurate knowledge of the service needs of maltreated elderly persons will become increasingly critical as the percentage of elders in the population continues to grow and as social services funding remains limited or is reduced.

REFERENCES

Anetzberger, G. J. (1990). Abuse, neglect, and self-neglect: Issues of vulnerability. In Z. Harel, P. Ehrlich, & R. Hubbard (Eds.), *The vulnerable aged: People, services, and policies* (pp. 140–148). New York: Springer Publishing.

Anetzberger, G. J., Korbin, J. E., & Austin, C. (1994). Alcoholism and elder abuse. *Journal of Interpersonal Violence, 9*, 184–193.

Belsky, J. (1980). Child maltreatment: An ecological integration. *American Psychologist, 35*, 320–335.

Bennett, G. J. L. (1990, July). Assessing abuse in the elderly. *Geriatric Medicine*, pp. 49–51.

Blakely, B. E., & Dolon, R. D. (1991). Area Agencies on Aging and the prevention of elder abuse: The results of a national study. *Journal of Elder Abuse & Neglect, 3*(2), 21–40.

Block, M. R., & Sinnott, J. P. (1979). *The battered elder syndrome: An exploratory study.* Unpublished manuscript, University of Maryland, Center on Aging, College Park, MD.

Blunt, A. P. (1993). Financial exploitation of the incapacitated: Investigation and remedies. *Journal of Elder Abuse & Neglect, 5*(1), 19–32.

Braun, K., Lenxer, A., Schumacher-Mukai, C., & Snyder, P. (1993). A decision tree for managing elder abuse and neglect. *Journal of Elder Abuse & Neglect, 5*(3), 89–103.

Burgess, R. L., & Conger, R. D. (1978). Family interaction in abusive, neglectful, and normal families. *Child Development*, *49*, 1163–1173.

Burston, G. R. (1975). Granny-battering. *British Medical Journal*, *3*, 592.

Cicirelli, V. J. (1983). Adult children's attachment and helping behavior to elderly parents: A path model. *Journal of Marriage and the Family*, *45*, 815–825.

Cornell, C. P., & Gelles, R. J. (1982). Adolescent to parent violence. *Urban & Social Change Review*, *15*, 8–14.

Eisenberg, H. B. (1991). Combating elder abuse through the legal process. *Journal of Elder Abuse & Neglect*, *3*(1), 65–96.

Filinson, R. (1993). An evaluation of a program of volunteer advocates for elder abuse victims. *Journal of Elder Abuse & Neglect*, *5*(1), 77–93.

Fins, D. L. (1994). Health care decision-making for incapacitated elders: An innovative social service agency model. *Journal of Elder Abuse & Neglect*, *6*(2), 23–37.

Gioglio, G., & Blakemore, P. (1983). *Elder abuse in Jersey: The knowledge and experience of abuse among older New Jerseyans*. Unpublished manuscript, New Jersey Division on Aging, Trenton, NJ.

Giordano, N. H. (1982). *Individual and family correlates of elder abuse*. Unpublished doctoral dissertation, University of Georgia, Athens.

Griffin, L. W., & Williams, O. J. (1992). Abuse among African-American elderly. *Journal of Family Violence*, 7, 19–35.

Hall, P. A. (1986). *Elder maltreatment items, subgroups, and types: Policy and practice implications*. Unpublished manuscript, Our Lady of the Lake University, Worden School of Social Service, San Antonio, TX.

Harbin, H. T., & Madden, D. J. (1979). Battered parents: A new syndrome. *American Journal of Psychiatry*, *136*, 1288–1291.

Harshbarger, S. (1993). From protection to prevention: A proactive approach. *Journal of Elder Abuse & Neglect*, *5*(1), 41–55.

Helfer, R. A. (1987). Back to the future. *Child Abuse & Neglect*, *11*, 11–14.

Hudson, M. F., & Carlson, J. (1994). Elder abuse: Its meaning to middle-aged and older adults: Part 1. Instrument development. *Journal of Elder Abuse & Neglect*, *6*(1), 29–54.

Hwalek, M., Williamson, D., & Stahl, C. (1991). Community-based M-Team roles: A job analysis. *Journal of Elder Abuse & Neglect*, *3*(3), 45–71.

Illing, M. (1977). Granny bashing. Comment on how we can identify those at risk. *Nursing Mirror*, *145*, 34.

Johnson, T. (1986). Critical issues in the definition of elder maltreatment. In K. A. Pillemer & R. S. Wolfe (Eds.), *Elder abuse: Conflict in the family* (pp. 167–196). Dover, MA: Auburn House.

Johnson, T. F. (1989). Elder mistreatment identification instruments: Finding common ground. *Journal of Elder Abuse & Neglect*, *1*(4), 15–36.

Kempe, C. H., Silverman, F. N., Steele, B. F., Droegemueller, W., & Silver, H. K. (1962). The battered child syndrome. *Journal of the American Medical Association*, *181*, 105–112.

Kosberg, J. I., & Garcia, J. L. (Eds.). (1995). *Elder abuse: International and cross-cultural perspectives*. New York: Haworth Press.

Lachs, M. S., & Pillemer, K. (1995). Abuse and neglect of elderly persons. *New England Journal of Medicine*, *332*, 437–443.

Longres, J. F. (1992). Race and type of maltreatment in an elder abuse system. *Journal of Elder Abuse & Neglect*, *4*(3), 61–83.

Matlaw, J. R., & Spence, D. M. (1994). The hospital elder assessment team: A protocol for suspected cases of elder abuse and neglect. *Journal of Elder Abuse & Neglect*, *6*(2), 23–37.

Milner, J. S., Gold, R. G., Curtiss, P., & Hawkins, W. L. (1989). *Analysis of epidemiologic disabled adult maltreatment data* (Vols. 1–4). De Kalb: Northern Illinois University, Family Violence and Sexual Assault Research Program.

Nadien, M. B. (1995). Elder violence (maltreatment) in domestic settings: Some theory and research. In L. L. Adler & F. L. Denmark (Eds.), *Violence and the prevention of violence* (pp. 177–190). Westport, CT: Praeger.

Neale, A. V., Hwalek, M. A., Scott, R. O., Sengstock, M. C., & Stahl, C. (1991). Validation of the Hwalek-Sengstock Elder Abuse Screening Test. *Journal of Applied Gerontology*, *19*, 406–418.

Njeri, M., & Nerenberg, L. (1993). We are family: Outreach to African-American seniors. *Journal of Elder Abuse & Neglect*, *5*(4), 5–19.

Patterson, R. L., & Dupree, L. W. (1994). Older adults. In M. Hersen & S. M. Turner (Eds.), *Diagnostic interviewing* (pp. 373–307). New York: Plenum Press.

Phillips, L. R. (1986). Theoretical explanations of elder abuse: Competing hypotheses and unresolved issues. In K. A. Pillemer & R. S. Wolf (Eds.), *Elder abuse: Conflict in the family* (pp. 197–217). Dover, MA: Auburn House.

Pillemer, K. A. (1986). Risk factors in elder abuse: Results from a case-control study. In K. A. Pillemer & R. S. Wolf (Eds.), *Elder abuse: Conflict in the family* (pp. 239–263). Dover, MA: Auburn House.

Pillemer, K. A., & Finkelhor, D. (1988). The prevalence of elder abuse: A random sample survey. *Gerontologist*, *28*, 51–57.

Quinn, J. M., & Tomita, S. K. (1986). *Elder abuse and neglect: Causes, diagnosis, and intervention strategies*. New York: Springer Publishing.

Ramsey-Klawsnik, H. (1991). Elder sexual abuse: Preliminary findings. *Journal of Elder Abuse & Neglect*, *3*(3), 73–90.

Ramsey-Klawsnik, H. (1993). Interviewing elders for sexual abuse: Guidelines and techniques. *Journal of Elder Abuse & Neglect*, *5*(1), 5–18.

Rathbone-McCuan, E., & Fabian, D. R. (1992). *Self-neglecting elders: A clinical dilemma*. Westport, CT: Auburn House.

Sengstock, M. C., Barrett, S., & Graham, R. (1984). Abused elders: Victims of villains or of circumstances? *Journal of Gerontological Social Work*, *8*, 101–111.

Steinmetz, S. K. (1988). *Duty bound: Elder abuse and family care*. Newbury Park, CA: Sage.

Straus, M., Gelles, R. J., & Steinmetz, S. K. (1980). *Behind closed doors: Violence in the American family*. Garden City, NY: Anchor Press.

Tatara, T. (1993). Understanding the nature and scope of domestic elder abuse with the use of state aggregate data: Summaries of the key findings of a national survey of state APS and aging agencies. *Journal of Elder Abuse & Neglect*, *5*(4), 35–57.

Tomita, S. K. (1990). The denial of elder maltreatment by victims and abusers: The application of neutralization theory. *Violence and Victims*, *5*, 171–184.

U.S. House of Representatives Select Committee on Aging. (1981). *Elder abuse: An examination of a hidden problem*. Washington, DC: U.S. Government Printing Office.

U.S. House of Representatives Select Committee on Aging. (1991). *Elder abuse: What can be done?* Washington, DC: U.S. Government Printing Office.

Utech, M. R., & Garrett, R. R. (1992). Elder and child abuse: Conceptual and perceptual parallels. *Journal of Interpersonal Violence*, *7*, 418–428.

Wasylkewycz, M. N. (1993). The Elder Abuse Resource Centre: A coordinated community response to elder abuse: One Canadian perspective. *Journal of Elder Abuse & Neglect*, *5*(4), 21–33.

Wolf, R. S., Godkin, M. A., & Pillemer, K. A. (1984). *Elder abuse and neglect: Final report from three model projects.* Worcester: University of Massachusetts Medical Center, University Center on Aging.

CHAPTER 17

Aging and Crime

Daniel P. Doyle

Starting in the 1970s, pundits, police, politicians, and professionals in the fields of gerontology and criminology began expressing fears that rising rates of crime were having a severe impact on the elderly. For example, a report prepared for the 1981 White House Conference on Aging noted, "Sadly, the elderly in our society suffer disproportionately from predatory crimes, and consequently, 'they are virtual prisoners in their own home and apartment because of fear of crime'" (White House Conference, 1981, p. 31). In 1980 criminologist Alan Malinchak wrote that "the elderly are victimized proportionately much more than any other age group" (p. 10). The victimization of the elderly has frequently been the subject of Congressional hearings (U.S. Senate, 1991, 1993, 1994). The image presented is one of a whole generation terrorized by criminals, taking refuge behind their deadbolted doors and burglar-barred windows, afraid to go to the grocery store.

Also during the 1970s and 1980s, the image of older persons as frequent crime victims was joined by another image, that of older persons as frequent criminals. *U.S. News and World Report* stated that serious crimes by persons 55 years of age or older had jumped 272% from the mid-1960s to 1980 and that old law-breakers were fast becoming a major problem for the police and correctional officials (New police worry, 1982). More recently, criminologist Peter Kratcoski was quoted as predicting the possibility of dramatic increases in criminal activity by older persons in the near future (Hopkins, 1995). There has been a dramatic increase in the number of articles on the elderly criminal in scholarly journals (Forsyth & Shover, 1986). And since the 1980s there have been several national conferences focusing on the older offender which have resulted in a number of books (McCarthy & Langworthy, 1988; Newman, Newman, & Gewirtz, 1984; Wilbanks & Kim, 1984).

As chapter 2 of this book clearly shows, our society is getting older. The question arises as to what effect these demographic trends have had or will have on the phenomenon called crime. Are we headed for a period of time when larger and larger portions of the population will be afraid to leave their homes for fear of crime? Will the police increasingly be unable to protect older persons from criminal victimization? Also, are we in the early stages of a geriatric crime wave? Will we see gray-haired persons knocking over convenience stores to supplement their Social Security?

Unfortunately, the mass media as well as the popular and academic literature have disseminated much information about aging and crime that is at best misleading and at worst completely wrong. Some of the research in the last few years has served to correct many misconceptions, so that we now have a better, yet still incomplete, picture of the relationship between old age and crime.

The purpose of this chapter is to provide an overview of the best research regarding two facets of aging and crime: (1) the criminal victimization of older persons and (2) criminal behavior by older persons. In looking at victimization, we will explore such issues as the extent to which older persons are victims relative to others, the pattern of crimes that are committed against them, and the consequences of such victimizations. In looking at criminal behavior, we will explore such issues as the volume of crime actually committed by older offenders, the kinds of crimes for which they are arrested, and increases or decreases in the amount of crime they commit.

THE CRIMINAL VICTIMIZATION OF OLDER PERSONS

The 1960s and 1970s was a period of increasing crime in the United States, and many came to believe that older persons were disproportionately bearing the brunt of these increases. Well publicized and often sensational accounts of vicious attacks and ruthless rip-offs targeting older persons spread the notion that older people were under a state of siege. However, prior to the mid-1970s, very few systematic data were available regarding who was most likely to be victimized by the various types of crime. The main source of crime information in the United States for many years has been the Uniform Crime Report (UCR), published by the Federal Bureau of Investigation (FBI). Although the FBI compiles information regarding reported crimes and arrests, it does not collect much information regarding the victims of crime. Further, because it is based only on crimes that become officially known to the police, the UCR significantly underestimates the volume of crime since much crime is never reported or detected.

An important breakthrough came in 1972 with the development of what is now known as the National Crime Victimization Survey (NCVS). The NVCS questions a large national sample of the population, presenting respondents with a list of offenses and asking them if they have been the victims of any of the offenses in the past 6 months. Details regarding the characteristics of the victim and the offender (if known) as well as the outcome of each incident are also recorded (U.S. Department of Justice, 1994). Carried out annually since 1973, the NCVS is the source of most of what we know regarding age and likelihood of victimization. Although the NCVS represents the best available data, it does have some limitations: Transient persons tend to be underrepresented in such household surveys, victims may have difficulty recalling the crime, victims may be embarrassed to admit victimization, victims may not even realize that they have been victimized, and the survey covers only a few types of crime (Alston, 1986).

The Extent of Victimization of Older Persons

Data from the NCVS show quite clearly that for almost every type of crime in the survey, persons 65 and older are the *least* likely age group to be victimized. Table 17.1 shows a comparison of the average annual victimization rate (per

TABLE 17.1 Average Annual Victimization Rates by Age of Victim and Type of Crime, 1987–1990

	Age of Victim			
Type of crime	12–24	25–49	50–64	65 and older
Total personal crimes	177.3	98.4	46.8	23.5
Personal crimes of violence	64.6	27.2	8.5	4.0
Rape	1.5	0.6	0.1[a]	0.9[a]
Robbery	10.0	5.3	2.4	1.5
Assault	53.1	21.2	5.9	2.3
Aggravated	18.4	7.5	2.2	1.1
Simple	34.6	13.7	3.7	1.3
Personal crimes of theft	112.7	71.2	38.3	19.5
Personal larceny with contact	3.6	2.4	2.2	2.6
Personal larceny without contact	109.0	68.8	36.1	16.9
Total household crimes	309.3	200.2	133.0	78.5
Burglary	121.3	66.6	43.3	32.4
Household larceny	153.4	111.9	73.3	39.5
Motor vehicle theft	34.6	21.7	16.4	6.6

Note: The personal crime victimization rate is the annual average of the number of personal victimizations for 1987–90 per 1,000 persons in that age group. The household crime victimization rate is the annual average of the number of household victimizations for 1987–90 per 1,000 households whose head is in that age group. Detail may not add to total because of rounding.

[a]Average annual estimate is based on 10 or fewer sample cases.

From *Elderly Victims* by U.S. Department of Justice, Bureau of Justice Statistics, 1992, Washington, DC: U.S. Government Printing Office.

1,000) for persons over the age of 65 versus those aged 12 to 24, 25 to 49, and 50 to 64. Contrary to what has been said and written, the best evidence available shows that in terms of both rates and raw numbers, the criminal victimization of older persons is relatively rare. The only exception is that those 65 and older have about the same rate of victimization as other age groups for the crime of personal larceny with contact (U.S. Department of Justice, 1992).

Patterns of Victimization of Older Persons

Crimes of Violence. Many believe that older persons are especially likely to be the victims of violent crime. Calculations based on Table 17.1 show that the proportion of total personal victimizations within each age group that are due to crimes of violence rather than crimes of theft is actually *lowest* among older persons. The proportion of personal victimizations that are violent in nature was 36.4% for persons aged 12 to 24, 27.6% for those 25 to 49, 18.2% for those 50 to 64, and 17.0% for those 65 and over.

Because it is relatively rare, murder is a violent offense that cannot accurately be measured in victimization surveys like the NCVS. However, the FBI UCR does record the age of homicide victims at time of death in the almost 99% of cases in which the age is known. Although persons aged 65 or over include more than 12% of the population, among homicide victims in 1993 less than 5% were aged 65 or over (FBI, 1994).

The pattern of violent victimizations for those 65 and older is somewhat different from that of younger persons (Alston, 1986). According to Table 17.1, among those 12 to 24, robberies account for 15.5% of violent victimizations; the remaining 84.5% are rapes or assaults. Among those 65 and older, robberies account for 37.5% of violent victimizations; assault and rape make up the remaining 62.5% (U.S. Department of Justice, 1992). It appears that in those few instances in which older persons are the victims of violent crime, the proportion of violent victimizations that are robbery rather than assaults or rapes is significantly higher for those 65 and older than for those under 65. This is consistent with a point made earlier: older persons tend to be the victims of property crimes rather than violent crimes. Robbery involves taking the possessions of someone through the use of or threat of force; thus, it has characteristics that make it a hybrid crime that includes elements of both violence and theft.

Although the likelihood of being the victim of a violent crime is low among older persons, the risk is not evenly distributed among those 65 and older. Certain factors are associated with higher violent crime victimization rates: being male rather than female; being Black rather than White; being divorced or separated rather than never married, widowed, or married; having a low family income level rather than a middle or upper income level; renting a residence rather than owning it; and residing in the central city rather than a suburban or rural area (U.S. Department of Justice, 1992).

Crimes of Theft. At any age one is much more likely to be the victim of a crime of theft or household crime than to a crime of violence. As has been noted, this tendency for victimizations to be crimes of theft rather than crimes of violence is most pronounced among older persons. Although their victimization rates are lower in all categories of crime, when older persons are victimized, the chances are greater than for young people that the crime will be a nonviolent offense.

Another difference between the old and the young is the relative frequency of victimizations for the crime of personal larceny with contact versus the crime of personal larceny without contact. Table 17.1 shows that personal larceny with contact, a set of nonviolent offenses consisting of nonforcible purse snatching and pocket picking, is the only crime covered by the NCVS in which older persons had victimization rates comparable to those of younger people. However, Table 17.1 shows that the proportion of personal theft victimizations that are larcenies with contact rather than larcenies without contact is significantly higher for those 65 and older than for those under 65. About 13.3% of the personal crimes of theft committed against those 65 and older involved contact, but only 3.2% of the personal crimes of theft committed against those 12 to 24 involved contact (U.S. Department of Justice, 1992).

As with crimes of violence, crimes of theft and household victimizations are not evenly distributed among those 65 and older. Higher theft victimization rates are reported for men, Blacks, divorced or separated persons, those who rent their residence, and those residing in the central city rather than a suburban or rural area. Except for personal larceny with contact, the victimization rates for crimes of theft and household crimes increase as income increases (U.S. Department of Justice, 1992).

Accounting for the Patterns

The NCVS data provide a fairly complete picture of the relative likelihood of victimization for the old and young with regard to an admittedly limited number of crimes. Less complete is our understanding of why we see the patterns that we do. Why is it that risk of victimization drops off so substantially with increased age? Why does risk of violent victimization drop off especially fast with increased age?

Several researchers have suggested that differences between older and younger persons in terms of lifestyle and day-to-day activities can help explain the patterns of victimization at different ages (Alston, 1986; Kennedy & Silverman, 1990). The "routine activity approach" (Cohen & Felson, 1979) in criminology hypothesizes that the likelihood that a crime will take place depends on three factors: the attractiveness of the target, the exposure of the target, and the extent of guardianship present (Alston, 1986). *Attractiveness* refers to the desirability of the target to the criminal: the potential financial gain, the emotional satisfaction he or she would enjoy, and the offender's perception of how easy a mark the victim would be. *Exposure* refers to the relative availability of a target to the criminal: knowledge of the existence of the target, visibility of the target, and proximity of the target to the criminal. *Guardianship* refers to the degree of protection present: someone or something that will increase the chances of the criminal getting caught (Alston, 1986). By examining the personal characteristics and lifestyles of older persons, it is possible to assess their likelihood of victimization in terms of attractiveness, exposure, and guardianship.

Contrary to the popular image of older persons, those 65 and older are not any more likely to be poor than those in the general population (Steffensmeier, 1987). Yet they do have a median income lower than that of the population as a whole. In this sense they are not especially economically attractive targets. However, older persons can be considered attractive targets in that they are often viewed as less able to resist. Although older persons today are as healthy as ever and there is considerable variation in the degree of physical decline present with age, on the average the ability to run away, summon help, or fight back lessens as one grows older (Alston, 1986).

Exposure to risk is lower for older persons, but the degree of guardianship is often higher. Most older persons do not live in the high-crime central city areas and are unlikely to associate much with persons in the crime-prone years (teens through early 20s). They do not go out at night as much and are less likely to frequent locations where victimization is most common: on the street, in parking lots, at parks, or similar areas (Alston, 1986; U.S. Department of Justice, 1993). In terms of guardianship, again, older persons are in a relatively good position. The majority live with one or more other people. Retirement means that older persons are more likely to be at home to protect their possessions (Alston, 1986).

Examining the opportunity framework for crimes against older persons provides a fairly good explanation of why they are unlikely victims of crime, especially violent crime. The opportunity framework approach can also help us to understand why older persons tend to be victims of particular types of crime. We saw that in those relatively rare instances when older persons are the victims of violent crime, the proportion of violent victimizations that are robbery rather than assaults or rapes is significantly higher for those 65 and older than for those under 65. With regard to crimes of theft, the proportion of theft victimizations that are larcenies with contact rather than larcenies without contact is significantly higher for those 65 and older than for those under 65.

Robbery and larceny with contact are actually similar crimes. The major difference is the degree to which the crime can be accomplished without the use of force. Conceivably, a personal larceny with contact could easily turn into a robbery (U.S. Department of Justice, 1993). For example, in a purse snatching (a larceny with contact), if the victim resists or the purse is being held in such a way that it is not easily grabbed, the offender may resort to the use or threat of violence and thus turn the offense into robbery. These crimes tend to take place away from the home, where attractiveness and exposure play relatively greater roles in the choice of target. We saw that of the three opportunity framework factors, the attractiveness of older persons as targets is probably most similar to that of younger persons. It is not surprising that when victimized, proportionately more of the victimizations of older persons tend to be robberies and larcenies with contact.

Victimization by Other Types of Crime

The data presented to this point show that, for the crimes shown in Table 17.1, older persons typically have the lowest victimization rates. Although NCVS crimes include those that most people view as the most serious offenses (U.S. Department of Justice, 1985), it is not an exhaustive list of crimes committed against older persons. Therefore, it may be true that older persons are being disproportionately victimized but by offenses other than those for which we have NCVS data.

Of particular concern to many researchers has been the extent to which older persons fall victim to various types of fraud. Some have noted that for a variety of reasons, older persons are more vulnerable to fraud (AARP, 1994). Although many have claimed that older persons are disproportionately victimized by fraud (AARP, 1995; Friedman, 1992), the best evidence shows that this is probably not the case. A recent fraud victimization study conducted by the National Institute of Justice using a representative national sample of the population showed that older persons are significantly *less* likely to be the victims of fraud and significantly less likely to have actually lost money in fraud schemes (Titus, Heinzelmann, & Boyle, 1995; U.S. Department of Justice, 1995).

There are other kinds of crimes for which anecdotal accounts would lead to the belief that older persons are specifically targeted. Unfortunately, the lack of systematic data limits what can be said about these problems. What follows, then, is simply an enumeration of other forms of crime of which older persons are thought to be frequent victims.

Aging is associated with certain chronic, sometimes painful, sometimes terminal, and often incurable diseases. Older persons, desperate for a cure, dissatisfied with conventional treatments, and/or uninformed regarding what is or is not effective treatment can fall prey to those promoting medicine, devices, and treatment plans that promise quick results (Alston, 1986; U.S. Senate, 1993).

The strong desire to remain in their own homes, coupled with the lack of physical ability to perform some maintenance and repair tasks, may make older persons more susceptible to home repair fraud in which they are overcharged for unneeded or substandard work on heating systems, roofs, driveways, exterior painting, tree trimming, and/or pest control (Alston, 1986; U.S. Senate, 1984).

Some purveyors of so-called medigap insurance, which is supposed to supplement Medicare coverage, have been accused of making large profits selling coverage that is unneeded (U.S. House, 1987).

The Consequences of Victimization

Older persons have low victimization rates for those serious crimes about which we have good information. But because the prevalence of victimization is lower is not to say that crime has little impact on older persons. The impact of crime on a particular age group is a function not only of the risk of victimization but also the susceptibility to damage of those who are victimized. Thus, even if the rate of victimization is lower, one could argue that crime has a more serious impact if those older persons who are victimized suffer more damage. This necessitates a discussion of the potential consequences of criminal victimization: physical injury, economic loss, and psychological damage.

Physical Injury. Because injury takes place in the context of violent crimes, the lower rates of violent victimization mean that, in general, older persons are very unlikely to sustain injury as a result of crime. But what happens to those few who *are* the victims of violent crime? Data from the NCVS shed light on this question. Table 17.2 shows the percentage of victims of violent crime who sustained an injury and measures of the seriousness of the injury. It is clear from this table that whereas those under or over 65 were about equally likely to sustain an injury, those 65 and older were more likely to be seriously injured (U.S. Department of Justice, 1992). It is not surprising that older persons may suffer more from their injuries. A broken bone may result in long-term disability for persons in their 80s but is unlikely to have the same impact on persons in their 20s. Again, older persons as a group tend to have more health problems and may be slower to recover from even minor injuries (Alston, 1986).

TABLE 17.2 Attacks, Injuries, Medical Treatment, and Hospital Care Received by Violent Crime Victims, by Age of Victim, 1987–1990

Crime characteristics	% under 65	% 65 and older
Injury	31	33
Serious	5	9
Minor	26	24
Received any medical care	15	19
Hospital care	8	14

Note: Serious injuries are broken bones, loss of teeth, internal injuries, loss of consciousness, rape or attempted rape injuries, or undetermined injuries requiring 2 or more days of hospitalization. Minor injuries are: bruises, black eyes, cuts, scratches, swelling, or undetermined injuries requiring less than 2 days of hospitalization.

From *Elderly Victims* by U.S. Department of Justice, Bureau of Justice Statistics, 1992, Washington, DC: U.S. Government Printing Office.

Economic Loss. A higher proportion of crimes that victimize older persons are property offenses. However, economic loss from crime involves not only the value of the property stolen but also the cost of property damaged, medical expenses due to injuries, wages lost because of injury, time spent making repairs, and time spent in contacts with the criminal justice system. The NCVS collects information on all of these aspects of economic loss by asking victims to estimate the monetary value of each. To calculate the adjusted net economic loss, the NCVS totals the losses sustained and subtracts the value of items recovered and insurance payments. Table 17.3 shows that among those who were the victims of crimes causing economic loss, there were no consistent differences with regard to net loss between those under 65 and those 65 and older (U.S. Department of Justice, 1987).

These data only partially address the question of the real impact of crime. Specifically, an economic loss causes more damage to persons with a low income.

TABLE 17.3 Adjusted Net Economic Loss, by Age and Type of Crime, 1980–1985

	Percentage of victims with economic loss			
Type of crime and age of victim	Less than $10	$10–49	$50–249	$250 or more
Crimes of violence				
Under 65	12	26	36	26
65 and older	9	24	40	27
Crimes of theft				
Under 65	17	36	34	14
65 and older	15	37	36	12
Household crimes				
Burglary				
Under 65	8	21	33	39
65 and older	13	27	30	30
Household larceny				
Under 65	16	36	35	13
65 and older	24	40	26	10
Motor vehicle theft				
Under 65	2	10	25	64
65 and older	3	12	23	61

Note: Percentages may not total to 100% because of rounding. Age of head of household is used for household crimes; age of victim is used for crimes of violence and theft. Data exclude crimes where there was no net economic loss or the net loss was not known or ascertained. Data were adjusted to 1980 constant dollars using the Consumer Price Index.

From *Elderly Victims* by U.S. Department of Justice, Bureau of Justice Statistics, 1987, Washington, DC: U.S. Governmet Printing Office.

One way of measuring the impact of economic loss is to calculate the loss relative to income. Using 1973 and 1974 NCVS data, researchers have shown that as a percentage of monthly income, those 65 and over sustained losses that were somewhat greater than those of most other adults (Cook, Skogan, Cook, & Antunes, 1978).

Psychological Damage. We have seen some evidence that victimized older persons sustain more serious physical injury and, to a lesser extent, greater economic loss. Somewhat less tangible is the psychological impact of crime. Most of this research has focused on the effects of victimization on fear of crime and the consequent impact on well-being.

Although it is not hard to understand why a person who has actually been the victim of a crime would be more fearful of crime than others, researchers who have studied crime victims have not always found this effect. Victims of crimes involving personal contact seem to be the most fearful, but often the effect of victimization is short-lived (Alston, 1986; Yin, 1985). Several studies have looked specifically at the psychological impact of crime on older persons and found that prior victimization was strongly correlated with anxiety in general and fear of crime in particular (Berg & Johnson, 1979; Lawton & Yaffe, 1980; Lee, 1983; Norton & Courlander, 1982). The few studies that have compared the impact of crime on younger and older victims suggest that the impact is somewhat greater on older persons (Berg & Johnson, 1979). This greater anxiety may result from the fact that older victims do tend to suffer somewhat greater economic losses relative to income. Further, actual victimization tends to emphasize physical weakness and vulnerability (Alston, 1986).

CRIMINAL BEHAVIOR BY OLDER PERSONS

As we have noted, reports in the popular media as well as in some scholarly literature indicate that crime by the elderly is relatively common and that it is increasing rapidly. This literature frequently presents a picture of isolated and impoverished senior citizens increasingly committing crimes ranging from murder to shoplifting in order to seek attention or merely survive (Cullen, Wozniak, & Frank, 1984). Other reports focus on the role of dementia, alcohol abuse, and adverse reactions to prescription drugs (Kossan, 1994). Although the kind of data needed to definitively assess these concerns does not exist, data are available that allow us to at least address these issues.

The most comprehensive source of information on the characteristics of criminal offenders (including age) comes from the FBI UCR arrest statistics compiled yearly for 29 offense categories. The general problems with UCR data have been well documented (Nettler, 1978). Analyses of the NCVS data show that only about a third of major crimes are reported to the police (U.S. Department of

Justice, 1993). Further, among the so-called Part I crimes (murder, forcible rape, robbery, aggravated assault, burglary, larceny-theft, motor vehicle theft, and arson), less than 20% of crimes reported are cleared by an arrest (FBI, 1994). Thus, those arrested represent only a small fraction of those committing crimes in any given year.

Questions can be raised regarding how closely the characteristics (including age) of those arrested match the characteristics of offenders in general. Many studies have concluded that although arrest statistics clearly underestimate the total amount of crime, they present a reasonably accurate picture of the relative likelihood of different subgroups of society to be involved in crime as offenders (Kercher, 1987). But some have suggested that older persons are less likely to show up in arrest statistics because the police and other criminal justice agents treat them more leniently. A number of studies have shown that age does not seem to have an effect on the decision of the police to arrest (Krohn, Curry, & Nelson-Kilger, 1983; Petersilia, 1985; Smith, Visher, & Davidson, 1984). Given these findings, it can be argued that although they are not without problems, the UCR arrest statistics provide a reasonable estimate of criminality in society as a whole.

The Extent of Criminal Behavior by Older Persons

The UCR arrest data establish quite clearly that very few of those arrested are 65 years of age or older or even 55 years of age or older. For example, in 1993 those 65 and older accounted for only 0.7% of total arrests, 0.6% of serious violent crime arrests, 0.8% of serious property crime arrests, and 0.8% of all other arrests (FBI, 1994).

Although the percentage of those arrested that are older persons is quite small, in order to systematically compare arrests across age groups, it is necessary to take into account the size of the population in each age category by calculating arrest rates within each age group. Table 17.4 shows the age-specific arrest rates (per 100,000) for selected offenses in 1992 (FBI, 1993). Looking at those over the age of 12, there is no crime in which those 65 or older do not have the lowest age-specific arrest rates. In general, the conclusion that older persons are relatively uninvolved in crime is supported by these data.

Table 17.4 shows not only that the arrest rates for older persons are quite low but also that the arrest rates follow a fairly predictable pattern with regard to age. For most crimes, the age-specific arrest rate increases precipitously after childhood, peaks out during the latter part of the teens, and declines steadily thereafter (FBI, 1993). With only minor variations, the same basic pattern can be found in looking at different types of criminality, different ways of measuring criminality, criminality in different cultures, and criminality occurring at different points in historical time (Hirschi & Gottfredson, 1983).

TABLE 17.4 Age-Specific Arrest Rates for Selected Offenses, 1992

Age group	Murder	Forcible rape	Robbery	Aggravated assault	Burglary	Larceny-theft	Motor vehicle theft	Arson
12 and under	0.1	1.5	6.0	14.7	40.9	154.6	7.3	6.3
13–14	4.9	23.2	150.5	241.1	543.5	1,941.6	318.3	40.5
15	15.7	32.0	280.4	397.2	785.6	2,440.4	631.1	36.2
16	29.8	39.2	345.8	524.7	857.7	2,606.0	666.2	31.7
17	41.2	40.9	352.0	567.2	813.2	2,392.3	550.9	26.5
18	52.0	50.2	371.9	617.8	829.9	2,262.0	439.2	21.9
19	44.8	42.6	297.6	570.0	641.5	1,734.3	318.4	16.8
20	38.4	41.1	247.0	525.7	490.2	1,419.3	236.6	14.0
21	36.0	40.4	222.1	526.9	416.0	1,265.9	194.2	12.1
22	31.1	39.5	199.3	527.7	370.2	1,153.9	167.9	10.7
23	27.8	35.1	185.4	508.8	339.7	1,092.2	152.6	10.9
24	23.3	36.0	178.3	495.8	316.7	1,091.4	139.3	9.3
25–29	17.0	31.5	141.0	434.1	273.2	950.2	102.1	8.4
30–34	10.7	26.1	90.9	345.7	200.2	797.8	65.8	7.0
35–39	7.8	18.9	51.5	255.0	130.4	616.8	40.9	5.5
40–44	5.6	12.5	25.3	167.7	70.3	420.1	23.2	4.1
45–49	4.6	8.3	11.5	113.6	35.6	270.7	12.5	3.0
50–54	3.3	5.7	6.3	79.3	18.2	194.7	7.5	2.2
55–59	2.2	4.0	3.0	51.1	9.0	138.8	3.6	1.6
60–64	1.4	2.5	1.4	31.5	4.2	103.6	1.9	1.0
65 and over	0.8	1.1	0.7	12.6	1.8	53.5	0.8	0.3

Age group	Forgery, Counterfeiting	Frand	Embezzlement	Stolen Property	Weapons	Sex Offenses	Gambling	Drug Abuse Violations
12 and under	0.7	1.7	0.2	5.5	7.9	7.6	0.1	3.2
13–14	14.9	54.0	1.6	139.4	180.8	89.3	4.1	170.2
15	35.9	122.4	2.2	249.9	311.3	98.1	10.4	469.3
16	62.5	92.5	5.9	299.5	395.9	92.5	17.3	783.5
17	95.8	133.4	12.5	326.6	436.1	88.3	21.2	1,044.2
18	140.6	268.3	15.4	359.9	492.6	91.0	22.5	1,460.5
19	148.3	353.1	17.4	286.9	414.2	84.5	20.3	1,458.2
20	147.7	417.6	17.6	230.5	349.6	78.2	17.3	1,372.2
21	128.0	444.9	17.7	192.7	330.4	79.6	16.1	1,340.0
22	129.5	452.4	16.3	167.8	295.8	79.9	13.4	1,317.6
23	114.0	457.9	15.2	149.0	262.3	78.4	12.9	1,266.3
24	117.7	462.9	16.6	137.5	230.6	81.0	11.5	1,222.2
25–29	99.6	401.3	12.0	107.5	168.8	78.3	10.2	1,077.4
30–34	76.0	310.5	9.6	75.1	114.0	71.9	9.2	846.3
35–39	53.0	242.8	6.6	52.7	80.8	57.7	9.4	581.6
40–44	32.9	171.8	5.2	33.4	58.4	43.8	9.2	341.4
45–49	18.5	110.7	4.1	18.5	41.8	36.4	10.4	173.6
50–54	10.3	70.5	2.2	12.2	30.8	28.5	10.4	93.6
55–59	5.6	40.5	1.4	7.0	20.9	26.0	10.3	48.1
60–64	3.1	23.8	0.8	3.9	13.4	16.9	7.0	23.9
65 and over	1.1	9.0	0.2	1.2	5.3	7.4	2.9	6.8

Note: From *Age-Specific Arrest Rates and Race-Specific Arrest Rates for Selected Offenses 1965–1992*. By The Federal Bureau of Investigation.

Explaining the Lower Rate of Criminal Behavior by Older Persons

It is clear that those arrested tend to be young rather than old, but it is not clear why this is the case. As mentioned above, it does not appear that older persons who commit crime are less likely to be arrested, but it could be that the lower arrest rate is due to "longevity factors' (Kercher, 1987). Those who are poor, male, Black, and undereducated have higher arrest rates and also shorter life spans. Thus, they are less likely to survive long enough to be arrested in old age. But evidence shows that the same basic age-crime pattern holds true when these factors are taken into account. In fact, Hirschi and Gottfredson (1983) argue that this relationship is invariant and that it holds true independently of (and therefore cannot be explained by) any of the variables now used in criminology.

Conceptually, several things could explain the lower arrest rate among older persons. If the lower rate is the outcome of aging, this implies that it could result from a drop in the prevalence of criminality with age, the incidence of criminality with age, or some combination of the two. A drop in prevalence occurs when individuals cease committing crime as they grow older, so the proportion of persons who engage in this activity is less for older age groups. A drop in incidence occurs when a more or less stable proportion of the population commits crimes throughout life but commits fewer acts of crime with advancing age. Although evidence is quite limited, longitudinal and other types of studies of the careers of criminals indicate that the decline in crime with age is primarily caused by a decline in prevalence (Farrington, 1986).

Many hypotheses have been put forth to explain the decline in prevalence of lawbreaking with increased age, yet few have firm empirical support (Fattah & Sacco, 1989; Hirschi & Gottfredson, 1983). Some explanations focus on the effect of biological changes that accompany aging. Physical strength or agility, which tends to decline with age, is needed to commit some types of crimes. For example, the ability to carry out a strong-arm robbery or to climb into a window to commit a burglary would presumably decrease as one approached age 65 (Farrington, 1986; Kercher, 1987). Evidence suggests that the decline in criminal behavior with age is steeper for these kinds of crimes (Kercher, 1987). Another biological theory says that for males, aggressiveness is linked to the level of the hormone testosterone in the body. This level peaks in the late teens or early 20s and declines thereafter (Farrington, 1986). Social psychological theories say that personality changes associated with "moral development" (Kohlberg, 1976) or "maturation" (Glueck & Glueck, 1940) explain the drop in criminality. Also, it is said that older persons are less interested in excitement, exercise more caution, and are more willing to defer gratification (Wilson & Herrnstein, 1985). However, it is not clear why these personality changes take place with age.

A number of theories attribute the decline in criminality with age to changes in the social environment (Farrington, 1986). A common finding in delinquency research is that having delinquent friends encourages unlawful behavior (Elliot, Huizinga, & Ageton, 1985). As persons leave early adulthood, marry, and take on jobs, they receive reinforcement for conformity from the workplace and the family, so the influence of delinquent peers decreases (Farrington, 1986).

An alternative view of the age-crime relationship says that the low arrest rates found among older persons are not simply the result of the effects of aging but rather that cohort and/or period effects also operate. A cohort effect would be operating if those who are old are less criminal compared to those who are young because the old were exposed to a set of values that more strongly discouraged criminality as they grew up, in comparison to those growing up in more recent times. A period effect operates if there are historical events that encourage or discourage criminality, affecting all age cohorts at a given time. It is difficult to disentangle cohort and period effects from aging effects, and researchers who have attempted to do so have had mixed findings (Farrington, 1986). Further, this research tends to focus on relatively young segments of the population. But in general, aging and to a lesser extent period effects seem to have the most impact on crime (Steffensmeier, Streifel, & Harer, 1987).

Is the Amount of Criminal Behavior by Older Persons Increasing?

Another often-mentioned assertion is that the amount of crime committed by older persons has increased in recent years and that a disproportionate amount of the increase has been for serious offenses. The number of persons arrested and the rate of arrests in all age categories has increased over the past 25 years. What needs to be examined is whether the increase in arrest rates for older persons is greater than the increase in arrest rates for the population as a whole.

Table 17.5 shows the age-specific arrest rates for those 65 and older and for the population as a whole for the FBI UCR Part I offenses from 1967 to 1992 (FBI, 1993). Also presented is the percentage change in arrest rates from 1967 to 1992. This table demonstrates once again that throughout the 25-year period, those 65 and older have always exhibited much lower arrest rates than other segments of the population. It also shows that the arrest rates for older persons have increased more slowly for some kinds of crime and more rapidly for other kinds of crime, compared to the population as a whole.

Looking at violent crime, the pattern is clear: violent crime arrest rates for those 65 and older have increased much more slowly than those for the population as a whole for essentially every type of serious violent offense. The one exception is forcible rape. However, the raw number of arrests of those 65 and older for rape is so low that even small increases in arrests greatly affect the rates.

Looking at property crime, the pattern is also clear: property crime arrest rates for those 65 and older have increased considerably faster than those for the population as a whole for every type of serious property offense. Again, for most

TABLE 17.5 Age-Specific Arrest Rates for Selected Offenses and Percent Change in Arrests, 1967–1992

Crimes	1967	1972	1977	1982	1987	1992	% Change 1967–1992
Violent crime							
All ages	124.4	173.3	207.7	236.9	233.9	307.5	+147.2
65+	11.6	13.3	13.9	13.9	12.6	15.1	+30.2
Murder							
All ages	6.5	9.6	9.3	9.9	8.3	9.5	+46.1
65+	1.5	1.8	1.3	1.2	0.9	0.8	−46.7
Forcible rape							
All ages	8.9	10.1	13.9	15.1	15.5	15.6	+75.3
65+	0.3	0.3	0.5	0.5	0.8	1.1	+266.7
Robbery							
All ages	40.9	60.5	67.6	73.8	61.1	74.0	+80.9
65+	0.5	0.9	1.0	0.7	0.5	0.7	+40.0
Aggravated assault							
All ages	68.1	93.1	116.9	138.1	149.1	208.4	+206.0
65+	9.3	10.3	11.0	11.6	10.4	12.9	+38.7
Property crime							
All ages	601.4	713.2	854.4	900.6	880.2	873.6	+45.3
65+	27.9	NA	50.3	69.9	62.0	56.1	+101.1
Burglary							
All ages	177.0	201.4	241.6	232.6	185.5	171.2	−3.3
65+	1.8	1.9	2.2	2.7	1.8	1.8	+0.0
Larceny-theft							
All ages	337.5	437.0	539.1	609.9	622.1	618.9	+83.4
65+	25.7	35.4	47.4	66.2	59.6	53.5	+108.2
Motor vehicle theft							
All ages	86.9	74.8	73.7	58.1	72.7	83.5	−3.9
65+	0.5	0.6	0.7	1.0	0.6	0.8	+37.5
Arson							
All ages	5.8	6.8	8.5	9.0	7.5	7.7	+32.8
65+	0.2	0.3	0.4	0.5	0.3	0.3	+50.0

Note: From *Age-Specific Arrest Rates and Race-Specific Arrest Rates for Selected Offenses 1965–1992*, by The Federal Bureau of Investigation.

of the offense categories the raw number of arrests is so low that it is hard to attach much significance to the rate changes. Most of the real increase in the rate of property crime arrests for older persons can be attributed to an increase in arrests for larceny theft. In 1993, the FBI UCR recorded 13,212 persons 65 and over arrested for larceny-theft. About 95% of the Part I property crime arrests for those 65 and over was for the crime of larceny-theft (FBI, 1994). Steffensmeier

(1987) found that the increase in larceny-theft rates was largely due to an increase in shoplifting and other petty thefts.

CONCLUSIONS

The evidence presented in this chapter shows that older persons are among the least likely to be involved in crime, either as victims or as perpetrators. Several writers have commented on the propensity within our society (including within social science) to create and/or exaggerate social problems, especially with regard to the victims and perpetrators of crime (Best, 1995; Forsyth & Shover, 1986; Steffensmeier, 1987). Any victimization of older persons is unacceptable, but by overstating the problem we run the risk of unnecessarily frightening those whom we want to help. Although crimes committed by older persons are a valid concern of society and an appropriate area of research, attempts should be made to keep the problem in perspective (Wilbanks, 1984).

REFERENCES

Alston, L. (1986). *Crime and older Americans*. Springfield, IL: Charles C Thomas.

American Associations of Retired Persons. (1994). *A report on the 1993 survey of older consumer behavior*. Washington, DC: Author.

American Associations of Retired Persons. (1995). *Telemarketing fraud victimization of older Americans: An AARP survey*. Washington, DC: Author.

Berg, W., & Johnson, R. (1979). Assessing the impact of victimization. In W. H. Parsonage (Ed.), *Perspectives on victimology* (pp. 58–71). Beverly Hills, CA: Sage.

Best, J. (1995). *Images of issues: Typifying contemporary social problems* (2nd ed.). New York: Aldine de Gruyter.

Cohen, L., & Felson, M. (1979). Social change and crime rate trends: A routine activity approach. *American Sociological Review*, *44*, 588–608.

Cook, F. L., Skogan, W. G., Cook, T. D., & Antunes, G. E. (1978). Criminal victimization of the elderly: The physical and economic consequences. *Gerontologist*, *18*, 338–349.

Cullen, F. T., Wozniak, J. F., & Frank, J. (1984). The rise of the elderly offender: Will a "new" criminal be invented? *Crime and Social Justice*, *23*, 151–165.

Elliot, D., Huizinga, D., & Ageton, S. (1985). *Explaining drug use*. Beverly Hills, CA: Sage.

Farrington, D. P. (1986). Age and crime. In M. Tonry & N. Morris (Eds.), *Crime and justice: An annual review of research* (pp. 189–250). Chicago: University of Chicago Press.

Fattah, E., & Sacco, V. (1989). *Crime and victimization of the elderly*. New York: Springer-Verlag.

Federal Bureau of Investigation. (1993). *Age-specific arrest rates and race-specific arrest rates for selected offenses 1965–1992*. Washington, DC: U.S. Government Printing Office.

Federal Bureau of Investigation. (1994). *Crime in the United States 1993*. Washington, DC: U.S. Government Printing Office.

Forsyth, C. J., & Shover, N. (1986). "No rest for the weary . . ." Constructing a problem of elderly crime. *Sociological Focus*, *19*, 375–386.

Friedman, M. (1992). Confidence swindles of older consumers. *Journal of Consumer Affairs*, *26*, 20–46.

Glueck, S., & Glueck, E. (1940). *Juvenile delinquents grow up*. New York: Commonwealth Fund.

Hirschi, T., & Gottfredson, M. (1983). Age and the explanation of crime. *American Journal of Sociology*, *89*, 552–584.

Hopkins, J. (1995, April 1). Older inmates strain system. *Cincinnati Enquirer*, p. B1.

Kennedy, L., & Silverman, R. (1990). The elderly victim of homicide: An application of the routine activities approach. *Sociological Quarterly*, *31*, 307–319.

Kercher, K. (1987). Causes and correlates of crime committed by the elderly: A review of the literature. In E. F. Borgatta & R. Montgomery (Eds.), *Critical issues in aging policy: Linking research and values* (pp. 254–306). Beverly Hills, CA: Sage.

Kohlberg, L. (1976). Moral stages and moralization: The cognitive-developmental approach. In T. Lickona (Ed.), *Moral development and behavior* (pp. 31–53). New York: Holt, Rinehart, & Winston.

Kossan, P. (1994, July 21). Old and in trouble. *Phoenix Gazette*.

Krohn, M., Curry, L., & Nelson-Kilger, S. (1983). Is chivalry dead? An analysis of changes in police practices of males and females. *Criminology*, *71*, 417–437.

Lawton, M. P., & Yaffe, S. (1980). Victimization and fear of crime in elderly public housing tenants. *Journal of Gerontology*, *35*, 768–779.

Lee, G. (1983). Social integration and fear of crime among older persons. *Journal of Gerontology*, *38*, 745–750.

Malinchak, A. A. (1980). *Crime and gerontology*. Englewood Cliffs, NJ: Prentice-Hall.

McCarthy, B., & Langworthy, R. (1988). *Older offenders: Perspectives in criminology and criminal justice*. New York: Praeger.

Nettler, G. (1978). *Explaining crime*. New York: McGraw-Hill.

New police worry: Old lawbreakers. (1982, March 29). *U.S. News and World Report*, p. 10.

Newman, E. S., Newman, D. J., & Gewirtz, M. L. (1984). *Elderly criminals*. Cambridge, MA: Oelgeschlager, Gunn & Hain.

Norton, L., & Courlander, M. (1982). Fear of crime among the elderly: The role of crime prevention programs. *Gerontologist*, *22*, 388–393.

Petersilia, J. (1985). Racial disparities in the criminal justice system: A summary. *Crime and Delinquency*, *31*, 15–34.

Smith, D., Visher, C., & Davidson, L. (1984). Equity and discretionary justice: The influence of race on police arrest decisions. *Journal of Criminal Law and Criminology*, *75*, 234–249.

Steffensmeier, D. (1987). The invention of the "new" senior citizen criminal: An analysis of crime trends of elderly males and females, 1964–1984. *Research on Aging*, *9*, 281–311.

Steffensmeier, D., Streifel, C., & Harer, M. (1987). Relative cohort size and youth crime in the United States, 1953–1984. *American Sociological Review*, *52*, 702–710.

Titus, R., Heinzelmann, F., & Boyle, J. (1995). Victimization of persons by fraud. *Crime & Delinquency*, *41*, 54–72.

U.S. Department of Justice, Bureau of Justice Statistics. (1985). *The national survey of crime severity*. Washington, DC: U.S. Government Printing Office.

U.S. Department of Justice, Bureau of Justice Statistics. (1987). *Elderly victims.* Washington, DC: U.S. Government Printing Office.

U.S. Department of Justice, Bureau of Justice Statistics. (1992). *Elderly victims.* Washington, DC: U.S. Government Printing Office.

U.S. Department of Justice, Bureau of Justice Statistics. (1993). *Highlights from 20 years of surveying crime victims.* Washington, DC: U.S. Government Printing Office.

U.S. Department of Justice, Bureau of Justice Statistics. (1994). *Criminal victimization in the U.S.: 1973–92 trends.* Washington, DC: U.S. Government Printing Office.

U.S. Department of Justice, National Institute of Justice. (1995). *Fraud victimization: The extent, the targets, the effects.* Washington, DC: U.S. Government Printing Office.

U.S. House Select Committee on Aging. (1987). *Hearings on direct mail solicitations to the elderly.* Washington, DC: U.S. Government Printing Office.

U.S. Senate Committee on Commerce, Science, and Transportation. (1984). *Hearings on consumer fraud and the elderly.* Washington, DC: U.S. Government Printing Office.

U.S. Senate Special Committee on Aging. (1991). *Hearings on crimes committed against the elderly.* Washington, DC: U.S. Government Printing Office.

U.S. Senate Special Committee on Aging. (1993). *Hearings on health care fraud as it affects the aging.* Washington, DC: U.S. Government Printing Office.

U.S. Senate Special Committee on Aging. (1994). *Hearings on uninsured bank products: Risky business for seniors.* Washington, DC: U.S. Government Printing Office.

White House Conference on Aging. (1981). *Report of the technical committee on the physical and social environment and quality of life.* Washington, DC: U.S. Government Printing Office.

Wilbanks, W. (1984). The elderly offender: Placing the problem in perspective. In W. Wilbanks & P. K. H. Kim (Ed.), *Elderly criminals* (pp. 1–15). Lanham, MD: University Press of America.

Wilbanks, W., & Kim, P. K. H. (1984). *Elderly criminals.* Lanham, MD: University Press of America.

Wilson, J. Q., & Herrnstein, R. J. (1985). *Crime and human nature.* New York: Simon & Schuster.

Yin, P. (1985). *Victimization and the aged.* Springfield, IL: Charles C Thomas.

CHAPTER 18

Death, Dying, and the Will to Live

Kenneth F. Ferraro

To many people, growing older is frequently associated with dying. There is good reason that many people think in these terms. As has been described earlier, there have been dramatic changes in life expectancy over the past two centuries. This is mirrored in contemporary societies by comparing life expectancy in third world nations with those in industrial or postindustrial societies. For instance, life expectancy in Bangladesh, Nigeria, and Uganda is still less than 50 years. In contrast, in the United States, Canada, and most of Western Europe, life expectancy is greater than 75 years.

What has accompanied the process of industrialization is a major change in when most deaths occur during the life course. In preindustrial societies, infant deaths were high, but deaths were also dispersed throughout the life course. Just going back to 19th-century America, death was much more likely to occur at earlier stages of the life course. Death in the first year of life was common, and about one third of the population died before age 20 (Uhlenberg, 1969). In more developed nations, there is still considerable risk of death in the first year of life, but mortality drops substantially after that first year and remains quite low for about five decades. Therefore, the highest death rates are manifest among older people.

Another way of thinking of this is that we have experienced a compression of mortality. Death for any individual, especially with special health risks, cannot be predicted; however, the general prevalence of death for modern nations is fairly localized (past the fifth and sixth decades of life). The successful public health improvements over the past century have raised average life expectancy to the point that older people are now the age group with the highest proportion of deaths, and mortality may become even more compressed due to public health and medical advances.

The compression of mortality over the past two centuries has led to a number of changes in how we view death and handle death and dying experiences. For instance, the timing of death and the social response to death at various points in the life course has changed. Because most deaths occur among older people, the death of a small child is often viewed as a greater loss than the death of an older person (Jecker & Schneiderman, 1994). Childhood deaths in modern societies are nonnormative, but death among older people is expected.

Another arena of change is the scene of most deaths. A century ago most people died at home and, as is still done is some cultures, "viewing" the body was also done in the home. Now the majority of people in modern societies die in institutional settings. Over 70% of all people die in either a hospital or nursing home (Kammerman, 1988; Kastenbaum & Candy, 1973). Thus, the experience of death is in many ways "hidden" from the public, especially because of the location of most deaths and the specialized occupations surrounding the death industry (e.g., morticians).

These changes are triggering a number of social and ethical decisions that we as a society have never before faced. A discussion of all of these contemporary issues is beyond the scope of this chapter, but a few of them are considered here. It is important to note, however, that many of the concepts and issues pertinent to a discussion of death and dying have already been discussed elsewhere in the book. Indeed, as we began the journey of considering what is a gerontological imagination, we noted that one must keep in mind that gerontology focuses on the aging process but that an awareness of how death may influence interpretations about aging is essential. Whether the application was terminal drop, social responses to widowhood, or anticipatory grief among family caregivers, death and dying have already been discussed at length in earlier chapters. This chapter briefly examines our conceptions of death and dying and how the will to live among older adults may be changing because of these conceptions. As Elias (1985) summarized the importance of these conceptions, "The image of death in a person's memory is very closely bound up with his image of himself, of human beings prevalent in his society" (p. 52).

CONCEPTIONS OF DEATH

At the most general level, scholars have attempted to describe how our conceptions of death and dying have changed. Probably the most widely cited of these analyses is offered by the French social historian Philippe Ariès (1974). Ariès devised a four-stage classification to typify the way in which death has been regarded from the Middle Ages to the present: Tamed Death (prior to 1200); Own Death (1200–1700); Thy Death (1700–late 1800s); and Forbidden Death (1900–present). One of the most astute observations from Ariès's work is how control has changed over this time.

Death in the Middle Ages was ever-present. Death struck people of all ages, often without much warning. As widely described in historical records for the Middle Ages, the individual often had some control over his or her dying—the last hours or days of life. Perhaps because the dying period was brief compared to that of modern times, the individual often had some control over the dying process. If at all possible, people typically lay down in bed and called others into reminisce, offer forgiveness or admonition, convey blessings, and perhaps pray. Indeed, cultural artifacts from the period include "popular manuals on how to prepare for death, called *artes morieni*" (Covey, 1991, p. 141). There were many customs and rituals for dying, but Ariès (1974) argued that the dying person exercised most of the control over the final hours or days.

During the second period, what Ariès (1974) called Own Death, images of death were modified to focus more on the self-assessment of one's life, and relatively minor changes occurred in the rituals associated with death. By the third stage (Thy Death), however, especially in the 1800s, major changes in the rituals occurred. First, death was often romanticized in this period, as manifest in artwork depicting angels and even erotic themes (Covey, 1991). Second, Ariès showed that the individual increasingly turned over control of the dying process to other people, especially family members. This latter change paved the way for specialized occupations taking control of death in the 1900s (Forbidden Death). The death industry grew, and funeral services were more controlled by persons outside the family, although the individual and the family often expressed their "wishes."

If one considers what has happened in the past three decades, it may be argued that people are desiring a return to greater control over dying. Medical intervention has provided new opportunities for extending the life of persons with highly impaired function. These "life extension" procedures are almost invariably offered in institutional settings and are often seen as "dying extension" procedures. Thus, social movements such as hospice and debates about euthanasia, assisted suicide, and life extension all seem geared to offering dying persons more control over their lives without unnecessarily prolonging the dying process. The questions surrounding these issues are penetrating.

What type of care is appropriate?
What should be done to extend life when function is so impaired?
Indeed, how much longer shall a person live?
Should food and water be withdrawn from dying persons?
Is withdrawing a feeding *tube* the same as withdrawing food to be digested?
And *who* should make each of these decisions?

There are no easy answers for these and a host of related questions in heterogeneous societies. Indeed, there are interest groups advocating answers on both sides of the issue for most of these questions (Sawyer, 1982). What we are left with is a series of public opinion polls, state laws, and judicial decisions that foster confusion and dissension as much as anything else. We see what has happened when the person has lost control over the dying process, but at the same time, we seek to control dying when we know that, ultimately, we cannot control it.

DEATH ANXIETY AMONG OLDER PEOPLE?

With all the changes in where and when death occurs and social confusion over the norms of dying, one wonders whether there is greater death anxiety today, especially among older people. Older adults are aware that their cohorts are shrinking and that the likelihood of death grows imminent. Might the awareness of this temporal localization of death in later life create or exacerbate fears of death and dying among older people?

Most of the research indicates that older people are more aware of their finitude but that they are not necessarily afraid of death (Kalish, 1985). Death of close family members and friends spur more contemplation about death throughout the life course. Thus, it should come as no surprise that older people *think about* and discuss death more often because they have lost more friends and family members to death. Thinking about death and being anxious are not the same thing, however.

All in all, age as a variable is not very predictive of death anxiety. For example, religiosity seems equally or perhaps more predictive than age. Previous research indicates that death anxiety is much lower among persons who are strongly religious or spiritual (Rasmussen & Johnson, 1994). Research on confirmed atheists is inconsistent. Some studies show somewhat lower death anxiety in atheists; others show them having high death anxiety (e.g., Jeffers, Nichols, & Eisdorfer, 1961; Kalish, 1985). Whatever the case, it is generally agreed that people who are uncertain about their religion or only sporadically participate in it have the highest levels of death anxiety.

There are also ethnic differences in death anxiety. In a study of older adults, Myers, Wass, and Murphy (1980) found that African Americans generally have higher death anxiety. They showed that older Black men manifest the highest levels of death anxiety and White men the least. They did not offer an explanation for these differences, but shorter life expectancy among minority groups may predispose them to greater concern. Or death anxiety may be just another manifestation of a more generally anxious orientation to life.

Men and women also think differently about death. Women have been found to be more concerned with the grief of others, the pain of dying, and what death does to the body. By contrast, men are typically more concerned about the termination of plans and projects (Kastenbaum, 1977). Based on these differences, the concept of death anxiety per se merits closer investigation in future studies, probably by examining the various dimensions of it.

The occurrence of death seems to concern most older people less than *how* they might die. High-technology medicine now means that life can be extended beyond the level of what most of us consider functional independence. In American society functional dependency is widely accepted in infancy and childhood but not during adulthood. Older people, therefore, face the specter of growing dependency and institutionalization due to chronic conditions such as stroke and Alzheimer's disease. Anxiety grows, not so much about the termination of life but about how the person's life is ended (Marshall, 1975). To put it another way, there is little evidence for widespread death anxiety among older people, but dying anxiety appears more prevalent and acute. Death is not typically conceptualized as the "ultimate failure" in modern societies; dependency is.

THE WILL TO LIVE

Although there may be some anxiety about dying in every person, most older people are not arrested by such fear in everyday life. What may be a more important question is whether they have the will to live. There is a fascinating body of research emerging on the significance for longevity of the will to live. Of course, a positive mental attitude and a sense of hope are widely understood as important to well-being. Yet a body of literature on the importance of wanting to continue life goes beyond positive mental attitudes. Some of this research grew out of studies of how people facing similar dire circumstances often handled the situation quite differently (Antonovsky, 1987). Whether in concentration camps or war or after natural disasters, some people endure these traumatic events and live years after them, whereas others who are in apparently good physical health simply die (Seligman, 1974).

Even more intriguing is the possibility that certain social or religious engagements may delay death. With data derived from biographies of famous people, Phillips and Feldman (1973) found that there are fewer deaths than usual before important events. Presidential elections, birthdays, and holidays apparently have a protective effect on life (see also Phillips & King, 1988). Idler and Kasl (1992) found similar results when studying religious observances among older people in New Haven, Connecticut. They found that religious group membership protected both Christians and Jews against mortality in the month before their respective religious holidays. This body of research stresses the meaning that these engagements have. Religion provides one with a system of interpreting the world and giving meaning to existence. The will to live, therefore, may ebb and flow while older persons face disability or bodily pain, but religious observances appear to aid the person's sense of coherence and purpose for living (Antonovsky, 1987). In addition, the role of religion in integrating people into social life has long been recognized in sociology (Durkheim, 1897/1951).

The will to live is related to a number of the questions raised earlier about euthanasia, assisted suicide, and the prolongation of life. Assisted suicide certainly reflects lack of a will to live. Yet even suicide (without assistance), although rare, reflects on these process of integration and meaning for older people in society. Could it be that if older people sense a loss of purpose in living and social integration, they may feel more inclined to consider suicide? Repeated thoughts about suicide are often used as indicators of depression. If depressed by functional disability and a growing sense of worthlessness, might older adults be predisposed to contemplate suicide seriously? Perhaps it may be useful to consider briefly the prevalence of suicide among older people as one indicator of how the will to live varies by age and over time.

To begin, it should be recognized that suicide has long been found to be related to social events and social organization/disorganization. The overall suicide rate in the United States has varied considerably during the 20th century. From a rate of 10.2 in 1900, it fluctuated widely over succeeding decades. The rates at the beginning of each decade from 1910 to 1960 were as follows: 15.3, 10.2, 15.6, 14.4, 11.4, and 10.6 (U.S. Bureau of the Census, 1975). There have been fluctuations over time across age groups as well. Figure 18.1 displays the suicide rate for the total population and three age groups of older people (U.S. Bureau of the Census, 1993, 1995). First, notice that suicide is much more prevalent among older people than in the total population. (The suicide rate for people 65 years and older is roughly double that for those 15 to 19 years old.) The rate was high for 65- to 74-year-old persons in 1970 and has since declined slightly. However, for persons 75 to 84 years of age and persons 85 and older, the rate has risen. How these rates may change in the future is hard to predict. Of course, demographers and epidemiologists have long understood that suicide

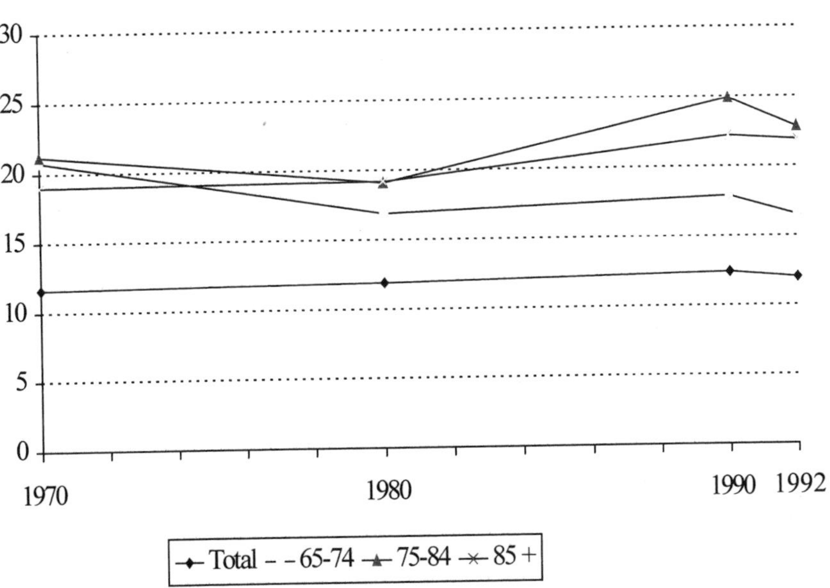

FIGURE 18.1 U.S. suicide rate for older adults since 1970 (rate per 100,000).

TABLE 18.1 Suicide Rates among Older People in Selected Countries by Sex and Age, 1990 (Rate per 100,000 Population)

	Men		Women	
Country	65–74	75+	65–74	75+
Australia	27.7	39.8	7.4	10.0
Austria	66.8	107.6	22.0	35.5
Canada	20.8	32.7	6.0	4.2
Denmark	47.3	76.7	30.2	32.2
France	52.9	107.2	20.2	25.7
Germany	39.4	75.6	18.2	22.7
Italy	28.3	47.4	9.7	11.1
Japan	36.6	62.9	25.3	48.6
Netherlands	21.1	29.0	13.4	10.8
Poland	28.0	27.3	7.2	7.4
Sweden	36.4	47.2	15.3	13.8
United Kingdom	13.6	19.4	6.1	6.2
United States	33.6	54.5	5.9	6.0

Rates for selected nations are for 1988 or 1989; Germany refers to West Germany in 1989.

rates are generally underestimates of the true rate because some suicides may be made to appear as accidents. Nevertheless, it is interesting to note that suicide grew more common during the past two decades among the older members of the elderly population, precisely when the effects of impaired function also grew among those 75 years of age or older.

Next, consider sex differences in suicide among older people. Table 18.1 presents the suicide rates for older people by sex and across two age groups for selected nations (U.S. Bureau of the Census, 1993). When these data are examined, it is apparent that suicide is much higher among older men than older women, and this relationship is quite consistent across the entire life course. Note also the differences between those 65 to 74 years of age and those 75 years of age and older. The United States and Canada are not alone in alone in this phenomenon of more frequent suicides among people 75 years or older. With a few exceptions, it is that group that has the higher rate of suicide, sometimes almost double the rate of those 65 to 74 years old. The very high rates of suicide in Austria and France are startling.

What do these suicide data mean? First, it needs to be kept in mind that suicide is a rare event. Despite all the difficulties faced in life, suicide is committed by a very small proportion of the population. Clearly, it gets considerable publicity because of the shock to families and acquaintances. Second, although rare, it is more common among older people than among younger persons. Teen suicide gets plenty of attention and rightfully so, but elder suicide is about twice as prevalent. Third, men are much more likely to commit suicide than women. One wonders if men's valuing of productivity and independence is part of the reason that they are more prone to suicide once retired and facing disability in physical function. Of course, women's social relationships are much more elaborate and supportive than those of men, especially when it comes to intimate relations, which are seen as critical to preventing suicide (Stack, 1982). It is too early to judge whether a social climate that embraces more aggressive use of euthanasia and assisted suicide will lead to more suicide. The data are limited, and no compelling patterns are evident.

The suicide data do speak to the role of integration of older people in modern societies, and gerontologists must remain vigilant in assessing how social policies may lead to an atrophy of such integration. Whereas the will to live is linked to social and religious engagements, it appears imperative to do what we can to ensure *social* communities that provide meaning and support for older adults. This may be more difficult in highly mobile societies, but the importance of doing so remains nonetheless.

FOCUSING UPSTREAM?

It is most reasonable to expect older adults to desire more control of how they are to die. Inasmuch as the process of succumbing to a chronic condition depends on a highly medicalized approach to living and dying, the dying process will often be longer in modern societies. Greater control for the older person may not appear feasible in the medicalized context wherein most deaths occur in such societies. Nevertheless, there have been attempts in recent years to return at least a modicum of control to the individual (e.g., California's Natural Death Act). What happens all too frequently in medical care of older persons is that advance directives, or "living wills," are prepared but not followed. This is sometimes due to the physician's concern over litigation for not implementing an aggressive medical regimen. More often, family members overrule the advance directives, thereby removing control from the older person as well. And sometimes it is the combination of physician concern over litigation coupled with family members' insistence on aggressive measures. Therefore, enhancing control over the conditions of death must include family education as well as limitations in medical malpractice litigation when advance directives are in place and were followed.

We need to focus upstream.

As a society desires to maximize individual choice over the conditions of death, there should simultaneously be efforts to assure older human beings of their intrinsic worth regardless of current function and productivity. None of us desires dependency, but dependency does not preclude a meaningful life for thousands of citizens, young or old, when their bodies do not function as intended or when they are smitten with what are called terminal diseases. Gerontologists need to be on guard against what Cohen (1988) calls the elderly mystique, a prejudice against disabled elders. The move toward more control over *how* one dies may lead to accelerating the dying process in unnecessary ways. Thousands of people who were diagnosed with terminal diseases have lived far beyond what medical personnel said was probable.

More generally speaking, too great an acceptance of control over one's death may latently lead to a devaluing of the individual's life. This issue of control over the dying processes poses a fine line for us to walk. Gerontologists need to value life and personal autonomy while emphasizing the life course contributions made by today's older people and the importance of *enhancing* life. If we do so, both death anxiety and dying anxiety may be minimized.

REFERENCES

Antonovksy, A. (1987). *Unraveling the mystery of health: How people manage stress and stay well.* San Francisco: Jossey-Bass.

Ariès, P. (1974). *Western attitudes toward death: From the Middle Ages to the present* (P. M. Ranum, Trans.). Baltimore: Johns Hopkins University Press.

Cohen, E. (1988). The elderly mystique: Constraints on the autonomy of the elderly with disabilities. *Gerontologist, 28*, 24–31.

Covey, H. C. (1991). *Images of older people in Western art and society.* New York: Praeger.

Durkheim, E. (1951). *Suicide.* New York: Free Press. (Original work published 1897).

Elias, N. (1985). *The loneliness of the dying.* Oxford: Basil Blackwell.

Idler, E. L., & Kasl, S. V. (1992). Religion, disability, depression, and the timing of death. *American Journal of Sociology, 97*, 1052–1079.

Jecker, N. S., & Schneiderman, L. J. (1994). Is dying young worse than dying old? *Gerontologist, 34*, 66–72.

Jeffers, F. C., Nichols, C., & Eisdorfer, C. (1961). Attitudes of older persons toward death: A preliminary study. *Journal of Gerontology, 16*, 53–56.

Kalish, R. A. (1985). *Death, grief, and caring relationships* (2nd ed.). Monterey, CA: Brooks/Cole.

Kammerman, J. B. (1988). *Death in the midst of life.* Englewood Cliffs, NJ: Prentice-Hall.

Kastenbaum, R. J. (1977). *Death, society, and human experience.* New York: McGraw-Hill.

Kastenbaum, R. J., & Candy, S. E. (1973). The 4 percent fallacy: A methodological and empirical critique of extended care facility population statistics. *International Journal of Aging and Human Development, 4*, 15–21.

Marshall, V. W. (1975). Socialization for impending death in a retirement village. *American Journal of Sociology, 80*, 1124–1144.

Myers, J. E., Wass, H., & Murphy, M. (1980). Ethnic differences in death anxiety among the elderly. *Death Education, 4*, 237–244.

Phillips, D. P., & Feldman, K. A. (1973). A dip in deaths before ceremonial occasions: Some new relationships between social integration and mortality. *American Sociological Review, 38*, 678–696.

Phillips, D. P., & King, E. W. (1988). Death takes a holiday: Mortality surrounding major social occasions. *Lancet*, *87*, 728–732.

Rasmussen, C., & Johnson, M. E. (1994). Spirituality and religiosity: Relative relationship to death anxiety. *Omega*, *29*, 313–318.

Sawyer, D. O. (1982). Public attitudes toward life and death. *Public Opinion Quarterly*, *46*, 521–533.

Seligman, M. E. P. (1974). Submissive death: Giving up on life. *Psychology Today*, 7, 80–85.

Stack, S. (1982). Suicide: A decade review of the sociological literature. *Deviant Behavior*, *4*, 41–66.

U.S. Bureau of the Census. (1975). *Historical statistics: Colonial times to 1970*. Washington, DC: U. S. Government Printing Office.

U.S. Bureau of the Census. (1993). *Statistical abstract of the United States: 1993* (113th ed.). Washington, DC: U. S. Government Printing Office.

U.S. Bureau of the Census. (1995). *Statistical abstract of the United States: 1995* (115th ed.). Washington, DC: U. S. Government Printing Office.

Uhlenberg, P. I. (1969). Study of cohort life cycles: Cohorts of native born Massachusetts women, 1830–1920. *Population Studies*, *23*, 407–420.

PART V

The Development of Gerontology

This final part of the book examines the questions of what gerontology is and what it is likely to become. Most agree that the field has experienced dramatic growth. The aging of our society has probably been a catalyst in the process. We want longer, healthier, and more independent lives. Gerontology is one field that is seen as being able to contribute much to understanding how we can accomplish these objectives.

Although it is clear that the field of gerontology is growing, there are several questions that fuel debates about how the field is growing. Among the issues that currently garner attention are: Is gerontology a discipline? That is, is there an emergent body of information that will enable the field of study we call gerontology to become its own discipline, independent of the current "parent" disciplines? To wit, will scholars be willing to set aside their disciplinary identity in biology, psychology, sociology, etc., to claim primary affiliations with gerontology, or, will they be hesitant to do so? Will the few programs offering doctoral degrees in gerontology grow and overshadow the certificate and minor approaches? Will gerontology become a profession? Should gerontologists be certified? There is no end to the questions about what gerontology is and what it should become.

In chapter 19, Ferraro and Chan do not attempt to answer all of these questions. Their objective is more modest. They seek to briefly describe the changes that gerontology has undergone, especially in recent decades, and attempt to document how much articulation and integration across disciplinary lines has developed. They do this by examining both scholarship and graduate education. While the terms multidisciplinary and interdisciplinary are often used interchangeably, they suggest a distinction. This distinction should help those interested in the field to better understand how far the field has moved in evolving into a discipline. They do not attempt to describe what gerontology should be, only to give an honest appraisal of how it has changed, thereby fostering sober reflection on what it might become.

CHAPTER 19

Is Gerontology a Multidisciplinary or An Interdisciplinary Field of Study? Evidence from Scholarly Affiliations and Educational Programming

Kenneth F. Ferraro
Su-Rong Chan

Gerontology as a field of study has witnessed dramatic growth, as evidenced by the proliferation of scholarly journals, professional societies, and educational programs. The field of gerontology is related to many disciplines, including the biological, behavioral, and social sciences, the humanities, and other professional fields (Achenbaum, 1995; Beattie, 1974; Cunningham & Brookbank, 1988). Whether or not there is growing interdisciplinary activity is related to several vital questions about the paradigmatic, scientific, and even disciplinary status of gerontology. Although there is much discussion of the value of multidisciplinary collaboration and interdisciplinary exchange, there is precious little evidence to test whether gerontology is becoming more interdisciplinary in character. The purposes of this chapter are to (1) briefly review the debate about multidisciplinary and interdisciplinary activity in gerontology and (2) examine evidence from scholarly affiliations and educational programming as indicators of such activity in recent years.

GERONTOLOGY: INTERDISCIPLINARY OR MULTIDISCIPLINARY?

A message on a T-shirt sold by the Gerontological Society of America a few years ago posed a question: "Gerontology: Interdisciplinary, Multidisciplinary, or

Undisciplined?" It was intended as a humorous reflection on the debate—at times heated—about what gerontology is and what it should be. As shown in chapter 1, there is considerable controversy over what paradigm governs this field of inquiry. What gerontology should be is clearly beyond the scope of this chapter, but we hope to contribute to this debate about the field and provide some evidence about how it has changed in recent decades.

In attempting to describe the current state affairs, it may be useful to first distinguish between the terms *interdisciplinary* and *multidisciplinary*. In practice, they are most often used interchangeably. We suggest a distinction. A *multidisciplinary* field of study refers to an inquiry involving a plurality of disciplines: disciplinary boundaries are maintained, and the unique contributions of each are highlighted. We refer to *interdisciplinary* as an inquiry similarly involving a plurality of disciplines: disciplinary boundaries are often muted, and the joint contributions of the synergy are highlighted. It may also be inferred, therefore, that multidisciplinary activity emphasizes collaboration among disciplines, and interdisciplinary activity emphasizes integrated, emergent approaches.

On the basis of these definitions, we begin this inquiry by assuming that gerontology is, by and large, a multidisciplinary endeavor. At times it shows evidence of becoming more interdisciplinary in character but, as of now, could not be generally characterized as such (Maddox, 1988). Statements by the Gerontological Society of America (1992) often stress the multidisciplinary character of that professional society: no discipline can claim more than 15.6% of the membership. It is possible that fields of study may evolve from multidisciplinary to interdisciplinary to disciplinary approaches (Hirschfield & Peterson, 1982; Ritzer, 1975). Indeed, Christensen (1964) and Burr and Leigh (1983) alluded to such a process in the development of family studies.

In reviewing the debate about articulation between disciplines, Achenbaum and Levin (1989) suggested that no consensus has emerged on either the definition of gerontology or its scope and boundaries. They speculate about future trends of developing a consensus in gerontology and note the hurdles involved in such progress (e.g., certification). The divergent agendas and worldviews of particular disciplines and gerontological institutions, as well as conflicts over both policy and territory among leading "gerontologists," will probably contribute to the difficulties in forming any intellectual or educational consensus in gerontology in the future (Achenbaum, 1995; Peterson & Bolton, 1980; Tornstam, 1992).

In discussing the development of gerontology into a science, Achenbaum (1987) addressed several of these issues and concluded:

> And although we engage in the more sophisticated discourse about esoteric theoretical and methodological matters than ever before, in fifty years gerontologists have not yet developed a satisfactory paradigm or established a uniform code of professional standards. Despite the fact that we have grown admirably more "scientific" in our study of aging, gerontology surely has not yet become a science. (p. 3)

At the heart of the changes in gerontology is the question of the paradigmatic status of the field (Tornstam, 1992). In the first chapter of this volume seven tenets of an emerging paradigm were identified, and it was suggested that two themes have dominated the development of gerontology as a science over the past few decades:

1. Gerontology is anchored in a normal-aging paradigm. Aging is no longer to be regarded by scientific researchers as simply "senile pathology" but as a "normal" stage of life (Rowe & Kahn, 1987; Shock & Baker, 1990).
2. Gerontology is recognized as a field of study involving more than one discipline (Achenbaum, 1987, 1995). The process of aging is complex; therefore, it is inadequate to simply study it from the perspective of a single discipline. Several disciplines will be "involved," but the nature of that involvement is what is in question.

Many scholars, educators, and policy personnel view multidisciplinary activity as essential to a vibrant understanding of aging. For example, most review panels for the National Institutes of Health that are related to aging are composed of people from varied disciplinary affiliations. Most gerontology education programs, especially the more developed ones, have for years required students to take at least some courses from multiple departments (Association for Gerontology in Higher Education, 1991; Seltzer, Sterns, & Hickey, 1978). It has been almost axiomatic that students interested in gerontology must take courses outside a single discipline (Association for Gerontology in Higher Education, 1989; Johnson et al., 1980).

Beyond multidisciplinary activity, there is clearly a move among some scholars toward interdisciplinary research and education. Interdisciplinary research is nothing new, but it remains relatively infrequent. Interdisciplinary education is still less prevalent but growing. Witness the growing number of graduate, including PhD, programs in gerontology, although several are qualified in one way or another. For example, one program advertises a PhD degree in "gerontology (public policy)." The idea behind these more interdisciplinary activities is that disciplinary boundaries are not essential and can be further muted as gerontology itself develops as a discipline. From this perspective, what is needed is more intellectual integration across the parent disciplines so that gerontology will emerge as a discipline.

On the other hand, there are arguments that do not reflect enthusiasm for growing integration in the field of gerontology. Some scholars are not troubled by the lack of interdisciplinary activity and may find value in maintaining multidisciplinary approaches. Science can exist in a low-paradigm state (Kuhn, 1970; Ritzer, 1975), and divergence in perspectives may be healthy for the field in fostering debate and innovation. According to this perspective, the growth in the field is beneficial, and further differentiation within the field of gerontology will probably be the main outcome—more differentiation generally means greater specialization and probably less integration. From this perspective scholarly differentiation and specialization are signs of scientific maturity, not of malaise in the field (i.e., it is not "undisciplined"). These disparate views have long been articulated in meetings and administrative discussions of the Gerontological Society of America as well as in other scholarly associations related to aging (e.g., the Association for Gerontology in Higher Education [AGHE]).

Although the value of multidisciplinary and interdisciplinary approaches merits discussion, this chapter does not argue for what gerontology *should* be. Instead, it is designed to consider recent social change in the field and characterize what gerontology *is*. Of course, it is a diverse field with many different approaches, but there are some observable patterns and trends in this growing field called gerontology. We consider changes from the 1940s to the present but give special attention to a key developmental period from 1977 to 1990. We believe that trends in scholarship and educational programming may reflect the movement from multidisciplinary to interdisciplinary activity, or vice versa, and, more generally, the process of paradigmatic change in gerontology over the past few decades.

SCHOLARLY PUBLICATIONS IN GERONTOLOGY

Scholarly publications in the field of gerontology have increased tremendously over the past three decades. It is also clear that the number of journals related to aging have mushroomed in recent decades. Katz (1992) lists more than 40 journals published in English and related to gerontology since the 1940s. Only two gerontology journals were created in the 1940s: *Journal of Gerontology* and *Geriatrics* (both started in 1946). Four journals were launched in the decade of the 1950s and four additional journals in the 1960s. Eleven journals were launched in the 1970s, but more than 20 were initiated in the 1980s. This is indeed substantial growth for the field, without even considering books, handbooks, and more popular publications. In considering this rapid growth, one wonders whether this proliferation and specialization of journals mean that gerontology has become more or less interdisciplinary? This is an intriguing question, but it probably cannot be answered just by examining the birth of new journals. The field has attracted scholars from many disciplines, and the more recent journals tend to be more specialized (e.g., *Geriatric Nursing, Gerodontics*, and *Journal of Religion and Aging*). Nevertheless, some journals appear to increase the interdisciplinary articulation (e.g., *Journal of Aging and Health*), whereas others are more clearly based in a single discipline (e.g., *Psychology and Aging*).

It may be argued that the evolution of the *Journal of Gerontology*—one of two official journals of the Gerontological Society of America—is an intriguing case study of the debate about multidisciplinary and interdisciplinary activity. Most gerontologists would judge it as the most prestigious journal in the field. At its

TABLE 19.1 Sectional Organization of *Journal(s) of Gerontology*

Year	Section
1946	None
1955	Biological Sciences and Clinical Medicine Psychological and Social Sciences, and Social Work Administration
1957	Biological Sciences and Clinical Medicine Psychological and Social Sciences, and Social Welfare
1961[a]	Biological and Medical Sciences Research in Psychological and Social Sciences
1963	None
1972	Biological and Medical Sciences Psychology and the Social Sciences Social Gerontology
1978	Biological and Medical Sciences Behavioral and Social Sciences Social Gerontology
1985	Biological Sciences Medical Sciences Psychological Sciences Social Sciences
1988	Journals of Gerontology: Biological Sciences Medical Sciences Psychological Sciences Social Sciences
1995	Journals of Gerontology: Series A: Biological Sciences Medical Sciences Series B: Psychological Sciences Social Sciences

[a] Inception of *The Gerontologist*, covering social welfare topics.

inception in 1946 the *Journal of Gerontology* had no sectional organization of topics but nonetheless published works from a wide variety of disciplines. The inaugural issue had articles ranging from basic science research on the age of neural stem tissue and the capacity to form roots to basic social science research on attitudes toward aging and the "aged" in traditional societies.

As displayed in Table 19.1, the sectional organization of the *Journal* has changed repeatedly. Although reviewers and editors have always been specialized, the presentation of the articles has varied considerably. Note from Table 19.1 that the *Journal* changed from no sectional organization of topics in 1946 to sectional organization in 1955. This pattern continued to 1963, at which time the *Journal* reverted to no sectional organization of articles. Sectional presentation of articles returned in 1972 and has remained in some form ever since. For over 40 years there was always an editor-in-chief, position; this was abolished in 1988, at which time each of the four sections named fairly autonomous editors. (Prior to this time all manuscripts were sent to the editor-in-chief, who would then send them to the sectional editors.) Also in 1988, the name was changed to the current *Journals of Gerontology*, with colons and sections following for the official citation; even pagination changed to signify the *sectional* journals. Thus, authors now cite one of the four journals rather than *the* journal.

The idea of physically splitting the journals was discussed for years and finally came to fruition in 1995 with the creation of two sections. One of the chief arguments was that the biological sciences needed more pages and more frequent publication than was feasible in the former format. Indeed, there is some consideration that all four journals will eventually be bound separately, with biological sciences moving from 6 to 12 issues per year. Some see these changes as evidence of growing differentiation and maturity in the field. Others view these changes, especially the most recent ones, as evidence of an atrophying commitment to interdisciplinary articulation and perhaps even multidisciplinary awareness. Some argue that binding the four journals separately may lead to less awareness of research activities and innovations in the sister disciplines.

Scholarly Affiliations in the *Journal of Gerontology*

One way to judge whether there is growing evidence of multidisciplinary and/or interdisciplinary activity in the field is to consider scholarly affiliations among authors in major publications. For this purpose, we analyzed the contents of issues of the *Journal of Gerontology* published in 1977, 1985, and 1990 to examine changes in the field. These years were selected as part of a larger project to correspond with the publication of the three *Handbooks on Aging* and the first, third, and fifth editions of AGHE's *National directory of educational programs in gerontology and geriatrics*. (The AGHE directories will be examined subsequently.) Affiliations refer to current departmental or center identification, not to departments from which people received their professional degrees.

Although several indicators of scholarly affiliations were considered, two were examined in detail: (1) *co-authorship from varied disciplinary affiliations*, signifying heterogeneous research teams, and (2) *frequency of joint or split appointments*, reflecting organizational change to accommodate multidisciplinary and interdisciplinary activity over time. For the latter indicator we also considered whether the joint appointment was with a gerontology or geriatric center or some other type of center.

Examining all issues of the journals in 1977, 1985, and 1990, it is clear that the number and percentage of articles that were co-authored (at least two authors) generally increased over time. The social sciences rate of co-authorship was about 70% in 1990, making it the least likely of the four sections for joint publication. The number of co-authors was generally highest in the biological sciences section (between 3 and 3.5 authors per article), but the medical sciences roughly matched that rate in 1985 and 1990. As shown in Figure 19.1, the percentage of articles co-authored by persons with varied affiliations peaked in 1985 for both the medical and biological sciences of the journals and declined slightly by 1990 (the rate for biological sciences was higher than that for medical sciences at all times). The percentage of varied disciplinary affiliations in the psychological sciences was fairly stable over time but dropped in the 1985 observation (40 in 1977, 32.1 in 1985, 41.9 in 1990). By contrast, the percentage of articles in the social sciences by authors with varied disciplinary affiliations showed continued growth from 33 in 1977 to over 60 by 1990 ($p < .01$). Although the medical sciences look less inclusive than other sections when it comes to

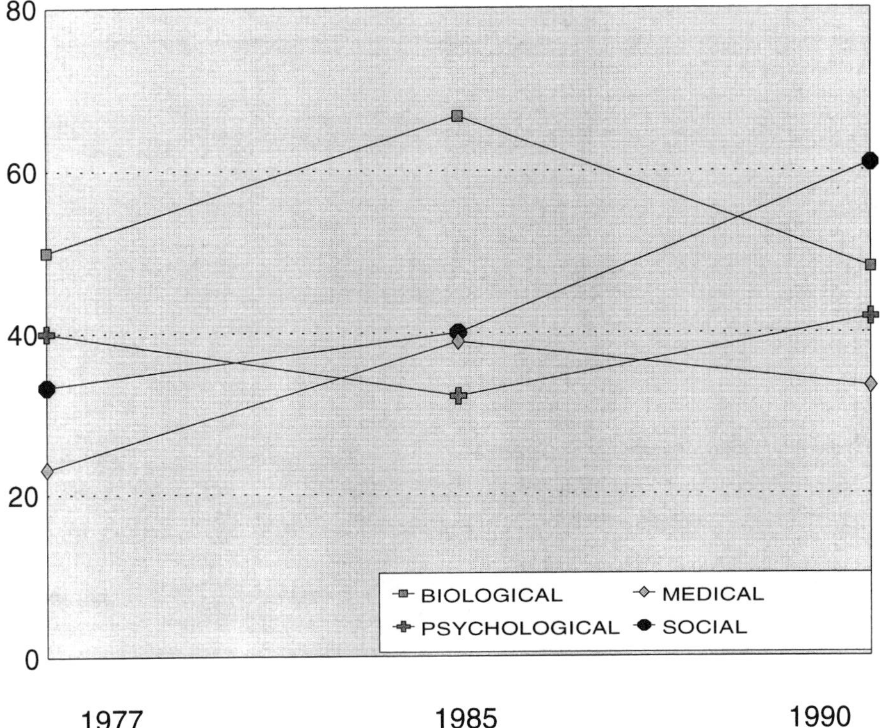

FIGURE 19.1 Percentage of varied affiliations of all authors of co-authored articles by section in the *Journal of Gerontology*.

working in diverse research teams, some caution is in order here because departments of medicine are generally quite large and may have such diversity within them.

The percentage of authors who named joint appointments is displayed for each section in Figure 19.2. Joint appointments grew dramatically over time in all fields except the medical sciences ($p < .01$). Over 15% of all authors in the biological sciences and nearly 23% of all authors in the social sciences named secondary appointments in 1990. Joint appointments in the medical sciences peaked in 1985, but the rate in 1990 was higher than in 1977. Many joint appointments were with units other than gerontology centers such as Veterans Administration, specialized medical (e.g., stroke research), population, and policy centers.

The percentage of affiliations with *gerontology* or *geriatric* centers among authors in the biological or medical sciences with a joint appointment never reached 10. For the psychological sciences, it actually declined, from 24% in 1977 to 9% in 1990. By contrast, the rate for such affiliations in the social sciences

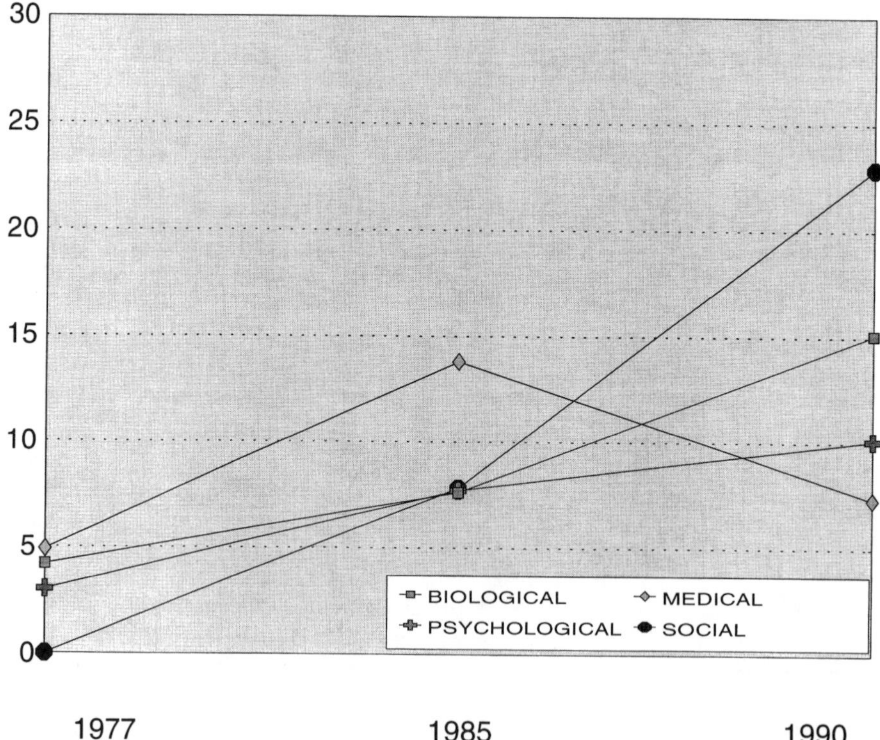

FIGURE 19.2 Percentage of authors naming joint affiliations, by section, in the *Journal of Gerontology*.

section of the journals rose from 11% in 1977 to 31% in 1990. Among all types of joint appointments, growth in affiliations with gerontology centers was observed only among authors in the social sciences (from 11% to 31%). Given the importance of laboratories to the biological, medical, and psychological sciences, split appointments with gerontology centers may not be very attractive unless they offer tangible research resources. For the social sciences, the cost of such appointments are generally modest or nonexistent.

To conclude, interdisciplinary activity increased over the 14-year period, but the rate of growth has been modest and varies across disciplines. Co-authorship generally increased over this time with some evidence of growing interdisciplinary activity among contributors to the flagship journal. The medical sciences did not manifest much change in this direction, and the trends do not approximate linear relationships, except perhaps for the social sciences. Joint or split appointments and affiliations with gerontology centers appear to have grown appreciably among social scientists contributing to the journals but remain modest overall. For other sections, some growth in joint appointments was observed but not necessarily with gerontology or geriatric centers. All in all, these data suggest growing interdisciplinary research activity among the biological, psychological, and social sciences, but institutional arrangements to support such exchanges in the form of joint faculty or research scientists' appointments have not progressed at the same pace.

EDUCATIONAL PROGRAMMING IN GERONTOLOGY

A second approach to assessing the degree of multidisciplinary and interdisciplinary activity in gerontology is to consider changes in higher education. Regardless of the research activities of leading scholars, changes in how educational programs are organized are important for this field of inquiry. Although there are over 1,000 educational programs in gerontology now, housed in over 500 institutions of higher education, the institutions offering graduate programs may be most likely to reflect the emergent structure and organization of the field (Bolton, 1988). Thus, content analysis of three editions of the *National Directory of Educational Programs in Gerontology and Geriatrics* was performed to examine basic changes in the both the structure of organizational units and the credentials offered (Association of Gerontology in Higher Education, 1991).

Table 19.2 presents basic information on the types, location, and control of colleges and universities offering some type of graduate education program. The type of institution is based on the classification scheme for differentiating universities as outlined by the Carnegie Foundation (Carnegie Council on Policy Studies in Higher Education, 1976). It is apparent from Table 19.2 that doctorate-granting and comprehensive universities were much more likely to offer educational programs in 1976. Since that time the number of institutions

TABLE 19.2 Type and Region of Institutions Offering Graduate Gerontology Programs in 1976, 1985, and 1991

	1976	1985	1991
Type of institution[a]			
Research university I	33.3%	19.3%	22.1%
Research university II	23.1	19.3	17.6
Doctorate-granting university I	7.9	14.5	14.7
Doctorate-granting university II	10.3	9.6	6.6
Comprehensive university or college I	0.3	26.5	30.1
Comprehensive university or college II	0	2.4	2.2
Liberal arts colleges	0	3.6	2.9
Theological seminaries	5.1	2.4	2.2
Medical schools or centers	0	2.4	1.5
Region			
Northeast	21.4	24.4	19.9
Midwest	26.2	31.1	31.5
South	31.0	33.3	34.9
West	21.4	11.1	13.7
Institutional control			
Private	21.4	30.3	28.1
Public	78.6	69.7	71.9
Total number of institutions	42	89	146

Note: Percentages may not add up to 100 due to rounding.
[a]Classified according to the Carnegie Council on Policy Studies in Higher Education (1976).

offering graduate gerontology programs has increased dramatically, especially among the comprehensive universities and colleges I. The patterns of change reflect the diffusion of graduate education over time, as one would expect in higher education. The southern region had the highest proportion of graduate programs over the three times, and the midwestern region had the second highest (consistent with active regional associations such as the Southern Gerontological Society and the Midwest Council for Social Research on Aging). As expected, over two-thirds of the programs were offered by public institutions.

The type of credentials offered by these programs is especially relevant to a consideration of the field of gerontology. One would expect that preferring an interdisciplinary over a multidisciplinary approach would be manifested in growth in degree programs. Figure 19.3 displays the types of gerontology credentials offered in 1976, 1985, and 1991 (first program named in the *Directory*). Indeed, there was substantial growth in degree programs over time—from only 5 in 1976 to 32 in 1992. Nonetheless, subtantial growth was also manifest for less integrated approaches, such as specializations, concentrations, and minors (i.e.,

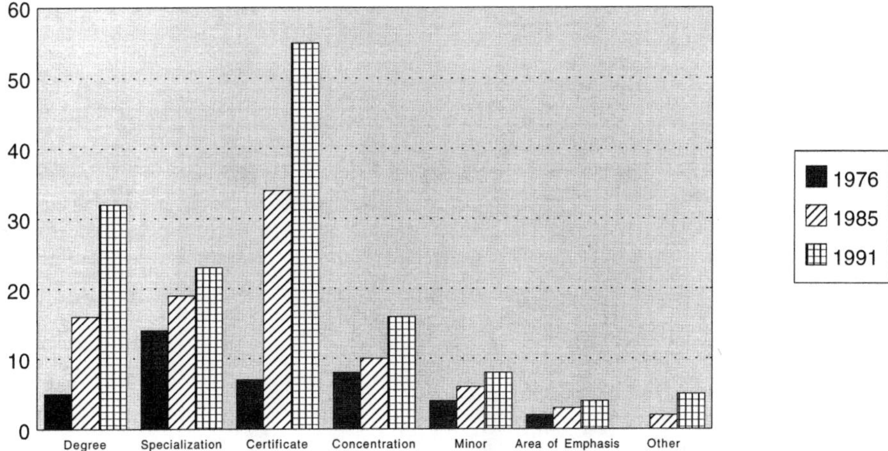

FIGURE 19.3 Gerontology credentials at the graduate level, 1976, 1985, and 1991 (first program listed in AGHE national directories). There were no programs classified as "other" in 1976.

multidisciplinary). What is most striking is the rise in the number of certificates offered, from 7 in 1976 to 55 in 1991. Looking at it another way, programs offering certificates represented nearly 18% of all graduate education programs in 1976 but nearly 38% in 1985 and 1991. Certificates are popular and have increased their share of the market, probably still reflecting the dominance of the multidisciplinary perspective.

The final indicator examined in the AGHE directories concerns the organizational structure of the unit offering the educational program. Figure 19.4 summarizes the major types of organizational structures over the three periods. Centers were the most popular type of organization in 1976, but programs are the now the most popular, accounting for over one-half of all such units. Schools and departments are those organizational units most likely to offer the degree programs, and as evident in Figure 19.4, they are still quite rare in the population of schools considered.

All in all, these data highlight the rapid and continuing growth of graduate gerontology instruction in American institutions of higher education (Peterson, 1986). Graduate gerontology instruction was largely confined to the research universities in the mid-1970s but has grown appreciably in the doctorate-granting and comprehensive universities and colleges in recent decades. Although the number of degrees in gerontology at the graduate level has grown rapidly, most of the existing programs are offered as master's degrees. Doctoral programs in gerontology are growing but still quite rare. Instead, the dominant credential offered at the graduate level is a certificate; specializations, concentra-

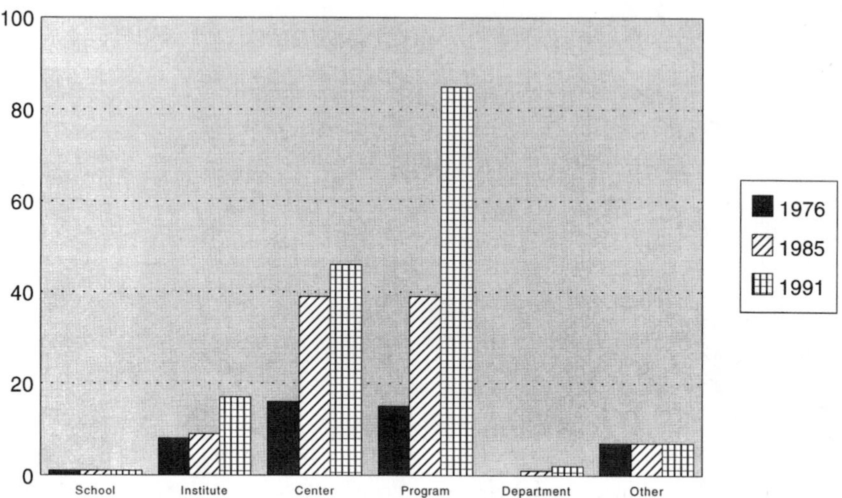

FIGURE 19.4 Organizational structures in gerontology graduate programs, 1976, 1985, and 1991.

tions, and minors also are becoming more prevalent (Peterson, Douglas, Bolton, Connelly, & Bergstone, 1987). These credentials are most often offered by multidisciplinary units referred to as programs, centers, and institutes. Taken together, these trends point to the overarching organization of gerontology as a multidisciplinary field of inquiry. There is clear evidence that interdisciplinary activity is increasing, but the multidisciplinary perspective seems to be the guiding framework for most programs.

GERONTOLOGY COMING OF AGE?

We asserted earlier that gerontology is principally a multidisciplinary field of inquiry. After reviewing change in the scholarly affiliations of authors to the flagship journal in the field and the types of educational programs offered by respondents to an AGHE survey, there is little evidence to refute the assertion of multidisciplinarity in the field today. Indeed, to summarize the conclusions from the data examined, two generalizations seem appropriate.

First, gerontology is squarely anchored in a multidisciplinary perspective. Despite specialization within various disciplines and the proliferation of journals related to aging, there is ample evidence that most "gerontologists" are sensitive to the importance of other disciplines' contributions. This is especially evident in the graduate educational experience as structured today. Thus, there is every reason to believe that this emphasis will continue and perhaps intensify in the future (Peterson & Wendt, 1990).

Second, interdisciplinary activities, in both research and education are growing. More research teams that span disciplines are being formed, and programs granting degrees are increasing. Thus, although the multidisciplinary perspective is dominant, the interdisciplinary perspective is alive and growing in both intellectual exchanges and educational endeavors. Moreover, in a community of scholars, most would agree that a multidisciplinary perspective is often a first step in the direction of growing integration in an interdisciplinary framework. The future may be bright for interdisciplinary approaches.

These developments are probably the result of influences both internal and external to the structure of the field. Most of the internal influences hinge on the interface of the participating disciplines. Gerontology is related to many disciplines, and this diversity has positive and negative consequences. Gerontological research benefits from a wider range of theories and perspectives, but this diversity probably also contributes to the struggle gerontology has had in attempting to define itself (e.g., debates between disciplines). On the other hand, external factors have influenced the development of gerontology as well. For instance, funding from the National Institute on Aging attracted outstanding scholars to the field who formerly were not specialists on aging.

Many university budgets were constrained during the 1980s, thus institutional development was often modest, especially in public or state-assisted universities. That gerontology could prosper at all on campuses that were cutting programs is a major testimony to the relevance and vitality of the field. Nonetheless, fiscal austerity often meant that growth was in the form of better organizing existing faculty and resources rather than creating new institutional entities. Other factors that must be considered in how gerontology will develop include employment opportunities for graduates of degree-granting programs and the current discussion among gerontologists about certification.

There is no doubt that gerontology is a mature field. It has its own journals, a body of research findings, and professional associations. Nevertheless, it is unclear whether the current developments of gerontology described here are the first steps along the predicted path for the field to arrive at an interdisciplinary framework. The future of gerontology may well depend on the willingness of traditional academic departments (e.g. psychology, sociology, biology) to cooperate in the joint gerontological enterprise. As Achenbaum (1995) concludes, "gerontology will continue to open new frontiers of knowledge as long as highly trained scholars are willing to cross the boundaries of their own scientific training and appreciate the rewards of broadening their fields of vision" (p. 268). We assert that "broadening the vision" is not the major problem but that "crossing the boundaries of their own scientific training" will keep gerontology in a multidisciplinary mode for years to come. Consider Kuhn's (1970) words in his analysis of science: the emerging paradigm in a field must be "sufficiently unprecedented to attract an enduring group of adherents away from competing modes of scientific activity" (p. 10). It may well be that where the field is headed will be shaped by how well gerontology departments and schools, espousing a truly interdisciplinary perspective, are able to hire and retain outstanding scholars as well as place their graduates in attractive positions.

For the sake of clarity, it may be useful to restate and extend our distinction between multidisciplinary and interdisciplinary approaches. As stated earlier, a multidisciplinary field of study refers to an inquiry involving a plurality of disciplines in which disciplinary boundaries are maintained and the unique contributions of each are highlighted. A multidisciplinary approach occurs when team members recognize the importance of contributions from other disciplines. An interdisciplinary field of study refers to an inquiry involving a plurality of disciplines in which disciplinary boundaries are often muted and the joint contributions of the synergy are highlighted. An interdiscplinary approach implies that team members are willing and able to develop and share a perspective that integrates the contributions of each team member's involvement.

Whether a multidisciplinary or interdisciplinary approach ultimately prevails, a solid argument can still be made that the next steps for gerontology hinge on clarifying the overarching perspective that guides the field, its analyses and interpretations: a gerontological imagination. Indeed, this book has attempted to better define and clarify the gerontological imagination and to add flesh to the basic tenets of such a perspective. It should continue to be an intellectually exciting task as gerontology comes of age.

REFERENCES

Achenbaum, W. A. (1987). Can gerontology be a science? *Journal of Aging Studies*, *1*, 3–18.

Achenbaum, W. A. (1995). *Crossing frontiers: Gerontology emerges as a science.* Cambridge: Cambridge University Press.

Achenbaum, W. A., & Levin, J. S. (1989). What does gerontology mean? *Gerontologist*, *29*, 393–400.

Association for Gerontology in Higher Education, Standards Committee. (1989). *Standards and guidelines for gerontology programs.* Washington, DC: Author.

Association for Gerontology in Higher Education. (1991). *National directory of educational programs in gerontology and geriatrics.* Washington, DC: Author.

Beattie, W. M. (1974). Gerontology curricula: Multidisciplinary frameworks, interdisciplinary structures, and disciplinary depth. *Gerontologist*, *12*, 545–553.

Bolton, C. (1988). Program standards and faculty development in gerontology instruction: A role for professional organizations. *Educational Gerontology*, *14*, 497–507.

Burr, W. R., & Leigh, G. K. (1983). Famology: A new discipline. *Journal of Marriage and the Family*, *8*, 467–480.

Carnegie Council on Policy Studies in Higher Education. (1976). *A classification of institutions of higher education.* Berkeley, CA: Carnegie Foundation for the Advancement of Teaching.

Christensen, H. T. (1964). Development of the family field of study. In H. T. Christensen (Ed.), *Handbook of marriage and the family* (pp. 3–32). Chicago: Rand McNally.

Cunningham, W. R., & Brookbank, J. W. (1988). *Gerontology: The psychology, biology, and sociology of aging.* New York: Harper & Row.

Gerontological Society of America. (1992, April). Elections are coming: Who are the voters? *Gerontology News*, p. 4.

Hirschfield, I. S., & Peterson, D. A. (1982). The professionalization of gerontology. *Gerontologist, 22*, 215–220.

Johnson, H. R., Britton, J. H., Lang, C. A., Seltzer, M. M., Stanford, E. P., Yancik, R., Maklan, C. W., & Middleswarth, A. B. (1980). Foundations for gerontological education (a collaborative project of the Gerontological Society and the Association for Gerontology in Higher Education). *Gerontologist, 20*, 1–61.

Katz, W. A. (1992). *Magazines for libraries: For the general reader and school, junior college, university, and public libraries.* New Providence, NJ: Bowker.

Kuhn, T. (1970). *The structure of scientific revolutions.* Chicago: University of Chicago Press.

Maddox, George L. (1988). The future of gerontology in higher education. *Gerontologist, 28*, 748–752.

Peterson, D. A. (1986). Extent of gerontology instruction in American institutions of higher education. *Educational Gerontology, 12*, 519–529.

Peterson, D. A., & Bolton, C. R. (1980). *Gerontology instruction in higher education.* New York: Springer Publishing.

Peterson, D. A., Douglas, E. B., Bolton, C. R., Connelly, J. R., & Bergstone, D. (1987). *Gerontology instruction in American institutions of higher education: A national survey.* Washington, D.C.: Association for Gerontology in Higher Education and Andrus Gerontology Center, University of Southern California.

Peterson, D. A., & Wendt, P. F. (1990). Gerontology instruction: Different models for different results. *Educational Gerontology, 16*, 359–372.

Ritzer, G. (1975). *Sociology: A multiple paradigm science.* Boston: Allyn & Bacon.

Rowe, J. W., & Kahn, R. L. (1987). Human aging: Usual and successful. *Science, 237*, 143–149.

Seltzer, M. M., Sterns, H., & Hickey, T. (1978). Introduction. In M. Seltzer, H. Sterns, & T. Hickey (Eds.), *Gerontology in higher education: Perspectives and issues* (pp. vi–vii). Belmont, CA: Wadsworth.

Shock, N. W., & Baker, G. T. (1990). Gerontology: The scientific study of aging, past and future. *Journal of Gerontology: Biological Sciences. 45*, B31.

Tornstam, L. (1992). The quo vadis of gerontology: On the scientific paradigm of gerontology. *Gerontologist, 32*, 318–326.

AUTHOR INDEX

SUBJECT INDEX